Portraits and Principles

OF THE WORLD'S

Great Men and Women

WITH

Practical Lessons on Successful Life

BY OVER

Fifty Leading Thinkers.

---✷---

DESIGNED AND ARRANGED BY

William C. King.

---✷---

WITH INTRODUCTION BY

REV. CHARLES H. PARKHURST, D.D.

---✷---

Over 400 Photo-Engraved Portraits.

---•·•---

THE KING-RICHARDSON CO.,

Springfield, Mass.

SAN JOSÉ. CHICAGO. TORONTO. INDIANAPOLIS.

Kessinger Publishing's
Rare Mystical Reprints

THOUSANDS OF SCARCE BOOKS
ON THESE AND OTHER SUBJECTS:

Freemasonry * Akashic * Alchemy * Alternative Health * Ancient Civilizations * Anthroposophy * Astrology * Astronomy * Aura * Bible Study * Cabalah * Cartomancy * Chakras * Clairvoyance * Comparative Religions * Divination * Druids * Eastern Thought * Egyptology * Esoterism * Essenes * Etheric * ESP * Gnosticism * Great White Brotherhood * Hermetics * Kabalah * Karma * Knights Templar * Kundalini * Magic * Meditation * Mediumship * Mesmerism * Metaphysics * Mithraism * Mystery Schools * Mysticism * Mythology * Numerology * Occultism * Palmistry * Pantheism * Parapsychology * Philosophy * Prosperity * Psychokinesis * Psychology * Pyramids * Qabalah * Reincarnation * Rosicrucian * Sacred Geometry * Secret Rituals * Secret Societies * Spiritism * Symbolism * Tarot * Telepathy * Theosophy * Transcendentalism * Upanishads * Vedanta * Wisdom * Yoga * *Plus Much More!*

DOWNLOAD A FREE CATALOG
AND
SEARCH OUR TITLES AT:

www.kessinger.net

Copyright, 1903, by
KING-RICHARDSON COMPANY
SPRINGFIELD, MASS.

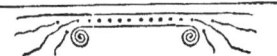

ALL RIGHTS RESERVED.

PREFACE.

LIFE to each of us is an ever-changing panorama. The sights of yesterday are old, the scenes of to-day are swiftly passing, and the pictures of to-morrow will be new. Each day comes freighted with greater opportunities and enlarged interests. To meet these constantly increasing responsibilities, our lives should be developed along practical lines. This volume points out and illustrates the principles which must govern the minds and hearts of those who would succeed and make the most of life and its possibilities.

The qualities of every noble life have their foundation in the truths unfolded in this volume, and, living these truths, men have made their lives grandly successful.

The great problem of the ages and the burning question of to-day is, "How to Succeed."

Every generation of the past has been confronted by this problem, and each individual is to-day asking the same vital question. The hopes and hearts of men are all alike. They may differ in degree, but never in kind. Your hopes are like mine. I wish for happiness, so do you. I desire to succeed, so do you. Our ideals of happiness or success may differ, but each is striving for that ideal we call success. No person in his right mind ever yet wished for ruin to his hopes.

How to bring our hopes to fruitage is the problem each one of us is laboring to solve. This volume solves the problem, and if it shall be the means of awakening aspirations for success along noble lines in the minds of the young men and women of our land, to whom it is especially sent; if it shall arouse greater zeal, or give new courage to any faltering traveler, or if it shall arrest any careless feet from going astray,—then the great aim and purpose of the book and its writers will be accomplished, and the noble men and women whose portraits, principles, and careers are here set forth, will live anew in other lives, bringing such blessings to the individual and to the world, as only eternity will fully reveal.

W. C. K.

Golden Links in the Chain of Life.

		PAGE
1—Our Noblest Birthright,		25
Rev. James W. Cole, B.D.		
2—The Meaning of Success,		29
Charles M. Gates, M.S.		
3—The Mainspring of Success,		36
Hon. Frederick Robie.		
4—Success Wrought from the Chaos of Failure,		41
Prof. George S. Forest.		
5—Selecting an Occupation,		44
Rev. James W. Cole, B.D.		
6—Value of Decision,		48
Prof. J. N. Humphrey, A.B.		
7—Danger of Being Side-Tracked,		52
Prof. James R. Truax, M.A.		
8—Singleness of Aim,		58
Rev. George A. Hall.		
9—Climbing the Ladder of Success,		68
John C. Dueber.		
10—Footprints of Failure,		73
Rev. James W. Cole, B.D.		
11—Dignity of Labor,		78
Rev. James W. Cole, B.D.		
12—Character as Capital,		84
Rev. B. O. Aylesworth, D.D., LL.D.		
13—Influence of Associates,		87
Rev. F. E. Clark, D.D.		
14—Fruits of Honesty,		91
Rev. James W. Cole, B.D.		
15—Not Above Your Business,		99
Rev. James W. Cole, B.D.		
16—Beginning at the Bottom,		104
Rev. James W. Cole, B.D.		
17—Results of Application,		111
William H. Scott, LL.D.		
18—Commercial Courage,		116
Rev. James W. Cole, B.D.		
19—The Man of Push,		119
Rev. George R. Hewitt, B.D.		
20—The Value of Tact,		122
William C. King.		
21—The Compass of Life,		130
Rev. Samuel Plantz, Ph.D.		
22—The Power of Perseverance,		136
Rev. James W. Cole, B.D.		
23—Earning the Capital,		143
Rev. James W. Cole, B.D.		
24—High School of Experience,		150
Rev. John Bascom, D.D., LL.D.		

CONTENTS.

	PAGE
25—Requisites for a Business Education, ...	154
Homer Merriam.	
26—Personal Independence, ...	159
Rev. James W. Cole, B.D.	
27—Importance of Self-Mastery, ...	170
Rev. James W. Cole, B.D.	
28—Doings Things Well, ...	176
Rev. M. Woolsey Stryker, D.D., LL.D.	
29—Self-Made, if Ever Made, ...	179
Prof. David Collin Wells, B.A., B.D.	
30—Personal Purity, ...	184
Rev. Edward Everett Hale, D.D.	
31—The Value of a Sound Body, ...	189
Rev. James W. Cole, B.D.	
32—Importance of Physical Development, . . .	194
Prof. A. Alonzo Stagg.	
33—Advantages of Difficulties, ...	199
Rev. William DeWitt Hyde, D.D.	
34—The Blight of Idleness, ...	204
Rev. George R. Hewitt, B.D.	
35—What Spare Moments Will Accomplish, . . .	207
Rev. James W. Cole, B.D.	
36—False Standards, ...	210
Henry H. Bowman.	
37—Rare Use of Common Sense, ...	213
Rev. James W. Cole, B.D.	
38—Ruin in Disguise, ...	219
Anthony Comstock.	
39—Chasing Fickle Fortune, ...	228
Rev. James W. Cole, B.D.	
40—Cutting 'Cross Lots to Success, ...	232
Hon. George F. Mosher, LL.D.	
41—Grandeur of Patience, ...	236
William C. King.	
42—Trading Opportunities for Failure, . . .	239
Rev. George Edward Reed, D.D., LL.D.	
43—Waiting for Something to Turn Up, . . .	245
Rev. A. B. Hervey, Ph.D.	
44—The Secret of Making Things Turn Up, . .	249
Rev. James W. Cole, B.D.	
45—Luck and Labor, ...	253
Rev. George S. Winston, LL.D.	
46—Reaping Without Sowing, ...	256
Rev. James W. Cole, B.D.	
47—Counting the Cost, ...	259
R. M. Armstrong.	
48—Wasted Energies, ...	263
Rev. John Cotton Brooks.	
49—The Chains of Habit, ...	267
Rev. James W. Cole, B.D.	
50—How and What to Read, ...	271
Rev. James W. Cole, B.D.	
51—Importance of Grasping Current Events, . .	275
Prof. Oscar J. Craig, M.A., Ph.D.	

CONTENTS.

	PAGE
52—Chimney Corner Graduates,	278
JAMES LANE ALLEN, M.A.	
53—Power of Concentration,	283
CHAS. G. D. ROBERTS, A. M.	
54—Helps and Hints on How to Think,	287
Rev. B. P. RAYMOND, D.D.	
55—Thought Reduces Labor,	291
Prof. GEORGE G. WILSON, PH.D.	
56—Eyes that See,	297
Rev. WILLARD E. WATERBURY, B.D.	
57—The Value of an Idea,	304
W. C. KING.	
58—Put Your Ideas into Practice,	306
BENJAMIN IDE WHEELER, PH.D.	
59—Importance of Being Punctual,	310
Hon. CYRUS G. LUCE.	
60—Delay Loses Fortunes,	316
Rev. H. A. GOBIN, D.D.	
61—Strive at Possibilities,	321
Rev. JAMES W. COLE, B.D.	
62—Practice Secures Perfection,	326
Rev. GEORGE R. HEWITT, B.D.	
63—Learning is Not Wisdom,	329
MERRILL E. GATES, LL.D., L.H.D.	
64—Power and Possibilities of Young Men,	334
JOSEPH COOK, LL.D.	
65—The Influence of Young Women,	338
Lady HENRY SOMERSET—FRANCES E. WILLARD.	
66—Woman's Work and Wages,	341
NELLIE E. BLACKMER.	
67—The Power of Mother's Influence,	350
Mrs. SUSAN S. FESSENDEN.	
68—Woman's Place in the Business World,	356
Mrs. FRANK LESLIE.	
69—Literary and Professional Women,	360
Mrs. MARY A. LIVERMORE.	
70—True Value of Character,	369
Prof. FRANK SMALLEY, M.A., PH.D.	
71—Reputation Is Not Character,	375
Prof. N. L. ANDREWS, PH.D., LL.D.	
72—Broken Promises,	379
Prof. JOSEPH K. CHICKERING, M.A.	
73—The Beauties of Simplicity,	383
Rev. CARTER J. GREENWOOD, M.A.	
74—The Value of Pleasing Manners,	385
WILLIAM C. KING.	
75—The Worth of Modesty,	388
Rev. GEORGE R. HEWITT, B.D.	
76—True Nobility,	390
HENRY K. BUTTZ, D.D., LL.D.	
77—The Breastplate of Self-Respect,	394
Rev. HUGH BOYD, D.D.	
78—Adapting Self to Circumstances,	399
Hon. EDWIN F. LYFORD, M.S.	

CONTENTS.

	PAGE
79—Individual Responsibility, Rev. W. C. Whitford, D.D.	403
80—Mental and Moral Growth, Rev. James W. Cole, B.D.	407
81—Motive and Method, Rev. George R. Hewitt, B.D.	411
82—Courage for the Duties of Life, Prof. C. A. Young, Ph.D., LL.D.	415
83—Duty Before Glory, Rev. George A. Gates, M.A., Ph.D.	418
84—Poverty Prepares for Wealth, Hon. J. H. Brigham.	421
85—Where to Get Rich, Homer T. Fuller, Ph.D.	423
86—Secret of Saving, Rev. James W. Cole, B.D.	425
87—Use and Abuse of Money, Rev. Washington Gladden, D.D.	429
88—Dangers of Riches, Prof. A. S. Wright, M.A.	434
89—Giving Enriches the Giver, A. M. Haggard, M.A.	438
90—True Magnanimity, Rev. George R. Hewitt, B.D.	442
91—Perils of Success, Rev. George R. Hewitt, B.D.	445
92—Whirlpool of Commerce, Rev. George R. Hewitt, B.D.	449
93—Gamblers and Gambling, Rev. H. O. Breeden, LL.D.	452
94—Wrecks of Wall Street, Prof. E. T. Tyndall.	458
95—The Balance Wheel, Rev. George R. Hewitt, B.D.	461
96—Use and Power of Faith, Rev. Lewis O. Brastow, D.D.	464
97—The Ministry of Trouble and Sorrow, Prof. J. M. Stifler, D.D.	471
98—Building for Eternity, Rev. H. B. Hartzler, D.D.	474
99—Our Great Ledger Account, Rev. George S. Goodspeed, Ph.D.	478
100—Life's Great Guide Book, Rev. P. S. Henson, D.D.	484

INTRODUCTION

BY

Rev. Charles H. Parkhurst, D.D.,

New York City,

THIS volume is minted from human experience and is made up of clippings from personal life. It is an attempt to put flesh and blood into black and white, and to coin heart-throbs into sentences. In this way the personal element comes well to the front and makes out the volume's worth and fascination.

Life is the only thing that counts,—generally speaking, in the material world, particularly speaking, in the moral and spiritual world. Even the Incarnation was first of all a divine attempt to get more life—personal life—into the world; and Whitsuntide only stands for another gigantic experiment of the same kind. Personality is the very substance and genius of all truth. Christ expressed this when he said, "I am the truth." Every one, in finite degree,—some more than others, some less,—is able to say the same thing,—"I am the truth." Truth is, in the first instance, personal; and becomes less and less truth according as the personal element is more and more wrung out of it. It is therefore that personality is the only real teaching power. Books are teachers, but only to the degree that they succeed in becoming an incarnation of their authors. Education, so far as it is authentic, is a process of personal interchange between teacher and taught. Teaching is the process of knocking down the wall of partition between two intelligences so that both combine to compose one apartment. All who have at any time passed under the baptism of some great loyal soul understand what this means. It is not necessary to undertake to explain the process, but it is not difficult to appreciate its reality. We can be made learned by studying things, but in order to become educated we have to draw from a supply that is kept flowing and ebbing with the tide of a personal pulse. So that the value of any teacher has to be estimated not by what he knows, but by what he is and by his communicableness; and the nearer a book can come to that,—the more it retains in it of the human pulse and the personal warmth of its author,—the more, in a word, it continues to be personal even after it has been cast into the form of printer's ink, the more it denotes as a book. There are books that are statuesque, and there are books that are picturesque, but, God be praised, there are also books that breathe: books that keep in them the life currents of the soul they are born from: like friths that still rise and fall with the impulse that is conveyed to them from out the distant deep; like sea shells that still murmur with the music they learned while yet at home in the sea.

Not only is person the only truth, it is also the only power. We have a way of saying that truth is mighty; but there is no might in truth except as in some way it is inlaid with the personal ingredient. The might of the Gospel is simply

INTRODUCTION.

another name for the personal might of Christ, who is the Gospel. It is not philosophy in the scholastic world, nor theory in the political world, nor doctrine in the religious world that have wrought effects; but men,—philosophy, theory, and doctrine held in personal solution. All of this was quite simply stated a good while ago by Schiller, when he said: "*Persönliches muss herrschen.*" What we mean will be made clear by saying that every doctrine deserving to be called such, was, in its earliest history, a bit of personal experience, a part of the life and being of the soul that gave it birth. The trouble with doctrines in their later history is generally, that the original pulse has ceased to beat in them, the life blood has dried out of them and they are no longer personal, but furniture for the herbarium or the museum. Indeed, we never call them "doctrines," or, at any rate, we never call them "dogmas," till their original personal blood is coagulated, and their remains have become archæological.

It is much the same thing to say that all progress is personal. History in its innermost genius is simply biography. You have read the history of Israel or the history of any other people when you have become personally acquainted with a dozen or a score of the men who were its successive centers of crystallization. Events do not go by show of hands. Arithmetic has very little to do with progress. Even in countries like our own where every man is supposed to count one, the ballot simply demonstrates to the public eye what has previously been personally settled by the larger thought and (let us hope) the wider plan of a few working centrally and controllingly.

Personality is also the natural pabulum upon which soul lives and thrives. The plant feeds upon antecedent vegetable; the brute upon antecedent animal; person feeds on person, first of all upon the Supreme Person, and secondly upon his human reproductions. Men live upon great souls that are and have been. Isolation is personal starvation. The power of a great soul over a smaller one is the outpouring of the Holy Spirit in miniature. We mean by that only, that its effect is baptismal, and that to that degree it pushes us along a line of ascent, awakens us out of our dreams, and actualizes our possibilities. That is the advantage of having great men and having them or their memories become the property of the people. Just as we need mountains in order to get rain, so we need mountainous souls in order that the average lowlands may obtain irrigation and cover themselves with verdure. No man can become bigger unless there is some being whom he looks up to. The greatest thing a great man can do is to stimulate the growth and encourage the stature of his contemporaries or successors.

Herein is the philosophy of all discipleship, whether it be the old Greek discipleship or the discipleship of Judea or of the later middle ages. The relation which discipleship indicates is an exceedingly earnest one, and an exceedingly prolific one, for it denotes on the one side the commitment of the higher to the lower, and, on the other, the surrender of the lower to the higher, and so insures the repletion of the lower: as Ontario drinks at the fountain of Erie, and Erie draws perennially from the upper lakes and the clouds.

PUBLISHERS' INTRODUCTION.

BOOKS that stimulate to high thinking produce, like good companionship, a noble life. For goodness is just as contagious as evil.

A noble life enriches both him who lives it, and those who come after him, who are made the better because of his example. For models are always more effective and valuable than mere rules. They teach both quicker and better. So Christ came and "left us an example that we should follow in His steps." What is true of the living man is also true of him when embodied in a book. Neither dies when he who lived the life, or wrote the book, passeth from earth. Not one of us *can* ever live or die unto himself.

Several of the authors of this volume are persons of national reputation, whose thoughts on other subjects are before the people. The others, while of lesser fame, are not unknown in their several localities. All of them have had wide observation and much experience in life, and they here offer many wise counsels as aids to the young in the forming of that finest and most important mechanism in the universe — character. They believe that there is just as much of true chivalry and heroism and devotion to the right in the world to-day, as in any past time. Neither goodness nor the love for it has yet perished from the earth. Many a young man and woman would do better than they are now doing, if they only knew how.

This book is designed to help such. While its writers cannot travel the road of life for you, and so give that *perfect* knowledge that can only be had by actual experience, yet next to that actual experience the most important thing in undertaking an unknown journey is a good guide book. Practical experience and good examples are the indispensable and only efficient aids in forming a noble character. The first each must get for himself. But it has been the aim of these writers to help you in respect to the last. We inherit money, we inherit examples, we inherit the facts of nature, but we do not inherit character, unless it be the bias toward one for good or evil. You have talents, ability, power, peculiar to yourself. Shall they bring forth a harvest of noble deeds, and so bring that highest of successes — a noble character? Character is greater than intellect, greater than gold, greater than the world.

Reading the "Lives of the Saints," made a Loyola. Reading the "Life of John Huss," made a Martin Luther. Reading the "Voyage of Capt. Cook," made a William Carey. Reading the "Life of Benjamin Franklin," made a Samuel Drew. Reading Cotton Mather's "Essay to do Good," made a Benjamin Franklin. May the reading of this volume inspire you to live worthy the opportunities the Creator has given you!

Authors of Portraits and Principles.

Rev. JOHN COTTON BROOKS, B.D.,
Rector Christ Church (Episcopal), Springfield, Mass.

(Brother of the universally beloved late Phillips Brooks.)
Graduated from Harvard in 1872, Philadelphia Divinity School in 1876. A devoted pastor.

Rev. GEO. A. HALL, D.D.,
Secretary of the Young Men's Christian Association for New York State.

Widely and favorably known for his untiring energy and great influence among young men.

JOSEPH COOK, LL.D.,
Noted Scholar, Preacher, and Lecturer, Boston, Mass.

Well known throughout the land for his vigorous thought and original style of expression.

Pres. GEO. T. WINSTON, LL.D.,
President of the University of North Carolina, Chapel Hill.

A graduate of Cornell University, 1874. A leader among the educators of the great South.

Rev. JAMES R. TRUAX, B.D., M.A.,
Professor of English Literature and Language, Union College.

Graduate of Union College in 1876, and from Drew Theological Seminary. Is a brilliant scholar and a forcible writer.

Rev. P. S. HENSON, D.D.,
Pastor First Baptist Church, Chicago.

Graduated in 1844, with the first class sent out from Richmond College; in 1855 founded Fluranna Female Institute, Va. For twenty years Editor of the *Baptist Teacher*. A brilliant leader in the denomination.

Rev. JAMES W. COLE, B.D., Northampton, Mass.

Graduated from Boston University. For many years was a leading thinker and preacher in New England. Ill health has prevented regular service for some time. His mental force and rare literary power is exemplified in the chapters he contributes to this work.

Prof. BENJAMIN IDE WHEELER, Ph.D.,
Of Cornell University, Ithaca, New York.

Graduate of Colby Academy, N. H., Brown University in 1875. Studied at Leipsic and Heidelberg, Germany. Professor in Harvard in 1885 and 1886. Called to Cornell in 1886.

Rev. CHARLES A. YOUNG, D.D.,
Of the College of New Jersey, Princeton.

Graduate of Dartmouth in 1853. In 1866 called to fill his father's vacant chair at Dartmouth, remaining eleven years. On account of scientific discoveries, has been honored with a medal from the French Academy of Science. Has become one of the leading astronomers of the world.

Rev. HENRY A. BUTTZ, D.D., LL.D.,
President Drew Theological Seminary, Madison, N. J.

Graduated from the College of New Jersey, at Princeton. Is a man of strong mental force.

Rev. A. B. HERVEY, Ph.D.,
President St. Lawrence University, Canton, New York.

A strong representative of the Universalist denomination. Widely known and possessed of great power and mental force.

Rev. B. O. AYLESWORTH, D.D., LL.D.,
President Drake University, Des Moines, Iowa.

Graduated from Eureka College. Dr. Aylesworth is an able preacher and one of the bright scholars and educational leaders in the Christian denomination

Authors of Portraits and Principles.

HOMER MERRIAM,

President of the firm of G. & C. Merriam Company, Springfield, Mass., publishers of Webster's International Dictionary.

Mr. Merriam has had a very successful business experience covering a period of half a century.

CHARLES MORTIMER GATES, M.S.,

President Creamery Package Manufacturing Company, Chicago.

Mr. Gates is a thorough business man; he organized his company, which is the largest establishment of the kind in America.

WILLIAM C. KING,

Of King, Richardson & Company, Publishers, Springfield, Mass.

This house was founded in 1878, and is among the largest and most successful publishing houses of this country. Mr. King is a self-made man, of strict integrity, keen business ability (a bank director), and known as an enterprising, successful business man. This volume is the result of his plans and execution, assisted by a large company of carefully selected men and women of broad experience and who have been successful in their various departments of life work. Is also prominent in the management of several large corporations.

Hon. J. H. BRIGHAM,

Ohio State Senator and Master of the National Grange.

Mr. Brigham is a practical farmer living at Delta, Ohio, and one of the leading men of his state. A devoted advocate of the rights of the farmer.

HENRY H. BOWMAN,

President of the Springfield National Bank, Springfield, Mass.

Mr. Bowman started in life as a bank clerk. Is now one of the leading business men of his city. Has the full confidence of the public, and is at the head of a large and successful banking house.

Hon. FREDERICK ROBIE,

President First National Bank, Portland, Me.

A practical farmer, an honored governor of his state, a successful financier, and holds the confidence of the people of his state.

Homer Merriam

Chas. M. Gates M.S.

Wm. C. King

Hon. J. H. Brigham

Hon. Frederick Robie

Henry H. Bowman

AUTHORS OF THIS WORK

AUTHORS OF THIS WORK

Rev. H. O. Breeden, Ph.D.
Rev. Samuel Plantz, Ph.D.
Geo. A. Gates, D.D., LL.D.
Prof. George S. Goodspeed, Ph.D.
B. P. Raymond, D.D.
N. L. Andrews, D.D., LL.D.
Lewis O. Brastow, D.D.
George E. Reed, D.D.
H. A. Gobin, D.D., LL.D.

AUTHORS OF THIS WORK

Mrs. Frank Leslie

Wm. DeWitt Hyde D.D.

Nellie E. Blackmer

M.W. Stryker D.D. LL.D.

Prof. E.T. Tyndall

A. Alonzo Stagg A.B.

Rev. Geo. R. Hewitt B.D.

Rev. Edward Everett Hale D.D.

Prof. J.K. Chickering A.M.

Frances E. Willard

Prof. J.N. Humphrey A.M.

Lady Henry Somersett

Authors of Portraits and Principles.

Rev. WM. De WITT HYDE, D.D.,
President Bowdoin College, Brunswick, Me.

Graduated from Harvard in 1879, and from Andover Theological Seminary in 1882, contributed to the *Forum* and other magazines. An able scholar and a man of great ability.

Mrs. FRANK LESLIE,
Proprietor and Manager of the Leslie Publishing House, New York City.

Mrs. Leslie is undoubtedly the foremost business woman of America. At the death of her husband, who had just made an assignment, she bravely took his place, and lifted a debt of $300,000, and has made a fortune besides. Her only inheritance was a tremendous debt and an opportunity.

Prof. E. T. TYNDALL,
Editorial Staff of the *Daily News* Philadelphia.

Graduated from National School of Oratory, 1887. Professor of Elocution, Drew Theological Seminary. In 1890 was given charge of the educational department of the Philadelphia *Times*.

NELLIE E. BLACKMER,
Head Stenographer with the Publishing House of King, Richardson & Co.

Was educated for a teacher. While teaching fitted herself without an instructor for her present position. A young woman of keen literary tastes and of rare business ability.

M. W. STRYKER, D.D., LL.D.,
President of Hamilton College, Clinton, New York.

Graduated from "Hamilton" in 1872 and from Auburn Seminary in 1876. Resigned his pastorate in Chicago in 1892 to accept present position. An educational leader.

Prof. A. ALONZO STAGG, B.A.,
Director of the Department of Physical Culture, Chicago University.

During college course became famous as the "great pitcher" for the Yale team. After graduation at Yale in 1888, spent two years in Yale Divinity School. In 1890 became physical director of the International Y. M. C. A. Training School, at Springfield, Mass. 1890 elected to present position. Mr. Stagg is the foremost educated all-round athlete of America.

Rev. GEO. R. HEWITT, B.D.,
An Able Scholar, Strong Preacher, and Brilliant Writer, Graduate of Harvard.

Rev. EDWARD EVERETT HALE, D.D.,
A Leading Divine, Thinker, and Writer, Boston.

The influence of Dr. Hale's voice and pen has made its impress upon both America and Europe

Prof. JOSEPH K. CHICKERING, M.A.,
Of University of Vermont, Burlington.

Graduated at Amherst College in 1869. A broad scholar and a very successful teacher.

FRANCES E. WILLARD,
President of the World's Woman's Christian Temperance Union.

Known, beloved, and honored for her incessant labor in behalf of humanity and reform.

Prof. J. NELSON HUMPHREY, M.A.,
Of the Wisconsin State Normal School, Whitewater.

Graduated at Milton College, 1879. A successful teacher, and author of a popular text book.

LADY HENRY SOMERSET of London.
President of the British Woman's Christian Temperance Union.

A woman of great refinement and culture, and devoted to the great needs of the common people.

Authors of Portraits and Principles

JAMES LANE ALLEN, A.M.,
Graduate of the Kentucky University.

Prominent literary contributor and author. Popular as a lecturer and platform orator throughout the South.

ANTHONY COMSTOCK,
Secretary of the Society for Prevention of Vice, New York.

Farmer boy, country store clerk, served in the 17th Conn. Vols. In 1867 accepted clerkship New York city. In 1872 began a vigorous campaign to suppress obscene literature, and has faithfully served the nation along this line for twenty-two years.

JOHN C. DUEBER,
President of the Hampden Watch Company, Canton, Ohio, and of the Dueber Watch Case Company, Newport, Ky.

Apprenticed as a watch case maker. Through diligence and push, backed by integrity of purpose and principle, this man has climbed the ladder of success. A self-made man.

Prof. OSCAR J. CRAIG, A.M., Ph.D.,
Professor of History and Political Economy, Purdue University, La Fayette, Ind.

Graduate of De Pauw University, 1881. Successful Institute conductor and literary contributor.

Rev. WILLARD E. WATERBURY, A.B., B.D.,
Pastor First Baptist Church, Clinton, Mass., and director of the Baptist Boys Brigade in New England.

Graduated at Syracuse University, and entered Y. M. C. A. as secretary at Concord, N. H., engaging in the ministry later. A strong preacher and popular, successful leader of young people.

Prof. GEORGE S. FOREST,
Of Ellsworth College, Iowa Falls, Iowa.

Farmer's son, educated at Cornell College, Ia. Has had a successful career as farmer, business man, and teacher.

HOMER S. FULLER, Ph.D.,
President of the Polytechnic Institute, Worcester, Mass.

Graduate of Dartmouth, 1864. Then became principal of Fredonia Academy, N. Y.; 1871 to 1880 principal of St. Johnsbury Academy, Vt.; 1880 to 1882 spent in study and travel abroad.

Prof. J. M. STIFLER, D.D.,
Prof. of New Testament Exegesis, Crosier Theological Seminary, Chester, Pa.

Graduated from college, 1866, and next from Crosier. Besides constantly preaching, has continually contributed to the religious press, prepared several books, and for many years been prominent in the preparation of the International Sunday-school lessons.

Rev. CARTER J. GREENWOOD, A.M.,
Pastor First Baptist Church, Iowa Falls, Iowa.

Educated at Homer Academy and Colgate University, New York. An able preacher and popular lecturer.

AUTHORS OF THIS WORK

- James Lane Allen A.M.
- Anthony Comstock
- John C. Deuber
- Oscar J. Craig A.M. Ph.D.
- Rev. Willard E. Waterbury B.D.
- Prof. G. S. Forest
- Homer S. Fuller Ph.D.
- Prof. J. M. Stifler D.D.
- Rev. Carter J. Greenwood A.M.

AUTHORS OF THIS WORK

- Prof. F. Smalley, Ph.D.
- Rev. W. C. Whitford, D.D.
- A. M. Haggard, A.M.
- Prof. A. S. Wright, A.M.
- Mrs. Mary A. Livermore
- Rev. Hugh Boyd, D.D.
- Mrs. Susan S. Fessenden
- Geo. F. Mosher, LL.D.
- Sec. R. M. Armstrong
- Hon. E. F. Lyford

Authors of Portraits and Principles.

Prof. FRANK SMALLEY, A.M., Ph.D.,
Professor of Latin and Literature, Syracuse University.

Educated at Northwestern University, and Syracuse University. Graduated 1874, A.B.; 1876 A.M.; 1891, Ph.D.

Rev. W. C. WHITFORD, D.D.,
President Milton College, Milton, Wis.

Graduate of Alfred University. Devoted many years to building up Milton College. Superintendent of Public Instruction in Wisconsin for four years.

A. M. HAGGARD, A.M.,
Corresponding Secretary of the Iowa Christian Convention, Ex-President of Oskaloosa College, Iowa.

Prof. A. S. WRIGHT, A.M.,
Of the Case School of Applied Science, Cleveland, Ohio.

Graduate of Union College. Studied three years in Leipsic and Paris. Called to the chair of Modern Languages, Union College, 1888.

Mrs. MARY A. LIVERMORE.

Organized the Sanitary Commission in 1862. Prominent in hospital work through the Civil War. A leader in temperance work. An able writer. Popular lecturer, favorably known throughout the land and beloved by all.

Rev. HUGH BOYD, A.M., D.D.,
Professor of Latin in Cornell College, Mt. Vernon, Ia.

Graduate of Ohio University, Athens. In 1883 elected president of Ohio University, but declined.

Mrs. SUSAN S. FESSENDEN,
President Woman's Christian Temperance Union of Massachusetts.

Graduated from seminary in 1855. Began teaching; became principal of her alma mater. An ardent worker on reform lines. A woman of high literary ability, and personal force in her home and in public life.

GEO. F. MOSHER, LL.D.,
President Hillsdale College, Hillsdale, Mich.

Graduate of Bowdoin College, Brunswick, Me., 1869. For some time editor *Morning Star*. Served two terms in New Hampshire Legislature. 1881, appointed by Garfield consul to Nice. In 1886 elected president of Hillsdale College.

R. M. ARMSTRONG,
State Secretary Y. M. C. A. for Massachusetts and Rhode Island.

Learned printers' trade. For many years employed with the *Traveler*, Boston. Six years superintendent Monument Square M. E. Sunday-school, Boston. In 1883 entered Y. M. C. A. work as secretary at New Bedford, Mass. Next at Springfield. Called to the State work in 1886.

Hon. EDWIN F. LYFORD, A.B.,
Member Massachusetts State Senate, 1894.

Graduate of Colby University, Maine, 1877. Admitted to Massachusetts bar in 1882. Member of Massachusetts House of Representatives in 1892 and 1893, and sent to the Senate in 1894.

AUTHORS OF THIS WORK

Rev. John Cotton Brooks.
Rev. Geo. A. Hall.
Geo. T. Winston, LL.D.
Joseph Cook, LL.D.
Rev. Jas. R. Truax, A.M.
Rev. P. S. Henson, D.D.
Rev. Jas. W. Coe, B.D.
Benj. Ide Wheeler, Ph.D.
C. A. Young, Ph.D., D.D.
Rev. Henry A. Butz, D.D.
Rev. A. B. Hervey, Ph.D.
Rev. B. O. Aylesworth, D.D.

LOYAL COLONISTS

Lieut. Col. Steele.

Hon. Dr. Borden.

Lieut. Col. Otter.

Capt. R. K. Barker.

Lord Strathcona.

LEADING BOERS

Gen. Piet A. Cronje.

Gen. Joubert.

Paul Krüger.

Pres. Steyn.

Gen. Sir George White V.C.
Lord Salisbury. 
Lieut. Col. R.S.S. Baden-Powell 
Cecil Rhodes 
Lieut. Gen. John D.P. French.  
Gen. Sir Redvers Buller. 
Colonial Minister Chamberlain 
Lord Kitchener 

ENGLISH LEADERS

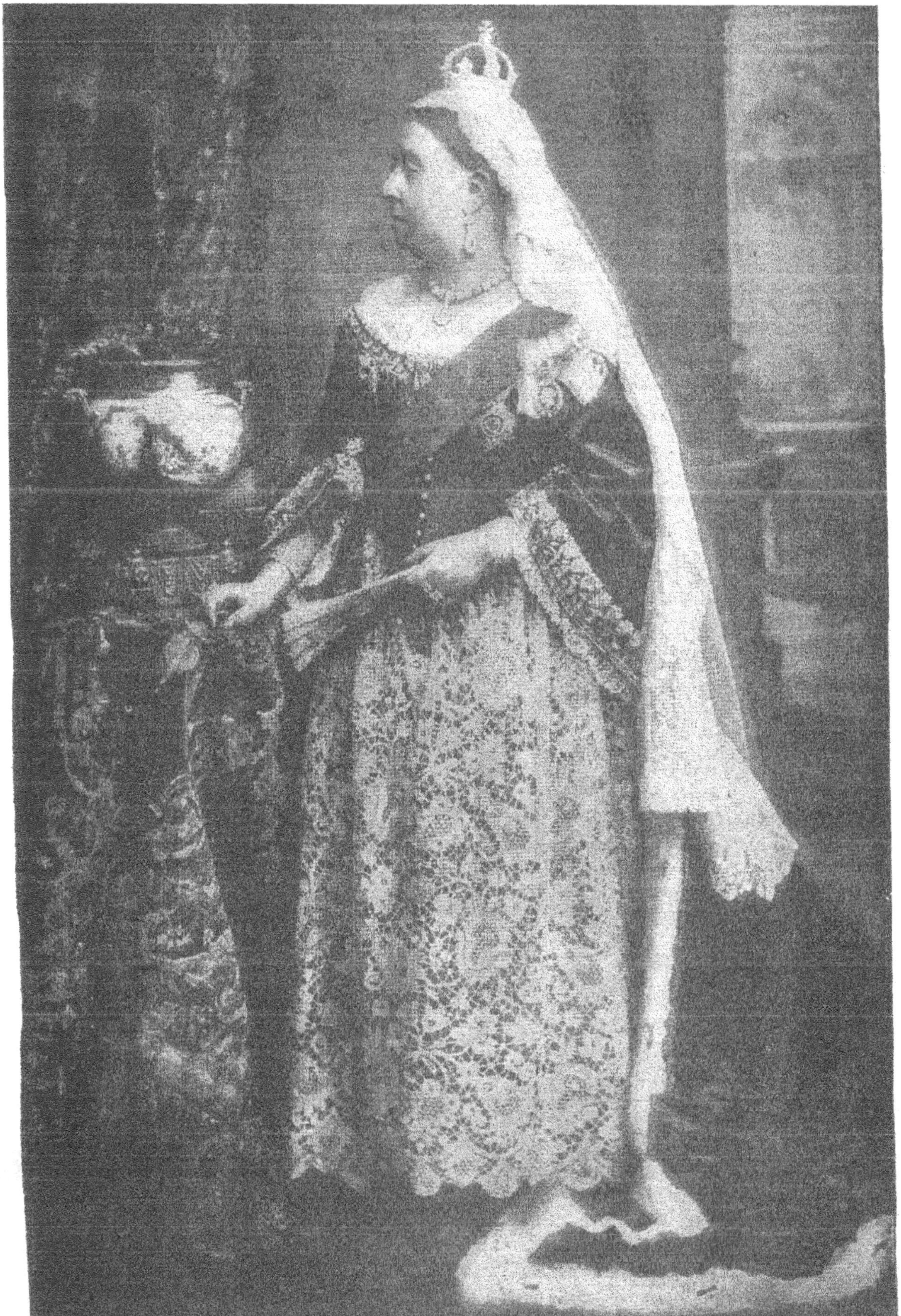

Leading Naval Officers.

Schley. Dewey. Sampson.

Vincent. Parkhurst. Bryan.

WELL KNOWN MEN

Founder Chautauqua Movement. Champion Silver Cause.

Dr. Parkhurst writes introduction to this work.

GREAT STATESMEN

Lewis Cass.

Stephen A. Douglas.

John A. Andrew.

Thomas B. Reed.

Thos. H. Benton.

John Hancock.

Patrick Henry.

George Washington.

Alexander H. Stephens.

John Winthrop.

John C. Calhoun.

Henry Clay.

24 A

GREAT STATESMEN

Charles Sumner
James G. Blaine
Edward Everett
Henry L. Dawes
Benj. Harrison
James A. Garfield
Grover Cleveland
Geo. F. Edmunds
Abraham Lincoln
Nathaniel P. Banks

24 B

GREAT STATESMEN

James Madison

James Buchanan

Millard Fillmore

Jno. Quincy Adams

Benj. Franklin

Daniel Webster

Thos. Jefferson

Martin Van Buren

James Monroe

John Adams

HONORED SOLDIERS

- John C. Fremont
- Admiral Farragut
- Gen. Custer
- O. O. Howard
- Geo. H. Thomas
- Phil. H. Sheriden
- U. S. Grant
- W. S. Hancock
- Winfield Scott
- W. T. Sherman
- Robert E. Lee

SOLDIERS

Steven Decatur. Oliver Cromwell. Phillip Schuyler.

Nathaniel Greene. Jos. Warren. John Stark.

Napoleon Bonaparte. Zachary Taylor. Geo. G. Meade. Wellington.

Geo. B. McClellan.

Winfield Scott Hancock. Gustavus Adolphus B. P. Lafayette.

24 E.

GREAT REFORMERS
Wm Lloyd Garrison.
John B. Gough.
John Howard.
Wendell Phillips.
Neal Dow.
Wm Booth
Francis Murphy.
Wilbur F. Crafts, Ph.D.
J. St. John.
Elihu Burritt.

EMINENT PREACHERS

Arch Bishop Hughs. D.D.
Chas. H. Spurgeon.
Theo Parker D.D
Henry Ward Beecher D.D.
T. Dewitt Talmage D.D.
Bishop Phillips Brooks D.D.
Richard Storrs D.D.
Wm. Ellery Channing D.D.
Lyman Abbott D.D.

PREACHERS AND WRITERS

Chas. G. Finney. John Bunyan. Cotton Mather. Roger William. Martin Luther. Savonarola. Isaac Watts. Richard Baxter. Lyman Beecher. John Wesley. John Wycliffe. Jonathan Edwards. Wm. Tyndale. Geo. Whitfield. Adoniram Judson. Charles Wesley.

MODERN PREACHERS And WRITERS
Rev. Edward Judson D.D.
Charles F. Deems D.D.
Russell H. Conwell LL.B
John Albert Broadus D.D. LL.D.
Dwight L. Moody
Wayland Hoyt D.D.
Cardinal Manning
Rev. B. Fay Mills
Robert Stuart McArthur D.D.
Rev. A. A. Miner D.D. LL.D.
Cardinal Newman
A. P. Peabody D.D.
Bishop M. Simpson

EDUCATORS

- Francis Wayland
- Maria Mitchell
- Eliphalet Nott
- Jas. Ferguson
- Horace Mann
- Andrew D. White
- Froebel
- Mary Lyon
- Pres. E. B. Andrews
- Prof. Drummond
- Pres. C. W. Eliot
- Gen'l Armstrong
- Mark Hopkins
- Wm. R. Harper

24 J

LAWYERS OF FAME

Benj. F. Butler

John G. Carlisle

Geo. F. Hoar

Henry Wilson

W. L. Wilson

John Sherman

Wm. McKinley

Wm. M. Evarts

Allen G. Thurman

Geo. D. Robinson

24 к

LAWYERS And JURISTS

Roger B. Taney

John Marshall | Franklin Pierce | John Jay

John N. Briggs | Rufus Choate | Joseph Storey

Aaron Burr | Horace Binney | Benj. R. Curtis

LAWYERS AND JURISTS

Elihu B. Washburn. Thaddeus Stevens. Sam'l J. Tilden. John M. Harlan. Chas Francis Adams. Chauncey M. Depew. Hannibal Hamlin. Sam'l S. Cox. John McClean. Schuyler Colfax. John A. Dix.

THINKERS & WRITERS

James Dwight Dana.
John Stewart Mill.
Matthew Arnold.
Sir Isaac Newton.
Prof. John Tyndall.
Louis J. R. Agassiz.
Prof. T. H. Huxley.
Thos. Carlyle.
Chas. Darwin.
Herbert Spencer.
John Ruskin.

AUTHORS & JOURNALISTS

NOTED JOURNALISTS AND WRITERS

Geo. W. Childs. Horace Greeley. Margaret Bottome.
J. G. Holland. Saml. Bowles. Geo. W. Curtis.
Whitelaw Reid. Mark Twain. Thurlow Weed.

MODERN WRITERS

- John Howard Payne
- Will Carleton
- John G. Saxe
- Elizabeth Stuart Phelps
- Maragret Deland
- Jean Ingelow
- Mrs. G. R. Alden (Pansy)
- Charles Dudley Warner
- Edwin Arnold
- James T. Fields
- Bret Harte
- James Freeman Clarke
- Edw. Bellamy
- Henry James
- T. Trowbridge
- James Parton
- Jules Verne

EMINENT HISTORIANS

Wm. H. Prescott.

John Fiske.

James Anthony Froude.

John C. Ridpath.

John L. Motley.

Geo. Bancroft.

David Hume.

Thos. Wentworth Higginson.

John Richard Greene.

Thos. B. Macaulay.

THE WORLD'S POETS

Schiller. Robt. Browning. Edgar A. Poe.
Alfred Tennyson. Shakespeare. John Keats.
Robt. Burns. Goethe. Milton.

FAMOUS NOVELISTS

Charlotte Bronte
Chas. Kingsley
George Elliot
W. D. Howells
A. S. Hardy
Wm. Makepeace Thackery
James Fenimore Cooper
Victor Hugo
Lew. Wallace
Walter Scott
Charles Dickens

24 T

AMERICA'S FAVORITES

Jas Russell Lowell.
Ralph Waldo Emerson.
Bayard Taylor.
J. G. Whittier.
Wm Cullen Bryant.
Oliver Wendell Holmes.
Nathaniel Hawthorne.
H. W. Longfellow.
Washington Irving.

24 u

TALENT AND GENIUS

- Emma Abbott Witherell
- Lawrence Barrett
- Charlotte Cushman
- Ole Bull
- Joe Jefferson
- Mary Anderson
- Edwin Booth
- Adeline Patti
- Paderewski
- P. T. Barnum
- Edwin F.

PROMINENT INVENTORS

Chas. Goodyear. John Ericson. Eli Whitney. Robert Hoe. Sam'l Colt. Richard Jordan Gatling. Gutenberg. Thomas A. Edison. Robert Fulton. S. F. B. Morse. James Watts. Elias Howe. Thaddeus Fairbanks. Cyrus W. McCormick. Geo. Stephenson.

PROMINENT MANUFACTURERS

John D. Rockefeller. Andrew Carnegie. C. C. Washburn. G. H. Corliss.

Hon. J. S. Pillsbury. D. B. Wesson. Peter Cooper. Ichabod Washburn.

Jonas Gilman Clark. Geo. M. Pullman. J. I. Case.

PROMINENT MERCHANTS

John Jacob Astor. John Hopkins. George Peabody. Wm. E. Dodge. Amos Lawrence.

Abbott Lawrence. Arthur Tappan. Jno. Wanamaker. Phillip Armour.

Marshall Field. Stephen Girard. Saml. Appleton. A. T. Stewart.

GREAT RAILROAD MEN.

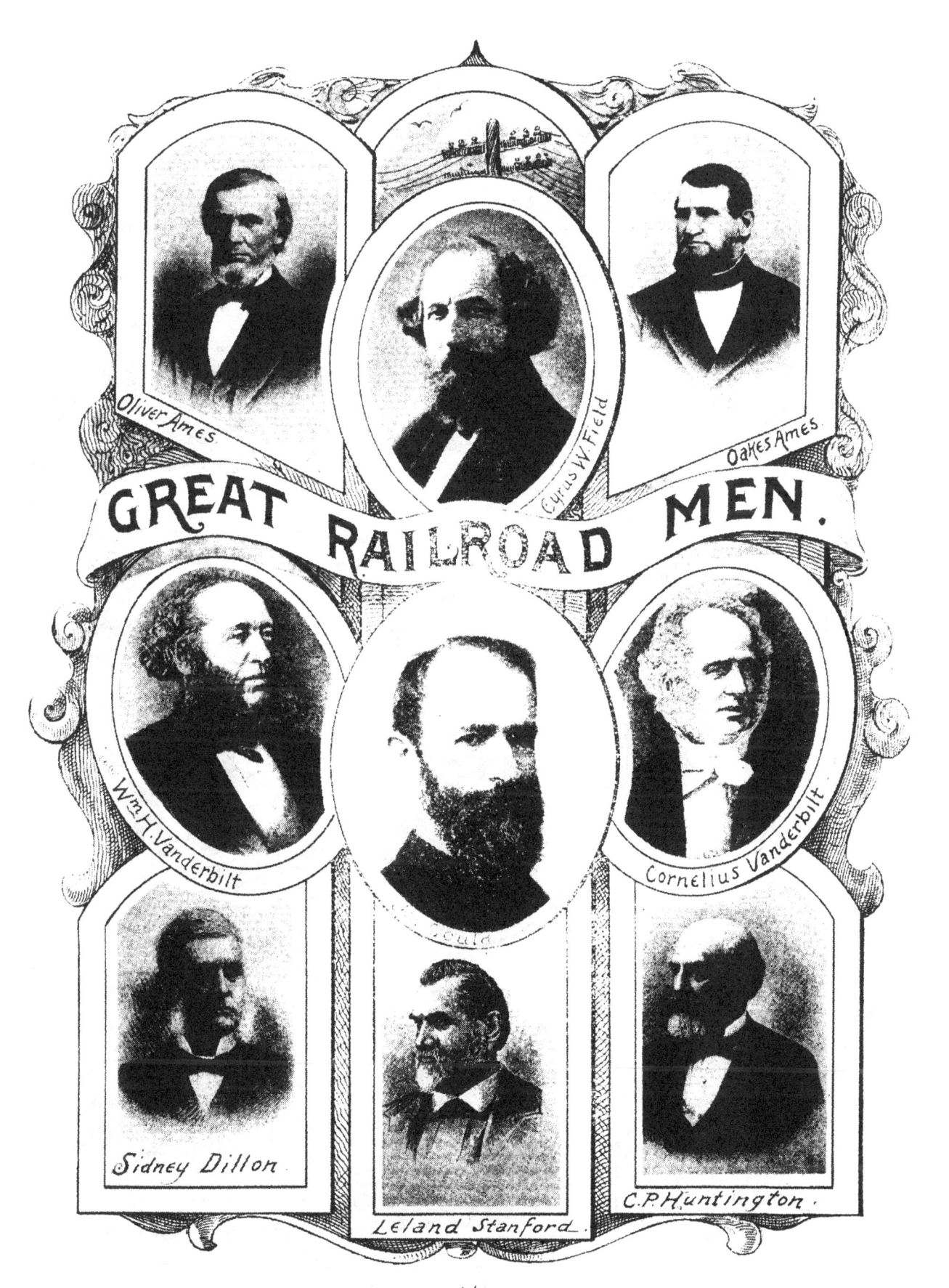

Oliver Ames. Cyrus W. Field. Oakes Ames.
Wm. H. Vanderbilt. Gould. Cornelius Vanderbilt.
Sidney Dillon. Leland Stanford. C. P. Huntington.

LEADING BANKERS

J. Pierpont Morgan. Geo. G. Williams. Lyman J. Gage.
James H. Eckles. H. W. Cannon. Alex Brown.
Henry Clews. Levi P. Morton. John Jay Knox.

SOME LEADERS OF THE NEW SOUTH

Rob't Taylor

Dr. Hunter McGuire

Gen. Fitzhugh Lee

Marion Butler

H. W. Grady

Thomas Watson

Matt Ransom

Benton McMillan

John B. Gordon

B. R. Tillman

Z. B. Vance

Gen. Wade Hampton

John W. Daniel

John T. Morgan

LEADING SOUTHERN WRITERS

Ruth McEnery Stuart

Mrs. Burton Harrison

Charles Egbert Craddock
Mary N. Murfree

Thomas Nelson Page

Joel Chandler Harris

James Lane Allen

Sam'l Minturn Peck

Sidney Lanier

Richard Malcolm Johnston

George W. Cable

FAMOUS WOMEN

- Louise Alcott
- Jenny Lind
- Susan B. Anthony
- Lucy Stone
- Christine Nilsson
- Harriet Beecher Stowe
- Mrs Potter Palmer
- Alice Freeman Palmer
- Elizabeth B. Browning
- Clara Louise Kellogg

FOREIGN STATESMEN

Lord Baltimore. Wm Pitt. Robt Peel. Francis Bacon.

Benjamin Disraeli. Sir Walter Raleigh. Wm E. Gladstone. Edmund Burke. John Bright.

Wm Wilberforce. Prince Bismark. President Carnot.

LIGHTS OF CANADA

Hon. Alexander Mackenzie.
His Excellency The Earl of Aberdeen.
Sir Charles Tupper.
Hon. Joseph Howe.
Sir Richard John Cartwright.
Sir Oliver Mowat.
Chas. G. D. Roberts, A.M. F.R.F.S. F.R.S.L.
Sir John Wm. Dawson.
Hon. Wilfrid Laurier.
Sir John A. Macdonald.
Hon. Sir John S. D. Thompson.

AUTHORS OF THIS WORK

Washington Gladden. D.D.

H. B. Hartzler. D.D.

Hon. Cyrus G. Luce.

Prof. David C. Wells. B.D.

Francis E. Clark.

George G. Wilson. PH.D.

John Bascom. D.D.LL.D.

W. H. Scott. LL.D.

Merrill E. Gates. Ph.D.LL.D.

Authors of Portraits and Principles.

Rev. WASHINGTON GLADDEN, D.D., Columbus, O.,
An Honored Pastor, Able Preacher, and Strong Writer.

Dr. Gladden's pen has brought him into close touch and sympathy with the readers on both continents.

Rev. H. B. HARTZLER, D.D.,
Director of Bible Study, Moody's Training School at Mt. Hermon and Northfield, Mass.

Strong pulpit orator, deep scholar, and fluent writer. A tower of strength and personal influence among the large company of young people who gather at these two schools, founded by the greatest evangelist of modern times.

Hon. CYRUS G. LUCE, Coldwater, Mich.,
Honored and esteemed for unswerving fidelity and personal sacrifice.

A practical farmer, served his State in the House of Representatives and the Senate, and twice elected governor. For twenty years a leading official in the grange and devoted friend of the farmer.

Prof. DAVID C. WELLS, B.A., B.D.,
Of Dartmouth College, Hanover, New Hampshire.

Graduate of Phillips Academy, Yale, and Andover Seminary. After spending some time studying in Germany, he served as instructor at Phillips Academy, Bowdoin College, and now at Dartmouth. A man of strong mental powers and a forcible writer.

Rev. FRANCIS E. CLARK, D.D.,
Founder of the Young People's Society of Christian Endeavor.

Graduated from Dartmouth in 1873. The name of this earnest, devoted Christian man is known and honored throughout the Christian world, for he set in motion an organization which has reached a membership of nearly two millions of Christian young people.

Prof. GEO. G. WILSON, Ph.D.,
Of Brown University, Providence, R. I.

Graduated at Brown, followed by study abroad. After filling several important positions was called to the chair of Political and Social Science at Brown in 1890. Professor Wilson has acquired prominence as a lecturer.

Rev. JOHN BASCOM, D.D., LL.D.,
Of Williams College, Williamstown, Mass.

Ex-President of State University of Wisconsin. For forty years a successful teacher of young men. Widely and favorably known through his able contributions to the press. A man of great influence among thinking men of America.

WILLIAM H. SCOTT, LL.D.,
President of Ohio State University, Columbus.

Educated at Ohio University, Athens; after graduating entered upon teaching. Ex-President of Ohio University. A man of broad culture and strong mental powers.

MERRILL E. GATES, LL.D., L.H.D.,
President of Amherst College, Massachusetts.

Graduated from University of Rochester, N. Y., in 1870. For eight years President of Rutgers College. In 1890 elected President of Oberlin College, and before accepting was elected President of Amherst. Dr. Gates is a man of unusual talent, tact, and force. As a practical educator of young men, probably has no superior. He is in constant demand as a lecturer, and contributes to literary journals. A leader in scientific, literary, and educational work.

Authors of Portraits and Principles.

Rev. SAMUEL PLANTZ, Ph.D.,
Pastor of The Tabernacle Methodist Church, Detroit, Mich.

College course at Milton College and Lawrence University, Wis. Completed theological course at Boston University.

Rev. HARVEY O. BREEDEN, Ph.D.,
Pastor Christian Church, Des Moines, Iowa, Editor *Christian Worker.*

Graduate of Eureka College, Eureka, Ill., 1878. A leading preacher of the Christian denomination and a popular platform orator and lecturer.

GEORGE A. GATES, D.D., LL.D.,
President of Iowa College, at Grinnell, Iowa.

Graduate of Dartmouth. Studied theology at Andover, afterwards studied abroad for some time.

Rev. GEORGE. S. GOODSPEED, Ph.D.,
Prof. of Comparative Religion and Ancient History, Chicago University.

Graduate of Brown University, 1880, of Morgan Park Theological Seminary, 1883. Post graduate course Yale University, Ph.D., 1891. For a long time editorial assistant to Dr. Harper on the *Old and New Testament Student.*

Rev. B. P. RAYMOND, D.D.,
President of Wesleyan University, Middletown, Conn.

Graduate of Lawrence University, Wis. (1870), and theological department of Boston University. Spent one year of study in Germany. Became president of Lawrence University and elected president of Wesleyan University in 1889.

Prof. N. L. ANDREWS, D.D., LL.D.,
Dean of the Faculty, Colgate University, Hamilton, N. Y.

Graduate of Colgate University, 1858, also graduated from the theological department of this institution in 1864. Spent much time in study and travel abroad. Has received the degrees of D.D., Ph.D., and LL.D.

Rev. LEWIS O. BRASTOW, D.D.,
Prof. of Practical Theology, in Yale University, New Haven, Conn.

Graduate of Bowdoin College, 1857. Studied theology at Bangor, Me. 1860 called to the pastorate South Congregational Church, St. Johnsbury, Vt. Served as chaplain of the 12th Vermont Regiment. In 1869 went abroad for study.

Rev. GEORGE EDWARD REED, D.D.,
President of Dickinson College, Carlisle, Pennsylvania.

Graduate of Wilbraham Academy, 1865, and Wesleyan University in 1869. In 1875 became pastor of the Hanson Place Church, Brooklyn, largest M. E. Church in the United States. Successful pastor, brilliant preacher, and widely known as a lecturer and platform orator.

Rev. H. A. GOBIN, D.D., LL.D.,
Dean of the School of Theology, DePauw University, Greencastle, Ind.

Graduate of the De Pauw University in 1870. In 1886 elected president of the Baker University, Baldwin, Kans.

Our Noblest Birthright.

Rev. JAMES. W. COLE, B.D.

WORK is the birthright of the human race. It is not a curse, but a benediction. It is not a mark of degradation, or of servitude, but an insignia of royalty. To work is god-like. "My Father worketh hitherto," said Christ; and all the universe bears witness to the fact. Intense, ceaseless activity is the law of life throughout all its physical and moral realms. He who would live must work. There can be no growth, or development, of body or of mind without it. When you cease to work you cease to live. Idleness breeds stagnation, whose only issue is corruption, decay, and death.

The progenitor of the human race, while yet sinless, had Heaven's sign manual, work, given him to do. Paradise was his, "to dress it and keep it." His subsequent sin and expulsion from Eden made no change in this fundamental law of his life. Thereafter, to him and his, work was different and harder and more profitless, but it was not a new thing to him; much less was it, as so often supposed, the result of sin.

All worlds are workshops. This of ours is no exception. Heaven is to garner at last the best productions of earth for its great universal exposition. "They shall bring the glory and the honor of the nations into it." But it is only "the glory and the honor" work that goes on exhibit there.

Are you and I now doing anything that "they" will think worthy of preservation? It is terrible to *do* nothing worthy; to *live* for nothing worthy; to *be* nothing worthy.

Endowed as we are with such godlike powers in embryo, and placed in a world that is fitted to develop the best that is in us to the highest point possible for us to attain in our present stage of being, what a shame it is to make one's life only a bitterness and a curse. Alas! how many are doing that! To prevent this worse than waste of existence, to help to nobler living here, to aid in the preparation for grander work in more glorious worlds,—is the purpose of this present volume. In it will be found words of wisdom from those who have attained, each in his own way and place, somewhat of success in this world.

They who now speak to you from these pages are soon to pass to the life beyond the scenes of time. Some of you must occupy their present places, must do their work; must, in your turn, help others as they now seek to help you.

Listen to their counsel and kindly words of advice. It may save you much of heartache and, perchance, despair hereafter. You too would succeed. It is not natural to wish to be a wreck, to be counted as "thorns" or "chaff." So it is safe to assume that you wish to make the life God has given you a blessing to yourself and to others. It is well, then, at the beginning of your career, to remember that there is no teacher like experience, nor any lessons so impressive and so costly as hers.

Very many, indeed, will learn at no other school, and all of us have, at some time, to take more or less lessons there. Yet it is neither wise nor safe to trust wholly to what you may learn of her, for you will find that the knowledge there gained, however valuable, often comes too late to be of benefit to you in this life, and serves only to remind you of your previous folly. Be willing, therefore, to learn from others.

Example is a better, more kindly, and less expensive instructor than experience, and the many life lessons here furnished will, if rightly learned, aid you in your effort to make noble use of the talents intrusted to your keeping. Whatever your position in life is, be assured, first of all, that all honest work, whether of hand or brain, is noble. It is the worker who dignifies the task, and not the task that ennobles the worker.

Christ, at the lowly carpenter's bench, was grander far than he who swayed Cæsar's scepter. If he had then aspired to sit on Cæsar's throne, he could not have been the Christ, for the only road from earth to heavenly glory lies through the valley of humiliation. Be not, therefore, ashamed either of your lowly surroundings, or of your humble and hard work. Are you poor and unknown? This certainly can be no barrier to your acquiring both wealth and honor. Rather, it should be an added incentive. For being now at the bottom there can be no fear of further falling, and the only direction is *upward*.

Unless one is low, it is impossible to ascend, and the higher one climbs, the more the glory, and the greater the strength of the climber. "Time and I against any other two," cried a heathen philosopher. You should have equal courage, for there is no stint of time in God's great universe. All the coming ages are yours. Resolve, then, to make something noble of yourself; to do something worth the doing. It will require hard work. But few persons have to struggle for success as did that world renowned missionary and explorer, Livingstone.

His parents were in such straitened circumstances that when he was but ten years of age he was put to work in a cotton factory as a "piecer," in order to eke out the family living. But the lad was hungry for knowledge, and with part of his first week's scant wages bought a small Latin grammar, and began to rise! He was required to be in the factory at work by six o'clock in the morning, and must work until eight o'clock at night, with but a brief interlude for breakfast and dinner. But undaunted he toiled on, hurrying at the close of his long day to an evening school, and then home to pore over his dictionary until midnight or later, or until, as he quaintly tells us, his mother would snatch away the candle from him in order to get him to bed.

In his brief account of his efforts to obtain an education, he says: "I never received a farthing of aid from anyone. My reading while at work was carried on by placing the book on a portion of the spinning-jenny so that I could catch sentence after sentence as I passed at my work; I thus kept up a pretty constant study, undisturbed by the roar of the machinery."

OUR NOBLEST BIRTHRIGHT.

For a dozen years he thus toiled, reading, he says, "everything I could lay my hands on, except novels."

He became proficient in the classics. He devoured all the books of science and of travel he could get. He studied practically geology and botany, roaming for miles in search of specimens. Becoming a Christian, he then resolved on being a missionary. When nineteen years of age, he was promoted to "cotton spinning," a kind of toil, he adds, that "was excessively severe on a slim, loose jointed lad; but it was well paid for, and it enabled me to support myself while attending medical and Greek classes in Glasgow in winter, as also the divinity lectures of Dr. Wardlaw, by working with my hands in summer."

The record of his life and labors as a missionary and explorer in Africa is a household tale. The story of how half the hearts of the world were moved to learn of his fate, the sending of the Stanley expedition to find him, and the opening up of Africa to civilization, as a result, form the now familiar romance of the nineteenth century. It was hard, persistent work that made David Livingstone famous. Concerning it, he said, "Looking back now on that life of toil, I cannot but feel thankful that it formed such a material part of my early education, and, were it possible, I should like to begin life over again in the same lowly style, and to pass through the same hardy training." That is the kind of spirit that makes heroes. Do not, then, shrink from *your* work, nor despair because of your lowly surroundings. Sterile soil, fierce storms, and rough winds develop the strong, toughened fiber of the oak.

God designed us for noble purposes, and put us in this trial-world to develop the best that is in us by giving each a work to do. Do not disappoint him and shame yourself by asking for easier tasks, but do the work now at your hand and do it well. Thus, step by step, you will be led up to nobler tasks and greater usefulness, with a name worthy of rank among the immortals.

Meaning of Success.

CHARLES MORTIMER GATES, M.S.,
President of the Creamery Package Manufacturing Co., Chicago.

IN these days of struggle and toil, of success and failure, in the midst of competition and strife, it is well for young men to pause at the threshold of their calling and ask "What is the meaning of success in life?" Yea, and far more important, indeed, is it for the man well started on life's mission, surrounded with all the temptations of business life and the immeasurable power of money and all its entangling forces, to ask frequently, "What is true success?" Shall these questions be answered according to the usual standard of the world, "Seek wealth and amass a large fortune, and you will never be lacking for friends and enjoyment," or shall they rather be answered from a higher and broader standard, which has its foundation in righteousness and its end and purpose in the well-being of man and his eternal welfare? Shall we enter and pursue life's mission for an altogether selfish purpose, which seeks to acquire all things by any means which may accomplish the end, or shall our dealings with men be tempered with justice and kindness, with some regard to what is right and fair, man with man? Shall our lives be measured altogether by the *dollars* we have gained or by the general *good* we have done in the world? Having been blessed with the good things of life, shall we appropriate them all unto self and its belittling ends, or shall we generously and wisely appropriate a portion at least to the needs and benefits of the thousands less prospered than ourselves? Shall not our lives be centered in a greater and a more far reaching end than self aggrandizement? Aye. Shall we not live that we may bless; gain that we may give; love that we may benefit mankind?

Who is not fond of life's stories when we think of the countless numbers of them that have been told, as well as the vast numbers unworthy to be mentioned since the advent of man? All history is but a story of human life. But what of the forty or more trillions of human beings that history has never deigned to mention, and whose names and life records have long since passed from the annals of time, their memorials having perished with themselves? Yet none would say that any of these vast numbers of human beings have lived in vain, but rather to no great end or purpose. 'Tis but the few names out of all those countless millions that have lived in the memory till our time. Not less than an hundred millions of men and women have lived and died in the United States since the discovery of America, yet out of this vast number the experts who compiled that extensive and most valuable "Encyclopedia of American Biography" could find, after a most careful and exhaustive research, but fifteen thousand one hundred and forty-two names among them all, and that, too, after taking in those now living who were, by inheritance or ancestral prestige, considered worthy of being so much as mentioned. Shall you and I be enrolled among the *few* or the *many?* If among the few, shall it be because of noble achievements, righteous deeds, and honorable acquirements, where the merits of our own worthiness make pre-eminence, or shall we be swallowed up in that innumerable horde of common oblivion?

'Tis a pitiful comment on human vanity and weakness that so few are found worthy to be mentioned, and that out of that number so few attain eminence through their own personal efforts, but shine from some borrowed light of inheritance. Some most noble names, indeed, are in the galaxy, names destined to glow with increasing brightness as the ages move on, names that the world will not willingly let die. But of others it can only be said that they serve as beacons to warn us, rather than as models by which we can build.

THE MEANING OF SUCCESS.

The Roman historian, Tacitus, that learned story-teller, says "The principal office of history, I take to be this: to prevent virtuous actions from being forgotten, and that evil words and deeds should fear an infamous reputation with posterity." He is right. Woe unto him who seeks eminence by dishonorable means. The success gained by evil doing forever endangers him who thus attains it.

There were tens of thousands of noble men in Rome in the days of Nero and Borgia; men who went unrecorded to their graves, while the names of those two persons stand out through the centuries livid with their owners' infamy. Better, a thousand times better, the waters of a Lethe, than such an immortality of shame.

What does success mean? To many, perhaps to most, it means the gathering of much of gold, of stocks, of lands. America has a multitude of such successful men. A half century ago there were but two millionaires in the United States. Now, New York alone has more than three thousand such persons. Thrice that number are said to be in this country,—some of whom reckon their wealth by scores of millions, while there are whole brigades, and even great armies of men in this fair land of plenty, who count their gold by the hundreds of thousands of dollars. Nearly all of them began life in poverty, and, reckoned by a commercial standard, they have been eminently successful men. Very many of them are noble specimens of Christian manhood, and are bravely carrying on the world's philanthropies, and in its *best* sense *are* successful men. Yet the experience of ages has demonstrated that it is never wise to take the mere accumulation of wealth as the standard of true success in life.

There are very many other things, much more valuable than riches, for which men ought to strive. The getting of great estates, the eager grasping after money, may ruin him who gets it. It is infinitely better to die poor than to get riches by any unjust means, however popular such means may be. For individuals who, like those of many empires of the past, gain wealth by despoiling others, like them, will sooner or later sink beneath the weight of their spoils.

He who gets riches as spoil taken from others, rather than as the product of his own honest efforts and skill, must always develop the baser elements of his nature, at the expense of his better and nobler faculties. And in such case his wealth is woefully expensive to him. What a curse money becomes to its owner, when it causes him to sacrifice all honor, all gratitude, all friendship, and love! In the sight of heaven, what consummate folly it is to seek to perpetuate a name by building up glittering piles of gold in a world of much ignorance, vice, and suffering, without ever lifting a hand to help, or giving a dollar to relieve earth's wretchedness. Do not understand me as decrying wealth. Not so! It is not in itself an evil but a good. It can only become an evil when its possessor hoards it, to his own and others' hurt. Wrong use will make of everything an evil.

The vices popularly ascribed to riches are due, not to wealth itself, but to the uses to which it is placed, and to the character and habits of those who acquire and possess it, or to the mode of its acquisition. He who makes his wealth a blessing to his fellow men can never have too much of it, while he who would use it solely for his own self-aggrandizement dwarfs his manhood and degrades the purpose for which he was created.

Experience has amply shown that the ambition to be enormously wealthy is as dangerous as the ambition to rule an empire. Both involve great temptations and tremendous responsibility to God and man. Either may be acquired by determination and long perseverance, but woe unto them who do not seek or use either end aright. He who has received the most of the products of his fellow men's toil is their greatest debtor. Happily, in this country, the man of many millions frequently carries on vast business enterprises, thereby giving employment to many men, and in this way becomes, to a greater or less extent, a benefactor. Men are always in need of work, and the great enterprises of the world supply it. Nevertheless, the man of millions needs to remember that his millions are not wholly his own. They are not, they cannot be, the product of his own toil. Life is far too short for him to have earned them unaided. Others have labored, and he has entered into their labors. He is their debtor and will ever be. Let no one be startled at this statement. It is easily proved.

Think a moment. The average wages of the toilers in civilized lands is not fifteen cents per day, and even in our own fair country it is not quite a dollar per day, and he who can earn ten dollars a day is a very great exception. Yet, if Adam had lived to this hour, and had earned ten dollars a day, and had worked every day, including Sabbaths, for all of the past six thousand years, and had never spent so much as a farthing of his earnings, either for himself or his family, or for his friends, he would as yet have earned but a quarter of Jay Gould's millions! But this man, and others like him, are said to have earned their scores of millions within a score of years. Preposterous! It can never be honestly done. Why, if you were to toil for fifty years, working every day, Sundays and all, for five dollars per day, a very good wage, and never spent a cent of it for rent, household or personal expenses, or charity, but saved it all, you would earn in those fifty years but ninety-one thousand two hundred and fifty dollars. Again, how long do you suppose it would take you to earn Jay Gould's eighty millions, if you were to work for two dollars a day without ever taking a rest on Sabbaths or holidays, and could save every penny of all your earnings? Just one hundred and nine thousand five hundred and eighty-nine years!

Whence, then, come such immense fortunes in so short a time to such men? Ah, largely from the pockets of other men. Listen now. Many a widow's and orphan's inheritance, and many a toiler's hard earned money, have been swallowed up in those depreciated stocks, estates, and bonds, the possession of which by these unprincipled men have given them such great riches. Verily, such are indeed humanity's debtors, for the inheritance and toil of others have enriched them.

THE MEANING OF SUCCESS.

He who was called the richest man in the United States recently died, leaving a stupendous fortune, aggregating, it is said, more than fourscore millions, and all accumulated within the brief space of forty years. For he died at fifty-six, and when he was fourteen years of age he sat by the wayside a penniless lad, weeping for lack of a dinner. As boy and man he was a model of industry and thrift. When a lad of thirteen he had invested the first half dollar he could call his own, in a book to fit him for a wished-for course in a village academy; and, entering the academy, he then worked for a blacksmith outside of school hours to pay for his board, often rising at four o'clock in the morning, and studying until time for his tasks at the shop to begin, in order that he might keep up with his studies. His academic career was soon cut short by his pressing poverty, and then he worked hard by day, and afterward studied hard by night, to fit himself for a surveyor.

When fifteen he began to run out village lots and township lines, and to make and sell maps of the surrounding territory. At seventeen he started to build, as a partner, a tannery, and a new town, and two years later he branched out as a local broker, then as a railroad speculator and owner of a line of railroad, buying the road at ten cents on a dollar. When twenty-two he sold out his interest in the town and bank for $80,000 and removed to New York, and was thereafter known throughout the land as a successful stockbroker, and railroad speculator, and, at length, the wizard of Wall street, and owner and operator of vast lines of railways that extended even from the Atlantic to the Pacific.

As a man, he was pure in his outer life, and temperate in his habits, using neither liquors nor tobacco; and in his family life, he is said to "have always been a model of purity and kindly affection." He has been often quoted and will yet be held up as an example of an eminently successful man. And yet truth demands that it should be said of him that he never earned the millions he called his own, nor were they justly gotten. To depreciate the investments of others, forcing them to sell at a great sacrifice; to enhance the price of gold at the expense of one's country and its starving poor, in order that one may be enriched thereby; to manipulate "corners" and "deals" in the market so as to squeeze out the money from others' purses into your own, may be considered legitimate among men, and be an evidence of one's great ability as a shrewd, sharp, brilliant financier, but such gold fearfully burdens its possessor at the gates of death, where all must pass.

Alas! when this particular man departed from the earth, he left all those millions simply to perpetuate his family name; while his soul entered the eternal realm, leaving no beneficent record to endear his memory to the affections of the world. Jay Gould succeeded in accumulating great wealth, but he did it at the expense of justice to others, and a dishonor to himself. His life was a colossal failure, judged from the standpoint of righteousness, and unworthy of emulation. Are you seeking the highest ambition and true success? Then note carefully these pages, and you will discern clearly the outline and principles of a real successful life. Let your aim be not riches as an end, nor pleasure and ease, for these are but the results of honest industry and application. Let your real purpose be exalted into the realm of righteousness and your goal the kingdom of heaven. To serve God and benefit mankind was the purpose and example of the Christ, which no man has yet exceeded.

The Mainspring of Success.

Hon. FREDERICK ROBIE.
President First National Bank, Portland, Me.

THE supreme agency for gaining success in any calling is the mind. It is sometimes said, and more often thought, that the greatest cause of success is labor — meaning energy of body, strength of muscle. It is often stated that muscular labor produces the wealth of the world. This is a great mistake. Intellect is mightier, and of more importance to success and the highest degree of happiness, than manual labor. Indeed, mere muscular energy does but a very small part of the world's work to-day. It is by no means the greatest or the most efficient agent in the production of wealth, or in gaining success in any worthy calling. The product of a few brains is now doing by far the richest, largest, and most important part of the world's work of this nineteenth century. What wonderful machinery for using the mighty unseen forces of nature the brains of a few men have produced!

We have in this country sixty-five millions of people. Yet in the United States, machinery, the product of brains, is doing an amount of work, day by day, that would require the utmost exertion of the muscles of more than a thousand millions of men to perform. Skill and power are not of the nerve, but of the mind. He, therefore, who teaches a man how to handle a tool effectively, or who produces a labor saving machine, is as much a producer of the world's food and wealth as he who uses them. Indeed, he is much more a benefactor to his fellows than he can be who simply employs his muscle in the production of food and wealth. A teacher, therefore, is, in the highest sense, as much a producer of the world's wealth and food supply as is the mechanic or the farmer. Nay, he is often much more so. He who taught James Watt the principles of mechanics that led him to that memorable walk around Glasgow green to evolve the "separate condensor," did more to enrich the world than any ten million laborers that ever lived. Now, just as a man may have great strength of body, yet do nothing worthy of it, so a man may have in him great mental sources of wealth, yet be very poor because he does not develop them. He may be richly endowed for the most eminent success, yet be a failure. The exhaustless well is in him, but he does not draw from it for his own and others' benefit.

It is a fact that every step of progress that has been taken since the world stood, has first been taken by some one man, or, at the most, some few men who were distinguished above their fellows by a superior energy, or foresight, or inventive faculty. Look over the chief events of history. Who caused them? Men of energy. Who were the actors in them? Individuals of energy, never the great masses of men. Who stand on the mountain heights as men of foresight or invention? Individuals, not the masses. Who climb the mountains? Only a few men of energy. The laggards are at the foot.

What is energy? Power in action. When not in action, power is not energy. Who talks of the energy of the stagnant water? But we do of steam; that is only the water in action. Have you inherent power? They who have it are sometimes, but not always, conscious of it. Often it needs the repression of poverty and the fires of adversity to develop it. Is that your condition? Then get up steam and use your power. Aspire after great ideals; great things; great men, of whom the world has not a few. Do not be content to be commonplace. Strike out for something worthy. The general level of humanity is yet very low indeed, even in our civilized lands. Determine to rise, and so elevate others. You can do it. Don't be discouraged by a sneer or a laugh. Commonplace folk too often seem to have a common interest in wishing all to be commonplace like themselves. But if humanity were reduced to a common level, either commercially, socially, intellectually, morally, or physically, what a world it would be! There is abundant work for you. Resolve to rise, therefore. Do not stay where you are. Reach out and up. If you would elevate others, climb to the heights yourself. Some one will be at the head and lead the van; why not you?

That keen intellectual scold, Carlyle, was wont to speak of the masses as the "plurality of blockheads." Whether it is an apt designation or not, you can perhaps tell; but, if you would reach success, you must give heed to Nature's laws, and use your brains and moral sense vigorously. Thrift and unthrift are not equal powers, nor will they ever be. One or the other rules you, and will ever rule you.

Whatever men of science may say as to action and reaction being equal in the physical universe, yet it is a fact that in the higher realms of the intellectual and the moral, Nature abhors an equilibrium and gives her chief honors to those who seek the heights. Success is not a matter of luck. Nature's laws cannot be neglected, nor defied with impunity. The laws which govern the production of wealth, or insure success in all worthy callings, are in the most absolute sense her laws, and the will of man can only be their servant and never their master. Do not for one moment imagine that because you may take no heed of Nature's laws in the conduct of your business, or in the government of your life, that therefore Nature will take no heed of you. Nature is never neglectful, lax, nor lazy; and she invariably demands interest on all her deposits. If she has given you power for success, you must use it, or forfeit it. It is her decree that power unused shall be dissipated. The heat and the steam that would drive an engine soon part with all their force if we do not use them. There is no mystery about success. Nature gives it to him who *wills*. The road to it is open to all who will take the journey, but, alas! that road is never crowded. There are tens of thousands to whom nature has given much of intelligence, very much of opportunity for success, but who, to the grief of their friends, never succeed because they neglect or refuse to put forth sufficient effort to gain the prize. Again and again you may see such men ignominiously distanced in the race by those who have but a fraction of their ability. Why? Because they do not "stir up the gift that is in them."

Look at what a single man of energy may do. In the archives in the Atheneum at Hartford, Connecticut, there is carefully preserved a small strip of poor paper that has a most wonderful interest for the thoughtful. To a casual observer it is nothing but a simple telegram sent to Baltimore from the Supreme Court Chamber at Washington, D. C., on May 24, 1844, by the daughter of the then Commissioner of Patents. In telegraphic symbols, it reads, "What hath God wrought?" It is but a bit of paper, yet it represents a marvelous story of many disappointments, of toil, privation, poverty, suffering, and a final triumph that revolutionized the business world; that multiplied immensely its stores of wealth, and brought the triumph of righteousness a thousand years nearer to us. That little paper is the first public message ever sent over the electric telegraph in the United States, by its inventor, Samuel F. B. Morse.

There were hundreds who listened to those lectures on electricity given by Prof. J. F. Dana before the New York Atheneum in the winter of 1826, but they were apparently and practically lost on all but one of his audience, the son of a clergyman, and a recent graduate of Yale, who was then earning a living and gaining some notice by painting portraits. The effect of that lecture upon him was to awaken a great interest in Franklin's discovery, to crowd out his love of art, and to set him about those long continued experiments that resulted in giving to the world its present system of telegraphy. It is not needful here to recount fully his twelve years of struggle, first to perfect and then to introduce his invention; of the scorn of his fellow men, who considered it a useless toy, and him a deluded, weak-brained enthusiast; of his fruitless journey to Europe to interest the stranger in it; of his return, when he wrote, "I am

THE MAINSPRING OF SUCCESS.

without a farthing in my pocket, and have to borrow even for my meals, and, even worse than this, I have incurred a debt for rents"; of his having to go twenty-four hours at a time without food, because of his great poverty; of his efforts to prevent the theft of his invention; of his oft-repeated and oft-denied prayer to Congress for aid to practically apply for public use his discovery on a larger scale than he could then do; of the grant, in jest, in the closing moment of the 27th Congress of an appropriation of $30,000, given largely to stop his begging; of the almost failure, and then the splendid triumph, to the utter confusion of the doubters; of the vexatious lawsuits by jealous rivals; of the public acknowledgment of his right to the invention; of the homeless father gathering once more under his own roof his motherless and scattered children; and then the nations of the world showering their gifts of medals, decorations, orders of knighthood, and purses of gold upon the shrinking, modest man, so long despised and rejected, who had annihilated space on earth for them, and made the antipodes to be their neighbors, and the secret of whose world-wide fame was his unconquerable energy that would not brook a defeat, much less despair of final success.

It is the example of such men, who, in spite of the mocking crowd, persist in yoking the forces of heaven to do earth's work, and tell her story, that should stir up the latent energies of your soul to a determination to win success, position, and honor, which lie within your grasp, and can be had by every one who is willing to pay the price.

Success Wrought from the Chaos of Failure.

Prof. GEORGE S. FOREST, Ellsworth College, Iowa Falls, Iowa.

GENUINE success is not a sudden outburst of what men call genius, but rather the result of continual, patient, common-place toil. The history of how success is missed often proves as instructive as the history of how it is won; and he who is found willing to learn from the experience of others will evade much hard toil, loss of time, and, perchance, escape a deal of trouble, sorrow, and regret. It seems very strange that so many young people are unwilling to profit by the experience of their elders. Though an inevitable result is found to attend a certain course of conduct, yet but few of them seem to care. There are multitudes who apparently prefer to learn by their own experience of disaster what they might have known without its sorrow and cost.

How often we see men of ripe experience nailing guide-boards of warning along the pathway of coming travelers! Yet the great masses of young people rush along with scarcely a glance at the multitude of danger signals waving from every point of contact in our daily experiences.

How much better, wiser, and richer we ought to be than our predecessors, for we have the multiplied experiences, accumulations, and inheritances of unnumbered examples before us. On every hand are brilliant examples of needless failure, and it is our privilege to heed the warning and steer our little craft clear of the shoals and breakers which have wrecked so many lives.

Why is it? When Euclid was explaining to Ptolemy Soter, king of Egypt, the principles of geometry, his patron inquired whether the knowledge could not be obtained easier. "Sir," said Euclid, "there is no royal road to learning." That statement is as true to-day as it was twenty-two centuries ago. There is no royal road to either wisdom or success in business. The path to them is not for kings alone. It is open to you and to me. You may win them, but to win requires a struggle, perhaps many a defeat. It is well it is so, for a victory is often harder to manage than a defeat, as many a noted commander has found.

If success were suddenly to come to you, it might find you wholly unprepared for it. The discipline gained, the habits required, in amassing a fortune, for instance, ought to fit him who has it both to value it properly and to use it rightly; while often experience has shown that the sudden acquisition of wealth utterly ruined its possessor, and what is true of wealth, is equally true of other things. So, then, if you fail in your efforts for success once, or twice, or many times, it is by no means a disgrace, and certainly is no cause for discouragement. But if you know the cause of your failure, and can remedy it, or avoid it, then it is a shame if you do not succeed.

When Franklin Pierce was a student at Bowdoin College, he neglected his studies, giving much of his time to athletics and military exercise, with the result that at the end of two years he stood at the foot of his class. Then, stung by shame, he resolved to redeem himself, and for the next two years applied himself constantly to his studies, so that he was able to graduate the third in a class which included such men as H. W. Longfellow, John P. Hale, and others of great fame. After his graduation, and after studying law for some time with somewhat of his old spirit of negligence, he attempted to address a jury for the first time, and broke down completely, making an absurd failure of it. But he knew the cause, and, when a friend attempted to condole with him over the episode, he replied, "I will try nine hundred and ninety-nine cases if clients continue to trust me, and, if I fail just as I have done to-day, I will try the thousandth one. I shall live to argue cases in this court house

(Amherst, N. H.) in a manner that will mortify neither myself nor my friends." And he did, for he became in a few years one of the most eminent lawyers of his state, and, at length, the President of the United States.

While circumstances do not always make the man (very many persons rising superior to and overcoming the most repressive environments), yet they have much to do with many in determining what the world calls their success. Many a one is counted as a failure, who, under different conditions, would be reckoned a brilliant success. General Grant plodded along, first an unsuccessful farmer, then tanner, then storekeeper, until the breaking out of the late civil war made him a great commander. At its beginning, so distrustful was he of himself that he doubted whether he had ability to command a regiment, but thought he might take charge of a company. The stress and circumstances of that dreadful war developed him. True, he had great natural abilities, but they were dormant, unsuspected even by himself, and it needed certain conditions to make a General Grant. There may be in you powers that can never be used save under the stress of mighty exigencies; and the defeats you now experience in your plans, the constant failure of your efforts, may be but the needed preparation for your final triumph. If there are an hundred steps to your ladder to success, and you have not reached it in traveling ninety-nine of them, do not conclude that the journey is a failure. All the other steps will be failures unless you take this last one. Press on and up. The prizes of life are generally at or near the end of the journey, not at its beginning, and not to go on is to miss them. Be valiant. Fear never gained a triumph. To cherish it is to lose your self-respect and the regard of the good. The most untoward circumstances, the most difficult obstacles, will yield to industry, intelligence, and courage. What seems a barrier to one's progress often proves to be but a new starting point, and may be so to you. Success belongs to him who dares win it; to him who knows that no defeat can be final, save the defeat of wrong.

Selecting an Occupation.

Rev. JAMES W. COLE, B.D.

HE who starts upon a journey should have a definite idea as to his destination, otherwise, he wanders about aimlessly like a vessel upon the great ocean, without chart or compass, or even a pilot, driven before every wind, and wrecked at last upon the shores of some unknown, barren country. Alas! and how many persons finally discover that life has been spent in vain, their energies and strength have been exhausted for naught; that the tree of life, which should have been laden with fruit, is barren, containing nothing but leaves.

Life is a journey, and he who would succeed should carefully consider its aim and end. Life is also a growth, and it should be developed along natural and noble lines. Every man endowed with the faculties and intelligence accorded to the great mass of people of this country ought to make his life a success, especially in the present enlightened generation, and in this, the best and greatest country of all civilized nations. It would seem that the only real excuse for failure must be either lack of intelligence or pure laziness.

Success is sure to crown the life of any person who possesses an average intellect, a high ideal, a disposition to work, who is ready to sacrifice if necessary and endure without flinching, and is willing to bear needful trials. And yet how few succeed. The world has ever been sharply divided into two classes,— the few who succeed, and the many who fail.

Why is it that so many fail while the opportunities are so great and the possibilities so vast? The answer is obvious. Men are not willing to pay the price of success, they turn a

SELECTING AN OCCUPATION.

deaf ear to the warnings of others; they ignore the lessons of experience, and, with eyes wide open, head their course straight for the rocks where thousands have gone down. Failure is the result of disregarding natural law.

Nature is not run on theory, or guess work, but is in accordance with unvariable facts. When our lives are molded in harmony with natural law, success is certain. Nature does not exist in vain. The universe is not a stupendous blunder. Some time, somewhere, God gives to every one a chance to win and wear a crown of victory.

One of the important facts of nature to be considered just here in this volume is that men are made to differ greatly in their natural endowments, in their fitness and aptness for particular pursuits, and, to a lesser degree, in their natural desires. We do not all desire the same things, nor all wish to do the same kind of work. Thus nature secures a variety of laborers for her various fields of toil.

In order, then, to succeed in life, one should early take an account of his stock in hand. For what is he naturally fitted? By this is not meant simply what one desires to do, but what can he do? For what has he an aptitude? Wishes, longings, impulses, however good, are not always the indications of genius, nor are they invariably a forecast of an adaptation for a special pursuit in life. If mere wishes could make men great, or rich, there would not be a poor or an insignificant person on earth. While, therefore, it is always advisable to aspire after the higher, one should not undertake what to him is impossible, nor should he fret out his days aping after the so-called great ones of the earth. Be yourself. You have your own special place and work. Find it, fill it. Do your work well. The world is in need of faithful, loyal workers. If your position is humble and lowly, strive for a higher plane. Larger positions await you as soon as you are prepared to fill them.

Lofty places and great deeds require great courage and great men. If you aspire after such places, make yourself worthy of them. It is always possible for one to lead an honest, noble, useful life, and that is success, and is as much within the reach of the humblest toiler as it is of the king on his throne.

Neither high office nor great wealth create virtue (though, alas, they often destroy it), and when we come to the end of life's narrow lane, virtue constitutes the only monument which will not crumble with our departure. We should early in life select some honest occupation, one that will help develop the nobler faculties of our being,—any occupation that is virtuous is honorable, however humble it may be. On the other hand, a business, whatever of eminence it may bring, or whatever remuneration it may offer, if it can be carried on only at the expense of one's better nature, can never be other than infamous.

Occasionally, early in life, a strong bias of mind toward some particular pursuit is manifested. It is nature's indication of a calling, and should be followed. Some notable instances are on record. The Rev. Isaac Watts, D. D., father of our modern hymnology, whose verses are sung in all lands where the gospel is known, and will be sung down to the end of time, and perchance in eternity, was born to poetry. His father, disgusted with the child's constant rhyming, is said to have tried, on a memorable occasion, to expel it from him by a whipping, an exercise that was, however, brought to an abrupt close by the little fellow wailing out amid his sobs, "Dear father, do some pity take, and I will no more verses make." The proceeding seems at this day strangely incongruous and out of place, inasmuch as the father himself was given to making "verses." And, when one time the father lay in prison for conscience' sake, the mother, too, had sat on the stones of the prison door with her child in her arms, consoling herself, as was her wont, with the words of Israel's immortal bard; and later she had stimulated the lad by offering in her boarding school a prize to the pupil who should compose the best "poem"; a prize the child once carried off by a somewhat saucy couplet when but seven years of age. So that by mere force of his pre-natal inheritance, as well as early example, Watts was born to be a poet.

Likewise, Benjamin West, when a child, robbing the tail of

SELECTING AN OCCUPATION.

his cat of hairs to make his brushes for painting, and with remarkable skill sketching with a bit of charcoal the sleeping face of his baby sister, to the delight of his mother, showed what nature designed him for.

Smeaton, while yet in bibs, making his little windmill and tacking it to the roof of his father's barn, foreshadowed the eminent engineer he was afterward to become. Indeed, the law of heredity indicated almost wholly for each of these their future. We are the product of our ancestors, and when once parents begin to pay heed to the great laws of nature governing the reproduction of the human race, there will be better and greater men begotten than in any age of the past.

Vast multitudes are now born into the world with a curse on them in the shape of inherited tempers, passions, tendencies, that make life a constant, and, at times, a fearful struggle. If, then, you have been well-born and well-bred, thank God. To you success ought to be easy. It will be an everlasting and unutterable disgrace if you fail. But we are not all blessed with a right and noble pre-natal inheritance, and to many success must come, not as the beautiful unfolding of a natural genius for it, but as the result of sustained, patient, commonplace, everyday effort against unfavorable influences. The question, therefore, "What shall I do?" is a very important one, and demands much careful consideration. Multitudes inherit their occupation as they do their disposition, from their parents, and so the child follows the business of the father simply because the father was in it before him.

While this course has very many advantages, it is not always the best. You may perhaps be able to do better things. If so, why should you do only what your forefathers have done? Life is full of opportunities. They are fairly hurled upon us. Look about you. This is an age of specialties,—in agriculture, in mechanics, in science, in art, in literature. You cannot do all, but you can do one thing well. You can surely find, then, the place and work for which you are adapted, and, having found it, stick. Life is far too short to be spent in roaming.

Value of Decision.

Prof. J. N. HUMPHREY, A.B., State Normal School, Whitewater, Wis.

THE decision of a single individual has more than once changed the current of the world's history; and that, too, not for an hour, but for centuries. Men now speak of such periods as epochs in the annals of time; they call their actors men of destiny. But they who lived in those periods did not know that the clock of the heavens had struck for a change on earth, nor did the actors realize that the centuries were to turn on them. The revolutions on earth, like those of the heavens, swing on unknown centers, and it is only when the periods are complete that men recognize the extent of the change.

Who of those who lived in the days of that poor Genoese wool-carder, Domenico Colombo, ever dreamed that the world's history and progress depended so much on that man's son, and would be so greatly changed by his seemingly wild decision to explore an unknown sea? Nor did that homeless and penniless sailor, as he wandered from place to place, begging now of grandees and anon of kings for the means to test his notion of a water route to the East Indies, and determine the possible existence of other lands on the way thither, ever for one moment suspect the momentous issues that depended upon his keeping that decision. But how much of the world's wealth, how very much of the world's progress toward better things, hung on that decision!

Who can yet tell how much the world has been influenced, commercially, politically, socially, religiously, by the existence and example of the United States? **How much has humanity**

VALUE OF DECISION.

gained by our free institutions, and our system of national government? What would be the condition of the world to-day without them? If Columbus had abandoned his decision, would another have soon made the journey? Or, would the world yet be in the depths of the superstitions and darkness of his time? Vain questions, perhaps, yet they give a faint glimpse of what was involved in that one man's decision, persistently maintained, to undertake an enterprise universally condemned and scoffed at by the men of his day.

Neither did that Wittenberg friar, Martin Luther, who in 1517 decided to publish his ninety-five propositions against the indulgence act just issued by Pope Leo X., have the faintest notion that he was then beginning the most memorable religious revolution of a thousand years. Nor did John Adams, two hundred and fifty years later, understand to what his decision to oppose the Stamp Act of 1765 would lead him and others. But nine years after that decision, it had brought him to write upon the eve of the assembling of the first Continental Congress, "The die is now cast; I have passed the Rubicon. Sink or swim, live or die, survive or perish with my country, is my unalterable determination." And then, two years later, with his indorsement, was passed that immortal resolution that "these united colonies are, and of right ought to be, free and independent states." At the birth of this new nation of the West, the world entered upon a new political era, and a new civilization, with the people as ruler.

History, as men know it, is almost wholly a record of the doings of such men of decision. It is they who rule the world. Difficulties and dangers are to them but new incentives to action. Defeats do not discourage them, but rather give them new wisdom wherewith to circumvent and conquer opposing forces. While others are lamenting that circumstances prevent their success, these men make of circumstances a ladder with which to reach success. They climb and conquer with them or over them. How grandly they tower above difficulties and glory over them!

VALUE OF DECISION.

See yonder stuttering, shrugging youth attempting to address the populace of Athens in the bema. What a miserable failure he makes of it! How the crowd jeer at him! Surely nature did not design him for an orator. He is weak of body, and insignificant in form. He is subject to fits of despondency that verge on madness. He is also excessively poor; for his guardians have defrauded him of his inheritance and turned him out on the world. Reason enough, surely, why he should fail. But the indomitable will within him asserts itself. The mocking crowd shall yet listen to him. See him now down at the seashore shouting at the roaring waves in order to accustom himself to hear unmoved the angry roar of his fellow citizens' voices in their oft turbulent assemblies. Hour after hour he gesticulates, with sword points at his shoulders to prevent that awkward habit of shrugging. Day after day he speaks with pebbles in his mouth to cure his stammering. His fellow men must hear him. And they did, for ere long, in his mighty philippics that "shook the arsenal and fulminated over Greece," he moved them as does the wind the forest's leaves, and they rapturously crowned him with the palm as the king of orators, —a title that twenty-two centuries have not yet taken from Demosthenes of Athens.

One hundred and sixty years ago, an English lad, scarce seven years of age, stood on a slight knoll looking out over one of England's many lovely landscapes. Daylesford Manor was spread out before him. The picturesque village with its thatched cottages, the old stone church with its coat of ivy, the magnificent park of ancient oaks and elms with its great herd of deer, the vast pastures with their fine herds of cattle, and the broad fields of waving grain, successively attracted his gaze. The lad's parents were dead. The grandfather with whom he lived was old and poor, and that grandfather had told him that there had been a time when all that magnificence had been the possession of his ancestors. No wonder the boy, as he looked abroad over that great estate, was sad. No wonder that the hot tears came.

VALUE OF DECISION.

But presently his eye brightened, his little form stood erect, as he formed a mighty resolve, and he stamped the soil proudly while he cried, "I will yet be master of this estate." From that moment his character took form. Slowly he pressed his way through poverty, hard toil, sore trials, and vast discouragements. Night and day he plodded and studied. He left his native land for India. He became eminent for his knowledge of that country's history, languages, customs, and literature. Slowly at first, but rapidly at length, he acquired wealth, and became at last the Governor General of the great British Empire of the East. But years before this the noted Warren Hastings had recovered and owned the home of his ancestors. That decision of his boyhood had governed and guided him like a star of destiny.

Decision is one of the conspicuous elements of victory in all our undertakings. The wavering mind rarely accomplishes anything. Decision becomes an incentive for action. With a purpose once fixed, victory will eventually crown our labor.

Danger of Being Side-Tracked.

Prof. JAMES R. TRUAX, M.A., Union College, Schenectady, N. Y.

THE expression "side-tracked" is ordinarily used by business men with a tone of vexation, to explain the non-arrival of expected goods. "Ought to have been here a week ago. Side-tracked somewhere. No telling when we'll get them now."

But why side-tracked? Why not moving forward on schedule time? Why have they lost their place in the procession? The possible reasons are various. The delayed freight may be of small relative value. Hungry populations are waiting for their supplies of dressed beef, and, when the rails are crowded, they must go forward, but rags and old iron can wait. The order in which interrupted railway traffic is resumed is instructive. First the limiteds carrying through mails, ingenious substitutes for actual personalities; or bearing living brains in such demand that an attempt is made to annihilate time and space to make them omnipresent,—the physician hurrying to a critical consultation; the lawyer to the defense of property, reputation, or life; the merchant to secure a coveted bargain; the manufacturer to gain a contract involving employment for thousands, or to obtain an invention that will revolutionize industry; the statesman to sway, perhaps, the policy of a nation;—many of the passengers, single factors in comprehensive movements, the success of which as a whole depends upon the dispatch of each. Afterward come the ordinary trains with the shoppers, and visitors, and minor workmen; then raw emigrant labor; then perishable freight, and, last of all, the bulk of common commodities.

DANGER OF BEING SIDE-TRACKED.

Side-tracking may also be the result of disability, due to structural weakness, to overloading, to premature start, to careless running.

Human life is a close parallel. There is the man who wants to do only very easy things, and who fails to realize that he thereby enrolls himself among the classes least in demand, and that when the ways are crowded he will be thrust aside. Students often think they act wisely in moving in the direction of least resistance, overtraining where nature has done most, and neglecting themselves where effort costs pain and so declares a need. They do not comprehend the truth that it is a full mental training that enables a man to adapt himself readily to varied demands and to novel situations, and that the ability to meet new emergencies by inventiveness is rarer and better paid than mere imitative skill. Two brothers of my acquaintance, the exact counterparts of each other in appearance, and of identical opportunity, separated on this line. One is satisfied with a small office, a clerk's routine, so much of the world as he can see in his daily walks between his home and place of business. The other is an organizer, has traveled over a large part of the globe, is an associate of the most stirring and influential, a developer of inventions demanded by an age of progress, and a rapid accumulator of wealth. There are young workmen who prefer easy piece work to a complete trade, but they gain no varied power and their life is subject to frequent fluctuations between employment and idleness. Young men would rather take a pleasant clerkship than put on the blouse and learn the details of a great manufacturing business, and so they grow gray-haired on the same stools, among scores of applicants for their seats, while the slowly developed superintendent, or manager, or master-mechanic advances in value and in independence with each added year. Lucrative political jobs seduce many a young man into neglect of himself and of opportunities for permanent success, and then like the magician's horse they vanish and leave the rider midstream to struggle alone against an overwhelming current.

DANGER OF BEING SIDE-TRACKED.

Some men are disabled by overloading; they marry too soon or undertake too many enterprises at once, and, moving sluggishly or fitfully, are in the way. Others are disabled by a premature start; they are overconfident, and enter upon professional life with sadly inferior preparation, so that every task means not only the visible performance, but the feverish effort to get in readiness. Their work at best is hasty patchwork, needing constant renewal. They are ever losing opportunities that cannot wait, and are outdistanced by younger competitors of no great initial ability.

Great numbers are crippled by intemperance, or by any indulgence that impairs mental or physical powers, or creates unreliability in performance. They can be found on white cots in hospitals, or moving about, languid and wan, with vital force nearly consumed, the dupes of mocking pleasure. They can be seen reeling homeward along busy streets, literally very much in the way of active men. The world scarcely heeds them except to remark "What a pity!" They are never included in any movement of business or wholesome recreation. In young manhood, they are retired far more completely than is the aged citizen whose mind is richly stored with experience even though the physical powers may be too weak for action. Sometimes they are set in motion for short runs, but only to break down more dismally each time, until finally they become an encumbrance even to a side-track, and are turned over the embankment to become covered with weeds and rubbish.

One of this class, who had heard of the recent wreck of another, saw, through the glass door of the saloon where he had been saturating himself, a sober acquaintance approaching. Hurrying out he met him and began, "Say—I want—to ask—you—a—question. Why—did—Smith—lose his place?" The gentleman addressed, wishing to be as considerate as possible, replied, "Really, I don't know all the reasons. You know he hasn't been in good health for a year or two." But without further delay and with drunken frankness, the inquirer remarked, "Say—do you know—he often lectured—me—for the—same thing?"

DANGER OF BEING SIDE-TRACKED.

"Well, it's a good thing to give it up, isn't it?" "Ye—es," with evident sincerity. But still, well-bred as he is, he will not give up. He will stay on the side-track.

Some men are weakened by flattery until they cease to cultivate their powers, cease to question facts, cease to heed honest critics, until some day they find themselves deserted, as weakness itself, even when they thought themselves to be storage batteries of exhaustless energy. On the other hand some are hampered by timidity. They side-track themselves, and deteriorate by disuse, while more confident men of less worth hazard more and gain strength and skill in service. Even Shakespeare would have been side-tracked if he had remained in Stratford instead of pushing boldly out for London, to make or mar his fortunes in that world of keen strife.

Some men are disabled by a misdirected competition, as a freight would be if it attempted to run on the time of an express. The poor clerk thinks he must keep up with his extravagant friends of superior positions. There are costly lunches, generous tips, fashionable clothing, expensive recreations, some gambling, neglect of home, putting off of creditors, shortage in accounts, disastrous speculation, despair, robbery, flight. Perhaps an influential friend succeeds in calling off the sleuth-hounds of the law, or in obtaining a suspension of judgment after arrest, but how shall he be put on the main track again? It is next to an impossibility to secure for him any place of financial trust. He is prone to be a borrower, a delinquent debtor, a gambler, in spite of his lesson. He is side-tracked for the rest of his life.

Distrust arises in various ways. A man who gains some ends by selfish scheming and underhand practice imagines he has found the key to success. At first it seems so, but a day comes when he is understood; his plausible words have no value; his essential falsity overbalances all his protestations, and even when he would be true, he is denied the chance, the doors are all closed against him, and he cannot be true even to himself because he has been false to all the world.

DANGER OF BEING SIDE-TRACKED.

There is a weakness that springs from a virtue in excess. Constant pressure destroys elasticity and overbears even rugged strength. There are students who, awake to the priceless value of time, anxious not to lose a moment, neglect rest and open air exercise, abridge meal hours, give up wholesome social relaxations, and, when the earnest work of life begins, the nerves give way; the overexcited brain will not be quiet; sleep will not come; the momentum carries on the mental machinery even when the throttle is closed; and a violated law of nature finally asserts its dignity. These are the well-built cars side-tracked because the journals are overheated. The wild dance of the steel atoms has never ceased; they have broken ranks and are destroying each other in their mad clash.

It would seem a thousand pities to conclude without a few words as to the possibility of avoiding dangers so imminent.

It is wisdom to delay the start until the preparation is complete. Unseasoned timber, untested iron, unguarded strains, may not reveal themselves to the unpracticed eye, but use brings out their real weakness.

Foregather, and discover the special needs of the generation to which you belong. Do not rigidly follow an old plan of campaign. Reconnoiter your special battle-field, learn the ground, the location, and resources of your particular foe. Learn to adapt yourself to varieties of situation. If you strive to do well everything you undertake, you will secure the best possible preparation for an emergency; namely, the ability to give your whole mind to it.

Mistakes are often remediable. Weaknesses can be foreseen and repaired. You find your knowledge defective, your methods antiquated. Do not force obsolete plans, and do not yield to discouragement. Give some of your spare time to supplying defects, and even without overworking you may still hold your right of way. Memory recalls a civil engineer, who, foreseeing opportunities far beyond the scope of the learning which he had brought from college, anticipated every demand by private study, and advanced with the progress of the work to its very consummation, always as its supreme director. Memory recalls the image of a man of misdirected powers, who in days of feebleness, caused by premature decay, roused his waning energies, held them to unflagging exercise, stayed the very progress of disease, until he had redeemed his past neglect, and had left to his children the heritage of a great name, and to the world the leaven of a great thought. Memory recalls another who by one fatal error hazarded the usefulness of his whole professional life. A wise charity shielded him. The dark secret was buried. The man never repeated his fault, but lives an honored, a trusted, a prudent, and sincere guide to many an earthly pilgrim.

You thought merit alone would succeed. You find envy blocking the way, or opening the switches. You have the right of way, but do not neglect caution, do not needlessly provoke opposition. Learn the supreme strength of great natures, *the reserve power of a masterly patience.* Heed cautionary signals. Keep up steam, but do not pull out the throttle until you are sure of a clear track.

Above all, remember that character holds attainments in place. It is seasoning, thorough temper, exactness of fit, that subdues all parts to their true function, so that wheel holds to axle; axle to journal-box; journal-box to truck; truck to platform; platform to its load; and all move as one to the single destination. Character is as unobtrusive as cohesion, and is therefore in danger of being slighted, but it is after all the master-force that holds every atom in its true sphere, and subordinates it to the main design. A life so built, so controlled, bides patiently its hour, but when the hour comes it is fully ready for the severest strain of use.

Singleness of Aim.

This chapter is strongly advocated by
Rev. GEORGE A. HALL, State Secretary Y. M. C. A. of New York.

SUCCESS is a relative term, and varies in its meaning with the nature of one's business in life. In a battle, to win a victory over the foe is success. If you start out on a journey, to reach the point of destination is success. The physician who saves his patients, the lawyer who gains his case, the political leader who obtains office, the merchant who profitably extends his trade, the manufacturer who widens commerce, the agriculturist who multiplies the product of the soil, the man of science or discovery who enlarges the sum of human knowledge, each, in his own sphere, reaches a success that is relatively, more or less, complete. And none the less surely does he succeed in life, who, it may be as an unknown and humble toiler, earns an honest living by useful labor, and by the uprightness of his life, example, and influence adds to the sum total of private and civic virtue. For to do good, and to become good, is the noblest pursuit of mortals. Goodness is everlasting, and rewards its possessor with its own length of days. He who has done his best to obtain goodness has reached the very highest success that the heavens know. Said Cicero, "Right is not founded on opinion, but in nature." And goodness is not of the earth, but of God, and he who gets it joins himself thereby with the Creator of all things, and *must* succeed. Not necessarily in this world, but somewhere, he must and will succeed. Here indeed it often happens that man's successful man and God's successful man have no resemblance whatever to each other. So much then as to what is implied by success. The word unfortunately is too often limited to the mere getting of wealth, or to the winning of a great name among men.

Having chosen your occupation, you of course wish to succeed in it. How can you best do so? By concentration of your efforts upon a single thing. Many persons engaged in business life spread their energies over too wide a field, with the result that while they might succeed handsomely in one venture, by undertaking too many they dissipate their powers of supervision, as well as of capital, and in the end fail to obtain the hoped-for success. And this, too, not because success is not there for them, but their force of time or means, or both, is too feeble at any one point to secure it, whereas, if they would concentrate on any one thing, they might conquer. It is not meant by this, that if a man has at his command more time or capital than he can well employ in his present business, he should not engage in another, but, if he has chosen the present business as the main work of his life, let him have a care that he does not weaken his force at that point. You should mass your force at that part of the line where the brunt of the battle is to come. If you have decided to win success in that particular business, stay there, and conquer. Many persons can make a grand success of one particular thing, but they cannot win in a dozen different undertakings.

In these days of constantly multiplying machinery and appliances, the tendency is to force men more and more into special lines of effort if they would succeed. The all-around physician, who treated man or beast for all their ailments, and as willingly and readily extracted your teeth as administered medicine to you, has departed (unless indeed you may find him on the frontiers of civilization), and in his place is another who gives sole attention to some special bodily organs, or diseases. So also the lawyer, who was once supposed to know and practice all kinds of jurisprudence, now confines himself almost wholly to one particular branch of it. The same thing is true also of almost all the mechanical trades. Garments, tools, machinery, shoes, etc., each go through the hands of many persons, who are expected to give attention to the making of their particular part. So in mercantile affairs, horticulture, gardening, and to an increasing degree in farming, the constant tendency is to some specialty. Whether this is a wise tendency or not, time alone can determine. One deplorable effect is already manifest, namely, making the operative to be but an adjunct of the machine at which he works, so that his brain too often partakes of the ceaseless, dull monotony of his machine. Many apparently know nothing beyond the apparatus at which they preside, and, alas for the good of the human race! they desire nothing more. If you have chosen to be a mechanic or specialist, you should be on your guard against this tendency to narrow the growth of the mind by this mere mechanical absorption. You should aim to make the very best development of yourself that it is possible to do. Strive to-day to make yourself fit for something better to-morrow. Resolve to grow mentally and morally. Concentrate your energies on it, and you will rise to better and nobler things.

See what a single aim will do in professional life. "This one thing I do," cried the great Apostle to the Gentiles; and he resolutely and steadily refused to be diverted from it by any possible consideration men might offer him. There were other apostles of the Christ also, but this single aim of Saul of Tarsus led him to "labor more abundantly than they all." But this "one thing I do," led him to use means for success, and to send for and make constant use of "books and parchments," and himself "give attention to reading," in order that such "profiting might appear to men," with the result that his influence over the thought of the Christian world to-day is greater than that of any other man that ever lived, save the Christ, whom he served so gloriously. A similar singleness of aim has put many a man in places of honor, or profit, in our land and time, and that, too, in spite of the most forbidding obstacles.

One such eminent American citizen, in one of his public addresses, said of himself and of his early trials, "I was born in poverty; want sat by my cradle. I know what it is to ask a mother for bread when she has none to give." At ten years of age, he says, he left his poor New Hampshire home to earn thereafter his own living as a bond boy to a neighboring farmer. He was to serve until twenty-one years of age; to have food and raiment, one month's schooling in the winter, and six sheep and a yoke of oxen when his time of service expired. He was so poor that up to his twenty-first year "a single dollar would cover every penny he had ever spent." But from his childhood he had an inspiration that did for him what a fortune could not have done without it. It made him great. This was an inspiration for knowledge, inherited perchance from his mother, who was "fond of reading." And so this poor bond boy began his service by reading over and over again a New Testament a neighbor had given him, and the few schoolbooks he could get, and then a lady, noticing the forlorn lad's fondness for books, began to lend him some volumes from her husband's library. And the boy toiled in the fields in summer and in the forest in winter, till the evening stars appeared, and then, when his work was done, he would crouch by the kitchen fire (for he had no money to buy lights), and read hour after hour, and, sometimes forgetting himself, he would read till the morning dawned. His employer never had cause to complain that he neglected his tasks, however hard they were, for the lad had good health, and was an industrious, willing laborer. At the end of his indenture he had read near a thousand volumes of the best American and English literature that he could borrow; works of history, philosophy, biography, and general literature. He sold his six sheep and yoke of oxen for eighty-six dollars cash, and that seemed a fortune to him, who up to that hour had never possessed so much as two dollars in money. He then worked a few months in the neighborhood for a small pittance, but his mind had grown, and he was restless to do better, and so he set out to look for a fortune elsewhere.

After he had become the vice-president of the United States, he told the citizens of Great Falls, N. H., when there on a visit, of this experience. He said: "I know what it is to travel weary miles on foot, and ask my fellow men to give me leave to toil. I remember that in 1833 I walked into your village from my native town, and went through your mills seeking employment. If anybody had offered me eight or nine dollars a month I should have accepted it gladly. I went to Salmon Falls, I went to Dover, I went to New Market, and tried to get work, without success; I returned home weary, but not discouraged, and put my pack on my back, and walked to the town where I now live, and learned the mechanic's trade. I know the hard lot that toiling men have to endure in this world, and every pulsation of my heart, every conviction of my judgment, puts me on the side of the toiling men of my country,—aye, and of all countries. I am glad the workingmen of Europe are getting discontented and want better wages. I thank God that a man in the United States to-day can earn from three to four dollars in ten hours' work easier than he could forty years ago earn one dollar working from twelve to fifteen hours. The first month I worked after I was twenty-one years of age, I went into the woods, drove team, cut mill logs, rose in the morning before daylight, and worked hard until after dark at night, and I received for it the magnificent sum of six dollars, and, when I got the money, those dollars looked as large to me as the moon looks to-night."

He spent a dollar and five cents in traveling that hundred miles on foot to Natick, Mass., twenty-five cents of it for a pair of slippers to ease his blistered feet. Then this future statesman agreed to work for five months for nothing, that he might learn the trade of making shoes. At the end of seven weeks, he found he had made a bad bargain, and, anxious to do something to obtain the education he had set his heart on getting, he bought his release for fifteen dollars, and began trade for himself, working sixteen hours a day, and often all night long as well. At the end of two years of such unremitting toil, he had saved several hundred dollars towards gaining an education for the practice of law, but now, in 1836, strength and health gave way, and, acting under the physician's advice, he went to Washington, D. C., for rest and recreation. Passing through Maryland, he saw for the first time what he had hitherto only heard of, the slave toiling under his taskmaster, and was told he must keep silence concerning it while in the state of Maryland. While in Washington, he visited the notorious slave-pen of Williams, on the corner of Seventh and B streets; saw men and women sold as cattle for the crime of having been given by their Creator a black skin; saw husband and wife, mother and child, separated, manacled, whipped, and marched off to a doom that was often worse than death; saw it done by authority of the Government. What the effect was upon him, he himself when United States senator has told.

In an address given at Philadelphia, in 1863, during the dark days of the civil war, he said, alluding to this visit: "I saw slavery beneath the shadow of the flag that waved over the Capitol. I saw the slave-pen, and men, women, and children herded for the markets of the far South; and, at the table at which sat Senator Morris of Ohio, then the only avowed champion of freedom in the Senate of the United States, I expressed my abhorrence of slavery and the slave traffic, in the capital of this democratic and Christian republic. I was promptly told that Senator Morris might be protected in speaking against slavery in the Senate, but that I should not be protected in uttering such sentiments. I left the capital of my country with the unalterable resolution to give all that I had, and all that I hoped to have, of power, to the cause of emancipation in America, and I have tried to make that resolution a living faith from that day to this. My political associates from that hour to the present have always been guided by my opposition to slavery in every form, and they always will be so guided. In twenty years of political life I may have committed errors of judgment, but I have ever striven to write my name, in the words of William Leggett, 'in ineffaceable letters on the abolition record.' Standing here to-night in the presence of veteran anti-slavery men, I can say, with all the sincerity of conviction,

SINGLENESS OF AIM.

that I would rather have it written upon the humble stone that shall mark the spot where I shall repose when life's labors are done, 'He did what he could to break the fetters of the slave,' than to have it recorded that he filled the highest station of honor in the gift of his countrymen."

With that single aim before him, he now returned to study at the Stafford (N. H.) Academy, laboring at his books with the same untiring industry that he had displayed in earning money for his education. Study meant business to him. His school life was unfortunately cut short by the failure of the man to whom he had intrusted his hard earnings, and he returned to Natick and began the manufacture of shoes on a capital of twelve dollars. He continued at the business ten years, employing at length over one hundred persons in his business. During all this time he never forgot his one purpose, but, by reading and the constant study of public questions, he pressed steadily towards the goal he had set.

When elected to the Legislature of Massachusetts, first as representative, and then as state senator, he stoutly and successfully battled for the removal of the unjust statutes that discriminated against the people of color in his Commonwealth. On the third day of February, 1846, he delivered before that body, when a member of the House, one of the ablest speeches ever made against slavery. In it, he frankly avowed, "I am an abolitionist, and have been a member of an abolition society for nearly ten years. I am proud of the name of abolitionist. I glory in it. I am willing to bear my full share of the odium that may now or hereafter be heaped upon it. I had far rather be one of the humblest in that little band which rallies around the glorious standard of emancipation than to have been the favorite marshal of Napoleon, and have led the Old Guard over a hundred fields of glory and renown." It took an uncommonly brave man to declare such sentiments, even in the state of Massachusetts, at a time when Methodist ministers were expelled from their conference and from their churches in that Commonwealth for simply attending an abolition meeting.

SINGLENESS OF AIM.

But this man, who, as a homeless and penniless youth, had entered the state but thirteen years before, had this for his political creed, "My voice and my vote shall ever be given for the equality of all the children of men, before the laws of the Commonwealth of Massachusetts, and of the United States."

In 1855, when forty-three years old, he was elected United States senator from Massachusetts to succeed Edward Everett, who had resigned, and at once he took his place by the side of his famous colleague, Charles Sumner, at a time when the halls of Congress were ringing with the fierce invectives, threats of personal violence, and oaths of fearful import, hurled by the men of the South against all who dared question the right of the demand of slavery to rule the land. Five years before, they had, by the passage of the fugitive-slave act, made the North one vast slave hunting field. But a year before they had compelled Massachusetts to give up the poor fugitive, Anthony Burns, and now, by the passage of the Kansas-Nebraska bill, their victory seemed complete; for had not a senator from Indiana publicly boasted in the Senate chamber, that in his free state they now imposed a fine upon the white man who even ventured to give employment to a free black man? Yet, in his first speech in the Senate, Henry Wilson boldly bore to these men this message as from the North: "We mean, sir, to place in the councils of the nation, men, who, in the words of Jefferson, 'have sworn on the altar of God eternal hostility to every kind of oppression of the mind and body of man.'" And when the same year, in a notable political gathering, a delegate from Virginia, with pistol in hand, approached him and denounced him as the leader of the Anti-Slavery party, he replied to him that his "threats had no terror for freemen"; that he was then and there ready to meet "argument with argument, scorn with scorn, and, if need be, blow with blow; for God had given him an arm ready and able to protect his head." It was time that champions of slavery in the South should realize the fact, "that the past was theirs, the future ours."

Those were the days of border ruffianism, when hundreds

SINGLENESS OF AIM.

of defenseless men and women and children were wantonly murdered in Kansas and elsewhere, by the defenders and propagators of slavery, for daring peacefully to resist their attempt to make of Kansas, contrary to the wishes of its people, and of the statutes, a slave state. But how bravely, mercilessly, because truthfully, Mr. Wilson exposed the weakness of the president who did not prevent those murders and outrages, and the fawning sycophancy of the politicians of the North who apologized for them, and how heroically he denounced to their faces the defenders of those crimes, and of the crimes of human slavery, in the Senate chamber, when one of their number, Preston S. Brooks of South Carolina, had made his dastardly and murderous assault in the Senate upon Charles Sumner.

Let the files of the "Congressional Globe" show his intense patriotism, his broad statesmanship, both before and during the progress of the civil war, and after its close, all of which is too well known to be here repeated. Massachusetts kept this man of single aim as her senator until he saw the liberation of millions of bondmen, and had witnessed the destruction of the most gigantic conspiracy against human progress that the centuries had known; and then when General Grant was elected president of the United States, in 1872, she gave him to preside as vice-president of the country over the legislative body where, for nearly a score of years, he had been the bravest, most patriotic, most hard working, and incorruptible member. So scrupulous had he been not to make his exalted position a means of worldly gain, that when this Natick cobbler, the sworn friend of the oppressed, whose one question as to measures or acts was ever, "Is it right, will it do good?" came to be inaugurated as vice-president of his country, he was obliged to borrow of his fellow senator, Charles Sumner, one hundred dollars to meet the necessary expense of the occasion. By his energy, his ability, and uprightness, he has shown to the poorest and humblest boy in the land that there are no barriers which can prevent his success if he enters upon his career with right principles and single aim.

SINGLENESS OF AIM.

It was said of William Wilberforce at his death, that "he had gone to God with the shackles of eight hundred thousand West India slaves in his hands," but Henry Wilson, the poor bond boy, had been one of the chief agents in breaking the shackles from four and a half millions. That purpose formed at the slave-pen in Washington was well carried out, not indeed as he had expected, but as God willed it.

Climbing the Ladder of Success.

JOHN C. DUEBER, President Hampden Watch Co., Canton, Ohio.

THAT famous English prime minister, George Canning, who, with Lord Brougham, was accounted the most famous political orator of the time, was born of poor parents. When but a year old, his father died, and the mother to earn her living became an actress. The wandering life of the mother worked disaster to her bright boy. He began to be dissipated when but a lad and would soon have gone to ruin if Moody, the actor, had not persuaded the boy's uncle, a man of property, to take him and educate him. The uncle consented on condition that he should abandon his waywardness, and at twelve years of age he was sent to Eton school. Here he took for his motto, "I must work if I would win," and applied himself with such diligence to his studies as to become the first scholar in his class, both in the schoolroom and in the debating society.

At eighteen he entered Oxford College, and, refusing to engage in the athletic sports of the school, he gave himself wholly to his studies, having, as he told a friend, a seat in the House of Commons in view. Graduating with high honors, he entered Parliament when but twenty-three years of age as an adherent and firm supporter of that eminent statesman, William Pitt. He became one of his secretaries and rose at length to be premier of the realm. He aimed at the top and by energy and application won renown and very early reached the goal he had set for himself.

At that same University of Oxford, fifty years before Canning's time, a poor lad had come like him thirsting for knowledge, and longing to rise. He entered the school as chore boy, and paid his way by blacking the shoes of the professors and students. He had been, he said, a vicious boy, but he at times had tried to help his mother (a widow who kept a small inn at Bristol) by sweeping and mopping the room. But one day Thomas à Kempis's book had fallen into his hands through some means, and it had changed the current of his life. The lad said he was not above hard work, and if possible he would like to work his way through college. So he blacked shoes and did chores for a living, and studied as he could.

The morals of the university were very low; infidelity ran wild among both professors and students, and this lad of sixteen, who insisted upon a strict religious course of life, was most mercilessly ridiculed by them.

The poor boy had set his mind upon being a great preacher, and undismayed he wandered out into the surrounding fields, where he would recite his sermons and meditate and pray. He had a marvelous voice, but not one of those who mocked at him ever for one moment dreamed that the bootblack was destined to become the flaming evangel of England and America and the most wonderful pulpit orator the world has yet seen, a man who could, as Garrick, the actor, said of him, make men laugh or cry by his intonation of the word Mesopotamia.

The majority of his fellow students were content with mediocrity and are unknown, while the name of George Whitefield, whose body awaits the resurrection morning in the old church at Newburyport, Mass., is held in loving remembrance by millions on both sides of the Atlantic as a very angel of God.

If you look over the line of great men of any age, you cannot but be impressed with this fact, that there was something within them that impelled them to rise. What was it? Superior mental endowments? Very rarely. Was it greater, or better, or earlier advantages of education? No, generally the opposite. Was it greater physical force? But seldom, if at all. What, then, was it? Almost invariably there is but one answer, viz., the power of *will*.

CLIMBING THE LADDER OF SUCCESS.

Men differ greatly in intellect, but will is not intellect. The natural appetite and desires of men, while nearly uniform, yet vary in intensity; but will is not appetite nor desire. The cause of a fact should not be confounded with the fact itself; and here is a fact, that the masses of men seem content to remain at a common level of desire and aspiration, which level is as yet at the bottom, where of necessity the competition must by the mere force of numbers be greater, while only here and there one out of the mass rises above his fellows. For instance, in business life there are many mechanics now in the industrial world, but few of them are what may be termed really first-class.

There are many lawyers, but very few are first class. Wherever you may go, a first-class orator, or reader, or teacher, or preacher, or merchant, is rarely found, and when found no one of them is exceptionally endowed with intellect above his fellow men. It is often found that many others had similar desires and aspirations, but they did not rise, while these few did. Why? Scan it closely, and you find that these *willed* to rise. They resolved to be masters of circumstances, while the masses drifted with those circumstances. Because their parents were poor was only to these a reason why they should not remain so. Difficulties were not obstacles, least of all were they a cause for discouragement or an excuse for a defeat. Why, difficulties and obstacles were the very things made for the will to combat and overcome! If not, what need of a will at all? What is will for but for combat and rule? Is the strife unequal? Then the more glory to the conqueror. Surely it is no great thing if Xerxes with his millions overcame Leonidas. Not to do it is a disgrace. But for Leonidas with his Spartan band of six hundred to overcome Xerxes's millions, ay, that were immortal renown! So these men of success set their will in array against the natural things made for wills to contend with and overcame them, and that is all there was to it. It was no mystery or fortunate combination of circumstances, though, as said before, these are often great aids to success, inasmuch as it is necessarily easier to overcome a little difficulty than a multitude of greater ones.

Two young men, students of Yale College, were one day discussing their future plans, when one of them declared it to be his purpose to become a member of Congress within six years. His companion generously laughed at what he imagined was a fond conceit. Said the other, "If I did not believe that I shall be a member of Congress within six years from to-day I would immediately leave college." He had decided on his plans; he was fitting himself accordingly. He had set his will to accomplish it if life and health remained to him, and within the six years John C. Calhoun became a member of Congress and was destined to wield an influence by force of his will, the evil results of which yet abide in our country.

Our minds are the vital force that deals with and governs to a large extent physical facts, and the will is the vital force of the mind without which mind seems useless and simply the creature of every whim of desire or gust of passion. Who can estimate the power of will?

But a little more than a hundred years ago the immense armies of Russia, Austria, and France, with their allies, struggled during the Seven Years' War to conquer the indomitable will of a single man, the flute player of Potsdam, and failed. Again and again they sought to overwhelm him with armies that outnumbered his three to one; armies led by veteran generals who had won many a bloody field. But the flute player knew that if he yielded the rising nationality of Prussia would be extinguished. He must conquer or perish. And so he set his mighty will in array and on the awful fields of Rossbach, Leuthen, and Zorndorf he heroically beat back his foes. They had eighty millions of people from which to recruit their armies while he had less than four. So it came to pass when the sun went down on the dreadful field of Kunersdorf, twenty thousand of his army lay dead and he had left scarce three thousand. What wonder that he was on the borders of despair?

But the wonderful will of Frederick the Great, held by the

stern necessity to conquer or die, rose up from this as from many another defeat and stalked forth defiantly, even menacingly, at the last, against the combined armies of Europe, and compelled them to forego their purpose to divide his little kingdom among them, and to recognize Prussia as thereafter one of the five great powers of Europe, a rank which since she has easily maintained. The will of Frederick II. made the Germany of to-day, and in it, and by it, he yet lives on earth.

Footprints of Failure.

Rev. JAMES W. COLE, B.D.

WHAT if you and I should make a failure of life? One of the lamentable facts about a failure is that it can never be a blank. Always somebody or something suffers loss by it. For our failures strike two ways,—backward and forward; backward to those whose hopes for our success are blasted, and whose pain we cannot measure, and forward to one's posterity, who will never cease to be affected by it. By far the worst part of a wrong act or course of life is its effect upon the future of those who were in no wise responsible for the wrong. What burdens are laid on others by our failures! "Gather up my influence and bury it with me," cried a dying man. As well ask us to turn back the stars in their courses. Why! the influence of the first man has not yet ceased on earth, though sixty centuries have elapsed since he departed.

And, then, very many failures might be so easily avoided if we only knew, or if we gave heed when we knew! He who has gone over a road can tell its dangerous places and bypaths; and, if he has placed danger signals there to warn fellow travelers, they surely ought not to neglect such signs and deliberately court harm and loss by ignoring his kind foresight and care for them. Yet, notwithstanding the many eminent examples of successful business life that have been furnished to them, it is said that ninety-three per cent. of the merchants of this country either become bankrupt, or fail to gain a competency, and so die poor. Why is it that so many fail and so few succeed? He who will solve this problem is surely a benefactor to mankind. In the city of Boston, for instance, it has been found that within a period of forty years nine hundred and forty-four out of a thousand business men either failed in their business, or died poor men, while again, taking the United States as a whole, not one man in four, at his death, ever leaves property enough to require a will, or an executor; and this, too, in the richest country on the earth!

Is man then made to toil in vain, or is there a cause for these failures? I know indeed that men talk of nature as being constructed and run only in accord with what they call "the survival of the fittest," and that all her rewards are to be given only to the few of mighty will or passion who rightly swallow up the substance, if they do not the person, of the many. I do not believe it. I do not believe that failure is the normal lot of man, no more than I believe that pain is his *natural* condition. Nature has made no provision in the human body for pain. There is no contrivance nor organ whatever for it. If pain comes, it comes as a result of violating nature's wise and beneficent laws for the well-being of the body. Man was not made for pain, and, be it noted, pain is always in the first instances caused by taking into the body an element foreign to it, and the sensation we call pain is nature's protest against its presence. Pain is not ingrained in nature, and, when it comes to us, it comes as a friend to warn us, or, at the last, as a sheriff to arrest the persistent transgressor.

You may carry the analogy if you please into business life. Man was made for success. Yet the multitudes fail. And then we say that success is the exception and failure the rule of life. Not so. The simple fact is that very many men enter upon a business career foredoomed to failure because they ignore the greatest of all laws, the law of righteousness.

Whether you believe it or not, this world was constructed according to righteousness, and the surest way to lose its gold is to forsake or ignore the God who made the gold for humanity's need. True, there are many who consider goodness as naturally and necessarily opposed to the accumulation of wealth, and who stoutly affirm that righteousness is not a factor to be considered in trade,—especially in Wall street, or at a horse mart. Yet, over against such teaching stands the mighty fact that all the world's great mines and all the vast resources of her material wealth are to-day in the hands of avowedly Christian nations, while more than five-sixths of all the property and of all the great money producing enterprises in England, and in the United States, are controlled and conducted by avowedly moral if not by professedly Christian men. Hence it is rather late in the ages to attempt to teach men that the sure way to obtain wealth is to forsake the God who created that wealth.

Why, if there is one fact that stands out like a mighty mountain peak towering over all others, it is this, that virtue is the indispensable condition among men for obtaining security of person and of property, and for maintaining peace, and for securing human happiness.

All the regulations for human society among civilized peoples are made to protect virtue, and to repress vice. And the more advanced the civilization becomes, the more indispensable, both to the individual and to society, is virtue found to be. Suppose, for a moment, that the regulations governing men were now reversed so that they fostered and protected vice, and punished and suppressed virtue; what a monstrous, inhuman condition of affairs it would be! Whose purity, property, honor, or good name would be secure? Indeed, who could gain wealth or a good name under such conditions? So, then, whether experience has taught men that virtue is a necessity of civilization, or whether virtue is imbedded in the very constitution of nature, still the one great fact confronts us, that in order to gain a success at all worthy of the name, we must be virtuous, that is, righteous, for that is the same thing. And it is because they ignore this fundamental fact of nature that so many men in every decade are financially and morally ruined.

Listen to this true recital. On the fourteenth day of September, 1836, at Port Richmond, Staten Island, an old man lay dying. He was desolate, friendless, hopeless, and poor, so poor as to have been in his last years dependent on the charity of a

FOOTPRINTS OF FAILURE.

Scotch woman who had known him in other days. Yet, this man had been born to fortune and to fame, for his father was a man of wealth and large attainments. But few, if any, young men have ever had better opportunities for obtaining eminent success. Nature had endowed this man with all her finest gifts. He was so brilliant of intellect as to be fitted to enter Princeton College at eleven years of age. His father had been president of that institution, and was one of the foremost men of his time, whether as educator, scholar, author, or preacher. His mother was the noblest daughter of the most renowned clergyman New England ever produced. His sister had, while living, been the wife of one of the chief justices of Connecticut, and this dying, forsaken old man had himself once been vice-president of the United States, and he might easily have been its president, honored and honorable in life and in death, if he had not despised the law of righteousness, and substituted intrigue and an iron will for moral principles wherewith to guide his life.

Do you ask how came he, who had been so nobly born, to make so fearful a mistake? He had stood one time at the parting of ways where God calls men, and another man had directed him wrong. It happened on this wise: When a student in college at the age of fifteen, his soul was greatly stirred by a religious revival then sweeping over the place, and the president of the college, to whom he went for advice in the hour of his soul's need, had called the religious fervor "fanaticism"; and, when still unsatisfied, some months later, he again sought instruction of another noted divine, similar advice was given him, and he believed them, and then Aaron Burr forsook the faith of his father and mother for the then popular and loose morality of Lord Chesterfield. It was the fruits of this apostasy that led men to distrust the most brilliant lawyer of his day, and caused his own political party to forsake him; and that then led him to seek to retrieve on the "field of honor" (!) his waning political fortunes by taking the life of his rival, Alexander Hamilton, at Weehawken, N. J., on that fatal early morning of July 7th, 1804. And then came in rapid succession his flight for safety from the wrath of his fellow men; his lurid dreams of an empire, and his long six months' trial for treason, with his after years of wandering in Europe as an outcast among men; and then the years of final recklessness and licentiousness, to the end. Oh, if the finger posts had only pointed right when he stood an awakened lad before Drs. Witherspoon and Bellamy! And yet the man who was so loved by such a daughter as Theodosia Burr could not be wholly bad. Young man, Solomon was right when he declared that "righteousness tendeth to life"; and Paul but wrote nature's law when he said that Godliness "has promise of the life that now is and of that which is to come."

The Dignity of Labor.

Rev. JAMES W. COLE, B.D.

ONE of the most important facts testified to by human experience in all civilized lands is this—that it is disgraceful not to work. Men in every age of the world have scorned the idler. They have sought to instruct him by example of industry; they have admonished him by the proverbs of the wise; they have railed at him in song; sought to reform him by law, and yet, like the poor, he is ever with them. Indeed, the poor are mainly his offspring, and, but for him, they would almost disappear from the earth.

The drones in the hive of human industry must needs eat, and so the toilers must produce, not alone for themselves, but for these cumberers of the ground. If labor was not so bounteously rewarded the world would starve, for there is at no time enough food stored within the houses of the earth to support its people for two years without a harvest. Hence the toilers must not only delve, and plant, and reap year after year, whereby to feed and clothe themselves, but they are obliged also to provide for these parasites on the body politic. This class of gentry, whether clothed in purple and fine linen, or decorated with rags, are fond of saying that "the world owes them a living,"—an assertion utterly absurd, and wholly untrue. It is bad enough to be a "do-nothing," but why add falsehood to shame by claiming assets never possessed? It is a law of nature that "if any man will not work neither shall he eat." Paul the Apostle did not originate that law. It is imbedded in the very structure of the world.

THE DIGNITY OF LABOR.

How wonderfully rich our country is in its material resources! You might put the entire population of the world in our own fair land, and easily support them all, so bountifully has God provided for this land. Yet for hundreds of years a few thousand Indians owned it all, and well-nigh starved to death in it, would have starved but for the wild beasts and birds they killed. Why? They were idlers, and shirked honest work. How rich this world might be if there were no idlers in it! In 1892 the cash value of the work produced by the toilers in this country alone in that one year was seven and one-half billions of dollars. If now the millions of soldiers, policemen, keepers of prisons and reformatories, throughout all lands, who have to depend upon the toilers for their bread while they are taking care of the mischievous and vicious idlers, could be released to do honest work, and together with the idlers each earned his own living, this would be a world of wealth and comfort.

God designed that men should be rich. So he stored the world underneath with uncountable treasures of gold, silver, iron, tin, lead, and gems, and vast reservoirs of fuel, and stocked the soil with great wealth-producing power, and crowded the seas and air with immense material for making it. Yes, the Almighty is immensely wealthy himself, and he would have his children so. Sin, the sin of idleness, makes them poor. If Mother Eve had been busily at work so that she had no time to gossip with the serpent, she and her husband might have stayed in Eden, and lived in luxury, but as it was in the beginning, so now, "Satan finds some mischief still for idle hands to do," and, if you neglect work in Eden, you may have to do a worse and harder kind outside. There is one thing which men and women have inherited, and it seems to have struck in very deep,—it is *laziness*. Surely, if you judge by the fruits of idleness, it must be a sin not to be doing some kind of honest work. What stores of wisdom, what nobility of knowledge, labor brings! And you cannot have it without labor, and hard labor, too. Learning is not an instinct, but an acquisition, and we shall never get beyond the need of having more and more

THE DIGNITY OF LABOR.

knowledge. Knowledge, like the Creator's works, is boundless in extent, and will continue while they endure. "Knowledge is power." Labor alone secures it. He who would *excel* must *work* for it, and by his labor he becomes dignified. If Michael, the Archangel, were sent from heaven to sweep the muddy streets of earth, the lowly work would not lower *him*, but how mightily he would elevate the task! How honorable thereafter street sweeping would be among the children of men! You have been given your work to do. It may be lowly. It may be uncongenial, but if it is for you to do, do it. Do it with your might. Do it the best you know how. By doing well the little, you will be fitted for the greater tasks and responsibilities of life; then the worker and the work alike become immortal.

By the light of torches in the early morning of March 9, 1791, an old man, eighty-eight years of age, was carried to his burial. He had been one of the most tireless workers this world has ever known. He literally defied death by his immense labor, and left the impress of his great personality in untold blessings upon the lives of more millions of men and women than any other one man has done since the days of Christ. He was the son of an English rector, whose life had been an unceasing struggle with poverty, who had been imprisoned for debt, and who died in debt, and so this boy was early inured to privation and toil. Twice the father's house had been set on fire at night by the rabble whom that father's faithfulness had offended, and the inmates by wading through flames had barely escaped with their lives. On the second occasion, this lad, then five years old, was forgotten in his chamber, and at the last moment, as the roof fell in, he was providentially rescued from the burning building by two of the neighbors. He was one of nineteen children, ten of whom lived to mature years. They constituted a most remarkable family. The celebrated commentator, Dr. Adam Clarke, says, "Such a family I have never read of, heard of, or known; nor, since the days of Abraham, has there ever been a family to which the human race has been more indebted. "John Wesley and his brother Charles were the product of noble ancestors. The man who has good, pure blood in his veins, ought to thank God for this inheritance, even though he leaves his parents' home without a farthing. To be well-born is in itself a fortune, and John Wesley was well-born. His father was an able, faithful, and talented preacher and a writer of note, but it was from his mother that John derived most of the great characteristics that made him so renowned. This woman, Susanna Wesley, was a marvel. She was not only the mother and nurse of her many children, but their schoolmistress and priestess as well. Her educational and religious system of instruction had some most extraordinary points, and was conducted solely by herself. The children, of whom there were thirteen at home at one time, "had the reputation of being the most loving family in the country."

Mrs. Wesley had a fine education and many accomplishments. She was beautiful of form and person, and a woman of rare energy, tact, good sense, and decision, and withal intensely religious. She so molded the character of her children in their childhood that when John Wesley finally left his parental home, at thirteen years of age, to become a student in a preparatory school, and then three years later to enter the University at Oxford, he had already received from his mother those prime qualities of method, punctuality, diligence, energy, and piety, which he afterward developed into that vast system of ecclesiasticism and doctrine now extended throughout the whole world, and popularly known as Methodism, so that Susanna Wesley has justly been called, "the mother of Methodism." As a clergyman, John Wesley "stands out in the history of the world unquestionably pre-eminent in religious labors above that of any other man since the Apostolic age."

A single great practical life has more than once changed the aspect of the whole civilized world. A single poor, drudging mechanic has by his invention of a machine, or by the application of a force, more than once doubled the energy and wealth of mankind. Steam was as mighty in the days of Abraham as it was when George Stephenson yoked it to his engine to do

THE DIGNITY OF LABOR.

the world's work. How it has since empowered, enriched, and blessed the nations! Electricity has been lying around loose, waiting for some practical mind to use it since the very dawn of the world, and, when the man appears, it is his fate to be first regarded, as Morse was, as a cracked-brained enthusiast, and later on as one of the great minds of the age.

So John Wesley, who was one of the most practical of men, was cast out from the churches and denounced as a wild visionary, and mischief maker, and a teacher of sedition and heresy, by the very men who, ere he died, came to regard him reverently as the instrument in God's hands for rescuing England from the "virtual heathenism into which it had lapsed"; and for saving the whole Reformation movement started by Martin Luther, from the "imminent ruin hanging over it," and for again reviving that vital "religion that was dying in the world," and they proclaimed him as the greatest mind that had appeared in the religious world since the days of the Apostle Paul.

For nearly sixty years he preached on an average fifteen sermons a week; he wrote incessantly with his pen, and published hundreds of volumes of books, tracts, magazines, treatises on almost all useful subjects, classical, moral, and religious; he traveled thousands of miles on foot, on horseback, by coach; he was often mobbed, and for years was constantly threatened with death by men of violence; his life was often in peril on land and sea; he had often the largest congregation to hear him that ever were gathered in modern ages, numbering sometimes more than thirty thousand.

He erected hundreds of schools, chapels, churches; educated thousands on thousands of his countrymen, and, though having an income from his books of many thousands of dollars, he religiously and constantly gave it away to the poor, and to spread the gospel he preached, and at his death he had barely enough to bury him decently. He was as saving of his time as ever a miser was of gold; each hour had its task. His favorite maxim was, "Always in haste, but never in a hurry." His

THE DIGNITY OF LABOR.

first rule for the conduct of the thousands of men he sent forth to preach was, "Be diligent; never be unemployed; never be triflingly employed; never while away time; never spend any more time at any place than is strictly necessary."

Circumstances have much to do with developing great men, but they do not create them. John Wesley turned the most unfavorable circumstances to bring about a revolution in the religious world, which by its beneficent results entitles him to be justly ranked among the great men of the ages.

This illustrious man affords a striking example of the dignity of labor. His greatness was the result of his incessant diligence. The world honors honest labor, but despises the idler.

Character as Capital.

B. O. AYLESWORTH, D.D., LL.D., Pres. Drake University, Des Moines, Iowa.

THE age still throbs, though not so painfully, with an eagerness for industrial wealth.

But a better age is coming, the age of Character. Already the unrest of the closing century is quieted by hope in the next. Great hearts have the pulse at last of the world's Great Heart. The capital of a too strongly competitive age is becoming the capital of a less selfish time, and will have vastly more intrinsic value.

We may profitably use the terms of the old idea with which to express the new.

Commercial wealth adds to one's personality. A man plus his farm, or his lands, is something more than the man alone. He is a combination of human and material potentialities.

A man with character is more than his natural endowments and their special training. He is these plus the wealth of integrity and uprightness of which he has become possessed in the world's struggle. Genius is not character.

Moreover, capital is the working force of its possessor. The idler and the tramp are men minus working force, and become a burden rather than an aid in carrying society's burdens. The active agency in modern society is wealth—except in the ignobly rich.

So, too, character is the vitalizing, reshaping, accomplishing, self-saving, and community-saving force which one must possess in addition to heredity and environment, often in spite of them, before he may become a solvent factor in the problem of

life. A stagnant pool, a dry mill-race, or a cinder is not a more forceless thing than a characterless man.

It is, furthermore, an attribute of capital that it multiplies itself when skillfully manipulated. This is the chief fascination of wealth. It bears its own legal rate of interest and under unusual demands often rapidly doubles and quadruples itself.

A character well begun not only steadily increases in purchasing power relative to the esteem and affection of one's fellows, but under great exigencies, and suddenly revealed opportunities, multiplies into the heroic, and into immortal worth.

If Lincoln, as a young man, could not have washed the "smartweed" from the face of the New Salem bully, whom he had soundly thrashed, having rubbed the biting weed into his pimpled face, he could not have become the most magnanimous foe any man or nation has ever known. The honesty that compelled him as a store-clerk to walk six miles after dark to make right a needy woman's miscounted change rather than wait for a chance to explain the matter later, made "honest Abe" the most conspicuous figure in the pantheon of human rights.

It is a unique function of wealth to cover the defects of a financial past, and reasonably secure its future. Losses are made good, and insurance established.

It is the noblest attribute of character that it atones for the lack or loss of itself in the years of weakness and rebellion, and increasingly fortifies against loss in more trying experiences still to come. God has compassionately established this law in his redemptive system. Yet we must not forget the psychology of grace. It is with more difficulty than in the world of commerce that lost character can be regained. But once regained it veils the past, and glorifies the future.

Men may destroy my reputation, but I must commit moral suicide before character dies. In this is its severer quality manifest. No truth, at first glance, seems so unwelcome, so crushing, as that of self-accountability. "I am to blame," are the hardest words our stammering speech ever knows.

Upon closer analysis, however, this same truth is the divinest part of man, the salt of his spiritual nature. It means that character may become mine in spite of what all men may do.

"I have achieved" are God's words. We are truly his offspring when we utter them. Who may not say them, if he will? Unlike the capital of marts, this capital of hearts, I, any resolute soul, may possess. A safer reporter than Dun & Co. compiles the list of the morally rich. No paper goes to protest when it has the indorsement of character.

The great Accountant invests this capital. Words vibrant with tenderness, deeds quick with unselfishness, sacrifices endured by pierced bodies, he puts at interest in the evolution of the race. When he strikes the balance, eternal life will be found to your credit. The true capitalist is a foe to poverty. So, too, the rich in character hate vice and seek to remove it in all the lives they touch. The richest merchant prince is the humblest man of his kind if he be a steward of God's wealth.

The noblest character is the poorest in spirit and, though he possess all the beatitudes, walks lowly among men, holding them to him the more closely. All greatness is meekness, for greatness comes through tribulation, as wealth through toil. The highest quality of true exaltation is humility.

Character lifts us up to God, and leads us down to men. Through it alone is the great discovery made that God is in humanity. To know that fact is not to fail of life or heaven.

> When the multitudes dead new-formed shall uprise,
> And with hurrying flight shall seek the great All,
> Not the boastfulest soul nor one overwise
>   Will hear his call.
>
> To some timorous plodder halting afar,
> With a glance of regret towards the old earth
> Where his pain and his faith had clashed in a war
>   That wrought his worth,
>
> The sweet voice of the life will come like the song
> Of a mother who croons her babe to its sleep.
> For his pain shall be peace, and love for the wrong
>   That made him weep.

The Influence of Associates.

Rev. FRANCIS E. CLARK, D.D., Boston,
Founder of Y. P. S. C. E., President of the United Society of Christian Endeavor.

THERE are two great forces constantly battling for supremacy in the lives of all young persons. Their success, happiness, and worth to the world depend very largely upon which of these forces governs their lives.

One by one, precious lives, the perpetually ripening human harvest, will surely be gathered either by the Evil One or by that gracious Husbandman who is always seeking to root up the tares and to encourage the growth of the good seed. Just as the head gardener on a large estate always has a corps of assistants to dig and weed and water and hoe, so the two great forces which are always striving for the possession of young hearts have their respective under gardeners, who are always busy.

These sub-gardeners are called "companions." They play dolls with the children in their infancy, and go fishing with them in their boyhood, and attend them to their first party in their girlhood. In fact, without ever suspecting that they are gardeners, that they are daily sowing, and nourishing, and training, they are, nevertheless, and under the direction of their respective masters, bringing forward this most tremendous product of the ages, the harvest of human character. Every boy who reads these pages is a far different boy to-day because Jack and John and Bob live in the same town with him, and every girl, though she does not herself realize it, is a far better or worse girl because of her friends Mary and Susie and Kitty.

THE INFLUENCE OF ASSOCIATES.

If I could transport all my readers forward fifty years, and could then with them look back upon their past lives, it would be easy, did not memory play us so many tricks and obscure so many events of importance, to show them how they had deviated from the straight line, how they had yielded to this temptation and to that, and how at times they had been led on to nobler and braver deeds than were their wont. In fact the track which their lives would make, would look not unlike the ragged, irregular line which marks the advent of a cold wave or of a storm sweeping from west to east, as shown on our weather reports. But every deviation from the ordinary line of travel, every indentation and curve to the right hand or left, almost without exception could be accounted for by the influence of one or more of those all powerful magnets, a good or bad companion.

Some years ago I spoke some words like these to the young people of my old church. I have never had them disputed, and I have had more and more occasion every year to believe that they are true. "I venture to say that not one boy in five hundred ever went into a rum shop alone for the first time. He went because he was asked to go. Because some companion took him by the hand and said, 'Let us see what is going on in there.'" Oh, if he could only know that the bad companion came to him direct from the Devil, if he could see the grinning face of Apollyon leering at him over that companion's shoulder, how he would start back in fright and dread! I know of young men who are going to the bad as fast as time can carry them, and I know the cause of their downward course. It is some evil companion from whom they have not moral courage to break away. They walk with him to school or business. They sit with him in church. They turn to him for his sneer or smile when the most solemn truths are urged upon them. The tears of mother, the warnings of father, the counsel of pastor, are of no avail because of this evil companion.

A number of years ago I asked a large number of the leading business men of Boston to tell me what in their view was

THE INFLUENCE OF ASSOCIATES.

the greatest enemy of youth. Very many of them, speaking out of their own experience, dwelt on the evil influence of bad companions.

I remember that one business man wrote, "Too few thumps and too much coddling makes the soul like dough, which shows a dimple for each touch of sin." It is my impression that the finger of the evil companion accounts for very many of these sinful dimples in a wayward soul. As the housekeeper's loaf shows every pat and pin prick, so the plastic souls of our boys and girls are dented and dimpled all over with the marks of good or evil companionship.

One of these strong business men to whom I wrote about the dangers of youth answered as follows: "When I look back at my own narrow escape from evil, of which I can hardly conceive the end, it brings tears to my eyes. I think the turning point of my life was going to California at the age of nineteen, and by that means breaking off the acquaintances I had formed. I was away so long that when I returned they had all scattered. I did not think at the time I was very bad, but still from my present standpoint it looks bad enough. I can look around me here in Boston and see many a man who is a perfect failure to-day who had the brightest prospects when young, and bad company was the first step downward."

Do you wonder that with these warnings from practical business men before my eyes I should say: Young men, if you feel that you have not the moral stamina to break with the companions who are dragging you down, if you feel that there is no other way to throw off this social chain, every link of which is a fetter for your soul, then I beg you to leave everything and flee for your life, though it be to California or Australia, or Alaska or Patagonia, though you leave father and mother and home and church behind you,—flee as you would flee from a pestilence. But the possibility of being dragged down by bad companions implies the equal possibility of being lifted up by good companions, just as night implies day and darkness suggests sunlight.

THE INFLUENCE OF ASSOCIATES.

It is not necessary for most young people to go away from home to escape bad companions, but simply to stay more at home, to get under the influence of the good. A gentle mother, a loving sister, a manly brother, and the other companions who naturally gather in such a home, are a better antidote for bad companions than any other medicine.

In this blessed influence of good companions is found one great benefit of young people's societies for religious and social purposes. If the religious element is kept predominant, if the spiritual idea is not lost sight of in the purely social and hilarious, all other matters will take care of themselves. Our social wants will not be neglected, our literary instincts will find scope and play, and then, so far as we can find them outside of the home circle, shall we find our best companions and our truest friends. I have no fear of the senseless sneer that is sometimes thrown at these organizations as "flirting societies," for the young man or woman who there finds a wife or husband will have taken the most important step of all in solving the great problem of youth, the question of a lifelong companion and associate, and will have taken it far more wisely than if such a partner had been sought at the ballroom or the theater.

Fruits of Honesty.

Rev. JAMES W. COLE, B.D.

THE bane of the business life of to-day is the constantly growing disposition to get money without earning it. Money is not merely a medium of exchange, but it is also a commodity like wheat, or corn, or iron, yet men who would die of shame if caught stealing wheat or corn do not hesitate to steal money whenever the chance presents itself. They would scorn to steal a bushel of wheat from their neighbor, and insist upon giving him full value for it, but to get money from him without paying dollar for dollar is quite another thing. To overmatch him in a bargain, why, that is trade. But why is it more a sin to steal wheat than to steal dollars? And he steals dollars who gets them of his neighbor without having earned them, or who does not give for them a full equivalent.

There is an almost insane desire abroad among men to get riches, not by the old-fashioned and slow steps of industry, perseverance, and economy, but by the quick road of speculation, regardless of whether that speculation is a legitimate and just one or not. There is such a thing as a righteous venture in a business transaction,—as when a man forecasts the prospective demands of the market of next month or next year, and arranges for the profits to meet his side of the transaction, supplying the honest wants of the community in an honest way. He buys at a fair price, and sells at a fair advance on the cost. He enriches himself by supplying the needs of the public, and not by plundering it. An honest man will not take bread out of the mouths of others to put it in his own. When he sells goods, he does not sell his soul with them. He consults his conscience in the countingroom quite as often as in the prayer meeting. He could swindle within the statutes, and get rich, but he will not do it. Happily for the race, there are yet such men, and such just methods of trade, but the tendency of the times is to be more and more dissatisfied with such honest ways of getting money. Young men vote them slow, and instead of climbing the successive rounds of the ladder of industry to reach the fortune at the top, they wish to go up by the quick, audacious elevator of the stock-speculator.

It is not yet accounted a reputable thing to be a Simon-pure gambler in business circles. Public opinion through its statutes has decreed that the gambler must ply his trade of plundering, if at all, in secret. He must get his hundreds, or his thousands, from his fool-victims behind tiled doors and carefully screened windows, subject to the accident of a swoop-visit by the police. For, forsooth, his business beggars children, and has on it the anathemas of wronged, deserted, robbed, and heartbroken wives and mothers. But the broker's boards and the stock exchanges, with their make-believe sales of things they do not own, their so-called purchases of things they never intend to have or pay for; who "bull" and "bear" the securities of honest folk; who can only make profits by constantly keeping values disturbed, and the business world in convulsions of uncertainty; whose constant effort is to induce mercantile men to become dissatisfied with slow and honest methods, and enter upon buccaneering expeditions to frighten *bona fide* owners of property to part with it at enormous sacrifices, that they may by securing it reap a rich (even if iniquitous) profit; why, such enterprises as these are carried on in the broad face of day, and protected by law, and accounted highly honorable business! But, pray, wherein do they differ from the old time gentry of the road, who were wont to present a pistol at your head, instead of a law book, with the same demand, "I have the power that gives me the right,—now your money or your life"? Can you define the distinction? Are not the men who get up corners in wheat, or who combine to raise the price of the necessities of life to the poor, as really highwaymen as the green-baize men of loaded dice and cunningly devised card? The one robs his victim because he has the skill to do it, the other robs his because the law gives him the power to do it. Both overreach and plunder. To protect either by law is to put a bounty on fraud, and proffer a premium for the demoralization and ruin of the public. There are men now operating in Wall street, New York, and in Chicago, and Boston, and many another city, who are rated at a score or more millions in cash, or its equivalent, and who have gained it all within a score or less of years, by just this kind of piratical stock-gambling and cornering of the markets. And lo! are they not all honorable men?

Now, it is not necessary to be either a gambler or a skinflint in order to amass a fortune. No man needs to strangle his conscience or harden his heart in order to gain a dollar, or a hundred thousand of them. He may be eminently successful pecuniarily without his money having the curse of his neighbor upon it, or the condemnation of him who hath warned us, "He that oppresseth the poor to increase his riches shall surely come to want," and "He that getteth riches, and not by right, shall leave them in the midst of his days, and at his end shall be a fool." Business *can* be carried on with astonishing monetary success by rendering a just and fair equivalent for every dollar it takes in. "A great cloud of witnesses" proves that. The great majority of those entitled to be considered the representative business men of this country for the past hundred years have been honorable, sagacious, and *honest* traders, whose success enriched the world as well as themselves. They prospered through causing others to prosper. There are benedictions, not reproaches, on their wealth, for their business has not been based on selfishness, and developed in greed, but has been so conducted as to prove that success in commercial lines is not opposed to one's highest advancement in goodness, and truth, and honesty.

Who of all the business men of his time was held in higher esteem than Boston's great merchant, Amos Lawrence, who

FRUITS OF HONESTY.

during his lifetime gave away in charities over seven hundred thousand dollars additional to the fortunes he left by will to his relatives? He was the soul of honesty. Those who knew him said of him, "His integrity stands absolutely unimpeachable, without spot or blemish." His history as a merchant from first to last will bear the strictest scrutiny. He seemed ever to have a reverence for right, unalloyed, unfaltering, supreme; a moral perception and moral sensibility which kept him from deviating a hair's breadth from what he saw and felt to be his duty. It was this that constituted the strength of his character, and was one of the great secrets of his success. It was this that secured him, when a young man, the entire confidence, and an almost unlimited use of capital, of some of the wealthiest and best men of that day. "His daily actions were guided by the most exalted sense of right and wrong, and, in his strict sense of justice, Aristides himself could not surpass him. He was a living example of a successful merchant, who, from the earliest period of his business career, had risen above all artifice, and had never been willing to turn to his own advantage the ignorance or misfortune of others. He demonstrated in his own case the possibility of success, while practicing the highest standard of moral obligation."

When a lad of fourteen years he was apprenticed to a merchant of his native town of Groton, Mass. "A sensible and pious father, aided by a prudent mother, had trained the child to become the future man," and, because of his integrity, he was soon intrusted with the chief control of the store. When twenty-one years of age, he went to Boston with his fortune of twenty dollars in his pocket, and took a position as clerk in the establishment of ———, and was soon offered a partnership in the firm, but he thought their methods of business were not strictly honest, and refused the offer. In a few months the firm failed, and he then began business for himself on credit, in a small way. Shortly after, his brother, Abbott Lawrence, came to him as an apprentice, and, at the expiration of the indenture, became his partner, and the firm of A. & A. Lawrence was known throughout the country for fifty years as one of the largest and soundest of mercantile houses. He was the chief founder of the manufacturing cities of Lowell and Lawrence (the latter named after him, as well, also, as Lawrence University and town in Kansas); he aided scores of young men to gain an education, and to start in business for themselves, and like his brother merchant, John Thornton, became known far and wide for deeds of benevolence, as well as for his great integrity of character.

In a letter to a young man just starting in life, he gives this as the *first* secret of his success: "In the first place, take this for your motto at the commencement of your journey, that the difference of going *just* right, or a *little* wrong, will be the difference of finding yourself in good quarters, or in a miserable bog or slough, at the end of it. To this simple fact of starting *just right* am I indebted, with God's blessing on my labors, for my present position, as well as that of the numerous connections sprung up around me. As a first and leading principle, let every transaction be of that pure and honest character that you would not be ashamed to have it appear before the whole world as clearly as to yourself." A second reason for his great success was his thorough familiarity with his business. "Supply and demand were as familiar to him as the alphabet. He knew the wants of the country, and sources of supply." Concerning this, he said, "The secret of the whole matter was that we had formed the habit of promptly acting, thus taking *the top of the tide;* while the habit of some others was to delay until about *half* tide, thus getting on the flats, while we were all the time prepared for action, and ready to put into any port that promised well." A *third* reason was a constant and careful supervision of his affairs. As to this he writes, "Among the numerous people who have failed in business within my knowledge, a prominent cause has been a want of system in their affairs by which to know when their expenses and losses exceeded their profits." A fourth reason he assigns was economy. "Most of the young men who commenced at that period failed by spending too much money, and using credit too freely. I made about fifteen hundred dollars the first year, and more than four thousand the second. Probably had I made four thousand the first year I should have failed the second or third year. I practiced a system of rigid economy, and never allowed myself to spend a fourpence for unnecessary objects until I had acquired it." Honest articles, sold only for what they were, and at only a fair profit, gave others confidence in the firm, and at length enabled them to reach a position to which few merchants attain. After more than thirty years of business life, Mr. Lawrence wrote, "I am not aware of ever desiring or acquiring any great amount by a single operation, or of taking any part of the property of any other man, and mingling it with my own, where I had the legal right to do so."

Up to the time of his death, December 31, 1852, no other man in this country had equaled him in the extent and amount of his individual benevolences, and while he does not give this as one of the reasons for his remarkable business success, it nevertheless was one, and by no means the least of them. While he exemplified the truth of the declaration of the Bible that "the hand of the diligent maketh rich," he was also another illustration of the truth of its statement that "he that hath pity upon the poor, lendeth unto the Lord, and that which he hath given will he pay him again." Three years before the close of his long business career, he wrote thus concerning his benevolence: "I adopted the practice ten years ago of spending my income. The more I give, the more I have," and thus he who had given seven hundred thousand dollars in charity to the poor had more than a million to leave for his relatives at his death.

A famous maxim declares that "honesty is the best policy," but if the mere getting of money be the object of life, the maxim is not true. A thief will beat an honest man in a trade, by very virtue of his being a thief, nine times out of ten. He will get more money in less time than any dozen honest men can get. If not, how comes it to pass in the United States that

FRUITS OF HONESTY.

less than thirty thousand men have possession of more than one-half of all the wealth of the country? Are none but them diligent? Are none but them economical? Are none but them intelligent? Are none but them honest? If "honesty is the best policy" for money getting, the above fact is a sad impeachment of the morals of the other sixty-five millions of the people of this country. They evidently have not pursued that particular "policy," for they have not that money. But, now, honesty is not a "policy." It should never be degraded to the mere level of a "management" or a "motive" for getting money. Honesty is worth more to man than any amount of dollars, or stocks, or bonds, or lands, can be. Honesty is a man's honor in action. His manhood is a trade, and he should prize it as a woman guards her virtue; he should part with life rather than be despoiled of it. How low indeed is he who bargains it for gold, or sells it for place or power! Young man, honesty, like virtue, is ingrained in us by our birth, if our parents are good. It is part of the material that enters into the wonderful thing we call character, or selfhood. Character is not an accident. We are not born with one, but with the material to make one. Character is a thing of slow growth, of development, like the body. Now as virtue or chastity has the first place, and the best chances in the social life market, so honesty has always a first mortgage on success of any or all kinds that is worth the having. True, you can get much wealth—the laws allow it— by parting with your honesty. So there are those who attain to much of ease and luxury (for a while) by forswearing virtue, but does it pay? Ask yourself that question when tempted by gold to dishonesty of act or word. Will it pay? Believe me there are better things, much higher, nobler things, than mere money getting. Howbeit, the very highest type of honesty, like virtue, is a help not a hindrance, to your getting on in the world, even in acquiring wealth.

David Maydole was a poor country blacksmith near Corning, N. Y., and was locally famous for his honest work, and for making, when the occasion required, an excellent hammer.

FRUITS OF HONESTY.

One day some carpenters from New York city came to the neighborhood to do a piece of work, and one of them needing a hammer had Mr. Maydole make it. His fellow workmen, pleased with its quality, bought some also, and, on their return, induced a dealer in New York to order a dozen, but the dealer found the price too high, and tried to induce Mr. Maydole to reduce it by using an inferior stock so that they might be sold in competition with those then on the market. He replied that he would not make a hammer unless he made it in the best manner, and of the best materials. The hammers the carpenters bought proved so superior to any others that they could get, that they asked for more. Gradually, as their quality became known, his trade increased in spite of the higher price, for the public soon learned that D. Maydole stamped on a hammer meant the best that David Maydole could make, and he came at length to have one of the largest manufactories in the country. His honesty did not hinder but helped him.

When that famous English merchant, Samuel Budgett, refused longer to adulterate his pepper, according to the universal custom of the trade of his time, with something that resembled pepper dust, but was not, and rolled out his casks of "P.D." and stove them to pieces, scattering their contents in the stone quarry, his bank account did not suffer loss, but it added immensely to his wealth of character. The inevitable tendency of all vice is to bring one down to its own low level, and when he refused longer to follow the lead of dishonesty by adulterating his goods, even with such a so-called innocent and harmless thing as "P.D.," and selling them for pure, instinctively men recognized it as a tribute to, and triumph of, the nobler elements of his character. For these little lapses from honesty are as fatal to character as are the little lapses from virtue. Said the poet, Dr. Young, "An honest man's the noblest work of God," and if you accept the reports of the health commissioner as to the extent of the adulteration now practiced in food products, he must be one of the rarest.

Not Above Your Business

Rev. JAMES W. COLE, B.D.

BY a law of nature, the faults indulged in our childhood become the vices of our mature years. The little purloinings and peccadillos of the lad become the embezzlements and rascalities of the man. The carelessness, vanity, and pertness of the maid develop into the extravagance, frivolity, and shrewishness of the woman. All the life of the oak lies hidden in the tiny acorn; and the sins and crimes of after years lie hidden in the faults of the child. All human experience has shown that it is far easier to prevent an evil than to remedy it. A child can destroy many acorns in a brief time, but the strength of many men is required for many days to uproot the forest of oaks, when those acorns are fully grown. All the men of violence and bloody crimes were once innocent children, and their deeds of atrocity that shock the world are the natural growth of evils nourished in childhood and youth. The boy who, as a child and lad, took huge delight in pulling the wings from flies and beetles, and impaling them on sharp splints, naturally grew into that Nero, who, as emperor, ordered the Christians of Rome to be wrapped in flax and pitch, and tied to stakes in his royal gardens, and then burned them as candles wherewith to illuminate the feasts at which he and his lecherous crew were wont to recline and shout and revel, the while his human, shrieking torches were slowly burning to their miserable sockets. If those childish evils had but been repressed, what a foul blot on civilized humanity would have been prevented.

Experience has amply proved that parents are responsible

almost wholly for the faults of the child, either transmitting them to him by heredity, or else cultivating them in him by indulgence, or by unwise teaching. In the first case, we become but the reproduction of our ancestors, and have, at times, to confess sorrowfully to ourselves, at least, that we inherit their vices, even if we are not heirs to their virtues. In the second instance, we are our parents repeated, plus the faults they developed in us. Our children of to-day are to be the parents of to-morrow, and whatever of faults we allow or plant in them, whatever of wrong ideas we give them, will inevitably bear fruit after its kind to trammel them later in their efforts for success in life, and it may be to work their ruin. Or should they win success in defiance of such faults, as some have nobly done, nevertheless those faults in some form and degree will be handed down to the coming generation, for no man ever yet has escaped from this law of heredity.

The seeds of evil, like the seeds of plants, always produce after their kind. It is with the hope of aiding you to avoid an evil already too extensive that this reference is again made to the great primal law of nature, heredity. Plant faults, and you will reap vices. Plant evils, and you will reap crimes. The future is in your keeping. You are to be the future men and women of honor, or of shame. You are to be distinguished for noble deeds, perchance for heroic daring, or you are to be the slaves of sensuality, and the purveyors, if not the creators, of vice. And which of these you become will be almost wholly determined before you are twenty years old. If, in those forming years, you are vain, inconstant, untruthful, and vicious, you will be likely to continue so to old age. On the other hand, should you have formed correct habits of life ere then, success is sure to come to you. This evil but just referred to is the growing disposition among the young to despise manual labor, and seek for a genteel living. In some homes, indeed, the young are taught by precept and by example the folly that only professional, or mercantile, or office work is respectable; that if one were to hold a plow, or drive a plane, or run a lathe or loom, or work in a kitchen, or preside at a washtub for a living, it would immensely lower, if not altogether ruin, one's dignity. In consequence, what are called the professions are crowded with those not fitted either by their natural gifts or by their acquirements, to succeed in them, and who by the very poverty of their surroundings are constantly subject to temptations to vice. If they were not so heavily burdened by dignity, they might soon be above the want or genteel beggary of their present positions, and pass their days in prosperity and usefulness by simply doing some honest, honorable, manual work. But too often their "dignity" forbids, and so some suffer in silence from want, and some resort to questionable, dishonest, and vicious methods to gain a livelihood.

Very much of the forgery and embezzlement of the day is due to the desire to maintain this false dignity of position without hard work. Men are being stimulated by the fabulous fortunes of a few men of note to despise the slow, plodding ways of the fathers of the republic, and they plunge into unwise speculations, hoping thus to amass a fortune quickly, or they tax the energies of mind and body to their utmost in the mad race for position, or wealth, and are wrecked in nerve and brain while yet in the flush of their manhood. The wise content with a frugal living and a modest competence has too largely departed, and in its place has come a feverish anxiety for much gold, and for luxury of dress and appointments, that is destined to undermine, slowly, perhaps, but none the less surely, the health and morals of the American people. It is time to call a halt, and to remember that there are other and nobler things to seek for than money. I would not have you despise money. It is a most useful gift of God to men. Yet who was ever satisfied with his pots of gold? If, however, that is what you are determined on seeking, bear in mind that it does not require a very high grade of brains or of morals to get it. Some of the most successful money-getters that the world has ever known never had an atom of greatness either in brain or soul, and, when the Almighty took away the money from them, he found only the skeleton of a man. The intellect was shriveled into a parchment for recording stocks and bonds, while the spirit had become simply a mummy's bag to take in gold. No, it does not take a first-class man to get money. A gambler can often get much of it; so can a thief; so can a rumseller. Indeed, such persons often get more of it, and in far less time, than an honest merchant, or a hard-working farmer or mechanic can. And the reason is very plain. *They are never above their business.* They could not succeed in it if they were. The business brings money, and all their energies are bent to the one thing of "getting on" by it. They may despise the business, and despise themselves for being in it, but the "easy money" it yields holds them to it. The instant they get *above their business*, that instant the business stops. *They must always be down to its level* in order to carry it on. And it is just so in all honorable lines of industry. No man ever makes much of a success in any one of them who *gets above* the business in which he is engaged. The moment he does, that instant his failure in it is certain.

The men of honor who amass honest fortunes by honorable means are never above their business. No part of it is so lowly as to be despised or neglected by them. They recognize the all-important fact in life that no necessary work can ever be dishonorable or degrading to any man. If you would get on in the world, never despise any honest, hard work, or worker. Pride, like modesty, is a most excellent thing in its place, but it is often assumed, and is sometimes counterfeited, and then it becomes grotesque, or contemptible. Many a young man is "too proud" to carry a bundle through the street for his employer, or even for himself, and orders it sent by the porter, but the same young man is not "too proud" to shirk work, and indulge in hours of leisure at his employer's expense, or to indulge in indelicate speech, or to fellowship vicious companions, any one of which things will lower his dignity more in an hour than it would to drive a dray for a twelvemonth. Peter the Great, though Czar of all the Russias, was never so great as when, in order to elevate his half-savage countrymen by inducing them to become shipbuilders, he laid aside his royal robes, and, disguising himself as an humble workman, entered the East India Company's dockyard at Amsterdam to learn the art of shipbuilding for their sakes, and lived in the lowly lodgings of his fellow laborers, and ate their kind of food, and was as one of them. Royalty's dignity was not tarnished by the deed, but how honorable shipbuilding became to all noble minded Russians when it was known that the Czar had learned it in order to benefit them.

John Marshall, for thirty-five years the chief justice of the Supreme Court of the United States, who had been general in the army, member of Congress, senator, and envoy to France, and his country's greatest constitutional lawyer, did not think it belittled him to carry from the market his family supplies. On one occasion, a pompous young fellow was loudly bewailing his inability to find an errand man to carry a turkey for him, when the chief justice, saying he was going past the young man's house, offered to take it home for him. The young man, who did not know Mr. Marshall, gladly accepted the offer, and contentedly trotted along by his side, and, when the house was reached, offered to pay him for the errand. When this was refused, the young sprout made inquiry as to "who that obliging old man was," and, when he was told, it began to dawn on him that there was a vast difference between dignity and dudism.

Boston's millionaire merchant and philanthropist, Amos Lawrence, once had a clerk in his employ who was requested to take home to a lady a small purchase, but he declined to do it on the ground that it would "compromise his dignity," whereupon Mr. Lawrence, hoping to teach him a lesson, carried it himself, much to the consternation of the fop, who had mistaken vanity for dignity. Unfortunately a few like him survive to this day, but they never get above a clerkship.

Beginning at the Bottom.

Rev. JAMES W. COLE, B.D.

PLATO, that prince of philosophers, lays it down as an axiom that whenever luxury (the product of wealth) prevails among a people, it invariably destroys the most mighty and flourishing of states and kingdoms. He also calls attention to the fact that persons born to wealth and greatness are almost unavoidably apt to become degenerate in vigor of body and in strength of mind; that the luxury of appetite, and voluptuousness of life, that great wealth induces, stifles the better nature of man, and renders him insensible to the grand motives of duty, of love of country, and zeal for the public good; that the soft and delicate life it brings subjects men to the dominion of a multitude of artificial wants and necessities, upon the having of which their happiness is found at length to depend to such an extent that, through fear of losing these conveniences and superfluities of life, they become timid, fearful, and cowardly, and are unfitted to undergo the fatigues and hardships and self-denials and struggles necessary for great achievements, either of conquest or of defense. And the historians of all ages and nations confirm the truth of the great philosopher's axiom. For, as nations have become greatly rich, they have been seen to become greatly corrupted, and to have perished of such corruption.

Is wealth, then, a foe to civilization and a hindrance to the development of man's better and higher nature? By no means. Wealth is the product of civilization. Savages are wretchedly poor. Wealth is the result of intelligence; the effect of the cultivation of one's nobler instincts; the creation alone of the virtues.

Vices do not produce it, although they often steal it. And this fruit of a good tree, the virtues, cannot necessarily, or naturally, be injurious. Poverty is a greater curse to humanity than riches ever were, and it is infinitely more to be dreaded. It takes an immense amount of divine grace to endure poverty. The Christ endured it, as he endured other evils, to show us that God could develop the noblest humanity even at humanity's lowest point of penury, but, nevertheless, poverty is not a thing to be desired. How it represses and perverts the finer, nobler instincts of man! To what low depths of beastliness it at length sinks him! How few, and how ignoble, are the ambitions of the great masses of the poor in almost all lands! How their poverty holds them down! While not a badge of serfdom, it is an occasion and a cause of servitude. While by no means a disgrace, it is the fruitful cause of many a shame. It is not a crime, but it is the nursery of a vast multitude of crimes, and no one should be content to remain in it who has the power and opportunity to rise above it. Men may talk as they please about the blessings of poverty, nevertheless there are but few natures who are capable of being ennobled by it if long continued. Ages ago the wise men declared that "the destruction of the poor is their poverty," and nature and human nature are the same to-day. Therefore, get out of poverty as quickly as you can; but get out of it nobly, by getting out of it naturally.

Nature makes no mistakes, and when she starts us at the poverty point, she does so for a very wise purpose. Poverty is the childhood period of mankind, and as the nations and individuals who compose them advance in the intelligence and virtue she designed for them, they naturally leave poverty behind them. With every increase in intelligence and virtue, wealth increases among all people. And yet, paradox though it be, it is generally a sad misfortune, as Plato estimates, to have been born of rich parents. To gain riches is to gain a certain kind of victory, and it is by many accounted the most desirable victory in life. Now a victory is often harder to manage than a defeat. It is sometimes far more disastrous than any defeat could be. Hence it has sometimes so happened that the acquisition of great wealth has proved to be only a mighty load to sink the possessor and all his in eternal infamy. They would have been better off if they had never been rich. It is a terrible thing to starve one's better nature simply to gain money that you must soon leave, perchance to ignoble souls, who can scarce decently wait for you to die ere they scramble after your pile of gold.

A recent writer has declared that not one in a thousand of the sons of very wealthy persons ever dies wealthy. The explanation is plain and easy. The sturdy virtues of economy, of thrift, and wise forecast that are needed to gain wealth, the necessity to labor, the abstinence from weakening dissipation and fleshly appetites, the constant vigilance required in the contest for it, are all lacking in the case of him who is born to it, and they are but seldom cultivated in him unless his parents are persons of rare good sense. The parents are generally either so occupied in acquiring their wealth that they neglect his education, or else they commit the task to hirelings, who teach him rather how to enjoy and spend money than how to earn and wisely use and care for it, with the very natural result that whereas the father began with nothing, the son often ends with nothing, or worse. Almost invariably the greatest kindness that can be done to young men or young women is to give them an opportunity to earn their own living, even though they are heirs to a fortune. Many a man has found that what seemed at first a hard necessity compelling him to earn his own living, was in reality a better inheritance than if he had been given scores of thousands of dollars without work.

The late United States senator, Simon Cameron, for a generation known as the "Czar of Pennsylvania politics," was left an orphan and poor when a child, and began to learn the printer's trade when nine years of age, and at twenty-three was the editor of the leading paper in Harrisburg. Afterward he became a banker and railroad speculator, and at length a man of great wealth, and a mighty factor in the politics of his state. When forty-six years of age, he became United States senator from Pennsylvania, which office he held for many years, until in 1872 he resigned in favor of his son, James Donald Cameron. Of this son, he said at one time, "He has been fortunate in one thing, he was born poor." The elder Cameron had come to know by experience that privation and hard work is one of the greatest blessings that can befall a young man. It develops the best that is in him by compelling him to cultivate virtue if he would get on in the world.

"Ill fares the land, to hastening ills a prey,
Where wealth accumulates and men decay."

One of the noblest and best governors that the state of Massachusetts ever had, and to whom she gave the phenomenal honor of re-electing him for seven consecutive years, was George N. Briggs, the son of a Revolutionary soldier, who was afterward a blacksmith. George was born at Adams, Massachusetts, April 13, 1796, and died of a gunshot accident at Pittsfield, Mass., September 12, 1861. When eleven years old, he was obliged to seek his own living, and was apprenticed to a hatter at White Creek, New York. Three years afterward, an elder brother gave him a year's schooling, for the lad, imbued with the idea of becoming a lawyer, was giving every leisure moment he could get from his work to study. Concerning this, Mr. Briggs wrote years afterward: "In August, 1813, with five dollars I had earned at haying, I left home to go to studying law. I had a brother living on the Hudson, whom I visited in September, and then, with my trunk on my back, came into Berkshire county, penniless, and a stranger to all except a few relatives and friends, most of them as poor as I was, and that was poor enough." But the penniless lad studied hard, and worked his way in every honest mode he could, and five years later was admitted to the bar of his native county, and soon took his place as a most eloquent pleader and keen debater. In 1830 he was elected to Congress as representative, and he served six terms, and then from 1843 to 1851 was governor of his state. During his governorship, the celebrated trial and execution of Professor Webster for the murder of Dr. Parkman took place, and Governor Briggs, believing that justice and the best interests of the people would be served if the law took its course, resisted the mighty efforts then made for a commutation of that sentence. After his retirement from the gubernatorial chair, he was for five years a judge of the Court of Common Pleas. He was a man of deep religious convictions, and at his death was president of the American Baptist Missionary Union, and of the American Tract Society at Boston, of the American Temperance Union, of the Massachusetts Sabbath School Union, and a trustee of Williams College, besides holding a membership in various other charitable and religious organizations, positions none of which, in all human probability, he would have reached but for the spur and incentive born of his early poverty.

The visitor at Lancaster, Pa., will find, in a large private cemetery at that place devoted to the burial of the poor of all nations and creeds, a tomb of the donor, who was buried there August 14, 1868, and on which tomb he caused it to be recorded that he had chosen that private spot, "not from any natural preference for solitude, but, finding other cemeteries limited by charter rules as to race, I have chosen it that I might be enabled to illustrate in my death the principles which I have advocated through a long life,—equality of man before his Creator." It is the grave of America's "Great Commoner," Thaddeus Stevens, the heroic leader of the patriots in the House of Representatives during the dark and troublous days of the Rebellion. He was born in Danville, Caledonia County, Vermont, April 4, 1792. His parents were in very humble circumstances, and Thaddeus was a sickly child, and lame, but intensely ambitious for an education. His noble, devout mother exerted herself to the utmost to aid him in his struggle, and by her help, and his own determined efforts, he was enabled at length to enter the University of Vermont. While there his father died in the war of 1812, and the university closed because of the war. He then entered Dartmouth College, from which institution he graduated in 1814. He became a teacher in the academy at York, Pa., and while there privately studied law, and in 1816 began to practice as attorney at Gettysburg, Pa., where for sixteen years he stood in the very front rank of his profession, helping many a struggling young man to an education, and fighting mightily to establish a free school system of education in his adopted state, in which for many years he was a member of the Legislature, and known everywhere as the unterrified champion of freedom, and of free speech and thought.

Living on the borders of a slave state, he was an ardent abolitionist, and rescued many a fleeing fugitive from being returned to bondage. As an instance of his kindness of heart toward the poor, despised black race, he stopped over night at a Maryland tavern when on his way to Baltimore to buy some law books for his scant library, in the early days of his practice as a lawyer, and a negro woman in great distress begged him to intercede with the landlord that her husband, a slave, who was also the landlord's son, might not be sold from her. Forthwith the young lawyer pleaded with the unnatural father in behalf of his humble daughter-in-law, but pleaded in vain. The "boy" should be sold, and he must have three hundred dollars for him, and no less. Finding entreaties all in vain, Stevens bought the landlord's son, and at once gave him free papers, and, abandoning his journey and the much coveted law books, returned to fight more fiercely than ever the barbarous system that degraded a man to the level of a beast.

In 1842 he removed to Lancaster, where he met with great success in his profession, and might have amassed much wealth but for his constant and lavish private charities. In 1848 he was elected to Congress by the Whig party, where he remained until 1853, when he retired and practiced law again for five years to repair financial losses with which he had met, and then in 1858 he was re-elected to Congress as a Republican,

BEGINNING AT THE BOTTOM.

which party continued him in office as its representative until his death. A master of invective, how he thundered against the rebels in Congress and out of it! Even in the thick of the fight, he rallied his countrymen to stand by Freedom's altar, never ceasing, never faltering, in his demand that all men should be free in limb, in thought, in speech; and he lived to see the land he loved so intensely delivered from the curse that for ages had rested upon it, for now man could no longer buy and sell his fellow man as though he were an ox. When Freedom writes up her heroes, chief among them will be found the name of Thaddeus Stevens, the grand old Commoner. An orphan asylum at Lancaster, for the poor children of both the white and black races, that he founded by his will, perpetuates his memory there.

The Results of Application.

WILLIAM HENRY SCOTT, LL.D., Pres. State University, Columbus, Ohio.

HOW much we shall accomplish in life depends on our ability, our opportunity, and our application. The first two are fixed quantities. Our natural ability was determined before we could exercise any agency or choice. Over what is now our acquired ability we once had a large determining power; but for our present use it too is fixed. However we may modify it hereafter, we can do nothing to make it at this moment different in one jot or tittle from what it is. The past was the time to mold the present, but the past is gone, and no man has any more power in it. We once held also a large determining power over what is now our opportunity. But that power has been exhausted, and at each occasion we must accept our opportunity, if we accept it at all, just as it is.

But the third factor is in our control. We may determine what amount of application we will join with our ability and opportunity. It is by our application therefore that the result, so far as we have any power over it, is always measured. The only question that concerns any man is, How should I use the gifts and occasions that I now have in order that I may perform my duty in life and attain my proper destiny? It is idle for him to complain that he has not been endowed with greater talents or favored with a better opportunity. Repining will only impair his present action. All that remains for him is to put forth his ability, whatever it is, in the improvement of his actual opportunity.

What results may he expect? Perhaps success in the outward thing that he aims at. Burritt, the blacksmith, began his career as a student of languages while he was working at the anvil fourteen hours a day. When his great acquirements became known and he was asked how he had made them, he wrote, "All that I have accomplished has been by that plodding, patient, persevering process of accretion which builds the ant-heap—particle by particle, thought by thought, fact by fact." Palissy, toiling in the face of poverty and failure to discover the secret of the white enamel, was so intoxicated with enthusiasm that men thought him a fool. God's fool he was, with a great hope at his heart for which he gladly suffered the loss of all things. His reward was success in what he sought and an immortal name. Tennyson, living apart, kept his mind brooding poetic themes, and through years of habitual retirement he nourished the thoughts and framed the expressions that made him the first poet of his generation. Gibbon has told us what years of research, reflection, and composition it cost him to produce his history—a work to which, with all its faults, we may apply the language which he applied to the empire itself—"a solid fabric of human greatness." Michael Angelo observed nature with a searching and critical eye. He studied human anatomy with extraordinary minuteness and thoroughness. He would begin a piece of work in the most elementary way, and develop it through each stage, often by repeated trials and always with the closest attention. While he was painting the Sistine Chapel he would not allow himself time for meals or to dress and undress; but he kept bread within reach that he might eat when hunger impelled, and he slept in his clothes. What were the results? Paintings, statues, buildings, military works of the first order, "miracles of genius" which have remained unequaled by any modern hand.

No less is it true in the pursuits of common life that by stern and laborious application each individual realizes the best results of which he is capable. Whatever your place, you can make the most of it by applying yourself wholly to it. In almost every case the best work is the result of the greatest application. It comes only at the last and as the effect of the final

THE RESULTS OF APPLICATION.

process. It is the exquisite product of all the resources and activities that can contribute to its perfection. It is the last and richest drop of the vintage.

Any work that is worthy of us has its difficulties. But what work is it whose difficulties cannot be overcome by heroic application? It is wonderful how the face of a dismal situation brightens when a calm and steady will confronts it. What seemed a mountain proves an airy phantasm. What seemed an impregnable Gibraltar is found to be penetrated with secret passages and stairways. But, however real and stubborn the obstacles may be, they almost always give way before a spirit of earnest application. Yet not always. The outward reward of even the most faithful endeavor sometimes fails. Either ability or opportunity, or both, may be wanting. Many causes may intervene whose existence and influence cannot be foreknown.

But there are other results that never fail. One of these is the growth of opportunity. Rigid for the present, for the future opportunity is elastic. Opportunity that is used opens the way to that which is greater. Press up to the boundary of the opportunity in which you now are, and it will be easy to step forth into the one that lies just beyond. Application is the path from lower opportunity to higher.

There are deeper and more abiding results. We may not aim to accomplish them. We may even be unconscious that they are forming. But while we are engrossed in pursuit of the outward object, the reaction of each effort that we put forth is impressing itself infallibly and ineffaceably in our nature. Our acts are recorded within us as if graven with an iron pen and lead in the rock forever.

The secret of self-improvement is that under the law of supply and demand strength comes by use. Every exertion consumes force, thus creating a want; and nature, wise economist as she is, immediately stores a surplus where the want arises, against future demands. The power to do grows by faithful doing, and our ability, though for our present need it is neither

THE RESULTS OF APPLICATION.

greater nor less than it is, can be made for the future indefinitely broader and more effective.

Application brings ease as well as strength. What we do often is done with less and less exertion. Learning is in great part but the process of acquiring ease by practice. The soldier, the penman, the musician, the orator, learn to perform the movements which their vocations require by repeating them till body and mind respond habitually and without effort.

Application produces skill. Up to a certain limit ease and skill increase together; but beyond that limit as the action becomes easier improvement is apt to cease. For while ease results from mere repetition, skill increases only by repetition that is conducted with attention and care. As attention and care decline, the performance becomes more easy but less skillful. Thus ease and skill, so far from growing in harmony side by side, become opposed to each other. Although the work as we performed it at first has become easy, the work as we ought to perform it is as difficult as ever; for all the energy that we are now able to save from the lower forms of effort through the ease which practice has brought us should be directed to more perfect achievement. Much of the mere routine of life we may turn over to habit and be content to get through it easily; but our real work should always command our highest intelligence and our fullest energy. In this we ought always to do our best; and if we do, we shall never cease to improve.

The hardest nature, apparently intractable by any force, will gradually yield to the influence of its own action; and thus an inner transformation may eventually be wrought. It is true, most men fail in their efforts at reform; but it is because their will is weak or because they do not wait with patience for results. These are the two requisites—time and an inexorable will. Given time enough, a will that knows no change can subdue the passions and develop the power and transmute the nature of the most degraded soul that breathes. No matter how weak a power may be, rational use will make it stronger. No matter how awkward your movements may be, or how

THE RESULTS OF APPLICATION.

obtuse your senses, or how crude your thought, or how unregulated your desires, you may by patient discipline acquire, slowly indeed but with infallible certainty, grace and freedom of action, clearness and acuteness of perception, strength and precision of thought, and moderation of desire. If you will apply your inner force to the achievement of a high and magnanimous life, you shall yet see with the imaginative eye and hear with the musical ear and think with the illuminated understanding and feel with the pure and serene heart. A transforming spirit will brood over you, shedding a slow diffusing light through your darkness and out of the chaos of your nature evoking the beauty and order of a new life. Steadfastly work and wait, and the secrets of science, of literature, of art, may one day lie open to your mind and you may rise to ranges of experience whose noble splendors surpass your present power to comprehend.

With persistent faith all can be done. Not in a day, not in a year. The results of application are a form of growth, and like all growth they proceed slowly and unconsciously. But by faithful application, doing each day what can be done in that day, by thoughtfulness, by aspiration, by patient, undiscouraged fidelity in every least thing as well as in every greatest thing, the sublime result will at last be realized.

Find your true end. Let the desire to attain it be to you as the breath of life. Let your application to it be steadfast and unremitting. Commit yourself to it in unreserved devotion. The results will assuredly be the largest measure of achievement, the largest measure of happiness, and the attainment of the noblest nature that are possible to your endowment and your opportunity.

Commercial Courage.

Rev. JAMES W. COLE, B.D.

IT is a misfortune to a man to have the path to success made smooth and easy to him; for in such case he fails to develop the sturdy virtues and personal resources that are alone the product of hard toil, economy, and thrift, and upon the development of these qualities depends the value of his manhood. True, the qualities may exist in him, but in such case they remain in embryo. The value of muscle depends not on its flabbiness, which is the result of want of exercise, but upon its strength and endurance, which alone come by use. Brains are valuable, not for their bulk, but for fineness, also due to use. And one's virtues or one's resources become valuable in proportion to their development. Use develops skill, aptness, strength.

The value of all victories depends not altogether upon the getting them, but upon *how* you get them. Sometimes a victory costs too much, and great wealth is often not worth the getting. If to gain victory you must part with honor, truth, manhood, then defeat is far preferable; for in such case the defeat becomes the victory when viewed from life's last hours. Honor and manhood outrank all wealth or position at that point, and beyond it. Many young men are apt to lose heart if their first plans and efforts for success miscarry; as though perfection were due to a first trial, or fruits were to be plucked before the seeds were grown. When a young man fails in business, he and the world too often think he is *ruined;* as though the first skirmish made or unmade the warrior; as though one chance for success were all that Providence gives us! Young man, ten thousand chances are before you. With the proper use of your present opportunities, new ones will appear. The due employment of your resources to-day will bring you new power to-morrow. Life is a constant unfolding of new opportunities, new resources, new powers. How much we have to-day that our fathers never dreamed of! And there will be more to-morrow. Neither nature nor human nature is exhausted.

A stout heart, a dauntless will, and a pure spirit are invincible everywhere. Nature yields her hidden treasures to him who dares seek them. Of her comes wealth; of her comes success,—but not to the faint-hearted. Fear keeps many a man poor, and often causes business men to fail. General Sherman tells us that he was offered corner lots in San Francisco in 1848 for $16 each, and could have bought gold mines for a few score dollars apiece, but was afraid to invest. In a few years thereafter they were worth millions. A man of very great wealth declares that he never made any money only at times called panics, when every one seemed possessed by fear. Then he bought, and when men recovered from their fear he was rich. Nearly every panic of these modern times is gotten up by men of daring to enrich a few individuals, and the moral is a very plain one—don't get frightened. You may lose money; but what matters it if you do not lose honor or health? All the capital of the world is simply the overplus of toil; that is, what is left after supplying the daily wants of mankind. If yours has departed, you can easily get more by toil, industry, economy, perseverance.

Never despair. Life is not solely for getting a living; it is for developing the perfect man, body, mind, and soul. And that is often better obtained through what men call failures and defeats, than by victories. Be brave. Cowardice is born of fear, and fear is weakness. Noble manhood and noble womanhood grow from resolute, determined spirits that take this life's vicissitudes to be, what indeed they are, the needful preparation for far more responsible and ennobling duties and employments in the life beyond. In this world's business affairs the man who refuses to consider himself defeated sooner or later wins success. He may not win the first battle, nor the second, nor the third, but, like Bruce of Scotland, he will fire his spirit in the hours of dejection that come to us all, with the perseverance even of the humble spider, and like him cry, "I, too, will yet conquer."

Sometimes a young man fresh from college, and full of its lore, gets discouraged if his brilliant talents do not at once put him in the highest positions; forgetting that skill is as needful to success as is knowledge of principles; and skill is born of toil. If you are but of good courage, you will find your place made for you, or make one for yourself. The world's great enterprises were not projected nor carried out by cowards. If De Lesseps had heeded the "It can't be done," of the world's faint-hearted croakers, there would now be no Suez canal. If Jay Cooke or Oakes Ames had taken counsel of the multitudinous prophets of fear, we should not now have our Pacific railroads. In all just, honest, honorable enterprises "I have" waits on "I dare."

The Man of Push.

Rev. GEORGE R. HEWITT, B.D.

PUSH, what is it? Our latest and largest dictionary* defines it as "persevering energy"; "enterprise." Definition, however, is hardly necessary. We Americans know full well the meaning of the term. We are the most pushing people on the face of the earth. As a nation we have more energy, enterprise, and go-ahead than any nation the world has hitherto produced. Says Emerson, "Import into any stationary district, as into an old Dutch population in New York or Pennsylvania, or among the planters of Virginia, a colony of hardy Yankees, with seething brains, heads full of steam-hammer, pulley, crank, and toothed wheel, and everything begins to shine with value."

There has lately come into colloquial use in our country a rather inelegant but forceful word which expresses exactly what we mean by a man of push. It is the word "hustler." To hustle is to push or make your way with difficulty through a crowd. To-day the thoroughfares of life are crowded; if a man would win a place in the ranks of professional or mercantile life, he must push for it. Push brings men of mediocrity to the front, and enables them to stay there. In these days of keen competition, a man without push is soon jostled aside and falls into the rear. Push is the passport to success. Push paves the way from poverty to wealth.

In no profession or pursuit is eminence achieved apart from push,—apart from hard, persistent work. "I find," said Livingstone, the great missionary explorer, "that all eminent men

---
* The Century.

work hard." We may be sure there has always been hard, earnest, persistent work somewhere before eminence has been gained.

"The heights by great men reached and kept
Were not attained by sudden flight,
But they, while their companions slept,
Were toiling upward in the night."

There is absolutely no substitute for that persevering energy which we call push. Scientists tell us that the various forms of energy manifest in the physical universe—light, heat, gravitation, magnetism, electricity—are all convertible into one another. But if a man has not mental energy, push, no other qualification he may have is convertible into it or can be a substitute for it. Nothing can take its place. Learning cannot. Talent cannot. Genius cannot. Genius is a dazzling thing, but it is not exempt from the law of labor. It must plod if it would win the prize. Genius is not a something that can dispense with toil, but rather a something that inspires the soul to persevere in needed toil. The world's greatest men have ever been its most energetic workers.

Genius, unless it have inherited wealth, must push and plod or it will die in the poorhouse.

History is full of splendid examples of what may be accomplished by energy and indefatigable push. Push led Columbus out from his Spanish hills across the western waves. In his journal, day after day he wrote these simple but sublime words, "That day we sailed Westward, which was our course." Hope might rise and fall, terror and dismay seize upon the crew at the mysterious variations of the compass, but Columbus, unappalled, pushed on due west, and nightly wrote in his journal the above words. A sublime example of push! It was push on the part of Knox that led to the reformation in Scotland; push on the part of the Wesleys that regenerated religious life in England. It was push on the part of men like Garibaldi, Cavour, and Mazzini that in our day has unified Italy. Push **is the word** that explains the marvelous career of Napoleon.

THE MAN OF PUSH.

Under all difficulties and discouragements whatsoever, his motto was, "I press on." When told the Alps stood in the way of his army, "Then there shall be no Alps," he said, and he built the road across the Simplon pass. Push is the word that explains all the wonderful achievements and triumphant progress of this nineteenth century. It has built immense cities where a few years ago were rolling prairies; it has girdled the globe with railroads and given us Cunard steamers for ancient shallops, so that we can go from Chicago to London in a week. It teaches us to raise our crops, and creates yearly more wealth than the Orient ever knew.

The man of push is a man of intelligence. He knows at what he is aiming, and works towards it like a Hercules. His push has a purpose behind it. His energy is not blind, neither is it fitful nor easily daunted. It devotes itself to a given object; is not drawn off to side issues; is quiet but incessant in operation; attends strictly to business; overcomes difficulties, not necessarily with noise and bustle, but one by one by steady pressure. Old Commodore Vanderbilt, being asked what he considered the secret of business success, replied, "Secret? There is no secret about it. All you have to do is to attend to your business and go ahead." Push is the application of mind to material conditions with wealth as the result. Your man of push sees where land will be wanted, clears it accordingly, lays it out, goes to sleep, and wakes up rich.

The man of push masters his circumstances and is not mastered by them. He believes that

"One constant element of luck
Is genuine, solid, old Teutonic pluck."

Circumstances have rarely favored famous men. They have fought their way to triumph through all sorts of opposing obstacles. Milton wrote Paradise Lost in blindness and poverty. His motto was,

"I argue not
Against Heaven's hand or will, nor bate a jot
Of heart or hope, but still bear up and steer
Right onward."

THE MAN OF PUSH.

Linnæus, the great naturalist, was at one time so poor as to be obliged to mend his shoes with folded paper, and to beg his meals of his friends. George Stephenson, the inventor of the locomotive, began life as a common collier, working in the mine. Nearly all the men who have risen to greatness began life under unfavorable conditions. Circumstances seldom conquer a man of push and determination. In the words of Tennyson,

> "He breaks his birth's invidious bar,
> And grasps the skirts of happy chance,
> And breasts the blows of circumstance
> And grapples with his evil star."

This chapter cannot be closed better than in the words of Sir Thomas Fowell Buxton. "The longer I live, the more certain I am that the great difference between men, the feeble and the powerful, the great and the insignificant, is *energy and invincible determination*—a purpose once fixed and then death or victory."

The Value of Tact.

WILLIAM C. KING, Springfield, Mass.

TACT is defined by Webster as being that peculiar skill and ready power of appreciating and accomplishing whatever is required by circumstances.

Men of great talents and profound wisdom are constantly being distanced in the race of life by those who have but a fraction of their attainments.

The latter have the faculty of using all the ability they possess to the best advantage.

Talent is mental or physical power, while tact is the ability to use talent skillfully. While the man of talent is getting under headway, the man of tact steps in and wins the race.

Wisdom will tell you what to do, while tact will show you how it is done; this is not because tact is wiser than his neighbor wisdom, but because he is more ready and apt. His vision does not take so wide a range as wisdom, but is more pointed and direct. The man of wisdom convinces, the man of tact persuades. The one overwhelms with his arguments, the other pleads or persuades. One uses logic, the other rhetoric; one appeals to the intellect, the other to the sensibilities, and, as the common people are not learned logicians, the man of rhetoric draws the crowds and pockets the cash. Talent gets high compliments, while tact carries away the prize. Men often ask why the man of wisdom does not succeed better in winning the laurels of life, and wonder why men of tact get so many of them. But there is no great mystery about it. Tact is ever on the alert for personal advancement, while wisdom seeks personal improvement. Tact has a keen eye for opportunities to win success, while wisdom is laboring hard to deserve it. Tact keeps its ear adjusted to catch all hints, while wisdom is content to give them. Wisdom has always something worth hearing, with but few listeners; while tact never lacks for hearers, whom it entertains if it does not instruct. Tact will adapt itself to circumstances, while talent too often ignores them. Wisdom is demanding in its claims, while tact will yield to conquer. Wisdom condemns the weaknesses of humanity, while tact ignores them or uses them to climb to place and profit. In a sentence, tact is the faculty of *adaptation* to the emergencies real or supposed of the present, while wisdom is for the permanencies of all time. The man of wisdom is not always the man of tact, while the men of tact are rarely noted for great learning. They are what the world calls "practical people"—persons who are more anxious to conciliate than to antagonize others. Hence men of tact figure among the most successful in business affairs, but they are rarely found among the ranks of the reformers. Reformers are men of different mold. Reforms come, however, but seldom, and the masses must have work and bread, and "practical" men must provide them. So it comes to pass that these men of tact constitute the life of commerce and of trade. Both commerce and trade are intensely conservative and will not willingly forego their dividends, therefore men of reform must be content to be "voices crying in the wilderness" until wrongs are no longer bearable; then the men of tact execute the reforms. That remarkable man of the 19th century, Abraham Lincoln, although the instrument in the hands of Providence for the liberation of four and a half millions of bondmen, was not by nature, habit, or education a reformer, and neither himself nor the political party electing him to the presidency had any thought of abolishing slavery.

Lincoln was a man of most wonderful tact. It was that tact which gave him immortality of fame and gave to his party a lease of power for thirty years, proving once more that men and parties will ever gain length of days through righteousness, his great distinguishing characteristic. He had good talents, but they were by no means of the highest order. He was surpassed in some respects by many men of his day, but he had industry, ambition, and a large stock of good common sense, ruled and directed by a tact that led him at moments of destiny to champion the cause of the oppressed, because on that side his tact taught him lay victory for himself and party.

With what adroit and well-nigh infinite tact he held his way through the stormy political campaigns that resulted in his election, and then through those fierce, troublous, and bloody days of the civil war! Other presidents have been as patriotic as he; some of them have been far greater statesmen, but as a political tactician he stands unrivaled, and, because of the peculiarity of the times in which he lived giving him great opportunity to exercise that tact, he has stamped the pages of history with a deathless impress. He never had a year's schooling. We quote from his own words regarding his parentage and early life.

"My father, at the death of his father, was but six years of age and grew up literally without any education. He removed to what is now Spencer county, Indiana, in my eighth year. We reached our new home about the time the state came into the Union. It was a wild region with many bears and other wild animals still in the woods. There I grew up. There were some schools, so called, but no qualifications were ever required of a teacher beyond 'readin', writin', and cipherin'' to the rule of three. If a straggler supposed to understand Latin happened to sojourn in the neighborhood he was looked upon as a wizard. There was absolutely nothing to excite ambition for education. Of course, when I came of age, I did not know much, still, somehow, I could read, write, and cipher to the rule of three, but that was all. I have not been to school since. The little advance I now have upon this store of education, I have picked up from time to time under the pressure of necessity. I was raised to farm work, at which I continued till I was twenty-two."

THE VALUE OF TACT.

He knew nothing of grammar, indeed, scarce understood what it means, nor did he study it until he had grown to manhood, when he wearily and alone plodded through the book, on finding that he could never hope to be a lawyer without the knowledge of constructing sentences. Yet how that tact of his led him in after days to say the right word at the right place! That is what tact does, and its possessor becomes renowned. Who quotes that learned and eloquent oration of Edward Everett, delivered at the dedication of the Gettysburg cemetery, November 19, 1863? But these few terse, tactful sentences of Lincoln's, written hurriedly on scraps of paper while going thither on the cars, on being informed that he would be expected to say something on that occasion, have already passed into fame as one of the rarest classics in the English language.

"Fourscore and seven years ago our fathers brought forth on this continent a new nation, conceived in liberty and dedicated to the proposition that all men are created equal. Now we are engaged in a great civil war, testing whether that nation, or any nation so conceived and so dedicated, can long endure. We are met on a great battle field of that war. We have come to dedicate a portion of the field as a final resting place for those who here gave their lives that that nation might live. It is altogether fitting and proper that we should do this. But, in a larger sense, we cannot dedicate, we cannot consecrate, we cannot hallow, this ground. The brave men, living and dead, who struggled here, have consecrated it far above our power to add to or detract from.

"The world will little note nor long remember what we say here, but it never can forget what they did here. It is for us, the living, rather, to be dedicated here to the unfinished work which they who fought here have thus far so nobly advanced. It is rather for us here to be dedicated to the great task remaining before us, that from these honored dead we take increased devotion to that cause for which they gave the last full measure of devotion; that we here highly resolve that these dead

THE VALUE OF TACT.

shall not have lived in vain; that this nation under God shall have a new birth of freedom, and that government of the people, by the people, for the people, shall not perish from the earth."

To what heights this poor backwoods boy had grown! On the first day of January of this same year he had as the chief magistrate of the land proclaimed liberty to the captives, and so by that action this man of tact, who in his struggle with Stephen A. Douglas for vantage ground in the coming contest for the presidency had chosen for policy's sake to give a quasi-support to the efforts of reformers against that hideous monstrosity and libel on humanity, slavery, had been driven at last by the hurrying feet of events to become himself a Reformer! Yet his tact even then led him in his message to the next Congress to base such official action as he had taken wholly upon the ground of public policy rather than upon righteousness, and then he went on to address them as a reformer might have done. Hear him as he pleads for the support of Congress.

"Fellow citizens, we cannot escape history. We of this Congress and this administration will be remembered in spite of ourselves. No personal significance or insignificance can spare one or another of us. The fiery trial through which we pass will light us down in honor or dishonor to the latest generation. We, even we here, hold the power and bear the responsibility. In giving freedom to the slave, we assure freedom to the free, honorable alike in what we give and what we preserve. We shall nobly save or meanly lose the last best hope of earth. Other means *may* succeed; *this could not fail.* The way is plain, peaceful, generous, just,—a way which, if followed, the world will applaud and God must forever bless."

His tact won the day again, and a year later he had grown so brave a reformer as to be able to say to Congress on December 6, 1864: "While I remain in my present position, I shall not attempt to retract or modify the Emancipation Proclamation; nor shall I return to slavery any person who is free by the terms of that proclamation or by any of the acts of Congress. If the people should by whatever mode or means make it the executive duty to re-enslave such persons, another, and not I, must be their instrument to perform it."

Brave words, bravely spoken! yet truth demands that it be said, however wise Abraham Lincoln was or might have been, if he had not had such amazing tact he would not, he could not, have succeeded as he did. For the records of his administration show that there was on more than one occasion a time of deadly peril to his country, and to himself as the leader of his party, when this tact alone had stood forth and seemingly rescued them from ruin.

What an inspiration to the poorest boys of the land his quaint, homely, successful life has become! Doubly dear to the world is he also, because at the last he was called to give his life a sacrifice on the altar of that freedom he had dared to proclaim to others. And so the thousand pages quarto of condolences preserved in the State Department at Washington that were sent from every civilized nation of the earth, when they had learned of his untimely death at the felon's hand, proves that this child of poverty, this man of many limitations but of great sensibilities, who had become the astute politician, the able president, and Treason's victim, had won humanity's heart at the last by being humanity's friend. Tact brought Lincoln to greatness; devotion to freedom brought him immortality of name.

But it is not alone in the professional life that this quality is found to be in the very highest degree necessary for success. Tact must be in constant exercise in business affairs if one would reach eminence. There is scarcely a great merchant or successful business man of to-day who is not an example of this desirable possession.

We frequently hear it said of a man, "He possesses great talent and exhibits little tact," meaning ability to adjust himself to conditions and circumstances and utilize his power and wisdom in securing practical, successful results.

THE VALUE OF TACT.

In practical everyday life tact towers far above talent.

Talent without the mellow, winning influence of tact would be like a sturdy forest oak without its luxuriant garment of green to shelter the weary traveler from the pelting rays of a summer's sun. Tact overcomes every difficulty and surmounts or removes every obstacle.

Every chapter of this volume represents a star in the great constellation of success, and the little star of tact lends brilliancy to many of her larger and more dignified neighbors. She holds within her hand the key to success, wealth, and honor.

The Compass of Life.

SAMUEL PLANTZ, Ph.D.
President Lawrence University.

IN that wonderful novel of Victor Hugo, "Les Miserables," there is one chapter which the reader will never forget. It is entitled "A Tempest in a Brain." Jean Valjean has been nineteen years in the galleys for stealing a loaf of bread and subsequently trying to escape from his imprisonment. He has at length been liberated but only to fall again into crime. By coming in contact with the saintly Bishop of D—— he has become not only transformed but transfigured.

Having assumed another name, he has established himself in an obscure village, intent on two things, hiding his real name and sanctifying his life by doing good. Here he has accumulated great wealth and won the profound respect of all who know him by his benevolence and humanity. But one day an old man who has stolen a bough of apples, by a case of mistaken identity, is arrested as Valjean, and is in danger of being condemned to the galleys for life. The question now comes before the true Valjean, shall he disclose his real name, and surrender himself as the escaped convict, or shall he allow the other man to go to the galleys in his place? He goes to his room, shuts himself in, and meditates on his duty.

The conflict between motives within him is fearful in its intensity. Expediency whispers to him of the toil of the galley service, of the loathsome companions he will have there, of the weight of the iron he will feel on his ankles and wrists. It points out how he will have to surrender his plans for helping the poor and sick, and above all how his ward Fantine and her child Cosette will have no one to assist them if he is gone. It

ACTING ON PRINCIPLE.

tells him that the old man is a thief at best, and probably deserving of all he would get. He makes up his mind not to disclose himself. "Just then," says Victor Hugo, "he heard an internal burst of laughter." His conscience burst the web of sophistry he was winding about it, and stood before him, and ridiculed him to his face. But he persists. He rises, burns the galley suit and other relics of his past life which he has had hid away, and will thus wipe out the last possible trace of his being Valjean. There is no one present. It is decided, he says. But again comes the internal burst of laughter,—"That is excellently arranged, you scoundrel!" He falls asleep. Voices speak to him. He awakes and walks to the window, but no stars are in the sky. A little longer the struggle continues. Then he arises.

He is calm now. The voice of expediency has been drowned. He is acting on principle. Right has arisen before him as more sacred than life. He enters a vehicle and drives as rapidly as possible to the place of the trial. As he enters the court room, he hears the condemnation of the old man. He is Jean Valjean, an ex-convict, and is to spend the rest of his days in the galleys. Then the real Jean steps forward and declares himself. By a mark on his arm he proves his identity. It was a sublime spectacle, that of a man of distinction denouncing himself that a poor old thief might not suffer unjustly in his place. The crowd in the court room felt in their hearts, says Hugo, that they had seen the shining of a great light, and so they had; for they had beheld, in a trying exigency, principle rising triumphant above expediency, a man choosing to sacrifice everything in order to do right.

Jean Valjean is a lesson to all of us. There can never be a compromise between a true man and his duty. The word *ought* is one against which nothing can be weighed. Put it in the scales, if you will, and see if it is possible to place anything on the other side which will outbalance it. Try wealth, honor, reputation. Will they outweigh it? No, they are like dust in the balance. Cast in pleasure, inclination, love of ease, tem-

131

ACTING ON PRINCIPLE.

poral interests, put your loves and your hopes in. Behold the word *ought* outweighs them all.

Here is a soldier with an empty sleeve. The day came when the question arose whether he should go to the front in the war. He had an aged father and mother to support, a delicate wife and young children who needed his care. He knew that the long march meant fatigue, and the battle field meant death; but in the scales of duty the little word *ought* stood firm against them all. This word *ought* is heavier than the word expediency, or desire, or danger, or parents, or children, or wife, or life itself, the preservation of which has been said to be the first law of nature. Says a brilliant writer and says it truly, "If you please, sum up the globes as so much silver and the suns as so much gold, and cast the hosts of heaven as diamonds on a necklace, into one scale, and if there is not in any part the word ought,—if ought is absent in the one scale and present in the other,—up will go your scale laden with the universe, as a crackling paper scroll is carried aloft in a conflagration, ascending towards the stars." Again, it has been said, "God is in the word ought and therefore it outweighs all but God." The same thought was present in the mind of Bacon when he remarked, "He who resolveth to do every duty is immediately conscious of the presence of the gods."

"What motive may
Be stronger with thee than the name of wife?
That which upholdeth him that thee upholds—
His honor: oh, thine honor, Lewis, thine honor!"

—KING JOHN, Act III., Sc. 1.

Stop a moment. Call the roll of the world's heroes. Who are they? Always and eternally the men who have obeyed the word *ought* crying out in the soul, those who have acted from principle. All greatness lies in motive, and no motive is great which is not rooted in conscience. A man cannot be a hero until he has sacrificed self to duty. Take John Maynard standing at the wheel of the burning vessel on Lake Erie, and holding her steadily toward the shore while the angry flames made a winding sheet of glory about him. What is the essence of

ACTING ON PRINCIPLE.

his heroism? He was acting on principle, seeking by sacrificing himself to save his fellow men.

So with John Howard, who enters the pesthouse of Italy to find the cause of the plague which is sweeping away hundreds of his fellow beings. Patriotism is simply acting on principle toward one's country; philanthropy is acting on principle toward humanity; and religion acting on principle toward God. All the virtues, chastity, temperance, forbearance, kindness, integrity, truthfulness, benevolence,—all these are only the effulgence of principle obeyed. This is the foundation of character in a man; for as Emerson has said, "A healthy soul stands united with the Just and the True, as the magnet arranges itself with the pole; so that he stands to all beholders like a transparent object betwixt them and the sun, and whoso journeys toward the sun, journeys towards that person."

There are men, and their number is legion, who try to tie principle to the apron strings of policy. Says one of Shakespeare's characters: "I, I myself, sometimes, leaving the fear of God on the left hand and hiding mine honor in my necessity, am fain to shuffle, to hedge, and to lurch." There are many such, men whose honesty is a convenience, and whose principles are shifted here and there for momentary advantage. They are "gentlemen who serve God as far as will give no offense to the devil," to use Wendell Phillips's cutting definition of a modern politician. When they think there is a slice of fat on the side of wrong, and only a slice of lean on the side of right, they traffic with their conscience, and pretend to be what they are not. They do not, as Emerson puts it, continually stand for a fact. We all know about the demagogue in politics, the stock-waterer in business, the bribe-bought legislator, and the smooth talking liar behind the counter who is all things to all men. These men have cast principle overboard and worship at the shrine of policy. And all of them are rogues, a menace to society, and a disgrace to mankind. Policy is never to be a motive. It is the antipode of right, which is to sit alone on the throne. Nor is there any gain in it in the long run. It is written in the laws of the universe with pen of iron that truth and truth alone shall prevail. Policy may win for a day, but man's life reaches out into eternity and up to God. The time surely comes sooner or later when policy has to sew fig leaves together to cover its shame.

Not so, however, with principle. No sins find it out. No risings of conscience trouble its breast. No obstacles hinder its final rewards. The man of principle will be the one on whose brow the golden crown of favor and esteem will finally rest. He may not obtain so much of material things as the man who, acting on policy, sells his soul for gain; but material things are not all. Lazarus, the beggar, may after all have more than rich Dives at whose gate he lies. There are spiritual as well as material values, and an ounce of the former outweighs a ton of the latter. It is a wise saying, for example, of the Preacher, "A good name is rather to be chosen than great riches." Even those who act on policy themselves esteem principle in others. Nicholas Biddle of Philadelphia, when president of the old United States bank, once dismissed a clerk because he refused to write business letters for him on the Sabbath. The young man was thrown out of employment by what seemed to some an over-nice scruple of conscience; but what was really true fidelity to principle. Not long afterward, however, Mr. Biddle, being asked to nominate a cashier for another bank, recommended this young man, mentioning what had occurred as proof of his integrity and trustworthiness, and adding, "You can trust him, for he would not work for me on Sunday."

Acting on principle gives character a peculiar savor, a kind of heavenly aroma which speaks out above one's acts. It makes the actor himself rise before us as greater than his deeds. It is said that those who heard Lord Chatham felt there was something finer in the man than anything he uttered. There was,—his moral tone. The depths of his being rippled on the surface. The fragrance of his spirit spread abroad. This is what we want in these days when so many men give a commercial value to morals, and the voice of conscience seems to be dying down to a moan. We need men who pitch their lives to the highest key, whose eye sweeps the whole horizon of duty, whose principles are as stable as the position of Gibraltar by the sea. We need men of moral nerve, whose first and sole inquiry is not, is it expedient, but is it right. Such men are God's noblemen. They walk the earth, in it but above it. Africa is growing greenest laurel, but she grows none green enough to adorn the brows of such men as these. South America has quarries of fairest marble, but none too white on which to carve the names of such sons of truth. Asia has sky-kissing Himalayas, but she has no peak high enough to pedestal the statue of those who are always sensitive and responsive to the voice of God in the soul. The cities of the earth have builded splendid mausoleums for their great soldiers, statesmen, and kings; London her Westminster Abbey, Paris her Pantheon cathedral, and Memphis her pyramids: but no mausoleums are rich and gorgeous enough to appropriately commemorate the memory of those in whose lives principle has ever been authoritative, and with whom to do what is right has ever been regarded as the supreme law.

"My conscience, hanging about the neck of my heart, says very wisely to me, * * * 'Budge not —' Budge,' says the fiend. 'Budge not,' says my conscience."
—MERCHANT OF VENICE, Act II., Sc. 2.

The Power of Perseverance.

Rev. JAMES W. COLE, B.D.

THE book of Nature is the oldest of all God's testaments to men, and the most important. On it are based all the others. But for it, they would not be. To render it a success, they are given. Not that the book of Nature is imperfect, but men are imperfect. The volume is yet too wise for them to understand it. Its pages have been open to be read of all men for thousands of years, yet they do not even now know how to train and care for their bodies so as to make of them a success. If they did, physicians would long ago have departed, and hospitals and asylums be unknown. And as to the best method of developing and using that one mighty and only instrument for gaining success, the mind, how wide is the difference of opinion among them, and what a lamentable failure many of them make of it! Happy is the man who can read Nature aright, and then obeys her instruction, for, "He that doeth these things shall live by them," is the promise. But multitudes of men misunderstand, or abuse, or refuse Nature's teachings as to the body, and disease and pain come, followed by the doctor with real, or assumed, antidotes and palliatives. Men overlook, or scorn, or are ignorant of Nature's mental laws for success, and in consequence the maimed, the wrecked, the failed, are everywhere, appealing both to the philanthropist and to the philosopher of morals for aid.

The most important of all things to you in this world is yourself. I do not mean your *selfishness*, but your *selfhood*, or, if you please, manhood. Or, as the good old Anglo-Saxon word "manhood" means, the kind, the quality, the manner,

[CHAPTER 22.]

of man you become. Nothing in the universe can ever take the place *to you* of yourself. What manner of man will you be, is therefore the all important question. On it depends your final, eternal success or failure. Now success, like life, is a most momentous thing. Things destined to endure are long in maturing. The success you seek for should accordingly always be worthy of you; for the testament of Nature, and the testament of the Bible, have the same foundation proviso, "Whatsoever a man soweth, that shall he also reap." In order to reap, one must prepare seed and soil. He must sow; he must cultivate; he must have long patience for it; he must reap when the harvest is ripe. He who will not do *all* these will not succeed. To do them requires much perseverance, for casual effort will not accomplish it.

See how some men of note won their success in life. It may not be the kind you desire, but this is the way theirs came to them. Elias Howe, the inventor and patentee of the first practical sewing machine in this country, received a royalty on his patents during his lifetime of over two millions of dollars. In 1844, after five years of apparently fruitless experimenting, he hit upon the present principle of the sewing machine,—that of a needle grooved, and eyed at the point, and two interlocking threads. Although unknown to him, Mr. Walter Hunt of New York had embodied essentially the same principle in a machine constructed ten years previously, but which Mr. Hunt had laid aside as useless.

Mr. Howe was by no means an extraordinary genius, nor a remarkable mechanic, but at the first a plain, plodding farmer boy, and later an everyday mechanic, and was considered rather dull brained by the neighbors. He was born in Spencer, Massachusetts, July 9, 1819, and died in Brooklyn, New York, October 3, 1867, three weeks after the expiration of his patent on the sewing machine. His father was a small farmer and miller, living in the south part of Spencer, and, when a small child, Elias had to help eke out the family living by sticking wire teeth into leather strips for cards (then made by hand) for

THE POWER OF PERSEVERANCE.

the woolen and cotton machines used in his own and neighboring towns. His schooling was very meager, being only that gained in the winter terms. When eleven years old he "lived out" at a neighbor's for a year. He then worked for his father awhile, and when sixteen he went to Lowell and worked in a cotton factory for fifty cents a day until the panic of 1837 closed the mill, and then he traveled to Cambridge, and obtained work in a machine shop, rooming with his cousin, afterward known as Gen. Nathaniel P. Banks.

In 1838 Mr. Howe went to Boston to work for a machinist, where he continued for some years, or until his interest in his "machine" led him so to neglect his work that he had to leave. That "machine" of his originated in this wise: shortly after going to work in Boston he chanced to overhear a conversation in which one of the speakers, a gentleman of wealth, offered to guarantee a fortune to the man who should invent a machine for sewing. Young Howe gave it no thought, but, in 1840, being of legal age, and then getting nine dollars a week, he took a wife, and shortly after found that his family needed more money for a comfortable support than he was earning. Besides, his work was hard and his health poor, and his wife not over strong, and discouragement was coming, and so one evening in 1841, as he sat watching his weary wife at her stitching, that remark about a fortune to the man who should invent a sewing machine flashed on him like an inspiration. Immediately he determined to make one, and thereafter gave every moment of spare time to thought and experiment on it.

When he had to leave his employer, his father, who had moved to Cambridge, made room for him and his family in the garret of his house. George Fisher, an old schoolmate of Elias's, then lived in Cambridge and had saved some money. To him Elias went, and had many a long conversation, trying to induce him to assist in the enterprise. At length Fisher agreed, for a half interest in the invention, to provide a home for Howe and his family and advance five hundred dollars, and more if needed, for tools and materials to make the machine, and, with his father's attic as a workshop, Howe set to work with great enthusiasm, unmindful of the laughter and ridicule of his acquaintances, who thought they were surely right in judging him to be "half witted." After many a failure he succeeded, in May, 1845, in getting a machine made that would sew more strongly than a tailor could, and then in July, to the intense delight of himself and partner, he made up on the machine two suits of clothes, one for each of them, and they thought that fortune was now at hand. Some further improvements were then made on the crude machine, and they began to make up some of them. But it then cost two hundred and fifty dollars to make such a machine, and they could not sell them to families at that price, and journeymen tailors denounced them as contrivances to take bread out of their mouths; so Mr. Fisher, whose one suit of clothes had now cost him over two thousand dollars, would do no more, and Elias had again to move his family to his father's attic, and begin work as a railroad engineer. He was unfitted for this, and had soon to give it up.

Mr. Howe's machine was patented in the United States, September 10, 1846, and, after many vain efforts to interest capitalists in it, he succeeded at last in sending one of the machines to London, England, by his brother Amasa, in October, 1846. The brother sold the machine to a corset maker, William Thomas, for fifty pounds, which included the sole right to control the manufacture of it in England. Mr. Thomas agreed also to pay a royalty of three pounds for each machine sold, and to pay Elias three pounds a week while fitting the machine for corset making. Amasa came to America, and in February of the next year returned with his brother Elias to England, where Elias entered the service of Mr. Thomas, and soon after sent for his wife and three children. At the end of the seven months Mr. Thomas concluded that he no longer needed the aid of the inventor, and soon made it so uncomfortable for him that Mr. Howe left.

Many months of great poverty now fell to his lot. Sickness

came to him; starvation looked in at the window. At length a charitably disposed acquaintance gave him a little help, and he set about to make and sell a machine. By the aid of relatives and friends and the pawnbroker, he at last got money enough to send his family home to America, and when he had completed the machine, although it was worth fifty pounds, he sold it for five, and took a note at that. Discounting the note for four pounds, he took passage for New York, where he arrived in April, 1849, with two dollars and a half in his pocket. Here tidings of the fatal illness of his wife met him, and, begging his way home to Cambridge, he arrived only in time to receive her dying farewell. Soon after news of the wreck, on Cape Cod, of the ship that brought his few household goods came, and the poor man literally sat amid the ruins of his family and his hope of a fortune.

But the clouds that so long lowered over him now began to lift, and he found that, though the capitalists would not buy his invention when he offered it to them, they had not hesitated to steal it while he was absent from the country, and that other inventors had combined his discoveries with improvements of their own, and sewing machines were rapidly coming into use. He succeeded in interesting a friend, George W. Bliss, who, taking as security a mortgage on Mr. Howe's father's farm, bought out Fisher's interest in the invention, and after Mr. Howe had succeeded in redeeming his original machine, and his letters patent, which he had been compelled to pawn in London, he began suit against the infringers, and in 1850 he commenced to manufacture his machine in New York, and thereafter was above want. In 1854 the United States courts decided the case against Isaac M. Singer and others for infringements, in Mr. Howe's favor. The infringers combined and paid him royalties that enabled him in 1855 to repurchase the rights he had parted with in the sad days of poverty and sickness, and Mr. Howe established a large factory at Bridgeport, Conn., for the manufacture of his **machine, and soon became a millionaire.**

THE POWER OF PERSEVERANCE.

Mr. Howe was intensely patriotic, and enlisted as a private in the 17th Connecticut regiment in the War of the Rebellion, and personally advanced the money to equip and pay that regiment at a time when the Government was financially embarrassed. He remained in the service until ill health compelled his retirement, and he will be gratefully remembered with Whitney, Fulton, McCormick, and the many other Americans whose perseverance and triumph over giant obstacles not only ennobled them, but enriched their countrymen as well.

John Hughes, Roman Catholic Archbishop of New York, was born at Annaloghan, Tyrone County, Ireland, May 24, 1797, and died in the city of New York the 3d day of January, 1864. His father tilled a very small plot of land called by courtesy a farm, and was very poor, and as soon as John could work he was set to planting potatoes, cutting and hauling muck for fuel, digging ditches, and anon "gardening a bit for the gentry." He then worked in a factory as a mill hand, dreaming all the while of sometime being a priest in his church, for his parents were devout Romanists and the lad's ideal was a priest. He had no education worth the naming and no influential friends, and his church did not then look out so eagerly as now for the education of its aspiring youth, so his prospects were very dark and unpromising indeed.

In 1816 his father emigrated to America, and settled in Chambersburg, Pennsylvania. The next year John landed in New York, a penniless young man. Here he worked at wharfage and at odd jobs, then, reaching his father's home, he worked as a day laborer, broke stone, jobbed around town, and toiled as small gardener for seven dollars a month, stinting himself and trying to save something towards getting that education for the priesthood of which he dreamed. After two years of struggle, and getting no nearer his goal, he was becoming discouraged, when he heard that at the Mount St. Mary's College of his church near Emmitsburg, Maryland, there were free scholarships. He started for that place, walking more than half the way from lack of money. When he arrived, worn, dusty, and

THE POWER OF PERSEVERANCE.

seedy in appearance, he was told, to his horror, that the free scholarships were all taken, and, alas! he had no money to pay for tuition. He hung about the place on the verge of despair. He had come so near his haven, and now to fail! Soon his little store of money was gone, and he was suffering, and in desperation he went to the president of the college, and begged for work to keep him from starving. The good man set him at gardening, and soon learned his story, and resolved to help him. He was far behind in book knowledge, but, when opportunity for study was given him, he applied himself most diligently, so that at twenty-nine years of age he was able to enter upon the priest's office that for fifteen years he had held before him as the prize of life.

He was a born fighter, and, beginning his ministry in a small parish in Philadelphia, he was soon in high controversy with the clergy of the Protestant faith. He wrote much, but very hastily, very diffusely, and not always correctly. He never became a scholarly man or a great thinker, but the controversial spirit, his untiring industry, and his zeal for his church built up his parishes and attracted attention to him, and when forty-five years old he was made Bishop of New York, and twelve years after was made Archbishop. While arbitrarily ruling his diocese, he was nevertheless a most adroit and skillful politician, and did more to build up his church in this country than any man had done before him. Americans remember him gratefully for his ardent devotion to the cause of the Union in the late civil war. He went, with others, at the request of Secretary of State Seward, to England and France, during a critical period of that war, to influence those governments to remain neutral during the strife. His lowly origin, the difficulties he triumphed over, the great eminence he attained in his church, the remarkable influence he had over men notwithstanding his limitations, are a striking instance of the *power of perseverance.*

Earning the Capital.

Rev. JAMES W. COLE, B.D.

WHAT is capital? Most writers on economics answer, "Capital is surplus; the storage of the labor of the brain and muscle; the overplus from the daily needs and uses of men." If this general definition be a true one, it can apply only to the outer, material forms of wealth. For one's wealth does not consist solely in the possession of money, however vast that sum may be. A simple definition of the word will show this. Strength is strongness. Length is longness. Breadth is broadness. Wealth is "wealness" or wellness; things that make for one's well-being. Is the miser a wealthy man? Do the millions of gold some men get tend to their well-being? Is it not true that the getting of money develops in some the baser elements of their nature, so that occasionally you may see persons whose riches have but served to make them meaner than the meanest poverty could ever make them? Can such persons be truthfully said to be wealthy or well-being persons? The word, you see, has broken away from its original foundation, and is by many persons regarded as simply synonymous in meaning with money. But money is not an end; it is a means to an end, and that end is nobly to live the life that is given you. If money or any other product of the earth will help you do that, then get it, get all you can of it; but if it would hinder you in your development of true manhood, then avoid it. Earn something else by your brain and muscle, if you would be wealthy.

When that noble man, the late Prof. Louis Agassiz, was asked why he did not use his great talents to gain money, when he was offered three hundred dollars each for a course of six lectures, he replied with lofty scorn, "I cannot afford to lecture for money." To him there were far more valuable and wonderful things in this world than money. Alas! that there are but few like him. The citizens of ancient Rome were wont to place the statues and images of their great ancestors on pedestals, and in the vestibules of their houses, in order to remind themselves and their children of those ancestors' virtues and glorious deeds, and to inspire them to emulate them; and for one hundred and seventy years they allowed no painted or graven image of a deity among them, with the result, as Plutarch tells us, that for two hundred and thirty years after the founding of Rome no husband deserted his wife, nor any wife her husband, and for six hundred years there was no parricide known, and for forty-three years, during the reign of Numa Pompilius, the temple of Janus, the god of war, continued closed, there being no war, nor sedition, nor conspiracy. Would that Americans could be diverted long enough from their worship of Mammon to cultivate some of the virtues of those old heathen! Perchance, then, they might, for the peace of their families and the good of the republic, imitate the example of that famous Themistocles of Athens, who, when two suitors, one a poor man and the other rich, sought for the hand of his daughter in marriage, chose the poor man, saying he desired as a son-in-law a man without riches, rather than riches without a man.

But now you are a man, and a man of business desires and wishes to succeed in some particular business. You have virtues and some talents, but, it may be, very little money, perhaps none. Can you succeed without money? Certainly. Some of the richest men in this country began their business life without a dollar. Nature is just as ready to help you to get riches as she was to help them. She will give as good returns to-day and to-morrow as yesterday. Money is but one of the numerous and valuable things to be found in her vast storehouses on land, and in the seas, and in the air, and in the sun, and you can get it out if you wish and will. Perhaps you have heard it said that "it takes money to get money." No, it doesn't. Money is not a loadstone, drawing its kind only. Money is only lumps of matter dug out of the ground, and shaped in certain forms and stamped with a design, and you can get an abundance of it without digging in the earth for it, and trying to catch it with another piece of the same kind. What! get money without capital? No, with capital. Why, man, you are a capitalist! Wages are only a form of income. An everyday laborer is a capitalist. Every person to whom God has given brains and a good body is a large capitalist. Your mind, your muscle, is your capital, and with them you may earn what you will. All the riches of the world is the product of the labor of brain or muscle. Your brain may be a veritable gold mine if you will but develop it.

In 1882, at Christie's rooms, London, a little daub of matter, only twelve by nine inches, that a brain had put on canvas, sold for thirty thousand dollars. It was Meissonier's "Napoleon the First in the Campaign of Paris." The same artist's "1814" was sold for one hundred and seventy thousand dollars; eight years later, Millet's "Angelus" brought one hundred and ten thousand dollars, and Murillo's "Conception of the Virgin" one hundred and seventeen thousand dollars. Great fortunes, you see, that the brain produced. The musician Paderewski spent a few weeks in this country a year ago, and then carried home with him one hundred and seventy-five thousand dollars, as the proceeds of his brain. Sir Walter Scott was a silent partner in the firm of the publishers of his books. The firm failed, and he was involved in debt six hundred thousand dollars in consequence. He was then fifty-six years of age. Summoning all the energy of his mighty brain to the task, he labored incessantly, by night and day, sending out volume after volume, until in five years he had paid it all by the product of his brain. Yes, brains are great money-getters, if you use them for that purpose. The son of a farmer in the state of New York, a sickly lad, Samuel J. Tilden, so used his brains as to bring him a fortune, by the practice of law, of five millions of dollars. A Swedish young woman, Jenny Lind, twenty-eight years of age, came to the United States with nothing but her voice, that her brain had cultured, and in ninety-eight nights she had sung out of the pockets of the American people seven hundred and twelve thousand dollars. Another Swede, Ole Bornemann Bull, so manipulated a violin as to draw out of the same American people in a single season more than a hundred thousand dollars; while an American-born lad of English ancestors, Edwin Booth, so used his brains while an actor, that in less than two months' time he had taken in from the people of San Francisco alone, over ninety-six thousand dollars. But why multiply instances in literature, art, oratory, music, the drama, all going to prove that your brain is your capital, and that all you need to do if you wish for money is to use it.

Brains, when combined with muscle, and used for mere money-getting, often yield fabulous fortunes. A German, John Jacob Astor, living in New York, so used his that in sixty-three years he had accumulated a fortune estimated at twenty million dollars. Two millions came from his trade in furs, teas, silks, and sandalwood, some millions from interest given him by the revenue laws, the balance coming from his real estate investments. He was born in the village of Waldorf, near Heidelberg, Germany, on July 17, 1763, and lived to be nearly eighty-five years old, dying in New York, March 29, 1848. His mother was a devout, hard-working peasant, of a close, if not penurious, disposition, whose soul was often vexed beyond all endurance by her shiftless, rollicking, beer-drinking husband (by trade a butcher, at which business John Jacob also worked when a lad). And so the home life, comfortless and stormy, early led John's three older brothers to go out into the world to earn their own livelihood. One of them, Henry, had settled in New York, and was also a butcher, and his letters telling of his thrift filled the lad with an unconquerable desire to go thither also. After his mother died, and the father remarried, the storms in the home waxed yet more furious and

EARNING THE CAPITAL.

continuous, so that poor John Jacob was often obliged to hie him to a neighbor's garret or outhouse, for refuge, and for a shelter for the night. He was poorly fed, and more poorly clad, and shrank from his boyhood companions for shame of his home and heritage.

When seventeen years old he succeeded in getting from his father a reluctant consent to join his brother in America, and the sturdy, well-built youth of iron frame, with two dollars in his pocket, set out to seek his fortune across the Atlantic ocean. Walking to the river Rhine, he hired as a raftsman and worked his way to the coast, and with the wages paid him went to London, where one of his brothers was living, and with whom he stayed two years, working like a galley slave, and living like a miser to save the money needed to carry him to the "New Land" of his dreams. When the Revolutionary War closed he bought a steerage passage to Baltimore, and with twenty-four dollars in his pockets, a small bundle of clothes, and seven flutes, bought as an investment, he sailed for the United States in November, 1783. On the ship a fellow German told him of his experience in America, how he had gone there penniless and friendless, and, beginning in a small way, had acquired quite a competence as a fur trader, and advised him to engage in the same business, giving him what knowledge he possessed as to the method of conducting it. They traveled together to New York, and, arriving at the brother's house, at once laid the plan before him; he advised that John Jacob enter the service of a furrier, to learn the business thoroughly. The next morning the three sallied forth, and at length found a Mr. Robert Bowne, a furrier of long experience, who engaged John at two dollars a week, and board. Here he beat furs, and sought all possible knowledge concerning fur-bearing animals from nature, from traders, and from savages.

He was soon made buyer for the establishment, and took long trips on foot with a pack of trinkets on his back, going north into Canada, and west to the frontiers, driving wonder-

EARNING THE CAPITAL.

fully sharp bargains with Indians and trappers to the enriching of his employer and himself. As soon as he had learned the routes and the business, he set up for himself, and began in 1786 to accumulate his immense fortune on this wise; after a few trips he took a small store in Water street, which he furnished with toy cakes and notions for Indians, who at that date brought in furs to New York. Anon, with his pack of trinkets on his back, he would leave the store in charge of the wife whom he early married, and would take long tramps on foot throughout northern, central, and western New York, buying his skins from settlers, trappers, savages, wherever he could find them, giving a dollar's worth of trash for a beaver's skin, which he would ship to London, where it readily sold for six dollars. With the six dollars he would buy goods that he could easily sell in New York for twelve. Soon he was able to employ agents, and multiplied his routes. Then he bought a ship to convey his goods to and from London. Shortly after he began to ship furs to China, then the best market in the world for them, and brought back cargoes of teas, and silks, and spices, frequently doubling his money. Accidentally he learned of the enormous value of sandalwood in China, and, loading tons of it at the Sandwich Islands for a mere pittance, he soon had a monopoly of the trade in that wood, and for many months fairly coined money. Often his profits on a voyage of each of his fleet of ships that he came to own amounted to seventy thousand dollars for each one.

During the War of 1812, and for many years, the United States tariff on tea was twice its cost in China, but the government gave a credit to importers on the duties due it of from nine to eighteen months, so that he could get two and three cargoes from China and sell them at enormous profits before he had to pay the duty on the first cargo. And for eighteen or twenty years, John Jacob Astor had what was actually a free-of-interest loan from the government of over five millions of dollars, a condition of things that admitted of getting rich very rapidly. As fast as his gains from his business came in, he

EARNING THE CAPITAL.

invested them in real estate by purchase in fee simple where he could, and where the owners would not sell, he got, if possible, long period leases of valuable property in what was soon the heart of the city. He bought Richmond Hill, Aaron Burr's estate of one hundred and sixty acres, for one thousand dollars per acre. Twelve years later, it was valued at one thousand five hundred dollars a single lot. Learning that certain lands in Putnam county were held by a defective title, he bought up what was then the worldly possessions and homes of seven hundred families, for one hundred thousand dollars, and then he compelled the state of New York to pay him five hundred thousand dollars for this land, to rescue the victims of the defective deeds from his grasp, and save to them their homes.

During most of his long life, his brain and body were simply a great and wonderful money-getting machine. He seems to have never known what real generosity was either in his business or out of it, and left his money at the end very unwillingly, and simply because he was obliged to do so. The love of it grew with his growth, but it never waned with his departing strength, and at the last dominated and ruled him with a relentless tyranny that was not only grotesque, but contemptible, because the victim delighted in it, and called it glory. He had a mind capable of far better things, and, while he was what the world reckons a thoroughly upright and honest business man, truth compels it to be said that he was not an admirable model, nor a safe one for you and me to follow. The one thing that keeps his name and memory green is his gift by will of four hundred thousand dollars to establish the Astor Library in the city of New York. His immense estate was left to his children and has been since continued in the family, and, like those of the Bedfords and Westminsters of England, consists to a very large extent in real estate, over a thousand valuable properties being now owned by them.

High School of Experience.

JOHN BASCOM, D.D., LL.D., of Williams College.

MY friend, Professor Perry, recently remarked to me: "Nothing is perfect in the world except the world itself as a school of discipline."

A knowledge of the world—that which the world teaches us—is the substance of all knowledge. No matter what ideas we entertain, or how we have come by them, they all need illustration and confirmation by experience. The world is many sided in its lessons, and these lessons, if rightly learned, all sustain and complete each other. Our most exact knowledge, which we designate as science; our daily gleanings of truth, which we term observations; our widest hopes of the future, which we call faith,—are all bound up in one volume, and that volume is the world. If the world, wisely rendered, gives us no warrant for our beliefs, our beliefs are null.

Moreover, it is not the world at rest but the world in motion that we are called on to understand, that is impressing upon us the greatest variety of convictions. We study the locomotive, even when it is standing still, in reference to its ease, velocity, strength, and safety of movement. It is a thing to be comprehended by virtue of its power to press forward with its loaded train. The world is to be understood in its progress and in reference to its progress. Leave it to stand still, study it as standing still, and we shall no more catch its true idea than we should the purpose of an engine, never having seen it speed along the track.

We all meet in the school of experience; and it is the school in which most of our acquisitions are made, and in which they are all tested as to their worth. What we term education is made up of a few antecedent suggestions which we are to verify in experience; a few of the most general forms of knowledge, like the knowledge of numbers, which we are to employ in experience. The quicker we get, fairly well equipped, at work on the world itself, the more actual and substantial our knowledge will be. The failure of education, so far as it has failed, has been that it has kept the mind back too long from the very facts with which it must learn at length to deal. We arm the young soldier so carefully that we forget to teach him his manual of arms; or we suppose that this manual will be an adequate substitute for the clear eye, the active thought, the firm mind, which are developed in conflict itself. We may hasten to the battle without arms, or we may be so long in arming that the battle may be over before we reach it. The true test of our preparation and our promptness—that which teaches us what preparation and promptness are—is the very struggle itself.

Experience, like all schools, has its defects, its difficulties. The man who has been taught by experience is very likely to be overconfident. To know how to do a thing, to be able to follow up the knowledge at once by doing it successfully, seem so certain and undeniable a power that its possessor may well enough pride himself upon it; may easily enough have a little scorn for one who, with apparently wider knowledge, hesitates and trips in its use. Experience readily begets a confidence that is closely akin to conceit.

The difficulty lies, not in the thing known, but in the fact that it is only one among many things that should be known. Knowledge won in experience is liable to be narrow. Overconfidence arising out of the clearness, and, at the same time, restrictedness of one's observation, is the danger of the man who is taught by experience only. We must broaden our thought through and with our fellow men. Our own experience must be corrected and completed by their experience. The world, therefore, in which we are all taught, in which we turn floating impressions into knowledge which gives power, must be the human world, quite as much as the physical world.

The man of business must deal with men and not with products merely; not with men in relation to products alone, but in the full range of their personal experience. This is the true world, the large world, the spiritual world, in which we are. One may fatally mistake men, touching them exclusively on the side of self-interest. He may win a shrewd, cunning form of sagacity that is very far removed from wisdom, and is by no means the truth which experience was ready to teach him. Simply because experience is so great a school, we must come to it with some greatness of mind, ready to be taught many things; and ready to review the things we have learned many times, that we may apprehend them more completely.

Looking on experience as a school, the first requisite is that we should take a liberal course in it, that the studies we pursue shall be fitted to correct, extend, and sustain each other. If we add, for instance, to the desire to obtain wealth or office or social position, the desire to attain and impart large and secure happiness, the schooling of the world will be instantly altered immensely thereby. Though the presence of the two things, we will say wealth and happiness, may in many respects concur, they will constantly modify each other; and the lessons which we should have wholly lost, or fearfully perverted, with the one notion, will be, by means of both notions, bound up in a fortunate, harmonious whole of truth. The world has many stands, and many wise men are rehearsing its varied instructions from them. If we would be well taught, we must listen to more than one speaker. The world is a broad world, and we must enter broadly into it.

We have said also that it is a world in motion; hence we can apprehend it well only as we see and share its movement. We must inquire not simply what are existing facts, but what those facts are fitted to bring forth. Here, a narrow experience signally comes short of wisdom. Many men, sharpened by a **most telling and real experience, nevertheless fail grievously** by virtue of their very successes. They have thought that the getting of something was sufficient, and have never once asked the world what would come of it when it was won.

Somehow or other, we seem to think, in a vague way, that it is faith alone that asks the question of fruits, and then gives us a remote and doubtful answer to it. Experience, observation, also ask this question, and give it a very immediate and final answer. We must study the world in motion if we would understand what is of real worth in it, what will abide in it, whither it and we are going.

We may well fellowship each other, and strengthen each other, for we are all in one school, and what we learn singly will be as nothing compared with the success of our common effort to render the world as a school of human life in terms of reason. A wide, penetrative, far-reaching outlook over the world is the labor, joy, and crown of our lives.

"Fie upon it, that experience should be so long in coming!"

Requisites for a Business Education

HOMER MERRIAM, Springfield, Mass.
Pres. G. & C. Merriam Co., Publishers Webster's International Dictionary.

I WOULD recommend at least a good common school education backed by good deportment and strict integrity. Then select a business with reference to natural fitness and preferences, not taking into account present wages so much as the probabilities of the future, whether it is a business that means only day wages all one's life or whether there will be opportunity for growth and expansion.

To bring out all there is in a man, he needs the planning, the thought, the mental training, involved in conducting a business for one's self. There are advantages in a college education if properly utilized; too often, however, the college graduate has not learned that close application of ten hours a day or more is needful to success, and he is not as a rule quite flexible enough to fall readily into full sympathy with beginning at the bottom and thoroughly learning the details from the foundation. After over fifty years of business experience and close observation, I think that as a rule, for education for business, the four years spent in college could be more profitably applied in mastering the details of some business.

Before selecting a business or securing a position, take a careful inventory of the moral surroundings, business integrity, and general character of employers and those in authority. These factors are essential to mental and moral growth, and also essential to true success in business.

If a desirable opening does not present itself, endeavor to secure a situation more or less akin to your choice, constantly watching for an opportunity for improvement. Thus employed,

A BUSINESS EDUCATION.

habits of application are formed and all that is learned will be more or less useful all through life.

A business selected and a place secured, then strictly begins the business education. It is generally best to take one of the lowest places in the establishment, giving mind and hand earnestly to the learning and doing the duties involved; doing all that is required and more if opportunity affords. While doing this, watch the places that are above you in the business, and learn all you can of the duties of such positions without neglecting your own, so that you may be ready to step up higher when opportunity offers. Then, when one above you is laid aside by sickness or otherwise, the employer will be much pleased if he finds that you are qualified to step into the place, and well perform the duties of the higher position. If you will follow this line, keeping to one kind of business, keeping your breath free from strong drink and tobacco, keeping your mind and body pure, you will be well educated for business, and will be likely to become a prosperous and successful business man.

Many years ago a publisher in New York having established a profitable business, not having firm health, wanted a partner as a worker. Among his customers was a young man in a comparatively small business in western New York, a diligent worker, with moral, religious, and business character all correct. For these, he was invited to become a partner with the New York publisher. The business grew until another partner was needed. A young man in a comparatively small business, selected for same reasons as the first, became a partner. The senior member of the firm died, and another partner was wanted. Some years before this, a firm in a small western city had failed and gone out of sight. Some of the creditors of that firm were now surprised at receiving from its junior partner an inquiry whether they would release him from the old obligations, on his paying ten per cent. of the same, saying that he had no means for paying, but had friends who would advance the ten per cent. if he could be released. The proposition was accepted and he at once became a member of the New York

A BUSINESS EDUCATION.

firm. He had gone to New York, obtained a situation with the house, and made himself so useful that he was wanted as partner. The three partners were selected not for capital but for character. The house was the firm of Ivison, Blakeman, Taylor & Co., for years the largest schoolbook publishing house of the country.

A young man was for several years clerk for the firm in which I was a partner. He learned the business, then went to New York and secured a situation with the house I have named. A while afterward I inquired of the senior partner of that house how well the young man filled his position. The reply was, " He is a pretty good clerk, as clerks go. If young ladies come in, he wants to stop and talk with them, he wants to dress well, he wants to stop work when the clock strikes; he is pretty good as clerks go, but as for being willing to take off his coat, and work as I am willing to work, he does not want to, and there are very few of them who do." I think that young man had as good a chance before him as did the one who came from the West and became a partner, but he failed to improve it and went downward instead of upward.

Some time ago I saw a gang of men at work on the street railroad; only one of them had his coat off, and that was the superintendent of the road.

Young man, if you desire to become superintendent, or proprietor, instead of being only a digger, work with your coat off, and work as if every dollar made in the business was made entirely for you.

Another young man came to us as clerk. After being with us some three or four years, he proposed leaving us, but he had made himself so useful that we could not spare him, and took him into the business as a partner, and now for many years he has been the head of the house, doing a large and profitable business. So it has been in many other instances; a clerk has made himself so useful that he could not be spared, and so must become a partner, but to do so he must put close work of hands and mind into the business, and plenty of it.

A BUSINESS EDUCATION.

There are always instances of prosperous men who have worked hard, are beginning to grow old, and want a young man as partner; they do not want money capital, they have enough of that, they want character, right habits, work, and these are the best capital a young man can have.

A merchant in Boston wanted a boy. One was recommended to him from the country, some twenty miles away. The merchant decided to try him, and sent a dollar to pay his stage fare to the city. On the day when he was expected the boy appeared, at a late hour. The merchant asked somewhat sternly, "Where have you been? The stage was in long ago." The boy meekly replied, "I did not mean to offend you, sir; it was the first dollar I ever had, and I wanted to keep it and so I walked." "You did just right," said the gentleman emphatically, "now go and get your supper and come to work in the morning"; and he said to a friend who heard it, "I would not take a thousand dollars for that boy." In process of time, the boy became a partner in the business.

Sometimes a single act or a single day shapes a young man's course and prosperity for life.

Many years ago I was traveling on the river St. Lawrence; on Saturday afternoon I stopped at a hotel on one of the Thousand Islands to pass the Sabbath. Several young men, commercial travelers, spent the day there. On Sunday morning all but one of them went out on the river and spent the day there. That one went to church and kept the Sabbath. He made himself known to me, was traveling for a relative of mine. Some time afterwards he applied for a situation to a large manufacturer, who wrote me that the young man had given a reference to me, among others. I replied that my knowledge of him was limited, but I gave the facts about that Sabbath. The young man obtained the situation, and he afterwards told me that he thought my letter decided the matter. The manufacturer's son, upon whom he relied, had died. He took the young man into his family and brought him forward in the business. In a few years the senior died; the young man was elected in

A BUSINESS EDUCATION.

his place as manager of the business, with a fine prospect before him.

Young man, there is abundant room for you in the higher and more responsible positions of life. You are needed. Will you rise to the emergencies and make yourself worthy of confidence and become qualified for responsibility? If so, be willing to do anything and everything that will advance the interest of your employer, and you will soon become too valuable to remain in the lower positions and will be asked to step up higher.

Make yourself worthy and the honor will come.

Personal Independence.

Rev. JAMES W. COLE, B.D.

MEN are not, as a rule, self-reliant and independent. They need props and aids both to stand and move. What are called the great men and women of any age or nation are the prize beings of the human kind, showing not the average of the race, but rather what can be done under certain conditions. The conditions, as well as the product, may be very exceptional, and so furnish no present wise criterion by which to judge. And he who under ordinary circumstances should attempt to imitate them would inevitably meet with disappointment, and perhaps loss. The times develop great men, and great men modify the times. Each of us has his appointed place and part in the economy of nature, and however insignificant we may be, or however low the place assigned to us, we may be assured that we are not made in vain.

Nature is not constructed or run at haphazard. The wisest of us do not yet know the plan on which nature is built; and the men of any generation can see but a very small part of the design unfolded in their day; so that it is useless for anyone to object to its wisdom, or to find fault with his particular place or time, or the kind of work in this world assigned to him. It is yet far too soon to find fault with anything of nature's handiwork or belongings. The all important question is, What ought I to do in life, and what is the best way to do it? Each of us must fill his own place and do his own work. If we refuse, or do the work illy, nature casts us aside as rubbish, as the "thorns" and "chaff" whose end is to be burned. Harsh, perhaps, but who can say it is not just? Now all thorns are perverted growths in nature, abnormal products of the natural world, and as culture increases they are eliminated, sloughed off, from the stock. They may have served a purpose as thorns in the then condition of things. But with the development of the plan of nature, they are then found to be no longer needful, and who can dispute the wisdom that discards them?

It is conceded that humanity is slowly progressing upward, but, however many ages there have already been, they are as nothing to those that await the race. We are as yet in the "first of the things" the Bible says, and nature confirms it, so that it is altogether too early to pronounce concerning "what we shall be" or what anything shall be in the ages ahead of us. But we may rest assured of one thing, that nature's highest and best product is not thorns; that, while the average of the race of men may yet be very low, the exceptionally great and good of the ages show the possibilities of the race even under present conditions. If the conditions improve, what may not the race become, more especially if the best predominates at last? There is infinite variety in nature. All lives do not run in the same channel. Even in the same family what diversity of forms, of features, of mental and moral characteristics are to be found.

Now nature is intensely individualized, and the momentous question before us is this: Is my type of individual to continue or to be sloughed off in the upward reach of the race? History shows that some types have already disappeared from this little planet, and others are now vanishing. Nature, with the advancing culture of the race, throws them aside as unworthy of perpetuation; or, having served their inferior time and place, they are not found adapted to superior conditions, and so disappear. In every age of the world there are seen to appear a few great men; men who tower above their fellows; men who are leaders; men who set the pace for a generation. Now, great men are either great blessings or great curses to their fellow mortals. Of whatever their greatness may consist, whether they are great in intellect, or great in riches, or great in position, or great in power, none others have such opportunities for good or ill; none others are so sovereign in blessing or in cursing to the world as they. Greatness of any kind is always a gigantic public trust, and woe unto him who defaults or misuses it. When nature endows a man with exceptional gifts of intellect, his fellows instinctively recognize it as their right, and his duty, that he use these gifts to uplift and advance them in goodness and truth. So doing, they perpetuate his name and fame as a benefactor. If he leads them astray or subverts their best interests, he is ultimately cast out, as a noisome thing, to rot.

Equally so when men with exceptional gifts to amass riches acquire them, it is no less their duty to use them to ennoble and bless their fellow men. Great wealth is also a great public trust to be used for the public good, and not merely for the owner's profit or pleasure. Men instinctively recognize this when a rich man dies clinging to the last to his pile of gold, or when he dispenses it for purely selfish or private ends. If our many millionaires of the present time fail to recognize their stewardship towards their fellows less fortunately endowed, history will ere long inevitably record another lesson which ought to have been taught the world thoroughly enough by the French Revolution. For the ability to get riches is as truly an endowment as is the ability to gain knowledge. The scholar is a debtor to his fellow men, and no less so is the man of wealth. The scholar and the man of wealth each may claim his knowledge or riches solely as of his own personal right or belongings. Nevertheless, all men recognize the fact that their duty is higher than their personal rights. The path of duty, and not alone the path of enjoyment, is the path of safety, and the true road to nobility. Property has duties to be performed, as well as rights to be protected, both in the sight of men and of God. Now the men who reach positions of eminence of any kind among their fellows must needs be self-guiding and directors of others, and cannot be of those who are nursed, sustained, and led by their fellow men. Their resources must be in themselves alone.

He who goes in advance, and thus leads, must assume and bear great responsibilities. He who leads must of necessity depend on himself; he must needs go alone, not with the crowd, but in advance of it. He must guide himself and others. And in order to do so he must be personally independent. By this is not meant oddity or impudence, or disregard of the opinion or wishes of others, but the just and wise use of his own faculties; the reliance on his own resources; the will and ability to stand alone, if need be; the purpose to win one's way, however long it may be, or whatever may be the obstacles in one's path. No one ever gets above the average of any community in which he lives, or above the average success of any particular business pursuit in which he may engage, who is not thus self-reliant. "I lead, let others follow," must be their motto, and by this nature specializes such, individualizes them for their leadership.

When that "man of destiny," Napoleon Bonaparte, had had himself proclaimed as Emperor of France, and the English government, ignoring the fact, continued to address him simply as general, he remarked to a friend, "They may call me what they please, they cannot prevent me from being myself." The being himself was what puzzled the men of his time. They could understand ordinary men, but this extraordinary individual, who would copy nobody, who would not follow custom or precedent, who would be himself alone, and who for fifteen years kept all Europe in an uproar and frenzy of fear, was a riddle that is not yet wholly solved. Whether his wild, inordinate ambition and wonderful personality combined to make of him a great military hero, or simply and only a monster of rapine and slaughter, will be permanently known when righteousness becomes the standard of judgment for the great men of the earth as well as for the small. In that day, I opine, the lowliest peasant who does "justly, loves mercy, and walks humbly with his God" will have greater reverence among men and angels than any or all of those who, like Napoleon, wade through seas of blood to sit their little hour on gilded pedestals called thrones, the while that fawning sycophants crown them with mock reverence and hollow praises.

This is a world and a universe of facts that sooner or later demolishes all theories and opinions of men that are not in accord with those facts. In the natural world it is found to be a fact that fruits of the very choicest and best kinds can be grown at less cost than is required for inferior sorts. So also the experience of mankind has abundantly shown that it costs far more to grow and care for a criminal, whether great or small, than it does to grow and care for an honest and useful citizen. Again, in horticulture, inferior fruits are grown not so much by culture as by neglect. It is even so with mankind. And the crying need of the age has ever been, as it is now, for the careful and systematic culture, not of a part, but of the whole, of the intellectual, moral, and spiritual nature of man. If the moral and spiritual nature of Bonaparte had not been neglected, what a saving to the world in blood and treasure it would have been! Merely intellectual culture made him a military prodigy, and a thing of horror. If to that military culture had been added the equal development of moral and spiritual nature, his church would have canonized him as a saint. To cultivate the intellect alone is to make a man either a very proud philosopher, or a prouder devil. Cultivate the whole man and you get a child of God. When this last is done on earth, the world will no longer take as its most illustrious models those men, however great, or wise, or rich, who have gained their eminence at the expense or by the ruin or destruction of their fellow men. When this is done, a new type of heroes and heroines will appear in the world's niches of fame,—the perfected fruit of the Perfect Man. For, believe me, the lowly carpenter of Nazareth, who, counter to the opinion and customs of his own and all other ages, taught both by precept and by his example that the only true, and the highest and best use of life was to "go about doing good," is an immeasurably grander, loftier type of man than the Corsican lawyer's son ever became by all his years of bloody military brigandage, notwithstanding that by his method he won a crown among men, while the Nazarene perished miserably on a cross. It cost the world over eighteen billions of dollars, and more than six millions of human lives to rear and maintain Napoleon, while the total expense to it of the entire human life of the Man of Nazareth was less than three thousand dollars, and the shedding of no blood save his own, given to redeem men.

If that huge sum of money, and the immense amount of human energy and effort continued through so many years to perpetuate a Napoleon, had but been given to the work of producing men of the type of Jesus of Nazareth, how much it would have ennobled, how much it would have enriched, how very much it would have blessed and elevated and advanced the world. He of Nazareth was wonderfully independent in thought and deed, and more autocratic than any other that ever appeared on earth, and he taught that no one should be called master save himself. But how vast the difference between the independence he taught men to have and to show forth, and that which is so generally called independence! And yet history shows that his kind is the only one that will bring you and me to the noblest, highest, and most permanent success and fame.

Said Martin Luther, "It is God's way, of beggars to make men of power, just as he made the world of nothing." Luther was himself one of the most remarkable instances of the truth of that saying. There have been men of mightier intellect, of far greater culture and refinement of character, of more religious fervor and zeal, and of greater force and wider influence in the molding of human opinions than he, yet Carlyle but voiced the sentiment of the Protestant world when he said of him, "I will call this Luther a truly great man; great in intellect, in courage, affection, and integrity; one of our most lovable and precious men. A right spiritual hero and prophet; once more a true son of nature and fact, for whom these centuries and many that are yet to come will be thankful to Heaven." The reader is doubtless familiar with the main lines, at least, of the life of this great leader of the reformation in Europe. What a wonderfully independent spirit he was! And how true to the life is the character sketch he gave of himself as being "rough, boisterous, stormy, and altogether warlike, born to fight innumerable devils and monsters, to remove stumps and stones, to cut down thistles and thorns, and to clear the wild woods." And right royally did he fulfill his mission.

This son of a poor miner was born on St. Martin's eve, November 10, 1483, at Eisleben, Saxony, and died when sixty-three years of age at the same place, on February 18, 1546. His father designed him for a lawyer, for which profession he seemed to think the lad's pugnacious spirit was best adapted; and so the noisy and mischievous boy was early sent to school, and received along with other lessons innumerable floggings at the hands of his teachers. Fifteen of these floggings he says he had in one forenoon. But he thrived on them, and was withal a ready learner. When he entered the school at Mansfield, his poverty compelled him, in company with some other scholars as poor as himself, to become a strolling musician, both in that place and in the neighboring villages, singing, as the custom of the day was, from door to door, and then begging for bread to support themselves at the school. There followed a year at a Franciscan school at Magdeburg, and later he entered the Latin school at Eisenach, still begging his bread as before by singing. But the life was a hard one, full of many sore trials. The fare, too, was poor; and the road ahead long and discouraging, and the poor boy was about to give up the struggle for an education, when a kind-hearted woman, Ursula Cotta, pitying him, undertook his support, so that he was able, when eighteen years of age, to enter upon a course of study at the University of Erfurt. At the end of four years he graduated as Master of Arts, in the year 1505.

During his student life a severe fit of sickness brought him to death's door, and a friend lost his life in one of the duels, then, as now, so common in German universities. Anon a bolt of lightning struck at his feet, and his somewhat naturally superstitious nature was aroused, and he resolved to become a priest instead of a lawyer. Accordingly, July 17th, 1505, he entered the Augustinian convent at Erfurt, and, after three years there, became a professor of philosophy at the University of Wittenberg. While at the convent he was noted for his devotion and self-denying labor. He was the sweeper, porter, beggar for the institution. Here he met with and studied for the first time a Bible, also the writings of St. Augustine, and Tauler's sermons, and was much helped to independent thinking by the commentaries of Nicholas de Lyra, and the counsels of Johann Staupitz, the superior of the order of St. Augustine. In 1510 he made that memorable journey to Rome as a penitent seeking pardon for his sins, and was slowly climbing on his knees the steps of the Scala Santa, opposite the church of St. John Lateran, when he heard an inward voice saying to him, "The just shall live by faith," and, rising, he there resolved to give up the vain endeavor to secure pardon by outward ceremonials, and to take it as a gift of God received by faith alone. Returning to his professorship, he was made a Doctor of Divinity in 1512, and for eight years thereafter he remained within the fold of the Catholic Church, laboring to reform the glaring abuses he found therein.

When Pope Leo X. engaged in the task of rebuilding St. Peter's Church at Rome, that prelate aroused the faithful of his flock by promising indulgence to all who should contribute toward the expense of rebuilding, and sent forth the Dominican monk, Tetzel, to dispense them in Saxony. Tetzel was uncommonly zealous both for the worthy father of his church, and for himself, and farmed out the indulgences promiscuously, even making an open sale of them as a quittance in full for future sins, as well as for those of the past, to the infinite disgust of the thoughtful, and the great scandal of the devout, among whom were the faculty of the University of Wittenberg. Ere long, Professor Luther protested against the indulgence sales of the monk by his famous ninety-five Latin theses, which he proceeded to post up on the doors of the Schloss-kirche at Wittenberg, on October, 31, 1517, and sent a copy of them to the Archbishop of Magdeburg, begging him to put a stop to the scandalous practices of Tetzel.

Immediately a storm arose and raged. The infant press took up the strife, and it spread throughout Europe like wildfire. In 1519 Dr. Eck and Dr. Luther held a public debate at Leipsic on the question, and the excitement spread faster and waxed fiercer. Professor Luther was supported by his University, and protected from civil violence by the elector of Saxony, Frederick the Wise. Leo X. at first considered the matter as simply a quarrel between the monks of the Augustinian and Dominican orders, but in June, 1520, when better informed, he issued his bull of excommunication against the heretic Dr. Martin Luther unless he recanted within one hundred days. But the mediæval professor had more "spunk" than some of our modern religionists or even that eminent scientist, St. George Mivart, has had, and so he not only refused to recant, but openly burned the Pope's bull before the Elstergate of Wittenberg, December 10, 1520, in the presence of the students and faculty of that university.

Now the war raged hot and furious, and soon Europe was in the throes of the mightiest revolution it had ever known. The frightened spiritual hierarchs invoked the aid of the civil government against the daring heretic, and a few months after the Wittenberg escapade, the young German emperor, Charles V., summoned him for trial before the Diet of Worms. The friends of the young professor, knowing his life was now at stake, sought to persuade him not to attend the Diet. But with the heroic answer that though there were as many devils there as tiles on the roofs of the houses he would go, he set forth, and was greeted on his arrival at that city by some two thousand persons who sympathized with him, and escorted him to his lodgings. On entering the hall where the Diet was held, the old commander, Freundsburg, tapped him on the shoulder, and kindly, warningly, said, "Monk, monk, thou art on a passage more perilous than any which I and many other commanders ever knew in the bloodiest battlefields. If thou art right, fear not, God will sustain thee."

At the Diet he was confronted by the haughty and mighty dignitaries of the Roman Church, by the Emperor of Germany, with the barons, nobles, and grandees of his empire, and a vast concourse of spectators, and when called upon to recant what they called heresy, he proceeded boldly to defend his doctrine, and in his defense he announced on April 18, 1521, his ever-memorable and ever-safe declaration: "Unless I shall be refuted and convinced by testimony of the Holy Scriptures, or by public, clear, and evident arguments and reasons, I cannot and will not retract anything, since I believe neither the Pope nor the councils alone; both of them having evidently often erred, and contradicted themselves, and since it is neither safe nor advisable to do anything against the conscience. Here I stand. I cannot do otherwise. God help me! Amen!" The Diet pronounced the ban of excommunication of the empire against him, as the church had previously done, and thereafter he was an outlaw, both before the church and the civil government.

The agents of Frederick the Wise protected him, and for ten months secreted him, under an assumed name, in the castle of the Wartburg, near Eisenach, in Thuringia. But the horrors of the Peasants' War were abroad in the land, and the wild vagaries of some of the Anabaptists; and the to him strange and erratic preaching of his colleague, Carlstadt, induced him to come from his retreat, against the advice of friends, in order that he might rescue the child of religious freedom of thought from being strangled in its infancy. And thenceforth, amid many perils, through all those turbulent and epoch-making years, he both gave and received many a sturdy blow, and made and alienated many a friend. In June, 1525, he returned to one of the ancient practices of the Roman Church he had left, and, to the surprise alike of his friends and enemies, he took to wife the ex-nun, Catherine Von Bora, in order, as he said, to please his father, to tease the pope, and to vex the devil, and continued thereafter to prize his "Katy above the kingdoms of France, or the state of Venice."

His habits, if contrasted with those of our modern times, would be considered rude and gross; but they were, like himself, the product of his age. He had a wonderful faculty of expressing, in the everyday speech of the people, the views he held. He lacked utterly the legislative faculty of John Wesley, and was far inferior to John Calvin and the Geneva reformers, both as a thinker and reasoner. He was impatient of contradiction, and of an imperious and overbearing spirit that he was never able to master, and he was mentally so limited that he could not willingly grant to others the right of conscience and of private judgment in religious things that he claimed for himself. He was often coarse in his thought and language, as were the times in which he lived. But he was emphatically a man of devotion, of faith, and prayer; and he lived in and with his Bible, as but few men have ever done. He put the energy of his being into his words and deeds, gave to the German race a translation of the Bible that is yet without an equal in that tongue, and which alone would immortalize his name. He compiled and wrote the catechisms of the church now called by his name. He compiled, translated, and wrote, books, tracts, and hymns, one of which last, the "Ein feste Burg ist Unser Gott," the famous war song of the Reformation, written in 1529, and based on the forty-sixth Psalm, is sung around the world by the men of all Protestant creeds. Though a fighter, and living in, and the child of, those times of blood and persecution, he came to his grave in peace, and has a name among the very chief of the world's reformers. A man of the people, his personal independence of character soon made him in those fierce, tempestuous times, a leader and spiritual ruler of the people; and to-day, after the lapse of three and a half centuries, no name is so revered by Germans the world over as the name of the once poor beggar boy, Martin Luther.

Importance of Self-Mastery.

Rev. JAMES W. COLE, B.D.

VICE is only another name for weakness and decay. Ages have proved that virtue alone can give us strength and life. Each person finds within himself, and everywhere he goes, the eternal contrast and the eternal choice between good and evil. If he choose the good, then strength of body, of mind, of character, comes to him, and ultimately the highest success of which he is capable. If he choose evil, the one inevitable result is loss of power to do the best work of which he might be capable, and, sooner or later, a collapse of his physical and mental force, and, finally, failure. In the business world, a poor workman always diminishes profits. And for this reason wages must be paid out of the profits of one's business, otherwise they must be taken from the capital, which can mean but one thing, the destruction of all business.

In the commercial world it is found that profits go with quality, not quantity; the higher the quality, the greater the profits; unless, indeed, one is dealing wholly with the ignorant, or with children, or savages, incapable of appreciating quality. A small good painting, or sculpture, or work of art is worth immensely more in the world's markets than far larger ones that lack their quality. Merit, not space, determines the price and the profits. Again, the best produce and the best goods are found to bring the best prices, they being in the end the cheapest because they are the best. He, therefore, who would succeed in business must perforce not be a poor workman. Nor, if he be an employer, must he use such workmen if better ones can be had. Poor workmen cheapen products; hence, the better the workmen, the greater the profits. Now, vice makes poor workmen. There are no exceptions in any age, nor among any people. True, some peculiarly vicious persons have attained to more or less of eminence in the world, and sometimes in business. But no sensible person will deny that such individuals would have been far greater and grander, and doing better, nobler work, if they had not been the victims of their vices. He, therefore, who wishes the highest success in life must shun the vices, whatever their name or nature, whether the generally recognized sins, or what men call the lesser evils, as the vice of idleness, or a disregard of others' rights, or of one's obligations, or the multitudinous petty wrongs that affect society. A man must be master over all evil, and not the victim or the slave to it, if he would reach the grandest success.

Society is surcharged with so-called small vices to which many young men succumb through their social instincts, and which vices experience has shown do effectually destroy all hopes of high success in life, whether such success be the best development of our character, or merely the acquiring of a fortune, or the winning of fame, or the gaining a position among men, or the doing good to one's kind. While these evils of appetite do not at once destroy life, and while they do not immediately impair the bodily or mental vigor, yet they do hinder immensely in the contest for the sublime success of which man is capable, and quite generally they prevent even a moderate degree of success in one's life.

Consider a very common illustration. According to official returns there is spent each year in the United States more than twelve hundred millions of dollars for intoxicating beverages, and more than three-fourths of this immense sum is spent by the poor of the land, who seemingly never stop to think that it is this and its kindred evils that make and keep them so poor and degraded. Blatant demagogues, moved with envy or self-seeking, are fond of declaiming against the possessors of large landed estates in this country as though they were robbers of

IMPORTANCE OF SELF-MASTERY.

the poor, and yet, every time they and their dupes swallow their worse than useless mug of beer, they each gulp down a square yard of as rich land as there is in the United States. That is to say, the mug of beer costs more than the present average price of land per square yard in the country. What landed proprietors the poor might become if they would but renounce such evils, and save their earnings! It is the nimble nickels that run away with the dimes and the dollars. He who saves them is a capitalist. He who uselessly, needlessly flings them away is a spendthrift whose poverty is of his own producing. The little savings are what make the capital.

The advancement of the human race must largely if not wholly depend upon their acquiring this habit of saving. The civilized nations of the earth are the only savers. Savages are notorious spendthrifts, and averse to labor, and yet they endure more privations to get a bare subsistence than any capitalist of the day has done to accumulate all of his gains. As a rule, the poor man who wastes his earnings toils harder and is compelled to endure more privations than our rich men have done to become possessed of their riches. Yet their wealth is wholly the result of saving, as all the wealth of the world is, and savings are always the product of toil. So, then, if you would advance in civilization, you must toil and you must equally as well save this beer money. And, further, we all know from observation, the use of intoxicants soon destroys a man's value as a workman. It is always the poor workman who is the first to be discharged when "hard times" come; and the first to "come on the town for support." It is poor workmen who fill the almshouses, jails, and penitentiaries, and who make up the vast army of tramps in all countries, who roam about whether the times are "easy" or "hard." Indeed, the poor workmen (made poor by their vices) are almost wholly responsible for the extent of the "hard times." But for him they would seldom if ever occur.

Once in about twenty years we have in this country what is called a "panic" in the business world. Manufacturing well-

IMPORTANCE OF SELF-MASTERY.

nigh ceases, commerce languishes, and "hard times" are on the people. Now the waste from and by the drink-traffic alone in these United States amounts at the end of that period to a little more than double the annual earnings of all the people of this country. In consequence, the commercial world finds itself overburdened; nature is exhausted and demands economy and rest. "Now," cry the demagogues, "there is an overproduction of manufactures and the products of the soil. There is no market for goods. We must have new outlets for commerce. Manufacturers are getting rich at the expense of the working man; and we must revise the tariff." Yea, verily. But why fume at the wrecks of the flood, while you leave unvisited and untouched the mighty fountains that produce the floods? It is true that there is no market for the products, and the savings, but why? Is it not simply because the great armies of the poor of the world, who far outnumber the well-to-do, and who need those products and ought to have them, whose physical and moral salvation depends on having them, have wasted and do so waste the products of their own and others' toil, for that which is not bread, that they are no longer able to buy, and in consequence your markets are glutted with goods, and panics come and "hard times" follow until such time as nature can recuperate the waste? He who wastes his substance in riotous living must come to want at last.

Make it possible for the toilers of the world to buy by removing the enormous annual waste to them caused by vices, and how the wheels of commerce would spin, and peace and plenty everywhere abound, and over all the weary lands come the benediction of Heaven.

The masses of the world in all lands are very poor. The bulk of the people in our own land are poor. It is not strange that they are so. The so-called petty vices bring them to poverty. There are tens of thousands of families in this country who have spent a fortune in chewing, smoking, and snuffing filthy tobacco, and they have nothing to show for it but disordered nerves, ashes, quids, and stench. A dollar a week

IMPORTANCE OF SELF-MASTERY.

is a low estimate for the cost of tobacco for many families. If saved and deposited every six months at seven per cent. compound interest, it would in fifty years amount to twenty-two thousand, four hundred and twenty-three dollars, and at the end of eighty years there would be a snug fortune of one hundred and eighty-one thousand, seven hundred and seventy-three dollars, so that but for these vices they might soon be well-to-do capitalists. In truth, the vices are all wonderfully expensive and ruinous, and if you would win your highest success you must avoid them; you must be master over them; not of one only, but of all of them. See how one of our noted Americans overcame them, and to what eminence it led him.

The late Admiral David G. Farragut, of heroic war memories, at the close of the late civil war in this country, gave this account of the cause of his great naval success and fame. "Would you like to know," said he to a friend, "how I was enabled to serve my country?" "Of course I should," replied his friend. "It was all owing," said the Admiral, "to a resolution that I formed when I was ten years old. My father was sent to New Orleans with the little navy we had, to look after the treason of Burr. I accompanied him as a cabin boy. I had some qualities that I thought made a man of me. I could swear like an old salt; could drink a stiff glass of grog as if I had doubled Cape Horn, and could smoke like a locomotive. I was great at cards, and was fond of gambling in every shape. At the close of dinner one day, my father turned everybody out of the cabin, locked the door, and said to me, 'David, what do you intend to be?' 'I mean to follow the sea,' I said. 'Follow the sea,' exclaimed father; 'yes, be a poor, miserable, drunken sailor before the mast, kicked and cuffed about the world, and die in some fever hospital in a foreign clime.' 'No, father,' I replied, 'I will tread the quarter-deck and command, as you do.' 'No, David, no boy ever trod the quarter-deck with such principles as you have, and such habits as you exhibit. You will have to change your whole course of life if you ever become a man.' My father left me and went on deck. I was stunned by the rebuke and overwhelmed with mortification. 'A poor, miserable, drunken sailor before the mast, kicked and cuffed about the world, and die in some fever hospital! That's my fate, is it? I'll change my life, and change it at once. I will never utter another oath, never drink a drop of intoxicating liquor, never gamble.' And, sir, as God is my witness, I have kept these three vows to this hour. Shortly after, I became a Christian, and that act settled my temporal as it settled my moral destiny."

What a wonderful uplift toward the noblest success in life vast multitudes of young men would at once receive, if they would but make and carry out similar resolutions. As vice makes poor workmen, and as poor workmen reduce and often destroy all profits, business interests require, even if there were no moral considerations, that you should be virtuous in order to succeed! But, believe me, not this world alone, but the universe itself, is set toward the production and perpetuation of the virtuous man.

Doing Things Well.

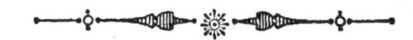

M. WOOLSEY STRYKER, D.D., LL.D., President Hamilton College.

THE word *well* is allied to the word *weal*. It has the notion of will and of wish. It suggests both an ideal and a purpose. One might write a book upon the immorality of carelessness. Whoever consents to less than his thorough best is neither shrewd nor good. To do things by halves or thirds, to put only a part of one's self into the given task, whether the tool is a pen or a pick, is to add to the general bulk of unrighteousness.

The old sculptor who said of his carvings, whose backs were to be out of all possible inspection, "but the gods will see," touched this matter to the quick. A result which one passes for his honest best, and which he knows is not that, is a kind of counterfeit. This felony has its reflex penalty in the slow effacing of the capacity to excel. It reacts in the deterioration of those faculties which gain by exactions, and dwindle by indulgences. Skill is wit plus will. To accept conventional estimates, to excuse one's self by averages, to let facility cheat thoroughness, to intermit that stern self-censorship, which both fidelity and farsightedness command, is to be always an apprentice, and never a master.

This adroit shirking when it becomes deliberate, or even chronic, puts a period both to mental and moral growth. Putty will for a while cover a multitude of sins; but, whether men discover the ill doer or no, the sins of superficiality will find the man out and wreak their inward penalty by making his soul shallower.

The genuine man, whether his product is books or boots,

DOING THINGS WELL.

whether he works by the year or by the day, will not willingly sacrifice quality to quantity. He will value the idea that lies in that keen German proverb, "The good is enemy to the best," which is to say that the passable blinds us to the perfect, and that offering a medium result we come to be incapable of the maximum. The so-called "pretty good" thus becomes the very bad.

The men who renounce mediocrity and uplift the average of the world are such as are never complacent with any present performance, and who by the energy of a great ideal first grasp and then tread every rung of the ladder. When a genuine and capable nature apprehends that slovenly performance is positively depraved, and that individuality is only another term for exceptional devotion to some line of effort, there breaks upon him vertical light.

Such a vision of what is possible to faithfulness and determination, will, if it is adopted into purpose, exorcise lethargy, indecision, procrastination, and all their fellow devils. The little idols of seeming and getting and all the inane pantheon will fall before the right-angled determination to do and never to be satisfied with half doing.

> "Heartily know
> That the half gods go
> When the gods arrive."

Doing well does not mean that we are to pause because we have done as well as another, nor because yet another's best is to us at present inaccessible.

It is not a relative but an absolute well-doing that God and men have a right to require at our hands. However, that is a noble discouragement which gauges its progress up by the topmost rather than midmost competitor. I have always found help in a wise paragraph of Richard C. Trench—"Fit, square, polish thyself. Thy turn will come. Thou wilt not lie in the way. The builders will have need of thee. The wall has more need of thee than thou hast of the wall."

DOING THINGS WELL.

"Seconds" may go cheap; but there is always a market for prime men. It will be found in the long run, and often in the short dash, that there is nothing more practical than a high and relentless ideal. And the ultimate and inestimable reward of work well done is the answer of a man's own soul in deep approval. Self-respect attends the outlay of one's total energy for worthy ends. The mere hireling, whether carpenter or king, is one who never tastes the pure springs of manliness. The solid soul who writes not alone on a crest, but on his heart, *ich dien*, attains "a peace above all earthly dignities." "In the morning," says Marcus Aurelius, "when thou art sluggish at rousing thee, let this thought be present, 'I am rising to a man's work.'"

And the Sage of sages speaks yet as he spake through the seer of Patmos, "*I know thy works.*" His "well done" will be the recognition and reward of all true men.

Self-Made if Ever Made.

Prof. D. COLLIN WELLS, Ph.D., Dartmouth College, New Hampshire.

IN July, 1870, the armies of France and Germany stood face to face upon the Rhine. Appearances favored France. She was richer and more populous; the organization of her forces appeared to be perfect. "On to Berlin," was the cry from Paris as the armies met. To the astonishment of Europe the French forces were cut in two and rolled into Metz and around Sedan like shore wreckage driven before a tidal wave. Within a few weeks, two great armies and the Emperor surrendered. Paris was taken, and German troopers paraded her streets. It was wonderful.

As men thought it out, they came to see that it was not France that was beaten, but only Louis Napoleon and a lot of nobles, influential because they bore titles or were favorites. Unhappy Louis Napoleon, the feeble bearer of a great name; Emperor, because of his name and criminal daring, upon the throne of his illustrious uncle, the man who made himself and the name! By a series of happy accidents he had gained some credit in the Crimean War, and at Magenta and Solferino. The unmasking time had come, as it always comes when sham, artificial toy-men meet genuine self-made men.

Such were the leaders on the German side. What a group they were, merely those four out of a great number,—every man the creator of his own greatness! King William, Bismarck, Von Moltke, and Von Roon.

William, strong, upright, warlike, and beloved by his people, "every inch a king." The German soldier, disciplined to perfection in the school and barracks, equipped and supplied by

SELF-MADE IF EVER MADE.

Von Roon, Minister of War, a master of administrative detail. Arms in perfect order, provisions enough and just where they were wanted, and a railway system so nicely organized as to handle the armies with utmost ease. Bismarck, the master mind of European politics, no miscalculation here. Above all, Von Moltke, chief of staff, who hurled armies by telegraph, as he sat at his cabinet, as easily as a master moves chessmen against a stupid opponent.

A rare man this Von Moltke! One who made himself ready for his opportunities beyond all men known to the modern world. Of an impoverished family, he rose very slowly and by his own merit. He yielded to no temptation, vice, or dishonesty, of course, nor to the greater and ever present temptation to idleness, for he constantly worked to the limit of human endurance. He was ready for every emergency, not by accident, but because he made himself ready by painstaking labor, before the opportunity came. His favorite motto was, "Help yourself and others will help you." Hundreds of his age in the Prussian army were of nobler birth, thousands of greater fortune, but he made himself superior to them all by extraordinary fidelity and diligence.

The greatest master of strategy the world has ever seen was sixty-six years at school to himself before he was ready for his task. Though born with the century, and an army officer at nineteen, he was an old man when, in 1866, as Prussian chief of staff, he crushed Austria at Sadowa and drove her out of Germany. Four years later the silent, modest soldier of seventy, ready for the still greater opportunity, smote France, and changed the map of Europe. Glory and the field marshal's baton, after fifty-one years of hard work! No wonder Louis Napoleon was beaten by such men as he. All Louis Napoleons have been, and always will be. Opportunity always finds out frauds. It does not make men, but shows the world what they have made of themselves.

On January 25, 1830, in the Senate of the United States, Hayne of South Carolina presented the Southern doctrine of nullification and state rights, in a powerful and plausible speech.

Webster proposed to answer him next morning. His friends protested that the time for preparation was too short. Next morning Webster delivered the greatest speech in American history. He had prepared for it all his life. "There is no such thing as extemporaneous acquisition," he once said. This opportunity did not make Daniel Webster; he had made himself, and responded naturally to the opportunity.

These examples from political and military life can be paralleled in every calling every day. Every obituary of scholar or millionaire tells the same story, that men are self-made if ever made. Francis Parkman, half blind, was America's greatest historian in spite of everything, because he made himself such.

It is the greatest glory of America that it is the land of self-made men. Here all is in free movement, and every one finds his own level. Fathers and grandfathers cannot long hold one up, or keep him down. Personal value here is a coin of one's own minting, one is taken at the worth he has put into himself.

This does not mean that every boy can make anything of himself. Natural talent and opportunities for using it are to be considered. Talents differ, and so do opportunities. What is meant is that upon one's self depends the use made of talents and opportunities. The finest talent can be wasted, as John Randolph wasted his by drink, or crowning opportunities thrown away, as Aaron Burr threw his away. If opportunities are earlier neglected, fine talents are never revealed, the world is poorer, the man is a failure.

This failure to make the most of himself may be, in one case, the failure to be a first-class carpenter, a master workman; in another, to be a thrifty, prosperous farmer; of still a third, to be a studious, growing doctor or lawyer. It is all relative to the start and surroundings. This does not condemn anyone to anything beforehand. Poverty and lack of friends did not condemn Lincoln and Garfield to ignorance and obscurity. In the United States, wealth and power are in the hands of men who have won for themselves. This is admitted, but it is often forgotten that the same rule is true all the way through society,— as true of the good blacksmith as of the railroad magnate. The man who, like Adam Bede, always drives a nail straight, and planes a board true, whom men always employ at good wages, is equally the maker of his own fortunes.

It is mostly a moral matter, an affair of character in its widest sense. This character building is delicate work. One has a dozen chances to spoil it in the making, every day and for three hundred and sixty-five days in the year; perhaps for seventy years, as in Von Moltke's case.

It is often a small thing that turns the scale. It may be that the favor of superiors or the public is lost by a hasty temper or a sour spirit; things within one's own control. Others train themselves to self-control and kindness, and win. This one may drink his first glass, and die a drunkard, or at best squander money that should be saved to noble uses. Another is an idler and wastes his time, with the result that he is ignorant when it is essential for him to know, or without resources when fronted with starvation or sickness. Another is a spendthrift and never gets ahead, however hard he works. Another yields to some weakness or passion, and finds himself heavily handicapped for life.

It is fundamentally true that one gets a better position, in the long run, only by filling well his present one. Fine qualities are perhaps better known to observers than to their possessors. The banker or the merchant notes them in subordinates; they are welcomed in the laborer; a doctor or a lawyer is employed because of them. Each one is his own best recommendation for promotion.

Advancement usually comes unexpectedly. One cannot prepare for it as if it were in the calendar. It is like the coming of the kingdom of heaven. The young officer, Von Moltke, mastered Russian as his fifth modern language, thinking it might be sometime useful, as it was. He perfected himself in every accomplishment and so was always qualified. It is the

SELF-MADE IF EVER MADE.

midnight oil that makes the great scholar. The pebbles in his mouth made Demosthenes, and the "well-stocked pigeon holes" made Daniel Webster.

All this means that one takes out of life only what he puts into it. If anything fine and noble is to be made of life, one must do it himself.

Personal Purity.

Rev. EDWARD EVERETT HALE, D.D., Boston, Mass.

THOMAS ALVA EDISON was once asked why he was a total abstainer. He said, "I thought I had a better use for my head." The answer is worth remembering by any young fellow who means to use his brains. A wonderful battery they make. Every morning they take up their work, and start us on our daily pleasure or our daily duty, if,—

If we have not undertaken to impose on nature's plan for them.

If we have not tried this stimulus or that stimulus, not in the plan for which they were made.

The young man who means to do the best possible work his body and mind can do, keeps his body and mind as pure, as clean from outside filth, as Edison keeps his brain.

This is what is meant when we are told to keep ourselves as pure as little children are.

The readers of this book are so well up to the lessons of this time that they know that the men who are trained for a football match, or a running match, or a boxing match, have to keep their bodies from any stimulus but that which is given by food prepared in the simplest way, so as to suit the most simple appetite.

It is not simply that a man's body must be in good order itself. What is needed is that a man shall be ready and able to govern his body. He shall say "Go," and his body shall go. He shall say "Go faster," and his body shall go faster. His will, his power to govern his machinery, depends on his keeping himself pure.

PERSONAL PURITY.

Three hundred years ago, a certain set of men and women in England earned for themselves the name of Puritans. That name was given them because they kept their bodies pure. Those men and women did this because the Saviour of men and all his apostles commanded them to do so. The New Testament insists on personal purity as the beginning of all training and all knowledge. "The wisdom from above is first pure," it says. And such men as Paul and Peter and the rest, who changed the world, insisted on personal purity. They meant that a man's body should be so pure as to be a fit temple of God. The Puritans of England believed in such instructions, and they kept their bodies pure. In his intercourse with women, in his use of stimulants, a Puritan gentleman earned his name by his chastity and his temperance.

The Cavaliers, the men at court, ridiculed this obedience to divine law. What followed on this ridicule? This followed: that, when the questions of English liberty were submitted to the decision of battle, when the fine gentlemen of the court found themselves in array against the farmers of Lincolnshire, led by Oliver Cromwell, the Puritan troopers, who kept their bodies pure, rode over the gay gentlemen who did not keep their bodies pure.

What happened on our side of the water was that the handful of Puritan settlers in Plymouth and in the Bay, who kept their bodies pure, were more than a match for the men of Massasoit and Philip, who did not keep their bodies pure. They could outmarch them, could outwatch them, could outfight them. They could rule their bodies. They could be firm to a purpose. They had at command such strength as had been given to them.

The young men who read this book probably know better than I do what are the temptations which now offer themselves in the life of an American boy. They are different in different places. I know that, not long ago, I was speaking on the need of immediate act if one would carry out a good resolution. I was in the largest theater in Boston. I looked up at the third gallery, which was crowded with several hundred boys and young men. I said, "Go home, and take down from the wall of your room the picture you would be ashamed to have your mother see there." An evident wave of consciousness passed over the hundreds of witnesses, as they turned to each other, as they smiled, or in some way showed that they knew what I was talking about. This is certain, that in the life of cities young men are the men solicited to throw away the purity of their bodies and to give up their self-control.

I say young men know better than old men what are the present temptations. If young men knew as well as old men do how much of the best life of every country is lost because the young men do not resist those temptations, they would pay more attention to what old men say to them. I was talking on this matter with a young artist the other day, and on the moment he named to me five of the most distinguished of the younger artists of France who had been lost to France and to the world by sensual habits. And anybody who knows the history of the tug of war between France and Germany twenty years ago knows what happened then. War tests all forms of manliness. It tests endurance and physical strength and patience under disappointment. We know who went under when the French troops, all rotten with the impurity of France, met the German peasants. The French Empire disappeared because of the dissoluteness of the French Empire. A court like that could not expect the support of soldiers any stronger than the officers of the headquarters-staff who marshaled them.

To a man deep down in licentious or intemperate habits, it is very difficult to prescribe the remedies for his cure. The trouble is that he has lost the power of will. It is very hard then to make him will or determine anything. The poor creature does not know what determination means. He says at night, "I will never touch liquor again," and the next day, when he passes a liquor shop, he says, "I have changed my mind, and I will take it again." Indeed, he has not changed his mind; he has almost no mind to change. He never made a resolution, because such a man cannot make a resolution. But we are not addressing him in this book; we are addressing young men.

For young men, the course is distinct, and not so difficult. The prayer, "Lead us not into temptation," states it very precisely. This is the reason why the men who wish to have our cities temperate wish to close the open saloon in the city. They want to save young men from a very fascinating temptation. For every young man who reads this page knows that, while he might go into an open shop with a friend to drink a glass of beer, to treat or to be treated, he would not so much as think of buying a bottle of liquor to carry it up to his own private room and drink it there. What we want, when we say we wish we could shut up all the liquor shops, is to save from temptation people who have not formed the habits of drinking. Just the same thing is to be said as to the temptations to unchastity. If you do not begin, you will not take a step forward. The moment that you find that a book is impure, or, as I said to those boys in the theater, is such a book as you would not show to your mother or your sister, that is the moment to put that book into the fire. Indeed, the mere physical act of putting it into the fire will be a good thing for you. It will be like one of the old sacrifices on the altar.

And if you want any reason which you can state to a friend or to yourself, for your taking such a course, the reason is, that you wish to keep mind and body in the condition in which it pleased God to make them. You mean to train yourself precisely as the trainer of a football team or a baseball team or a boat crew trains his men. You mean that your hand shall be steady, your feet quick, your arm strong. And, more than this, you mean to have these powers in immediate command, so that they shall do just what you, the living man, want to have done.

Let me say a word from personal experience. All intelligent young men are, and ought to be, interested in literary work. They are all interested in the authors whom they love to read. I should like, therefore, to close this paper by saying that I have known most of the American literary men of my time. I have

PERSONAL PURITY.

known many of the ablest American physiologists of our time. Such men will differ, I suppose, as to the question whether, after men begin to die, a physician might recommend a stimulant for waning powers, when a particular effort was to be made. A man begins to die when he passes the age of forty-five. But even if you grant, what certainly is not proved, that after men begin to die, a glass of beer or a glass of wine may be sometimes recommended in certain lines by medical advisers, I think nobody pretends that this is done for any other reason than to resist for a moment, more or less, the decay of declining life. This book is written for people who have not begun to die. It is written for young men in the fullness of their power. To such men I want to say, what I have said again and again in public, and what has never been challenged. I have worked side by side with other men, on the newspaper press, in my own profession, and in various public cares; and from what such men have said to me, and from my own experience, I know that the brain of man works most accurately and most steadily, and therefore most reliably, when it is never plagued or perplexed by the influence of liquor. I know that the literary man who is a total abstinent comes back to his desk every morning most easily and most readily. On an emergency he sticks to his work for four and twenty hours, if it is necessary, most cheerfully. And in that four and twenty hours his work is best worth reading. You may ask any newspaper man you choose, or any literary man of fifty years' experience who has known the other literary men of his time, and they will substantiate my answer. You may ask any trainer of athletes, and he will sustain my answer. For absolute physical exertion the point is conceded. The riflemen who take the prizes in England are total abstinent men. And Greely told me himself that if he were to take another party to the North Pole he would take no man if he was not a total abstinent by habit and principle. In point of fact, the great exertion by which the American flag was planted nearest the **North Pole was made by men who had no regular spirit ration.**

Value of a Sound Body.

Rev. JAMES W. COLE, B.D.

THE immense advance of this age over preceding ones is due not to our superiority in our natural powers of body or of mind, but to the construction of fine implements whereby the range of the bodily senses has been so greatly enlarged. What stores of knowledge, what sources of material wealth, have been opened up to men by the telescope, the microscope, the spectrum, the minute delicate balances of the chemist, the choice instruments of the physician and surgeon, and the marvelous appliances of the mechanic and the inventor, whereby the hitherto hidden forces of nature are put to use for the comfort, welfare, and enriching of mankind! If our bodily senses had not been so enlarged by these things, in what branch of knowledge would we be superior to the men of other generations?

Whatever may be the conditions of existence in other worlds, it is certain that in this one the mind of man is not only located by his body, but developed by the body; so that our body is, to the highest degree, a necessity to the well-being of our minds. When the body is defective, through lack of organs, the mind is limited by being shut up in that direction. Persons born blind, or without hearing, or speech, are not naturally defective in mind, but the mind is shut up through lack of organs of manifestation and use.

That marvelous thinker, Bishop Butler, suggests that the mind of man may have many hidden, undreamed-of powers, not now used because of a lack of bodily organs for their development, so that to a degree our present bodies may be a

VALUE OF A SOUND BODY.

limitation to the mind, repressing its energies! However this may be, it is certain that whatever of value our bodies here possess is due to the indwelling mind. The body without a normal mind is not only a useless thing, but a burdensome thing, as is manifest in the case of idiots and the insane. But in these cases the defect or impairment of mind, whereby the body becomes a burden to be cared for by others, is primarily due to a defect or impairment of the body's functions or organs, and when that impairment is remedied the mind renews its normal condition.

How, or by what, mind and body are connected, or by what agency they act or interact on or through each other, none can as yet tell. We only know that the body is as necessary to constitute a man as the mind is. We know, too, that whatever impairs the body limits, by that impairment, the mind. We also know that vice corrupts the body; and we also know that this vice depraves through the body (if it does not deprive) the powers of the mind. Now, mind is the developing, governing, enriching factor in this and all other worlds. Without the mind the body is dead, inert, useless. Of what possible value were a universe of matter without mind? Further, in all beings (unless, indeed, the uncreated Being is an exception) the mind must of necessity be localized and centralized in a body if individuality exists. Of what use were your mind or mine if it were uniformly distributed throughout infinite space?

That we shall individually exist hereafter is to me not a doubtful problem, but a demonstrated certainty. And that we shall have a body is also sure. To what extent it may differ from our present bodies, I may not now speak. But this I wish here to emphasize. *No one questions that the mind can be and is depraved through and by means of a vicious bodily life. No one can reasonably question that if the mind exists the moment after leaving such vicious body, it exists in its essentiality just as it existed the moment before leaving that body— i. e., depraved.* Take now the doctrine of the Scriptures as to the resurrection of the body (a teaching unfortunately in these days held in abeyance if not openly repudiated, yet to me one most natural and accordant with nature and her unfoldings), and the value of a *sound* body becomes a thing of tremendous import. Here, as just now noted, a defect in bodily organs limits by deprivation the mind. Here a vicious bodily life depraves the mind, and so also limits the mind. How feeble is the mind of the drunkard and the licentious! How ignorant, and gross, and poor, and vile this world would be if all were such! The mind gross but a moment before going out of this world is a gross mind the moment after,—for transmigration is not transmutation.

The Scriptures teach the same doctrine that nature does, to wit, that like assimilates to like throughout the universe. Even the atoms of matter will unite, or coalesce, only under certain conditions, or in definite proportions. Vice transmutes the powers of mind and by that transmutation impairs it. Vice transmutes the powers of the body, and by that transmutation impairs it. The drunkard, the debauchee, changes by his life of vice the very character and constituency of the blood corpuscles on which the growth, development, strength, and efficiency of the body depend, so that at last the body breaks down and disintegrates.

"There shall be a resurrection both of the just and of the unjust," taught the Saviour of men, and unless it can be shown that the mind dies, this must have reference alone to the body of man. That the mind does not, cannot die, is to me a certainty. Now, "with what *manner* of body do they come" in the hereafter? Each with body fitted to the place it is to fill,— *matched to* the mind it embowers! Why, that is simply carrying onward the present course of nature. And yet men cry out against the Bible teaching that hereafter the filthy mind shall be seen and known by its filthy body resurrected and conjoined to it. All created minds are necessarily centralized in a body. Nature makes her environment after the manner of the thing interned. Worlds are fitted for the beings that inhabit them. And minds and their bodies are not merely co-related,

VALUE OF A SOUND BODY.

but conjoined each after its manner and kind. Even as to the holy and the blessed of men it is written, that, like as "one star differeth from another star in glory, so also is the resurrection of the dead."

Young man, this ought to give you a solemn pause when you are tempted to vice. Experience here shows that vice will not merely impair but destroy your prospects in this world, because of its impairing and destroying power on the body and mind. And nature and her Creator forewarn you that it will have equally deleterious and unchangeable effect in the life to come. One is greatly hampered in this life if born with a corrupted or deformed body, however strong or brilliant and noble the mind may be. But to carry an inherited deformed body and an imbecile mind in this world is a trial indeed. Nature here, by locking up the mind, abates the affliction to the innocent victims of others' wrongdoing. Will she be equally sympathetic hereafter to those who here consciously work evil to themselves? Does she not here give such "the reward of their own hands"? What if she carries it out hereafter and it come to pass as prophesied of old, that those "that sleep in the dust of the earth shall awake, some to everlasting life, and some to shame and everlasting contempt"? Here we pity those who inherit idiocy; and we blame while we pity those who by vicious ways bring idiocy upon themselves, and then,—well, we can't help it, we are forced to put them away from us for care and keeping; if we did not they would so hinder us in our own better life, and then they serve as warnings to us to beware of vice.

Young man, young woman, are you to be only a beacon of warning hereafter, instead of nobly serving him who gave his life for noble ends? This, you, and not another, must determine. To do work effectively here one must have both knowledge and proper tools, and the efficient tool for all our work is the body. A weak, sickly, or defective body puts one at a disadvantage. You should therefore as carefully train, develop, and discipline and use your body as you would the

VALUE OF A SOUND BODY.

mind; for through the body the mind is enlarged, and through it, it is yet to be perfected. A great part of our present life is necessarily taken up with the growth and care of the body. Some of the Greek philosophers contended that the body through its appetites hindered right thinking; some of the ancient Hebrews held, as do many moderns, that it hinders right doing and so they seek to make its desires an excuse for an evil life. But the Creator did not make a mistake when he gave us this body. It is a most wonderfully made instrument for doing and learning most wonderful things. But like all his good gifts it must be rightly used. The best bodies, like the best minds, when perverted become the worst and most depraved. For the higher the height, the farther and deeper the fall. A sound body, rightly used, is the best help to the unfolding of the mind here; and upon the proper development of that mind depends the future body we shall have. "Each in his own order," saith the Word. What order shall you and I be in?

Importance of Physical Development.

Prof. A. ALONZO STAGG,
Director of the Department of Physical Culture, Chicago University.

THERE is nothing more interesting in the world than watching the growth of things, and noting their development. We plant our garden with many kinds of seeds. Eagerly we watch for the appearance of the tiny sprouts, and as eagerly observe their growth. We organize a society or a business scheme and are interested heart and soul in its progress. A baby comes into the family, and we are intensely wrapped up in him. We watch his daily progress and note each sign of increasing intelligence and strength. "My! how you have grown, my lad, since I last saw you. How tall are you, and how much do you weigh?" are questions frequently asked of a growing boy. So the world takes note of the hundreds of thousands of growing youths. Development in any good form is what people are on the watch for, whether mental, moral, or physical. But it is physical growth which calls forth most frequent comment. Everybody can see that. The evidence is presented to their eyes. See the slight form of a girl developing into the symmetrical form of a woman, or a lanky boy filling out into the full vigor of manhood. "How strong he is getting to be also! He can almost wrestle his father, or carry his mother in his arms, or handle a bag of meal." There are a thousand and one things for which a boy needs strength. If a boy, a man surely.

Yes, physical development is what most of us boys are interested in. We want to be as strong or stronger than our fathers. We want to be taller and heavier, to be able to lift more and walk farther. But, my lad, none of these things can be brought

IMPORTANCE OF PHYSICAL DEVELOPMENT.

about unless you are willing to work for them, or play for them, if you will. The large frame, the full, deep chest, the strong muscles, do not grow unless they have work and exercise to enlarge and strengthen them. Of course food is necessary to the body also, but we all get that. What we do not all get, however, is proper exercise to develop the physical part of our being to its fullest limit. Some of us have reasons for not taking the proper exercise, but in most cases, if the truth were known, the person has plenty of opportunity to get the exercise, but is either too indolent or too indifferent to take it. Does this hit any of you, my readers?

Now for a word on *importance*. The importance of anything is measured by its usefulness. The telegraph and telephone have become important because of their service to mankind. Stretch a wire across the continent and attach no transmitter or receiver to the ends of your wire, and it becomes of no practical use, only a resting place for swallows. Build a ship complete in every detail out on the prairie apart from its place of service, and as an aid to mankind it is as useless as Noah's Ark upon the top of Mt. Ararat. The things which are of use to man, the theories which can be crystallized and put to service, the thoughts which assume practical forms,—these are what the world demands, and in the long run these are the only things to which the world will hold fast. Let a Bell invent a telephone, an Edison an electric light, a Froebel the kindergarten method, and prove their utility, and the world will not give them up until another telephone, or electric light, or child-training method has proved its right to supplant the first. Physical culture has proved itself important and necessary, no matter what differences of opinions as to methods may exist in the minds of educators, and the time has now come when no boy or girl should be able to say like Topsy, "I just growed," so far as his or her physical condition is concerned. But in order not to say this, most young men and young women will need to take the matter of fitting themselves with a fine physique into their own hands. Some states make mental training

IMPORTANCE OF PHYSICAL DEVELOPMENT.

compulsory, but as a rule they leave the physical training, which should supplement the intellectual, to be worked out by the children themselves.

But now I want to say a few words on the *importance of developing the body.* It is important, first, because the body is the home of the mind, which every one is trying to develop to the greatest degree. The body has the most intimate relationship with the mind, and in great measure is its servant, and obeys the command of the will. The will speaks to the body through its motor nerves, and the body responds according to the sharpness of the command, and its ability to obey. But the body influences the mind in an important way, also. A puny body means a small supply of blood, which means limitation in mental endurance, and in recuperation after prolonged mental effort. The brain is fed by the blood, which is also its scavenger, carrying away the waste matter produced by the process of thought. Now, it is as apparent as the fact that one and one make two, that, other things being equal, the man who has the largest supply of rich, pure blood will be able to give more sustenance to his brain, to cleanse it better and more quickly of its waste, to work longer and produce better thoughts, and to recover sooner after the work, than a man who has a smaller supply of blood, and that not so pure. There are other influences, however, which affect the mental powers, otherwise the man who has the largest quantity of blood within his body would have the greatest mental development. There are great differences in the quality of brains, some being much more highly convoluted and sensitized than others, but, given such a brain, it would many fold increase its power if assisted by a plentiful supply of pure blood.

Further, health and vigor of the body in all its organs affect the health and vigor of the mind. Full health and vigor can only come when the body is developed in all its parts. Man is a unit made up of a complexity of parts, which bear a sympathetic and helpful relationship to each other and to the whole, according as these parts are in a healthy condition.

IMPORTANCE OF PHYSICAL DEVELOPMENT.

An abused stomach or an exposed nerve is sufficient to set aside mental application for the time being.

It is easy to see how important, how absolutely necessary, it becomes for man to possess a good physical development. If force of circumstances, or ambition, or unwise living, enter into his life in such a way as to tax his body severely, then his life becomes full of trouble and exhaustion. Yes, and how often is one's body taxed in the ordinary affairs of life. We must catch a train. It is necessary to run in order to do this, sometimes to run fast. If our body is in proper physical condition no harm will result, but if otherwise we run at a great risk of a serious strain, for we have never subjected ourselves to enough exercise to strengthen properly the heart and lungs. Walking along the street one falls on the ice. If the muscles of the body are in proper condition nothing serious will result, but should the accident befall a poorly developed person, the shock and bruises may seriously affect his health. But there are a thousand and one ways in which a fine physique is found necessary in a lifetime. Much of the tired feeling, and nearly all the collapses of middle life, can easily be avoided by giving proper attention to physical training in our younger days. One so developed is not subject to this languor, and is almost unconscious that he possesses a body.

We should be proud of our physical development. The young man with a fine physique walks along the street knowing and feeling his strength, and with the consciousness that he can take care of himself. His muscles fairly ache to rescue some one from danger; to stop a runaway team, or to perform some other heroic deed which seems in keeping with his fine physical development and muscular prowess. And what lad is there possessing such muscular powers who does not think of such things, and is not constantly on the alert for just such opportunities for usefulness? Such a young man will be quick to act when emergencies come. He will not be confused, for he knows his capabilities and can quickly bring them into service.

IMPORTANCE OF PHYSICAL DEVELOPMENT.

Yes, every boy and girl, every young man and woman, can well afford to give time and attention to acquiring a healthy and vigorous body. It is time to call a halt on puny, sickly, hollow-chested and weak-kneed men and women. There are enough such people in the world now, who are moaning with pain and sending forth their sad complaining, and you, my boys and girls, you, my young men and women, are the ones to call the halt. Develop that body which God has given you. Run and romp and play games; skate and ride your bicycle; row and swim; play baseball and football and tennis; engage in all the sports of youth in fact, and then, in addition to doing these things which take your fancy, take gymnasium work under a good instructor, and you are well started toward a happy and successful life.

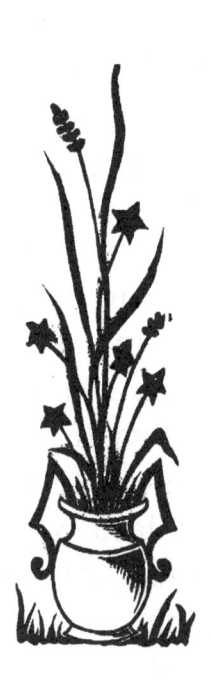

The Advantages of Difficulties.

Rev. WILLIAM DeWITT HYDE, D.D., President Bowdoin College, Maine.

THE philosopher Kant remarks that a dove, inasmuch as the only obstacle it has to overcome is the resistance of the air, might suppose that if only the air were out of the way, it could fly with greatest rapidity and ease. Yet if the air were withdrawn, and the bird were to try to fly in a vacuum, it would fall instantly to the ground, unable to fly at all. The very element that offers the difficulty to flying is at the same time the condition of any flight whatever.

The chief difficulty which a locomotive has to overcome in moving a train is friction. Yet if there were no friction, the locomotive could not move the train a single inch. The resistance of the water against the prow is the chief difficulty that the steamship has to overcome; yet if it were not for this same resistance of the water against the blades of the propeller, the ship would not move at all.

This same law, that our difficulties are the conditions of our success, holds true in human life. A life freed from all difficulties would be a life shorn of all its possibilities of power. Mind, like matter, is plentifully endowed with inertia. Powers not called into active exercise lie dormant. And powers suffered long to lie dormant die. Difficulty is a spur that wakes us up and compels us to exert our powers. And the exertion gives us new power; and so out of our difficulties is born our strength. The child of luxury, whose wants are gratified, whose faults are overlooked, whose whims are indulged as fast as they arise, has no occasion to develop self-control, self-reliance, self-support. Hence he grows up without them; and when the time of

THE ADVANTAGES OF DIFFICULTIES.

trial comes he is found heartless, helpless, hopeless, in the face of conditions which the sons of poverty and toil master with perfect ease.

This is the reason why the average country boy so easily outstrips the average city boy in the keen competitions of city life. The city boy has hosts of acquaintances and friends; while the boy from the country is an utter stranger. The city boy has polished manners; while the boy from the country may be awkward and bashful. The city boy is given a good start in the office; while the country boy has to begin out in the factory or warehouse. The city boy has friends on the lookout to secure him chances of promotion; while the country boy has to work his own way by his own exertions. This goes on perhaps a dozen years; and to all appearances the city boy has altogether the best of it. At the end of that time there is a change. A man is wanted who thoroughly understands the business from top to bottom; one who can put into it energy and force; one who will give his days and nights to its development and extension. It is no longer a question of granting favors to this or that individual. It is now a question of urgent need. The business must have the right man or fail. The firm turns to these two young men. One has been in the office all these years; comfortable and contented; he has saved nothing, not taking the trouble to familiarize himself with the petty details of the business or to cultivate the acquaintance of the men who are actually engaged in the rough, hard work which it involves. He does very well where he is. He is a good bookkeeper. But he is not qualified to take the control of the actual work. The workmen would take advantage of him. Customers would get the best of him. He will not do. The firm turns to the other young man. He has learned the processes peculiar to the business. He knows the men with whom he has had to deal. He has had a small salary, but has saved a portion of it every year. He understands the business better than anyone else. He wins the promotion he deserves. The boy who has had to earn his living knows the value of a dollar as the boy who has always had his spending money given to him never can. The young man who has been knocked about in the world appreciates kindness and love as those who have always had plenty of friends and favors too often fail to do. The man who has been misunderstood and criticised and condemned unjustly acquires a firm reliance on his own integrity of purpose which the popular man is very likely to lose.

Even the severest physical defects and limitations have their compensations. There is no misfortune which a resolute will may not transform into an advantage. A closer acquaintance with the inner life of men of large achievement seldom fails to reveal the presence of some early privation, some bodily infirmity, some sore bereavement, some bitter disappointment, which has served as a secret spur to their endeavors. Out of hundreds of such cases I will cite two American historians: William H. Prescott, and Francis Parkman. In earlier days the order at college dining tables was not perfect; and frequently a "biscuit battle" followed the conclusion of the meal. In his Junior year, as Prescott was passing out of the Commons Hall after dinner, he turned his head quickly to see what the disturbance was, and was hit in the open eye by a large, hard piece of bread, which destroyed the sight of the eye. On his return to college after the resulting illness, he "now determined to acquire more respectable rank in his class than he had earlier deemed worth the trouble." A year and a half later the other eye became inflamed and affected with rheumatism. For weeks at a time he was compelled to remain in a room so dark that he could not see the furniture; and here he walked hundreds of miles from corner to corner, thrusting out his elbows so as to get warning through them of his approach to the angles of the wall, from which he wore away the plaster by the constant blows thus inflicted on it. He was compelled to abandon his chosen profession of law. At the age of twenty-five he found himself with greatly impaired eyesight, and with no accurate knowledge of the modern languages. Yet he chose as his life work history, which more than any other line of literary work requires eyesight; and a branch of history which required the constant use of the languages of Southern Europe. He at once set about the training of his memory; and persisted until he could prepare, work over, revise, correct, and retain in his memory the equivalent of sixty pages of printed matter; which he would then dictate to his amanuensis. In the face of these difficulties he produced the history of Ferdinand and Isabella, the Conquest of Mexico, and the Conquest of Peru. And later, when he could use his one remaining eye only one hour a day, and that divided into portions at wide intervals, he prepared his history of Philip II. As President Walker of Harvard University said, "We lamented the impairment of his sight as a great calamity; yet it helped, at least, to induce that earnestness and concentration of life and pursuit which has won for him a world-wide influence and fame."

Francis Parkman, in his college days, at the age of eighteen, devoted himself to the history of the French settlements in America. In order to understand the life of the Indians, who played so large a part in the history which he was determined to write, he went and lived among them in the far West. In doing this he greatly impaired his health. His eyesight was affected so that he could not read or write but a few minutes at a time; and his general health would not permit him to apply himself to study more than half an hour at a time. Yet, like Darwin, who could study but twenty minutes at a time, and that rarely more than twice each day, he has left us a splendid monument of work done so thoroughly that no one will ever need to do it after him.

The men who succeed best in the end are frequently the men who have most difficulty at the start. The greatest orators, from Demosthenes to Webster, have made wretched failures of their first attempts. During the years he was at Phillips Exeter Academy, Webster, although he committed piece after piece to memory, was so overcome when called upon to speak that he never was able to leave his seat. Difficulty may come, as in these cases from excess of power, which is at first uncontrol-

THE ADVANTAGES OF DIFFICULTIES.

lable, but is the condition of great achievement when control is gained. The colts which are hardest to break make the best horses to drive.

No young man should be discouraged by difficulties; for nothing worth doing was ever free from them. They are the stuff success is made of.

> "Then welcome each rebuff
> That turns earth's smoothness rough,
> Each sting that bids nor stand, nor sit, but go!
> Be our joys three parts pain!
> Strive, and hold cheap the strain
> Learn, nor account the pang; dare, never grudge the throe!"

The Blight of Idleness.

Rev. GEORGE R. HEWITT, B.D., Springfield, Mass.

WE live in a day when the poet and the philosopher have combined to sound the praise and dignity of labor. Idleness is no longer deemed honorable or genteel. Work is the new patent of nobility. "The latest gospel in this world is," says Carlyle, "Know thy work and do it."

No man, rich or poor, has any right to be idle if he is able to work and can find work to do. Every man born into the world is bound to perform his proportionate share of the world's work. He cannot, unless he is a hermit, live by and for himself alone. He is born into society, stands included in society, derives unnumbered benefits from society, and so is morally bound to make some contribution to society.

Work is the law under which men live. Fish do not leap from the lakes into our frying pans, nor loaves of bread drop down from the skies; forests and clay banks do not shape themselves into dwellings, nor the mines automatically give up their treasures; and so long as they do not, the life of man on this planet can have no other law than that of unremitting toil. Let the world play holiday for a year and famine would reign from pole to pole. The world is always within one year of actual starvation. We really live from hand to mouth, and the world's incessant toil is all that keeps its fourteen hundred millions alive.

Since work is the law by which men live and society exists, the lazy man who will not work is a nuisance and a burden to society. Somebody else must do double work that he may live without doing any. An able-bodied, healthy man who spends his days in idleness, refusing to contribute his share of work, manual or mental, for the maintenance of the world's life, is a fraud and a cheat. A man who shuns work defrauds and disgraces himself.

Idleness if it became general would bring a universal blight over the earth's surface. If the world to-day wears a different look from what it wore when Adam walked in it, if foul jungles have been cleared and waste places reclaimed, if stately cities have arisen and the desert been made to rejoice and blossom as the rose, it is all by reason of the labor that has been bestowed upon it. Man by his work has "stamped the brute earth and the raw materials taken out of it with the signature of mind." Let labor cease and the earth would revert to a wilderness. Industry and civilization go hand in hand. Indolence and barbarism are invariably linked together. By idleness it comes to pass that instead of the fir tree comes up the thorn, and instead of the myrtle tree comes up the brier. Says Solomon: "I went by the field of the slothful, and by the vineyard of the man void of understanding; and, lo, it was all grown over with thorns, and nettles had covered the face thereof, and the stone wall thereof was broken down. Then I saw, and considered it well: I looked upon it, and received instruction."

But idleness brings a blight not only on the earth and on man's possessions; it also brings a blight on man himself.

(1) It blights his powers. Man is a bundle of latent powers and capacities. Labor, in its varied forms muscular and mental, is the divinely appointed way by which our powers and capacities are to be quickened and unfolded. But an idle man's powers, being unexercised, remain undeveloped; and not only so, they even wither and shrink. Capacities unused waste away. We read in Scripture that the man who hid his talent lost it. Every member of the body and every faculty of the mind has a function to fulfill. Let them lie in idleness, and feebleness and atrophy ensue. A man needs work, then, not only for work's sake but for his own sake. He thereby perfects himself. Toil is a great teacher. Daily work is a daily school of patience, punctuality, fidelity, honesty, truthfulness, and all the virtues. Idleness is a school of nothing but vice.

THE BLIGHT OF IDLENESS.

It is a tomb in which a living man shuts himself. It is the blight of every talent, the paralysis of every power.

(2) Idleness blights a man's happiness. There is joy in work well done. The humblest mechanic who accomplishes a given piece of work experiences a pleasure the idle man never knows. No bread eaten by man is so sweet as that earned by his own labor. No man can be happy who is living a useless life. Everybody despises him, and in his inmost heart he at length comes to despise himself. Self-respect wells up in the heart of a man whose powers are employed for useful ends.

(3) Idleness blights character. "Satan finds some mischief for idle hands to do." It was when King David tarried in idle luxury in Jerusalem, instead of taking the field in person and leading his army to battle, that he fell into the double crime that is the only blot on his otherwise fair fame. A man is never so well fortified against evil as when he is busy. The bicycle is kept upright by its own velocity. When it stops it falls. Regular employment is a moral safeguard. "Doing nothing is an apprenticeship to doing wrong." When you find a young man doing nothing, the chances are ten to one that he is drifting to the bad. Satan finds his recruits largely among loafers. Idleness is the mother of crime. Some time ago a young man was sentenced to the state prison of Connecticut for forgery. As he was changing his own for the prison suit, he remarked to the officer, "I never did a day's work in my life." The officer sagely replied, "No wonder, then, you have brought up here." The devil tempts all other men, but an idle man tempts the devil. The idle brain is the devil's workshop.

Dream not, then, young man, of a life of idleness. "One monster there is in the world," says Carlyle, "the idle man." Honorable toil is the road to health, wealth, and happiness. Idleness will prove a curse to you and an injury to those with whom you come in contact. It will blight your powers of mind and body and at last it will bring you down

"To the vile dust from whence you sprung,
Unwept, unhonored, and unsung."

What Spare Moments Will Accomplish

Rev. JAMES W. COLE, B.D.

MIND rules this world. The day of government by mere brute strength and numbers has departed. Machine guns and needle guns conquer and keep in quiet not merely the savage but the civilized races of men. Mind is rapidly making "grim and horrid war" to be a civilizer and peacemaker by reducing war to mere butchery and so by making it too costly, making it unpopular. Mind is also making the grosser passions of men too dreadful to be tolerated. Even those seemingly omnipotent passions of gain and lust will soon be subdued, either by reason, or by dynamite. Some misguided souls are even now undertaking to do it by the last process.

But, is there not a better way? Mr. Andrew Carnegie, himself many times a millionaire, has well and truthfully said, "The man who dies rich dies disgraced." It will yet be changed to read, "The man who lives rich while any of his fellows shiver and starve, lives disgracefully." It may be too early to preach this, but it will yet be popular; for not only is mind abroad, but hearts are coming.

Mind and heart rule the next life and make it an endless joy to those fitted for it. They should rule this world, and may sometime. When they do, "swords will be beaten into plowshares and spears into pruning hooks." When they do, life on earth will not be, as it is now, for the great majority of its inhabitants, a mere pitiful scramble for an existence in which the poor have no leisure and the rich have too much, but earth will have, as heaven has, its days of play and times of jubilee.

WHAT SPARE MOMENTS WILL ACCOMPLISH.

Men have to work there as here, but life was never intended to be an everlasting treadmill grinding out food merely to keep the body alive. God is good enough and nature bountiful enough to make this world a paradise. But things are yet much awry. I have my notion as to *how*, and *why* it is so, but this is not the place to utter it, and seeing we are yet obliged to be on the go most of the time to keep the wants of the body supplied, I am asked to tell how the mind can manage to get its share of good things. The reply is indicated in the title of this chapter. "Spare moments" will do it. They have done it for others, and will do it for you.

The bulk of mankind get their mental food—what little they have—at second-hand shops and are yet in their minority, holding to what their fathers held, and doing what their fathers did. Should an original thinker arise among them they usually label him "heretic" or "fool" and then calmly wait for the next generation to pronounce him philosopher or saint, and deplore their fathers' folly. You should, by God's grace, rule your own kingdom of brain, and "call no man your master." But you will never do it unless you cultivate that kingdom, and for this you must have time. The choicest ideas, like the choicest fruits, do not grow without culture. But give them culture, and, lo, how by God's grace they flourish and enrich the world! How prolific they sprang, from Moses "skilled in all the learning" of that one university country of his time, Egypt; and from that mighty and grand Paul, "brought up at the feet of Gamaliel," president of the famous school of 1200 students at Jerusalem, longing even in his old age and nigh the gates of paradise for "books and parchments"; and from Augustine blessed with all that the schools of his day could give him; and from that poor German miner's son fresh from the University of Wittenberg, whose brains flashed fire over the dark ages; and from John Milton, the best scholar of his time; and from John Wesley, the Oxford graduate; and from Jonathan Edwards, the Yale collegian, not to mention the hosts on hosts of their fellow men, eminent in religion, in science, in art, in literature, who, whether they were blest with the schools or without them, fed the brain by knowledge culled in their moments of leisure, and scattered it abroad to elevate and ennoble mankind.

Get but one new thought or idea a day, and you will be rich in fifteen thousand of them in forty years, and be a learned man. Give but an hour a day to careful, thoughtful reading for forty years, and you will have read seven hundred and thirty volumes large duodecimo. How proficient in many a branch of learning you may become with but an hour a day! Robert Bloomfield, a poor boy deprived of schooling, shut up to caring for hogs and sheep, and then to the shoemaker's bench, became, by diligently improving the few leisure moments he could get while at work, one of the most learned Biblical scholars of his or any other age, and ranked among the best educated men of his time in other branches as well. Elihu Burritt, a poor fatherless boy apprenticed to a blacksmith and toiling twelve hours a day at the forge, studied mathematics, Latin, and Greek at the anvil, and after the day's work was done studied while other boys played or slept, and so became in thirty years, the marvel of his time, and is known in many a country as "the learned blacksmith." Gideon Lee was so poor in his boyhood that he was compelled to go barefoot, even in winter, but, working hard and improving his leisure moments in storing his mind with useful knowledge, he became at length a rich merchant and mayor of New York city. Literally, thousands of men whose names blaze on the world's roll of honor have done the same, and have risen by saving the time which others flung away. If you will, you can do likewise and become rich in stores of wisdom.

False Standards.

HENRY H. BOWMAN, President Springfield National Bank, Springfield, Mass.

SOME one has said, "Show me the companions, the habits of life, the present tendencies of a young man, and I will foretell his destiny." The task is not difficult, "as a man thinketh in his heart so is he." There is abundance of sound truth in the language of the old darky, who, to the objection of his grandson that hell could possess no reality because the supply of brimstone would be insufficient, replied, "Why, bress you, honey, dey takes deir brimstone wid 'em."

A noble or an ignoble character are alike results, and the forecast of the end of a present course in human life is not impossible, nor strange, nor difficult. "Do men gather grapes of thorns, or figs of thistles?" No, never! Yet many young men are careless in the discharge of the duties of their positions, loose in their choice of companions, unwise in their habits, and wonder why they do not get on, why promotion does not come to positions of greater trust, and they comment harshly upon their "hard luck." There is no "luck" about it; it is a result, the cause lies in themselves, and is entirely within their control.

Some years ago a boy entered a store in Chicago as the youngest clerk; he was told to be on hand at eight o'clock each morning, and immediately inquired if there would be objection to his coming at seven, that he might have more time to see that everything was in order. He was ambitious not to discover how *little* he could do and retain his place, but how *much* he could do, and he labored early and late to make himself necessary to his employer. He succeeded. Such service is bound to win success; no other fruit grows in that soil. That boy, now a man in middle life, is a leading manufacturer in a New England city. There is no mystery about it. "Whatsoever a man soweth that (that only) shall he also reap."

Success! What is this thing all desire, few comprehend, and less are willing to pay for? Many young men think, or seem to think, the coveted prize will fall to them without effort, but it will not. If it were something external to the man, it might be so. Possibly men might then wander aimlessly, drifting with the tide, shifting with every changing breeze, and gather success as a sort of side issue while lounging along the highway of life. But it cannot be so acquired; it is not for sale upon those terms; it is no accident, but a result; it does not come by chance, but as a reward of long and patient effort.

Success in its highest expression is making the best of one's self; it is doing with steadfast, unremitting fidelity the homely duties of everyday life; it follows closely upon an unwavering recognition of the fact that the surest guarantee of advancement is the faithful discharge of the duties of the lower place, the filling the subordinate position so full of honest service that in the nature of things promotion must ensue. It was the man faithful over a few things who was made a ruler over many. In a word, success is *character*. Young man, make the best of your talents, your opportunities, *yourself*. Beware of false standards in your conduct and methods of life. Imitate not him whose moral life has the slightest taint either by associations or personal conduct. Follow not the example of anyone whose methods of business are at all questionable. Keep your life and character free from blemish or stain. Aim high. Low motives, inferior aspirations, any attainment less than the best you are capable of, are all unworthy of you. The world was not called into being for your exclusive benefit, others have rights as well as you. Believe, and let the belief have expression in your life, that when the Saviour of men said, "I am among you as one that serveth," he was an abiding example to all who should come after him. That is a miserably false standard in life, a low and utterly unworthy view of its possibilities and its importance, that, moved by no high purpose, walks blindly and with ill-considered steps along the King's highway. That life alone fulfills its obligations that is earnest and helpful, strong and true.

> "To thine own self be true;
> And it must follow, as the night the day,
> Thou canst not then be false to any man."

Rare Use of Common Sense.

Rev. JAMES W. COLE, B.D.

THE fish in the waters of the Mammoth cave have places for eyes but no eyes, their eyes having been lost through disuse, due to the absence of light. Nature gave them eyes, but they found themselves in conditions where the eyes could not be used, and so perished by inactivity. Use would have saved to them the faculty of sight. Three-fourths of the days of the average civilized man must be spent in work for the support of himself and society. Work is as necessary to his welfare as morality. Yet many men take work as they take bitter medicine, under protest or with a grimace. But it is work that develops manhood, and the perfected state of man will appear when each individual of the race does his appropriate work. There is more work done in the world to-day than ever before; more work of brain and more of muscle. Just as fast as men become Christianized they must work; for to a Christian, work is as much a duty and a privilege as is worship. By means of work and worship, God is developing the perfect man. Laziness and sainthood never dwell together.

All our faculties are given us to be used. Use strengthens and develops them. Misuse and neglect will weaken and ultimately destroy them. The absence of light will destroy your eyes. You must use them if you would keep them. So as to this faculty of "common sense," you must use it if you would keep it. Many persons seem to think that the business of all others can be and ought to be carried on according to the dictates of common sense, but successfully to manage affairs like their own requires extraordinary sense, and so, by neglecting to use this faculty, they fail. The majority of men are not deficient by nature in this sense; else how can it be "common" to men? It would be a misnomer to speak of the existence of "common sense" if it is only possessed by a few individuals of the race. The famous aphorism of Rev. Dr. Emmons, that "common sense is the most uncommon kind of sense," is very wide of the mark. The good doctor is often quoted as an example of the absence of the faculty, because though a very learned man of his time he did not know how to do so commonplace a thing as to harness a horse; nor would he ever undertake it though having several horses on his farm; nor would he even unharness them, and when at an unfortunate time he was obliged to get his faithful old family horse from the chaise, unaided, he did it by taking the harness entirely to pieces by unbuckling every strap he could find. He was not an "unfortunate," lacking common sense, but was simply one of the very numerous class who neglect to make proper use of the sense God has given them. His ignorance of common things was due not to a lack of ability to learn them, but to a lack of inclination to use that ability. Negligence or laziness made him, as it has made many others, the butt of their fellow men. He could have learned, and with his abundant opportunities he ought to have learned, and not to do so was a disgrace. He who stumbles at the head of the stairs is very apt to go to the bottom, and the worthy and learned parson, by refusing to use the faculty God gave him wherewith to know common things, came dangerously near being classed as a fool by the average man. But as the combined folly of all fools never yet resulted in wisdom, but only served to make wisdom the greater contrast, so the very general neglect to use this sense called "common sense" has so magnified it that when a man does by its aid accomplish his purposes, others who at the first derided him for what they called his folly, end by admiring what they call his genius; whereas genius is nothing in the world but common sense at work for noble ends, and refusing to be discouraged.

Charles Goodyear was for the greater part of ten years gen-

erally considered woefully lacking in common sense because he persisted at the task which he had set for himself, namely, to discover how to vulcanize rubber. Friend and foe alike dubbed him "the India rubber maniac." But neither the ridicule of friends nor the worse suffering of his family, reduced by his constant experiments to the direst poverty, and to the necessity at one time of selling even the children's schoolbooks to provide them food, could deter him. Hungry and well-nigh naked, penniless and well-nigh friendless, he toiled on, and succeeded at last because his common sense had been so developed as to notice the trivial accident of a fragment of his compound falling upon a hot stove, and the change produced in it by the heat. Noticing that gave him his great discovery and fame. But he would not have noticed it if his sense had not been educated. He lived to see his discovery applied to more than five hundred different uses, and giving employment to more than sixty thousand persons, and greatly adding to the comfort and welfare of mankind on sea and land, in war and peace. And although at his death, in 1860, he was yet in debt, he had made a multitude of men rich by his unrequited toil, and came to be acknowledged as one of the world's benefactors, and was at last given medals and decorated with honors as one whose good sense had enriched and ennobled mankind. But if he had not succeeded, the common herd would yet be calling him a fool. Was he?

Inventions have produced the great bulk of wealth of this wealthiest age of the world (nine-tenths of it, it is claimed) and have added immensely to the well-being of man; but the great majority of those inventions were due, not to the use of extraordinary sense, but to common sense. It was a plain common sense woman who nailed some shears to the edge of a board by one of their blades, and then, connecting their loose blades by a wire, showed the operation to the elder McCormick. Out of that common sense device came the present mowing and reaping machines, to lighten toil and increase the food supply and wealth of the nations. The common sense of Ames put an extra plowshare on the other side of a plow, and the world had the first sidehill plow, and he a fortune.

After being buried for three centuries there was dug up in 1865, the oven and some other relics of Bernard Palissy, the potter, who for sixteen years toiled night and day in a poverty that compelled him to burn even the floors and furniture of his humble home to carry out his numberless experiments made to discover the art of enameling pottery. Though denounced as a devil, he succeeded, and now the work of that humble potter, who was by far the first chemist of his age, is to be found alike in the humble houses of the poor, and the palaces of kings.

Coal, considered only as a black stone, lay under the ground and on it for ages, until common sense used it for fuel; and now it gets out of it not only heat and light, but the many beautiful aniline colors, and paraffine, and there are yet other things to come.

Who can estimate the value to the world of the spinning frame for carding, drawing, roving, and spinning cotton goods, calico, and flannels? Yet the poor barber, Richard Arkwright, was declared to be in league with Satan while he was perfecting and testing his machine, and was considered bereft of common sense by the mob, who destroyed his mill and machinery. Yet this very mob afterward came to acknowledge that this man who toiled while they slept, and whose family often suffered for lack of food while he worked at his "machine," and who became so ragged that he could not go abroad in the daytime, was a wonderful friend to them, in that he vastly multiplied their comforts and increased their wealth, by multiplying work for them while he lightened their toil. Even so was his contemporary, Hargreaves, the inventor of the spinning-jenny, who was denounced and his machine destroyed by a mob; and the weaver, Joseph Marie Jacquard, inventor of the pattern weaving machine for silks, carpets, etc., whose house was pillaged by his fellow workmen, his looms destroyed, and frequent attempts made to take his life as one who was bringing them to starvation and ruin. Yet they soon after lauded him as a hero, when they saw that he was multiplying work for them, and so increasing their wealth and comforts. When Arkwright and Hargreaves were given the order of knighthood, and Jacquard the cross of the Legion of Honor, and a statue to his memory in his native city, where he had been mobbed, men gently acquiesced, and said it was well; these were men of common sense.

That once poor Danvers boy, George Peabody, who became the world's greatest philanthropist, both in the extent of his charities and the magnitude of the money he gave to help the poor, said in a public address when on a visit to his native place, "There is not a youth within the sound of my voice whose early opportunities and advantages are not very much greater than were my own, and I have achieved nothing that is impossible to the most humble boy among you." But they seem not to have believed him. For while since then many of her young men have been supported at the public expense in jail and poorhouse, Danvers has had no other George Peabody. Why? Said the Duke of Argyle, "The ideals that men worship, the propensities they indulge, the habits and manners they allow to grow up among them, the laws and institutions which embody their conceptions of political authority and of social obligations,—all these are the very seat and center of the causes which operate upon the rise, duration, and decline of wealth." ("The Unseen Foundation of Society," chap. 6, p. 163.)

Many a man is to-day cursing what he calls his "ill-luck," and talking as if he believed a malignant destiny had thwarted his every effort to succeed, whereas it is his own vices that have defeated him; and he who is now destitute, it may be, might have lived in competence if not in wealth, if he had been industrious and prudent at the beginning of his career. A few indeed are foredoomed at birth, by their inheritance of vicious tendencies, to be held in thrall by poverty, unless the grace of God rescues them. But the average man's wealth and advancement depend upon himself, upon his opportunities, and the use he makes of them. It is good work that brings good luck. A productive machine cannot remain productive if it is constantly being damaged. You are a productive machine; both your body and mind are such. Why make them useless by neglect, or a vicious use of them, and so become at last yourself a burden on others? Why should thrift be taxed for the support and sole benefit of the idle and vicious? Surely to live on the industry and property of others, when you can support yourself, is both an indecency and an outrage. You may, if you choose, look on the necessity to work that is laid upon man as a wrong. Nevertheless, it is not so.

"Right," said Cicero, "is not founded on opinion, but in nature." If it is right to have a stomach, you should work to fill it if you can, or else go hungry. Why should another, perhaps not so able as yourself, work to put food in your mouth? Every refusal to obey the law of right is a folly and a crime against your own good. It is right that you should work. He who despises the right despises him whose likeness the right is. No man has ever yet been able to build an enduring structure on the foundation of a lie. Sooner or later his edifice tumbles into ruin. Now it is a lie that any success worth the name can be had without work, and hard work, too. A victory that is worth the naming must be fought for. And the victory that is offered you and me is of such magnitude and far-reaching results that it is an honor to be chosen of God for such a fight. Don't despise it, and be an idler. Don't despise it and compromise it away by an unwise or a vicious use of the powers given you. Many a young man and young woman fancy they may have a gay time in their youth, and ofttimes in places when vice is made splendidly attractive in order to wean the people from righteousness, and then after they have sowed their few wild oats, they can settle down in life and achieve success. Poor simpletons! they follow folly as the donkey does the grass which the driver offers him, but always an inch from his nose. And, like him, when they would return it is too late, and their strength has fled.

Ruin in Disguise.

ANTHONY COMSTOCK,

Secretary of the Society for the Suppression of Vice, New York City.

"The labor of a day will not build up a virtuous habit on the lines of an old and vicious character." —BUCKMINSTER.

THE folly of youth is, oftentimes, the ruin of future prosperity. The psalmist of old cried out because of the effect, in after years, of the sins of his youth. Ephraim "smote upon his thigh" and cried out bitterly because of the curse flowing from the sins of his youth. Job said, "Thou writest bitter things against me, and makest me to inherit the sins of my youth."

The sins of youth, or, to use a common expression, "the sowing of wild oats in youthful days," brought a harvest of bitterness into the lives of these men of old.

It is not my purpose, in this article, to discuss the causes that have led to the decay of cities, fortresses, or castles, nor search for the secret that has overturned nations in the past.

Rather, we discuss the work of destruction to health and morals that is going on in our very midst.

The lives of men, like the history of cities and nations in the past, are for our example, instruction, and warning. We need not go back to ancient history, however, to ascertain the cause of decay and destruction that is going on about us. We must look facts, unpleasant though they be, in the face. We must take the world, to-day, as it is, not as we would wish it were.

People who live in our large cities, and are actively engaged in the busy world of manufacture, trade, and commerce, are making life a rapid transit, and are being whirled along at a pace that kills.

A fair illustration of the nerve-grinding process may be witnessed during the business hours at any of the stock, produce, manufacturing, or mercantile exchanges, where transactions, embracing thousands of dollars of stock or produce, are opened with a shout and closed with a nod of the head or gesture of the hand from the party fortunate enough, in the confusion, to catch the seller's eye.

Fortunes amounting to millions of dollars are made in a few brief years by sharp and unscrupulous men. But these fortunes cannot bring peace, happiness, and security into the home. They oftentimes smother conscience and torture the soul. Wealth and position cannot prevent death from entering the home, nor curb the appetite for strong drink and unclean living.

Too often wealth is misapplied to furnish those things which an inherited appetite suggest, or which unhallowed passions and tastes crave and demand.

For every effect there stands a cause.

For every harvest there has been a seed sowing.

What is the cause, to-day, of the downfall and **ruin of so** many youth?

What is the cause of so many scandals in high life?

Why are there so many houses of prostitution and **dives in** our great cities, and why are they steadily on the increase?

If diphtheria appears in a tenement house, if a case of yellow fever or smallpox is discovered in the community, immediately the health officers seek to quarantine the disease and discover its source. In like manner, let us look for the cause of the moral leprosy existing in our land. Our young men and maidens are falling like autumn leaves upon every side of us. Many are stricken down by a contagion that destroys character, blasts future prospects of happiness, and mortgages the soul to the devil.

Much of the sorrow and misery, squalor and want, moral leprosy and sin, that now curse the human race, and are leading so many to ruin and destruction, is to be charged up to the four great crime-breeders of the day: —

Intemperance, gambling, evil reading, and infidelity. The first three, like marauding guerrillas scattering missiles of death, are destroying thousands and tens of thousands. Their victims are struck down in the homes of the wealthy and through all grades in society to the hovels of the most wretched. Sons and daughters are stricken with a moral pestilence in the home. Guardians and parents are mourning over the loss of their children. Parents' hearts are broken, and schools, seminaries, and colleges are disgraced by the discovery of evils growing out of debauched minds.

Many evils sting to death in secret, while others stalk forth in open day.

The policy shop, lottery office, gambling hell, pool room, and race track gambling receive the patronage of some so-called respectable men, and are allowed by a deadened public conscience to conduct their business in open day, in defiance of law, order, and morals.

Intoxicating liquor is on tap in the land. Collected into one stream, and allowed to flow into one river, it would almost outrival Niagara's mighty flow.

Evil reading is the miasma of the moral atmosphere, which poisons the soul. Much of it is disseminated broadcast, and frequently enters the home where children dwell, with the tacit consent of the parent.

Outside of a very limited circle of earnest, devoted, and heroic men and women who have supported the work of the New York Society for the Suppression of Vice for the last score of years, there are very few in the community who have any idea of the blasting influences and the appalling effects flowing from the devil's printing press.

Many of the books are of a character so degrading that no human mind can be brought into contact with them without feeling a shock; while imagination receives an indelible stain that nothing but the grace of God can remove.

RUIN IN DISGUISE.

Many of these publications reach innocent childhood and youth without the knowledge of parent or teacher.

The bloom of youth fades; the eyes become sunken and lusterless. The spirit is broken. The will becomes paralyzed, the conscience seared, the heart hardened, and the soul damned by these corroding influences, which, like wild beasts of prey, are hunting our children in secret to destroy them.

Two hundred and twenty-nine different books, many of them of the vilest possible character, have been published in this country during the past last half century. Like a moral pestilence they have swept over the land. Many and many a home has been shrouded in misery; many a young life quenched because of the fatal stab that has come through the tainted pages of such publications.

The catalogues of schools, colleges, and seminaries have been collected by these moral cancer planters, and the names of innocent boys and girls, thus obtained, have first been used to send the circulars and advertisements of the party first obtaining them, and then these names and addresses are sold as a matter of merchandise to other scoundrels, in order that they, too, may bid for the moral purity of these innocent ones, by sending their advertisements of corrupt enterprises to defraud and ruin.

The New York Society for the Suppression of Vice have seized more than one million of names and post office addresses found in possession of persons raided or arrested by them.

Again, schools and seminaries are invaded by miscreants who copy with a pen some short sketch from a foul book, or some poem or doggerel of a filthy character, and then, getting it into the hands of one bad boy or debased girl, a whole school will be defiled.

A young lad, a few weeks ago, was found in an institute with some of the foulest pictures, which he was in the act of showing to a number of his schoolmates when detected.

Another institute of learning was visited by the agent of the Society for the Suppression of Vice, and every boy in the school had, or had had, the vilest possible matter; copies of which had been made by boys and girls and passed from one to the other, until, not only all of the boys, but a portion of the girls, had been infected with this deadly virus.

One instance brought to the writer's attention, a young man, one of seven children, his father a minister, was found with twenty-one varieties of these matters, which he had been copying with his own hand and sending to boys in a school on the Hudson. When his father's attention was called to the fact that his son had possession of these things, some of which he had had for a period of seven years, with tears streaming down his furrowed cheeks, he said: "This explains it all. This explains why Willie is not converted. All of his brothers and sisters have been brought into the fold of Christ except him. We have prayed in the class room, at the prayer meeting, and family altar for his conversion, but nothing would seem to touch him."

Again, the "blood and thunder" story papers are breeding youthful criminals. Many and many a boy who has been arrested for larceny, dishonesty, highway robbery, or for murder, has traced his downfall to the fascinations and allurements of the half-dime novel, or "Boy and Girl Story Paper" of modern days.

One young man was arraigned at the Tombs police court recently for manslaughter, who, after reading some of these stories, had purchased a revolver and when in dispute over a gambling game (doubtless learned from the same source), having been told that he lied, deliberately arose from his seat at the table, drew his revolver, and with the braggadocio of a dime novel hero said, "Johnnie, that has got to be wiped out with blood," and shot his associate down.

Three young men were committing a burglary. One of them shot and killed the proprietor of the store thus being raided. When arrested and told that the man was dead, he says, with the unction of a dime novel fiend: "I must be a 'tough' now. A fellow is not a 'tough' until he has downed his man."

Intemperance, gambling, and evil reading sow to the wind

and reap the whirlwind. They each create crimes where they do not exist, and nurture them wherever they exist.

Infidelity, an apologist for free license to do as you please, would remove the restraints of religion and morals from the propensities of the wicked.

Intemperance has so branded its victims in society, that the government in taking the last census discovered "*one million habitual drunkards.*" From other sources we find that from *seventy-five thousand to one hundred thousand drunkards die each year.* Nine hundred millions of dollars are spent annually in the liquor business. There are about 65,000,000 inhabitants in the United States. This means one in every sixty-five is an habitual drunkard. But nearly or quite one-third of our population are twenty-one years of age or under. As few minors or children are habitual drunkards, we have a proportion of about one to forty-four of our adult inhabitants, habitual drunkards.

Then, sad thought! the majority of these million habitual drunkards are parents, bringing a tainted race into the world. Many of the children of to-day, then, have inherited appetites for strong drink. With open saloons upon every side, and a weak public sentiment against the drink curse, a free, open bid for the ruin of these birth-cursed ones is made in open day.

These figures and facts, awful though they be, are silent as to the harvest of crimes, poverty, and want flowing from this seed sowing of intemperance and folly. No word is mentioned of the hundreds of thousands of homes wrecked, or the women degraded by squalor and shame. The millions of children of these drunken parents seem to awaken no voice in their behalf. The chivalry that strikes for helpless women and innocent, defenseless children has been palsied by the mockish sentiment that "the drink curse has come to stay, and nothing can be successfully done to remove its ravages." Many professing Christians will not refrain from the use of wines and liquors as beverages for their brethren's sake, although the curse of intemperance enters the very fold of the house of God, to number its victims. The reckless saloon-keeper is encouraged, shielded, and sustained by the patronage of so-called reputable citizens; while political bosses stand in the shadow of death to collect assessments out of this blood money.

Let political bosses take their hands off of the superintendent and police force, and leave them free to enforce the law, and the manly instincts of the entire force would soon drive these crime-breeders into dark corners and narrow limits. Instead, the corrupt saloon is a pap for politicians to fatten upon. Assessments must be paid regularly, from saloon, dive, gambling hell, and disorderly house, to enable political bosses to live without work, and carry each election for party ends, and against the rights of the people.

The gambling hell takes its place beside the saloon, oftentimes within the very precincts of the saloon. Brothels surround the saloon and the low playhouses, even as "the mountains are round about Jerusalem."

The policy shop and the pool room are doing tenfold more harm to the rising generation than all the faro banks and roulette tables in the country. Into the poisonous air of a policy shop, children from tenement houses, wives of laboring men (crazed with the idea that they can make something in these haunts of crime), drop their pennies to enrich this meanest of all mean gamblers. Our young men are drawn in, to associate with some of the worst elements of society, by the offers of great return for small investments. The policy shop, pool room, and race track are taking from the hands of the poor the money that should buy bread for starving children.

In raiding policy shops in the city of New York, it is no uncommon sight to see little girls and boys, hardly as high as the counter over which the policy writer does his business, come in with a piece of paper with numbers upon it, which some crazed man or woman desires to bet, and a few pennies accompanying this play, tightly clasped in their hands; and I have more than once seen these little tots reach up and deposit their numbers and money into the hands of men whom we were about to arrest.

RUIN IN DISGUISE.

The curse of horse-race gambling is worse to-day in our land than the poisonous miasma of the Louisiana lottery. More homes are wrecked, more young men ruined, more embezzlements, more defalcations, thefts, robberies, breaches of trust, suicides, and murders result each year from pool gambling and betting on horse racing than ever were known to exist in the palmiest days of the Louisiana octopus, which for a quarter of a century hung suspended over this nation.

Easy-going citizens may shut their eyes, if they will, to the awful harvest gathered by this nation from the corruption of youth by intemperance, evil reading, and gambling.

Simply because people will not stop and reflect, because they will not admit what is apparent to every thoughtful man and woman, does not remove the curse, nor make the harvest of these crime-breeders any the less terrible to this nation. Nor does it stop the dread consequences of the future or its awful results. To sum it up in a word, the tolerating of these crime-breeders is every year calling for more judges and courts to try the criminals created by them, more grand juries, and longer terms of service for each session of the court. Each year there must be an additional tax to provide for more police officers — more peace officers. Annually there must be an enlargement of reformatories, penitentiaries, states prisons, jails, hospitals, alms-houses, while paupers' graves multiply.

What mockery! what absurdity! what short-sightedness it is to employ in a great city a large army of peace officers, and then, by the same token that appoints these officers to power, that uniforms them and pays their salaries, authorize crime-breeding establishments to open their doors to tempt our young men from paths of virtue and honesty; and to lay traps for the feet of those who have been cursed by an inherited appetite for strong drink, or tendency to wrongdoing.

In other words, to appoint a policeman to patrol the sidewalk, and then line his beat with saloons that degrade manhood, dethrone reason, fire the brain and passions, and turn men from sober, industrious, bread earners, to victims crazed by the drink curse, who, when fired out of the saloon upon the officers' beat, are either taken to jail, to be provided for at public expense, or sent home in this mad condition of mind to vent their wrath upon the noble women and helpless children that dwell beneath the roof which they once provided as a home for their loved ones.

Intemperance, gambling, and evil reading are as parasites that are boring into the hull of the ship of state. They are microbes of contagion, and are sending more deadly disease into the community than can be charged to smallpox, scarlet fever, Asiatic cholera, or any other of the dread contagions against which this nation has wisely quarantined its ports.

Because of the seed sowing of these crime-breeding monsters, we are growing up an undergrowth of criminals. Children are born into the world with criminal propensities.

Over and above each of these foul and vicious monsters — outgrowths of man's greed — comes the shriek of the infidel, removing the restraints of religion and morals from the propensities of the wicked; blasphemously crying out, "No God," "No hope of heaven," "No eternity."

The remedy for all these calamities that are growing up in our midst, casting a dark shadow over the future of this nation, is the cleansing of the heart of man by the blood of the Lord Jesus Christ, the turning of this nation unto God, and the exalting of his word in the hearts of the children. With the conversion of sinners unto God must also come, as an imperative duty and necessity, the stopping of the devil's seed sowing for evil. We must prevent the crushing out of moral and religious sentiment, through the saloon, gambling hell, and by the devil's printing press. If we would stop crimes, we must stop crime-breeding. In order to prevent a criminal harvest, we must stop that seed sowing which germinates crime.

"Be not deceived; God is not mocked; for whatsoever a man soweth, that shall he also reap."

Chasing Fickle Fortune.

Rev. JAMES W. COLE, B.D.

IT is often a great misfortune to have a fortune. "They who seek for riches fall into temptations and snares, and many foolish and hurtful desires which drown men in ruin and destruction. For the love of money is a root of all evil." It is too often reckoned the chief end of life to get much of it. Men search sea and land to find it. They endure untold privations to obtain it. Women are eager to marry it. Health is sacrificed for it. Morality is flung away to gain it. Honor is counted as naught in the wild rush for it. It is the century's badge of heraldry, the insignia of rank, the key that opens the doors of privilege and preference. Men look at all things through gold-suffused eyes. Everywhere the multitudes are clamoring for gold. "Give us gold," is the well-nigh universal cry as attested by the universal seeking. America is pre-eminently a land of gold. But great wealth in the hands of a few invariably breeds trouble.

Money is a concentrated and centralized power in politics, while the power of the masses is too often scattered, diffused, and dissipated. As a result, wealth often elects its legislators and enacts laws favorable to itself, and is now steadily reducing government to a science for making money. In consequence we have now in this country two wide extremes of society, the millionaire and the tramp. Deep poverty is as unfavorable to morality as great wealth. And when these two extremes of the body politic,—the tramp and the millionaire,—become hopelessly diseased, the body must die. The mortification at the extremities will destroy life at the center. To oppress men, whether by law or custom, sinks them to a low level. To pamper them is equally ruinous because equally corrupting. The specially privileged classes never willingly renounce their privileges. America, therefore, needs to dread these two men,—the millionaire and the tramp. Neither should be especially cultivated by process of law.

Money, however, is as essential to the development and welfare of mankind as are light and heat. While not bread, it is the great agency in bringing bread to the world. While not raiment, it is the essential factor in producing it; while not education, culture, advancement, progress, yet each of these largely depends upon it; where it is lacking, they decay. The more abundant it becomes, the greater the prosperity and happiness of mankind. Whence, then, is the wrong of its getting, whether it be by one man or the million? There is never any wrong in it, in itself. It is the wrong use that makes it an evil.

Wealth, like light and heat, is one of nature's products, and designed, like them, for man's well-being. But for heat and light we should die. Yet a man may get so much light, or he may use it so improperly, as to destroy his eyes. He may get so much heat as to burn his body to a crisp, or he may use either or both these material agents to another's wrong. If a man so monopolize nature's store of light and heat as to compel his fellows to sit in cold and darkness, he commits an outrage, albeit he do it by means of a superior knowledge or skill not given to them. Light is as essential to human welfare as eyes are. Eyes do not create light, but they use it. Without eyes, light would be useless. Light and eyes give us knowledge and enjoyment of the objects in nature, but they do not create those objects. The unwise use of objects frequently destroys the eye. A wrong use of light will also destroy it; so that the very things for which the eyes exist may prove to be their destruction. Nevertheless, those things are not evils. So, also, money is a good thing in itself; a very necessary thing for man's well-being. Without money, he would cower like the savage in cold and darkness. Yet, what multitudes of men and women are debased and destroyed by money. Thus the best things in the world if taken out of their places or uses may become the worst things. He who makes the gratification and cultivation of his natural appetites the main pursuit of his life becomes a loathsome debauchee. The most intense love for the virtuous does not become unholy, because the unclean choose to pervert nature to their own destruction. But he who seeks appetite for appetite's sake inevitably destroys both it and himself. So man's natural desire for wealth may be turned into the great instrument of his woe.

Money is not a sin, nor the desire for it guiltiness, any more than our natural appetites are sins. It is the perverted use, the undue seeking for these things, that brings guilt. He who makes it the chief business of his life to "seek" money, lowers and debases his nature by that seeking, and so falls into temptations and snares, and foolish hurtful desires. Nevertheless, money is a necessity to man. All men need money, need it for their highest good; need to use it, not abuse it. He who unduly seeks it, abuses it. He who gets it unjustly abuses it. He who seeks it for his own selfish ends abuses it, and then, like all perverted things, it becomes a curse instead of a blessing.

Seven persons, at different times, each drew the first prize of one hundred thousand dollars in a government lottery, with this result: The first to win was a paying teller in a bank, a quiet, industrious young man. On receiving the fortune, he resigned his position at the bank, began a career of extravagance and dissipation, and in two years was reduced to beggary and died in a public hospital of diseases engendered by his vices. The second to draw the grand prize was a man in middle life, having a fine family and a good business situation. When the money was paid him, he also became a spendthrift, a drunkard, and a debauchee, and soon spent his fortune with the harlots he had chosen in place of his family. Then he borrowed money on his reputation for wealth, became a bankrupt, and spent his later years in prison for debt. The third was a merchant not inclined to extravagant habits or vice. He was doing a good **paying** business. With his enlarged capital of one hundred thousand he now greatly extended his business with a purpose to become one of the merchant princes of the land. But while he could conduct his little business well, he was not adapted to work his enlarged field, and, making poor investments, he soon became bankrupt, and was subsequently obliged to seek work as a clerk in the very store of which he had been the former owner. The fourth to whom the fortune came was a poor widow unblessed of suitors. She at once became "very attractive" to a swarm of admirers, one of whom she soon married. He was a gay, dashing cavalier and spent the fortune for her in an amazingly short time. Then they separated. Then came a divorce, and she was left far worse off than when a "poor, lone widow woman." The fifth fortunate owner of the prize was a noted singer in his country, who had already earned a small competence by his talent. He gave up his profession and launched out as a banker and broker, intent on becoming a millionaire. But he quickly found others more skillful than he, and they soon took from him the hundred thousand and the little fortune, and he had to begin life over again. The sixth to win was a poor, laboring man of naturally penurious habits. When the gold came to him, he hoarded it most religiously, loaning it only at exorbitant rates, and constantly fretting lest some of it should be lost or stolen. He became a sordid, miserable miser, living for and gloating only over gold, and was at last meaner than the meanest poverty could make him. While his stock of gold increased, his soul grew smaller and smaller, and he died as many another has done, shamefully, wickedly rich,—but only in gold. The seventh to whom the fortune came, led, like most of the others, the spendthrift's short, gay life to poverty and misery and ruin, and lost his all when he parted with righteousness to gain the unhallowed gold.

If the time, energy, ingenuity and perseverance exercised by the thousands in trying to make a fortune quickly and by illegitimate means were turned into an honest channel the world would be infinitely better, happiness and prosperity more general, and there would be less poverty, vice, and crime.

Cutting 'Cross Lots to Success.

GEORGE F. MOSHER, LL.D., President Hillsdale College, Mich.

IT is generally not a good thing to attempt. Napoleon III. tried it at Sedan and was ignominiously defeated. Grant fought it out "on this line," counting neither time nor effort as too costly for the end in view. From the time of Alexander, who desired his preceptor to show him some shorter and easier way to learn geometry, men have found that the shortest cut to success has been the patient pursuit of a toilsome and possibly tedious way.

But the "short cut" has a siren voice and mien. It especially tempts the business man. If three-fourths of the men who enter business make a failure of it, it will be found that three-fourths of the failures are among those who have tried the short cut. Tweed and his famous ring tried it. Winslow, since 1876 in hiding in some quarter of the globe, tried it. The staked-out towns in our western country, with more vacant than occupied lots, and with more grass than traffic in their streets, are signs of it. If any of these have succeeded, it has been because patient industry and conservative capital have centered there and furnished the conditions which have made the boom a bargain, and given the corner lot its value.

The foundation of business prosperity may be laid in some crucial moment, as when one resists some great temptation to be dishonest, and masters the evil tendency; but the building of the structure itself is a long task. "There is nothing," said Beecher, "like a fixed, steady aim, with an honorable purpose."

An esteemed citizen of Massachusetts died in 1893 leaving an honorable name and thirty million dollars. The beginnings of both his wealth and his good name lay in the purpose rigidly adhered to by his grandfather "to make a little better shovel than anybody else,—in fact, the best shovel that can be made." "I know of no short cut to wealth," said the elder Rothschild, "but I have generally found it to be a good rule to buy when others wanted to sell, and to sell when others wanted to buy." "Take care of the cents," said Stephen Girard, "the dollars will take care of themselves." "No abilities, however splendid," said the great merchant prince of New York city, "can command success without intense labor and persevering application." "This one hundred dollars shall gain me one thousand," the writer heard a young man say at Monte Carlo in 1882. He played, lost a fortune of seven thousand dollars in twenty-four hours, and then sent a bullet through his brain in the garden of the gambling hall. The Bible did not contradict sound business experience in pronouncing a woe on those "who make haste to be rich."

The same temptation is also strong for the student and the professional man. Two or three hours on a given lesson when one may "cram" the text into the mind in an hour or less; seven years in the college course and the professional school when one might buy a diploma at a trifling cost of money and almost of no time, seem like great obstacles to the young man or woman impatient of discipline, or delay. The preacher who buys or borrows his sermons, the lawyer who works for fees rather than to protect truth and justice, the editor who drives his brain with stimulants, the physician who is willing to violate law and morality because "there is money in it,"—all these are examples of the prevailing desire to win success suddenly,—and of its failure. They are the men who are "plucked" at commencement time, who soon come to be known in the newspaper offices as "penny-a-liners," and who are designated by the honorable and painstaking members of the other professions as "quacks," "plagiarists," and "pettifoggers." Wasted energies, a discredited name, public distrust, poverty and shame,—these are among the penalties to those who try to win success at the expense of virtue and honor.

After all, it depends mainly on the true nature of success, and whether it lies in the direction of the short cut or not. That is not success which is not essentially worthy of achievement, and a worthy end is spoiled if it be sought by base means. Given the worthy end, and sometimes the dash wins it. It was thus that Napoleon I. added another kingdom to his empire at Marengo, and that Sheridan won a victory at Winchester. It is the quick move that often decides in business ventures. "Be an off-hand man; make your bargains at once," was the advice of the great English financier to his apprentice. But that implies genius, and even genius somebody has defined as being "infinite patience." The fable of the hare and the tortoise still has its message for this rushing age. "Prayer and provender," says the proverb, "hinder no man's journey. There is no time lost in sharpening the scythe."

Even if there be such a possibility as "cutting 'cross lots to success," it is only in exceptional cases, and doubtless in those cases somebody's care and persistence have gained what somebody else's smartness has seized. It is Goodyear in his rude laboratory enduring poverty and failure until the pasty rubber is at length hardened; it is Edison biding his time in baggage car and in printing office until that mysterious light and power glows and throbs at his command; it is Carey on his cobbler's bench nourishing the great purpose that at length carried the message of love to benighted India;—these are the cases and examples of true success.

Macaulay describes the boy Warren Hastings, then a lad of seven, lying on the banks of the stream which flowed through his ancestral estates, and vowing in his poverty and weakness to regain that lost domain. That purpose never forsook him. He pursued it with that calm but unyielding will which was one of his characteristics. In India ruling fifty million people, amid all the distracting cares of war, finance, and legislation, through all the turns of his sad and eventful career, this end was never lost sight of, and before his long public life, so singularly checkered with good and evil, honor and shame, was ended, he had become Hastings of Daylesford, and when at length he died, it was to this home of his fathers that he was borne for burial.

Most real successes are won that way. It is the old route of patience and labor. It is lesson after lesson with the scholar, it is venture after venture with the merchant, it is trial after trial with the inventor, it is voyage after voyage, even against mutiny and tempest, with the discoverer, it is picture after picture with the painter, even failure after failure with the poet and writer, that at length wins this prize that most men are seeking. If now and then, with Byron, some one awakes to find himself suddenly famous, yet the majority of people find, with the Duke of Wellington, that "the secret of success is firmly doing your duty in that station of life to which it has pleased God to call you."

The Grandeur of Patience.

WILLIAM C. KING, Springfield, Mass.

PATIENCE is one of the grandest virtues of the finite being, and to it may be credited greater achievements and nobler results than the world has yet acknowledged. It is that peculiar quality of mind and heart which seals all complaining lips, soothes the wounded heart, and simply abides the time for the accomplishment of a purpose. To act is a noble thing, but to wait patiently exhibits a nobler and a higher power of manhood.

It is not always an easy task to wait patiently while we feel that we are approaching the object of our desire, yet seem to see it receding from us.

One of the serious barriers to thoroughness in the education of the young men and women of our land is the feeling that the highest triumph of life is to complete their education before reaching twenty.

The boy looks out upon life, and, seeing men vigorously engaged in their various pursuits and callings, he feels that the years devoted to study and preparation are largely thrown away. He resolves to hasten through, and take a short cut across the field of knowledge. Consequently he rushes blindly into the arena of life's activities but illy prepared for the great combat.

It has been stated that only about seven per cent. of business men succeed in life. No doubt this large percentage of failures is due to the impatience of youthful years. Young men do not appreciate the true value of a thorough preparation for life's work, but enter upon business or professional life before they are sufficiently matured either in education or in years, hence they lack the stamina essential to success.

By reading the biography of some great man who won fame and honor, a young man is fired with a desire to become great and honored also, and he at once sets about to reach the goal. He does not stop to analyze the life of this great man and follow him from the cradle of poverty, through long years of hardship and struggle, years of discouragement and thwarted plans, years in which there were, by far, more cloudy days than sunshine, but he sees only the brilliant crown studded with stars of success. He ignores the element of time in reaching the goal of greatness. He sets aside the factor of life's developing hardships and forgets that true greatness is built upon a foundation laid deep, broad, and solid, requiring time and patience. The would-be great man is too impatient to master the elements of his chosen theme, but, on the principle of the greater including the less, he plunges into the very heart of his subject, and soon becomes bewildered, discouraged, and with shame and humiliation abandons his wild notion of leaping upon the platform of greatness.

Many great and useful men, it is true, have completed their college course while very young, but nature smiled upon them in a generous manner. Their peculiar aptitude for acquiring knowledge enabled them to pursue their course at a rapid pace, without impatient haste. Some pronounce a man of this class a genius, forgetting that genius consists of a special aptitude for performing great labor,—patient, persistent, incessant labor.

Nature furnishes us with the grandest example of patience in the whole realm of the universe. Her patient hand is seen on every side. From the tiny acorn she slowly rears to full stature the mighty oak of the forest.

"Through what long and weary ages has nature pounded on the granite doors of giant mountains, pleading for crumbs that fall from rocky tables, that she may bear them down to the vales, to feed the hungry guests that wait in the halls below. Through countless ages she has stood with patient hand and sifted into river beds and ocean depths the fine alluvial morsels that she begged from miser mountains."

Patience has produced the grandest results in the achievements of man. As one writer beautifully expresses it:—

"There is no shining goal of human glory too bright or too remote for patience. No height can tire its wing. Strike from the firmament of human greatness every star that has been placed there by the hand of patience, and you cover that firmament with the veil of midnight darkness. It is patience that has crushed mighty evils and wrought sublime reforms in human history; patience, that dared to stand up and meet the taunts of ignorance and bigotry; patience, that has calmly walked back into the shadow of defeat, with 'Thy will be done' upon its lips; patience, that has breathed the fiery smoke of torment with upturned brow."

Patience is one of the grandest representatives of the Creator. Truly has it been said:—

"Patience comforts the poor and moderates the rich; she makes us humble in prosperity, cheerful in adversity, unmoved by calumny, and above reproach; she teaches us to forgive those who have injured us, and to be the first in asking the forgiveness of those whom we have injured; she delights the faithful, and invites the unbelieving; she adorns the woman and approves the man; she is beautiful in either sex and every age."

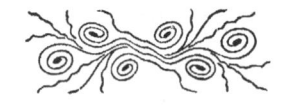

Trading Opportunities for Failure.

REV. GEORGE EDWARD REED, D.D., LL.D.,
President Dickinson College, Carlisle, Pa.

GEORGE COOKMAN, one of the most distinguished preachers of the earlier portion of the century,—once chaplain to the Senate, and finally lost in connection with the foundering of the ill-fated "President" in the year 1841,—used to say that were it to be given to him to live his life over again, and were it possible, also, for him to choose the particular portion of the world whereon his re-advent should be made, together with the date thereof, the country which of all others he would select as the theater of his re-appearance would be the United States of America, and the time the latter half of the nineteenth century. Then, as it seemed to him, would life be most worth the living.

What man living to-day, what one cognizant of the wonderful progress of an age grander in achievement, more prolific in opportunity, in every realm of human striving, more exacting, too, in its demands, than any similar period of time in history, will for a moment question that George Cookman was right?

If, as one of our poets has said,

> "In an age on ages telling,
> To be living is sublime,"

then, surely, is it sublime to be living to-day. Never, certainly, was the march of the human mind more majestic, never opportunities more generous and inspiring, never rewards more ample and satisfactory.

Congested as may appear the market for unskilled labor, whether in business, mechanical, or professional life, it yet

TRADING OPPORTUNITIES FOR FAILURE.

remains true that nowhere is the market for skilled labor overcrowded; nowhere the supply of competent men, of competent women,—men and women who are achievers, who can do things, who can bring things to pass,—equal to the demand.

The demand, however, let it be observed, is for *competent* men; of incompetents, the number is legion.

A thousand pulpits vacant, in a single religious denomination, a thousand preachers standing idle in the market place, while a thousand church committees scour the land for men to fill those same vacant pulpits, and scour in vain,—is a sufficient indication, in one direction, at least, of the largeness of the opportunities of the age, and also, of the incompetency alleged.

Why this state of affairs? Why this splendor of opportunity, coupled with failure, so widespread, and so alarming, to measure up to the height of the same?

The heading of the chapter indicates, as fully, perhaps, as any other of this book, the answer,—namely, *the trading of opportunities.*

Of what avail the wealth of openings for successful work, if there be not in men the spirit which induces to the right using of the same? Verily,

> "There is a tide in the affairs of men,
> Which, taken at the flood, leads on to fortune;
> Omitted, all the voyage of their life
> Is bound in shallows, and in miseries.
> On such a full sea are we now afloat;
> And we must take the current when it serves,
> Or lose our ventures."

Of the truth of these familiar words human life, whether high or low, furnishes ample illustration. Opportunity comes to every man; success only to him who has the wisdom, energy, courage, and determination promptly to grasp and utilize the same.

A few years ago in a town of Connecticut, the writer saw a young man driving a dump-cart through the streets, an occupation honorable enough in itself, but to him dishonorable in the extreme. All looked at him as he passed, and all with a sense of indignation. His story was known. Two years before there had come to him, by inheritance, a fortune of twenty thousand dollars, to one of his antecedents a fortune princely indeed. With the twenty thousand dollars came, also, one of the finest farms of that region. When he drove by that day, every dollar was gone. Fast men, fast women, fast living, carousing, gambling, drinking, had done it all.

The splendid opportunity had been traded away, "for so much trash as may be grasped—thus." He wanted pleasure —the wild, loose life—and he had it, for two years; then the dump-cart!

"Take my name from your church book," said a young man, standing by my side, by the altar of a city church. "Strike it out. I want my liberty." Up to that hour that young man had been steadily rising in the esteem of all who knew him. The church had been to him as a ladder assisting him to the heights of popular regard. The prospect before him was as fair as human heart could wish. Then came the tempter, whispering of "unnecessary restraint," of "freedom from ecclesiastical strait-jackets," of "larger liberty," of "repudiation of old-fogyism," and he fell; disappearing, as did the young man of the Scriptures, "sorrowful because he had great possessions," because he could not make the sacrifice demanded by the faith he had avowed; because he had neither the wisdom nor the courage to stand in the life which, thus far, had so powerfully contributed to his success. Appeal was useless, and with a sinking heart we watched him going out, like another Judas, *into the night*.

"J. died last night. Come and conduct funeral service." So ran the telegram. As we read it, there rose before us the form and face of one of the most brilliant and promising young men of our acquaintance, one once a member of a Christian church, honored by all, "excellent and of good report" in every way, a fond husband, an affectionate father, a successful man of business—afterward, an agnostic and a failure. Death had come and there remained but a shadowed grave; shadowed by the remembrance of a life wasted, of powers misused, of influence perverted in the advocacy of ideas repudiated, it is true, on the threshold of eternity, but repudiated too late to counteract the evil of those wasted years.

These are but samples from the ever-unfolding book of human experience. Everywhere about us, in the churches, in the shop, the mill, the office, the trading goes on.

It goes on, too, in colleges and schools, no less than in the ordinary walks of life. Every year hundreds of young men are sent home from halls of learning, branded with a reputation sure to follow them through life. Before them have been the great possibilities for education and mental development open to the youth of America as to the youth of no other land of earth; behind them fathers and mothers willing, at any cost of personal sacrifice, to furnish the means wherewith to afford to their children privileges, the like of which they were never permitted to enjoy; about them instructors, abounding in the learning of the schools, and rich in stores of practical wisdom, ready to act as counselors and friends; all that anyone could ask, in the way of opportunity, within their grasp. Young men, working their way amid poverty, privation, and want, looked upon them, envious of their condition, angered, almost, at the contrasts presented in their respective conditions and experiences. The verdict was, "expelled." Opportunities of acquisition of knowledge, of mental discipline, of preparation for useful service, of winning fame and fortune, all counted as nothing, when laid over against the delirious pleasure of a single forbidden hour.

Opportunities lost, generally speaking, are lost forever; they come not back again.

> "A thousand years a poor man watched
> Before the gate of Paradise;
> But while one little nap he snatched,
> It oped and shut. Ah! was he wise?"

A few years ago there arose in the West a congressman, a man who flashed and flamed for a brief day athwart the horizon of our political life; then, like a meteor, he disappeared. In an unlucky hour a letter so full of grotesque spelling that even Mrs. Partington would have blushed to own authorship thereof, found its way into print, with the congressman's name attached. The country burst into a laugh, and the man was doomed, literally laughed out of the court of public opinion. Not even his pitiful plea that some one had "mucilated" his letter could avail. The glamour was gone and, with the glamour, the ambitious politician.

Deficiencies of like character have robbed many a man of distinction which otherwise might have been his. Never stopping to think of the value of opportunities for the gaining of education; refusing to believe that they would have anything to do with manhood, too late, they would have given fortunes for the acquisitions those lost opportunities would have afforded. Yet the trading goes on. Everywhere the gambling spirit prevails.

"Trading in futures," men term those transactions where they buy and sell that which, as yet, is not, and that which, likely, may never be, but of all "tradings in futures" none are so frightful in their outcome as those in which honor, reputation, good name, respect of men, hope of success, everything, is bartered for the pleasure that simply destroys; that happiness that perishes with the using. Looking out over the wrecks of human lives, lining, in every direction, the coasts of human experience, marking the fallings of men and that which ruined them,—how significant become the solemn, and, as some think, almost mocking words of one who, favored with opportunities such as have come to but few of any age, or clime, yet turned aside to vanity, dying at last of weariness and vexation of spirit. "Rejoice, O young man, in thy youth; and let thy heart cheer thee in the days of thy youth, and walk in the ways of thine heart, and in the sight of thine eyes; but know thou, that for all these things God will bring thee into judgment." Seize, then, the chance that comes to you.

Do as did the dying Garfield when told that there was but

TRADING OPPORTUNITIES FOR FAILURE.

one chance out of a hundred for him to live. Say with him, *"I will take that chance!"*

> " Be wise! The tide is at its height,
> Which now may waft thee to the wished-for shore;
> Thy home 's away, and swift the moment's flight;
> The goal, the crown 's right on, thine eyes before;
> The trumpet calls to gird thee for the fight;
> Hark! now it sounds, but soon shall sound no more!"

Waiting for Something to Turn Up.

Rev. ALPHEUS BAKER HERVEY, Ph.D.
President of St. Lawrence University, Canton, New York.

THIS was the motto of that extraordinary man, whose interesting biography we owe to the pen of Mr. Charles Dickens, the late Wilkins Micawber. If closely pressed, we should have to admit that his career was not especially distinguished by what we call success. As a business man he does not shine forth an example to the world. It does not appear that Her Majesty ever selected him, as she did Bessemer, and Mason, and many others, for knightly honors, as a recognition of his great services to the wealth-producing activities of the nation. He was often deeply concerned in business transactions, and was justly celebrated for the number and variety of the legal papers which he signed and executed. Few in his day were more familiar with the stamped paper on which subjects of the British Crown record their contracts. His were always contracts to pay certain sums due, for value received. Though a distinguished man of affairs, his sense of *meum et tuum* was that obscure or defective that he considered himself to have fully discharged a debt when he had signed one of these bills. In consequence, those having the misfortune to be his creditors, taking a different view of the matter, and not finding these bills passing current like those of the Bank of England, subjected this great "financier" to endless troubles, by means of writs, and civil processes, and deputy sheriffs, and debtors' prisons, and things of that sort. Indeed, one can hardly read the story of this remarkable man, whose history so brilliantly illustrates our theme, without coming to see that it requires almost as much genius, and quite as much trouble, to manage "to live on nothing a year," as Thackeray phrases it, as it does to earn an honest livelihood.

Mr. Micawber is the type of a class of "dead beats" which infest every community. They are great humbugs, but they probably humbug themselves even more than anyone else. They are selfish and ignoble, and mean-spirited to the last degree. But they are also preternaturally conceited. They have such lofty opinions of their merits and abilities that they think Providence, or Fortune, or whatever rules the world, is bound to make great things turn up for them. There is a proverb, long current, that "God takes care of the lame and the lazy." I suspect it originated in the philosophy of those who are always "waiting for something to turn up." Of course these people are always disappointed. They deserve to be. They come to nothing but disaster and disgrace. It would be an impeachment of the wisdom and justice of Providence to suppose it would bestow special favors on men of this kind. Things do not "turn up" in this world. They are turned up. It is the active not the passive voice in such matters. There is an endless chain of efficient, natural causes running through life. Nothing comes from nothing. Multiply even billions by a naught and a naught is the product. There is also a law of equity. Men get what they deserve. Victory is won only by strenuous, brave battle. Success is gained only by effort, by labor, by self-denial, by skill and patient long-continued struggle. "Waiting for something to turn up" is waiting for moonbeams to turn into silver, for magic and chance to take the place of natural law in the universe. It is the philosophy of the shiftless, the refuge of the lazy, the excuse of the improvident.

But perhaps my readers will ask, "Are there then no favoring circumstances and conditions in life?" "Is there no tide in the affairs of men which taken at its flood leads on to fortune?' Yes, doubtless; but only for those who work and wait, not for those who lie and wait. They are for those who are out in the midst of life's activities, "doing their level best" under all conditions and circumstances, not for those who skulk and shirk. The best chances come only to those who take all the chances, good and bad, and make the most of them. The big fish, as well as the little, are caught by those who go a-fishing, not by those who stay at home.

The best of all opportunities are those which arise out of a strong, resolute, earnest, faithful man's own character and personality. It was a part of the philosophy of the younger Disraeli, that "man is not the creature of circumstances, but circumstances are the creatures of man." His own remarkable career is a strong proof of the truth of the maxim.

Much is said now about "environment" and its important relations to the evolution of life. This is only a new name for old things, viz., circumstances and conditions, the things standing round about the life. But the life, not the environment, is the really important factor in the case. That is power. That transforms, shapes, uses, the crude elements standing around. So the living man in the world is the only source and center of original power. In him is life, transforming force. Circumstances are plastic in his hands and yield themselves to his touch. He changes them by contact with himself, from crude, lifeless elements into inward living force. Obstacles tower before him like mountain chains, stopping his path and hindering his progress. He surmounts them by his energy. He makes a new path over them. He climbs upon them to mountain heights. They cannot stop him. They do not much delay him. He transmutes difficulties into strength, and makes temporary failures into stepping stones to ultimate success.

In his great epic, Vergil sang of "arms and a man." In our modern epics we sing of "man and his machines." But in the new time as in the old, the man is infinitely more than either arms or tools. He it is, if he have the manly spirit, if he have courage, if he have ambition, if he be a man and not a dolt, or a block of wood, who will go forth and with a masterful hand turn the world about. He will not weakly and meanly "wait for something to turn up."

WAITING FOR SOMETHING TO TURN UP.

Search the history of the world through and you will find that all the great captains of industry, as well as of war, the mighty men of action and influence in the world, in art, in science, in invention and discovery, in philanthropy, in statesmanship, are men who do not "wait for something to turn up," but who take hold of the world's work and do it. The duty of doing is for all and each, both small and great, in the proportion of his ability and strength. It is, beyond all expression, ignoble, unmanly, and cowardly to sit down in this great busy world idly "waiting for something to turn up."

The Secret of Making Things Turn Up.

Rev. JAMES W. COLE, B.D.

"The heights by great men reached and kept,
Were not attained by sudden flight,
But they, while their companions slept,
Were toiling upward in the night."

SOME of them were, but not all. Some persons have stumbled into great places for a time, or upon a great fortune, and so have gained a name and fame that could not be said to be either of their making or seeking. They simply happened to be there at the auspicious time and place and were lifted into greatness. Some have inherited special conditions favorable to gaining a fortune or fame; but outside of or without those conditions, they would have been only ordinary persons in ordinary circumstances of life. Others have attained to great fortune and eminent distinction regardless of the most unpromising circumstances of birth and life. Yet even these last were not independent of place, and time, and education for their success. Indeed, it may be truthfully said that no man is wholly independent of circumstances; and that his environment will determine both his place in history, and his degree of success in life. Would Shakespeare have been Shakespeare in any other age or country? If Dante had lived in our time, he could not write "The Inferno," neither could Milton now write "Paradise Lost." The progress of thought since their day would prevent. Alexander the Great could not now conquer the world; nor should we have the famous names of Wellington, Grant, or Sherman, if they had lived in more peaceful times. What other age, or what other country, could produce the present enormous number of American millionaires? Great names as well as

THE SECRET OF MAKING THINGS TURN UP.

great riches are sometimes due to other causes than an overmastering intellect, or "the hand of the diligent."

The owner of a corner lot in San Francisco, California, traded it for a suit of clothes. The lot is now worth over a million dollars; but it was not "the hand of the diligent" that made its present owner the millionaire. In Melbourne, Australia, in 1837, a corner lot was sold for one hundred and sixty dollars. Fifty years later it was worth $2,466,500, and its owner a rich man, but not by his own "diligent hand."

The founder of the house of Rothschild was a poor Jewish clerk in Hanover, Germany. He afterward began business in a very small way as banker at Frankfort, and became distinguished for two things, his shrewd good sense and unswerving integrity. When the French army invaded Hesse-Cassel in 1806, compelling the Elector William to flee the land, William deposited with Mr. Rothschild for safe keeping for eight years, the sum of five millions of dollars without interest, or security other than his integrity. It was the judicious investment of this huge sum left to him without interest, and not merely the "hand of the diligent," that was the prolific source from whence came the present colossal fortune of the house of the Rothschilds. When Meyer Anselm Rothschild died, his heirs continued to pay the Elector an annual interest of two per cent. on the five millions, until in 1823 they paid the principal to William's son and heir.

So, likewise, the vicissitudes of the war of 1812 gave to Stephen Girard the bulk of his millions, just as the civil war enabled other men to amass their present great fortunes. Said the old Celtic-Breton law, "There are three periods at which the world is worthless,—the time of plague, the time of a general war, the time of a dissolution of spoken promises." But in each of these times a few persons become greatly rich. While our late war wasted hundreds on hundreds of millions of dollars, and hundreds of thousands of human lives, it also developed hitherto unsuspected resources of wealth and methods of getting rich, together with a surprising energy of mind that

THE SECRET OF MAKING THINGS TURN UP.

made some men very wealthy and others greatly famous. Nevertheless, war is robbery; war is infamy; or, as General Sherman tersely, truthfully, put it, "War is hell." Mankind will yet come to see that slaughtering one's fellow man is the most unremunerative industry ever devised on God's green earth; and, like all forms of injustice, it is sure to bring either sooner or later, its own dire, evil effects. When righteous laws shall prevail, then cannon shall remain silent.

Man never would have emerged from barbarism if he had not sought out and made use of the hidden wealth of the land. And to do it successfully, men require and must have freedom, intelligence, and morality. Wherever tyranny prevails, the people are poor. Few under absolute monarchies are rich, and their riches, like that of the governments themselves, were due to plunder taken from others less powerful. Education is necessary to obtain wealth. Coal, electricity, sunlight, water, and air have been in the earth since man was created, but ignorance got no wealth out of them, nor ever would. Men educated to desire only the bare necessaries of existence never make a market for anything but those necessaries. Educate them to appreciate and to desire other things, and you increase both their wealth and the wealth of the world. Not only is education thus necessary to increase wealth, but the best educated man has the most chances for success in life. The editors of the Dictionary of American Biography, who diligently searched the records of living and dead Americans, found, as elsewhere stated, fifteen thousand one hundred and forty-two names worthy of a place in their six volumes of annals of successful men, and five thousand three hundred and twenty-six, or more than one-third of them, were college educated men. One in forty of the college educated attained a success worthy of mention, and but one in ten thousand of those not so educated, so that the college-bred man had two hundred and fifty times the chances for success that others had. To particularize: Medical records show that but five per cent. of the practicing physicians of the United States are

THE SECRET OF MAKING THINGS TURN UP.

college graduates; and yet forty-six per cent. of the physicians who became locally famous enough to be mentioned by those editors came from that small five per cent. of college educated persons. Less than four per cent. of the lawyers are college-bred, yet they furnished more than one-half of all who became successful. Not one per cent. of the business men of the country were college educated, yet that small fraction of college-bred men had seventeen times the chances of success that their fellow men of business had. In brief, the college educated lawyer has fifty per cent. more chances for success than those not so favored; the college educated physician forty-six per cent. more; the author, thirty-seven per cent. more; the statesman, thirty-three per cent.; the clergyman, fifty-eight per cent.; the educator, sixty-one per cent.; the scientist, sixty-three per cent. You should therefore get the best and most complete education that it is possible for you to obtain.

Morality, integrity, and education constitute a triangle of power for turning possibilities into realities. A man may succeed without much of an education, but his chances of success are immensely enhanced if he possesses a good education. We do not mean by this that a man must spend years within the walls of a college. A person may become well educated and never see the inside of a college or even a high school.

The present day affords opportunities for gathering knowledge which lies within reach of everybody, and he who would gain knowledge need not remain ignorant.

Knowledge, then, is one of the secret keys which unlock the hidden mysteries of a successful life.

Get knowledge, be strictly honest, be diligent, and persevere, and you have the secret of turning things up and making your life a success.

Luck and Labor.

Rev. GEORGE T. WINSTON, D.D., LL.D.
President University of North Carolina, Chapel Hill.

LIFE is full of golden chances, but only wisdom sees them and only labor reaps their harvest. "Luck comes to those who look after it," says a Spanish proverb. "Luck meets the fool, but he seizes it not," says the German.

The great Napoleon declared himself a "Child of Destiny" and professed to believe in luck. After Waterloo he confessed his real belief. "Providence," said he, "fights on the side of the strongest battalions." God helps those who help themselves.

Among the Greeks and Romans luck was worshiped as a goddess. But even in that age of childish superstition and scientific darkness, wise men saw the folly of worshiping what we ourselves create.

> "*Nullum numen habes, si sit prudentia; nos te,*
> *Nos facimus, Fortuna, deam caeloque locamus.*"

"O Luck, thou hast no existence, if we were only wise; it is we, it is we that make thee a goddess and place thee in the skies."

Genuine sons of fortune are always self-begotten. From the obscurity of doubtful birth and life in a cabin, Abraham Lincoln rose to the height of human power and fame. Fortune was ever at his side to make him or to mar. He took her gently by the hand and made her his servant. What Clay and Webster, what Chase and Seward, what Everett and Douglas, could not accomplish was done by the humble rail-splitter. The same opportunities came to them all. Lincoln seized them and held them with such wisdom and power that he seemed almost to create them. Fortune knocked at his door and he did not keep her waiting. His career was guided by unerring wisdom. He was no accident. The political wisdom of the century was embodied in his life. His oratory is the voice of humanity.

Wisdom and labor are the parents of luck; for only wisdom can see opportunities and only labor can use them. "Labor conquers all things," said the poet Vergil. "Diligence is the mother of good fortune," said Cervantes. "The gods sell everything for labor," says an ancient proverb. "'Tis in ourselves that we are thus or thus. Our bodies are gardens, to the which our wills are gardeners; so that if we will plant nettles, or sow lettuce; set hyssop, and weed up thyme; supply it with one gender of herbs, or distract it with many; either to have it sterile with idleness, or manured with industry; why, the power and corrigible authority of this lies in our wills."

Bernard Palissy, the celebrated potter, spent the labor of years and much substance in seeking to produce enamel. In the final experiment he spent six days and nights without sleep at the furnace. His supply of fuel being exhausted, he pitched into the furnace his garden palings, his household furniture, shelves, and doors. "Poor crazy fool," said wife and neighbors. But the great heat produced the enamel, and now Palissy was a "child of fortune." Wisdom and labor had made him great.

"Nil sine magno
Vita labore dedit mortalibus."
"Life gives nothing to mortals without great labor."

For more than fifty years John Wesley preached fifteen sermons a week. Great men are all great laborers. Even genius is only infinite capacity for intelligent labor. No great product is spontaneous. Webster's finest outbursts of eloquence were carefully elaborated in his study. His energy and his capacity for labor were truly Herculean. Sidney Smith aptly called him "a steam engine in trousers."

Patrick Henry's immortal speech in the Virginia House of Delegates was not only carefully composed but the very gestures were studied and practiced with the patient skill of an actor. Professor Moses Coit Tyler, in his life of Henry, shows beyond question that the orator's career was wrought out by toil and labor—as well as by talent.

There is a task for every man in life. No lucky throw of the dice will ever win the golden apples in the garden of Hesperides. Only the toil of Hercules can gain them. "Wherefore I perceive that there is nothing better, than that a man should rejoice in his own works, for that is his portion."

> "Let us then be up and doing,
> With a heart for any fate;
> Still achieving, still pursuing,
> Learn to labor and to wait."

Reaping Without Sowing.

Rev. JAMES W. COLE, B.D.

THERE are some things in the world, the uses of which are not yet perhaps discovered, that need no cultivation by us, but grow spontaneously, as, for instance, weeds, thorns, noxious plants, poisonous insects, destructive reptiles, and animals. But useful things, pleasant things, valuable things, must be cultivated. To do this requires opportunity, time, means, and toil. The first three God furnishes bountifully, the last he requires us to supply. He might do it all for us, but, with our present natures, that would be a great misfortune.

In Honduras, and in some other tropical countries, nature is so prolific, that with a fortnight's toil one can get a food supply for a year. But thus, through a lack of stimulus to labor, the natives have become most degraded beings, some of them, both men and women, according to the statement of the late Bishop Simpson, who witnessed the scene, having become so lazy that they lie on their backs under the banana trees, eating the fruit from the branches, too indolent to stand and pluck it. Ten thousand such creatures would not be worth one stirring Yankee. But the Yankee might become such if you took away from him the necessity to toil.

For another to help you to a living makes you a dependent, and by taking away the necessity and stimulus of doing for yourself enfeebles you, and sooner or later unmans you. He who is too weak, or too lazy, or too proud, to help himself to an honest living by doing honest work is doomed to failure. To desire exemption from the necessity of work; to wish for learning without the task of acquiring it; to covet ease with nothing to do but "enjoy yourself," by wealth, however great, or by pleasure, however intense, is to desire corruption, decay, and death. The bodily senses become satiated, palled, sickened, and turn at length into instruments of torture through mere pleasure, as many a glutton and reveler and debauchee have found to their horror, while mere idleness undermines and at length pulls down both soul and body. How inane, and feeble, and vapid are the idlers of the world!

The beginning of all excellency lies in the determination to make the best use of one's self. To help yourself, to earn your own living, to win your own fortune, to make your own way in this world, is the only means possible by which your powers of body and mind can be developed; and, upon their proper development depends your highest, best success, here and hereafter. No other can develop them for you. You alone can do it, and to teach you how to do it is the purpose of this book.

There are altogether too many persons anxious to live upon the toil and profit by the fortunes of others rather than to earn their own. Do you know what that means? It means to be a thief and a vagabond. Does that sound harsh? Read this testimony from the chaplain of one of the large prisons of to-day: "From my experience of predatory crime, founded upon a careful study of a great variety of prisoners, I conclude that habitual dishonesty is to be referred neither to ignorance, nor to drunkenness, nor to poverty, nor to overcrowding in towns, nor to temptation to surrounding wealth, nor, indeed, to any one of the many indirect causes to which it is sometimes referred; but, mainly, to a disposition to acquire property with a less degree of labor than ordinary industry." If they had been willing to earn their own living, to give honest work for honest dollars, they would not have been there. He who is not willing to do his work well and honorably, save when his employer's eye is on him, is a dishonest man. He who is not willing and does not strive to give a just equivalent for what

REAPING WITHOUT SOWING.

he receives is a thief. He wants to get something for nothing in return. He is a first cousin to the "gold-brick," "salted mine," and "doctored oil-well" people. They are only after a little larger something for nothing, perhaps, than he.

To get by unfair means the toil or the wealth of another will never be any other than a misfortune to him who gets it. Even when another gives you a fortune you did not earn, it proves in general a misfortune by arresting the development of your own powers of manhood, that need and must have work in order to grow. Say you that a great fortune is a very desirable and good thing? True, but it is by no means the best thing. The value of a good thing is determined by the length of time it will remain good. If its goodness vanishes in a moment, can he be called wise who gives his life for that moment's gratification? Is it not a large waste of this life to seek only for those things that must end with our present existence, and this life is but a moment? Was Jesus of Nazareth a lunatic or a philosopher when he bade us, "Lay not up for yourselves treasures upon earth, but lay up for yourselves treasures in heaven"?

You must make your own fortune on earth if you would be honest, and honorable, and gain a well-developed manhood. Luck will not bring it to you. Cunning or petty scheming will not secure it for you. Depending upon the patronage of others will not gain it, but your own industry and fidelity to the right will. Even so in heaven. If you would have treasure there you must lay it up. No other can do it for you. It is not there awaiting your coming, else why the command to "lay up for yourselves." There is no reaping there the benefit of another's sowing, but "whatsoever a man soweth *that* shall he reap." What kind of seed are you sowing? Will the reaping make you honorable hereafter and well-to-do? Poverty here has many a burden and sorrow, but to be poor hereafter is to be poor indeed.

Counting the Cost.

R. M. ARMSTRONG, State Secretary Y. M. C. A. of Massachusetts.

NO man, as the Great Teacher has told us, enters upon any worldly project, begins to build a tower or to wage war against an enemy, without first sitting down and counting the cost. To do so would imply folly, and invite shame and disgrace. We have been endowed with the power of thought, and to go through this world without exercising this power is to abdicate the throne of reason, and bring ourselves down to the level of the brutes that act only from impulse.

No prudent man will enter any course of conduct without first reckoning what such a course is likely to cost—both to himself and others. This would be both foolish and perilous.

"Whatsoever a man soweth, that shall he also reap," and he will reap much more than he sows. Would that young people might have this passage of sacred writ burned into their souls! Almost any day, unless he stop to think, a man may do some act that will cast a blight over his entire life, and perhaps determine his destiny. A man would be almost as safe in mid-ocean on a rudderless ship, or on a flying train that had no engineer, as in living in a world like this, and in an age like the present, without thinking.

If young people would but look about them, they would see in so many families, and certainly in every community, wrecks —men (and women too) who failed to count the cost, and after a few years' of sowing to the flesh, have reaped the whirlwind. Young men and women, *think*. Take warning from the far too numerous examples all around you.

Youth is proverbially thoughtless. It is full of ardor, energy, and enthusiasm. All things wear for it the charm of novelty and freshness. It sets out on the voyage of life with "hope at the prow and pleasure at the helm." While all this forms the strength of youth, it at the same time exposes it to many dangers. Just because of its ardor and whole-heartedness, it is liable in a thoughtless moment to enter upon some path, the end of which means ruin and disgrace.

Youth has had no experience in the evils of life, knows not the pitfalls that lie in the way. Many a pathway opens on either hand, which to a young man seems inviting and pleasurable, but which is extremely hazardous. The first steps in the way of sin are always attractive. "There is a way which seemeth right unto a man, but the end thereof are the ways of death." Forethought is imperative. Before taking the first step in any path that opens, think of the end. Sit down and count the cost. Act not in haste.

Among the evils into which young men fall are the following:—

Social Drinking. It is estimated that more than 60,000 persons in this country annually go down into drunkards' graves—an exceeding great army. Not one of this number ever intended to become a drunkard. The expression, "I can drink, or let it alone," is often heard. Reader, if you are in the habit of drinking moderately, try to do without stimulants for a week, yea, for a day. Many have tried this, and found to their amazement that they were slaves to the drink habit. Every drunkard is a person who tried to be a moderate drinker, and failed. The only safety is in letting the vile stuff alone.

Gambling. This is one of the most fascinating forms of vice, and young men unthinkingly become entangled in its meshes. A social game of cards, with a small stake "just to keep up the interest," is played—and then the larger stake follows. Defaulters and suicides are on every hand as a result of this modern curse. The only safety is—never begin. Count the costs.

Sensuality. Universal experience proves that sensuality

does not pay. Misery and crime follow in its wake. God stamps it with the mark of displeasure. The very countenances of those who indulge in it are changed. Our insane asylums are filled with its victims, and homes which might be happy, were it not for this seductive evil, are homes but in name. A deadly inheritance is handed down to the children. Oh, that men would but think before taking the first step away from virtue!

Evil Associates. To voluntarily go in bad company is to court the society of the devil. A man usually takes on the moral and mental complexion of the company he keeps. The forming of a new companionship frequently marks a turning point in a young person's life. Advice of good people should be taken in the matter of choosing associates. We sink or rise to the level of those with whom we mingle. No one can afford to associate with those whose companionship will drag him down. It costs too much. Resolutely turn away from the mean, the profane, the impure, the skeptical. Choose the good, the true, the pure, the manly. If the companionship is what it should be, the vices referred to will be avoided without much effort.

Trashy Reading. When the taste for impure and exciting reading is once acquired, it is no easy matter to break away from it. A freshet of vile reading matter floods the country. Young people purchase indiscriminately. Many a young man of promise has been side-tracked by indulging in sensational and impure reading. The books cost little, but if one counts the cost to his manhood the purchase will never be made. Seek the advice of wise counselors, who will gladly assist in the selection of healthy literature.

Worldly Success. That which is often called success in life is not worth the price paid for it. "Not slothful in business, fervent in spirit, serving the Lord." Oh, how can men forget the direct command of God! A man says, "I am going to give my undivided attention to business for the next twenty years. I will not give time or money to benevolent objects now. I will give much time and thousands of dollars by-and-by." That man will never give either time or money. He will grow more mercenary as the years go by. Men grow prematurely old in their greed for wealth. They lose their interest in and love for all that is good and true. Man pays too dear for so-called success when it is purchased at the expense of intellectual, moral, and spiritual development. Man is more than money, his soul greater than the world, eternity greater and more enduring than time.

Count the Costs. Use your reason. Take warning from the failures on every hand. What is the universal experience? What is the natural outcome of indulgence in the above-mentioned evils? Young men, if you enter a life of sin and forgetfulness of God, you have no valid reason to believe that you will fare better than the thousands who have preceded you, and have been swallowed up in the maelstrom and are forgotten.

Wasted Energies.

REV. JOHN COTTON BROOKS, Springfield, Mass.

WASTE in any particular means diminution of absolute possession in the world of that which counts for something in life, the absence of which is an actual loss to the world, and to its possessor. As the world goes on becoming more and more intelligent about itself, and the number of its possessions and their value, it becomes more and more aware of its waste, and the most successful man in all departments of life is he who can lessen waste. The prevalent aim now is not to add to our present resources so much as to make the very most possible out of them. To find out uses for the persons or things which are now wasted in life is to be the glorious work of the men of the next generation, and that which will contribute most to their enrichment.

If what we have said be true, the waste, therefore, of anything begins when it does not find the end of which it is worthy, and that end, it being a possession of man, evidently must be the highest possible service of man, or, rather, the service of the highest part of man. This is all expressed in those words of the Disciples about the ointment which the woman was pouring on Christ's head, "To what purpose is this waste?" Blind spiritually though they were, their argument yet rightly takes for granted the fact that lack of purpose means waste, and they challenge her to show her purpose in dealing with this valuable commodity of the world, of which, although nominally her own, she is responsible to the world for the use. The necessity, therefore, in avoidance of waste, is the thorough knowledge of one's nature and needs, and the purpose for which one lives, and then the appreciation of the adaptability of the various possessions of one's life to satisfying those needs, and the fulfilling of that purpose. We can see from this that a purposeless life, or a life of low nature, is sure to be a wasteful life.

Now let us take this special possession of energy and see its possibilities of waste. Let us not think now of what we are usually afraid of wasting, our money, or time, or thought, or love, but of this alone. In the first place, what is it? I should say that we should best describe it, though it is not easy to do so in any words, as power in action. The reason that we find it so hard to define is, I think, that it is one of those things which shows itself in its results much more than it does viewed by itself. Indeed, it amounts to nothing if it is not acting, it cannot be said really to exist at all then, as our description of it implies power in action. It is living only when it is active; then, I can have power and yet not be accomplishing anything, but I cannot have energy without doing something. This shows us very plainly the value of energy in the world. It takes up the power that there is in a man and turns it to account, makes it *applied* power, able to reach results. It stands midway between the force and the work, and brings them together by reaching out a hand to each. What can be comparable with this energy as a human possession? It creates money, it saves time, it carries out thought, it satisfies love. It is the engine which takes the steam of the boiler and gives it in activity to the waiting machinery of life to fill the world with finished products. The waste of such a thing as this, the greatest of the world's necessities, is most serious to contemplate, and our subject grows in magnitude as we proceed. The question of option in regard to it gives place to that of duty. The interests of the world are involved in the economy or waste of the energy of the individual.

And here we have discovered one great means of waste of this precious thing in what we have said. For we have seen that energy ceases to be when it ceases to act. Do we not perceive, then, what a loss of it may and does come constantly from its non-use? Scientific men tell us that it takes an additional five per cent. of fuel to raise a body of water again to the boiling point when it has once been suffered to fall below it. How carefully should we consider, therefore, the causes which in any way may tend to diminish the use of a man's energy, and especially in his early life. The conditions of body and mind which prevail in him have a bearing on this important possession of his life, which we rarely stop to consider. The breakfast which he eats this morning and the exercise which he takes will have a large share in deciding whether he is to be energetic or not to-day. And we cannot say that that is all, and that each day's life is complete in itself, for we know that the wrong diet and habit of a man, continued day after day, have a cumulative effect upon his constitution, which steadily wastes all the energy that he originally possessed. And another cause, little thought of, is the neglect of educational advantages in early years, which, if faithfully acquired by study and reading, bring a man's mind into intelligent sympathy with the interests and needs of the world about him, and also take away that restraining self-distrust which keeps many a one from use of his best energies, and therefore the achievement of the best results, from lack of confidence in his powers and abilities as compared with those of others. And, far deeper still, and more serious in their influence, are the faulty spiritual conditions which are suffered, ofttimes unconsciously, to grow up in our natures. Self-complacency, if indulged, tells a man before long to let well-enough alone, and not to exaggerate the need and requirement for action on his part in life. Jealousy, and its companion or cause, lack of love for others, shuts the energy of life off from its healthiest range of operation, and takes away its best motive. Finally, saddest of all the deadening influences in a human life, the root and spring, indeed, of these others, loss of faith in God, and consequently in man, for the last cannot exist without the first, absolutely kills out all energy by robbing it of its vital principle, belief in life of any kind as a reality at all.

WASTED ENERGIES.

But now to go on and think of the other form of waste of energy which comes from the misuse of it. This leads us straight to the thought of purpose in life, for the results of energy and not the mere employment of it is that wherein alone lies its value. An energetic person who is so only for the mere enjoyment of the physical or mental excitement of being so, however pleasurable that may be, is completely wasting his energy. And even if the emotion which moves the energy gets further with it and reaches some end, if that end be nevertheless unworthy of the employment of so great and precious a factor in the world's life, by reason of its being immoral as designed for the injury of the interests of some fellow man, or else narrow and selfish as concerned only in the welfare of the man himself, again we have a terrible waste of that energy for which every one who possesses it is accountable to God and the rest of mankind as joint owners with himself. It is in this idea of responsibility that we can alone arrive at any intelligent estimation of the real waste of energies in life. Unless we regard energy everywhere, in every shape in which it presents itself, and in every man in whom it is found, as a trust, and the use of it as a religion, it will be sure to be wasted, just as life itself in a vast number of cases is being unconsciously wasted every moment. Any energy which is not consecrated energy is thrown away and lost, however much it is used. And the saddest part of it is that it is not only lost, but (as waste, we have seen, always signifies) the man robs God, the world, and himself of it when he so uses it. All existence is dealt with dishonestly, and is the poorer for it. This is what makes this subject of vital moment in every life, and shows us the awful significance of wasted energies.

The Chains of Habit.

Rev. JAMES W. COLE, B.D.

"THE Chains of *habit*" (from Latin *habere*, to have), i. e., "the chains of *having*." Having what? In civilized lands no person of sense speaks of there being such things as the chains of honesty, the chains of truth, the chains of purity, the chains of honor, the chains of righteousness; but they do speak of the chains of dishonesty, of falsehood, of vice, of dishonor, of sin. Why? Because each recognizes that the first are in strict accord with the best interests and the highest development of men, and so are not chains but are our natural belongings, and that the latter only debase and ruin man. From whatever source this knowledge may have come to them, whether by experience, or tradition, or revelation, they hold that to have the first of those things is to be free, and to have the last is to be a slave, and they have embodied that thought into both their language and their law.

We were designed for freedom. Slavery of the body was felt to be and is now recognized by all civilized nations as an abhorrent thing, not to be tolerated, but to be abolished. They will yet hold that slavery of mind is worse. The laws that govern the physical world are no more wise and immutable than are those governing the mental. In accord with the first the body was designed to take in foods, not poisons. Yet a man may so accustom his body to the use of the deadly and violent poisons of alcohol, of tobacco, of opium, etc., as to become in soul and body their most abject slave, and be led to commit the most atrocious crimes while under their influence, or in order to obtain them. In such case, their fellows speak of them as being diseased, and the victims of the alcohol, tobacco, or opium *habit*, etc. First, they had the drink, or the tobacco, or the opium, or the lust of pleasure or of gold, and could have left them. Now the drink, the tobacco, the opium, the lust, the gold, have them and they are eternal slaves, and who shall deliver from that bondage?

So likewise the mind was designed for the knowledge of truth, and not error. Yet a man may so accustom himself to error as to become its most devoted slave, and be led to commit the most fearful crimes in order to defend it, or to propagate it. The dungeon, the rack, the gibbet, and the stake, bear witness to this in earlier times, and the dynamite bomb of the anarchists in these modern days. But does truth, any more than virtue, need violence to propagate it, and make it flourish? Does not the use of violence disprove the claim to be either virtue or truth? A sober man does not commit the awful deeds that dehumanize the drunkard, nor will the man of truth persecute, torture, and kill his fellow men, to establish the truth. Truth never needs that.

How do men come to be drunkards, or slaves to the vices? Sometimes by inheritance—their parents before them being such; by dalliance with them; sometimes by education by another; more generally by forming the habit in childhood and youth, by sipping cider, wine, beer, etc. Acts repeated make habits. No man ever became a drunkard by one drink. It was keeping at it that at last made him a slave. And then how abject he is. Listen, while an ex-slave, John B. Gough, tells of it. "Oh, it is pitiful, it is pitiful—the appetite for intoxicating liquors when it becomes a master passion! one of the most fearful that man was ever subject to! And not only is it amongst the low, as we call them, and the illiterate; not only amongst those whose first words they heard were words of blasphemy, whose first words they uttered were words of cursing; but it also holds the man a slave who stands in front of the counter and pleads for drink: 'Give me drink. I will give you my hard earnings for it. I will give you more than that. I married a wife, and promised to love and cherish her and protect her—ah! ah! and I have driven her out to work for me, and I have stolen her wages and I have brought them to you—give me drink, and I will give you them! More yet; I have snatched the bit of bread from the white lips of my famished child—I will give you that if you will give me drink! More yet; I will give you my health! More yet; I will give you my manliness! More yet; I will give you my hopes of heaven—body and soul! I will barter jewels worth all the kingdoms of the earth—for "what will a man give in exchange for his soul"—all these for a dram! Give it to me!'" Young man, water never made a man such a slave as that. No drink nor food in nature ever wrought such evil to men. It is only the poisons that work such havoc; and it will yet come to pass that the community or state that licenses the making of such slaves of men by the drink traffic will be deemed to be in league with hell.

How do men become slaves of error? How do men become thieves, liars, lecherous beasts, and men of violence and blood? By the teachings of parents or others, it may be—more generally, however, by little acts of dishonesty; by slight deviations from truth; by hearing or telling stories they would blush to their finger-tips to have their mother, sister, or a virtuous maiden hear; by little acts of cruelty and robbery repeated till the heart is hardened and conscience is stifled, and the brain inhabited by unholy, cruel, and foul things, and the nature finally sets wholly to evil.

Acts form habits; habits form *character* (from the Greek *charassein*, to cut furrows, to engrave); and character tends constantly and swiftly to fixedness. And when the plastic mind of the child and youth has hardened into the man of evil, what can change him? When he is old he will not depart from the way in which he was trained when a child; unless it be that some miracle of grace *somewhere* arrest him, and the Infinite One change the "heart of stone" again to one "of

THE CHAINS OF HABIT.

flesh." But will he? and where? and when? We see here how quickly the folly of the child becomes the vice of the youth, and then the crime of the man. When each of us shall enter upon the next state of our being, shall we find the law of that life to be what the Scriptures forewarn us—to wit, " he that is holy shall be holy yet more—and he that is filthy shall be filthy yet more"? If so, how fearful to enter it in chains to evil habits of whatever name or kind!

How and What to Read.

Rev. JAMES W. COLE, B.D.

FENELON declared, "If the riches of the Indies or the crowns of all the kingdoms of Europe were laid at my feet in exchange for my love of reading, I would spurn them all." Would you? Think for a moment what it means. On the one hand it means to have more wealth and worldly grandeur and power than any one man has ever had. And for it you are asked to give up the "love of reading." Would you do it? Stay a moment,—what does that involve? An ignorant, belittled, besotted soul, for time and eternity! The mind, the soul, can no more live without knowledge than the body can without food.

There are three sources of knowledge,—experience, conversation, reading. How exceedingly limited would be one's experience and conversation, without one's reading, or the reading of others. Books contain the experience, the conversation, the investigation, the thoughts, the deeds of the world's men and women. Books contain the knowledge of the ages concerning other worlds and beings, and our duties or relations to them. Books feed the mind, develop the soul. How few, and feeble, and absurd, and childish, are the thoughts and deeds of the peoples who have no books! How they wallow in ignorance and mere animalism! Of what benefit then would the world's wealth be to such a savage or an ignoramus who would not read, but preferred the world's gold to reading? Books are the world's ages of wisdom, stored for the benefit of coming peoples. What infinite misery and suffering we should be saved from if we but heeded their story!

HOW AND WHAT TO READ.

Books are the world's phonographs of the dead, who speak to us in them of their lives, their loves, their thoughts, their times and deeds. Here you may call up the shade of Xenophon and hear from him the graphic story of The Retreat of the Ten Thousand, or Plutarch will come at your bidding, and tell anew the deeds of the ancient worthies. Cæsar will recite for you his campaigns, or Demosthenes or Cicero deliver in your hearing their great orations. Euclid will come from the dust of Egypt and repeat the problems with which he puzzled Ptolemy two thousand years ago, and Socrates and Plato speak to you on the mighty problem of the hereafter, and holy Paul and John will tell of the glories that await in heaven. Or you may hear the long silent voice of David sing again in your ears the holy songs of earth and of Zion, or Moses shall repeat over the commandments that God gave to him for you and me. Aye, out of this phonograph you may hear "words of life" from the lips of the Saviour himself. Here Galileo, Newton, Herschel, come to show us the amazing wonders of God's universe, that their eyes have looked upon, and here come the toilers and travelers of all ages and climes on earth and sea,—poets, philosophers, sages of science, romancers, reformers, prophets, priests, kings, each ready to tell us, through the books, of what they knew or could hear, of things that then were, and of nations long dead, or of things that are yet to come.

Verily he who is not fond of reading is poor indeed. There are letters yellow with years that the wealth of this world could not buy,—simply letters written by fingers now turned to dust In them, surging through them, I hear again the melody of a voice that made one life at least a diapason, and reading them they prompt to nobler living and the getting of a spirit meet for the time when life again shall throb with harmonies that shall be eternal. So you should read all books. Read them to be made stronger, better, wiser by them. Shun as deadly virus the reading that lowers or weakens your manhood. There are antidotes for many bodily poisons—but "who can minister to a mind diseased"? You would not willingly associate with one taken with infectious disease—why take to your spirit a leprous companion in the shape of a false or vicious book? Read slowly all books that are worth reading. Many books are only froth; an ocean of them would furnish no nourishment. Don't get them; or if you have them don't waste time over them. Many books are sweets; most novels aim to be such. If you take them at all, take them very sparingly and only the choicest and purest. In large quantities they fearfully impair digestion. Our public libraries are making a multitude of young mental dyspeptics, who will feed on nothing else but these sweets, some of which are poison. Aim to read books that will make you think. Some books do not, because there is no thought in them; the maker could not give what he had not.

We give you a list that will help to thinking, and thinking is what you need in order to grow. Food must be digested and turned into bone, sinew, muscle, to be of benefit to us. And you must turn mental food into fiber if you wish to grow. You must take time to think. One cannot be always eating even good food unless he wishes the dyspepsia, or means to die early. So do not be always reading. One good strong book thoroughly digested is worth a dozen dainty tid-bits nibbled at constantly. When you read, do it with pencil in hand to mark the places suited for your digestion that you may come there again. Neither minds nor stomachs are all alike, but some relish one thing, some another. There is an abundance for your liking, and such as will nourish you. Don't read simply as a dissipation, *i. e.*, "to kill time." You cannot "kill time," and such an effort will only kill you. Don't gormandize. The glutton as well as the fool shall come to want.

Read to grow, and grow to read; and, to do it, you must above all else read, mark, and inwardly digest the book of all books—the Bible. I know there are some who dissent from this last, persons who seem to take a sort of gruesome delight in thinking they were "*born orphans*," and that if the Father of the universe ever existed he is now dead, and his burial place has been discovered by them. Nevertheless he is intensely alive,

HOW AND WHAT TO READ.

and in his phonograph, the Bible, you may hear him speaking words that never man spake, which if you heed and obey will make you "meet to be partakers of the inheritance of the saints in light."

Many of the great leaders in the world's history were self-educated.

It is astonishing what a broad education may be secured through a systematic course of reading.

The following list of books forms a wide range of practical knowledge which may be mastered in a year, and lay the foundation of a comprehensive education.

A valuable course of reading, FIFTY-TWO VOLUMES, *including every department of literature :—*

HISTORY AND BIOGRAPHY—Outlines of Universal History, *Dr. G. P. Fisher;* Shorter History of the English People, *Greene;* Fifteen Decisive Battles of the World, *Creasy;* Leading Events of American History, *Montgomery;* The American Commonwealth, 2 vols., *Bryce;* Our Country, *Strong;* The New Era, *Strong;* Life of Washington, *Irving;* Life of Lincoln; Life of Garfield.

TRAVEL—Bird's Eye View of the World, *Reclus;* Due West, *Ballou;* Over the Ocean, *Curtis Guild.*

RELIGION—The Bible, especially John, Mark, Proverbs, Acts, Psalms, I. and II. Timothy, James; History of the Christian Church, *G. P. Fisher;* Manual of Christian Evidence, *Rev. A. Row.*

SCIENCE—Physical Geography, *Russell Hinman;* Physics, *J. D. Steele;* Political Economy, *Ely;* Walks and Talks in the Geological Field, *Winchell;* Recreation in Astronomy, *Warren;* Chemistry, *Appleton;* Introduction to Botany, *Steele;* Hygienic Physiology, *Steele.*

ESSAYS, etc.—Sketch Book, *Irving;* Outline Study of Man, *Hopkins;* Self Reliance, Manners, Friendship, Love, *Emerson;* Self Help, *Smiles;* Ethics of the Dust, *Ruskin;* Hand-Book of Universal Literature, *Botta;* Makers of Modern English, *Dawson.*

POETRY AND DRAMA—Paradise Lost, *Milton;* Hamlet, *Shakespeare;* Julius Cæsar, *Shakespeare;* Lady of the Lake, *Scott;* Marmion, *Scott;* Tennyson, Whittier, Longfellow.

FICTION—David Copperfield, *Dickens;* Vanity Fair, *Thackeray;* Hypatia, *Kingsley;* Kenilworth, *Scott;* John Halifax, *Miss Muloch;* The Pilot, *Cooper;* Adam Bede, *George Eliot;* Ben-Hur, *Wallace;* Pilgrim's Progress, *Bunyan;* Scarlet Letter, *Hawthorne;* Tom Brown at Rugby, *Hughes;* Uncle Tom's Cabin, *Mrs. Stowe.*

Importance of Grasping Current Events.

Prof. OSCAR J. CRAIG, A.M., Ph.D., Purdue University, Lafayette, Ind.

THIS is an age of activity and advancement. The one who succeeds will do so because of his ability to enter into competition with others and win success by his own energy and acuteness.

There is not a profession but has many followers. There is not a business that does not apparently have as many engaged in it already as can pursue it with profit. There is not an occupation that does not seem to lack room on account of the numbers that have chosen it. In order to insure success under these circumstances it is not enough that one is willing to work, to plan, and to economize. Something more is required than simply earnestness, thrift, and attention to business.

The man or woman who would succeed in this age must be able to take advantage of every circumstance. To take advantage of circumstances they must be understood. Things happen and afterwards we know their meaning. This will not suffice. We must be able to give the interpretation at once. If we do not some one else will, and will also reap the benefit.

Not only is it a requisite of success that we be able to interpret the meaning of facts as they occur, but we must know that which is likely to occur. The man who succeeds must not only be equal to the emergency, but must be able to create an emergency where none exists. Men are not so much the product of the times as the times are what men make them.

It is not possible for one to isolate himself from the present and give his whole attention to his business to the exclusion of surroundings. True, there are many who attempt to do this, but they never attain to more than a respectable mediocrity and spend their lives in a fool's paradise without knowing it.

These things being true, it is of the utmost importance for one to know current happenings. Further, in this age of papers and periodicals, it is inexcusable indolence not to be informed concerning current events. The current events of to-day become history to-morrow, so that he who grasps the present as it comes has also the immediate past at his command. There is but one way of forecasting the future and that is by understanding the relation of the present to the past. The one who fully comprehends the present must also know how the past is related to it. There is not an isolated fact in history, neither is there an isolated current event. Every fact bears definite relation to some other fact, and so every current event has its relation to some other event, as cause, effect, or corollary. Happy is he who is able to grasp these relations, for he holds the promise of success. The one who is not able to do this fails to win. He stops to wonder. He is surprised that others succeed and blames his own lack of success on his evil stars or the machinations of an enemy.

The successful man of to-day is the wide-awake man. He not only knows his own business well, in fact, a little better than anyone else, but he knows something of life around him. It is this that has given the characteristics of the present age. Newspapers abound, filled not only with current news, but with current knowledge. We have magazines and periodicals with their rich stores of material. Books are on every hand and on many subjects, but predominant will be found some reference to the present.

History and economics are receiving more attention than ever before because men want light on present problems. The greatest problems of to-day are political, social, and industrial. The trend of education in the present age is another argument in favor of a knowledge of the present.

The question is no longer, What do you know? but, What can you do? The expression "Knowledge is power" is an old adage, but to-day it is a back number. Power is only in the ability to apply knowledge, and so we find a class of schools gaining in favor that not only furnish knowledge but train their students in the application of it.

In these technical schools it is the present that must take precedence, although viewed with all the light the past can shed upon it. Not the ancient history of the steam engine is demanded, but the ability to construct the most modern and complete form; not the story of how Franklin discovered the relation of the lightning to the electric fluid, but the ability to design and construct the dynamo that will run the greatest number of lights at least expense; not how the subject of alchemy has developed into modern chemistry, but how to conduct manufactures, prepare fertilizers, and compound pharmaceutical preparations with the least possible waste.

These things are possible to those only who know the present, and, fully comprehending current events, are able to turn them to proper account in the routine of daily life.

Chimney Corner Graduates.

JAMES LANE ALLEN, Noted Lecturer and Writer, of Cincinnati, Ohio.

HUNDREDS of young men in this country, because they cannot go to college, give up the thought of ever becoming educated, relinquish the happiness, honors, and usefulness which education alone can bring, and enter upon early manhood as self-accepted failures. I should like to link my arm within that of each of these young men and walk out with him some night when the heavens are clear. Then for every star that he could point out to me, beginning with the brightest, I would undertake to point out for him some shining name among the living or the dead, who, without college or teacher, transformed his inner darkness into light, his ignorance into knowledge, and is now set, either as a greater or as a lesser light, in the firmament of the world's benefactors. The dawn would break and we should still be talking; and for nights to come there would be no end for the names, as there would be no number for the stars.

Not lack of schools and teachers, nor want of books and friends; not the most despised rank or calling; not poverty nor ill health nor deafness nor blindness; not hunger, cold, weariness, care, nor sickness of heart, have been able to keep men in this life from self-education. What is it that you want to learn and cannot? Is it writing? Remember Murray, the linguist, who made a pen for himself out of a stem of heather, sharpening it in the fire, and for a copy book used a worn-out wool card. Is it English grammar? Remember Cobbett, who learned it while he was making sixpence a day, often with no light but winter fire light, and often crowded away from this and reduced almost to starvation if he spent but a penny for pens or paper. Have you no money to buy books? Remember More, who borrowed Newton's Principia and copied it for himself. Is it the multiplication table you wish to learn? Remember Biddle, the poorest of boys, afterward known throughout the world, who learned it up to a million by means of peas, marbles, and a bag of shot. Is it music? Remember Watt, inventor of the steam engine, who, with no ear for music, mastered harmonics for himself because he had determined to build an organ. Is it Latin? Remember the son of a poor jeweler, afterward Sir Samuel Romilly, who learned it untaught. Is it Greek or Hebrew? Remember the dull carpenter apprentice, Lee, afterwards master of many tongues and professor at Cambridge, who began by buying a Latin grammar, sold his Latin books and bought Greek ones, sold his Greek books to buy Hebrew ones, always teaching himself. Is it geology? Remember Hugh Miller, who learned in a stone quarry. There is little taught in the school that men have not taught themselves amid difficulties and despite obstacles greater perhaps than you have ever known.

Are you hindered and disheartened by your position in life and the sort of trade you follow? Well, what then, in heaven's name, are you? A barber? So was Arkwright, founder of the cotton manufacture of England, who began by shaving people in a cellar at a penny a shave. Are you a coal miner? So was Bewick, founder of wood engraving. Are you the son of a poor farmer? So was Sir Isaac Newton, the sun itself in the heaven of science. A bricklayer? So was Ben Jonson, one of the most illustrious names in English literature. A tailor? So was brave Hobson, admiral of the navy. A butcher? So was Wolsey, the most illustrious cardinal of England. The fireman on an engine? So was Stephenson, inventor of the locomotive. A shoemaker? So was Edwards, the profound naturalist. A bookbinder? So was Faraday, afterwards lecturer on chemistry before the Royal Institution. From every human craft men have started out in quest of knowledge and found wisdom.

CHIMNEY CORNER GRADUATES.

You say, Ah! these were extraordinary men; I am ordinary and cannot do what they did. Certainly not. You miss the lesson: do what you can with your powers and opportunities as faithfully as they did what they could with theirs. Then perhaps you will find yourself no longer ordinary. For what made these men extraordinary? Genius? Don't you believe it. If you could collect them into one august company and bid each rise and state the secret of his success, perhaps not one would say, my genius. One would say, my patience; another, hard work; another, energy; another, perseverance; another, memory; another, common sense; another, self-reliance; another, the habit of attention; another, not wasting time; another, the capacity to take infinite pains. All the answers would be the simplest; and these are the old, old answers that have been given since the world was made and must be given while the world shall stand. Nor can anything new be said to you that has not been repeated to every generation seeking knowledge this side of the youthful priests of Egypt and the calm scholars of Greece, except this one thing, that self-education is more practicable in the United States at the present time than in any land in the past; for four reasons: books are cheaper than ever before; text-books are now made simple and easy to meet the wants of students at home; much of the knowledge taught in the universities is now put within reach of the chimney-corner student in a popular form through newspapers, weekly and monthly publications; and in every village, so widespread has education become, will be found some persons to whom the solitary, earnest toiler can apply for suggestion and guidance. These advantages the self-educated men of the past never enjoyed. What is your further necessary outfit? It is very simple: a few hours of leisure out of every twenty-four; a little money; and the determination to act as teacher to the powers of your own mind.

Yes, that is the whole truth; teach yourself. You can; if ever educated, whether in college or not, you must. For what is a college? A place where a set of men will train the powers of your mind for you and require you to absorb knowledge? No. I was thrown with many hundreds of young men in my university; afterwards I taught hundreds of others. It is my firm conviction that the greatest number of those who failed did so from this mistaken idea of a college as a place where they would be trained and be taught. But a college is mainly a place where you train yourself and teach yourself—under guidance and with certain advantages. In a gymnasium who carries on your muscular education? You. You tug, you expand your chest, you push, pull, strike, run. A teacher in a college no more trains your mind than one in a gymnasium trains your body. He gives out from day to day mental work for you to train your powers upon. You go off to your chimney corner and do this or not. Then you go back to him and he finds out what you have done; whether you have trained memory, patience, self-reliance, attention, capacity for work, and capacity to take pains. But all the teachers in the world cannot train these powers for you. They only guide, encourage, inspire, as you draw these things out of your own nature, toiling in some chimney corner of solitary effort. But if you must train them in college, can you not train them out of college? Life is the answer. Life, the world, trains every power to the highest exercise and efficiency in persons who never saw a college or had a teacher.

Here, then, perhaps, we reach your greatest difficulty; you believe you can attend to the training of your powers, but for guiding them in the pursuit of knowledge a teacher is indispensable. True. But now make your greatest discovery of the goodness and wisdom of nature, who realized that while few of the myriads of her human creatures could ever pay for a teacher, all of them needed to be taught, and so bestowed upon the human mind not only the power to learn but also the power to teach itself. She has made you to yourself both pupil and teacher, school child and school master. If you will only learn well all that your mind can teach you, your education will never lack breadth and depth and sublimity. Who taught the first astronomer? Who the most advanced one living to-day? Who taught Gray American botany, or Audubon American ornithology, or Franklin science, or Edison invention? Who in every age and land has taught those who knew more of any subject than all others? Who taught these teachers in colleges? All have been taught by the teacher you possess—the teacher within. On going to college a young man's first astounding discovery is often this: that every teacher there sets him to teaching himself. The better college student you are, the more independent you will be of every other teacher than yourself. If in college you cannot teach yourself at all, you fail and education becomes impossible.

But if you have to teach yourself in college, cannot you do this out of college? Life is the answer. Life, the world, is self-taught in a thousand cases where it is college-bred in one. Thus, whether you go to college or not, all education is essentially self-education; and in the truest, noblest sense of patient, energetic self-reliance every graduate is a chimney corner graduate.

The Power of Concentration.

CHARLES G. D. ROBERTS, A.M., F.R.S.C., F.R.S.L.
The Popular Canadian Writer, Fredericton, N. B.

OBSERVE two rivers, each delivering a great volume of water to the sea. The one, after rushing with the fresh force of youth from its mountain birthplace, spreads itself out upon the low-lying lands. Lacking the wholesome restraint of firm shores, of fixed limits, its currents split, wander all abroad, and waste themselves. Losing its native energy, it soon lets drop the burden of silt or débris which it carried at first without effort; and wide shoals presently form to further choke its course. The rich plains which it should have opened up to the service of mankind are turned by its misdirected flow into pestilent marshes. Its power is either wasted or become a curse.

With a force perhaps less joyous and less abounding, the other stream sets out on its career. Its source may be less high, less unsullied, its tributary rivulets more laden with refuse and scourings. But when it reaches the great plain it is held within bounds. Its banks are high enough and strong enough to curb its impulse. With the vigor of its current undissipated, it now cuts itself a channel deep and clear. Its undivided force bears easily onward the burdens wherewith its start was handicapped. Its full and steady flood becomes the feeder of great cities, the highway of enlightenment and progress. Its power, concentrated and controlled, is one of the benefactors of mankind.

Let us change the figure, since no one figure can do more than present a single view of the complex attribute of human action which we are considering. The sunlight on a winter's day may stream down upon us ever so copiously, and yet, perhaps, not raise by the fraction of a degree the temperature of the flesh exposed to it. But let these diffusive rays gather themselves into the focus of a convex glass. The result is significant. The concentrated beam of force impresses itself now with a fiery insistence. It will take no denial. In a few seconds it will scorch the flesh. It will set fire to the dry wood of the window-sill, though ice be forming all about it.

From the world of daily experience we might draw many more such parables of the power of concentration. In a word, concentration is that which makes force speedily and directly effective. Who has not seen the small man of nervous organization, acting under stress, accomplish feats of strength that baffle men of twice his muscular development? He was able, when spurred on to it, to concentrate all the force of his muscular system at the one point where it was just then needed,—the arm, or the leg, or the back, or the shoulder,—and so for the moment that one member attained an astonishing strength. The moment, perhaps, was a vital one. That man's strength, because he had the power of concentration, became great for the great emergency.

Who has not seen the boy or girl of merely average brains, but with a clearness and persistency of aim, distance competitors of thrice the original endowment? The clearness of aim gave concentration; and this concentration made the lesser volume of force the more effective.

And who has not seen the brilliant student, with capacity to learn all things, with sound principles, with ripe culture, with refinement of taste,— equipped, in a word, for the richest conquests of life and fate,—who has not seen such a one fall pitifully short of achievement, by reason of a wasteful or wavering dispersion of his gifts? His powers lacked the burning-glass of one clear purpose. They were never brought to a focus.

"Jack of all trades, master of none." This is the plain aphorism into which the world has crystallized its contempt for the man who lacks the power of concentration. Brains, talents, capacities, this man has doubtless had them, from the earliest days of human society. Without them he could never have been even a "Jack" of more than one trade. But the stream of his force has ever spread itself thin. And so he dwells in the world's scorn, who might have been enrolled in the temple.

Seeing that the power of concentration means success, we cannot take too much pains to cultivate this power, we cannot too prudently and too tirelessly guard against a wanton dispersion of the currents of our force. When discipline and education, applied upon the base of our native gifts, have more or less adequately equipped us for the work of life, it is of the highest importance to make haste and set ourselves a worthy aim. Happy indeed is he who never needs to pick and choose a purpose, but who, instead, has his purpose born within him, or is early seized upon by an impulse whose authority and worth are beyond denial. But many of us must select our aim in life, making a cautious appraisal of our own preferences and capacities; while others again are constrained to take whatever course is in view, fitting themselves to this as best they may.

To the first class, those whose purpose draws them as the pole draws the needle, concentration comes of itself. A great impulse, a consuming zeal, and their energies are bent all one way, as the wind bends a field of wheat. By the second class, however, concentration must be sought with prayer and fasting, for it is most sharply repulsed by circumstance. With a little leaning this way, a little talent that way, an extrinsic preference for some quite other goal, and an opportunity, perhaps, close by, yet not congenial to the venturer's gifts and uses, it will be hard to choose one course, and still harder, when trials come, to avoid repenting of the choice. Yet, the choice once made, concentration will speedily deepen the channel into which we have turned our currents. Concentration will soon stimulate to the dimensions of a talent that which was at first, perhaps, no more than a scarce perceptible tendency or fancy. Concentration will give to all the secondary or mechanical operations of our effort the ease and exactness of habit, setting free so much more force for initiative, originating power, all that which thrusts a man to the front in his vocation. Concentration, too, will excite the growth of that enthusiasm (the French call it *le cœur au métier*), without which one can never be a master in his craft.

Workers whom an inexorable destiny has placed in the third class may often find themselves launched upon a career for which they are naturally as unfitted as a colander for the uses of a bucket. Their daily task may leave all their best powers unemployed, while calling for the exercise of those very faculties with which nature has been least careful to endow them. The situation is indeed a hard one. Despondency plucks at the sleeve of him who stands in it. There seems to be no way out. But even here concentration offers the best hope of escape. It has the virtue to so encourage and conserve the feeble capacities in their forced exercise, as to make possible at length that scanty measure of success which may avail to open a door of escape into less trammeled activities. The best way to convince your world, be it a big world or a little, that you can do triumphantly well the thing that you are fitted for, is to do with concentrated fervor and fidelity, *when it is your duty*, the thing you are manifestly *not* fitted for. Keep hammering away at one spot long enough and you will make your mark there, be the hammer no bigger than a toothpick.

Hints on How to Think.

Rev. B. P. RAYMOND, D.D., President Wesleyan University, Middletown, Conn.

WE are always safe in questioning nature, and when we are sure of her answer, we may depend upon it with the utmost confidence. How does nature deal with the innocent, beautiful, unthinking babe? For the babe that is born into that home among the hills of New England is not yet a thinker. It has powers that will enable it to think when properly brought into exercise. Indeed, it is not yet properly a person; it has capacity to become a person, that is, a being that thinks and wills. It is an *it*, and we very correctly call it an *it*. We say, "Is *it* not beautiful?" but we never say *it*, of the boy or girl ten years of age. It has become a person, and we say he or she is beautiful. How does nature bring about this marvelous transformation? She receives this helpless giant from the arms of its mother, and begins its training by compelling the boy to ask questions.

Go out with the boy that has a really living mind after this transformation has been carried on for a few years, and see how nature treats him. She sets up interrogation points along the roadside, and he runs into them. He asks, "What makes it dark?" "Does the sun go to rest because it is dark?" "What makes the moon run with you when you run, and stand still when you stand still?" "Who made the stars?" "Who made God?" "Can God see me in the night? When the gas is out? When I am asleep?" "When does God sleep? Does he not get very tired?" Nature has set up question marks in every empty bird's nest, in every ghostly shadow that goes creeping over the mountain side, in the stars above, set deep and mysterious in the blue dome, and in the rocks beneath. Nature has filled the world with wonders, and her interrogation points become interrogations naturally and necessarily in the mind of every healthy boy and girl, man or woman.

One question answered is a hundred planted, and they spring fresh and green like living shoots about the roots of a great tree. The answer that nature makes to the query how to learn to think is, "Ask questions." If a man observes the rising and setting of the sun as the ox does, without reflection, he will know no more about it than does the ox. He may feel a sense of comfort in the warm light, and may lie down to chew his cud, much as does the ox. His intellectual life will be about as near zero as it is possible for an intellectual being to be.

There is a great deal of mental dissipation in the reading of weak books, books that lead neither to thought nor to action. James Freeman Clarke once gave this advice, "Read much, not many books." He expounded his text by urging thorough reading of the best writers. Some books are worth reading a half dozen times, and many not at all.

We need not be afraid to be ignorant of many of the books of our time, if we know something thoroughly concerning a few great books of the time. Even though a young man may have few opportunities in the schools he may become an educated man. Let him consult some educated man who he knows will be glad to help him. Select books along some serious line of solid reading, and then by a little determination adhere to a plan to read in that line every day for a year. One will be surprised at himself as he looks back over the ground covered by an hour a day of real work. He will begin to find himself at home among thoughtful men on that subject. He will grow in intellect, in self-respect, and will find himself related to the kind of men and books that quicken thought. Every great science is more or less intimately related to every other science. "Read much, not many books." Learn something well.

This habit of asking questions of nature, of great books; the habit of looking through nature and books for the mighty forces

HINTS ON HOW TO THINK.

which explain nature and history, calls out the reflective powers of the soul, trains the man to think, and he reaps his reward in increased possessions and enjoyments of the best things.

The man who is passive and who reflects not at all upon nature, man, God, or destiny, knows next to nothing. The man who reflects little, knows little, and the man who summons himself to reflection that is vigorous, searching, sustained, and extensive, knows much. This power cannot be inherited. It cannot be put on and taken off like a suit of clothes. It is a power gained by mental gymnastics. Swing the clubs of reform. Think! Race with the swift-footed ideas as they run through the course of history. Think! Wrestle with the problems of politics, morals, and religion. Think! Do not be in a hurry, but think, conclude, and act. This is the philosophy of mental growth in a nutshell.

The North American Indian who lives in our great West does very little thinking; he does not summon himself to the task of asking and answering hard questions. He stands at the confluence of two mighty rivers, and only sees a promising pool for fish to supply his physical need, or a beautiful stream on which to dream while he floats his birch canoe. He sees upon the prairie only the buffalo herd, hears the thunder of its wild rush, but thinks only of buffalo skins to keep him warm when the winter moons return. He sees the mountains, but thinks only of the wild turkey or the fallow deer. He does not summon his thoughts to anything deeper or worthier than the supply of his physical necessities. The white man's mind acts upon this scene in quite a different way because he has trained himself to think. He sees the same streams and the same prairie and buffalo herd with its stalwart leader, but he thinks little or not at all of fish, or birch canoes, or buffalo meat, or skins; he sees the promise of a great city at that favored center. He sees the support of teeming millions in the vast prairies which lie fat and rich and wide about him. He sees the mountains, but no wild turkey; the fallow deer do not attract him, except it may be for a passing moment. He sees in the mountains the coal and

HINTS ON HOW TO THINK.

copper, the iron, silver, and gold which make civilization possible and powerful. What is the difference between him and the North American Indian? Just this: the white man thinks, he applies his mind to the phenomena about him, asks a thousand questions, turns nature around and looks at her on every side, sees her in manifold relations, knows her, loves her, wooes her, wins her, and what a bride she becomes to him! We may learn to think by thinking. Ask questions and then answer them, raise difficulties and then remove them.

Thought Reduces Labor.

Prof. GEORGE G. WILSON, Ph.D., of Brown University.

HOW is it that man accomplishes so much? Some animals are larger, have more strength, can move faster, can follow a trail, may live on land or in water, do not need so tender nor so long care in infancy, do not require clothing, shelter, and many other necessities for man's existence.

Such being the case, one might at first think the greater possibility of development would be in some other animal than in man. The ants work faithfully; the bees are examples of diligence; the beavers show much intelligence in the construction of their dwellings, yet all these manifest practically the same characteristics, and live the same life generation after generation. Little of the past enters into their lives. Sometimes the same nest, cave, or hole may serve as the home of several generations; but little of what those preceding saw, knew, or did affects those that come after.

One of the great hindrances to the progress of most animals is the lack of thought, or, if there be any well developed thought, the lack of a means of registering and transmitting it to others. Some animals by instinct or foresight provide for the future, yet even these repeat the same labors year after year without the application of improved methods.

How does man gradually become superior to nature's forces, while most animals find in them the same obstacles year after year? It is true that God in the beginning commanded that man should be "fruitful, and multiply, and replenish the earth, and subdue it; and have dominion over the fish of the sea, and over the fowl of the air, and over every living thing that moveth upon the earth." Here were great forces, animate and inanimate, to be brought under man's power. The labor of primitive man, or of man in uncivilized countries, even now brings little more than food and shelter, and these often of the poorest sort. Even existence must often be a struggle. An uncivilized man's hardest labor may bring only an extra fish or two; indeed, his dreary round of life may differ little, so far as civilized man can see, from that of lower animals. A few simple implements, a monosyllabic language, a limited range of action and thought, usually characterize man in his lowest stages.

Yet it is this power of thought that gives him superiority over other animals. His cunning plans entrap them; his intelligence shows him how they may be trained and used. Over "the fish of the sea," "the fowl of the air," and "the living things upon the earth," man has obtained a measure of dominion; even the great whale has felt his keen lance. The cow, the horse, the dog, and many other animals serve him.

From the other animals man differs greatly in his power over thought. Through his ability to express it in language, he becomes acquainted with the acts of others. The thoughts of early days were handed down by tradition. A great step in advance was taken when thought was expressed by means of symbols. These symbols were rude in the beginning, like the picture writing of ancient peoples, or the figures on Dighton Rock.

When letters came to be used, there was a still greater step even though these letters must be slowly written by hand, but when John Gutenberg, about the year 1450, showed the civilized world how this labor might be lessened through the use of movable type, another wonderful advance was made. Man was no longer dependent upon what he could hear from the mouth of others, or upon the slow process of recording thought by hieroglyphics, or even handwriting. By printing, many copies of a page could be far more easily made than a single one formerly was. The thought of the past could be preserved with that of the present. The hard labor once needed was no longer required to make the thought of one age a basis for the action of another.

It is very easy to see how this preservation of thought of the past in books and language of the present reduces the labor of man from day to day. A single table of logarithms abridges the labor of mathematical computation; the nautical almanac greatly lessens the labors of the seafaring man; a cook book does the same for the housekeeper; a single set of rules, the result of the thinking of some learned man, makes difficult undertakings easy for men who but for these rules would never dare attempt such labor.

The compounding of many valuable substances, or even the manufacture of gas for illuminating purposes, is a simple labor for those who are acquainted with the principles applied by William Murdoch in 1798. The labor of those who have come after him has been lessened by his thought. A library in a town or city may contribute much to the progress of the town or city by reason of the thought stored upon its shelves.

Communication between man and man has been greatly enlarged through language in the forms already mentioned, yet other forms of expressing thought have been found in modern times. The telegraph and telephone are the most marked examples of such means.

Man has put his thought in other forms than spoken, pictured, or written language. By use of some of the forces of nature, he has made other forces his servants. Carlyle called man a "tool-using animal." It is through tools and machinery that man has been able to multiply the efficiency of his labor. The savage increased his power by the use of the rude stone hammer. The civilized man brings to his assistance the giant steam hammer of the great machine shops and foundries. The early farmers labored long to do the work of a single mowing or reaping machine. The Massachusetts shoemaker of a few decades ago used but simple tools. Now the complicated machinery directed by a workman here and there does the work of many an olden shoemaker. Weaving is something far different from the long process of the eighteenth century. The stored thought of Whitney, Arkwright, Slater, and many others enters into the production of cloth.

Invention, the flower of thought, has made possible what but a little while ago was thought impossible. Large populations are supported on small areas, or in sections formerly thought uninhabitable. The inventions of Watt and Stephenson have opened up vast territories, and made their resources available. Where, in the middle of the nineteenth century, slowly moving wagon trains carried men and supplies to the far West, vestibuled trains, luxurious in appointment, and fast freights, fifty years later, perform the same services. "Time-and-space-conquering steam," as Emerson names it, under the direction of thought, has revolutionized the world of labor.

The application of electricity bids fair to accomplish even greater wonders than steam. These are not new forces, but thought has harnessed them to do the work of man. Years of testing are sometimes necessary for the final discovery of the best means of governing force. The arc light was known to Sir Humphry Davy from his study of electricity in 1813, but it needed the Brush system of 1878 to make it practical for street lighting. The incandescent principle of electric lighting, long known, awaited an Edison to make it feasible for general purposes. Edison's inventions are in no sense the product of chance, for he says, "I never did anything worth doing, by accident." In his own words, his rule is, "When I have fully decided that a result is worth getting, I go ahead on it, and make trial after trial until it comes." Cyrus W. Field on one side of the Atlantic, and Sir William Thomson on the other, worked long and faithfully before their thoughts were realized in the great Atlantic cable.

How wonderful these great inventions are, those who live in daily contact with them hardly realize. There is needed such a contrast as between this and the preceding century, or as between the conditions of the civilized and uncivilized countries of the present day. It is easy for those, who, a few years ago, wondered at the first telephone, to appreciate the feelings of the savage warriors of Lobengula, king of the Matabele, when on a visit of investigation in England. It was not impossible for them to believe that the English could make a machine which, by some means, to them mysterious, might speak English, but when one of them at one end of the telephone line heard the words of his friend at the other end, in the dialect of the Matabele, his wonder knew no bounds.

Not alone has electricity, once so feared by man in the lightning, been chained by the thought of man and made his servant, but many other of nature's forces do his will. Carlyle questions of powder, "The first ground handful of nitre, sulphur, and charcoal drove Monk Schwartz's pestle through the ceiling: what will the last do?" Where man once labored years to produce but slight impressions upon the face of the mountains, now by powder or dynamite the same labor is done almost in an instant. Hills are leveled, and through the hearts of mountains, once considered impassable, dynamite has opened tunnels for the commerce of the world.

There seems to be no place in life where thought will not reduce labor, not only in the mammoth undertaking, but also in the trivial daily duty. The schoolboy hastening through his essay, careless of moods and tenses, fumbling several books for apt illustrations, opening the middle of the dictionary for a word beginning with *c*, finds next day his work must be entirely rewritten. To the one who thoughtfully plans the labor of the day, the tasks are easier, and both labor and laborer are dignified. As Emerson says, "No fate, save by the victim's fault, is low."

Thought is one of the most valuable forms of property, since it makes possible the greatest achievements. Yet "thought is the property of him who can entertain it, and of him who can adequately place it." Applied thought accomplishes far more than years of labor. As the thought-bulk of the world becomes daily greater and greater, man obtains a wider and wider dominion over the forces of nature, and thus by the application of mind to matter will he, in the language of Carlyle, "achieve the final undisputed prostration of Force under Thought, of Animal courage under Spiritual."

Eyes That See.

Rev. WILLARD E. WATERBURY, B.D.
Pastor Belmont Avenue Baptist Church, Springfield, Mass.

"FOR I am fearfully and wonderfully made; marvelous are thy works." As I write, my eye takes in the paper before me, then the various objects in the room, in their form, color, direction, and distance. I next look from my window and see the dwellings, factories, business blocks, and church spires, and the hills stretching far away into the dim distance, while over all the clouds, like phantom ships, go sailing in the sea of blue. All these things I take knowledge of by means of a little spherical mechanism less than an inch in diameter. The objects on my desk or about the room I may touch and handle; the far-away hills with their mottled coverings of forests and snow I also touch, though not with the hand. I cannot go to them except by a journey of many hours, but I open my eyes and they are brought to me on the wings of light. Yes, I find they have been knocking at the curtain of my window with the coming of the dawn, and when I close my eyes for a day dream they are gently tapping at the closed portals, and wait to reveal unto me their mingled majesty and beauty.

Eyes that see,—" The eye sees what it brings means of seeing. To Newton and his dog Diamond, what a different pair of universes!" And many a man goes through life with open eyes indeed, but with a brain behind the eye so sluggish that he sees little more than does the dumb brute by his side. The eye is, after all, but an instrument of the brain, and what we urge is that the brain be taught to use with more skill this delicate mechanism. We need educated eyes, trained powers of perception and reproduction. Walk through the streets of the city with a companion, look at the same show window for an instant, and then ascertain which can give the fuller account of what he has seen. The eye is capable of being trained to a process of instantaneous photography, which will afford both pleasure and profit to the possessor.

As children we begin with laboriously grasping a word at a time in silent reading, and some never get beyond that stage; others gain power to read a line at a time; still others are known to have attained such proficiency as to grasp the thoughts expressed on an ordinary book page at two or three glances. These readers are not necessarily superficial, nor indeed do they always read at this rate, any more than one who is swift of foot always runs. But we have possibilities of development, which, if brought out, would add greatly to the sum total of our worth.

The difference between the success of this one and the failure of that one, is often simply in the use of the eyes. One sees and seizes that at which the other but idly glances. The successful man indeed sees more than the facts or objects which come under his notice. He sees them as doors of opportunity which wait to be pushed open and give him access to something better beyond. In reading the lives of inventors and discoverers we often come to this expression, "He noticed that—" and then follows the account of how some commonplace thing, which others had repeatedly passed around or stumbled over, became his stepping-stone to success.

The opening of the mouth of the Mississippi by Captain J. B. Eads is a case to the point. The great river is constantly bringing down great quantities of sand and mud, which gradually fill up the mouths of the stream. The sand bar thus formed had so increased that it finally blocked up the passage to such an extent that large and heavily loaded ships could pass over it only with the greatest difficulty. On one occasion over fifty vessels were seen lying north of the bar, waiting for an opportunity to get to sea. Sometimes they were delayed for days or even weeks, and were obliged to be at great expense for steam tugboats to haul them through. The national government and the state of Louisiana had expended millions of money trying to remove the obstruction, with but partial and poor success. Captain Eads noticed that where the river was narrow the current was strong, and so deposited but little mud to fill up the channel, and he was convinced that by building new banks on each side near the mouth of the river, thus narrowing and greatly increasing the velocity of the stream, the mud and sand would be swept out to sea. And then if the bar were dredged out it would not form again.

Congress was slow to give consent for trying the experiment, as nearly all the civil and military engineers opposed it. But finally permission was given and Captain Eads set about his task, and in four years what he had seen in possibility others saw in realization, so that now large ocean steamers pass up to New Orleans or out to sea without difficulty. Two millions of dollars per year are thus saved, and the commercial importance of New Orleans has been greatly increased.

We must not suppose that discoveries and inventions are ordinarily the result of chance. We are correct in saying of discoverers and inventors, "they noticed," but we should be far from the truth in saying, "they happened to notice." They noticed because they had cultivated their powers of observation, they had eyes that saw. What seemed a stroke of luck to their fellows was in fact a result of pluck in going through the world with eyes open rather than sauntering on in dreamy idleness. Sir Isaac Newton worked out the statement of the law of gravitation, and discovered that the same force that caused the apple to fall from the tree in his mother's orchard kept the moon in its orbit. Other men had seen apples fall and the moon move onward in the heavens, but he was the first to see the connection between them. While in the University of Cambridge he was so close a student that he often sat up the entire night working on some difficult mathematical problem, and in the morning would seem to be as much refreshed with his success as though the hours had been given to sleep. It was in the summer of 1665, while at home, that, seated in the orchard and seeing the ripe fruit drop, he fell into one of his profound meditations on the nature of the force which caused it to fall. The train of thought seemed to have been something like this: 1. These apples fall in a direct line toward the center of the earth. The same force causes a cannon ball to *curve* toward the same point. Everything in the world is drawn and held by it. 2. If these apples fell from a tree half a mile high they would not the less seek the earth's center. 3. Suppose an apple should fall from the moon—then what? He saw that the movement of the moon in its orbit around the earth is really a constant falling toward the earth; that it is constantly drawn by the earth from a straight line in which it would move by its own momentum, were it not for the attraction of the earth. But not until 1682 did he complete the problem, and give to the world the solution.

For true success there must be not only the general powers of observation, but a specialized training of those powers, so that we shall be searching for our specialty. Yonder stand three men upon a hilltop. The first is a dealer in real estate. His trained eye enables him to estimate the fertility of those broad acres in the valley, and the value of those forest-covered slopes, or the possibilities of making the sightly eminence upon which they stand a suburban settlement, where men may build homes away from the noise and smoke of the city. The next is a geologist. His eye takes in the nature of the soil, the rock formations, the scattered bowlders, the outlines of hills and valleys and courses of rivers, and he sees how through unmeasured ages the forces of nature have been bringing to its present form the region of country which is spread out at his feet. The third is a painter. For the possibilities and utilities of the valleys and hillsides, or the processes by which they came to their present form, he cares but little. He looks with an artist's eye, and his soul swells with an artist's joy, and he longs to capture for his canvas these valleys of verdure, the **river which like a silver ribbon seems carelessly thrown down** among the green, the wooded hills which rise one behind another and grow blue in the distance, the white houses away up the valley yonder, which seem like scattered pearls in a setting of emerald, and the hazy sky which throws a veil of dreamy softness over the whole landscape. Each of these men has eyes that see, but the eyes of each have been differently trained, and so each sees his specialty.

The true poet must have eyes that see. He is more than a maker of rhymes and meters. He must see and show to us what ordinary eyes have not detected. For example, one of our poets, in giving a picture of the Netherlands, writes:

> "The sails of windmills sink and soar
> Like wings of sea-gulls on the shore,"

and we are thrilled with the aptness of the comparison. Of the Lighthouse he says:

> "It sees the ocean to its bosom clasp
>   The rocks and sea-sand with the kiss of peace;
> It sees the wild winds lift it in their grasp,
>   And hold it up, and shake it like a fleece.
> The startled waves leap over it; the storm
>   Smites it with the scourges of the rain,
> And steadily against its solid form
>   Press the great shoulders of the hurricane."

The incoming tide and the plashing waves are fittingly called the "clasp," and "kiss of peace." The white fleece of foam from which the waters are shaken out and fall back, we also see after the poet has shown it to us. The "startled waves" leaping over the barriers at the shore we recall, and we remember that they came rushing in swifter than the wind, as though seeking to escape from some pursuing enemy. The "scourges of the rain" picture the many lashes, each numerously loaded and all wielded by the wrathful wind. And when this does not avail, the wind, which has now become a hurricane, presses its mighty shoulders against the tower of stone, causing it to quiver indeed, but not to yield.

EYES THAT SEE.

We usually find what we search for. He who is looking for evil motives and deeds in his fellow men will be quite likely to find them. And some seem to make this their wretched specialty. They pride themselves on their insight into human nature, but for any good they do you will look in vain, they are detectives rather than physicians. There should be a care not to develop the eyes to see evil, since we inevitably become transformed into the likeness of that which we have as the object of our attention. A man's object in life will surely bend and mold him into conformity to itself. An old whaler said that he had for more than a score of years sailed the seas for the capture of sperm whales, and he supposed his heart would be found by a post mortem examination to be in the form of a whale.

While we should not be searching for sin, we should train our eyes to see danger signals, and make sure that we have not become morally color-blind. It seems strange that some persons should be unable to distinguish red from green. Dalton could see in the solar spectrum only two colors, blue and yellow, and having once dropped a piece of red sealing-wax in the grass, he could not distinguish it by its color. Dr. Mitchell mentions a naval officer who chose a blue coat and red waistcoat, believing them to be of the same color. Color blindness is usually in relation to red, and yet red is the universal danger signal. Young people often say, "I can't see the harm of this or the wrong in that," and, refusing to take the word of others that the signal shows red and indicates danger, they rush on to ruin.

As color blindness is the occasion of many wrecks and ruins, so nearsightedness is the cause of many sad failures. The trained eye of the sailor will detect a sail out on the horizon, when a landsman would see but the meeting of sea and sky. The eye should be trained to long distance seeing, for often we must pass through defeat to victory. Temporary loss may be the gateway to permanent gain. In most enterprises there is at first a necessary sinking of some capital, but this becomes the out-of-sight foundation upon which the superstructure may be solidly reared. The farmer, the merchant, the manufacturer, look ahead, often a long way ahead. They have eyes that see. The chess or checker player who sees but one move ahead will seldom win unless he plays with another who is equally stupid.

But finally in all our seeing and seeking let the object be a noble and worthy one. I have read of a man who found a valuable gold piece, and from that time forth he walked with eyes upon the ground searching for gold pieces. He would not lift his eyes, lest he should overlook some money lying in his path. In the course of his life he did find several pieces, but meanwhile his soul was becoming narrower and more sordid. He saw not the blue skies, the fleecy clouds, the rainbow arch, the stars brighter than gold, the crescent or full-orbed moon. He had eyes to see, but better far for his soul had he been blind. I read of the great leader and law-giver Moses, "He endured as seeing Him who is invisible." And more than we need the power to find gold dollars or eagles, or to see stars and moon and sun, do we need to have this promise as our possession: "Thine eyes shall see the King in his beauty; they shall behold the land that is very far off."

The Value of an Idea.

WILLIAM C. KING, Springfield, Mass.

THE true value of an idea is beyond the power of computation. The world is not governed by gold, but by ideas. The man who works without ideas becomes a mere machine, stupid and void of either mental or physical growth. The man whose mind is kept in a condition of healthy activity, becomes an intellectual power. He is constantly evolving ideas which are of value to himself and the world.

Gutenberg was a young man whose mind was active. He was familiar with the laborious and difficult task of producing manuscript volumes. He conceived the idea of making movable type and thus of making books by printing instead of by the slow process of writing. As we look upon the vast product of the printing press, and consider the immeasurable influence it has exerted for four centuries, who can estimate the value of this one idea? If it had remained in the closet of darkness hidden from the world, the common people of the present generation would be but slightly, if any, emerged from the intellectual night which had hitherto enveloped them. Gutenberg was a thinking man. He communicated his ideas to his wife and received from her a smile of approval and encouragement. He at once began to put his idea into tangible form, and, as a result, we to-day have the art of printing with a wide diffusion of its products, and consequent intellectual stimulus and influence throughout the civilized world.

The idea of bridling the electric current and sending it across the continent and around the world at a speed of lightning, freighted with thought and intelligence, is beyond the power of human computation in point of value to the world.

THE VALUE OF AN IDEA.

To-day we sit in our office and audibly speak with persons a thousand miles distant, recognizing their voices as distinctly as though in the same room. If the idea of the electric current for conveying sound had never been put into practical use, what a loss the world would have sustained!

James Watt little realized the value of an idea as he was experimenting with his mother's teakettle. Had the power of steam never been developed, we should doubtless still be traveling by the old stage coach and on horseback. What a blessing has come to our homes, and to the world through the idea of the sewing machine, conceived by Elias Howe! Although he became almost swamped in the mire of difficulties and discouragements, he was possessed of a wonderful tenacity of purpose; every obstacle was trampled under the ponderous foot of determination, and the result is known to the civilized world.

The wonderful advances made in mechanical devices and in science are the result of ideas. Men have studied, wrought, and labored diligently to reduce these ideas to practical use. As a result we see on every hand the gigantic strides of improvement and progress. Nowhere on the face of the earth is there greater incentive for the development of ideas and their application to practical use than in our own country.

The opportunities for advancement and improvement are by no means exhausted. We have scarcely read through the primer of inventive genius. In every department of life's activities large rewards are offered for ideas.

What is your occupation or particular line of work? Is there not some part of your daily toil which could be simplified and its accomplishment facilitated by the introduction of an idea?

The worth of an idea should be apprehended by every young man and woman, as an appreciation of its value will exert a strongly beneficial influence upon the choice of occupation, companions, and books.

Seek to gain ideas from others and to develop them from your own resources. Their possession and use will make you wise to know and to do.

Put Your Ideas into Practice.

BENJAMIN IDE WHEELER, Ph.D.
President University of California.

"WHAT does, what knows, what is; three souls, one man," so the doctrine of John reads in the words of Browning. Doing, knowing, being; action, intelligence, character; these three are the trinity of life, and how can either be spared? The mere knowing of things does not make character, any more than the rules and canons of an art make skill. Acquaintance with the conventionalities of society does not make a gentleman. On the other hand, mere busyness is not being. Bare locomotion does not generate soul power. The restlessness of the house fly yields, we suspect, no fruit, either in knowledge or wisdom. Character is begotten of intelligent acts. It is the resultant of choices. What we are at any time is the product of all our deliberate acts. We are what we have done. Every single act of the will yields its insensible but none the less certain contribution to the sum of character. Elevation of moral character comes only through the furnace fires of moral testing and struggle. The half-reformed pickpocket, who, on seeing a handy purse in the outside pocket of his neighbor on a street car, prayed for strength, and changed his seat, made a gain of strength thereby. He could have made greater by sitting it out.

The supreme end of life is not found in knowing or in being. That were selfishness. The possession of character or knowledge is no end in itself. Character that does not act is dead. Action is its oxygen. The death is by asphyxiation. Knowledge that does not take shape in deeds, that does not apply itself to life, that does not take the life-form, is rubbish. Be-

PUT YOUR IDEAS INTO PRACTICE.

tween true learning and pedantry there is a deep gulf fixed. The one has a purpose with reference to the life of man, and is transmutable into acts; the other is an end to itself, is selfish, and takes hold on death.

The supreme end of life is not found in knowing or in being, but in putting knowledge and being into action. Personality is the active form of being. Herein lies the contrast between Christianity and the great Hindoo religions. Christianity looks to the development of personalities,—personalities that live and act the beneficent life of God, and so become the sons of God. The Hindoo religions look to the annulment of personality. Life is all sorrow. Desire, effort, action, is the great sin. Release from personality and absorption into the world-all is the true salvation. The one is the religion of optimism and action, the other of pessimism and quietism.

How natural it is to convince one's self that this is a perverse and hopeless world, and to shrink back into quiet with one's self, and let things drift. The dubious man is seldom a man of action. He will criticise the action of other people freely, but he will not take the responsibility of action upon himself. In council he will evolve a dozen reasons against a proposed plan, but will not formulate a substitute. His work all goes into the breeching and not into the traces. It is preeminently the men of hope, of outlook,—the optimists,—who act. Action is creative, and the motive power of creation is faith.

Distrust, then, is the first ground of inaction, and the second is like unto it,— cowardice. How we stand shivering and dawdling before the bath, afraid to take the plunge. Action involves responsibility. Assuming responsibility is bravery. The heroes, the great leaders of men, are the men who take upon themselves the responsibility of action. The world is always waiting for men to lead it, men who have the courage of their convictions, are willing to select a course of action, take the risk, and start upon it. The men who forever stand counting the cost and estimating the disgrace of failure, they cannot be leaders. They are cowards.

PUT YOUR IDEAS INTO PRACTICE.

Cowardice is the second ground of inaction, and the third is akin to it,—moral laziness. The will is weak. The fuse goes out before it reaches the charge. The case was clear, the opportunity apparent, but the will would not act. Knowledge would not transmute itself into action. "A little more sleep, a little more slumber, a little more folding of the hands to sleep." Half the sloth is moral sloth. More men fail through debility of will than through intellectual or physical debility. Force and energy are largely matters of the will.

Another ground of inaction is confusion of purpose. Men do not think the matter through. They do not grasp the essentials of the situation. They wallow in its details. They fail to gather all the conditions within a single field of vision, so that perspective is possible. Various possibilities of action stand in confused conflict. The mind is a jumble. Now one course, now another, seems good. It is a great thing for a man to know what he wants. A house divided against itself cannot stand. Conflicting and unsteady purposes throttle action.

Elaborate theorizing often proves in practical life a check upon action. Theorizing becomes an end to itself. It affords in itself a distinct satisfaction, especially when the theorizer is not troubled with any responsibility for their enactment, or with any relation to the actual vulgar state of things in life. Some minds are natural generators of schemes and theories. There is steam enough in the boiler, but it never goes to the cylinder. It never makes the wheels go round. So it becomes merely a question of explosion and ruin or of the safety-valve and waste. Generally it is the latter.

Thought that is to go into action must know life. Theologies that are constructed in seclusion from life are not likely to touch life. They can be rehearsed and defended and subscribed to, but men do not usually live by them or die by them.

The best test of a theory or an idea is to put it into practice. If you are convinced that political conditions are not what they should be, and have an ideal of a better way in mind, do not think you are justified in hiding your ideal in a napkin and

PUT YOUR IDEAS INTO PRACTICE.

yourself in a monastery. Do something. Attend the caucuses. Go there with a plan of action. Organize support for your idea. Push for nomination and election men who represent your idea. Secure a place on a political committee. Propose a definite plan. Do not spend yourself in criticism of what other people are doing. Do something. One chief reason why politics are what they are is that the people who have the higher ideals prefer to put them into laments rather than into action, and people who have low ideals put them into action rather than into laments.

Put your ideas into practice. It is better for the ideas. That is what they were intended for. Exercise is their hygiene.

Importance of Being Punctual.

Hon. CYRUS G. LUCE, Ex-Governor of Michigan.

THERE is no teacher so wise as the Creator of the universe. There is no model so perfect. There is no other example that can be so safely and profitably followed. In every movement of the entire universe, the importance of punctuality is taught. He who knows all things, and controls all things, is so observant of its necessity that the sun, moon, stars, as well as the earth, move on, each in its own orbit, for thousands of years, without once being behind time for a single moment. So punctual and accurate is nature's machinery, so prompt is the engineer, that astronomers can determine the rising and setting of the sun and moon, and the eclipses that will occur, for centuries to come. But none can calculate the consequences of a failure on the part of any of the heavenly bodies to be on time.

Reliability and punctuality furnish the foundation upon which the whole structure of creation rests. So far as the plans of the Creator relate to the world in which we live, they are centered in the population that have in the past, do now, and shall in the future inhabit the earth. In order to accomplish the highest purposes of life, rules must be adopted for the guidance of conduct, and when good rules are once adopted they must be adhered to with religious fidelity.

While the duties that fall to the lot of any one individual are so small when compared to those which affect the whole creation that they are scarcely discernible by the naked eye, yet every one, no matter how humble, has functions to perform that affect not only one's self, but one's associates. Punctuality on the

IMPORTANCE OF BEING PUNCTUAL.

part of a boy or girl when first attending school adds materially to the comfort and profit of all who attend in the same room. The laggard who enters the schoolroom late not only suffers a personal loss, but inflicts a wrong upon the teacher and entire school. This is just as true as it would be if some little star should be tardy in its movements, thus throwing the entire universe at least into temporary confusion. Very early in life we form habits good or bad which go with us to the end. The habit of being behind time in entering the schoolroom, unless broken off by a determined purpose and firm will, will affect life's work all along the years. There is no line of life work where punctuality is not a necessity. However lofty may be the aims and aspirations of individuals, in ninety-nine cases out of a hundred they cannot be realized without this cardinal virtue.

The men whose names adorn and honor the pages of history have been renowned for the possession of this one trait of character as much as or more than for any other. On time, on time, has been their motto from the beginning to the end of their career. But we need not look alone to the lives of the distinguished. Perhaps it is wiser not to do so, for but very few live the lives of the distinguished, and even these few need no prompting; they understand the importance of punctuality. In everyday life it is just as essential. The clerk in the store, bank, or commission office will never rise or become a necessity to his employers unless he is in season and out of season.

On time! on time! This must become a part of his very life. Unless he does this, upon him neither his employers nor their customers can rely. And the rule that applies to the employee must be well learned and practiced by the employer. The bank whose doors do not open promptly at the accustomed hour is heralded as a broken bank. A minute late casts suspicions; five minutes late and a bank failure is announced, and all of its attendant evils afflict the community.

The same rule, to a greater or less extent, though not so forcibly illustrated, applies to all the callings in which men are engaged. The farmer sometimes acts as if he thought that his

IMPORTANCE OF BEING PUNCTUAL.

calling was exempt from an application of this unerring rule that applies to all things in heaven and on earth, but no greater mistake ever entered the head of mortal man. The farmer is engaged in the most important occupation known to the head or hand of man. Upon the products of the soil all rely for their anticipated prosperity. If the farmer does not lay broad and deep the foundation, other structures beside his own must crumble and fall, and to fill the demands that are properly made upon him, he, like the great stars, must be punctual in the orbit allotted to him in nature's economy. He must plow, plant, and cultivate on time, or the burdens imposed upon him at harvest time will be light indeed, and thus will be destroyed one of the main pillars of the edifice that sustains commerce, manufactures, and trade throughout the world. No more important lesson can be taught to the farmer's boy than is found in the everyday life of the successful, practical farmer. Every hour presents an object lesson. Every year many of these are presented to the mind of the close observer, and the central idea of all these is found in the two words, *thoroughness* and *punctuality*. Without this virtue, a high permanent success seldom comes to the tiller of the soil. Hence farmers and farmers' sons can learn that they and their business prove to be no exception to the general rule that affects men in all other legitimate occupations. Punctuality for them means not only greater prosperity, but lighter labors, and more leisure, more frequent opportunities for social enjoyments, and intellectual improvement, fewer failures, heavier crops, and frequently better prices.

Boys on the farm, be punctual, and prosperous and happy as a result. A good lesson in punctuality is taught to all men by the news gatherers for daily papers. The fierce competition between publishers, and their keen anxiety to be the first to promulgate and scatter broadcast important events, induce them to employ none as reporters but the most prompt and punctual men in the market. These men will chase a phantom as well as a reality. They will face the winter's cold, and the summer's heat. If a burglary is committed, they are there. If rumors of a murder

IMPORTANCE OF BEING PUNCTUAL.

reach their ears, no night is so dark, no danger so great, as to deter them from a punctual appearance on the spot, and, as a reward to the one who shall first reach any scene of disaster, a rise in salary is a certainty, while the laggard loses his place. These men in the prosecution of their calling teach lessons that should be indelibly impressed upon the minds of all. Their success as well as failures ought to stimulate to activity all young men everywhere. With them punctuality is an absolute necessity. But *how* to be punctual is a question that confronts all, and torments many. In response to chiding or prompting, the most common reply or excuse is, "I had no time." The close observer of men and things is impressed with the fact that it is those who perform the greatest tasks who are the most punctual, and it is they who do the least who the most frequently disregard all rules relating to punctuality. The men who do the most seem to have more time to assume new duties. The hardest worker of the present century was Horace Greeley. From 1840 to 1870 he was the great editor of the greatest newspaper of the times. He wrote longer and stronger editorials than any other writer during all these years. Still he was, or always seemed to be, ready to do an unlimited amount of outside work. He traveled abroad, and he compassed our own continent from ocean to ocean. He lectured in scores of places, at home and abroad. He wrote and published a large volume on "What I know about farming," and later he wrote and published two large volumes upon the "American Conflict." All this time he was discharging the exacting duties that devolved upon the editor of a great metropolitan daily and weekly newspaper. How did he perform all of these herculean tasks is a question that comes home to all of us. The answer is found largely in the fact that he was always punctual. He not only practiced this virtue, but enforced it upon his employees, and others with whom he was associated. Again, he was methodical; this is a twin brother to punctuality. Without this men cannot achieve great victories over obstacles, nor climb high on the ladder of fame, fortune, and honor. In order to be

IMPORTANCE OF BEING PUNCTUAL.

punctual, one must be methodical. Just so much time must be allotted to a discharge of the various duties assumed. Failure is stamped upon the brow of him who permits his work to chase him during the hours, days, weeks, months, and years of a lifetime. This is especially true of one who undertakes to do much in the world. Just a little may be accomplished without method. We should all be possessed of an ambition to do much, not a little, with life's opportunities. The misfortunes which arise through want of method and punctuality are recorded on almost every page of the world's history. For the want of it, battles have been lost, and national banners have trailed in the dust. Both history and observation bring to our attention the awful results of being a moment too late. The opportunity comes and passes by, never to return. We may grieve over the fatal consequences that flow from our want of punctuality. We reflect upon the failure of darling objects, but are, when too late, powerless to avert the disaster. Of all the men on earth who should in season and out of season be punctual in the discharge of every duty, it is the men who run the trains over the bands of steel that checker this whole country from ocean to ocean, and from the lakes to the gulf. The remorse and anguish which often follow as a result of being one moment too late in the performance of a duty as engineer on a railroad locomotive are fearful to contemplate. As these words are penned, there comes back to us fresh recollections of fearful disasters that recently occurred in Michigan and Indiana. It was during the height of travel to and from the Exposition at Chicago, that a train heavily loaded with excursionists from the fair was standing on the main track at Jackson, Mich., when another equally heavily loaded train overtook the first section, wrecked two cars, and killed fourteen human beings. The engineer applied the brakes one moment too late. A fast express was hurrying to Chicago over the Wabash road. A freight train was side tracked at a small station in Indiana. The brakeman was thirty seconds too late in turning the switch. The rapidly moving passenger train crashed into the freight, and precious human lives were lost. Later and sadder was an accident that occurred at Battle Creek, on the Chicago and Grand Trunk railway. The engineer was two minutes too late in stopping his train. As a result twenty-seven valuable lives were lost; communities were shocked; mourning was carried into many a household. The engineer suffers in sadness and sorrow, and all of this because he did not promptly and punctually obey orders. We will not harrow the reader with further recitals. These are only given to emphasize the importance of being punctual. Yet less painful and important results come home to all of us as we review the experiences and observations of a lifetime, and we think if we had been there on time, it might have been different.

"For of all sad words of tongue or pen,
The saddest are these: 'It might have been!'"

Delay Loses Fortune.

Rev. H. A. GOBIN, D.D., Dean of De Pauw University, Indiana.

SOME virtues seem to be opposed to each other. Energy is quite unlike patience, caution stands over against courage, and independence is not suggestive of humility.

But this opposition is more in appearance than in reality. Each of these qualities keeps the other in proper limits. An excellency can easily be perverted into a fault. An excess of courage becomes rashness. An extreme caution is timidity. But where courage is restrained by caution, and caution is quickened by courage, then symmetry and force of character are produced.

Energy, courage, and independence are positive qualities. They incite to activity. They generate and sustain great enterprises. Modern civilization is the product of these characteristics. The passive virtues—humility, patience, and meekness—would have no value if not associated with the above positive traits. Even justice and equity would have no existence if there were no heroic spirits to define, illustrate, and maintain them.

The absence of positive traits in any life is sure to work disaster. No advantage of birth or position can be a substitute for them. When the Prince of Coburg was engaged in his war with the Turks, he commanded, in person, an army of thirty-seven thousand men. He was defeated by an army of twenty-eight thousand. About nine miles distant was his general Suvoroff with an army of twenty-two thousand. When Coburg was defeated, he sent the following sorry message to Suvoroff: "I was attacked this morning by the Turks. I have lost my position and my artillery. I send you no instructions what to do. Use your own judgment, only let me know what you have done as soon as you can." Suvoroff immediately sent this stinging reply: "I shall attack the Turks to-morrow morning, drive them from your position, and retake your cannon." Suvoroff kept his word, and before the next night Coburg had his old position and his artillery. Coburg was a prince by heredity, but Suvoroff was more than a prince by achievement. Coburg would have lost everything by his irresolution and delay had it not been for the alertness and vigor of Suvoroff.

Human life is an incessant conflict. Hence the constant use of military illustrations to represent the qualities and conditions of a successful life. The Prince of Peace said, "I came not to bring peace but a sword." Peace as an ultimate condition is the result of a victorious conquest. Even divine love meets the resistance of the human cross in coming to the hearts of men. In some cases a crown comes to a brow by the accident of heredity. But the crown represents some preceding conflict. The crown was first worn by a conqueror before it could be transmitted. The world will soon insist that crowns can be worn only by those who achieve them. There will be no transmitted crowns. Heredity is losing all its advantages as a basis of preferment. This is true not only in the political world, but in every walk of life. The supreme question is not, who is his father? or, what is his family? but, who is he? What has he done? What can he do? Fortunes are lost by delay not merely as to acquisition on the part of the low born, but fortunes are lost by delay as to retention on the part of the high born. In our public schools the sons of the richest sit side by side with the sons of the poorest. They study the same lessons; they recite to the same teacher. Their tasks are the same. It will not do to say to the poor boy, "Be spry, my lad. Work quick and fast. No time for delay. You have your fortune to gain, your crown to win," but to the rich boy say, "How happy you are! You don't need to study. Your fortune is made. You are rich by inheritance."

DELAY LOSES FORTUNES.

All observation shows that as much tact and energy are needed in keeping fortunes as in gaining them. A most conspicuous scene in every community is the decay and wretchedness of rich families. Scarcely a neighborhood but that an example can be found of a fortune lost by the delay to acquire the mental and moral traits necessary in the safe conduct of business affairs. It will not do to charge these misfortunes to "bad luck." Addison wrote in the *Spectator* his view of this apology respecting the decline of English families: "I may here as well as anywhere impart the secret of what is called good and bad luck.

"There are men who, supposing Providence to have an implacable spite against them, bemoan in the poverty of a wretched old age the misfortunes of their lives. Luck forever runs against them and for others. One, with a good profession, lost his luck in the river, where he idled away his time a fishing, when he should have been in the office. Another, with a good trade, perpetually burned up his luck by his hot temper, which provoked all his customers to leave him. Another, with a lucrative business, lost all his luck by amazing diligence at everything but his business. He gave his golden hours to games, races, and yarn-spinning company, and came back to his books and accounts with brains dull and heavy as lead. Another who steadily followed his trade, as steadily followed his battle. Hundreds lose their luck by indorsing, by sanguine speculations, by trusting fraudulent men, and by dishonest gains. I never knew an early-rising, hard-working, prudent man, careful of his earnings and strictly honest, who complained of bad luck. A good character, good habits, and iron industry are impregnable to the assaults of all the ill luck that fools ever dreamed of."

This description, written at the beginning of the eighteenth century, is just as appropriate for the close of the nineteenth.

"Bad luck" is generally a fool's apology for his incompetency and indolence. The chief reason why more men and women do not make a better success of life is not because they are ignorant of the true conditions of thrift, but because they delay to put these conditions into immediate and constant use. A Spanish proverb says, "The road of 'by and by' leads to the town of 'never.'" The wild boy and frivolous girl say, "Time enough to be sober minded when I get old; now is the time for fun." But the days are flying by; even the years are going too fast, and the unfortunate youth is getting more and more of a dislike for serious work. Fun is a just and delightful relaxation after hours of steady employment. But fun as a business becomes a sorrowful task. Fun is the condiment which gives more relish to solid meats; but who could become healthy and strong on a diet of pepper sauce and bonbons? The first meaning of the word relaxation is a release from tension and confinement. It can only be a luxury when it is the rebound from the girding up in noble toil. If one should ask, "How can I get the sweetest sport, the richest fun, the finest pleasure?" the answer would be, "Put the most of your time to solid labor and then, when you unbend for amusement, you get the full flow of enjoyment unrestrained by a consciousness that you are neglecting important duties."

If the evening of life is to be an occasion of rest and congenial society, then the forenoon must be given in a worthy manner to a worthy business. What affliction is more distressing than poverty in old age! When the old are poor, they are generally lonely, or worse than lonely, by the frowns and tones which indicate that they are an incumbrance. But if they have a competency in property and income, they will not need for pleasant friends. It is not worth while to get angry at such a condition of things, and rave and vituperate that none are so deserving of comfort and friends as the aged who are poor. Complaining will only increase the solitude and wretchedness. Instead of attempting to reconstruct society in order to adapt it to your future misfortunes, better construct your life so that you will enjoy good fortune to the end of your days. The best way to do this is to get the best possible wisdom of earth and heaven and without delay put this into your mind and conduct. The wiser the early morning, the sweeter the shades of evening.

"Shun delays, they breed remorse;
　Take thy time while time is lent thee:
Creeping snails have weakest force;
　Fly their fault, lest thou repent thee.
Good is best when sooner wrought,
Ling'ring labors come to naught.

"Hoist thy sail while breeze doth last;
　Tide and wind stay no man's pleasure!
Seek not time when time is past,
　Sober speed is wisdom's leisure;
After-wits are dearly bought;
Let thy fore-wit guide thy thought."

Strive at Possibilities.

Rev. JAMES W. COLE, B.D.

VERY much of time, effort, and culture is needed to perfect the choicest things of nature. Many unpromising seeds and stocks have, by culture, been developed into the most beautiful of flowers, and the most delicious of fruits and foods. Culture brought out their latent, unsuspected powers and virtues and established their value. Many things now called mere useless weeds would, if cultivated, prove most valuable flowers or foods. The generally used and very valuable potato of commerce bears but a slight resemblance to the insignificant tuber, the product of which Sir Walter Raleigh had such difficulty in getting his countrymen to try three hundred years ago. In Cato's time oats were considered only a weed, and rye was not grown, and corn and rice were unknown to the civilized world, and silk was thought to be a thing scraped from the mulberry tree.

It has taken centuries to bring the world up to its present state. We are the fruitage of many generations, and yet the perfect man has not come. But in due time he will appear. You and I may hasten his coming by making the most of ourselves. Richter said, "I have made as much out of myself as could be made of the stuff, and no man could require more." Yet the masses of men and women seem content with mediocrity. But few realize their capabilities, and fewer yet seem to care.

The schoolmaster was wont to say of one of England's noted statesmen in the lad's boyhood, "he is a dunce," and, years after, when the boy grown to manhood, attempted to speak in

STRIVE AT POSSIBILITIES.

Parliament and made a most ridiculous failure of it, the sneers, laughter, and taunts of his fellow members seemed to confirm the teacher's estimate of him. But though humiliated and shamed beyond endurance, he exclaimed as he sat down discomfited, "It is in me, and it *shall* come out!" And it did. For Richard Brinsley Sheridan became the most brilliant, eloquent, and amazing statesman of his day. Yet if his first efforts had been but moderately successful, he might have been content with mere mediocrity. It was his defeats that nerved him to strive for eminence and win it. But it took hard, persistent work in his case to secure it, just as it did in that of so many others.

Said James Parton, "Men destined to a great career, I have observed, generally serve a long and vigorous apprenticeship to it of some kind. They try their forming powers in little things before grappling with the great. I cannot call to mind a single instance of a man who achieved success of the first magnitude, who did not at first toil long in obscurity." This witness is true; the world's great names were not made in a day. It took John Milton forty years of toil to produce "Paradise Lost," and William Cullen Bryant rewrote his "Thanatopsis" more than a hundred times, and then he was not satisfied with it, feeling that he could yet do better. David Hume labored thirteen hours a day for many years before his great "History" was prepared, while Noah Webster toiled for thirty consecutive years to produce his dictionary. Bishop Butler rewrote his immortal "Analogy" twenty times, and Gibbon his "Memoirs" nine times, while Burke rewrote parts of his great speech against Hastings thirteen times.

True, these men were men of great abilities. But the beginnings of talent or of genius are, like the other things of nature, very small, and, if uncultivated, they remain dwarfed or disappear; and if the world's great men had not so persistently worked, they would never have been heard of. President Wayland, of Brown University, was accustomed to say to his students, "Young gentlemen, remember that nothing can withstand day's works." And Daniel Webster declared that it was this, not genius, that gave him his fame, when he said, "I know of no superior quality that I possess unless it be the power of application. To work, and not to genius, I owe my success." Charles Dickens is called a man of genius, yet this is his testimony concerning himself: "I have tried with all my heart to do well; and whatever I have devoted myself to, I have devoted myself to completely. In great aims and in small I have always been thoroughly in earnest. I have never believed it possible that any natural or improved ability can claim immunity from the companionship of the steady, hard-working qualities, and hope to gain its end."

Another of the world's great men, Sir Walter Scott, who was also a tireless worker, in a letter to his son, admonishes him on this fashion: "I cannot too much impress on your mind that labor is the condition which God has imposed on us, in every station of life. There is nothing worth having that can be had without it. . . . As for knowledge, it can no more be planted in the human mind without labor, than a field of wheat can be produced without the previous use of the plow." Believe me, the poorest, most insignificant boy or girl never dreams of the great reserve of power, the immense capabilities of the human spirit. If they would but seek to develop it within themselves, what deeds of high renown they might accomplish.

Said the eminent Dr. John Kitto: "I think that all the fine stories about natural ability, etc., etc., are mere rigmarole, and that every man may, according to his opportunities and industry, render himself almost anything he wishes to become." His witness is entitled to great weight for he had a cruel, drunken father, who reduced his family to great suffering and beggary, and John, losing his hearing by an accident, was sent to the poorhouse to be taken care of. But the sorrowful lad thirsted for knowledge, and his progress in his boyish studies astonished the authorities. At length a benevolent man took him from the poorhouse and sent him to school. Though deaf for life, such was his untiring industry that he became one of the most

STRIVE AT POSSIBILITIES.

renowned Biblical scholars and writers of his age, and his works are read to-day with great profit and delight in Christian homes throughout the whole world.

The average man or woman content with commonplace attainments sometimes wonders at the progress of men like these, but this progress serves only to give us an inkling of the yet undeveloped and unknown powers of men. These did not reach the highest point of expansion. They had latent capabilities undreamed of. The Scriptures declare, "It doth not yet appear what we shall be." Very many buddings of our nature do not even appear in this "the first of the things" for mankind. There yet awaits transformation "from glory unto glory" in the on-coming ages.

Two young students of Williams College sat by a hayrick discussing their future, when one said to his companion, "You and I are little men, but before we die our influence must be felt on the other side of the globe." And it was, for then and there was born the great American Foreign Missionary Association's work for the salvation of the heathen world. Those students were poor and humble young men, but the fire of divine love for the perishing moved them to action and they did what they could.

You may be very little, but you can make your influence felt not only in this little world, but also in other grander and nobler worlds in the "ages yet to come," by making the very best and most of yourself in this life. This is God's design for us. Listen to his word, "To the intent (Gr. "for this express purpose") that now unto the principalities and the powers in the heavenly places, might be made known through the church the manifold wisdom of God, according to the eternal purpose which he purposed in Christ Jesus our Lord," "that in the ages to come he might show the exceeding riches of his grace in kindness toward us in Christ Jesus." You may have been born and are now living under what you consider great disadvantages of poverty or of inherited weaknesses. But these should be goads to spur to new diligence rather than excuses for idleness.

STRIVE AT POSSIBILITIES.

"To start in life with comparatively small means seems so necessary as a stimulus to work," said Samuel Smiles, "that it may almost be set down as the *secret of success.*"

Look around you on the world's most successful men and see if it is not true, and then strive at the great possibilities before you "It is not that which is done for a young man that is most valuable to him and others, but that which he is led to do for himself." Aim at the eternities to come and develop the very best of yourself for the nobler work and being that there await us.

Practice Secures Perfection.

Rev. GEORGE R. HEWITT, B.D.

IT is a truism that forms the title of this chapter, but it is none the less important on that account. There is only one way to learn how to do a thing, and that is by doing it. No art, no pursuit requiring skill, is mastered at once. It must be wrestled with long and patiently before it gives up its secret.

A man can learn how to saw wood in about fifteen minutes, and can then earn a dollar a day at that business the rest of his life. It is a useful occupation, but demands neither skill nor long training for its successful prosecution. Muscle with a moderate degree of intelligence is all that is necessary.

It is very different with pursuits demanding dexterity, skill, and brains. Years are required to gain the mastery over them. "How long did it take you to prepare that sermon?" asked some one of Dr. Lyman Beecher. "Forty years," was his prompt reply. Giardini, when asked how long it would take to learn the violin, replied, "Twelve hours a day for twenty years." It would be very pleasant if we could learn to play the violin or piano by inspiration. But the great musicians did not learn in that way. Incessant practice was the price they paid for their proficiency. Not by sudden inspiration but by painstaking cultivation are dexterity, mastership, and facile power of any kind acquired. Nothing is done easily, not even walking or talking, that was not done with difficulty at first. Practice in any line of action brings to our aid the law of habit, a law which reigns in the muscular and mental no less than in the moral realms of action.

PRACTICE SECURES PERFECTION.

Do anything a sufficient number of times, and you acquire facility in doing it. Every action tends to repeat itself; repeated action begets habit, and habit is second nature. All the powers and possibilities within us lie subject to this law of habit. Practice puts the law in operation, evokes latent possibilities, and calls into action powers which would otherwise have lain ingloriously dormant.

A child has all the organs of speech that the consummate orator has, but he has not acquired the power of using them. That power was gained by practice. Gladstone was once a prattling, stammering boy, but by practice his vocal organs became flexible, and adapted to all the intricacies of expression, until at length listening assemblies sat charmed by the music of his resounding periods.

Listen to a great pianist like Paderewski, whose touch is marvelous, whose fingers glide over the keys as if instinct with life, and it seems as though it must always have been easy for him to play; but on inquiry you learn that it was by practice, incessant and severe, from early years to manhood, that he acquired that exquisite skill.

"Those who are resolved to excel," said Sir Joshua Reynolds, "must go to their work willing or unwilling, morning, noon, and night; they will find it no play, but very hard labor." Some one has said that no great work is ever done in a hurry. With equal truth it may be said that the power to produce a great work is never acquired in a hurry. No-one ever wrote an immortal poem, painted a great picture, or delivered a famous oration without serving his apprenticeship, and doing what we may call the drudgery of his art. It may have been in secret that the drudgery was done, but done it had to be. Vasari relates in his "Lives of the Painters," that Giotto could with his hand draw a perfect circle, but he does not tell us how many imperfect ones he drew before he made a perfect one. Even Titian and Raphael had to begin by drawing straight lines; Beethoven and Mozart by picking out the notes one by one; and Shakespeare himself had to learn the alphabet before he wrote

PRACTICE SECURES PERFECTION.

Hamlet and King Lear. Little by little these things are learned. "There is no such thing," said Daniel Webster, "as extemporaneous acquisition." Perfection is not gained, any more than heaven, "at a single bound." "We build the ladder by which we rise."

Charles J. Fox was a gifted man, but his gifts had to be gradually developed by practice. He made it a point to speak in Parliament every night for his own improvement. Henry Clay's advice to young lawyers was not to let a day pass without exercising their powers. His own early practice of the art of speaking is well known. At the age of twenty-seven he began and for years he continued the practice of daily reading and speaking upon the contents of some historical or scientific book. These offhand efforts, he says, were sometimes made in a cornfield, and not unfrequently in a barn with only horses and oxen for his auditors. Not sudden inspiration or illumination while speaking, but careful cultivation, he gives as the secret of his oratorical power.

Be not discouraged if progress seems slow. Time and toil will work wonders. Practice is the prelude to the song of victory. Do your best every time. Remember Beethoven's maxim, "The barriers are not erected which say to aspiring talents and industry, 'thus far and no farther.'"

Learning is Not Wisdom.

MERRILL EDWARDS GATES, LL.D., President Amherst College, Mass.

"To what purpose should our thought be directed to various kinds of knowledge, unless room be afforded for putting it into practice, so that public advantage may be the result!"
—Sir Philip Sidney.

IN certain moods you may spend an hour in turning over the leaves of a dictionary when you are not "using" it. But you will hardly call a dictionary interesting reading! Why? Not because there is too much learning in it, but because the knowledge contained in it is not alive. There is no such orderly arrangement of facts, no such systematic unfolding of principles, as marks the scientific treatise. It lacks the interest that attaches to the progress of events in a history, to the growth of character, the unfolding of plot in the novel. The dictionary is a mass of knowledge, valuable for reference; but it presupposes a man with intelligence, purpose, and will, to use this knowledge.

For the successful conduct of life, mere learning is not enough. We do not undervalue learning. All knowledge has a certain value. Probably the danger that least of all threatens your life is the danger of knowing too much! But it is possible to be very learned, and yet to be singularly destitute of the ability to make learning of any use, to one's self, to one's friends, or to the world at large. Learning is not wisdom. In order that learning may be intelligently acquired, even, there must be a wise appreciation of the ends for which it is to be attained, of the relations which the knowledge you are acquiring bears to other departments of knowledge, to the conduct of your own life, to the thought and the life of your fellow men. It is not merely a question of what you know. To what purpose do you know it? How much do you see in it? To what use will you put it, for others or for yourself?

The knowledge that comes of itself through the mere experience of living is not enough to make one wise. How many men and women you know who have been beaten upon by all the stormy experience of fifty years, and sung to by all the beauty and joy of life for fifty years, who still seem none the wiser for it. One does not grow wiser by mere passive existence. If experience is to be of value, it must be reflected upon, it must be reacted upon, by the self within. You must learn your own lessons from experience, with conscious effort, and with the determination to learn them and to use them, or you will never be wise, even in the lowest sense of the term.

Nor is the knowledge that is strenuously worked for, that is won by severest effort, in itself enough to make one wise. It is not always true that "knowledge is power." Sometimes acquired knowledge is only the cause and the evidence of exhausted and wasted energy. Learning that is consciously labored for, as well as the knowledge that comes from experience of life, if it is to contribute to true wisdom, must be seen and used in the light of a higher vision. Knowledge must be directed to the attainment of ends higher than mere acquisition, whether of learning, or money, or fame and selfish power.

The knowledge which you have worked severely to acquire, furnishes a presumption that in thus working you have acquired power of will and the habit of the intelligent application of all your powers to the task that immediately confronts you. To this extent, the possession of knowledge creates a presumption in favor of your possessing wisdom. But it does not prove that you are wise.

Do you recall some of the elementary definitions of the science of mechanics? "*Work* is the production of motion against resistance." "*Energy* is the power a body has of doing work." "*Potential energy* is the power to do work which belongs to a body by virtue of its position," as, *e. g.*, to the tightly coiled spring, to the uplifted hammer of the pile-driver; these bodies by virtue of their position are in possession of potential energy, of energy which may or may not be used to accomplish wise ends. Learning is at best but potential energy. If wisely used, if intelligently directed to right ends, learning may become "kinetic energy," power actually put forth in useful work.

Learning alone will not make your life productive of good. There must be right feeling and strong willing before results follow. Knowledge ought to lead to right feeling. But knowledge does not always result in clear vision, right feeling, and right action. When it does we call it wisdom.

> Knowledge is proud that he has learned so much;
> Wisdom is humble that he knows no more."

Perhaps there is less of the conceit of learning among American scholars than in Europe. But we sometimes see traces of that conceit, which is always the mark of the petty soul. There is the conceited pedant. There is the dilettante in learning, finical in his moods and his intellectual habits,—a "man who thinks himself supreme or precious, and spends his life in turning pretty phrases, when not engaged in admiration of his own exclusive intellectual possessions."

The wise man, with his learning, has the intelligence that teaches him how to use his knowledge. He has true views of life;—right ends, and the skill to attain them. He is unselfish in his aims.

> "Here the heart
> May give a useful lesson to the head,
> And learning wiser grow without his books."

No man can be called truly cultured, truly wise, until his relations to his fellow men and his power to serve them fill a larger place in his thought and effort than does his wish to advance his own interests, to press for his own selfish advantage.

To be wise, then, you must have a right aim in view, the true end of life clearly before you. It is no accident that in the Bible wisdom always includes morality and the willing service of God. All the world's great poets, too, speak to us always of morality, and the unselfish service of our fellow men, as characteristic of the highest wisdom. There can be no true view of life where the highest ends of life are ignored. Always, however much of learning he may have acquired, the man who "says in his heart, there is no God," shows himself destitute of true wisdom, — "the fool" of Proverbs, and, in the light of philosophy and poetry, always "the fool."

If you are wise, you will ask yourself seriously, "For what, for whom, do I intend to live?" Two answers are possible: "I mean to live for myself"; "I mean to live for God, and so for my fellow men." Every man's life, whether he is conscious of it or not, vibrates full and strong to the keynote of one or the other of these two answers.

He who lives for God will find himself irresistibly impelled to the best and widest service of his fellow men. He who lives for self, however he may strive to strengthen his position by maxims of worldly prudence, fails of all the highest ends of living.

Reckon from self as a center, and your fellow men are your hated rivals in the struggle for existence and advancement. Ambition's law of life becomes the blood-stained "survival of the fittest"; and the highest glories life can yield you, in their hollow and transitory splendor will be yours but for a tremulous moment, until the younger, the more vigorous, the more fortunate competitor shall thrust you aside, and for his brief moment wear the bauble for which you strove until your selfish life went out in nothingness.

Reckon from God as the center, and your fellow men become your brothers, infinitely worthy of your loving interest, since one Father has made all our spirits after his own image, and one Saviour has died to redeem from sin and restore to God-likeness all who will turn to him, even the most debased. Thus reckoning from God as the center, the law of self-abnegation, of loving service, becomes the law of your life.

"But I have a duty to myself; I am under obligation to make the most of my own life," you say. Unquestionably! And you will do the best for yourself, intellectually and morally, when you subjugate yourself to the service of God in the service of your fellow men. Thus living, the feverish strain will be taken out of life; its hot, panting rivalries you need not longer know. The success of all good and true men will be your success. The spirit of Him who came not to be ministered unto, but to minister, will possess your soul; and failure for you will be impossible.

The very effort for others' welfare, and for the maintenance of righteousness, which may exhaust your vital powers, will still assure your deathless victory — your true success!

Herein is wisdom, — that you learn much, and put your learning and your life to the highest uses.

The Power and Possibilities of Young Men

JOSEPH COOK, LL.D., Boston.

ALL thoughtful young men have many day dreams of the important and noble things they will do, and the men of power they will become in after years. These imaginings are more or less colored, as all our dreams are, by their local associations and surroundings. Those of us who have come to maturer years, on looking back over the track of experience, see that many of these fond fancies of youth might have had fulfillment, if the dreamers had but had proper instruction as to the use of the powers given them by nature. You mean to make a success of life — what is needful to attain it? May one who has had much observation of his fellowmen be permitted to outline the things that in his judgment go to make up a successful life, and to indicate briefly how they may be secured? Five things, at least, are necessarily included in all true success.

(1) Self-support; to obtain which a good degree of health of mind, certainly, and also more or less of bodily vigor and industry are required.

(2) A good education, *i. e.*, a wise training of head, hand, and heart; all of them, and not, as is so often attempted, the culture of but one or two. All are necessary to make the perfect man, and all should be educated aright.

(3) A good occupation, whether mechanical, agricultural, or professional, and one in which you should be proficient to a degree that removes from it all of irksomeness. So far as possible the occupation should be one suited to your individua endowments, and to your home and school training. It should be one in which you can do good and get good.

THE POWER AND POSSIBILITIES OF YOUNG MEN.

(4) A home in which to anchor the heart and garner the fruits of toil. It may include simply a wise, cheerful, single life, or the wife and children given you by Heaven.

(5) And chief, a saved soul and a pure body. This means certainly as much as a deliverance from the love of sin, the guilt of sin, and the filth of sin. Having these things, life may be said to be successful. Lacking any of them, it is to a greater or less degree a failure.

These United States are pre-eminently the land of young men, and for young men. They conduct the business, and control the affairs of this country, as do the young men of no other nation on the globe. Our institutions develop the youth of our land very quickly, and bring them to the front early, and your opportunities must soon be met. The hour to secure the very best success of which you are capable will shortly arrive. Shall your powers be developed to meet it? Will you make the best possible use of them? This is for you to determine. Shall yours be among the noblest and best of lives? You can make it so. Do you inquire how? By developing aright the mind as well as the body.

There is a best way to live, and it is certainly wise to live that best way. How can it be done? In order to live the bodily life well, one must have needful food, and use it properly. One may starve his body in the midst of plenty if he does not take and eat of Heaven's bounty. The mind, the heart, or affectional nature can no more grow without appropriate food than the body can. One of the chief uses of food for the body is to promote the growth of bone, nerve, and muscle for work; food is not to be taken solely for the amusement of the appetite. Food when not followed by work, *i. e.*, exercise, will in time impair the body it was meant to nourish and develop.

Bodily athletes are made by food and work. The mind needs mental food; but it must be digested and assimilated by work, and, when so used, what prodigies men may become! Look out over the ages and see the long line of heroes, grown, all of them, from small beginnings. Are your powers feeble? So were theirs, but they developed them. Are your possibilities unknown? So were theirs, but they grew and expanded them. And you may. As one should get the best and most nourishing food for the body, so of the mind.

Avoid cheap things. Shun slops. Poverty may compel one to live on cheap bodily food, albeit it hinders growth and impairs strength, but surely in this country, and in these days, one need not starve the mind. But get the best. Then use it, work by it, live by it. An ounce of solid truth, well used, is of more worth to you than would be a planet's weight of any knowledge which you do not put into deed, or incorporate into mental fiber.

Avoid mercilessly all second rate, or worse, matter. You will get a new body by and by, but the mind, the soul, the selfhood, lives forever. Therefore, put mainly the best and choicest into it. Do you ask which is best? The world has very many good, but there is only one *best*. Do you inquire which it is? Ask the Covenanters, Puritans, Pilgrims, blessed martyrs, apostles, prophets of all time, what gave them strength for such heroic deeds and hallowed deaths, and there will be but one answer.

Do you know of a book in all the world that you shall wish to pillow your soul on when the body is dying? Very well; that is the one for you to cultivate and feed your mind on now. There is but one such, I repeat, in all the wide world. It is the book that has made, and yet makes, more noble men and women than any or all other books or things combined, the book from whence comes all other excellence. It is the book that can alone make your life and mine a complete success. That book is the Bible. While not neglecting the many other good and valuable books of the world, you should, above all others, read this. Study it. Transmute it into deed. Become obedient to its truths. Follow its directions, and you shall become at length *the perfect man*. It gives and develops power as no other does, and it alone prepares man for the tremendous possibilities of this life, and those of the life that is to come. As a song of life I venture to dedicate this hymn to you young men and to entitle it—

THE BATTLE CRY OF SUCCESS.

Now the Lord hath spoken to me,
May no evil day undo me;
    Lies before me clear and fair,
    Pathway up a mountain stair,
    Sunlight in the upper air.

Many years Thy Whisper moved me,
Many years Thy Right Hand proved me;
    Thou afar didst see to-day;
    All the noontide hidden lay
    In the morning dim and gray.

Many lands and many oceans,
Many peoples in commotions,
    Thou hast shown me as a sign
    That Thy Whisper is divine;
    May Thy purposes be mine!

Evermore by Thee enshrouded,
In the azure sky or clouded,
    Let me follow Thy behest.
    Without hasting, without rest,
    As a star moves toward the west.

Thou my Helmet, Falchion, Leader,
Lord and Saviour, Interceder,
    Both my left hand and my right,
    Fill with javelins of light
    And with ten archangels' might!

The Influence of Young Women.

LADY HENRY SOMERSET, London.
President of the British Woman's Christian Temperance Union.

MISS FRANCES E. WILLARD,
President of the World's Woman's Christian Temperance Union.

IT is within the present province of mankind to develop nature but not to improve on it. All the present deliciousness of fruits or flowers was contained in the original seeds out of which they were developed. Men have added nothing to nature. Now the normal condition of men and women is that of the family. Without one's family, what were all else of life? Without them would life be worth the living? How could there be love, and hope, and ambition, without the family? There might be lust of appetite, of acquisition, of conquest, for mere existence, but how could holy love exist without the family relation? And love is *life*. In the Bible the words are almost interchangeable in meaning.

Now men are ruled by their appetites, and women by their affections, until education has taught them the proper uses of both. As the highest relation is the family, the highest position in that highest relation is given by nature to women, to wit, the care and culture of home and children. She holds in her keeping the happiness and the welfare of the world.

As a rule the first seven years of life determine the future of the child and so of the man. If the home-life is cheap, frivolous, impure, unintelligent, its product will be such. Not only a man, but a man's children, are what his wife will let them, and him, be. If she is socially, naturally, his superior, she can elevate him. But if she is socially inferior to him, her condition fixes his status: for, however good or great a man may be, he is always degraded and humbled in his own sight and in that of the world, when he has to blush on account of or make apologies for his wife.

The young women of to-day will be the matrons of to-morrow, and while they never can make over the young men whom their mothers have made years ago, they can almost wholly determine the character of the next generation, by wisely using their influence with the present one. What kind of associates, what kind of companions, will you choose among men? Fate will not fix it for you, but you must determine it. There are serious vices among men, foul blots on humanity that impair its energies, that bar all upward progress of the race, that are steadily dragging it downward to bestiality and diabolism,—vices that breed crimes, natural, unnatural, and preternatural, by which and from which woman has been and is the silent, greatest sufferer,—shall they be perpetuated? On its answer hangs the destiny of the ages. Shall the vice of the father be fastened on your innocent child through you? That is the problem you are to solve. Over against the world's misery stand the young women of the day with power not merely to assuage it, but to blot it out. Will they do it? Do you ask how? By resolutely refusing to be the medium for its perpetuation. Demand purity of thought, purity of purpose, purity of deed inexorably of the young men with whom you consort. How long would the vice of drink, the filth of tobacco, the delirium of gambling, the leper-seeking of lust, dwell in this world, if the young women in it were to refuse fellowship with any young man tainted by them? Not a generation.

How often one may see on the public thoroughfares, intelligent, refined virtuous young women in company with gentlemen acquaintances who so far forget the honor of the lady's company as to belch forth the smoke and stench of the cigarette and cigar, or the lesser filth of the quid? Would they do it if they knew they should forfeit the lady's favor? No young lady wishes to go through the Golgotha of suffering of the drunkard's wife—yet how few have courage to refuse association with a young man who takes his wine, if he be a man of wealth, or position? No young man of sense would take for a consort one whose impure life would entail nameless sufferings on himself and offspring. Why should not a young lady be equally prudent and exacting? Demand of your gentleman friends both the purity of life and of speech they require of you. Believe me, there is no young man whose acquaintance is worth the having who will not respect and admire you more for refusing to fellowship what he may call his petty weaknesses, than he will do if, for the sake of his company, you quietly ignore vices you would not think of cherishing in yourself. You know and he knows that a woman's social condition, aye, her eternal condition, is determined, not by her wealth, nor by her beauty, but by her moral and mental qualities. Will the eternal balance be less exacting in his case? If not, why do you seek to make it so in this life by smiling on his vices?

The young women of the world must redeem it of its vices, or doom it. Nature—no, he who created nature—has given them an influence that would regenerate the race if they would but use it aright. Nature's great decree is that man shall seek his mate, not the mate the man. If he come unclean of body or of soul shall he find the pure equally as ready as the unclean to welcome him? Shall there be no distinction? Is it not time that the pure young women of the land face toward the future, and demand a noble, virtuous companionship? It will come, but only at their bidding. To have it come, frown down intemperance, the tobacco evil, profanity, impurity of deed and speech, idleness, and dudishness. Insist on the cultivation of mind as well as brawn, of godliness rather than covetousness, of gentleness as well as genteelness, of truth rather than tricks in trade. Have it understood that respect, courtliness, and kindness toward one's own mother and sisters is as great virtue in a young man as vows of love to his sweetheart. Make it known that honor is greater than gold, and that the heart outweighs and outranks the brain.

Woman's Work and Wages.

NELLIE E. BLACKMER, Springfield, Mass.
Head Stenographer King, Richardson & Co.'s Publishing House.

> "I stood up strait and worked
> My veritable work. And as the soul
> Which grows within the child makes the child grow,—
> So life, in deepening with me, deepened all
> The course I took, the work I did."
> —Elizabeth Barrett Browning.

NEVER since "Adam delved and Eve span" has anyone questioned woman's right to work. She has fed and clothed the world, she has given unremittingly of strength of body and of soul; but the wage-earning woman is distinctively a factor of the complex problem of our modern life. Rapidly woman has worked her way into the wage-earning world, with a remarkable facility and power of adaptation entering every industry which does not require the exercise of great physical strength. This is well. The outlook of woman has been widened, her dormant capacities quickened and developed, she has been removed from the humiliating position of a dependent, she is valued as never before; and, as an indirect result, both men and women have come to understand more clearly that the welfare of the human race depends as much upon the position and welfare of woman as upon that of man.

Never yet has any great tidal wave of progress swept up the shore of time without carrying before it something of value that had been builded with patient care, destroying, only that more beautiful and enduring structures might be raised on firmer foundations. This change in the industrial world has taken place so quickly that the times have not kept pace with it. Equilibriums have been disturbed and complicated social problems arisen that will require time and patient thought to adjust. But it is plain that the advantages to woman and to the world at large of this change are inestimable, while the disadvantages may be overcome, not by yielding any of the ground gained, but by a steady pressing forward to a surer footing on heights beyond. Although this change in affairs has brought about evils and difficulties which did not before exist, it has set us free from dangers and difficulties still greater. The strong cords of tradition and custom by which woman was bound have been broken and she is free to do whatever she *can* do. With an unswerving purpose to exalt womanhood and secure its rights in the world of industry, never sacrificing principle nor yet arousing needless antagonism, the stronger helping the weaker, let every self-supporting woman stand in her place, proud to be a help, not a hindrance, a producer as well as a consumer, and glad to take her part in a forward movement involving the welfare of woman and so of the race.

If any working woman to-day feels that her lot is a hard one she may well be thankful she was born no earlier. But little has been written about the common women of the early and middle ages. In every age there has been a class of women highly favored. Born to wealth and the heritage of a noble family, endowed with beauty and that indescribable power called "charm," men have been ready to serve them, to fight for them, and, if need be, die for them. Who has not been thrilled by the stories of the knights "without reproach or fear," who, bidding farewell to the ladies they left protected by castle walls, rode away "redressing human wrongs?" But what proportion of the women of those days, think you, were "ladies," and what proportion the slaves, not the queens, of men?

Up to the opening of the present century there was small place for a woman forced to self-support. In colonial times wages in this country were about what they were in England, and a woman might earn a shilling a week by weeding or possibly two shillings by a week's work in the harvest field.

Domestic servants received about $30 a year, but there was small demand for them. During the first quarter of this century women school teachers were paid $1.00 a week and "boarded 'round," teachers of especial skill receiving as high as $1.25, which was considered great wages for a woman. In those days every one was comparatively poor and both food and clothing coarse and plain. All manufacturing was of the simplest character and done in the homes. The farmer raised the sheep and the farmer's wife and daughters carded and spun the wool and made the garments the family wore. Linen cloth was made at home from the flax raised on the farm. Cotton cloth, being something they could not make themselves, was not used, and they alternately shivered in linen and perspired in woolen, both kinds of cloth being coarse and heavy compared with the machine-made goods of to-day. Coarse shoes were made at home by the men, the women "binding" them, and the women braided from coarse straw the hats then worn.

With the building of the factory and the introduction of the manufacture of cotton cloth, a new era opened for the women of our land. To be sure, the days were unmercifully long and the pay small, but the girls who gladly thronged into the factories from the New England homes were inured to hardship and accustomed to long days of toil without pay. Small wonder they considered it a privilege to work but little harder and to receive in return that magic medium of exchange they had sometimes seen in the hands of their fathers, but rarely in the hands of their mothers, and of which few had ever possessed as much as a dollar. Lucy Larcom's charming book, "A New England Girlhood," describes perfectly the change in the life of the times brought about by the cotton factories. The average wages of the workers were about sixty cents for a day thirteen to fifteen hours long, while the most expert could earn from six to eight dollars a week. But they had good board at the corporation boarding house for $1.50 a week and saved money.

Following the establishment of the cotton mills came the

shoe factories, the paper mills, the straw shops, and, as the country increased rapidly in wealth and industries of various kinds multiplied, women were employed more and more, as female help was more plenty as well as cheaper than male help.

Whenever a new industry or calling has been opened to women the pioneers have had to bear more or less unpopularity and scorn; but they have made the way easy for those who have followed them until it is almost universally conceded that a woman's sphere is wherever she can render efficient service.

The labor reports state that about four hundred kinds of manual labor are now done by women in the United States, and Miss Penny in her encyclopedia of occupations open to women mentions five hundred and thirty-one suitable employments for women in the arts, sciences, trades, professions, agricultural and mechanical pursuits, and these may be increased by subdivision. Statistics show that not less than seven per cent. of the population of the United States are women engaged in gainful occupations.

It is found that the average age of the working woman is twenty-five years and that she begins work at the age of seventeen. The average wage paid to working women in this country is $5.75. The highest average is in Massachusetts, $6.68—the lowest in New Jersey, $5.00. These figures are perilously near the living point, $6.00 a week being the smallest sum on which any girl living in a city can feed and clothe herself respectably. Yet hundreds of women and girls are working for $2.50 or $3.00 a week. Occupations calling for education and some degree of mental work command about the same wages as skill and dexterity in manual labor—from eight to fourteen dollars a week—while positions calling for responsibility, business ability, and experience, yield correspondingly larger wages.

The query is often raised why women receive less pay for their work than men. There are many reasons, the most obvious one perhaps, being, that they are in no position to make terms, self-support being a necessity, and the applicants more numerous than the places. They have here and there combined to keep up wages artificially, but this is a poor makeshift, assisting the few to the detriment of the many. In addition to every limitation that women have to meet they have the limitations of their sex, and to this we must add the resistance of men workers and, until recently, the loss of caste with their own sex. One writer states that the reason women receive less pay than men for the same work is because they are "less self-reliant, less ready to cope with sudden emergencies, and more easily overcome by difficulties." Very likely. Suppose a wise, able man of affairs should be taken from his environments some summer day and placed in charge of a hot kitchen, with a baking in process and a dinner to be prepared. Put a crying child in his arms, and then watch for signs of his superiority. How would he compare with a woman in "self-reliance and the ability to cope with sudden emergencies"? By the changes of the times woman has been placed in a new environment and it is not strange that she does not at once rise to the level of man in what has always been his chosen field.

Years ago it was argued that it would not answer to open the field of labor to women, as they would become so enamored with the pleasure of earning their own living and the independence it would give them, that they would not be willing to marry. While this argument shows slight knowledge of the human heart it suggests one of the greatest of the many advantages that have come to woman through her ability to be self-supporting. The average woman who has mingled with men and women in the working world a few years as a rule has too little sentimentality and too much common sense to marry, merely from fancy, a man who is unworthy of her or unable to support a family; and, being able to support herself, she is relieved of any temptation to marry "for convenience," for a home, for bread. As this tends to fewer marriages but more harmonious ones, and so to the elevation of the race, let us rejoice. A social condition which makes it easy for every woman to take the stand that she will marry no man she cannot love, honor, trust, and live with harmoniously, is an emancipation, the magnitude of which can only be appreciated by comparing it with the varying position of woman from the time she was considered property and bought and sold like cattle down to the present time.

While this change in the social and industrial status of woman is an advantage and thousands of women are now happy in earning a comfortable living for themselves, many helping to support others as well, there is a phase of working life that is anything but hopeful. The revelations made by those who have patiently investigated the condition of the lower class of working women in the large cities—the sewing-women, the cigar-makers, the great army of the unskilled—are appalling. Merely to read of the hardships these women undergo in the awful struggle for a bare existence makes the head swim and the heart fail. The interference of legislation here and there and the strenuous efforts of philanthropists are measures ridiculously insufficient to cope with the flood of poverty, degradation, oppression, and wickedness. These terrible conditions seem to be principally the result of unrestricted emigration and of overcrowding in the large cities. There, where existence is worth the least, the struggle for it is the fiercest.

Under the present system of competition can we blame a starving woman for underbidding her neighbor on work, that she may have the wherewithal to buy bread? Can we blame the manufacturer for buying his labor in the cheapest market? Yes. Better starve than snatch the bread from a starving sister. Better die in poverty than to make money out of the suffering of a fellow creature. But this is high doctrine and few can attain unto it. But what of a social system under which such alternatives are inevitable and which is daily crowding helpless women further down in want and misery in spite of all efforts to help and uplift? It is doomed. How will a change be wrought? Peaceably, we have reason to hope. By force, we have reason to fear. What will it effect? A social condition in which every man or woman willing to work shall have a chance to live.

WOMAN'S WORK AND WAGES.

One obvious lesson to be drawn from a hasty survey of the field of woman's work is that every woman who desires to be self-supporting should aim to attain skill in her chosen work. She should learn to do whatever she has to do as well as it can be done. If in a place where there is no chance for advancement, no opportunity to do better work and to earn more money with the passing years, it will be worth a present sacrifice to place herself where she will have such opportunities. This will take time and strength for those who have drifted into the wrong channel, but it will pay.

For those who can choose their calling and prepare for it the field is wide. Time and money spent in fitting for a congenial and useful occupation is a good investment for every woman who can possibly compass it. The questions every woman seeking employment has to meet are, "What do you know?" "What can you do?" This demand for competency is growing more imperative daily. It is those who *know* and who can *do* who have employment and good pay. The welfare of all demands that every worker shall do the best that is in her, as every step upward leaves a place below to be filled by another and lessens by so much the state of congestion among the unskilled.

Not to every woman is it given to be a preacher or a teacher, not all can organize and plan, but there are numberless humbler tasks that as truly meet the world's need. The less inspiring the work in itself the greater the need of carrying to it the best qualities of the worker. The manner in which some women dignify every kind of work they do is a revelation. What we deem commonplace or menial becomes noble under the touch of their interest and enthusiastic effort. The oft-repeated statement that it necessarily lowers a woman to enter the working world and to toil side by side with men is an unwarrantable assumption and a libel on both men and women. A refined, dignified, gracious woman will carry those qualities with her wherever she goes, while a rude, silly girl will be quite as unrefined and frivolous in the home as in the shop or office. In the business world there is no room for childishness, peevishness, or willfulness, and in the discipline of working life many a woman has learned self-control and a certain consideration for the rights of others she would otherwise have missed.

In order to make her own way a woman needs to have a stout heart. She must not be easily overcome by difficulties nor expect that her path will be smoothed by poetic justice. She must learn to take people and things as they are instead of fretting because they are not as she would like to have them, and if she is wise she will cultivate the habit of looking on the bright side. She must realize that superficial knowledge and hasty, imperfect, slipshod work will not do, that weariness and disgust before the battle is half won will not do, that nothing but application and patient, thorough work will bring her satisfaction or success.

It is to be deprecated that since it has become common for young women to become self-supporting, the greed of gain has so taken hold of some that girls are willing unnecessarily to sacrifice an education for the work that will bring them a few dollars a week pin money, leaving the school for the store, factory, or office. Parents ought to realize, if the girls do not, that for working people the only time to obtain an education is while young, and that two or three extra years spent in acquiring knowledge will broaden the girl's outlook for life and make her a happier and wiser woman. The working girl's life is a crowded one. Many "keep house" in a small way and make most of their own clothing in addition to their daily work of from eight to ten hours. Unless the love of knowledge and the taste for good literature is gained in school there will be little time or desire after working life begins for the pursuit of that culture which has been so well defined as knowing "the best that has been said and thought in the world." With such a taste an active force, no life is barren, no matter how full of monotonous toil. The poorest are rich in the legacies of mind and heart left for mankind by the thinkers and poets of all ages. The pity is these legacies so often go unclaimed, while the toil and the care of life and the *deceitfulness of poverty* narrow the mental and spiritual vision until the worker fails to see that "the life is more than meat and the body than raiment." The habit of church attendance, although kept up with difficulty and at a sacrifice, will serve to keep a door open into the intellectual and spiritual world, and thousands of working women can testify to the uplift received from their weekly glimpse of truths that at once rest and stimulate.

It would be well if every worker could carry into the daily routine the inspiration of these words of Carlyle's:—

"The situation that has not its Duty, its Ideal, was never yet occupied by man. Yes, here in this poor hampered, despicable Actual, wherein thou even now standest, here or nowhere is thy Ideal: work it out therefrom; and working, believe, live, be free. . . . O thou that pinest in the imprisonment of the Actual, and criest bitterly to the gods for a kingdom wherein to rule and create, know this of a truth: the thing thou seekest is already with thee, 'here or nowhere,' couldst thou only see!"

NOTE.—Different phases of this subject are fully treated in the following books:—

Women Wage-Earners, by *Helen Campbell*.
Prisoners of Poverty, by *Helen Campbell*.
Woman's Work in America, by *Annie Nathan Meyer*.
How Women Can Earn Money, by *Victoria Penney*.

The Power of Mother's Influence.

Mrs. SUSAN S. FESSENDEN,
President Woman's Christian Temperance Union, of Massachusetts.

PROFESSOR Drummond, in his lecture on "The Evolution of Motherhood," says, "All the machinery, all the preceding work of nature, is to the end that she may produce a mother. The work itself is one of the most stupendous processes of nature. The mother is the ultimate object of the evolution of the animal kingdom. Nature has never made anything higher."

At last, from the lowest form of life, at the command and according to the law of the Author and Controller of evolution, a mother exists. It yet remains for the world to evolve a higher and still higher type of motherhood. The sweetest, purest, strongest, most unselfish relationship in life is that of mother. God intended that this should be so. To this end is the little infant laid so helpless, the most helpless of all the animal creation, into the arms of a mother, who has gone down into the depths to receive it, and who should rise to the mount of self-purification and self-abnegation that she may promote its prosperity and happiness.

That is a thrilling little story of the mother who was lost upon the mountain. When the snow fell and the fierce winds howled, and the cold penetrated,

> "She stripped her mantle from her breast
> And bared her bosom to the storm,
> While round her babe she wrapped the vest,
> And smiled to think her child was warm."

POWER OF MOTHER'S INFLUENCE.

It is, however, an act that finds its counterpart in kind, differing in degree, in the life of every true mother. The thought of self is eliminated when the interests of "my child" are involved. All the laws of nature are planned in infinite wisdom to strengthen this bond. Because there are exceptions to it, because there are selfish, loveless mothers, is no proof against the law, nor any demonstration against the wisdom of it. There exists no law without exception. Much, however, that appears to be in defiance of this law is only the present incomplete evolution of motherhood, which has as yet, by no means, reached the highest. Mothers and sisters have been greatly hampered in their growth and influence by the condition of subordination in which woman has been held. No character can reach its highest possibilities in a position of subordination. Responsibility, accountability, personality, are discounted and the individual is correspondingly weakened. Before the best influence can be established, the completest character must exist, and that can come only when this vestige of heathenism disappears in church and state. In this way only can God's purpose concerning the womanhood of the world be brought to pass. In whatever other relationship in life woman might or might not find a representative in man, in this he must utterly fail; he can never represent her motherhood. These maternal rights, duties, and obligations she delegates to none. In this, her crown of motherhood, woman stands peculiar, alone. The sweet joy, the strong tie, the unquenchable love, the untiring solicitude that swells with the first consciousness of a new life, and life of one's own life, and ends not in time nor eternity, is such that only experience can reveal, and even experience cannot understand. Awe, reverence, adoration, are emotions not too strong with which to stand in the holy of holies of motherhood. This it is that makes the various Madonnas the most universally, reverently loved of all the works of art. It appeals to every thinking, feeling being.

" A mother is a mother still,
The holiest thing on earth."

POWER OF MOTHER'S INFLUENCE.

The influence of this maternal love re-acts upon the child from the hour of conscious existence. Nature, who has permitted no two leaves to be alike, has given a still greater diversity to human souls. To meet the necessities of this infinite variety, she has given to each a mother. No child has a fair chance in life who fails to be well born and well mothered. An ideal mother is still a thing of the future. A wise appreciation of the good of the race and the influences that tend most rapidly and surely for the uplift of humanity would recognize, as the initial force, the betterment of mothers. The education of the child begins before any conscious forces have been brought to bear upon it.

Through all the ages, the higher virtues have become more and more the vital moving forces in private and public affairs in proportion as the mother element has been respected and utilized. Our country to-day needs just this; it needs mothering; it needs to have the power of love for humanity transcend the love of wealth, or position. Mothers need the largest development, the utmost freedom and dignity, to enable them rightly to meet the demands of creating and educating the race.

Ben Jonson ascribed all his early impressions of religion to his mother's piety. She was a woman of distinguished understanding. Once when some one was asked whether Mrs. Jonson was not vain of her son, the reply was, "She has too much good sense to be vain, but she knows her son's value." How characteristic of motherhood! "She hid all these things in her heart." The world owes much to the early influences on the heart and life of the child. God pity the child who has an ungodly, worldly, frivolous mother! Mothers have special need of the power of the invisible, mighty love of the Divine to shed a softening charm. They need that protecting, all-embracing love that does not forsake its object because of weakness or sin. It is the mother who loves, and trusts, and hopes when all the world condemns. Mother's room, mother's heart, means home to the prodigal. When all other influences fail, this will often suggest the infinite love of God, and bring back the wanderer, worn by passion and the antagonisms of life, to the paths of purity and truth. Timothy was admonished that he should lead an exceptionally pure life because of the pious influence of his "grandmother Lois and his mother Eunice."

Hugh Miller derived from his mother his extraordinary genius for narrative. She possessed imaginative faculties, a creative power of fantasy that, with training and education, would have made her a power in the world of literature, either in poetry or romance. Untutored, these powers led her into the endless vagaries that were so powerful among the unlettered people of her day. Her son, surrounded with this weird atmosphere, early imbibed the uncanny notions, and they powerfully influenced him through life. He suffered paroxysms of terror in childhood. The influence of these early impressions, all his subsequent scientific education and research could not overcome. There is little doubt that eventually his early death was caused by this nervous strain. How important it is that mothers should be educated! Errors can be discovered only by intelligent thought. The mind must be trained to reason, to create ideals, to regulate imagination, to direct and modify emotion; all this can be accomplished only by education. What a shortsighted policy was that which established schools for boys before these opportunities were afforded girls!

Mothers should have piety and education; they should also have strong characters, devoted to some mighty ruling purpose. The pettiness of some women is the bane of their children. Consecrated strength and nobility will mold the character that comes under its influence. What a charming illustration of this power do we find in the Booth family, where all the children followed in the path of self-renunciation so faithfully trodden by the parents.

Mothers should have strong bodies as well as carefully trained minds. To these should be added spiritual force and aspiration, for the influence pre-natal and post-natal is immeasurable, not less on mind and soul than on body. A mother whose waist is compressed, impeding the action of vital organs, cannot have a healthy child; neither can a mother whose mind has been compressed, circumscribed to a round of petty thoughts, be expected to influence her children to intellectual power. Like produces like.

All influence, good or bad, springs from the character and thought. This influence makes its way through an infinite variety of channels. The tone of the voice, the expression of the eye, the pressure of the hand, the unpremeditated act, all make indelible impression on the plastic heart of the youth. Each has its influence on the formation of character. "The world wants men," yes, and women, too. To obtain these, we must have the highest type of mothers. Happy the woman, who, like the mother of the Gracchi, can point to her children and exclaim with joy, "These are my jewels."

Frederick the Great, when he heard of the death of his mother and sister Wilhelmina, exclaimed, "This loss puts the crown on all my sorrows. My spirits have forsaken me. All gayety is buried with the loved ones to whom my heart is bound."

No position in life is superior to the influence of a mother's love. One of earth's noblemen said, "All that I am, all that I have been able to do, I owe to my mother."

There was once a mother whose beautiful, cherished daughter was called in the early days of budding womanhood to the higher service of heaven. In looking over her papers, her mother found these words in her journal, "As I have watched the daily, hourly life of my mother through the years of mingled cloud and sunshine, I feel that I must be true indeed to be worthy of such a mother." Could any music of oratorio be so sweet?

What a proud moment to the mother of James A. Garfield, when, at the pinnacle of earthly honor, his first thought was of the joy his promotion would give that true and faithful heart, and he turned and kissed his mother before addressing himself to the waiting multitude. It was a tribute to the influence that had made his life worthy of honor.

POWER OF MOTHER'S INFLUENCE.

Cowper in his touching address to his mother's picture shows how great a power is exerted in the early years of childhood, and how indelible is the impression of the tender touch of a mother "passed into the skies." Love is indeed a simple fireside thing, whose quiet smile warms earth's poorest hovel to a home, and whose influence radiates from this center to earth's remotest bounds.

Woman's Place in the Business World?

Mrs. FRANK LESLIE,
Proprietor and Manager Frank Leslie Publishing House, New York.

NOT many years ago had this question been propounded to a circle of business men, the answer would have been unanimous in the negative. Within our memory woman had *no* place in the *business world,* and, indeed, seemed, in the opinion of multitudes, to have no sphere of usefulness outside of the kitchen, nursery, and society.

A woman's judgment upon financial matters began and ended with her power of getting her money's worth out of the drygoods merchant, the market man, and the grocer; also, in a good many cases, it was proved in her skill of abstracting money on various sly pretexts from her husband's unwilling pockets.

The husband, adopting the creed of his father, treated his wife just as he did his children, supplying her wants liberally if they seemed to him rational, and denying her wishes with more or less good nature if they seemed to his superior wisdom exaggerated.

After all, the principle is a sound one, that the money getter should be the money keeper and dispenser; it is in the line of justice, and that is the best law of the world in all matters purely worldly, like money earning and money spending.

Perhaps a consciousness of this "eternal fitness" in the matter has been one of the great incentives to woman's wonderful progress in these lines. Her wants have increased tenfold since the days of our meek, domestic grandmothers, and have far outrun any increased facility on the part of our natural protectors, and providers for meeting them. Women saw more and more clearly that to live as they wished and expend as they liked they must have money of their own, and not depend upon the caprice or the capacity of some man's pocketbook.

Besides those who had the choice, there arose more and more prominently into view that great class of women unattached to any man; or, if attached in the sentimental sense of the word, unable to reap any practical or monetary advantages from that attachment; these, too, must live, for even blighted affections do not suffice in lieu of bread and butter.

"Men must work, and women must weep," sings the poet, but unfortunately for woman, her need of weeping does not preclude her need for work, and more and more does that necessity become obvious and pressing.

Woman's first advance into the business world was timid and tentative; she begged humbly to be allowed to do a man's work for half a man's wages, and she received uncomplainingly reproofs and sneers, and criticisms and impositions, that few men would have offered to a fellow man, and few men would have borne or remained under.

But public opinion, that most powerful of "governors" in the great engine that runs our world in this country, began first to murmur, and then to speak aloud, and at last to shout, that this style of things was both ridiculous and unjust, and therefore untenable. Public opinion announced that work should be paid for, not by the sex of employee, but by the value to the employer. If a woman puts on male attire, goes to a counting-room and does the work of a man satisfactorily and steadily, why as soon as her sex is discovered and she puts on feminine garb is she to be cut down a third or a half from her former wages? But an inborn prejudice is very hard to kill, especially in the minds of those who profit by the perpetuity of that prejudice, and all classes of employers, although not all employers in any class, still persist in the mean discrimination of sex in their payments for work equally well done by male and female employees.

A friend of my own, a woman of singularly fine and logical intellect, wrote several articles for a magazine. The correspondence was at first carried on under her initials, and the publishers, supposing her to be a man, made liberal payment for the two papers, at the same time requesting more. Another paper of equal merit in every way was sent with the mention that the writer was a woman. Payment was made in due course, but of just two-thirds the amount paid for each of the previous papers.

But woman's courage and perseverance already have conquered many obstacles to her success, and will in the end conquer all. She has "come to stay" in the business world as surely as in the world of home and of society, where her place has always been conceded.

More than this, the timid employee, underpaid and slighted, although the pioneer of the advancing army, no longer stands alone or unsupported. Women of capital, of position, and of a sublime faith in themselves and their ability, have come to the front, and taken up their position as leaders and commanders. The old sneer and smile have died off the lips of even conservative men, and few will now deny that woman is a power to be considered not only in the world at large, but in the world of business especially. And why not? Most women have keener insight, quicker perceptions, readier resource, and more fertile brains than most men. Women of the class likely to undertake the lead in business are, as a rule, braver than men, that is to say have more faith in themselves, and are less liable to panic.

"Pretty bad times just now, but we shall come out all right in the end," said a business woman to me the other day, and, before the hour was out, a man gloomily remarked, "I see nothing but ruin ahead, and, if it were not for the disgrace, I would end it all to-night."

Perhaps at present this optimistic faculty in woman may make her a little rash, a little headstrong in business enterprises, but this is a fault which will mend itself with experience. Woman is quick to learn, and not too proud to abandon a mistaken course as soon as she perceives her mistake; she is at once more daring and more cautious than man, and hence one of her most important positions in the business world, especially of the future; she can and she will open paths on which men would never have ventured, but will stanchly follow so soon as he is convinced of their safety.

A heavy fieldpiece is very effective when securely planted, but the light cavalry are the guides who will test the ground before the artillery ventures upon the possible morass.

Woman's place in business, do you ask? It is at man's side, as in every other relation in life. Her mission is to bring her delicate perceptions, her quick intuitions, her inherent conscientiousness, into the arena where they have been sadly needed and often wanting. She can lead and she can follow with equal facility; she will set herself and her sex upon a vantage ground they have never yet occupied in this world's history, and she will at once elevate and diversify the monotonous levels and unhealthy swamps of business ways and walks.

Her place is like the place of the air—everywhere, and of vital need to everybody, diffusive, penetrative, universal; never obtrusive, except when unjustly opposed, and then a power which, although soft and intangible to the grasp, can overturn the steam engine, which has always seemed to me a very type of masculinity.

Literary and Professional Women.

Mrs. MARY A. LIVERMORE, Melrose, Mass.

IF the women of the early century, in America, could have looked down the years with prophetic vision, their lonely and unsatisfied souls would have been amazed at the quantity and quality of the literary work of the women of to-day. For American women have attained a phenomenal prominence in literature at the present time, and many of them stand in the front rank as writers of ability. One of the most successful magazine managers declares that "of the fifteen most successful books published in the last two years, eleven were written by women."

Miss Hannah Adams, born in Massachusetts, in 1755, was the precursor and the pioneer of the literary woman of to-day. From her "Autobiography," published in 1832, when she was seventy-seven years old, we are made acquainted with the difficulties that hedged up her path to authorship, which were even more serious than those surmounted by Harriet Martineau, the foremost literary Englishwoman of the last century. In addition to these, she believed so completely in the mental inferiority of women, as announced by men at that time, that she was almost broken down by an abject depreciation of her sex. Her "History of New England," written in the stiff and formal style of the day, is in many of the older libraries—a book which nearly cost her her eyesight, but which yielded her very little in the way of pecuniary compensation.

After Miss Adams, and near the close of the eighteenth century, came Miss Catharine Sedgwick, and Mrs. Lydia H. Sigourney. The former wrote mild novels, illustrative of New England life; the latter was a most prolific versifier, a writer of sketches, of "Letters," of books of travel;—fifty-seven in all, preachy, flowery, garrulous, and sentimental. Both were public favorites, and were widely read. Mrs. Sigourney was called "the Mrs. Hemans of America," and both helped bring in the larger education and the broader life now enjoyed by women.

Lydia Maria Child was unlike either of them. She was endowed with a decided genius for literature and art, but her conscience compelled her to enter the anti-slavery reform at its most unpopular stage, and just at the outset of her career, and public favor was withdrawn from her. Her literary work was of superior quality, and she wrote between thirty-five and forty books and pamphlets through every one of which runs a high moral purpose, as steadily as a trade wind blows.

The entrance of Margaret Fuller into the literary world marked an epoch for woman. With a larger and more thorough educational equipment than any of her predecessors, she aspired to the loftiest ideals, and possessed inexhaustible insight and unflinching moral courage. Her "Woman in the Nineteenth Century" rang out like the blast of a bugle, compelling attention and summoning women to strive for something higher, holier, and better than anything they had yet achieved or attempted. Its effect was immediate, and its influence has extended to our day.

Then came Harriet Beecher Stowe, a genius, a member of a rarely endowed family, who leaped at a bound to world-wide popularity, through her famous anti-slavery novel, "Uncle Tom's Cabin." It achieved a success in America and Europe never before attained by any book,—and it was written by a woman. It entered the anti-slavery lists like an army with banners. It silenced the sneers at "female writers," and gave to women an impulse and a courage they have never lost, and their tendency to literary study and work soon swelled into a passion.

It is not possible, within the limits of this article, even to paragraph worthily the leading literary women who have since appeared. Rose Terry wrote faithful sketches of New England life. Harriet Prescott fairly dazzled her readers with "The Amber Gods," "Azarian," and other brilliant short stories. Elizabeth Stuart Phelps, with passionate out-going of the heart towards women, wrote novels into which she artistically wrought her pity for human pain, her longing for a nobler social life, and her intense demand for justice. Mrs. A. D. T. Whitney wrote sketches of early womanhood, which entranced and stimulated her young readers to the lofty thinking that lies behind noble doing. Louisa M. Alcott brought the whole world of girlhood to her feet by "Little Women," and other stories, published as fast as the steam-worked press could throw them off. Frances Hodgson Burnett captivated the readers of two worlds, as she wrote from both an English and American standpoint. Constance Fenimore Woolson made us acquainted with the social life and physical characteristics of any section of our country where she chose to locate her sketches. Helen Hunt uttered in "Ramona" her passionate protest against a century of national wrong-doing and dishonor.

There is no space to speak of the brilliant writers who are at the front to-day—Margaret Deland, Miss Murfree, Sarah Orne Jewett, Mary Hallock Foote, Amelia E. Barr, Agnes Repplier, Lillie Chace Wyman, Octave Thanet, Olive Thorne Miller, Mary E. Wilkins, and others, each working distinctively in a field of her own.

The great magazines, which publish much of the best literature of the day, have been friendly to women writers from the very first. "Five hundred women have contributed articles to the Century Magazine from its organization under the old name of 'Scribner.' Three hundred women have contributed to Harper's Monthly, fifty-five to Scribner's Magazine, two hundred to the Magazine of Poetry, and from seven to eight hundred to the Ladies' Home Journal, in the nine years of its existence. A year's number of that journal represents the work of about one hundred and forty women. Twenty-two women have contributed to the Forum, and fully two-thirds of the contributors to the New England Magazine are women."

Some of the most successful editors of magazines are women, Mrs. J. C. Croly, Mrs. Frank Leslie, Mrs. Mary Mapes Dodge, Mrs. Ella Farnum Pratt, and the late Mrs. Martha J. Lamb, editor of the Magazine of History, established by herself, being prominent examples. The women editors, and associate editors of journals and newspapers, as also the women journalists of the day are too many to catalogue.

The development of women as poets has kept pace during the last half century, with their evolution as writers of fiction, and a steady gain is perceptible all along the years. Their verses vary as do their novels, in style and excellence. Mr. R. H. Stoddard tells us that "there is more force and originality—in other words, more genius—in the living women poets of America than in all their predecessors. There is a wider range of thought in their verse, and infinitely more art."

Among the women poets of the first half century were Mrs. Frances Sargent Osgood, whose verse was extremely graceful, if somewhat fanciful; the sisters Alice and Phœbe Cary, who sang as the bird sings,

> ———"that, lighting on a twig,
> Feels it give way beneath her, and yet sings,—
> Knowing that she hath wings!"

Mrs. Anne Lynch Botta, the *morale* of whose song was always elevating, and whose thought was deeper and more profound than that of many of her contemporaries; Miss Lucy Larcom, the friend of Whittier, whose early themes were pastoral and domestic, but who, with increasing years, soared to the loftiest heights of aspiration and trust; Mrs. Julia Ward Howe, who, richly endowed with a rare gift of poesy, has achieved earthly immortality with her "Battle Hymn of the Republic," which breathes the most fervent patriotism.

Many of the sonnets of Mrs. Helen Hunt are worthy of a

place beside the best written by Mrs. E. B. Browning. Mrs. Celia Thaxter sings of the sea, and you taste the salt spray, and hear the roar of the waters in a storm, or the rush of the waves up the beach, as you read her poems. Edith M. Thomas delights her readers with the perfect finish of her work, and the subtle beauty that pervades her verses. Louise Chandler Moulton, who is best pleased with minor music, writes exquisitely, if mournfully, of the pathetic sadness that runs through human life, like a warp of black in a woof of white. Others there are, a goodly company of them, like Mrs. James T. Fields, Mrs. Piatt, Edna Dean Proctor, Louise Imogen Guiney, and others for whose names we lack space, who are elevating the general tone of American literature by their perception of the fine details of life and nature, and by visions of beauty which everywhere meet them, which are woven into unaffected and inspiring songs.

The advancement of women in professional life has been less rapid and pronounced than in literature. It was not till the middle of the century, 1849, that a woman was allowed instruction and graduation from a medical college, and not till 1850, that the Woman's Medical College of Pennsylvania was founded. Men physicians and medical schools stoutly opposed the training of women for medical practice, and also their admission to the profession, even when duly qualified. Nevertheless women were so deeply in earnest for medical instruction, that, in 1859, Dr. Elizabeth Blackwell, the first woman who received a diploma from a medical school, and entered the profession, estimated "that about three hundred women had managed to graduate somewhere in medicine." But their instruction was entirely inadequate.

It was absolutely necessary that medical schools should be founded for the education of women, and hospitals established for their clinical training, conducted by women. To this work they bent their energies, and in about a quarter of a century they have established six such hospitals, and founded four women's medical colleges. In the West many medical schools of the highest standing have been opened to them, which are largely co-educational. Then came the struggle on the part of women physicians to obtain official recognition in the profession. It was a prolonged and acrimonious crusade against intolerance and medical bigotry. In 1872, Dr. Mary Putnam, of New York, returned from France with a medical diploma from the Paris École de Médecine,—the first ever granted to an American woman. She was speedily admitted to the Medical Society of New York without discussion — and the question of the "official recognition" of women physicians was settled.

More than twenty women are now serving as physicians in insane asylums. The census of 1880 records about 2,500 women practitioners in the United States. In the census for 1890, this number will certainly be much increased. "What women have learned in medicine," says Dr. Mary Putnam-Jacobi, "they have in the main taught themselves. And it is fair to claim that, when they have taught themselves so much, when they have secured the confidence of so many thousand sick persons, in spite of all opposition; when such numbers have been able to establish reputable and lucrative practice,—to do all this shows an unexpected amount of ability and medical fitness on the part of women."

The struggle of women to obtain legal instruction, and admission to the profession of law, has been equally tedious and bitter. The common law of England becoming the law of America, its women have been regarded as ineligible to admission to the bar, until within the last quarter of a century. There was one exception. This was the case of Margaret Brent of Maryland, the kinswoman of the first governor, Leonard Calvert, who died in 1647, leaving Mistress Brent as his sole executrix, and as his successor as attorney for the second Lord Baltimore. The records show that "she not only frequently appeared in court as his lordship's attorney, but also as attorney for her brother, Captain Giles Brent, prosecuting and defending causes for him. Also as executrix of Leonard Calvert's estate, and in regard to her personal affairs, nor is there any record of any objection being made to her practicing as attorney on account of her sex."

The first woman since those days to ask for and obtain admission to the bar of this country, was Mrs. Arabella A. Mansfield of Mount Pleasant, Iowa, in 1869. Her husband was admitted at the same time.

Mrs. Myra Bradwell of Chicago, who had studied law under the instruction of her husband, Judge J. B. Bradwell, was the next to apply for license to practice law. But the Supreme Court of Illinois, in 1869, refused her application, on the ground that she was a woman. She carried her case to the Surpeme Court of the United States, but, in 1873, it affirmed the judgment of the state court. Mrs. Bradwell never renewed her application for a license, although the Legislature of Illinois enacted that "No person shall be precluded or debarred from any occupation, profession, or employment (except military), on account of sex." She founded the *Chicago Legal News*, which she edited, and in 1890 the Supreme Court of Illinois, on its own motion, granted to Mrs. Bradwell "a license as an attorney and counselor at law."

The next court case was that of Mrs. Belva A. Lockwood, of Washington, D. C., who graduated from the law school of the National University in 1873, and was admitted to practice in the Supreme Court of the District of Columbia. She sought admission to the Court of Claims, with a client, and also to the Supreme Court of the United States, and was denied admission to both. She immediately took steps to secure the passage of a statute by Congress, which would give her admission to these courts, drafting the bill herself, and in two years had the satisfaction of seeing it enacted, and of obtaining admission to the courts that had refused her. Since then ten other women lawyers have been admitted to practice in the highest court of the land.

Thus, step by step, women have made their way into the legal profession, and one by one, the law schools have been opened to them. The number of women lawyers in the country is estimated at one hundred and fifty. In different parts of the country, women have acted as "police judges, justices of the peace, grand and petit jurors, federal and state court clerks and deputy clerks, official stenographers and reporters for federal and state courts, special examiners or referees, court appraisers, court record writers, notaries public, legislative clerks, deputy constables, examiners in chancery, and examiners of applicants for admission to the bar, and state and federal court commissioners, when many cases have been tried before them."

The admission of women to the theological schools and to the ministry is still hotly contested, and they have made less advance in this profession than in the others. In the West, the theological schools of the Unitarian and Universalist denominations admit women, and grant them ordination when they graduate.

The theological school of St. Lawrence University, Canton, N. Y., is open to women, and has graduated many. Its first woman graduate was Rev. Olympia Brown Willis, who was previously graduated from Mt. Holyoke Seminary, and from Antioch College, in the days when Horace Mann was president. Mrs. Willis was the second woman minister in the United States.

The Methodist denomination admits women to its theological schools, but denies them ordination. The Quakers, or "Friends," as they prefer to be called, have always given women equal freedom to preach with men. There are about three hundred and fifty women preachers among the Friends at the present time, in our country. The Free-will Baptists also admit women to the ministry. There are indications that the orthodox Congregationalists are moving towards the admission of women to the clerical ranks. More than forty years ago, Rev. Antoinette Brown, a graduate of Oberlin, was ordained to Congregationalist ministry, by a council called for that purpose. Rev. Louise L. Baker, of Nantucket, Mass., was ordained by the deacons of her church, two of the four deacons being women. Later, Rev. Mary Moreland, of Illinois, and Rev. Amelia A. Frost, of Massachusetts, have been ordained and installed by a ministerial

LITERARY AND PROFESSIONAL WOMEN.

council, according to the established usages of the Congregationalist church.

Rev. Augusta J. Chapin, now of Omaha, Neb., who was associated with Rev. Dr. Barrows in the management of the "Parliament of Religions," which was held in Chicago during the World's Fair, is the only woman minister of America who has received the degree of D.D. It was worthily bestowed. A graduate of a Michigan college, she was ordained to the ministry of the Universalist church more than thirty years ago, has been a settled minister ever since, receiving meanwhile, for work done, the degrees of A.M., Ph.D., and now of D.D. About fifty women have been ordained in the Universalist church, and twenty more or less in the Unitarian church.

Women have an especial fitness for the work of the ministry and the call for their service is most pressing. They constitute three-fifths of the membership of the Christian church to-day, and occupy many pulpits as lay preachers, or evangelists, where they are welcomed by resident pastors. The world has already lost much by the enforced exclusion of women from the work of the church, and it is beginning to comprehend this and to demand that they shall, in the clerical profession, as in others, be given an equal chance with men.

True Value of Character.

Prof. FRANK SMALLEY, Ph.D., Syracuse University, New York.

IF we were required to name four men who should represent both ancient and modern times and different nationalities, men whose lives and character are now a part of the history and heritage of the race, whom could we name that would better fulfill these conditions, and at the same time illustrate the theme of this chapter, than Lincoln and Gladstone, Seneca, the Roman philosopher, and Solon, the Athenian legislator? Mr. Gladstone's ability as a wise statesman may be passed over, and he may stand here as a type of intellectual brilliancy. No person who is acquainted with the writings of the great premier, and has read his speeches, will question the estimate that classes him among the greatest intellects of his generation. This will indeed contribute to his fame, but can anyone doubt that it is an insignificant factor in comparison with the spotless character that will be a potent inspiration to young men to the end of time?

Seneca, philosopher, also tutor and counselor of Nero in the early and only honorable part of the reign of that prince, was one of the wealthiest men of his day. He, too, was a man of large intellect, and, being imbued with the elevated sentiments of the Stoic morality, he has embodied many of these in permanent literary form. Seneca, however, is not remembered for his wealth, but for the high ideal of character manifest in his literary productions, and exemplified in his life. The former was an incident, and so considered by him; the latter has immortalized him. Abraham Lincoln is a type of the noblest manhood in the highest station attainable to man. In him is conspicuously apparent the compatibility of political supremacy with the most unimpeachable integrity. Lincoln accomplished a great work. He was a man of wonderfully clear vision, of the highest qualities of statesmanship, of great wisdom in plan and action. But is it chiefly because of that work and of these qualities that he will always be held in affectionate remembrance by this nation? No. It is because he was "honest old Abe," and was always actuated by motives of the highest honor, that his memory will be a blessing, and a benediction to posterity.

The Roman poet may lament in his plaint that men thrive by crime while integrity shivers with cold and goes hungry, but, if his philosophy would but penetrate a little more deeply, he might find a solution of his difficulty like that found by the Hebrew poet when, in similar strain, he avers and deprecates the prosperity of the ungodly. Nor need we go so far as he, to consider the end of man; for a true estimate of the popular respect for honor and truth will convince one that it is not yet time to despair of the human race. Down in his heart every man admires honesty and candor and condemns guile and insincerity. The popular notion of the sterling honesty of a certain man prominent to-day in public life is a more effective cause of his advancement than all the arts of the politicians, and has once and again baffled the efforts of wily opponents in his own party to keep him in obscurity. It pays even to have a reputation for honor, but it pays far better to have the article itself, for in the end men generally find their true level. "Honesty is the best policy."

Six hundred years before the Christian era, lived and labored Solon, the wise and popular lawgiver of Greece. His popularity was not that of a temporizing demagogue. It rested on the considerate judgment of the better classes which silenced selfish dissatisfaction, and it became so great that his fellow citizens willingly took an oath to abide by his laws; so much did they confide in his wisdom and motives. But his real greatness did not appear so clearly when he was basking in the sun of popular favor, as when, in old age, he staked his life on his character in opposing the arts of a tyrant, then incipient, later fully developed. His constancy, courage, and patriotism neither favor could enhance, nor tyranny abate.

Four men have now passed in review, men noted respectively for great talent, large wealth, high position, and public favor. It is clear that it was not this distinction that was the cause of their renown, but something beneath it all without which all these would have been of trifling value. It was in fact the talent of character, the wealth, elevation, and stability of character, whose natural effect has been to render these names illustrious and enshrine them in the hearts of men.

An idea of the proper estimate of character is thus obtained. It may be said to be measured by candor and honor, integrity and conscientious devotion to duty, and it may be defined as the one thing about us that abides; as personal identity; *who* we are, as well as what we are; the moral status, and of much greater importance than the social status, a talented mind, or a gifted person.

Character is a coin that passes current and at par value in all countries. It is like a gold monetary standard whose value is universally recognized. Posterity estimates men not so much by what they did as by what they were. It honors and reveres those who, under severe strain, have maintained their integrity, whose devotion to principle is their legacy to man, and their highest claim to perpetuity of fame. It holds in lasting contempt those who have betrayed their country, have taken the bribe, or have resorted to unscrupulous methods for party or personal advantage; in a word, men devoid of principle.

It must not be inferred from what has been said, that wealth, talent, and popular regard are not desirable. They are indeed desirable, and are often of great service, but they are of secondary importance. The ancient Stoics made a distinction of relative values that is worthy of a modern philosophy. Their conception of virtue quite coincides with the estimate of character herein presented. As its elements they named justice, temperance, courage, and prudence, whose union in the same individual constitutes the sage — the type of perfect character. Wealth and power, beauty and health, popularity and fame, can neither add to manhood nor detract from it, and were therefore esteemed as matters of indifference. This is a philosophic distinction that accords with a common sense distinction, although one need not go the whole length with the Stoics and claim absolute perfection for the man of honor and of character.

But let the mind return from these reflections to a further brief study of the men whose names have been mentioned. Was it easy and natural for them to be what they were? Were they subject to no temptations? Did it cost no struggle to incorporate into their lives that which shall abide, and which constitutes them models of integrity and true manhood? We are very prone to idealize our heroes and to forget that they were human like ourselves, and subject to like passions. The world is full of men of the grandest endowments who fail because they lack the needful character. Were it not for this, many of them in due time would take their places in our list of heroes.

To answer the questions proposed above, it must be affirmed that temptations are peculiarly severe to those who in some respects excel their fellows. It is a shrewd saying of one of the seven wise men of Greece that "the possession of power will bring out the man"; and power here may have a broad application. For a brief illustration, take first its most obvious application. Nero was a wise ruler for five years; Domitian was a model emperor for a brief period after his accession; Caligula gave promise of bringing great relief to a people oppressed by the morose tyranny of his predecessor. But in each case the consciousness of almost unrestricted power and of full opportunity, without the conserving grace of high motive and patriotic purpose, resulted in a rapid downward career and ultimate ruin. High station demands peculiar stability of character.

TRUE VALUE OF CHARACTER.

But to make a broader application of the aphorism of the sage quoted above, and to make still clearer the true value of character from historical illustration, set opposite the names of the four men who were proposed as its worthy exponents, those of other men similarly gifted or favored, but of quite different character. And it might add interest to the contrast, and render clearer the lesson of the illustration, if, antithetic to each, another of the same nationality were named. Who could then be more fittingly selected than Bacon the Englishman, for intellectual brilliancy, Crassus the Roman, for affluence, Aaron Burr the American, for high station, and Themistocles the Athenian, for popular favor?

Why does not the talented Bacon shine by the side of the "grand old man" of these later days? Why must he forever occupy a lower pedestal? The answer may be found in the historical stamp that he bears and must ever bear. The characterization of Pope that is inseparably connected with his name will bear evidence to the latest generation of the fatal defect in his character.

> "If parts allure thee, see how Bacon shined,
> The wisest, brightest, meanest of mankind."

Would any discreet young man ask for the nobility of Bacon's intellect if it must be accompanied with the curse of his character? If wealth constituted character as it does create social respectability, the Roman Dives and usurer would rank with the philosopher Seneca, and a nearly contemporaneous barber would outrank even him. But the wisdom and stability of the Roman sage, the beauty and moral elevation of whose sentiments are worthy to be compared with the precepts of the great letter writer of the New Testament, give him unquestioned claim to an honorable immortality, while the vulgar triumvir is remembered only for his money, his joint usurpation of power, and his unsuccessful generalship.

If character were estimated by political preferment, Aaron Burr would rank next to the highest, whereas such good qualities as he did possess are powerless to save him from perpetual dishonor, and are easily forgotten in disgust at his baseness. If popular favor were the patent of this true nobility, Themistocles, immediately after the battle of Salamis, would be a famous exponent, but instability and insincerity wrought his ruin in disgraceful but merited exile. Who would venture now to name him in the same breath with his fellow countryman Solon, or Burr with Lincoln, Crassus with Seneca, Bacon with Gladstone? And the reason for this just verdict of the popular jury is clearly manifest.

The tests of prosperity are perhaps even more severe than those of adversity. Both are valuable; both operate to effect an equitable adjustment, howsoever fortuitous circumstances may have misplaced men in the shaking of the lots. The assurance, however, is gratifying, that although genius may be the gift of the favored, integrity is never exclusive and is denied to none, and while few acquire wealth or attain distinction, a spotless character — more royal than any endowment or distinction — is the privilege of all.

Reputation is not Character.

Prof. N. L. ANDREWS, LL.D., Dean of Colgate University.

WHAT is reputation? Etymology answers that it is an estimate, a repeated and so an established judgment. As computation gives arithmetical values, so reputation is an estimate of human values.

The word character is even more luminous in suggestion. It signified first a graving-tool for marking upon stone or metal. Next it was a mark thus made, then a symbolic or alphabetic sign, and again some distinguishing feature of an object. Most naturally, then, it has come to denote that combination of qualities and traits, both intellectual and moral, which marks a personality. Who has impressed them upon us? First of all, our ancestors. No one may deny the effect of heredity. There is a race-character, and a family-character. "If you wish to reform a man, begin with his grandfather." Environment, also, is potent. By conduct, by speech, even by look or by gesture, the people with whom we associate impress us continually. But let us not exaggerate these hereditary and external forces. The sharpest graving-tool, most constantly in use, most efficient to form character, is in our own hands.

What is attributed to us makes our reputation; what we are, constitutes our character. Is not the latter obviously more important? Yet reputation has more votaries. Witness on every hand the straining to gain public attention and to make a name. But men cannot escape the world's daily testings. On some wall or other is ever appearing the handwriting, "Thou art weighed in the balances, and art found wanting." Many are the true and good, who often, without public notice, endure life's tests. But how frequently in public relations, in business, and in society, reputations fall like trees before the blast. Usually character failed long before. The stock of the tree was decayed within. Any moral standing, and any estimation for ability, untrue to fact, are disappointing.

Let us suppose that one's character is overrated. An adventitious reputation, due to happy accident, or the favor of unwise friends, is singularly insecure. Socrates illustrated this by supposing an incompetent man desirous to be reputed a flute player. He purchases a beautiful instrument, and procures persons to praise his skill. But what a calamity befalls him if a good judge of such music invites him to play! His only safety, and that a ridiculous one, is in declining. And if one has not the kind of ability that answers to his reputation, his capacity in any other line is likely to be distrusted, and so an overrated man may become underrated.

A thoughtful preacher once said to some college students, "What belongs to a man will come to him." Most of them challenged the proposition, but not a few have lived to see in it a large measure of truth. Given rightly directed effort, and good work is sure of recognition. Without effort, nothing belongs to us. Marked efficiency in any line needs no self-blown trumpet to proclaim it. Successful men have earned success. If a great business passes to a second generation without the training which adapts them to maintain it, prosperity is rarely continued. Our only safe rule of self-judgment, with all allowance for exceptions, is that men get what is due them. It is a sorry sight when one is found complaining that he is not appreciated. The trouble probably is that he is not taken at his own estimate, but measured at his real value. In fact, he is appreciated. Let us leave it to an Iago to say that "reputation is an idle and most false imposition; oft got without merit, and lost without deserving." Believe rather that the estimate of our fellows is usually just.

Reputation has undue emphasis ever as the reward of virtue. Plato marvelously portrays two opposite characters, the one completely just, and the other completely unjust, but each esteemed the contrary, and so receiving rewards exactly transposed. Which would one rather be? He insists that the good man thus misjudged is better off than the bad man enjoying the social advantages of a supposed virtue. His goodness is an internal harmony, preferable to every external benefit. Surely the consciousness of moral integrity is a fountain of abiding self-respect. Fortunately for human weakness, actual life does not apply a test so severe. Misconception and passion may inflict temporary loss of popularity, but, in the end, reputation vindicates character. Not desire for a great name, but self-respect, fidelity to principle, and loyalty to duty most need cultivation. A gentleman giving his idea of dress said that he would have the best goods nearest his person; that if any must be coarser and cheaper, it should be his outer garments. So self-respect, and the respect of those nearest to us, should stand first. A reputation in keeping with these is an added but secondary good. The thing of prime consequence is what a man is to himself, for he cannot escape his own company.

Moral worth will pretty surely be made manifest, and reputation correspond some day to character. Not simply in a future life, but usually in this, "There is nothing covered that shall not be revealed, and hid that shall not be known." In such disclosures that startle society, how painful the contrast between what men have seemed to be and what it is now found they are! Those who have been nearest to them are not always so much surprised, for some slight indication of real character has already impaired confidence. Morally sound men and women of experience often feel the character of others in subtle, indefinable ways. Quite commonly it impresses its unmistakable marks upon the countenance.

The wise man will desire the reputation which comes without the seeking. Let the methods of architects instruct us. The old-time builder was likely to decide the exterior form of a house, and then to divide the space within as conveniently as this general shape permitted. The architect of to-day sits

REPUTATION IS NOT CHARACTER.

down with the family for whom the house is to be built, and studies internal convenience and comfort. This done, he conforms the exterior of the house to its inner plan. Such is the true relation of character and reputation. We have seen children blowing soap-bubbles, and have noticed how likely they are to collapse, if one blows too hard. Apart from reality, "the bubble reputation" is unsubstantial and transient. The man of genius, ability, honest attainments, and sterling character need not concern himself about his name. He will be content to think with old Richard Bentley that "no man was ever written out of reputation but by himself."

Broken Promises.

Prof. JOSEPH H. CHICKERING, A.M., University of Vermont, Burlington.

"WHAT accounts," said one wise man to another, "for the lack of integrity in the social, political, and business life of our time?" "The failure," was the reply, "rightly to estimate the value of one's word; the popular belief that people do not mean what they say, or only half mean it. If anything is worse," he added, "than the way in which promises are broken, it is the way in which they are made, obligations being readily assumed by those who must know they can never discharge them."

This conversation set me to thinking on the causes which had brought about this condition of affairs. In thought, I followed the child from his earliest education in the home and the school to his entrance upon the active duties of life. I seemed to hear the parent threatening a punishment that is never inflicted; the teacher promising a reward that is never bestowed; the employer holding out a hope of advancement that is never realized. And then I saw how the child, putting upon a promise the same value that he sees his superiors put upon it, is soon copying their example. "I will surely," he says, "be back by five o'clock;" "I will, without fail, learn my lesson for to-morrow;" "I will not leave the office until it has been thoroughly swept." Promises thus readily made are as readily broken. The next step, from matters of little to those of large importance, is a very easy one. The young man borrows money, engaging to pay it at a certain time; the promise is forgotten, and the day passes by. He pledges himself to provide for a destitute family; something takes his attention, and the needy are neglected. He makes a marriage engagement very hastily and inconsiderately, sees some one else he likes better, and throws his promise to the winds. The process of moral decay is a simple one. The man is not overpowered in a moment by a sudden temptation; the habit has grown with his years, until it has become a part of his very being. No obligation now has binding authority. He breaks faith with himself, with his fellow men, with his Maker—for he takes upon himself the most solemn vows one can take, with little idea of their real meaning and little conception of the sin of violating them.

I have not, I am sure, drawn a fancy picture; I have simply set forth a state of affairs that is causing the deepest anxiety to all lovers of their kind, to those—and, thank God, they are many—to whom loyalty to their assumed or implied obligations to the family, to society, and to the church, is a matter, not of convenience, but of principle and duty.

If, now, it be asked, what is the remedy, at least two distinct answers present themselves. The first concerns itself with the individual, with you and with me. Suppose every man, woman, and child, whose eye meets these lines should take as his motto that adopted by a business man of large experience and success: "Make few promises, but keep those you have made, at all hazards." What a difference it would make in the relations of parent and child, of teacher and scholar, of master and servant. The merchant would no longer be in doubt whether the note would be paid the day it was due; the judge would not fear that the jury would return any but a true and righteous verdict; the clergyman would not wonder whether his church members would fulfill the solemn obligations they had assumed. The dawn of a new day of confidence and hope would surely be near.

The second remedy, and the only other one I shall mention, will be found in holding up and emphasizing, in all possible ways, illustrious examples of the virtue in question. Leonidas and his three hundred at the pass, Horatius and his companions at the bridge, Casabianca alone on the deck, are figures as interesting as familiar, and will never be outgrown or forgotten. But we need not go back to ancient days, or fly to foreign shores; our own time and our own country furnish them in abundance. Where can we find a better example, in political life, of loyal devotion than in Charles Sumner, who, having once espoused the cause of the slave, never deserted it to the end of his long and arduous life, bearing obloquy, misrepresentation, even personal violence, without a murmur of regret? In a less conspicuous position, whose record is brighter than that of John B. Gough, the apostle of temperance, who, having taken the pledge, fought a long, unwearying struggle against the power of this habit in himself, and died with words of good counsel on his lips? In military life, who has a better title to fame than the great leader in our civil war, who declaring that he would "fight it out on that line, if it took all summer," kept his promise and saved his country?

But there are examples nearer home. Many a neighborhood, many a family, has its own hero, unknown to fame, but with record on high. Let me tell you of one.

In the study of a friend there hangs, just over his desk, a pen-and-ink sketch that has always excited my interest. Only lately has he told me the story. The picture represents a boy, perhaps a dozen years old, struggling in the midst of a swollen torrent, to reach the opposite shore. The result of his effort seems doubtful, and the words underneath, "Faithful unto death," increase our apprehensions. It seems that, many years ago, my friend, then a young man, was lying sick with a fever. His condition was critical. The doctor needed to be with him every moment; but there were too many sick in the village to make this possible. A distant relative of my friend, a lad of thirteen, was staying in the house, and, as the physician left to make another visit, he called the boy to him and said, "If at midnight there seems any change in Harry's condition, I shall expect you to let me know. I shall be at my office by that hour, and, if there is need, I will return here at once. Can I depend upon you for this service?" "Yes, sir, you can," was the simple reply. Midnight came, and the need was urgent. The boy ran a few rods down the road, only to find that the bridge, at the other end of which stood the doctor's house, was gone. In its place, an angry flood was sweeping everything before it. But he did not hesitate; he was sturdy and strong, and the life of another was hanging in the balance. Plunging in, he battled long and manfully to reach the other side. At last he gained the bank. The doctor was summoned, and, by help of a bridge half a mile down the stream, crossed in safety, and, in all probability, saved the life of my friend. But alas for the boy, so brave and devoted! The exposure was too severe, and he survived it but a few months. He had kept his word, he had saved the life of another at the cost of his own. He had fought and overcome. In that family, his name is a household word, held in lasting remembrance, an inspiration to lofty deeds and self-sacrificing devotion.

It may not be ours to render any such service, to attain any such distinction; but we may each, in his own place, however humble that may be, do something to make social intercourse truer and better, something to make faithlessness appear in its genuine deformity, something to deserve the blessing promised to him that "sweareth to his own hurt and changeth not."

The Beauties of Simplicity.

Rev. CARTER JAY GREENWOOD, A.M., Iowa Falls, Iowa.

BEAUTY and simplicity are not incongruous terms. The most beautiful things are not necessarily complex; neither does it follow that ugliness should accompany simplicity.

An apple blossom is a simple flower, and yet it is beautiful in design and color. And, as Beecher says, "An apple tree puts to shame all the men and women that have attempted to dress since the world began." Solomon "in all his glory" was outrivaled by a common lily of the field. And yet, the lily in its modesty and artlessness is the very personification of simplicity. Nature has a fashion of constructing the most beautiful things from the simplest elements. She gathers up refuse animal and vegetable matter and it comes forth reanimated in other forms of life. Out of the calcareous rocks that the builders have rejected she rears domed cathedrals frosted with stalactites and paved with stalagmites. From swamp and stagnant pool she snatches the liquid putrefaction, and distills it into crystal dewdrops. Into her wonder-working looms she thrusts her old and worn-out garments, and, behold, there come forth new fabrics of finest texture and softest colors. With deft fingers and the most consummate skill and tact she blends, softens, subdues, and harmonizes, everywhere avoiding glare and gaudiness. From snow-capped mountain to dew-decked violet, Nature has emphasized the fact that beauty of the highest order is the child of simplicity.

As Nature is the expression of God's thoughts, so Art is the expression of the thoughts of man. The more closely Art patterns after Nature in simplicity of design, the more beautiful will be her creations. Nature abhors affectation. When Cicero

THE BEAUTIES OF SIMPLICITY.

inquired of the oracle at Delphi what course of study he should pursue, the answer was, "Follow Nature." We should all do well to take the advice of the oracle. Our actions are the most beautiful, not when the most eccentric, but when the most natural. "We are never rendered so ridiculous by qualities which we have, as by those which we aim at," says the French proverb. If we would acquire beauty of style in speech and composition we should use simple language. The hymns, "My Country, 'tis of Thee," "Home, Sweet Home," and "Nearer, My God, to Thee," are very simple in musical construction, but the beauty of these old-time melodies thrills us when we weary of the classics by the great masters. As models for constant study and contemplation, one prefers the less obtrusive tints of Titian to the glaring colors of Rubens. The most beautiful queens of earth have not figured in courts and palaces. The Man of Nazareth—the most beautiful character in human history—was simplicity *par excellence.*

It might be a wise provision to establish in every educational institution a chair for cultivating the beauties of simplicity. We should seek to be adorned with those graces imparted by culture rather than by the clothes made by the tailor. It was a magnanimous act on the part of that wealthy girl graduate who induced her companions to join with her in appearing on the platform clad in plain calico gowns in order to place a poor classmate on an equality with themselves. If the college gown is a means by which the beauty of simplicity is sacrificed for show, then it should be abolished. In line with this suggestion Beecher furnishes these pertinent words: "A tallow candle does not become wax by being put in a golden candlestick. If there is no difference between you and other people, except that you wear drab and they wear broadcloth, then there is no difference." Strive not only to be simply beautiful in every word and act, but endeavor to be beautifully simple, which is the most difficult art.

The Value of Pleasing Manners.

WILLIAM C. KING, Springfield, Mass.

A PERSON'S manners generally indicate his character. They are an index of his tastes, his feelings, his temper, and reveal the kind of company he has been accustomed to keep.

There is a kind of conventional manner, a superficial veneer, a "society cloak," used by some people on special occasions which is of but little importance, of no practical value, and as transparent as it is worthless.

Artificial politeness is an attempt to deceive, an effort to make others believe that we are what we are not; while true politeness is the outward expression of the natural character, the external signs of the internal being. Thus a beautiful character reflects a beautiful manner.

There is a vast difference between "society customs" and genuine good manners. The former is a bold but fruitless attempt to counterfeit a noble virtue, while the latter is the natural expression of a heart filled with honest intentions.

True politeness must be born of sincerity. It must be the response of the heart, otherwise it makes no lasting impression, for no amount of "posture" and "surface polish" can be substituted for honesty and truthfulness.

The genius of man may for a time hide many defects, but the natural character cannot long be hidden from view; the real individual is bound sooner or later to come to the surface, revealing his imperfections, natural tendencies, and personal characteristics.

Good manners are developed through a spirit imbued with

unselfishness, kindness, justness, and generosity. A person possessed of these qualities will be found gentle and polite. Good manners should be essential factors in our education, and cannot be too strongly emphasized when we realize that they are but the outward expression of inward virtues, and like the hands of a watch indicate that the machinery within is perfect and true. A noble and winning daily bearing is the outgrowth of goodness, sincerity, and refinement, and is the fruit of a practical application of the golden rule, the crowning perfection of a noble character.

Among the qualities which contribute to worldly success, true politeness takes first rank. It is said of A. T. Stewart, the merchant prince of New York, that he owed his success largely to his genial bearing and graceful manners.

History is crowded with examples illustrating that in literature it is the delicate, indefinable charm of style, more than thought, that immortalizes the work. So in the business world it is the bearing of a man towards his fellow men, that often, more than any other circumstance, promotes or obstructs his advancement and success in life.

The address and manner of a man generally determine his success or failure. How often we are compelled to do business with a person whose very presence is repulsive; he appears to be utterly void of noble, manly qualities, while, on the other hand, we come into contact with those whose personality is like the pleasant rays of a June sun, warming and gentle.

The friendship of a man of genial character is courted and sought, while the one who is cold and gruff is shunned or his presence endured no longer than is absolutely necessary. We are all creatures of conditions and circumstances, and dependent more or less upon each other in all the walks of life.

In this day and age, under the brisk competition for patronage in every department of human activity, the expression of the nobler qualities of mind and heart counts much for capital in trade.

The person whose heart and life are right will exhibit those manly, winning qualities so universally admired, and will secure the cordial approbation, the general good will, and hearty support of friend and stranger. There is no field of labor where good manners are out of place, no condition of even a depraved nature which is not influenced more or less by the exercise of a kind heart and genial air. Even the brute recognizes and shows an appreciation of kindness. These qualities of mind and heart, cultivated and woven into the fabric from daily life, will yield a harvest of rich fruitage.

Pleasing manners constitute one of the golden keys which turn the bolts of the door leading to success and happiness.

The great motive power of our conduct is the heart; it is the fountain head of all action. This truth is illustrated by the calm words of Sir Walter Raleigh, as he was led to the block and the executioner was trying to adjust his head to a comfortable position: "'Tis more important that my heart be right than my head." The heart is the great reservoir from whence flow the issues of life. When the heart is right the life will be right, and success in all of its completeness will be the fruit.

The Worth of Modesty.

Rev. G. R. Hewitt, B.D.

NOTHING is more worthy of cultivation than simple and unpretending manners. Hardly anything else is so attractive. Modest behavior wins friends, while pomposity and pretension drive them off. Modesty is not a weakness, though many young men seem to think so. On the contrary, it is perfectly compatible with strength, and as a matter of fact is generally found in men of uncommon ability and force of character.

Modesty is not self-disparagement, but rather the appraising ourselves at our true value. The derivation of the word is instructive. It comes to us from the Latin, and is derived from *modus*, a measure, and so comes to mean the measuring faculty. Modesty, therefore, means not underestimating ourselves, but correctly estimating ourselves. It avoids self-disparagement on the one hand, and on the other it prevents us from thinking "more highly of ourselves than we ought to think."

Modesty is not to be confounded with diffidence or bashfulness. Diffidence is self-distrust. The diffident man is either ignorant of his powers, or distrustful of them, and so shrinks from undertaking what he may be perfectly competent to perform. The modest man is neither ignorant nor distrustful of his powers, but he does not vaunt himself because of them, and is not puffed up. Sir Isaac Newton solved one or two problems that no other human intellect could solve, but, as Ruskin says, he did not on that account expect all men to fall down and worship him. He was modest withal and likened himself to a boy

THE WORTH OF MODESTY.

who had picked up a few pebbles on the beach, while the great ocean of truth lay undiscovered before him.

Genuine merit is always modest. The truly great man is ever the most humble. He is aware that for everything he can do there are a hundred things he cannot do; that for everything he knows there are a thousand he does not know; and that if he is possessed of some good qualities, there are others he lacks. Ignorance alone is vain and boastful. It is the empty ear of grain that proudly holds up its head; when filled, it bends modestly downward.

The great charm of all power is modesty. The pomposity of many people is an attempt to impose upon the world by passing for more than they are worth. It is due to fear that they will receive no more attention than their scanty merits deserve. Cheek is not an "infirmity of noble minds," but afflicts only persons of inferior powers. It deserves to fail as it usually does. Brag, at the best, can be but a very brief substitute for ability. Brass makes a bigger noise than gold, but it is gold men are after, and they commonly know it when they see it. In the long run, every man passes at his true worth. To try to pass for a person of greater importance or ability than you really are, is not only absurd, but also dishonest. It implies deceit, as well as conceit, and is therefore a fatal defect in any character. True merit cannot be hid, and needs not to sound a trumpet before it. If there is anything in you, depend upon it somebody is going to find it out. If there is nothing in you, you cannot by swagger and bluster cheat the world into believing that there is.

Avoid brag; it will bring you down in the eyes of those whose good opinion you most desire. Cultivate simplicity in action and in conversation. Promise little, perform much. Neither talk loud nor dress loud. Modesty is beauty's crown, admirable alike in old and young. It adds a grace to every virtue, and furnishes the finest setting in which ability of any kind may shine.

True Nobility.

Rev. HENRY A. BUTTZ, D.D., LL.D.,
President of Drew Theological Seminary, Madison, New York.

THE highest eulogy which can be paid to anyone is to say that he is noble. It is comprehensive of all the virtues and of all the graces. There is no one word representing character and esteem which is so all-embracing. There are some words for which no adequate definition seems possible. The feeling of their meaning is deeper than any impression which language is able to convey. Such a word is nobility. If one were to attempt the substitution of some other word for it, such as goodness, benevolence, justice, he will find that neither separately nor collectively do they fully express its meaning. It can only be stated by circumlocution, and even then inadequately.

It is first of all a feeling. The appeal which is made to a noble person is answered almost before it is presented, because his consciousness of the needs of others is so acute that the meaning is comprehended intuitively. Nobility is the expression, not of the intellect so much as of the soul, not merely of the mind but of the heart. It is often, indeed generally, expressed in the face, for a really noble person, however much he may strive to do so, cannot conceal from others the benevolence which controls his life.

The nobility of feeling involves sympathy with all that is true and good. It is the condition of a person who looks with dissatisfaction upon everything low and degrading and is conscious of entire harmony with that which is elevated and pure. Such feelings have animated all those who have been recognized among the choice characters of the world.

Then there is also nobility of character. The feeling has become habit, and forms what is known among men as character. It is not a mere emotion, but a mode of life in which all the powers and attainments are subordinated to the highest aims and plans. The noble character finds itself so intrenched in desires for the welfare of all, that temptations in the opposite direction cease to be effective. In other words, his whole being has become ennobled.

Nobility of feeling and character are always accompanied by nobility of action. Character and action are harmonious, and cannot be in conflict. There may be good actions performed spasmodically or as the result of impulse by those whose souls are not noble, but a steady, sustained life, doing noble deeds, is only possible when connected with those emotions and conditions which naturally and necessarily produce them. A life that is noble is always the result of inner forces and not of external incitements. The topic under consideration is not merely nobility, but true nobility. This word is employed by lexicographers and in literature in different senses. It is applied to nobility of descent, *i. e.*, to hereditary nobility, in which the title descends from generation to generation. It is a title of rank and has no necessary relation to personal character. While some such noblemen have true nobility, there are others to whom it is entirely wanting. There have been men of loftiest worth who have worn the highest crowns of rank or station, while others who are officially designated by such titles have shown themselves unworthy to wear theirs. Of Lord Byron it may be said that he was a great poet and a nobleman, but not a noble man, while of Lord Shaftesbury it must be said that he was alike noble in rank, in character, and in works, thus combining in himself the highest qualities of manhood.

The real nobility, however, has already been indicated, viz., that which consists in personal worth. One may be truly noble, and recognized as such though destitute of learning, scholarship, office, or rank. Indeed, it is frequently found in persons of the humblest worldly circumstances. Almost every day we read of acts worthy of heroes, done by those whose names are scarcely known in the community in which they dwell. Instances to justify this statement will meet daily the readers of current literature.

The qualities then which must be sought in order to secure true nobility are a lofty purpose, deep sympathies, and absolute self-sacrifice. Neither is sufficient without the others. What then is the purpose which must enter into and constitute a noble life? It must be both general and particular. It desires to make the best of the whole world and the best of each member of society. It, however, must save the whole by saving each part of it. It serves the whole society by serving the units of which it is composed. Hence nobility does not neglect little things or to do good in what seems small and insignificant ways. Nothing is too small and nothing is too large for a noble soul to do. In statesmanship and patriotism both George Washington and Abraham Lincoln were truly noble. How lofty their aims, how earnestly they sympathized with struggling humanity and how unselfish and complete were their sacrifices!

How much nobility is found among business men! How many are doing business, not for their own aggrandizement, but to benefit their fellow men! A gentleman of extensive business told the writer of this but recently that he did not expect to make any more money. What he made hereafter was for others.

The same is true also in professional life. In the ministry, in law, in medicine, are to be found men, not a few, whose aim is not wealth or fame, but who desire to serve "their generation according to the will of God." It were easy to make a catalogue of men and women in all ages who represent to the world this type of character. They are the choicest treasures of our world, more precious than mines of gold and of silver. To enumerate even a few of them would be impossible here.

The one noble character which rises above all others is the

world's Redeemer, the Lord Jesus Christ. He is the highest specimen of true nobility the world has ever known. Every trait illustrating it was found in him and the attainment of it will be best secured by the study of his life and teachings and the imitation of his example.

True nobility is possible to all and everywhere. It matters little whether one be in public position, or in private station, in a royal palace or in a humble cottage, in professional life or in daily manual labor. There is no place where it will not have opportunity for exercise. Wherever generosity, purity, self-sacrifice, truth, and fidelity are found, there will be found that for which all the people of the world should seek, true nobility.

> "Be noble! and the nobleness that lies
> In other men, sleeping, but never dead,
> Will rise in majesty to meet thine own."—LOWELL.

"Be noble in every thought and in every deed."—LONGFELLOW.

The Breastplate of Self-Respect.

Rev. HUGH BOYD, D.D., Cornell College, Mt. Vernon, Iowa.

IN the olden days of the arrow and the spear and the battle-ax, before the invention of the more destructive weapons of modern warfare, the trusty knight rode forth to battle, or took his place in the lists of the tournament, armored from head to foot. A wonderful contrivance was that armor, consisting of many parts and of various construction, some parts of solid iron, others of interwoven links, or of interlocking plates of steel. The helmet, to withstand the blows of the battle-ax, and the breastplate to protect the vital organs, were some of the most important parts.

Beautiful and befitting as was this armor in its day, it is to us but an obsolete curiosity from a past age. The gayly caparisoned knight of the middle ages, clad in burnished steel and bedizened with gold, would hardly excite our admiration. His image would be to us but an interesting spectacle from a page of ancient history.

> "The knights are dust,
> Their swords are rust,
> Their souls are with the saints, we trust."

We fear no more the hurling of the spear or the whizzing of the arrow. We have come into that condition of mind in which we look with indifference on the weapons that inflict only bodily injury, as compared with the keener, and more destructive, agencies that impair the moral character and maim the soul. True, the bullet of the madman, the dagger of the desperado, the poisoned stiletto of the assassin, are thoughts from which we recoil in horror when presented to our minds by a near-at-

THE BREASTPLATE OF SELF-RESPECT.

hand tragedy. But, in general, they are looked upon as only a remote contingency. On the other hand, we know the sources of moral contamination are as pervasive as the air we breathe. Against these we must defend ourselves as best we may. No material defense will turn aside the onset of moral pollution. No armorial coat of mail can preserve the integrity of the human heart. Not by external defense but by an internal power is the soul made strong to resist its foes.

In the poverty of human speech we still speak of the new defenses by the old terms. By such insensible degrees have we passed from the barbarism of brawl and battle to the arts and practices of civilized life, that we are not conscious of any incongruity between the terms we use and the ideas we represent. Though battles be no more, we still shall fight the battle of life. We still speak of the helmet of salvation, the armor of righteousness, the sword of truth, the battle-ax of reform. We strike, we cleave, we ward. We stand on guard, we lead the forlorn hope, we push the battle to the gates of the enemy.

The transition from the old life to the new has left upon its line of march the most enduring of all historical monuments in the very words we use. A breath of air, thrilled by the perishing organs of human speech, passes by an unseen medium to the human ear, passes on its invisible way from generation to generation, and from age to age, and stands a more enduring memorial than marble or bronze.

In that defensive condition arising from a consciousness of moral rectitude, arising from a belief in the native dignity of one's own soul, from the feeling that nothing mean, or low, or groveling is consistent with its own power and purpose, we may say that the soul is defended by the Breastplate of Self-Respect.

That soul is weak that has no self-protection. It feels exaltation only when greeted with the favoring shouts of the multitude. When the impetus of popular applause has spent its force, it suffers a corresponding dejection. It is serene in the sunshine, but perturbed in the storm. It flames with ardent joy when fanned by the hot breath of flattery. It freezes in the cold atmosphere of neglect. Without power to sustain itself in and of itself, it shrinks in abasement beneath the weight of unjust calumny. Slights and sneers and innuendoes torture it with keenest pain. It goes down in the dust before the hot shafts of ridicule.

It is not well that any soul should be thus defenseless and exposed to all adversity.

But there are yet greater perils; more to be dreaded than the things which are merely disagreeable, or aggravating, or painful to the sensibilities are the things which bring some moral defilement to the touch, or inflict some ugly wound in the fair fabric of the soul's integrity.

Enticements to evil courses beset every pathway. They lie in wait for the careless and timid. They even dare to meet the self-confident and the strong. More especially do they challenge to life combat every generous, high spirited, ambitious youth. We may exalt in our thought "the power that makes for righteousness." We cannot overestimate the magnitude or the might of that power. But in order that the race may triumph, the individual must suffer. "To him that overcometh," is the word of holy writ. "The gods sell everything at a price," is the reflection of a pagan philosopher. We may ponder the universal scheme of all human life and see that the "Eternal Goodness" is ever at work toward beneficent ends. We cannot paint the picture too beautiful or too true. But to make it beautiful and to make it true, the individual life must fight its way through, or go down in an ignominious failure to an inglorious fate.

For this omnipresent conflict is there not some armor of truth and righteousness that will protect the wearer, or enable him to ward off the destroying agencies that are aimed at his life? Is there no defensive weapon with which to meet the enticements to evil, the trend to idleness, to greed, to rapacity, to unjust dealing, to low living, and foul thinking? We do not mention here that supreme moral awakening that enthrones man's higher powers, and makes all the beatitudes regnant within him. There is a sentiment, a force. within us and upon us; a force, a sentiment, sometimes but dimly felt. It is the consciousness of selfhood. It is an enlargement of the feeling of personal identity. It is a recognition of the soul within us as being not our own but ourselves, not as being wise, or rich, or great, or strong, but as being our very selves, to be defended and kept if large and mighty, to be no less defended and kept if small and weak. The soul is its own armor. To the enthronement of this feeling as an active agency in the protection of character, we give the name of self-respect, a name that by light and trivial applications has lost some of its force. Let us revivify its import, while we are kept by its gentle, invisible power.

Self-respect, that clothes the soul as with a panoply, is an endowment within the reach of all. It is the native covering of every soul, sensitive and tender, but strong and defensive. It increases in protecting power through its own use, or it may be weakened by the carelessness of the wearer, if he allow some secret arrow of evil to pierce between the joints of his armor. It is not self-appreciation, for it may exist in the highest degree, with a distrustful undervaluation of one's self. It is not respect for one's self as the possessor of great riches. That is the worship of wealth, an abject sentiment. It is not respect for one's self as the possessor of great beauty. That is vanity. It is not respect for one's self as being finely or fittingly dressed. That may be a proper feeling, but it does not rise to the dignity of moral quality. It is not respect for great learning. It is not respect for excellent endowments of mind. That is pride of intellect, the most unlovely of all pride. It is not respect for lofty position, for offices, for honors, for notoriety, or for fame. That is to grasp the shadow and disregard the substantial entity. In proportion as feelings like these gain the mastery, in that proportion all true self-respect shrivels and withers and dies.

In the earliest days of man's earthly existence, his infant thought looks upon everything, even his own form, as external and foreign. He gazes in mute wonder at his hands, but does not know these are a part of himself. Evidently he thinks they are foreign bodies. But, into the frail palace of the infant soul come unnumbered messages of pleasure, or of pain. From hand and foot and face and finger-tip come messages of joy or pain, that by some mute, mysterious logic, are traced to their source. By some experiences of pain or pleasure, the infant man has grasped the idea of externality and self. The frail network of nerve and filament and interlacing fiber that enfolds his body has become a monitor and a guide. Even through its frailness and sensibility to pain, it becomes a protection and a defense. The infant man learns to avoid danger, and, after a while, even to ward off peril by sturdy blows.

By a process equally slow, in years a little later, we rise to the moral consciousness of selfhood, and attain the instinct of the self-preservation of the soul. Not through feelings hardened to the stroke of evil, but by a supersensitiveness to the pain of injustice and untruth, we become strong to resist, and firm to oppose. The day of our defenselessness is the day of our power.

In the daily strife between truth and falsehood, in the daily contest between the good and evil side, in the face of the cowardly suggestion to do a little wrong that great good may come at last, in the still more cowardly suggestion to do wrong for a little while because the supreme good is unattainable, in the covert and insidious approaches of evil as well as in the fierce onsets of temptation, the soul that has arrived at a consciousness of its own supremacy, that has come into the feeling of fidelity to itself, stands,—firm, erect, and true.

Time would fail to tell, how, without arrogance or pride, the native covering of self-respect is broadened and brightened, made lustrous and strong, when, to the native vision of selfhood and its instinctive protecting power, there is added some transcendent vision of moral excellence and beauty in the soul itself, self-seen.

For now in every moral conflict no less than in every physical conflict of tournament and battle in the olden time,

> "What stronger breastplate than a heart untainted?
> Thrice is he armed that hath his quarrel just;
> And he but naked, though locked up in steel,
> Whose conscience with injustice is corrupted."

Adapting Self to Circumstances.

Hon. EDWIN F. LYFORD, State Senator of Massachusetts.

"BE independent of circumstances, adapt them to yourselves, make them for yourselves," is the boastful advice of the self-made man.

There is in this, however, no great encouragement to the average citizen, who, like the unfortunate Mr. Dolls, is sure to feel that there are circumstances over which he has no control. For his comfort be it said, that it is not always safe to rely implicitly upon the statements of the man of self-manufacture, especially with reference to his own mode of construction and operation.

It is true that in a sense we may often be said to control and alter our circumstances, but the change is rather in, than outside, ourselves. He who moves into a new house alters his surroundings, but he it is who has changed position, while the house has neither burned down nor moved away. We enter into different circumstances rather than alter the circumstances themselves, and it is worthy of note that any advancement and improvement we may thus make, is due very largely to a careful adaptation to our present surroundings and a ready and judicious use of the opportunities about us. While, then, the stubborn facts may not be altered, we can conform to them, and by so doing make them serve our ends. He who thus adjusts himself to circumstances makes them his friends that hasten to help at every turn, while he who fails so to do is surrounded by enemies that continually annoy and attack.

In society, that man "gets on," is popular, and makes a success who knows how to adapt himself to the people whom he

ADAPTING SELF TO CIRCUMSTANCES.

meets. This does not require him to be two-faced or double in his dealing, nor that when "among the Romans, he should do as the Romans do," without regard to his own sense of right, but it does demand the use of good sense in rendering his conduct appropriate to the places and people in which and among whom he is for the time placed. He who should wear crape at a wedding or crack jokes at a funeral, would very soon have no weddings to attend and no funeral but his own to enjoy. On the other hand, he who is ever quick to respond to the feelings of those about him, becoming a child with children and a man among men, possesses not only the strongest element of popularity, but a means of accomplishing untold good.

The business man must continually adapt himself to his surroundings. As the nature of trade changes, as times are good or bad, as customers are easy or hard to please, and as the numerous chances of business are every day presented to him, he must be ever on the alert and quick to adjust himself to all these and the thousand other circumstances of his business world. The exercise of this power of adaptation or, in other words, business sagacity, insures success; to neglect it, means failure. The manufacturer who should still insist on turning out flintlock guns, instead of conforming to the changed condition of affairs, would find no market for his wares, and he who should undertake to run a line of stages from Boston to New York would be quickly taught that he had failed to understand the requirements of the present day.

The teacher, the lawyer, the doctor, and the minister must learn to adapt themselves to the characters with whom they come in contact. The teacher who instructs all his scholars in the same unvarying manner, without regard to their individual peculiarities, fails to understand the first principles of his vocation. The lawyer and doctor are obliged to suit themselves to their cases, their clients, and their patients, and even the minister must deal differently with the lambs and sheep of his flock, and preach very different sermons on Thanksgiving and Fast day.

ADAPTING SELF TO CIRCUMSTANCES.

From the countless minor adaptations to circumstances required in change of place, of scene, or in society, a positive pleasure is often derived. The person who constantly presents to his own view but one phase of his character will soon tire of the prospect. In adapting himself, however, to various people, the changing moods of the same people, and to different situations and circumstances, he becomes aware of a certain variety in his nature which gives an interest and zest to life.

Many a one who supposed himself suited to his ordinary surroundings and nothing else has been agreeably surprised to find that, under altered conditions, new capacities have developed and powers been manifested of which he had not dreamed before. Much of the pleasure of travel and the summer vacation is due not merely to new sights and sounds, but, largely and especially, to learning to adapt ourselves to these changed conditions. He who is fond of camp life finds a keen enjoyment in his plain and primitive quarters, not only because they are so different from those at home, but also because he feels a peculiar delight in the discovery that he can live and be happy, though the floors are not carpeted nor the streets paved. His food also has an added relish when, in adapting himself to his summer environment, he has discovered a hitherto unsuspected ability to prepare it himself.

In the greater vicissitudes of life, in the often sudden changes from poverty to wealth, from obscurity to renown, from health to sickness or the reverse, an ability to adjust one's self to the new conditions saves many an annoyance, lightens many a bitter disappointment, and makes conquest possible, when without it defeat would have been inevitable. Many a man fallen "on evil days" has, by adapting himself to the change, succeeded in rising again, while had he shunned companionship and, keeping aloof from others, merely sighed for past glories, he would have grown still poorer. On the other hand, he who bears suddenly acquired wealth or popularity without undue elation is justly counted worthy of his good fortune.

ADAPTING SELF TO CIRCUMSTANCES.

Modern science proclaims the doctrine of the survival of the fittest. It tells us that those forms of life which are best adapted to their environment are most likely to endure. It is no less true that in society, in business, in life, the man who has learned most perfectly to adapt himself to his surroundings, and to conform to the circumstances in which he is placed, will succeed, while he who has neglected to learn this lesson will continually struggle and continually fail.

Individual Responsibility.

Rev. W. C. WHITFORD, D.D., President Milton College, Wisconsin.

"I WILL be somebody," exclaimed a country lad to himself, as he, seventeen years of age and walking towards a village in Central New York, first caught sight of the buildings of a flourishing academy in the place. He had come from a school district then in the backwoods, and from a home scantily supplied with even the necessaries of life; and was determined to become, if possible, a student in that institution and to complete in it a course of its hardest studies. He was clad in rustic garments woven and made by his mother, was blessed with a robust body and a large brain, and had formed habits of patient industry and serious thinking.

The teachers were at once pleased with his rugged, honest face and earnest spirit, and saw that he possessed natural abilities of no inferior sort, but undeveloped. Admission to the lower classes was granted him; chances to pay his expenses by working at odd jobs fell in his way; and at the end of four years, a diploma was handed him as the best scholar among a dozen graduates of the school at the time.

Afterwards he finished elsewhere a college course with great credit to himself; some years later he returned to the old academy as its efficient principal; and was finally elevated to the presidency of a leading theological seminary in the West. Hundreds of youths enjoyed his ripe instruction in each of these positions, and were incited and guided by him to engage in most active and useful labors. Thus he filled out a distinguished career, relying upon his own powers, and giving full scope to a worthy ambition to rise in the world by cultivating to the utmost these powers and by improving assiduously the superior advantages he found.

It is true that a large majority of the youth of our country, as was the case with this lad, cannot by wealthy parents, family influences, or persons in power, be lifted into the desirable places in business, society, or the government. At the best, only moderate help can be rendered them, such as must be gauged by the limited means accessible in rearing them, and by the other humble conditions attending their early days. Surely, to them there is no royal road to success in the higher walks of life, only a common, well-beaten path along the valleys and over the hills of persistent and wearisome effort. They gain the coveted rewards, climb to the pinnacles of usefulness and renown, only by depending entirely or very largely on their own individual strength and purpose. They must show the resolution of a miner, who is represented in an old device as standing alone before a high ledge of rocks, with a raised pickaxe in his hands, and saying, "As I do not find a tunnel here, I will dig one to the bed of ore myself."

Alas! very many of our youth will not attempt a vigorous struggle to honor best their own existence and to aid in a large way their fellow men. With the most favorable incentives to exertion constantly before them, they are content to remain in the lowly, inconspicuous places wherein they were born and reared. They drift in the current of the everyday events that occur around them. The most prospered of them spend their lives like that dependent idler who is fitly described by an English novelist as having "his plate of chicken and his saucer of cream, and frisked, and barked, and wheezed, and grew fat, and so ended." They leave nothing behind them to be added to the world's storehouse of good. But now and then some one belonging to this class of youth, disgusted with his aimless conduct and his frivolous amusements, or weary of the humdrum and drudgery of his lowly toil, breaks away from his environment, and starts out seriously and bravely to better his state and standing among his fellows.

INDIVIDUAL RESPONSIBILITY.

As a notable and yet not a single instance, a thriftless, grown-up boy in a New England town, sitting with several associates by the roadside, observed a stranger riding by in a fine carriage drawn by spirited horses and receiving the hurrahs of a crowd of people; and the boy turning to these companions, and springing from the ground, with his face ablaze with a new animation, said to them, "I'll do that thing myself sometime." Over a score of years afterwards, he was welcomed and cheered by the citizens of the same place, as he, a leading member of Congress, rode through its principal street on a visit to the humble home of his childhood.

The sympathy and the helping hand of really thoughtful and well-to-do persons are seldom withheld from the boy or the girl that earnestly strives to overcome the hindrances of poverty, and sometimes the unreasonable opposition of relatives and others without ambition, and to become qualified to work in the more remunerative or serviceable positions. In many cases such encouragement acts as a most effective motive in these youth, and often forms the only solid basis on which they can reach forth and attain the object desired. It certainly increases in all of them the responsibility to make the most of themselves, their time, and their opportunities. The pressure of this obligation should remain and grow stronger in them; it will bring about most beneficial results. "May the Lord bless you and help you to be a noble man," said a great-hearted deacon of a church to a homeless, neglected, and keen-eyed urchin, as he placed his warm hand on the flaxen head. This prayer, this benediction, was signally answered. A sudden inspiration changed the course of the thoughts and feelings of the sad and sensitive boy; a most active and brilliant career was subsequently opened to him; and at his death thousands blessed his memory.

Some one has said that the best education is gained by struggling for a living. But add to this a determined purpose to acquire wealth, to sway political power, to become an adept in some trade or profession, or to assuage the sorrows of men, and the culture of the needy and diligent youth will assume the style of a much higher development. Not only will he learn the ordinary lessons of industry, frugality, foresight, and independence of character, but he will possess the invaluable sense of manliness, larger freedom, skillful personal force, and broader usefulness in the chosen pursuit of his older years. He will attempt to perform deeds and to exert influences vastly above those conceived as possible by a man of common training. As a rule, he will surpass the sons of the rich in ability, in grade of work, and in enjoying the confidence of the world. Of necessity he has done immeasurably more to strengthen his body and mind, to have complete control of their activities, and to understand in a practical way the masterful adaptations of the best means to the best ends of life, to avoid failures and to win successes in his plans and operations. He is like the young eagle that, when full-fledged, is driven by its mother from its nest to hunt for its food. It strengthens its wings and acquires a daring flight, not only in such a search, but also in gaining a higher crag on the mountain side, where it finds a perch of greater safety to itself, and has a wider view of the tangled woods and the adjacent fields beneath, in which may be hidden its prey. At length it succeeds in reaching the tallest peaks near its former home, and finally in soaring among the clouds a monarch over all other kinds of birds it meets in its excursions.

Mental and Moral Growth.

Rev. JAMES W. COLE, B.D.

FOOD is necessary to the growth and well-being of the body, both in this world and in all worlds where there are bodies. Only the Self-existent and Eternal Being is self-sustaining. All others must live by and be continued on his bounty. To obtain the unhindered growth, and the proper development of the body, it is a necessity that it shall receive the right kinds of food, at suitable periods, and in proper quantities. If it be given wrong material as food, the body is poisoned, the growth is hindered, and sickness or death ensues.

Of the sixty-eight elements now known to compose the solids, liquids, and gases of the material world, but fifteen enter into the composition of our bodies. Growth and health can therefore be had only by taking as food substances that contain those elements. If we take any outside the fifteen, they are at once cast out, or, if retained, they poison the body. Again, the body is weakened if suitable foods be given in too small quantities, or at periods too far apart; so likewise the body is impaired if suitable foods be taken in too large quantities, or too frequently.

To grow, therefore, we must give attention, to what, how, and when, we eat. We must eat to grow. We are designed to grow. Not to grow is unnatural. Whatever hinders growth should be avoided. Whatever helps to a sound growth should be sought for. There may be life without growth—as in dwarfs. But it is a sad misfortune to be a man in years and a child in body. Such are at a great disadvantage in this world, shut out from many an avenue to success, and deprived of many of life's choicest blessings, and generally of family and social ties.

MENTAL AND MORAL GROWTH.

Dwarfs in nature are due to an arrest of growth, and this is frequently due to a lack of food at the right time for growth, or to use of wrong materials as foods; dwarfs are not always due to accident, but may be deliberately produced. Men produce dwarf trees, and plants, and animals, under nature's laws. So likewise they produce dwarfed intellects and souls under nature's laws.

You have seen men and women with fully grown bodies, but with the intellect of a babe. You call them imbeciles. The body grew but the mind did not. While nature mercifully shuts from them a sense of their condition you see it is a very great misfortune not to grow mentally. So also you have seen men and women with well developed bodies, and strong, well grown minds, but who in soul were infants. They knew no more of God in mature life than they did when babes, and the reason was their moral nature did not grow. Giants often in intellect, in their spiritual nature they remain dwarfs. There are mighty philosophers in every age, who are totally ignorant of the simplest divine things that even "babes in Christ" know fully. To them alas! the future abuts on darkness, not on radiant glory. The explanation is a very simple one—they have not grown in their moral nature since they were born. Why? Food is necessary to growth. They fed the body, they fed the mind, but starved their souls. Their parents first for them, they afterward, sought out and obtained the food needful for the growth of the body, and took it regularly, and in proper quantities; they avoided starvation and gluttony, they shunned poisonous substances, and so grew vigorously; then their parents first, they afterward, cultivated and developed the mind by daily instruction, and study, through precept, example, and investigation, while the soul was left to grow of itself if it could, or starve.

Men produce dwarfed trees, plants, animals, deliberately, under nature's laws, and parents produce dwarfed souls in their children by shutting out God from them, by feeding their souls on the "husks" and "vanities" of earth, or by deliberately

MENTAL AND MORAL GROWTH.

teaching them to use the poison of sins, that dwarf and ruin the soul. It is a sad thing to have a child come to years of manhood and be a dwarf, or be deficient in bodily organs; it is infinitely more sad to have him grow to the stature of a man and be a fool through a defect of intellect; but when you are transferred to another world, it will be found to be the saddest of all things to enter it dwarfed in soul.

He who is deficient in bodily organs or growth, or who is deficient in or neglects the culture of his intellect here, finds himself sorely hindered in this life in his efforts to succeed, and generally becomes a dependent upon the charity of others more favored. If such disaster comes to them through these defects of body, in this the *bodily* life, what loss may not come in the *spiritual* life to those who enter it maimed, halt, or sickly, through a neglect to culture the soul, or through feeding it on the poison of sin? The soul, like the mind, like the body, was made to grow. Not to grow is to be unnatural. You cannot feed the body on ideas, those are for the mind. You cannot feed the mind on strawberries or terrapins, those are for the body. The body will not grow if fed on arsenic, or even on gold or silver. They are very useful in their place, but that place is not the body. You will not grow very much mentally by chasing a ball or trundling a bicycle, or flipping an oar, or tripping the toe, however useful they may be for bodily development, neither will Euclid put fat on your bones. The mind as well as the body must have suitable food, in suitable quantities, at suitable times. It, like the body, can be dwarfed, poisoned, starved, or overfed; and with equally as disastrous results. But properly fed and cared for, what may not the mind accomplish. Likewise you can feed the mind on logarithms, the differential calculus, and a study of earth alone, but not the soul. That "crieth out for God, even the living God." The body will only grow by giving it its components; the intellect develops only by its appropriate pabulum: and the soul, being of divine essence, can only be nourished and developed by divine substantialities. Then it has life—"and this is life eternal, that they may know Thee the only true God, and Jesus Christ whom Thou hast sent." Not to know them is to be dwarfed forever. See to it, then, that with your growth in body and in mind you also "grow in the grace and the knowledge of our Lord and Saviour Jesus Christ, whose is the glory both now and unto the day of eternity. Amen."

Elizabeth Cady Stanton,
Organizer of the First Woman's Rights Convention.

Motive and Method.

Rev. GEORGE R. HEWITT, B.D.

BY the term motive here is meant the ideal object or end toward which our life is consciously directed. The word is used not in its primary sense of the determining impulse within the man, but in its secondary sense of the object desired and aimed at without the man.

In this sense every man has, or should have, some controlling motive in life, something he lays to heart and lives for, and which is the most potent agent in calling forth his powers. No one ought to live an aimless life. It is the glory of man that he is a creature of motives, that he can set before himself some end or object, then direct all his energies to the attainment of it.

In our time and country the most powerful motive with men is the acquisition of riches. We are a money-loving and a money-getting people. With us, wealth is almost esteemed a virtue and poverty a crime. The whole movement of our social life seems to point to riches as the chief good. The rich are deemed happy and the poor miserable. Hence the all-impelling motive with men to-day is the acquisition of wealth.

Now, while wealth is far, very far, from being the most worthy motive that can actuate a man, it is yet a perfectly legitimate motive. It is no sin to get rich or to be rich. On the contrary, it may be the duty of some men to get rich, provided always that they get their riches by proper methods and use them for worthy ends. One man's wealth does not necessarily imply another man's poverty. It is possible to grow rich in business and at the same time enrich all parties concerned in the business. Such being the case it is, as we have said, not only legitimate, but it may even be the duty of some to become rich. Wealth is needful for the fullest life and the highest well-being of any community. There can be no high civilization without it. As one writer well says, "There is not a single feature of our civilization to-day that has not sprung out of money, and that does not depend upon money for its continuance." Morse may invent the telegraph, but wealth must be forthcoming before a cable can be laid 3,000 miles beneath the sea, connecting the old world with the new. Stephenson may invent the locomotive, but without wealth no track will be laid nor train run from New York to Chicago. Edison may invent the telephone, but it requires wealth to stretch the wires from street to street and city to city, converting the whole continent into one vast whispering gallery.

Wealth, like knowledge, is power, but whether a power for good or for evil depends upon the possessor. When rightly used it is a good thing, but, like every other blessing, it is liable to be abused, and then it is an evil thing. As J. M. Barrie has finely said, "Let us no longer cheat our consciences by talking of filthy lucre. Money may be always a beautiful thing. It is we who make it grimy."

There is nothing inherently wrong, then, in having as a motive the acquisition of wealth, provided it be gained in right ways. The danger is, however, when money-making is a man's ruling motive, that in his haste to be rich he shall be led to adopt methods that are not right. What are some of these methods? Much has been written on the subject of commercial immoralities. Space will allow only the briefest glance at some of them.

(1) There is that commonest of all wrong ways—misrepresentation on the part of the seller. This may be done directly by false statements or false advertisements, or indirectly by suppressing the truth as to certain defects in the goods offered. **Inferior material, imperfect workmanship, deficient measure, adultera-**

tion, are all forms of misrepresentation. It is possible to lie by a label as well as by the lip.

(2) There is the way of grinding the faces of necessitous workmen. Compensation should always be just and sufficient to afford the workmen a decent living. To pay a workman starvation wages on the ground that if he does not work at that figure others will is robbery, whatever political economists may say about it.

(3) There is the way of speculating with borrowed capital. The wrong here lies in putting the property of another without his knowledge or consent where it is insecure. The venture may turn out well, but it may not, and if it does not the owner is the loser.

(4) There is the way of trading in futures, which is nothing but gambling. No honest equivalent is given for gains. It is merely betting that the prices of certain commodities will be higher or lower at a given future date than they are now.

(5) There is the way of taking advantage of bankruptcy laws. A man by legal technicalities may evade the payment of his just debts. Not to pay honest debts when you are able to pay them, on the plea that you have been legally released from them, is a species of stealing.

These are but a few of the crooked ways into which men enter in their eagerness to be rich, to say nothing of "cornerings," "watering of stocks," and other questionable methods resorted to by corporations, trusts, and "combines." The danger is, when a man has money-making as his ruling motive, that he will be tempted again and again to traverse the principles of morality. "They that desire to be rich," as the Apostle truly says, "fall into a temptation and a snare and many foolish and hurtful lusts, such as drown men in destruction and perdition."

We sometimes hear it said that if strictly honest in business a man will never be rich. Then be poor. There are some things better than money. Manhood, honor, integrity, are better than money. "A good name is rather to be chosen than great riches." To gain wealth at the expense of character is to barter jewels for gewgaws. Riches got by guile are thrice cursed. They are cursed in the getting, in the keeping, and in the transmitting. To gain the world and lose yourself is to make a poor bargain.

The Lawrences, Abbots, Dodges, Moores and Budgetts, and other merchant princes, were rich in character as well as in money. Their business methods were honorable to the last degree. By industry and enterprise, by fair dealing and genuine politeness, by punctuality and promptitude, they amassed great wealth. They lived noble and benevolent lives. When wealth flowed in upon them they hoarded it not for themselves, but held it in trust for God, and used it to bless mankind and further every good cause. They are true models for a business man to follow.

Do not be in haste to be rich. It is full of peril. Be willing to wait. You may be happy without being rich. Provide things honest in the sight of all men. Remember the noble words of George Washington, "I hope I shall always possess firmness and virtue enough to maintain what I consider the most enviable of all titles, the character of an 'Honest Man.'"

Courage for the Duties of Life.

CHARLES A. YOUNG, Ph.D., LL.D., Princeton College, N. J.

I SHOULD not like to maintain that courage is the noblest and most admirable of human qualities, but in men it is certainly the one that is most applauded; the faint-hearted and cowardly are looked down upon by all. The lack of courage makes any high success impossible. There are in history many instances of men who were pre-eminent in other qualities, but failed to reach the goal for want of this; they were unrivaled in their power of organization, in their accurate perception of the condition of affairs, and in their ability to penetrate the designs of their opponents, but at the critical moment they had not the nerve to cope with the occasion, and missed the chance, if nothing worse—failed in accomplishment, if they did not suffer actual overthrow.

Courage alone of course is not enough, for unsupported by prudence and wisdom it would often bring disaster. But it is indispensable. It is needed constantly in the performance of duties that appear to be dangerous, or are even merely disagreeable,—as, for instance, in standing out for the right in opposition to the prevailing sentiment of the community, or in going counter to the wishes of those on whom we are dependent for comfort or support, or in denying ourselves indulgences known to be injurious to the cause we have at heart. Indeed, it is in such internal conflicts that true courage meets its most trying tests; these battles are in the dark; we fight with foes invisible, without any support of admiration or applauding shouts. Then, too, in business of every kind, as well as in statesmanship and war, there come continually times when risks must be taken.

COURAGE FOR THE DUTIES OF LIFE.

One may have made his preparation with the most prudent care, may have provided, so far as possible, with far-reaching foresight for all contingencies; but there will still be adverse chances and possibilities, and they must be faced unflinchingly if one is to gain any eminent success. As a rule the greatest difference between ordinary men and those who have accomplished great things lies largely in the courage with which the latter have accepted responsibility and taken reasonable risks.

The courage requisite for life's ordinary duties is not so much physical as moral; not that the former is to be despised, for it is often greatly needed. But more frequently what one most wants is that stout-hearted loyalty to the right which accepts the claims of duty, plainly seen, as paramount to all others, and does not inquire as to the ease or agreeableness of its performance, nor hesitate for any dread of consequences. This makes a man energetic and efficient, and if he is clear sighted as to right and wrong, and has tact and skill in action, he becomes powerful for good. Undoubtedly if he is muddle-headed and ethically obtuse, this very force and fearlessness makes him a dangerous fanatic: one sometimes wishes that all fools were cowards.

There is no doubt that courage is a quality greatly to be desired, and the question comes, how can it be attained and cultivated? To a great extent, certainly, it is a matter of natural temperament; some are born brave, and from the first delight in conflict, and enjoy the stimulus of difficulty and danger. Others are chicken-hearted from infancy, and, though they may be very wise in recognizing what ought to be done and how to do it, they are afraid of shadows; they see frightful lions in every path, or walls they have no pluck to scale. The naturally fearless man is fortunate indeed, unless his bravery is mere stupidity and blindness. Life is easy for him in what for others are its hardest struggles, and his keenest delights are in experiences that are martyrdom for them. But the man not so gifted by nature can to some extent repair his defect by learning to look at things philosophically, especially by considering the import of human action in its relation to character-building, and to the life to come. He will consider that in the highest sense no real harm can come to one who is in the line of duty; he may suffer for the time being, but pain thus met and rightly borne is the very hand of God, molding and forming the human soul,—we are "made perfect through suffering." One will consider also that the "duty" for which he is responsible consists only in honest attempt, and not in successful achievement; the final outcome depends on many things outside ourselves, and must be left to Providence. This idea grasped firmly gives freedom from the paralyzing power of fear of failure. It was just this in President Lincoln that made him so brave, with a sad, strong courage that flinched at nothing. He had learned that the only thing for him was to do "the right as it was given him to see the right," leaving the consequences to the powers of heaven. To one thus loyal to what is highest within him, nothing that is clearly duty seems impossible or hard, for he draws upon the power of God himself.

Over the door of the great hall of Rugby school are written the noble words of Emerson:—

> "How nigh is grandeur to our dust,
> How near is God to man!
> When Duty whispers low, "Thou must,"
> The youth replies, "I can."

Duty Before Glory.

Rev. GEORGE A. GATES, B.D., Pres. Iowa College, Grinnell, Iowa.

> "Not once or twice in our rough island-story,
> The path of duty was the way to glory."
> —Tennyson's "Ode on the Death of the Duke of Wellington."

IT is a shrewd remark of Dr. Holmes that "fame comes to most men when they are very busy thinking about something else. It rarely comes to those who say, Go to now, let us become a celebrated individual." To set out for such a goal as glory is an altogether cheap ambition. To pursue such a phantom is better than to have no ambition, unless it be the seeking of glory at the sacrifice of all else, which is simply devilish; but the deliberate choice of such a purpose is almost sure to fail of its achievement or to end in notoriety rather than true, hence abiding, glory. Napoleon is a good example of this at its worst; a man like Disraeli at its best. To the highest natures, the pursuit of glory is a most arrant absurdity. It is just ridiculous. It is something for a man to laugh over until his diaphragm aches, even as over the performances of Don Quixote.

The older the world gets, the more it builds its monuments to those who have rendered the race conspicuous service. This was not always exclusively so, for the reason that standards of greatness have not always been as true as we flatter ourselves they are now. Ages which worship power will honor those who manifest power of some sort. But the world at its best has learned that power is not the highest, but sacrifice.

Duty nearly always means crucifixion of some sort. There is a philosophical reason for it. Ignorance resents instruction; wrong resents righting; privilege dreads liberty; intrenchments in rights yield slowly to calls to duty. So that a leader out of ignorance into wisdom, a fighter against wrong, an uncompromising defender of right, a devastator of oppressive privilege, establisher of liberty, the prophets little careful of right but an infinitely insistent on duty, are sure enough of curses and may go to the cross; hence the duty which brings abiding glory is nearly always for the time utterly inglorious. This is the price; few there be that will pay it. It is a hard saying; few will hear it. Some of the prominent ones among those few who have heard the call, and who have obeyed the call and paid the price, have been enshrined permanently in the world's memory. They are verily the glory of the race. For the obscure ones who have done their part as well, it is the privilege of faith to believe that their reward shall not be finally wanting.

Whom of the past do we call glorious? Men like Buddha, Moses, Luther, Cromwell; in our own land, Washington, Lincoln. On what does their glory rest? Is it not in their cases unselfish and efficient service rendered to their fellow men? Compare the standards by which we judge them and give them glory with the current standards of ambition among men. With what office was Buddha honored among the people? What salary did Moses or Luther get? What estates did Cromwell own? How much did Washington accumulate? Was Lincoln a rich and prosperous and comfortable man? Let us remember that the earthly rewards of Jesus were summed up in the death of the cross.

Is it not plain when we think of the true glory of mankind, how trivial are many of our current ambitions? Whom, then, of our time will be held glorious by future generations? We cannot tell that. But we are perfectly sure of some who will not be so held. The ambitious, rich, powerful, prominent leaders of human society, institutions, and politics? No, no. Not many such are called. But some will be remembered who now are comparatively obscure, who have been so busy just doing their duty that they have had no time even to think of glory, much less pursue it.

DUTY BEFORE GLORY.

Indeed, glory is a word which will pass out of use. It is of a low grade of civilization. As the race becomes divine, other ambitions than to win glory will take possession of the human spirit. Not so much right and duty, but love and self-sacrifice, precede and proclaim, nay, verily constitute glory. The world builds temporary monuments to the merely conspicuous. But the race has its abiding monuments of the heart only for those of quite another sort; they are doers of their duty, lovers of their kind, sacrificers of themselves. These are they who lost their lives, and they have found them.

The only true glory which anyone can ever have will be not the glory which he seeks, but that which is thrust upon him. Duty can never be done for the sake of winning the reward of recognition; it instantly becomes contemptible pride, and must ultimately fail of glory.

The path of duty is the way to glory. There is only one supreme duty, and that is, forgetting all about such things as glory or self in any way, to fling one's self with divine abandon into whatever service he can render to his fellow men. This service itself is its own glory. To want any other is evidence of an unredeemed life. There has been but one perfect example of such a life on earth. We shall do well to follow him who "made himself of no reputation." Because he, out of love to man, perfectly did that, his place is on the throne of the world for all time.

Poverty Prepares for Wealth.

Hon. J. H. BRIGHAM, State Senator of Ohio.

WE do not write of extreme or hopeless poverty such as is sometimes found in the wretched dens of our large cities. Children who survive such surroundings are more likely to gravitate towards the prison or almshouse than to become respectable and wealthy citizens. Still there are cases where children raised under such unfavorable conditions have become successful and honored members of society. I shall confine what I have to say on this subject to those who have none of the luxuries of life, except good plain clothes and food, and who find it necessary to practice rigid economy, and cultivate habits of industry in their childhood days. They thus learn the cost of a dollar, and how to get its worth when they part with it. Having no property, or very little, they are not likely to contract that worst of all methods of business, buying on credit. Necessity compels them to "pay as they go," and they soon realize that they have discovered the "philosopher's stone." It is time that they may depart from this safe business rule when they do have credit, and suffer the consequences, but the habit of "paying as you go" once formed is not likely to be abandoned, and is one of the best preparations for wealth. I do not of course refer to credit obtained in purchasing a farm, a house, or the necessary outfit for business, or work, but to purchase what is consumed, or what cannot be made to produce or save money.

The absence of wealth compels thought and planning to get along without that which we are not obliged to have, or leads us to devise ways and means of supplying our wants without reducing our working capital. The young man who has no money is not sought after by associates who would like to help him spend it. He is not urged to visit the saloons and gambling houses, as he has no feathers to pluck. Being obliged to work, he learns to be independent and self-reliant. And when the day's work is ended, nature demands rest, and he is likely to heed the demand, and thus avoid the temptation and danger that hide in the darkness, and lead many boys into the downward road that ends in extreme poverty, if not in crime. As poverty does not furnish means to be wasted in idling away time in school, the poor boy is generally diligent, and forms the habit of improving every moment that can be spared for study, and thus another step is taken on the road that leads from poverty to wealth. The poor young man has no time to waste in the society of frivolous young women, and is not a favorite even of his parents. He therefore avoids that drain which has impoverished many young men.

It would be an easy matter to furnish many examples of poor boys who have become very wealthy, but it is not necessary. An investigation will show that a very large majority of the men of wealth in this country were comparatively poor in their youth. On the other hand, boys who have been reared with all the surroundings of wealth are often unable to add to what they inherit. Many of them, in fact, sink into poverty simply because they have never been compelled to learn the value of money by earning it by their own labor, and have never been taught by stern necessity to economize and save their substance. I do not say that what is true in the United States is true everywhere. I believe it is a difficult matter for the poor in the old world to advance from poverty to wealth. What I have written, therefore, is intended to apply principally to the land of glorious opportunities, the United States of America.

Where to Get Rich.

HOMER T. FULLER, Ph.D., Pres. Polytechnic Institute, Worcester, Mass.

ONE of the ancient philosophers said, "Give me where to stand and I will move the world." By this he meant not place, but principles; not locality, but a basis for thought and conduct. A young man once said to a friend, "I am ready to begin the practice of my profession if I can only find a place." "It is all place," was the reply. "You can start anywhere if you have in you the marrow of success."

For the securing of a competence, there are but three external conditions, viz., a temperate climate, a just government, and a country which has fair natural resources. These conditions exist in almost every part of the United States, and almost everywhere it is possible for a man to acquire wealth. The proof is found in the fact that there are to-day men of wealth in every state in the Union, and in smaller towns as well as in larger cities. Indeed, a large proportion of the richer residents of our cities began life in country towns, laid there the physical and mental foundations of their prosperity, there their accumulations, and removed to cities either for greater convenience in the prosecution of their business, or for the enjoyment in a new sphere of society of the fruits of their acquisitions.

It is said that Portland, Oregon, has more millionaires than San Francisco; Portland, Maine, more rich men in proportion to its population than Boston, and that the owners of two of the largest estates in New England have spent nearly all their lives in towns of less than five thousand inhabitants. The founder and endower of a New England University began his business career in one of the most rugged hill towns of the Bay State,

WHERE TO GET RICH.

and one of the largest capitalists in New Jersey has resided fourscore years in an upland village. Men have created towns, and so the whole social atmosphere which has environed them. The Fairbanks of St. Johnsbury, Vermont, bought a water power, invented scales and the machinery for their manufacture; developed a world-wide trade; built up a village, and established and endowed an academy, a library and art gallery, and a natural history museum.

The Cranes of Dalton, Massachusetts, the Cheneys of South Manchester, Connecticut, the Slaters of Rhode Island, Mr. Andrew Carnegie at Braddock and Homestead, Pennsylvania, Mr. George M. Pullman in the Illinois town which bears his name, and many others have made place and occupations for themselves and thousands of their fellows. They did not find it necessary to adopt the advice of Horace Greeley and "go West." Indeed, they often chose most unpromising sites, but by their energy and perseverance overcame obstacles, and made rocks and sands and clay-banks and even mud their servitors. In every region of our broad land, there are undeveloped resources. Within ten years a small town in Vermont has more than trebled its population and increased its wealth many fold by quarrying granite; other towns in the same state mine marble, or slate, or soapstone. There are millions yet in scores of mineral deposits in the Eastern United States; and there are millions more in the raising of fruit and vegetables right hereabouts where we live, for a near market. But we must study ourselves more, nature more thoroughly, the laws and methods of business with a keen eye and an earnest purpose, put our whole heart and our entire strength into the work we choose, and, under ordinary circumstances, we cannot fail of measurable success.

The Secret of Saving.

Rev. JAMES W. COLE, B.D.

WASTE makes men poor. Waste keeps them poor. Not so much the great wastes, the wars, the pestilences, and the famines, although the wealth destroyed by them during the centuries has been enormous, exceeding many times the present wealth of the nations of the earth; but it is the lesser and constant wastes that so impoverish mankind. Even among the most advanced nations this waste is immense. In England during the last six years there have been, according to the writers of "The Land," more than a thousand million dollars swallowed up in investment companies, and various banking schemes. Much more than that amount has been sunk in the United States within that period through various speculative enterprises. The many stock and produce exchanges have become almost wholly speculative concerns, if not gambling institutions. In a single year the Cotton Exchange, of New York City, sold over thirty-two million bales of cotton, when the entire production of cotton in this country for that year was less than six million bales. In that same year, the Liverpool Cotton Exchange so speculated and disturbed the market that fifteen million spindles, giving employment to thousands of men and women, were forced to stop work, causing a loss of hundreds of thousands of dollars to manufacturers, and a yet greater loss to their employees. In that year the oil wells of the United States produced nearly thirty million barrels of oil, but the New York Petroleum Exchange alone sold during the year two thousand million barrels of oil, and somebody had to lose by the gambling. In consequence of this speculation in products and stocks, ten men in the city of New York in that year gathered an aggregate of eighty million dollars, getting it almost wholly from the gudgeons who bit at their hooks hoping to get rich thereby.

The Louisiana Lottery took in millions of dollars from its dupes, who sent it to them in driblets of a dollar or less, the contributors being to a great extent the laboring men and women of the country. Reference has already been made to the great waste caused by the drink and tobacco habits. If now you add to these the improvident expenditures for luxuries of food, of clothing, of amusements, and kindred extravagances, the waste becomes incalculable, and one need not wonder that so many are poor. I am not speaking of the extravagance of men who have inherited enormous fortunes, like the present Rothschilds, one of which family paid in 1890 one hundred and sixty-eight thousand dollars for an old historic clock not worth for service as much as a Waterbury watch, or of that other man of wealth who, at the Siston library sale in 1884, paid fifteen thousand dollars for a Mazarine Bible that was not nearly so good as the seventy-five cent ones of the American Bible Society, nor of the "swells" who pay twenty-six thousand dollars a year for a suite of rooms and board at some of the famous hotels in New York. And yet those rich spendthrifts were not a whit more extravagant in their way than multitudes of working men are in theirs. It is true that the wealth of the world is very unequally divided. But if it was equally divided among men and women to-day, inequality would begin among them before the sun set. Their acquired or inherited appetites, passions, prejudices, and habits would soon produce as great inequality as now. The same waste would produce the same poverty.

What huge sums of money are now being wasted by the laboring man through his "brotherhoods" and their frequent "strikes" and "lockouts!" And he has continued it for generations, and always with the same disastrous results. The guilds and brotherhoods of the Middle Ages had precisely the same paralyzing effect on prosperity as those of to-day have, and for the same reason, namely, they sought to make their power felt through the "strikes" alone, thus scaring enterprise and capital, and, by stopping production and trade, impoverishing themselves. If, instead of interfering with the inception and management of industries they did not and could not originate, and cannot manage successfully because of a lack of training or ability, they were to exert their power to insure stability of industry rather than to prevent it, they would be immensely better off. Why should not these industrial combinations that so often beggar rather than enrich their members by wasting their capital (*i. e.* dues, fees, and labor) invest it in industrial enterprises themselves, and likewise become the much denounced and much envied capitalist? In proportion as they feel the risks, anxieties, and hopes, and see the difficulties to be encountered and overcome in order to gain success, in that proportion will they learn that it takes more intelligence profitably to employ muscle, and more wisdom successfully to save and invest its products, than it does to labor with one's hands alone. Good profits, if they came, would show them the conditions for successful ventures; and the losses that are sure in some way to come through the incompetency or dishonesty of others, would show them how dependent all men are on each other's well-doing and well-being, both for their daily bread and for profits for their toil.

Capital is only one of the tools that thinking men use in originating their designs and carrying on their enterprises. It takes a higher order of brain to develop and conduct the business, the commerce, and the inventions of the day, than to work at the loom or the forge. Such a brain must watch for opportunities of investment, devise plans to take advantage of them, provide the means to do it, calculate the costs, determine the risks and overcome them, and on the doing it successfully depends all the laborer's work and wages. The laborer's wages are his wealth, and that wealth stands on precisely the same footing as all other forms of wealth do; and, like them, depends on the general prosperity and advancement in intelligence and culture of society.

THE SECRET OF SAVING.

Some day the laboring man will learn that his monopoly of labor by means of "strikes" is just as disastrous as any other monoply, and that he himself is responsible for many a collapsed industry, many an abandoned enterprise, and much of the idle capital he complains of, which would be invested for mutual good, if his "strikes" did not make capital timid. No false teaching can be of any real value to anyone, and the sooner the man of to-day accepts it as a fact that his existence, his advancement in society, and his increase in wealth depend upon his intelligence, industry, and freedom from vicious associations and habits, and the wise use he makes of his opportunities, the better it will be for him and for the world.

Ignorance is waste. Vice is waste. Sin is waste. The universe is made up of little savings of atoms. This old earth is but the saving of particles of sand and rock and mineral. The great seas are but the savings of tiny drops of vapor. Your wealth, if you get it, is made up of little savings. More than one man's fortune has been due to the first five dollars he put into the savings bank. More than one rich manufacturer will tell you that his wealth came to him by what most persons would call petty savings of materials, or of time. I would by no means have you penurious, neither is it needful to gnaw morality to the bone as some are doing in order to get rich.

The great reason why you and I should be saving is not merely that by so doing we shall increase our store of wealth, and so increase our comforts and happiness, and add to the welfare of the world, but our habits are made, like savings, by little acts, and these habits form characters, and character is the only possession which we take with us to the next world. It is a dreadful thing to bid farewell to this life either as a miser or a spendthrift. Happy is he who gets all the money he honestly, honorably, can, spends it liberally for his own and others' welfare while he lives, and leaves it without regret when his stewardship of it is at an end. Such a man can walk the streets of the New Jerusalem without having to shudder at the thought of a **former deep debasement to that city's paving materials.**

Use and Abuse of Money.

Rev. WASHINGTON GLADDEN, D.D.

WHAT shall we do with our money—with what we inherit, with what is given to us, with what we earn? How shall we use it? What principles shall guide us in keeping it, or in parting with it?

I have put these questions to several wise men and women of my acquaintance, and I have received various replies.

"Spend less than your income," answers one sententiously, "even if your income be very small." This may be said to be the first principle of personal economy. No man's life can have any comfort or peace in it until he has learned to build on this good foundation. He who lives by this rule may know what self-respect is, and what is independence, and what is manliness; he who despises this rule is always at war with himself, and is often subjected to unspeakable humiliation and embarrassment.

"Early learn the lesson of frugality," answers a merchant. "I have now in mind a number of men, some of whom I have employed, who, to my knowledge, have earned enough to have lived well, and at the same time to have made themselves possessors of good homes, and who to-day are miserably poor, simply because they never learned to save."

This is not a deep saying, but it has a broad application. I have had plenty of opportunity to verify it, in a ministry extending over thirty years, in several towns and cities, with a large number of poor families always under my eye—families with whose habits and circumstances I have been, of course, much more familiar than most of their neighbors were likely to be. It is the result of my observation that the greater proportion of the poverty of this country is due to foolish habits of spending money. You may often find two families of equal income and equal necessary expenses, one of which will be well-fed, well-clad, and well-housed, with a slowly growing surplus in the savings bank; while the other will be always destitute, and poverty-stricken, and often knocking at the poor-master's back door. The difference is solely due to the fact that the one family expends its income wisely, and the other squanders its income on all manner of small luxuries and diversions.

Most of the poverty of this country is the fruit of extravagance. Nine hundred millions of dollars are expended every year for intoxicating liquors. Of this certainly one-fourth must be spent by the men who work for wages. Putting aside the physical and moral injury occasioned by strong drink, the extravagance of this expenditure is deplorable. If alcohol is a food, as some physiologists maintain, the amount of nutrition contained in it is infinitesimal. It must be classed as a luxury. The same thing must be said of tobacco. And when we know that the people who work for wages spend probably four hundred millions a year on these two luxuries, the voice of their complaint loses much of its impressiveness.

I write these words in the midst of a vigorous effort, on the part of the benevolent people of my own city, to meet and relieve the destitution existing among us. We are told that there are some thousands of families for which charitable aid must be provided. Yet I dare say that if all the money which has been expended during the last year by these families for strong drink and tobacco were now in their hands, half of them, at least, would be able to pull through this depression without aid, and without serious discomfort. I have not dared to say so much as this to my neighbors who are organizing this relief work, for I do not wish to dampen their enthusiasm; but I am as sure of it as I can be of anything. There is another fact to which I have not thought it wise to call the attention of my neighbors at this juncture. A pretty well informed man, who knows quite a number of our liquor dealers, told me the other day that the universal testimony of these gentlemen is that their business is not suffering in this depression. Such facts are very discouraging to men of good will who wish to do what they can for the improvement of the condition of the wage workers.

There is, however, a great deal of extravagant expenditure, aside from the money which goes for strong drink and tobacco —expenditure which is simply foolish or childish—for the gratification of a silly vanity or a morbid craving. And the extravagant people in this country are not all working people; those who never earned a cent in their lives are apt to be utterly unprincipled in their use of money; young people in school and college, and the idle and dangerous classes who inhabit the avenues and throng the watering places, very often exhibit a plentiful lack of intelligence and conscience in their dealings with money. The reckless use of money is characteristic of Americans; in no land is it gained so easily; in no land is it flung away so profusely. Our young people early become addicted to this vice of extravagance; it is a vice by which myriads are ruined.

Money furnishes a constant test of character. He who uses it wisely; who spends it when he ought to spend it and saves it when he ought to save it; who gets money's worth for it, in the truest sense, when he parts with it, and makes it always serve his highest interests,—to him money is an unspeakable good. In spending money rationally many of your best powers come into play, your foresight, your judgment, your conscience, your benevolence.

Give one young man a thousand dollars a year to spend, and he will gain largely by the expenditure. In the first place he will have something precious and permanent in the way of material possessions to show for it at the end of the year—good books, choice pictures, useful furniture, and, perhaps, certain instruments of culture, such as microscopes or natural history specimens, by which his future improvement will be assisted. But this is the smallest part of his gain. He has accustomed himself, day by day, to use his judgment in buying or in refusing to buy; in considering what was needful and judicious expenditure; his will has gained firmness; his moral sense has been educated in resisting temptation; in every way his character has been solidified and broadened. The value of this kind of discipline is quite beyond estimation. It is by just such a regimen that the sturdy virtues are nourished and confirmed.

Give another young man one thousand dollars a year to spend, and he will lose heavily by the expenditure. At the end of the year he will have nothing left to show for his money except a few partly worn garments, swiftly going out of fashion, and a few valueless trinkets; his money has gone for livery bills and suppers and cigars and theater tickets and all sorts of fooleries; he has been ruled, in all this outlay, not by his reason and his judgment, but by his appetites, his vanities, his lower cravings; every day he has known that the money was going foolishly, and he has cursed himself for making such improvident and unproductive use of it; and these weak self-indulgences have steadily lowered his self-respect and confused his judgment and enfeebled his will. Let me tell you, young men, that there is a great deal of manhood to be gained or lost in the spending of your money!

The duty and discipline of saving is a more familiar theme to you; you get well lectured about that, and some of you need all you get, and more. The importance of keeping your expenses within your income and of accumulating thus, by your prudence, some capital for business and some reserves for a rainy day—all this is not to be gainsaid. You ought to be saving something every year; and if you do not begin now there is danger that you never will begin. The habit of living up to and beyond his income is a habit that grows on a man; and it makes little difference whether his income is one dollar a day or ten dollars a day; the man who spends the whole of the smaller sum will, in nine cases out of ten, spend the whole of the larger sum when he gets it, and run in debt in the bargain. The habit of saving is one that you ought to form at once; and there is good discipline in that, as you have often been told.

But I want you to see that there is also good discipline to be gained in spending money; in wisely using it, as well as in keeping it. You can buy with a small income, if you know how to handle it, something better than rubies, something more precious than fine gold,—yea, durable riches and righteousness.

There is only one word to add. The right use of money implies not only prudence and economy, but also benevolence. No man in this world rightly liveth unto himself. Money is power, and all power is for service. Every man is under obligation to use his money not only productively but also beneficently. Some of your best gains will come through giving. No man gets more money's worth for what he spends than he who knows that his outlay has gone to relieve suffering, or to give help and comfort and happiness to his fellow men. If you never spend any money except for your own benefit—unless you can see that it is coming back to yourself in some form of personal satisfaction—your money will be a curse to you, I care not how you get it. So far as your own soul is concerned, you might just as well be a miser and hoard it all, as to spend it all, no matter how shrewdly, and put no love into the spending.

Dangers of Riches.

PROF. A. S. WRIGHT, A.M., School of Applied Science, Cleveland, Ohio.

IT would be interesting to know just what our over-sea visitors of last summer now think of us. Are we still *parvenus?* Is Dives, proud of his bank account and his showily furnished house, still the typical American citizen? Possibly our friends have gleaned some new facts during their summer outing. They may have learned that there are more than five thousand public libraries in the United States, that the best English works are more widely read here in proportion to the population than in the mother country, that our average citizen is more intelligent than the average Englishman, Frenchman, or German. As they gazed upon that dream of the ages by the lake-side, they may have realized that æsthetic taste, nobility of conception, poetry of soul, were qualities not alien to the American spirit; at the meetings of the Congress of Religions, they may have perceived that other divinities than Mammon claim some measure of our homage.

And yet, in the seclusion of our homes, we will admit to our foreign friend that our rapid acquisition of wealth has not exercised an altogether salutary influence upon individual or national character.

That simplicity which was the proud distinction of New England life is no more. Walthen Fürst, the type of the true Swiss nobleman, naïvely remarks: "Why, soon we shall need to put lock and bolt upon our doors." Few of us would care to return to the time when there was nothing in the house worth stealing; many of us regret that so many burglar alarms are necessary. We with modest incomes are quite willing to change the style of our hats,—the hats we now buy wear out,—but furniture, no! Wealth has created false standards, false tastes. Many a youth of the avenue wastes enough annually on his shoes to add a fine section to his library, a fine collection to his natural history museum :—alack! this youth has neither library nor museum. The Harvard student spends five times as much as the Leipsic student; the latter is fivefold more enthusiastic in his search of knowledge. Books rather than rugs is his principle; ours, rugs first, books if the money lasts. Money-worship destroys the scientific spirit. Science like religion will have none but pure devotees. The American boy's first question is: "What will it cost?" his second: "What will it sell for?" The study for which his natural gifts best fit him, which will broaden his mind, stimulate his emotional nature, quicken his spiritual faculties, is spurned for one which is practical, which has a market value. Scientific research demanding self-sacrifice, the study of the humanities which liberalize and strengthen, are abandoned for cash and trash studies. The business college supplants the college of liberal arts. Such students, called possibly, later, men of science, are in fact bookkeepers. The skill they possess, they sell as their butcher sells meat.

The criticism of Buckle in his "History of Civilization," that while "the average intelligence of the American people is above that of any other people, America has fewer first-rate scholars than any other nation," is a just one, and the reason therefor is the utilitarian spirit of our land and time. Inventors, it is said, seldom reap the financial fruit of their labors. Let us hope that the time may come when they will not care to do so, when great humanitarian purpose may be the motive spring of intellectual effort, when the joy of noble thought and noble accomplishment may seem reward that richly rewards.

It is to be feared, too, that the greed for riches is gradually destroying those finer emotional and spiritual qualities which are our best gifts. Mr. Sydney G. Fisher in a recent number of the *Forum* has pointed to the fact that nearly all of our great writers—Longfellow, Whittier, Bryant, Hawthorne, Poe, Emerson, Irving, Prescott, Motley, Lowell, Holmes, Channing, Taylor—were born before 1825. He has sought an explanation in the decline of a national spirit caused by immigration. Doubtless immigration has been hostile to the growth of literature. But literature—certainly that of poetry, romance, oratory, philosophy—is a child of nature. It must breathe pure air; that of the mart stifles it. Wall street furnishes no inspiration to the poet. Poetry and spirituality are freeborn. They bear their own reward. Goethe has beautifully expressed the thought in his poem, "The Bard." The bard, who has just sung his most soulful melody in presence of king and courtier, refuses the chain of gold offered by the king. Handing back the precious gift he exclaims:—

> "I sing as sings the bird
> That in the branches dwelleth,
> The song itself, its own reward,
> From deepest soul it welleth."

No nation can afford to lose its ideals. Our republic was born of a noble thought, was cradled in an atmosphere of liberty and religion, gained the strength of youth through deeds of self-sacrifice. The best heritage of our people is its love of truth. Truth sits enthroned in man and nature; back of both is the Divine. Science, literature, music, sculpture, painting, are the outward expression of an inner soul. In touch with the Divine man grows divine. Our best gifts are intellect and soul—both divine. If we cultivate them, we receive the best rewards. The æsthetic grows only in contact with nature, the intellectual in contact with men of thought and books of thought, the spiritual in contact with God.

To barter the music and poetry of the soul for a chain of gold is ignoble. The chain will fetter to earth. Mammon is a mundane spirit. Listen to the poet:—

> "Mammon, the least erected spirit that fell
> From heaven; for even in heaven his look and thoughts
> Were always downward bent, admiring more
> The riches of heaven's pavement, trodden gold,
> Than aught divine or holy else enjoyed
> In vision beatific."

DANGERS OF RICHES.

Neither intellectual, emotional, nor spiritual enjoyment has any cash value. The great danger of wealth is that it tends to dry up the springs of pure enjoyment. The stagnation or deterioration is gradual and insidious as is the loss of physical power. The intellect starves, the emotions wither, the spiritual nature dies. The possible giant becomes a pigmy. Awakening—there is none; the dead emotions are never resurrected. The immortal has put on mortality.

Giving Enriches the Giver.

A. M. HAGGARD, A.M., Ex-President Oskaloosa College, Iowa.

TWENTY years ago, in a Wisconsin town, two boys were schoolmates. One was from a poor family; the other from a family more fortunate. The principal of the academy had suggested the organization of a cricket club. Both boys were very active in the various committees of preparation. In due time the first game was called, the captains were "choosing up." Frank chose Fred, who had not signed the constitution because he was unable to pay the prescribed fee. Frank had paid his dues, and entered his name as a member, but Fred would not believe it until the book was shown him. The boys are now men. Fred declares that nothing in all his life ever made a deeper impression on his heart. What will he not do for Frank? He would cross the continent at his call. He would risk health and life itself for his friend. He would do for Frank's children what David did for the son of Jonathan, his deceased friend. What has Frank gained? In Fred he has an account upon which he can draw unlimited drafts; a bank where no draft will be dishonored; a balance which can never be overdrawn.

This is but one incident from one life. How poor and barren most lives would be without such deeds! Strike out the gain of giving, and you destroy the core of history, the soul of oratory, the beauties of literature, the glories of poetry and song, the heroism of patriotism, the divinity of religion, and the hope of eternity.

He who wins the choicest gains of life must give. This is THE LAW. It is written upon the face of a world of dead matter. The crude, unsightly carbon must give itself upon the rack of nature's secret inquisition, if it would shine in diamond beauty, or adorn a royal crown. It is written upon the pages of living matter. The seed cannot refuse the darkness and decay of its field sepulcher and yet receive the enrichment of a glorious harvest. We cannot avoid the cross and yet wear the crown.

It is written in God's Word, "Give and it shall be given unto you, good measure, pressed down, shaken together, and running over." God himself honors this law by filling it full. He is the giver of that "unspeakable gift"; the giver of all good; the giver of all givers. All across the wide, wide sweep from the dust of the ground to the throne and heart of God, this law reads always the same, *Giving is gain.*

Is it right for the giver to think of his gains through giving? Does not such thought color his giving with selfishness? Jesus of Nazareth not only harbored such thoughts but was borne up thereon as by eagle's wings. "For the joy set before him he endured the cross and despised the shame." It is not wrong; it is not selfish. "God loveth a cheerful giver," and it is good to think on that love. It is good to know that "whosoever shall give to drink * * * a cup of cold water only in the name of a disciple * * * shall in no wise lose his reward."

Unselfish Giving is not a giving devoid of self. To eliminate self from giving is as impossible as to eliminate the glory of God from the universe he has made. What then is selfish giving? It is the wrong adjustment of self. It may be so placed as to help, or destroy. Make the centripetal force predominant and you destroy not only the orbits but the planets themselves. Subordinate this force and you lay the foundations of the starry dome, and fill the universe with order and law. In like manner, self made predominant renders true giving impossible. Self subordinated is incense upon glowing coals. The gift without the giver never filled the temple of the soul with the precious aroma of love. No holy place, no high priest in royal robes, no golden censer though enriched with diamonds, can atone for

GIVING ENRICHES THE GIVER.

the absence of incense, and that incense is self rightly placed, self subordinated or sacrificed.

> " He gives no gift who gives to me
>   Things rich and rare,
> Unless within the gift he give
>   Of self some share.
>
> " He gives no gift who gives to me
>   Silver or gold,
> If but to make his own heart glad;
>   Such gift is cold.
>
> " He gives me gifts most rich and rare
>   Who gives to me,
> Out of the riches of his heart,
>   True sympathy.
>
> "He gives best gifts who, giving naught
>   Of worldly store,
> Gives me his friendship, love, and trust.
>   I ask no more."
>
> —*Laura Harvey in Demorest's.*

In giving the benefit may be transferred in many appropriate forms. That form which first recurs to most minds is money or property. At present there is manifest a wave of benevolence. The endowment of educational institutions, the furthering of benevolent enterprises, and the enlarging of missionary undertakings is characteristic of this quarter of our century. Our multi-millionaires are doing themselves credit in these fields. A host of men and women of smaller means are adopting the ten per cent. rule in their giving. Personal inquiry, well directed, will surprise many readers; first, at the number voluntarily practicing this method; and, next, at the wide range of condition covered by these givers, some being very limited in means; and, in the third place, at their testimony in answer to our proposition, "Does giving enrich the giver?" If you have never had communion with these witnesses, gain it at once. Or, better yet, try the method for yourself. It is *an inspiration* to meet a nineteenth century business man who

GIVING ENRICHES THE GIVER.

puts into his ledgers the faith of the prophets and the fervent zeal of the reformers. Such can tell of gain through giving as no man can write it. The shadow of such persons is sufficient to make one feel that "it is more blessed to give than to receive."

But money is by no means essential to giving. In fact, cash values often dwindle into utter insignificance in the greater giving. Money is powerless in the expression of such a gift as Arnold von Winkelried gave to Switzerland and to the cause of freedom. The blood of our Revolutionary fathers, and the more precious blood of Christ, are valuable beyond the expression of figures and dollar marks. Who has not known some one, perhaps an elder sister, naturally talented, who has given up her classes and her prospective college course with everything which usually inspires young womanhood, in order to care for a large family of motherless brothers and sisters? Thus to grow old and go alone down life's further slope is often the divinest giving. Did not James A. Garfield receive from an elder brother such a gift? And if so, which is now the richer? In home life, in social and political circles, and in the business world are mines of wealth which open to none but the true giver. Darkness can find its way to the sun more readily than the selfish heart to these gold mines of God.

One more question, What proportion exists between a gift and its recompense? It is the ratio between Paul's "light afflictions for a moment," and his "eternal weight of glory." It is the ratio between a few cheering words one dark night spoken on the street, and John B. Gough as he is known and as he is yet to appear. It is the ratio between three-sixteenths of one cent, and that place here and hereafter given by God's books to the widow who cast in the two mites. It is a godlike ratio. It is clothed in his infinity.

True Magnanimity.

Rev. GEORGE R. HEWITT, B.D.

MAGNANIMITY is sufficiently defined by its name. Literally it means "greatness of mind." And that is just what it is—capaciousness of mind and of heart. It may properly be regarded, therefore, not merely as a single virtue but rather as a state of mind out of which all the virtues grow. It is a spirit to do and to bear great things. It bears trials without sinking beneath them, faces danger and death without flinching; can smile benignly on the face of a foe and rejoice in a rival's success; is serene under great provocations, and endures with a steadfast heart both perils and privations for the sake of great principles and the common good.

One of the finest descriptions of a magnanimous man to be found in all literature is Emerson's brief characterization of Abraham Lincoln: "His heart was as great as the world, but there was no room in it to hold the memory of a wrong."

It is in our treatment of those who have done us wrong that our magnanimity, or the lack of it, most conspicuously appears. The magnanimous man bears no grudges, does not enter in the ledger of memory an account of injuries or slights received, but takes a generous view of all enemies, adversaries, and competitors.

Cotton Mather was wont to say he did not know of any person in the world who had done him an ill turn but he had done him a good one for it.

Pericles, the renowned Athenian, was once waited upon by a scurrilous fellow who reviled him to his face. As he was leaving, Pericles called a servant and told him to take a lamp and show the man the way home.

TRUE MAGNANIMITY.

Magnanimity towards friends is touching and beautiful, but towards enemies it is sublime. There is a spiritual grandeur about it that shows man at his best. The union of lofty self-control and self-sacrifice which it displays is the thing that impresses us.

In the Franco-Prussian war a French soldier was brought into the operating room of the hospital at Metz with a fearfully shattered hand. The chloroform had begun to give out, and the local druggists had tried in vain to make it. "Well, my friend," says the surgeon, "we shall have to have a bit of an operation. Would you like to be made insensible?" "Yes. I have suffered so much all night that I don't think I could stand it."

"Are you particular about it?" asked the surgeon.

"Why, is that stuff scarce now that puts you to sleep?"

"We have scarcely any left."

The brave fellow reflected a moment, then replied, "Keep it for those who have arms and legs to be taken off, but be quick." He stuffed his cravat in his mouth, lay down, and held out his hand. "Did it hurt much?" said the surgeon, when the operation was over. "Oh, yes; but what can you do? We poor fellows must help one another."

The classic instance of this kind is that of Sir Philip Sidney. Sidney was the contemporary of Shakespeare, Bacon, Ben Jonson, and other brilliant lights of the Elizabethan era. He was admired for his learning and genius, the friend of the queen, the favorite of the court and of the camp. But he is best known and endeared to posterity by the fact that as he lay dying on the battlefield in Flanders and his attendants brought water to cool his fevered lips, he bade them give it to a soldier stretched on the ground beside him, saying, "Thy necessity is greater than mine." Nothing is so regal in man as magnanimity. Man is likest God when he is magnanimous.

Every man should vigorously strive to cultivate this tranquil self-control, this breadth of mind and heart, which are the main elements of magnanimity. One of the best ways of doing so is to familiarize yourself with the lives and deeds of the heroes of the world. Walk down the aisles of history in the company of the great and good and you will catch something of their spirit, on the principle that "he that walketh with wise men shall be wise."

Without a measure of magnanimity a man is in a fair way to become a wretched self-tormentor as he grows old. He will be narrowed by selfishness, soured by envy, and crushed by the disappointments of life.

The magnanimous man like the contented man has in himself a continual feast. He can say:—

> "My mind to me a kingdom is;
>   Such present joys therein I find,
> That it excels all other bliss
>   That earth affords or grows by kind.
> Though much I want that most would have,
> Yet still my mind forbids to crave."

Perils of Success.

Rev. GEORGE R. HEWITT, B.D.

WE have not the slightest expectation of saying anything on this subject that will have one feather's weight of influence in deterring anyone from striving to attain success. Whatever its perils, they will eagerly be braved for the sake of reaching the shining goal. All risks will be run if only the coveted prize may be grasped.

What do we mean by success? What would probably be the reply of four out of every five men whom you should meet on the street if suddenly asked what they understood success to be? They would say success consists in gaining wealth, or at least a competence. This, of course, is not the highest idea of success, but it is the current idea. The age is materialistic, and success like everything else is estimated in terms of dollars and cents. Such being the case we shall take success in the present chapter to mean simply becoming rich or becoming eminent, either in business or in professional life, as the case may be.

In this acceptation of the term, then, what are some of the perils of success? They are by no means visionary. Though, perhaps, not so obvious as the dangers attending failure they are none the less real.

I. There is the danger of pride. As Dr. Robert South very pithily puts it: "Who is there whose heart does not swell with his money-bag, and whose thoughts do not follow the proportions of his condition? What a difference sometimes in the same man poor and preferred! His mind like a mushroom has shot up in a night. His first business is to forget himself, then his friends. When the sun shines the peacock displays his train."

The peril of prosperity is that it is very apt to make a man "think more highly of himself than he ought to think." Addison has said, "'Tis not in mortals to command success," but the successful man is prone to forget this, and to take all the credit of his success to himself. He fails to make sufficient allowance for favoring circumstances, for the element of chance, or luck in business, or for a smiling Providence. As Nebuchadnezzar at the height of his prosperity and pride said, "Is not this great Babylon which *I* have built by the might of *my* power and for the glory of *my* majesty?" so the prosperous man to-day is apt to give the pronoun "I" a large place in his conversation. His thoughts are likely to be filled with himself, with what he has, and what he has done more than others. Such a man is apt to stop his ears to the entrance of reproof or advice. A man of his capabilities is too wise to need the assistance of another's wisdom. The wealthier a man is the wiser he is in his own conceit. Thus prosperity begets pride, and success gives birth to a feeling of self-sufficiency.

II. Another peril of success is that of failing to make a right use of it. The danger attending all good things is that they will be abused and so become evil things. Money always brings with it the possibility of its misuse. The sudden accession of wealth, therefore, is a perilous thing for a man unless he is under the power and guidance of high moral principles. He will be tempted merely to hoard it or use it for himself, to think his one business now is to enjoy his wealth and not to do good with it, to take his ease and pamper himself instead of making himself helpful to society. How many men of prosperity to-day stand surrounded by persons and objects on which they might bestow their wealth with the greatest advantage to giver as well as receiver, yet they give not. The idea that wealth should be held and administered for the necessities of the world never seems to have entered their minds. Poverty and suffering, the cause of education, religious enterprise and many other claimants stand around them stretching out their hands in mute appeal, but they either do not see or, seeing, heed them not.

The late George W. Childs of Philadelphia, so well known for his splendid generosity, tells in a volume of recollections published some time before his death, that during the war he asked a very rich man to contribute some money to a certain relief fund. The wealthy man shook his head and said: "Childs, I can't give you anything. I have worked too hard for my money." Mr. Childs goes on to say that being generous grows on a person just as being mean does, that he himself had worked hard for his money, but always gave in proportion as his ability to give increased, until he found his greatest pleasure in doing good to others.

They that are strong, whether physically, mentally, or financially, are strong not for themselves alone, but ought to share the burdens of the weak. As Shakespeare has said:—

> "Thyself and thy belongings
> Are not thine own. . . .
> Heaven doth with us as we with torches do,
> Not light them for themselves."

The successful man is in danger of forgetting this. When lifted up to a point of prosperity above his fellows he is apt to think that it is that he may shine for his own sake, and not like the sun, for the necessities of the world.

III. Our limited space will allow the mention of only one more peril attending success, and that is, that in attaining it a man is liable to stunt and dwarf himself. Competition to-day is so keen, the struggle to "get on" is so intense, that a man who goes into business with the purpose of succeeding must go into it over head and ears. The absorbing and feverish devotion which business exacts to-day as the price of success is a serious menace to the highest life of the nation or of individuals. In gaining success it may be questioned whether a man does not lose more than he gains. A recent able writer has said: "The world is full of men who are atrophied on every side except that through which they are gaining their daily bread—men who have sacrificed to success about everything that makes life worth living." They have no time for books, no time to bring their souls into contact with the best that has been thought and done in the world, no time for travel, no time for friends, no time for religion, no time even for the sweet amenities of home. Their interests are narrowed, their souls are warped and crippled by thinking of only one order of facts, which order is summed up in the word "business." If the time comes for such men to retire *from* business they find they have nothing to retire *to*. Literature, science, religious and philanthropic interests have now no charm or refreshment for them. In the fierce struggle for success the door has been closed that opens upon these fair realms, and now the key cannot be found, or, if found, is so rusty it cannot be used. It is easy for us to see the reason underlying the fact to which President Eliot refers in his address on "The Disadvantages of Present Rich Men," when he says: "I observe that the life of the rich man who has got his money and is a little out of the struggle to get it, becomes dull, monotonous, and uninteresting."

Success in scientific or professional life is likely to be accompanied by the same narrowing process. The case of Darwin, the eminent naturalist, may here be cited, who about the age of thirty lost all pleasure in art, music, and poetry. Shakespeare became so intolerably dull that it nauseated him. "My mind," he says, "seems to have become a kind of machine for grinding general laws out of large collections of facts, but why this should have caused the atrophy of that part of the brain alone on which the higher tasks depend, I cannot conceive." It may well be questioned whether in very many cases the price exacted for such success is not more than anyone can afford to pay.

The Whirlpool of Commerce.

Rev. GEORGE R. HEWITT, B.D.

COMMERCE is a wide word. In its broadest acceptation it includes every kind of trade or business, from that of the importer of silks and laces to that of the tin-peddler. Wherever there is an exchange of one commodity for another, or for money, there is commerce.

The origin of commerce is not far to seek. It was born of men's necessities. One man had that which another wanted, and for which he had something to give in exchange. From this want on one side and the spirit of accommodation or of acquisitiveness on the other sprang trade or commerce.

To-day trading has become the great business of the world. Man is a trading animal. He takes to trading like a duck to water. If he has no other commodity to dispose of, he will trade jack-knives with his next neighbor.

The object of all trade to-day, of course, is gain. No man would embark in any business enterprise without the hope of reaping some profit from it. And when a man is once fairly engaged in business it is astonishing how seductive it becomes. The appetite for trading grows by what it feeds on. From small beginnings a man is tempted to branch out indefinitely until he soon comes to have more on his hands than he can comfortably handle; and at last his whole life and thought have to be surrendered to commercial transactions and the making of money. Hence we see the fitness of the title of this chapter. Commerce is like a whirlpool. The danger that besets a man is that he will be drawn deeper and deeper into the whirling vortex of trade, until his business, which should be a means to an end, becomes an end in itself.

THE WHIRLPOOL OF COMMERCE.

Said a young business man to the writer not a great while ago: "I almost envy you your opportunities for study and thought upon high themes. I dislike to be obliged to think incessantly about money-getting. But once in you can't get out."

A man begins by making a little. It seems very easy. Straightway his ambition enlarges. The thought presently floats into his mind, "Why am not I one of those born to be millionaires?" At first a few thousands would have satisfied him, now nothing less than hundreds of thousands will do.

If a man is doing a business of $50,000 per annum at five per cent. he thinks he might increase it to $100,000, and so double his profits. Or if he is doing a $100,000 business he aspires to do a $200,000 business, or if a $200,000 business nothing short of $500,000 will satisfy him. Accordingly he borrows capital, enlarges his plant, employs extra help, puts additional drummers on the road, and by every means endeavors to double his sales. But he soon finds that to keep his enlarged plant running he must offer his goods, or bid for contracts, at a lower figure than formerly. This, coupled with the additional cost of maintaining the larger plant, cuts into his profits; and so it comes to pass that many men find after doubling their sales they have only increased their cares, but have not materially increased their profits. Inordinate ambition to do a big business and get rich quickly wrecks a great many men both physically and financially. Better a small, old-fashioned business with some leisure, contentment, and peace of mind, than a big business with anxiety, excitement, wakeful nights, and nervous collapse.

Not content with a rapid extension of their own business, men, in their eagerness to make money, are too easily seduced into side ventures. They are induced to put a little money into this enterprise and a little into that. Notwithstanding that for every one that grows rich by mere speculation a hundred are made poorer, yet men will invest hopefully in the most doubtful ventures.

THE WHIRLPOOL OF COMMERCE.

One thing a young man should do early in his business career is to resolve to steer clear of a life of speculation. It brings demoralization and ruin to thousands. Moreover, if he is wise he will think twice before investing the profits of his own business in outside enterprises of which he has no personal knowledge. The Honorable William Whiting, one of the most successful business men in Western Massachusetts, a man of wide experience and observation, in a recent article on "Business Failures" has these words: "The man does best in the long run who sticks to his own business, is chary of outside responsibilities and schemes, and invests his surplus that must go outside safely at six per cent."

In conclusion: A man had far better make less money than become so involved in business that he can think of nothing else, and at last break down of nervous worry. Beware of the tyranny of trade. Beware of its tightening hold upon your spirit. Trade so as to become more of a man thereby, and not less. The commercial world is a splendid arena for the development of manhood. Men make trade, but trade also makes men. But alas! for one that is made by it five allow themselves to be unmade or marred by it. See to it that commerce does not cramp your soul, nor crush out the nobler sentiments. See that it leaves no disfiguring marks upon you after you have done with it forever. Give manhood the supremacy. Keep business subordinate. Remember the Frenchman's epitaph: "He was born a man, and died a grocer."

Gamblers and Gambling.

REV. H. O. BREEDEN, LL.D., Editor Christian Worker, Des Moines, Iowa.

THE spirit of gambling, like the terrible breath of a noisome pestilence, pervades society. It is the blighting curse of modern American life even as it was the bane of English society in its halcyon days. Charles James Fox, and even Wilberforce, did not escape it. From the palatial mansion of the wealthy gambler in the chamber of commerce, to the thoughtless if not unprincipled young man that throws dice at the cigar counter; from the "bookmaker" at the fashionable club race track, to the ragged, smutty urchin who flips coppers in a back alley, the gambling spirit is the same, and the gamblers are identical, save in raiment and acumen, unless, indeed, we attribute to the first mentioned, a much larger degree of moral turpitude.

The genus gambler is a hydra-headed monster. In his vulgar trappings, he is the common "three card monte man" who traps the unwary at county fairs, or on railway trains; or the roulette and faro manipulator in gilded dens whom everybody looks upon as a dangerous foe to society, and a dethroner of morality. He appears to be what he is, and is what he appears to be. The professional gambler is under the ban of society. He receives no sympathy from the community. His gambling is not respectable; it is outlawed. His work has its penalty.

But the gambler presents another head. He is not now the ignoble, "outlawed professional," but the "speculator in commerce." He is clothed in "purple and fine linen." The ordinary gambler, who advertises his profession, is put off the "smoker," while the gambler in stocks and grain rides on a pass in a Pullman palace car. Justice is blindfold when the "monte man" is before her. His offense is indictable; but when the board of trade "angel" appears, she lifts the blind, sees who it is, and lets him pass.

The common gambler observes a strict code of honor that spurns the use of "loaded dice," but the commercial gambler congratulates himself on shrewdness in receiving "points" that enable him to "corner" the market on breadstuffs.

But the monster exhibits another head, and now he is a "pool gambler." He is an accessory of the race course and the baseball diamond, since these offer an arena for his cupidity and love of excitement. Last year he paid one hundred and seventy-five thousand dollars for the "exclusive" bookmaking privilege at the Washington Park races in Chicago. The race track and its adjunct, the city pool room, is probably the second most formidable and dangerous institution in America to-day. Its legitimate offsprings are deceit, concealment, forgery, embezzlement, and theft. Young men steal their employers' money to bet on the races; young girls sell their virtue for money to wager and for "tips." Married women leave their families and rob their husbands at the bidding of the "pool." It is a veritable "Pandora's box, from which issue all moral evils and social disasters, only hope is not in the box."

Still another form of the gambler appears, this time in the drawing room, arrayed in richest gowns, cut décolleté and bedecked with jewels or clad in evening "full dress." He is now the society gambler. Cards, notwithstanding their bad history and evil associations, are his instruments. Progressive euchre and sometimes poker are his games. It is not money he seeks now, but excitement and the indulgence of a passion. The prizes are offered only to add spice to the diversion, just as opium in the cigarette, or the salacious and libidinous in the modern theatrical performance, — "the spice of hell." Sometimes he tries to hoodwink the uninitiated into believing that playing for "prizes" is not gambling. But the strongest moral microscope ever known, will fail to discover the least difference between them. In the drawing room, at the fashionable evening party, a young man receives his initial lessons, and a passion is called forth and developed which demands gratification. Indulge it he must even though it takes him among vilest associates and into most disreputable places. The downfall and utter ruin of many an otherwise noble young man dates its beginning from the decisive hour when he was seduced by the mistress of some elegant home into playing progressive euchre in the social circle.

But the gambler sometimes enters the sacred portals of the church, clothed as an "angel of light," and opens up his paraphernalia at the church fair or bazar, directing a "raffle" or organizing a "lottery." He often deceives the "very elect" with the specious plea that the end sanctifies the means, and the holy place transforms the "creature." A hog, of animals most unclean to a Mohammedan, strayed into a mosque and polluted the temple, driving the priests almost wild with consternation. But one, shrewder than the rest, solved the difficulty on the spot. The temple was so holy that when the hog crossed its threshold it was transformed into a pure and innocent lamb. Even so the animal they call a "tiger," in his lair down in the tough district of the city, undergoes a radical if not "miraculous" change and becomes a sportive, stainless lamb, "when Mary leads it into the church."

The church that tolerates, for the sake of filling its coffers with dishonorable dollars, the unhallowed methods of the lottery and raffle, deserves the curse of God and man. It is an ecclesiastical gambling den and ought to be dealt with as such. It is more "a school of vice, and instructor of incipient gamblers, an apologist for immorality," than a church of the Lord Jesus Christ.

Gambling is associated with and followed by a whole brood of dire evils and flaunting vices. It provokes the thirst for strong drink. The terrible reaction of an exciting "winning," or a destructive and heavy "loss," calls for a stimulant; this "enemy in the mouth" not only dissipates depression, but "steals away the brains," and goads its unreasoning victim to return to the gaming table. It not only calls for stimulants but entraps its victims in other meshes. The gambling hell and the variety theater are mutual supports. The saloon, the "tiger's lair," and the brothel constitute the devil's vile trinity of breeding and nesting holes of sin and vice in protean forms. Gambling is not only a menace to, but a withering blight upon, the home. When it becomes a rooted passion in the heart, there is no room for the flowers of domestic joy and peace. The "fires of all the finer feelings become embers" upon the hearthstone of the home which contains a devotee of the "black art."

It has been said that a woman can forgive her husband a hundred libations on the altar of the jolly Bacchus or the blind god of fortune with vastly more ease than one foul sacrifice at the polluted shrine of lustful Venus. But women should understand that in seven cases out of ten, virtue is first dethroned, the will made weak, and passion strong by slavery to gambling and drink. Why is it that gambling has obtained such a foothold in American life and flourishes almost unhindered, in its terrible sway from palace to hovel, from plutocrat to pauper? Because nearly everybody believes in it. It is certainly within bounds to say that the real root of the difficulty in suppressing this evil is that a great many people in our best society and in our churches are not convinced that there is anything really wrong in gambling. They ask, "Is it not lawful for me to do whatsoever I will with my own?" The answer from a moral standpoint should be most emphatically "No." In small matters as in great, a man is only a trustee of the property he calls his own, and his title is only valid when he uses it equally for his own good and that of his fellow man. He is not at liberty to appropriate his own property to useless and malevolent ends, to waste it foolishly, much less to use it for promoting vice. No man has a natural right to stake one penny upon a game of chance, no more than he has the right to take the loaf of bread which at the time he does not want, and tread it in the mire in the presence of a hungry child. But gambling is intrinsically evil and only evil. The indictment against it is fourfold.

First — It fosters belief in luck and chance and superstition. It offers a premium upon witchcraft and voodooism.

Second — It insults labor and destroys motives to honest industry. The young man who won one hundred dollars on the races by risking only one dollar, or the servant girl who drew fifty dollars by a lottery ticket for which she paid but fifty cents, are both now thoroughly disgusted with the slow and conservative but honest methods of earning a living. "Why work like a slave for fifty dollars or twenty dollars per month when one can win twice that sum in an afternoon?" The first winning of a young man constitutes the most unfortunate event in life, for it weakens all laudable ambition to achieve success on skill, merit, and economy as a business man. It begins in a desperate attempt to get something for nothing, and usually results in getting nothing for something.

Third — It corrupts the whole manhood, and prostitutes the noblest faculties of the soul to basest uses. Its poison is insidious.

Once in the system, like malaria, it chills and fevers and unfits for life and shatters the constitution. It begins by demoralizing the powers of application. It then spoils men for the plain duties and rational enjoyments of everyday life. It blunts the sense of right, until the gambler comes to regard the most sacred things, even the manhood of man, and the virtue of woman, as purchasable. It feeds the passion for nervous excitement by bringing together the greatest number of demoralizing stimulants. These are intensified as the stakes increase, and the habit grows until a desperate mania, or a horrible insanity, robs character of purpose, piety, and purity, and brings the end of a blasted life.

It is the unanimous testimony of ministers of the gospel that it is far more difficult to lead a man who has become infatuated with the gambling mania to a life of uprightness and virtue than to lead a drunkard from his cups.

GAMBLERS AND GAMBLING.

The wretched man upon whose soul the powers of darkness have secured a mortgage in the game of chance will leave his family in semi-starvation, even in sickness unto death, and hasten like a moth to the candle of destruction.

Fourth — But the chief indictment against it is written in a very old book, in the words, "Thou shalt not steal." There are two possible ways by which one may get money or property from another honestly. First, he may receive it as a gift. Second, he may render an equivalent. The gambler who acquires money by purchasing a chance in the "pool" by a wager, a raffle, or securing a "prize," gets it in neither of these ways. He has simply won it. The money lost, is lost contrary to the desire, design, and therefore to the proper consent of the persons losing it. And the winner holds it by no better right according to the interpretation of strict morality than the thief or robber.

Gambling leads directly to dishonesty. The connection between gambling and stealing is so natural and intimate that prudent business men refuse to employ gamblers in positions of responsibility. There are indications that a thoughtful and conscientious people are taking steps looking toward the suppression of this measureless evil. Great Britain has recently formed an anti-gambling league, and courageous leaders of Christian thought, and molders of moral sentiment, in New York city have projected a "National Anti-Gambling Society" for the protection of the young and the manhood of America.

When once the American people realize the enormity of this sin, they will drive it from the land with the besom of destruction. In the mean time it is the imperative duty of the press, pulpit, and platform, to agitate.

May the agitation go on and increase in volume and velocity until the reign of devils is summarily cut short — until this cloud, one of the darkest that ever dropped over the earth's fair face, is lifted and dispersed.

Wrecks of Wall Street.

Prof. E. T. TYNDALL, Editor Daily News, Philadelphia.

ONE of the most fascinating spots in this country, and especially in New York city, for the young speculator, is on the floor of Wall street stock exchange. Although each day new additions are made to the numbers of wrecked fortunes and blasted lives, yet each succeeding day adds new plungers to the list. This alluring den occupies a large portion of the block bounded by Broad, Wall, and New streets, and Exchange place. When the excitement waxes warm even the older members on the floor have difficulty in keeping their heads, and the inexperienced take headstrong risks in the turmoil and soon find that, instead of realizing the fond dream of immense wealth, they are ruined and penniless. And it is not only the inexperienced who are wrecked financially, not to speak of the physical and moral influences of those gambling places.

When the immense influence which Wall street exerts on the trade of to-day is considered, the conclusion is, to say the least, alarming. Millions of dollars are involved in these daily speculations, and experience has taught that a panic there means crash followed by crash, as most of the largest speculators are directly or indirectly connected with large financial concerns elsewhere. One of the first and greatest failures on Wall street, known as the "Western Blizzard," occurred in 1857, when the Ohio Life and Trust Company, a gigantic concern, with millions invested in stocks, failed. Business was for a time paralyzed, as many banks, which had advanced this supposed-to-be stanch company large sums of money for speculating purposes, had to suspend, and the hard-earned savings of

WRECKS OF WALL STREET.

thousands of honest men and women were sacrificed, because of the recklessness of those gamblers. In the panic of 1873, made famous by the issuance of $7\tfrac{3}{10}$ Northern Pacific Railroad bonds by Jay Cooke, hundreds more were ruined. Then followed "Boss" Tweed's failure in 1872, and later the panic of 1884 precipitated by Ferdinand D. Ward and James D. Fish; and "Black Friday" will not soon be forgotten by the speculators of Wall street. George I. Seney, once president of the Metropolitan Bank of New York, invested millions of dollars in Wall street stocks, failed and dragged down with him, his own bank, a Brooklyn bank, in which he was director, and also a Brooklyn insurance company which had loaned Mr. Seney large sums of money. James R. Keene, one of the brightest and most fortunate speculators ever on Wall street, rolled up a fortune of several millions in a comparatively short time, but later through rash speculations lost it all.

And so the story runs. Success may smile upon the speculator for a time, but misfortune is almost certain to follow; then comes a wrecked life, and the unfortunate dupe is a thousandfold worse off than if he had never made a dollar by gambling. His nervous system has been in a constant state of excitement and his physical constitution is more or less impaired by the strain. A more serious impairment, however, results from the dwarfing and stultifing of the moral sensibilities. No person can gamble in any form without the moral nature being affected thereby, and speculating in stocks is one of the worst forms of gambling, as they are bought and sold on margins. If the market goes against the speculator, he must have more money to cover the shrinkage and hold his stock, and there is just where the rash young man who has access to money, not his own, is tempted to appropriate his employer's means, with the hope of making large gains and returning the money thus used, without any person, but himself, knowing that it was ever taken. But, alas, how often is he swamped, disgraced, and ruined for life! and this, too, is not the worst feature of the case. Perchance a mother or a sister is involved in the downfall and caused to suffer agony of mind, a thousandfold worse than death itself. In many cases a promising young man with means is anxious to rank among the millionaires of the day and steps into one of those gambling shops and soon in the excitement has his all at stake. Anxious days and sleepless nights are passed as stocks waver. Finally a crash comes, ruin instead of wealth is the result, and, being driven to desperation and willing to meet death rather than penury, a self-destroyed life is the painful outcome.

These are only a hint at the evils which result from speculating on Wall street. Blasted hopes, ruined homes, broken hearts, distracted wives and mothers, once happy children cast upon the world with an indelible stigma resting upon them, and untimely deaths, follow regularly and surely in the train of misfortunes emanating from this den of gambling.

The Balance Wheel.

Rev. GEORGE R. HEWITT, B.D.

EVERYWHERE in the material universe we behold steadfast order and beauty as the result of equilibrium between opposing forces. In the movements of the heavenly bodies stability is due to the beautiful balance between two forces, one of which tends to make the whirling worlds fly apart, and the other of which tends to make them fly together. In like manner, in the structure of our living bodies, stability is the result of equilibrium between the vital force which builds the molecules together and the chemical force which tears them down.

As in the realm of matter so in the realm of mind and of morals, stability and order are the result of a proper balance between conflicting powers. We frequently hear it said of certain men that "they lack balance," or that their "mind has lost its balance." They are unsteady. They act sometimes in a way that seems strange and unaccountable to their fellow men. Socrates used to say that all men were a little insane, for they all at times did things that seemed ridiculous and strange to others.

A perfectly sane or sound mind is a perfectly balanced mind. Man needs a balance wheel that his movements may be regular, orderly, and steady. Whatever serves for the regulation and co-ordination of movements is figuratively speaking called a balance wheel.

(1) Such a balance wheel in the practical conduct of life is *good common sense* or sound judgment, or in other words discernment of the proper thing to do and to say and of the

proper time to do and say it. Common sense is not nearly so common as the name implies. There are people who, as we say, always "put their foot in it." Even if they do the right thing, they do it in the wrong way or at the wrong time. They mar whatever they attempt by overdoing it. How frequently a public speaker spoils an excellent speech by saying some unnecessary things! He weakens what he insists upon by insisting upon too much. Essentials and non-essentials seem to have equal prominence in his mind. He "slops over." He loses his balance, and is carried into some extravagances of statement which cause him to be less esteemed than he otherwise would be.

Such persons fail to see things in their proper relations. They may be learned and sympathetic, but they lack practical wisdom, which, as Arthur Helps says, "acts in the mind as gravitation does in the material world, combining, keeping things in their places, and maintaining a mutual dependence amongst the various parts of the system."

There was good old Bronson Alcott, for example, who had both a soaring intellect and a tender heart, who was always full of great schemes for the advancement of the human race, but, as a recent writer says, "Alas for his family! He would sit on his piazza expounding to visitors his plan for the emancipation of women, while his wife was tugging a pail of water from the distant spring as a step toward providing dinner for the host and his guests." There was a lamentable lack here of perception of the eternal fitness of things.

Some philosophers like Locke hold that sound sense, the perception of the fitness of things, is not acquirable, but must be born in a man. With this opinion Dr. Witherspoon, at one time president of Princeton College, would seem to agree, for he was wont to say to incoming classes of students:—

"Gentlemen, if you have not learning this university is the fountain; if you have not piety the grace of God will give you that; but if you are wanting in common sense, may heaven have mercy on you."

THE BALANCE WHEEL.

(2) As common sense is the balance wheel in practical life, so conscience is the balance wheel in the moral life. Conscience is that power in us by which we discern the moral qualities of actions. It warns us before we do wrong, remonstrates with us while we are doing wrong, and fills us with self-reproach after we have done wrong. If, for example, a chance to enrich myself in some crooked way is presented to me, conscience at once warns me that it is wrong to cheat, makes me feel that I ought not to cheat, then, if in spite of its warnings, I go on and do the wrong, it chides me and fills me with a sense of guilt and shame.

Without a conscience man is like a machine without a regulator, sometimes too fast, sometimes too slow, seldom just right. Amid the innumerable variety of actions, choices, impulses, feelings, likings, habits, and passions, which are possible to man, conscience is the natural regulator and monarch. It presides over them all, and subjects all to its jurisdiction. We may not obey its behests, but we cannot silence its reproaches.

Do nothing against conscience. To disobey it is to destroy the peace and equipoise of your inner life. An approving conscience is a priceless treasure. It is really the smile of God. What conscience indorses God indorses. What conscience condemns God condemns.

Conscience is prophetic of a future life and of our accountability there for the deeds done in the body. Were this life all, conscience would be an incumbrance. We should be over-freighted for the voyage of life. A canal boat has no need of a compass. A compass argues deep sea sailing. A conscience argues eternity beyond the river of time. He who lives by conscience lives for two worlds. He who lives for this world only needs a balance wheel. We should call a man who could sit on a barrel of gunpowder smoking a pipe, a rather unbalanced sort of man; so is the man who lives in this world thoughtless of the next.

The Use and Power of Faith.

Rev. LEWIS O. BRASTOW, D.D., Yale University.

OUR conception of the value of faith will depend upon our conception of its significance. Let us therefore at the outset understand what is meant by it.

In theological discussions faith has often been made synonymous with belief. But faith is surely more than belief. Belief is pre-supposed, but the two are not identical. Faith is the larger word. Faith may include belief, but belief does not as a necessity include faith. Belief is a response and a committal of the mind to an object that is recognized as real or true. Faith is a response and a committal of the entire inner self to an object that is recognized as good. It involves a docile and believing attitude of mind, but it includes also a certain responsiveness of feeling and of conviction and a concurrence of will. In such attitude of self-responsiveness and act of self-committal, faith always recognizes its object as good. It may attribute to its object a good that does not belong to it. That is, knowledge of the object may be defective. But faith always attaches itself to what it conceives to be good. No one trusts what he recognizes as bad. All genuine faith therefore has a certain ethical significance. It is the object of faith that conditions the nature and scope of such ethical significance. The object may possibly be one's self. There is a reasonable and a worthy self-trust. If it be normal, that is, if it be neither too large nor too small, neither too arrogant nor too degrading, neither the self-assertion of pride nor the self-depreciation of conscious self-degradation, it is right and good. Every man should be able to believe in and trust himself. Entire self-distrust is irrational and immoral. God put strength into manhood and meant that it should be an object of confidence. No one can fight successfully the battle of life otherwise. To distrust one's self in an emergency is to invite defeat. A habit of self-distrust undermines strength. It is never safe to suspend one's self in the uncertainty of self-distrust. A reasonable, well balanced self-trust, held within the limits of a dependent life, is moral. The object may be one's fellow men. No man can stand alone. The world crushes the one who attempts it. It is the necessity of life to believe in and trust one's fellows. It may often prove a misplaced confidence. In so far as it is, it may be irrational and morally defective. But faith cannot be called irrational, in so far as the necessity for it is given in the constitution of the human soul, and in the ordering of human life. To claim that faith, exercised in entire independence of the demonstrations of reason, is irrational, is to impeach the rationality of life itself. Faith in man is rational and it is moral.

The object may be the world in which we live. It is an instinct of faith that impels us to assume the order of the world, and to commit ourselves to it. The world was made to be an object of confidence and we are set over against it with a faith-capacity corresponding, by virtue of which it becomes a constitutional necessity to intrust one's self to it. When this confidence in the world becomes an intelligent self-committal to it, as involving a moral order, it enters the ethical domain. It may thus possibly attain even a religious significance. All sound faith in self, faith in fellow men, faith in the order of the world, may possibly involve a latent or implicit faith in a higher power above all, which is more and other than all, in whom centers the life of man and the constitution of the world. Certain it is that when we bring this question into consciousness, and begin to think rationally and morally, we are obliged to postulate the reality of God as the basis of all rational confidence in the reality and significance of the universe. It is faith as related to this higher object, faith, therefore, not in its technical and theo-

THE USE AND POWER OF FAITH.

logical but in its ethico-religious significance, that I have in mind. And it is the object of this chapter to discuss its use and power in life.

And, first, in mental life, or in the domain of thought and knowledge. We begin to think in the realm of faith. All thought that influences life presupposes faith in thought itself and in the mind that produces it. We trust ourselves before we know ourselves. Indeed, we trust ourselves in order to know ourselves. Faith belongs to that part of our being that operates to a large extent below consciousness and to a still larger extent independently of knowledge. We take ourselves seriously and on trust when we begin to think, and when we attach any significance or worth to the products of our thought. We commit ourselves in good faith to the workings of our own intelligence, and following its lead reach what we believe to be knowledge. And all knowledge is won only on a basis of faith. We commit ourselves also to the faculties that lie below intelligence, and believe that their witness, too, leads to knowledge.

So also do we trust what lies without ourselves. All objects external to ourselves become objects of knowledge only because we are so constituted that we must believe in them. We do not prove them to be valid in order to believe in them and intrust ourselves to them. We believe in and trust the world before we know it. Knowledge of the world and of man is never the measure of our trust in them. All external objects of knowledge are approached along the pathway of faith. Not even a beginning in knowledge is possible without an attitude of good faith in what lies beyond the power of experimental or logical demonstration. And this attitude is necessary at every step and stage of the process up to the end. We assume the reality of the external world. We do not demonstrate it. "By faith we know that the worlds were made." We assume the order and unity of the world before we prove them. Knowledge that comes through the understanding is necessary to correct and regulate faith, but faith is necessary to the knowledge with which the understanding begins and completes its work. We know God before we prove his existence. We must assume his existence before proof is possible. Knowledge of his reality is given in an experience that is more than rational experience, and it is the knowledge of faith. Thus we know the God of redemption. We see and know nothing as it is until we see and know it from the standpoint of a right relation. We know ethical realities only as we are ethically responsive to them. We know purity, justice, grace, only as we commit ourselves to the objects in which they inhere, become subject to them and test their reality and validity by experiment. Thus we know God in redemption. We believe and trust in order that we may know. Christianity is a revelation from without, but Christianity as a religion is revelation transferred into the domain of experience, and such experience is the experience of faith.

Secondly, its use and power in emotional life, or in the domain of feeling. Life needs uplifting. It needs to be greatened. It is greatened from within. It is the expansive power of noble emotions that exalts our manhood. Largeness of heart is necessary to largeness of manhood. Great things must be felt in order to be known as great. Mental life is dependent upon emotional life. The best intellectual interest in the truth is dependent upon an emotional interest in it. Feeling is an avenue of revelation. We see clearest when we feel deepest the realities of the invisible. The inspired man is he whose whole soul is moved by the power of invisible realities that fill and enlarge him with great emotions. This is the prophet. Are there not exalted states of feeling in which we come to new self-knowledge and to new knowledge of reality external to ourselves? Who can know himself or the world in which he lives, or the God which is in it and behind it until he has felt himself lifted into some height of feeling that is large enough to measure his possibilities? Who can know the grandeur of life until he has been made to feel it? Who can know God until he has been filled with a sense of his greatness and glory? There are emotions that crowd the soul, such, for example, as may have been experienced upon a mountain summit, of such vastness and such masterful power that the whole wide universe seems new in its awful grandeur, and God gives us, as in a moment, a new revelation of himself and of our existence.

Life needs ennobling. What takes hold of our capacity for noblest enthusiasm in the largest, strongest, and most practical way, must be one of the chief interests of life. Well, now, it is faith that conditions such uplifting of soul. It is this capacity to take in influences from the realm of the invisible and eternal, influences that touch deeper depths of being than the realm of thought, and to commit ourselves to what we recognize as native to us, remote though it often seems, that enlarges us into surprising greatness.

A great religious joy is conditioned by the presence and fellowship of the living God realized in experience through faith. One may prostrate himself in abject humility before the resistless might and majesty of a godless universe, but the soul cannot thus be exalted. Religion greatens the soul because faith brings one into living fellowship with God. The man of faith is always the man of inspiration. The sad lives are the self-centered lives that exalt themselves within the cloud limits of a world from which God has been dismissed. Over against the lives that refuse to bow themselves in trust to a God who has come in redemption, we may set the lives of those who yield themselves even to an illegitimate authority. The Church of Rome can point to lives that have been lifted to great heights of joy by self-surrendering trust. And there may be great elevation of soul in trusting submission to a power which one mistakenly believes to represent the authority of God. Better this than the godlessness that plunges thousands of the poor and degraded, such as this great church once reached, into hopelessness and despair. The isolation and the pride of an age that would dismiss God from the universe are sure to produce a mighty reaction, and men will bow themselves to a church that they may in self-defense rescue their lives from the hardness and impoverishment of a godless secularism. Look at the lives of the masses who have lost faith in God and in the redemption that is preached by his church. The fountains of joy are dried. What a church can do for faith, God, who is not adequately interpreted by any church, can do far better. It is not faith in a church, but in a God who has redeemed us, that can save the joy and nobility of life. Enlargement of the capacity for intelligent faith will become tributary to the happiness of the world.

Thirdly, its use and power in practical life or in the domain of action. Faith lies at the root of all practical virtues. Christianity in making faith central in ethical life interprets all best ethical experience. The men of achievement have always been men of faith. What men need, when the difficulties of life crowd upon them, is what the disciples needed and asked of their Master, increase of faith. He whose faith is strong is strong enough to support the faith of others. Faith is the root of fidelity. He who trusts and is strong is the one whom others will trust. He who finds his own foundation sure and rests upon it will make a foundation upon which others may rest. This, too, is the patient man who endures when hardships come. Faith takes hold of an object which it recognizes as good, and having taken hold it holds on. And faith holding on to the good in the midst of evil is patience. Patience is self-perpetuating trust. It is faith enduring to the end. True faith is moral steadfastness. "Steadfast by faith" is the Christian's definition of patience. In it the soul keeps itself to the object of its trust. Doubt is a parley with difficulty. Despair is surrender to it. Faith, holding firmly to the good that lies beyond all earthly difficulty and barrier, is the patience that insures victory. Who is he that endures but the one who trusting the good he cannot see, a good that is not the less real though it be unseen, waits for it? And this, too, is the courageous man who is not only strong to wait but strong to achieve. Faith is vantage-ground for the fight. He who fights well must feel that he has something under and about him that he can trust. Hardship brings a man to a stand. It throws him back upon something that will stand by him. He who rallies against the onset of gigantic difficulties must rally from the basis of something to which he is self-committed in mental and moral confidence. No man can fight difficulties in the air. Perpetual doubt or distrust is moral imbecility. In the presence of difficulty one sees as never otherwise how necessary it is to believe in something. Faith that takes hold on God and redemption is at the foundation of the loftiest courage this world has ever seen. What Christianity has done for the courage of the world can never be adequately estimated. Faith as a working force in the battle of life is a theme that demands a treatise. What is left of the optimism of modern life allies itself with this working force that Christianity has brought into and left in the world.

In a final word, then, the modern world needs more faith in faith. It is a simple thing, but it is a power that removes the mountain barriers of life. Man is weak, but the power that made and upholds and redeems is committed to him, and will see him safely through. The wisdom and the strength of life are in self-committal to Him.

The Ministry of Trouble and Sorrow.

Prof. J. M. STIFLER, D.D., Crosier Seminary, Chester, Pa.

THERE is no house without a roof; no part of the house so carefully kept in repair. For the summer's sun scorches the unprotected head, and storms of rain and snow and hail are sure to come. He who enters life with no shield against sorrow and trouble has moved into a house without a roof.

The heart that never aches is not a human heart. Pain is inseparable from mortal life. It may not be constant, but it is inevitable. The mind struggles with mysteries which it cannot solve; bereavements bruise and cut the tendrils of affection; the body suffers from disease; the will is racked by disappointments, and the conscience is often blistered by remorse. And while one has a mind to think, a heart to love, nerves to feel, a will to determine, and a conscience to speak for God,—that is, while one is a man,—he is exposed to suffering on every side. Job had lived long and was prosperous. He said, "I shall die in my nest." But he bitterly learned his mistake, for as there is none that lives and sins not, so there is none that lives and suffers not. The origin of suffering may be mysterious and its object in particular cases far from certain, but of the fact there is absolutely no question.

But if no good came from it, pain would disprove the benevolence of God. The swamps and marshes that breed fevers and malaria grow also lilies, and some of the sweetest of them grow nowhere else. The bitter loss of Jacob's favorite son was the only means of restoring him to the patriarch a prince. The hammer that breaks the hull of the nut gives you its sweet kernel. The diamond cannot shine until it is cut. And it is

THE MINISTRY OF TROUBLE AND SORROW.

diamonds that are cut, not pebbles. And so no pain is malignant. It is not always even a penalty, but the price without which excellence cannot be bought.

> "Heaven is not mounted to on wings of dreams,
> Nor doth the unthankful happiness of youth
> Aim thitherward, but floats from bloom to bloom,
> With earth's warm patch of sunshine well content.
> 'Tis sorrow builds the shining ladder up,
> Whose golden rounds are our calamities,
> Whereon our firm feet planting, nearer God
> The spirit climbs, and hath its eyes unsealed." —LOWELL.

Now, he who does not expect to be exempt from pain, who also believes that in some way it is beneficent, has a covering to which to resort in the storm. "The whole wisdom and magnanimity of life consist in a will conformed to what is, with a heart ready for what is not." Pain is often wisdom's handboard pointing to a better, safer path. Sorrow is homeopathic. We are given little doses to cure us of greater ills. The loss of a hand spares us the loss of the arm. There are griefs that no prudence and no forethought can either avoid or avert. But there are others also which none but fools suffer more than once.

Sorrows and disappointments influence character tremendously. Nothing has more weight on the aim of life. Much of our thinking and planning goes to shun what is considered life's woes. The weak man often succumbs before these, and with the slander against the Creator in his heart, that life is not worth living, gives way to melancholy, moroseness, despair, or suicide. The stoic is little better. He receives his own ills with clinched teeth and defiant indifference, and looks with tearless apathy on those of others. Hearts were made to ache, and it is divinely intended that they may improve by the pain. Solomon says, "By the sadness of the countenance the heart is made better." And of a greater than Solomon we read, "Though he was a son yet learned he obedience by the things which he suffered," and was made "perfect through sufferings." Failure and disappointment have generally taught the earnest man his choicest lessons. One of these, an American poet, says:—

> "Nor deem the irrevocable past
> As wholly wasted, wholly vain,
> If rising on its wrecks at last
> To something nobler we attain."

Bereavement makes the heart tender and sympathetic; confidence betrayed leads to wiser caution; sickness suggests more care of health; failure in business teaches better methods, and sin, unless one loves it, by soiling the conscience leads to the Cleanser.

Sorrow confers a value which nothing else can give. Value is more than the product of labor. There are price marks higher than any ever reached by toil. Men esteem highest that worthy thing for which they have suffered most. Christ not only died for men because he loves them, but he doubly loves them because he died for them. Liberties, political, social, religious, are so precious because they were all bought with blood. The sufferings of the early colonists and of the Revolutionary fathers at Valley Forge endear this nation to their children. Dollars are but dust, and nothing that dollars can buy is worth much. The precious things of life come to men only through pain—pain of body, brain, and heart.

Sorrows give an excellent opportunity for the exercise of the highest virtues. It was the lepers of Molokai that made Father Damien a hero. If the traveler going down from Jerusalem to Jericho had not fallen among thieves, the priest and the Levite would not have lost their reputation and the good Samaritan would not have made his. He who lives only to escape or to surmount his own allotted sufferings may be a prudent man but he is basely selfish. He who can bear another's griefs is like him who was the normal man, who suffered much himself that all others might suffer less.

Building for Eternity.

Rev. H. B. HARTZLER, D.D.,
Bible Teacher, Moody's Training School, Mount Hermon, Mass.

"WHEN a man builds his home," says T. DeWitt Talmage, "he builds for eternity." The saying is true; yet the home itself is only for time, and not for eternity. It is only a part of the scaffolding on which the builder for eternity is doing his work of raising up the imperishable walls of human character. When the work of time is done, the scaffolding falls away, and only the spiritual structure remains, "a house not made with hands," indestructible and eternal. Looking out from the home window, upon the whole wide realm of the material world, with all its latter-day wonders of science, art, and discovery, and all its bewildering variety and complexity of appliances, we see but a larger part of a vast system of temporal scaffolding, upon which the builders for eternity find temporary footing and facility to carry on the real, abiding work of life.

One of the greatest of men, who had an experience perhaps never paralleled in human history, in being permitted to pass the line of the unseen and return again, with untranslatable visions and experiences in his heart, to climb the earthly scaffolding and carry his unfinished work to completion, declares that "the things which are seen are temporal; but the things which are not seen are eternal." So the testimony of God, through all ages, has been that this material, temporal frame of nature is to serve a temporary purpose, for a season of time which to him is but as "one day," or as "a watch in the night," and then shall fall away, as the husk from the ripe corn, as the scaffolds from the finished building, disclosing the great structure in all its details, on which all the generations of men have wrought, and of which they form constituent parts.

When Jesus, the Divine Teacher, draws the line of division between the wise and the foolish, he puts on one side all those who build their house on the sand, for time only, and on the other side those who build on the rock for eternal security. Paul emphasizes the supreme importance of bedding one's life-work on the one immovable, imperishable foundation—"Other foundation can no man lay than that is laid, which is Jesus Christ." He carries the thought farther, from the foundation to the superstructure, and distinguishes between the perishable and the imperishable materials which the human builders use, with the solemn warning, "Let each one see how he builds on it," for, says he, "if anyone buildeth on this foundation either gold, or silver, or precious stones, or wood, or hay, or stubble, the work of each will be exposed to view; for the day will expose it; because it is to be tested by fire; and the fire will disclose the work of each, of what sort it is. And that builder whose work shall endure will receive his reward. And he whose work shall burn up will suffer loss; yet himself will escape; but it will be as from the fire."

The really valuable, precious, durable materials, represented by gold, silver, and precious stones, which enter into the structure of a life that shall stand approved for eternity, are all unseen and spiritual. Christ specifies some of them when he calls the roll of the blessed ones—the poor in spirit, the mourners, the meek, the hungerers after righteousness, the merciful, the pure in heart, the peacemakers, the sufferers for righteousness' sake. Peter admonishes the builders for eternity to add layer to layer on the walls of character—faith, virtue, knowledge, temperance, patience, godliness, brotherly kindness, love. Paul's specifications are almost identical, showing that both had learned the art and science of spiritual architecture from the same Divine Master. They are these—love, joy, peace, long-suffering, gentleness, goodness, faith, meekness, temperance.

BUILDING FOR ETERNITY.

A structure built on the foundation of Christ, of such materials as these, is fire-proof, storm-proof, time-proof, judgment-proof, eternity-proof. It shall stand, when the "wood, hay, and stubble" houses shall have gone up in smoke, "a house not made with hands, eternal in the heavens." Not less true than beautiful is the thought expressed by Frederick W. Robertson in these words: "Feelings pass; thoughts and imagination pass; dreams pass; work remains. Through eternity, what you have done, that you are. They tell us that not a sound has ever ceased to vibrate through space; that not a ripple has ever been lost upon the ocean. Much more is it true that not a true thought, nor a pure resolve, nor a loving act, has ever gone forth in vain." Even so, for they have all gone into the solid structure of character that is eternal.

Says Dr. J. G. Holland, "Labor, calling, profession, scholarship, and artificial and arbitrary distinction of all sorts are incidents and accidents of life, and pass away. It is only manhood that remains." As Apelles, the famous Grecian artist, wrought with painstaking care upon his pictures, he said, "I am painting for eternity." But the artist laid down his brush over two thousand years ago, and only the man remains.

Building for eternity! How startling and soul-arresting the thought! It can be done only in time, and all the eternity of the builder hangs upon the character thereof. It must be finished before the material footing of time gives way, and the scaffolding of the body, with its related world timbers, falls. The work is great and wonderful. The time for its performance is short. Nothing else, amidst all the contending claims of life, is of equal importance. Christ, who knows all about both worlds, sets this work on the forefront of all endeavor, as the supreme and all-embracing object of the highest, holiest ambition. The man who reverses this order is branded as a fool, who loses his eternity and himself in the poor, perishable gain of a few fleeting years—buying the self-indulgence of an hour with the price of a soul and an eternity of unmeasured possibilities of blessedness and glory.

BUILDING FOR ETERNITY.

For this great work of life God has not left the poor, groping, blundering builder to his own wit and wisdom. He has not thrown him back upon his own resources of human nature. He himself has drawn the plan and given the specifications. In the Bible he has put it all down so plainly and simply, that even the fool, with that wonderful manual in his hand, need not err. He even offers to come into lowly partnership for co-operation in the work, to give power, to make his strength perfect in human weakness, to take the heaviest burdens himself. He has given his solemn pledge that not one thing of all that is necessary to the completion and perfection of the work shall fail on his part.

One by one the workmen, the builders for eternity, are dismissed from their work. How unspeakably sad and heartbreaking will it be to the foolish builders to see the work of a whole lifetime, of every toil and care, vanish in the testing fire of the day of God! "Wood, hay, stubble!" Time, strength, talent, painful application, all wasted and lost! Houseless, homeless, hopeless for evermore!

But how glorious, builders, will be the day that shall declare the work of a lifetime approved by God, and reveal the perfected temple of character, unhurt by the fire, "found unto praise and honor and glory at the appearing of Jesus Christ"! Oh, blessed fullness of compensation for all the toils and tears, the sacrifices and sufferings, of this little life! To be forever with the Lord! To have a permanent place in that "city never built with hands, or heavy with the years of time; a city whose inhabitants no census has numbered; a city through whose streets rushes no tide of business, nor nodding hearse creeps slowly with its burden to the tomb; a city without griefs or graves, without sins or sorrows, without births or burials, without marriages or mournings; a city which glories in having Jesus for its King, angels for its guards, saints for citizens; whose walls are salvation, and whose gates are praise."

Into that city of God, with life's work well done, may writer and reader at last have an abundant entrance.

Our Great Ledger Account.

PROF. GEORGE S. GOODSPEED, PH.D., of the University of Chicago.

THE evening hour is approaching. The day's work is almost over. We have made many entries during the busy hours, but have not found time to sum them up and compare debit and credit, to know where we stand. It is well to do so now before we go home. Rest will be sweeter and the evening hour undisturbed, if we have made out the balance sheet. Then to-morrow we can go back to our work refreshed, with no unfinished tasks lying in our onward pathway. And if we should die, there will be no errors for our successor to correct, and no ugly snarls for the expert to unravel.

Not every one of us keeps accounts. There are some very careful people, who, in their family life, are extraordinarily systematic and laborious in the reckoning of their receipts and expenses. Then there are others so constituted that they do not know where the money goes, or whence it comes, and they do not care. But in one sphere we are all bookkeepers, and our library, if it has no other book in it, has a ledger, which we are at work upon every moment of our waking hours. It is the book which we open from the first day of conscious responsibility and close only as the night of death draws down. Then, indeed, we take it with us where we can take nothing else, and, on the last great day, we bring it before the great Master Accountant when "the books are opened," and we read out from it the record of the past, the balance sheet which determines the place and manner of our future activity through the endless ages. This kind of accounts we cannot avoid if we would, and, even when we are most heedless and thoughtless, we are still going on with the record. Is it not worth while, then, to take down the book before the final entry is made, to look over the accounts, and cast up trial balances to find out where we stand? Come with us, each with his own record, and as our present volume draws to a close, open life's ledger, examine its most important accounts, ask how they stand, and, in the light of the facts they disclose, forecast the future and prepare for it.

The parties with whom you and I deal in life are, as individuals, many and various, but in this ledger of ours they may be summed up under three heads, *Self, Society,* and *God.* With these three persons, many, yes, all our transactions are held, and, as many as are the spheres and modes of dealing with them, they, after all, are the principals. In the brief word of counsel and conference which we are to have together, these three accounts will occupy all our attention. Let us be frank, sincere, seeking only to know how we stand with these three all-encompassing factors of our life.

The account with *Self*, our nearest neighbor, our constant companion—how full that is in all its specifications! Here is your body, which the highest authority has called "the temple of God." It is wonderful in structure, exquisite in mechanism, of extraordinary endurance, unequaled flexibility, an illustration and the seat of the most stupendous as well as of the most minute of the natural forces. You have been given the charge of it, its governance. You are engineer of the finest mechanism in existence. How have you handled it? Have you made it the "temple of God" or the hall of Satan? Has it been purified or degraded?

There are your thoughts. They are part of your account with Self. Its figures are known only to yourself—and God. You do not tell your nearest friend all your thoughts, but "He that searcheth the heart, knoweth the mind of man." This is a most important element in your life's business. Are those thoughts clean and sweet? Do you think on that which is most noble and worthy? A high aim and steadfast endeavor after character is everything. Are you master of your purposes so that, whether you sail over rough seas or smooth, whether your way lies in the light or the darkness, you are pressing onward toward the higher goal, never giving up though bruised and battered? A high moral purpose in one's own soul makes the difference between true life and mere existence. The one has a harbor to make. The other is like a chip on the stream, the sport of current and storm. The one lays up treasures in heaven. The other is an eternal bankrupt. What does the ledger say—gain or loss? a worthy ambition or heedless, careless improvidence? This account with Self may well make us ponder and beware.

You turn on a few pages and come to the account with *Society*. Man enters into relation with himself first, and with his fellow men next. Social relations bring obligations, and the obligations fulfilled or unfulfilled appear in the book. What is the home life? Have the children seen the father and mother quarreling? The attitude of the son or daughter toward the parents is the subject of a great commandment of God. What responsibility is assumed by the father of a family, by the mother of children!

What is the business life? The real meaning and value of the money you have made or lost, by fair or foul dealing, you estimate at its true value in the ledger. Here it is charged up for or against you. Other men may think you progressive, but perhaps you write yourself down here as a cheat. Other men may think you dull and slow, but your deeds inscribed on that page show instances of self-sacrificing kindness that would shame your slanderers. The records of your property and its actual worth appear here. What you have given, you possess. What you have selfishly made, you have lost. This ledger is a great corrective of the everyday dealings of man with his neighbor. And the record is made by himself.

Let us look at this account with society from two general points of view,—in terms of speech and influence. The physi-

OUR GREAT LEDGER ACCOUNT.

cian says to the patient first, "Let me see your tongue." What have his words contributed to the debit or credit of a man with his fellows? It has been estimated that one says in a week what, if printed, would be an octavo volume of three hundred and twenty pages. In thirty years this would amount to an extensive library of one thousand five hundred and sixty volumes. How little of it is available and uplifting material, and how much is silly and corrupting! The great evil in our common conversation is that so large an element of it is idle, extravagant, injurious. How much time is consumed in gossip more or less slanderous! How much vulgarity and worse than vulgarity is vomited forth from some men's mouths! On which side of the account does all this go? "By thy words shalt thou be justified, and by thy words shalt thou be condemned."

Even more comprehensive and vital is your obligation to society in the matter of influence. It appears not as promissory notes written on paper, but in the human hearts impressed for good or ill by your example. The marks of influence are ineffaceable, and yet its meaning and effect are easily overlooked. Look around you on your associates and ask yourself, "How am I paying the debt I owe them? Does my example point them upward? Do my words call their better natures into action? What kind of a mark does my life leave upon men?" Influence is as subtle as the atmosphere, but just as penetrating and powerful. Here are father and mother. As a great preacher has said, "They have the marking of a child's heart. They are writing that child's history because they are living it. They are branding its life with shame or sealing it with glory." Who can realize the debt of young womanhood in this matter of influence, and how grandly may she redeem all her obligations. Young women, if they would and dared, or desired, could transform the characters and aspirations of the young men of our generation! Are they meeting their obligations?

Oh, this influence of ours, how poorly are we redeeming our opportunities and paying the debts which are incurred through its possession!

> Is there then no death for a word once spoken?
> Was never a deed but left its token?
> Do pictures of all the ages live—
> On nature's infinite negative?

This is what influence—that potent power of every human life—really means. And the debts incurred through its possession will be known in their entirety only when the secrets of every human heart and the outcome of every human life shall be revealed.

Only a word more about the last and greatest of these ledger accounts,—*God*. This really sums them all up. If God "is, and is the rewarder of those that diligently seek him," then in him we live and move and have our being. We owe everything to him, and what we have to pay to balance every account, comes at last to him. What then are we doing to help ourselves in squaring our obligation to him? How far short comes the best endeavor! There are some who even overlook or repudiate their debts to him. Even of those who acknowledge his claims, how few do more than give him a beggarly hour or two in the week, and begrudge it if they are called to make sacrifice on his behalf. Ought there not to be a toning up of our sense of obligation in relation to God? Should not our lives show at least some sort of acknowledgment of dependence on him? We cannot hope to pay our debts. God has put us under obligation not only by providing for our wants, surrounding us with comforts and opportunities, but also by helping us in the midst of trials and difficulties into which we have fallen by our own obstinacy and ignorance, and has given us a revelation of himself in the Bible and in his Son, Jesus Christ.

But there is a brighter side. God has given man the privilege of paying his obligations and satisfying the divine claims by a wonderful method,—agreeing to take man with all his debts into the firm, making him a partner in the concern. All this is on one condition, that you and I will enter the business, and make it our one aim, our chief purpose, to forward the enterprises which God has in hand. These enterprises are the highest and noblest known to man. They involve the love of God and man, the upbuilding of character and righteousness, the bringing of the divine kingdom of peace and good will toward all. Shall we agree? Then we can close this ledger to-night with good hope. For he who is our principal Creditor cancels the indebtedness and places at our disposal a capital the like of which we never had before.

Shall we refuse? Then I know no way of escape from bankruptcy. False entries cannot deceive the Eye that looks through all deceit. Even other men will find out at last that you are a sham, and your own self will clamor for its due in vain, and you will loathe yourself. And then you will come before the great white throne, and "the books will be opened," where all the great debt is revealed, and you will not find from God above, society about, or self within you wherewith to cancel it. There will be seen as in letters of fire streaming through these accounts the secret cipher of your past and the solved riddle of your future.

This ledger of life is an important volume, the most important you have in your library. It may not be encouraging to turn it over and behold how tremendously the balance inclines to the opposite side. Yet to open the eyes, and fairly to face the problem, is the beginning of its solution. And with God, the principal creditor, as the friend and helper of man, we need not fear. With his aid and in his service, we shall succeed in paying our utmost obligation to self and to society, both in thought, in word, in deed, and in influence. We shall have the honor and satisfaction of laying up treasures in heaven, where moth and rust do not corrupt, and where thieves do not break through and steal.

Life's Great Guide Book.

Rev. P. S. HENSON, D.D., Pastor First Baptist Church, Chicago.

THE first recorded word of God is, "Let there be light." He covereth himself with light as with a garment. He "dwelleth in light which no man can approach unto." He is "the Father of lights," and "in him is no darkness at all." Heaven is all ablaze with the light of his countenance. The celestial city "hath no need of the sun, neither of the moon to shine upon it, for the glory of God doth lighten it." And that makes heaven.

"In his presence there is fullness of joy." Removal from that presence means utter darkness, and that makes hell.

Earth swings midway between heaven and hell, and hence, though not involved in rayless gloom, it is shrouded in darkness that may be felt; and men grope about upon it very much as did the men of Sodom, when they sought Lot's door on the night of doom.

The light that once bathed it has been eclipsed by the intervention of sin's dark shadow. Some little things that lie very near we may be able to discover, but the great things, far-reaching as eternity, and tremendous as the judgment, we cannot see at all. Upon the most momentous questions that ever engaged a human soul there is absolutely no light shed by earthly philosophy. What am I? and Whence am I? and Whither am I bound? and What is my duty? My danger? My destiny? These are questions before which all the oracles of earth are dumb. In the innermost chamber of the human soul a faint and flickering light is shining, and we call it conscience, but it is like the smoking lamp in a miserable Lapland hut, that only makes the darkness visible. Some moral sense is left, enough to make us responsible subjects of moral government, but so confused is it in its judgments, and so weakened in its motive power, that if we are left to it alone we shall never clearly know the truth or thoroughly do the right. In the absence of any higher authority man is bound to obey his conscience, even though he have reason to believe that he cannot trust it. And that conscience is anything but infallible is only too palpably proved by the contradictory judgments it has registered in different lands and ages, touching almost every moral question.

One is bound to follow his conscience whether right or wrong, and yet if the conscience be wrong the act is not made right because it was performed conscientiously. Surely this a sad dilemma for a human soul, and one that would seem to make pathetic appeal for the intervention of a God of tender mercy. He has proved himself graciously regardful of all the lower needs of our lives. Surely he will not be utterly indifferent to the highest. Beautiful and beneficent provision in point of fact he has made to guide us in our perplexity, and to rectify the registering of our sin-perverted consciences. Conscience is like the pocket watch of the engineer who runs the locomotive of a railway train. He has a time-table and a timekeeper, and by these he must be governed. But in the careless handling of his watch, we will suppose he has let it fall. When he puts it to his ear he finds it ticking still. Possibly it has been damaged, but how much he cannot tell, and he still must be guided by it in his movements on the road. And yet if it be out of order he is in imminent danger of disastrous collision. Now to guard against such perilous possibility the railroad company has hung up at the stations along the line, chronometers that are supposed to keep accurate time, and with these he must compare his watch as he pauses for a moment for the purpose. But these chronometers are regulated from Washington, and the time at Washington is governed by the stars, for nothing below the stars can be relied upon to run exactly right.

THE BIBLE THE LAW OF LIFE.

Our individual conscience is like that engineer's watch. It has had a fateful fall, and is sadly out of order, and if we absolutely rely upon it we are sure to come to grief and shame. But God in great mercy has provided an infallible standard by which to rectify our private judgments, and if we fail to make the rectification, then the failure is at our peril.

That standard is his holy Word—which is the standard for all men and for all time, for the nineteenth century no less than the first, for the world has not outgrown it and never will outgrow it while the ages roll.

Talk of "The Light of Asia"—it is only a "will o' the wisp" in comparison with this. No code of ethics that the world ever saw is for a moment comparable to this. "A lamp to our feet" is this indeed. Not such a "search light" as that which during the Columbian Exposition in Chicago used to flash fantastically across the heavens, lighting up the very clouds, or in its lower range illuminating towers and spires. What we practically need is not a thing like that, but "a lamp to our feet."

Our pathway lies amid bogs and pitfalls, and we are strangers and pilgrims on the earth. A single misstep may land us in ruin, or involve us in a maze of perplexities and perils from which we shall be extricated, if it all, only with tears and blood. God has given us a book "to which we do well to give heed as to a light shining in a dark place." And there is not a single dark place that it does not illumine—not a single question that it does not answer—not a single relation in life, with respect to which it is not an all-sufficient guide. Man has a body, fearfully and wonderfully made, capable of exceeding enjoyment and exquisite pain, of splendid service and of deepest degradation—full of appetites that clamor for gratification, and which if allowed to have full swing and sweep will make the immortal soul their slave. What to do with that body—how to gratify it and yet to govern it—this is a question of utmost moment, and one whose perfect answer is to be found nowhere outside the Bible.

"Know ye not that your bodies are the temples of the Holy

Ghost?" "Keep thyself pure." "I beseech you, therefore, brethren, by the mercies of God, that ye present your bodies a living sacrifice, holy and acceptable unto God, which is your reasonable service." A man upon whose heart these Scriptures are engraven will be likely to make the most of his body without allowing it ever to be uppermost.

Obligation arises from relation, and very various are the relations that we sustain to one another, and very delicate, and intricate, and perplexing are the obligations that confront us. Just how to discharge them is the thing that it mightily concerns us to know, and nowhere shines so clearly the light of truth and duty as in the pages of Sacred Writ. If husbands and wives would only read, and mark, and inwardly digest, we should hear no more of the vexed question of woman's rights, for love would be the fulfilling of the law. Every right would be accorded without the necessity of political conventions, and the divorce mills would cease to grind their horrid grist. If parents and children would only ponder and practice the wise and tender precepts that are given for their guidance in God's old book, there would be fewer wild and wayward boys and girls, and fewer gray hairs brought down in sorrow to the grave.

"Children, obey your parents in the Lord: for this is right. Honor thy father and mother (which is the first commandment with promise), that it may be well with thee, and thou mayest live long on the earth.

"And, ye fathers, provoke not your children to wrath: but nurture them in the chastening and admonition of the Lord." This summarizes the whole parental and filial code, and obedience to this law would make every home a little heaven below.

Man is not only a member of the family, but belongs to that wider sphere which we call society. And society has its conventionalities, its amusements, its interchanges of good offices, its fashions, and its politics, all of which are permeated by perplexities and moral obligations. How shall these perplexities be wisely settled and these obligations thoroughly met?

THE BIBLE THE LAW OF LIFE.

No man who has any common sense, or moral sense, or self-respect, can afford to resign himself to the current, and allow himself to be dominated by what is denominated the spirit of the age, which as often as otherwise is the spirit of the devil.

"Be not conformed to this world, but be ye transformed by the renewing of your minds that ye may prove what is that good and acceptable and perfect will of God." Not the edict of fashion or the mandate of a party, but the will of God, this is the only infallible rule of life, and he who walks by it shall find that wisdom's ways are ways of pleasantness, and all her paths are peace.

And man is meant not merely for the pleasurable enjoyments of society, but for the sterner battles of business. And a very trying experience is it when a young man whose life has been all of sunny hours, devoted to physical enjoyment and light educational employment, wakes to the realization of the hard necessity of undertaking the struggle for his own existence.

Every man for himself seems the motto of the world, and the novice in business, no matter how generous his natural impulses, is tempted very speedily to adopt it for himself. Eat and be eaten is the law of the animal creation, and cheat and be cheated would appear to be the law of business. Your neighbors will adulterate, and misrepresent, and undersell, and overreach. Will you allow them to take away your custom, break up your business, and beggar your family, or do as they do? Very likely the latter, unless firmly rooted in moral principle and securely fortified by the word of God.

"Wherewithal shall a young man cleanse his way? By taking heed thereto according to Thy word."

There are many who suspect, if they do not openly declare, that a man cannot do business upon the strict ethical principles enumerated in the Scriptures. They are very beautiful, they say, in theory but impracticable in business; they may do for the pulpit, but not for the market place and the commercial exchange. It is thought that one must give his conscience a little leeway and conform to the conventionalities of trade, or he never can succeed.

And, yet, we maintain that the Bible was not made simply for old times, but for the new as well, and that no better business manual has ever been devised, or will be till the world shall end. Of "the man whose delight is in the law of the Lord," and who so delights in it that he meditates on it day and night, it is written that "whatsoever he doeth shall prosper."

The knave may, indeed, have a certain brief appearance of prosperity, but the curse clings to him and his fortune, and sooner or later it will burn into his very flesh like the poisoned shirt of Nessus.

There is no incompatibility between business and religion, and cannot be, seeing that the Lord has called us to both. And we are exhorted to be "not slothful in business, fervent in spirit, serving the Lord." And among the very foremost business men of our time, and of all time, have been those whose Bibles were as indispensable in their counting houses, as daybook and ledger.

"Trust in the Lord and do good, and so shalt thou dwell in the land, and verily thou shalt be fed." That is the most stable business house in which God is a silent partner, and yet is constantly consulted. Piety and prosperity go hand in hand. Fools think to take short cuts, but making haste to be rich they fall into a snare. "They shall eat of the fruit of their own doings, and be filled with their own desires." But even were it otherwise, even were poverty the appointed portion of all that strictly follow the precepts of God's holy word, it would be worth one's while to suffer it, for there are some things of greater value than what the world calls riches.

"Happy is the man that findeth wisdom, and the man that getteth understanding. For the merchandise of it is better than the merchandise of silver, and the gain thereof than fine gold. She is more precious than rubies, and all the things thou canst desire are not to be compared to her." What we are here for is not to gather a heap of decaying matter with a muck rake, but to develop manhood of the noblest type, that shall worthily wear the crown of glory that the Judge of all the earth will place upon the brow when the conflicts of life are happily over. Well may we join with the Psalmist in saying, "Blessed are the undefiled in the way, who walk in the law of the Lord." In every earthly relation it is, indeed, "a lamp to our feet and a light to our path."

And this last clause suggests a longer look and a wider view than that which concerns the little details of one's life to-day. We are so constituted that we are bound to stand on tiptoe, anxiously peering into the great beyond. Whither am I bound? And what is my destiny? And wherewithal shall I appear before God? These are questions that will not "down," and yet they are such as no oracles of this world can answer.

"Search the Scriptures," was the voice of the Great Teacher, "for in them ye think ye have eternal life, and they are they which testify of me." The world is full of teachers saying, Lo, here, and, lo, there, and there be many that are ready to follow them even to their own undoing!

Even Christendom is divided into warring sects, that mouth their shibboleths, and confound honest inquirers with their discordant cries. "To the law and to the testimony; if they speak not according to this word, it is because there is no light in them."

If our Saviour's prayer for the unity of his people is ever to be realized, as surely it ultimately will be, the consummation so devoutly to be wished will be attained not by cowardly or conscienceless compromise of truth, but by the surrender of the authority of all earthly standards, and the absolute submission of the minds of men to the infallible authority of the word of God.

Successful Men and Women.

The Story of Trial and Triumph.

WRITERS AND THINKERS.

Louis John Rudolf Agassiz, naturalist, educator, born in Motier near Lake Neufchatel, Switzerland, May 28, 1807, died in Cambridge, Mass., December 14, 1873. Father a Protestant clergyman. Studied medicine at Zurich, Heidelberg, Munich. Perfecting himself in study of fossil fishes, he was appointed professor of Natural History at Neufchatel in 1832, and spent summers in Alps studying glaciers. Published five volumes of "Researches on Fossil Fishes" (300 plates), 1832–42 and a work on "Glaciers," 1840, " Systeme Glaciaire," 1847. In 1846 he came on a scientific excursion to the United States, where he then determined to live. Appointed professor of zoölogy and geology at Harvard, 1848, and published that year " Outlines of Comparative Physiology." 1865 conducted expedition to Brazil, exploring lower Amazon and tributaries, discovering over 1800 new species of fishes, and published in 1868 " A Journey to Brazil," mainly written by his wife, and that year became non-resident professor of natural history in Cornell University, Ithaca, N. Y. In 1871 went with the Hassler expedition under Professor Pierce to South America and Pacific ocean, and established a summer school of science in 1873. He loved knowledge for its sake, and attracted students by his intense personality, originality, and earnestness as but few have ever done. A thorough believer in special divine creations, he rejected the theory of Darwinism and gave notable lectures against that theory. No other man of his day, unless it be Hugh Miller, made science so popular and attractive as he, or was so immense a scientific force.

Matthew Arnold, poet, author, born 24th Dec., 1822, in Laleham, near Staines, England, and died in Liverpool, England, April 16, 1888. He was the eldest son of Dr. Thomas Arnold, later the head master of Rugby School. At his birth the father was a private tutor at Laleham, and after his removal to Rugby and when Matthew was twelve years of age he was sent to Laleham to the private school of Rev. J. Buckland (brother of the celebrated Prof. Buckland). Two years later he studied at Winchester under Dr. Moberly and in 1837 entered his father's school at Rugby. In 1840 he won the open scholarship at Baliol College, Oxford, and entered that institution the following year. In 1842 he won the Herford scholarship prize, and in 1844 the Newdigate prize, and in 1845 became fellow of Oriel College. Two years later, in 1847, Lord Lansdowne, the Whig leader, gave him the post of private secretary, and in 1851 he married a daughter of Justice Wightman and resigning the secretaryship accepted the post of lay inspector of the British and Foreign School Society, a position he held for a quarter of a century, visiting in the performance of his duties all parts of the kingdom and making several visits to the Continent in the interest of his school work. He also held the chair of professor of poetry at Oxford College from 1857 to 1867. In 1885 he visited the United States, giving a course of public lectures in the leading cities, one of which, lecture on Emerson, provoked much adverse criticisms from Emerson's friends. Of his ten volumes of published works, two are poems, two essays, three religious criticisms, and three general literature, the one on "Literature and Dogma "(1872) having perhaps the widest circulation, and awaking many replies.

Thomas Carlyle, author, born in Ecclefechan, Dumfriesshire, Scotland, 4th December, 1795, died in (Chelsea) London, England, February 5, 1881. His father was a small farmer in humble circumstances. Thomas was a precocious reader from childhood, and designed by his parents for the ministry, and educated at the parish school, then at Annan grammar school, and when fifteen entered the Edinburgh University, and, being undecided as to his future at his graduation, he became mathematical tutor at Annan in 1814, and two years later went to Kirkcaldy as assistant to Edward Irving, then conducting a school there. But Carlyle did not like teaching, and having contracted the chronic dyspepsia, that tinged all his after work in life, he abandoned teaching in December, 1818, and having saved some $400, he now resolved to study law rather than divinity, and went to Edinburgh University for a further course, supporting himself by writing for Dr. Brewster's encyclopedia, and at length gave up the law for literature. To help toward this purpose he became tutor to the two sons of Mr. Buller at a salary of $1,000 a year, and having the evenings to himself he translated Legendre's Geometry, adding to it his chapter on proportion, and being one of the finest German scholars of his age and an omniverous reader, he at this time, translated also Goethe's "Wilheim Meister," and wrote his "Life of Schiller," publishing the latter in installments in the *London Magazine*. In June, 1824, he went with the Bullers to London, and in the autumn left their employ but remained in England until January, 1825, when he returned to Scotland and wrote for the *Edinburgh Review*, and other periodicals. October 17, 1826, he married Miss Jane Baillie Welch, and lived in Edinburgh till the next May when poverty drove him to reside on his wife's estate at Craigenputtoch, a lonely, dreary spot, where he stayed for six years, studying, writing for Reviews, publishing translations of Jean Paul, Tieck, Musaus, Hoffmann, and other Germans of note, till then unknown in the English world, and preparing some forty notable biographical sketches for the "Edinburgh Encyclopedia." In July, 1831, he had completed his "Sartor Resartus" (*i. e.*, stitcher restitched) and went to London to find a publisher, but after many efforts failed, and in 1833 he published it in fragments in *Fraser's Magazine*. In 1834 (February) having then saved $1,000, he suddenly resolved to remove to London (Chelsea), where he resided till his death. In 1837 appeared his "The French Revolution, a History," the first of his works to which he affixed his name, and he had by it become famous. Of the thirty-three volumes composing his complete works, the greatest is his "Oliver Cromwell," and his "Life of Frederick the Great," the latter published in 1865, and the result of fourteen years of research and prodigious labor. In November, 1865, he was chosen rector of Edinburgh University, and the following March gave there his celebrated address "On the Choice of Books," and then in April, while absent at the university, his wife died suddenly in her carriage at Chelsea, and stricken with grief and remorse he prepared those "Letters and Memorials" of her that have immortalized the gifted woman who for so many years heroically crushed out her own heart longings in order that her husband might gain his renown.

Charles Anderson Dana, journalist, born at Hinsdale, N. H. Aug. 8, 1819. His boyhood was spent in Buffalo, N. Y., where he worked in a store until eighteen, studied Latin and prepared himself for college and in 1839 entered Harvard University, but was obliged to leave at end of two years, and was afterwards given his degree. In 1841 he became a member of that famous ill-starred socialistic experiment in which so many notable persons engaged, known as "Brook Farm," Roxbury, Mass. When it collapsed he did editorial work on newspapers in Boston for two years, afterward joining, in 1847, the editorial staff of the New York *Tribune*, and the following year spent eight months in Europe, and on return became one of the proprietors and the managing editor of the *Tribune*, a position which he held for fifteen years, when disagreeing with Horace Greeley as to the conduct of the civil war, and that editor's course concerning it, he resigned April 1, 1862, and was at once employed by Secretary of War Edwin M. Stanton in special work for that department and in 1863 made assistant secretary of War Department, spending much of the time in the field with the armies. At the close of the war went to Chicago, working on a new paper, *The Republican*, till its failure, when he came to New York in 1867 and organized a stock company and bought the then moribund *Sun* and became its editor, making it a renowned and profitable journal. Mr. Dana and George Ripley were the planners and originators of the American Cyclopedia (D. Appleton & Co.), working on it from 1855 to its completion in 1862, and together with General James H. Wilson published the "Life of General Grant" in 1868. Another noted work of his, "Household Book of Poetry" (1887), has gone through many editions.

James Dwight Dana, scientist, educator, born in Utica, New York, 12th Feb., 1813. His father was a man of means, and the son was given the advantages of the schools of his native town, and at seventeen entered Yale College (attracted thither by the fame of the renowned scientist, Prof. Benjamin Silliman) and graduated with much honor in 1833, and after his graduation was appointed an instructor of mathematics in the United States Navy, and visited various seaports in France, Italy, Greece, and Turkey. On his return from this voyage he was appointed mineralogist and geologist to United States Exploring Expedition to be sent to the South Pacific, but as the expedition did not sail until August, 1838, he spent the time from 1836 to 1838 as assistant instructor in chemistry with Prof. Silliman at Yale College. In 1838 he sailed with the expedition and was wrecked on a sand bar at the mouth of Columbia river. During his absence of three years and ten months, he had charge in addition to mineralogical and geological departments of that of zoölogy, especially the crustacea and corals, and for thirteen years after his return he was employed in studying the materials he had collected and making the drawings and preparing the reports for publication, of which the government issued three volumes with plates, publishing one hundred copies of each volume. From his return in June, 1842, to 1844, he resided in Washington, D. C., but in the latter year he removed to New Haven, Conn., where he has since resided, and in that year he married Miss Henrietta Frances, third daughter of Prof. Benjamin Silliman. In 1850 he was appointed Silliman professor of natural history and geology at Yale, but did not take the chair until 1855; and in that year (1850) he became associate editor of the *American Journal of Science and Arts* (founded by Prof. Silliman in 1819), and after the death of his father-in-law he became its senior editor. In 1854 he was elected president of the American Association for the Advancement of Science. In 1872 was given the Wollaston medal by the Geological Society of London, and in 1877 the Copley gold medal by the Royal Society of London. He is also a member of the Institute of France, of the Royal Academies of Berlin, of Vienna, of St. Petersburg, of the Royal Academy of the Lincei of Rome, and of many scientific and learned associations in his native land. Besides the many hundred articles he has written for scientific journals he has written some half dozen books of science of very wide circulation that not only have given him much fame but which have become accepted as standards in their departments, as, for instance, his Manuals of Mineralogy and of Geology.

Charles Robert Darwin, naturalist, author, born at Shrewsbury, England, February 12, 1809, died at Down, England, April 19, 1882. Was fifth of six children born to his father, who was a physician of marked individuality and an attendant and adherent of the Unitarian Church. Charles's mother died when he was eight years old and his training fell to his elder sisters; at sixteen he went to Edinburgh University to study medicine. This was distasteful to him and after two years he went to Cambridge to study for the ministry, was a poor student standing tenth in his class; was fond of natural history. Read Humboldt's "Personal Narrative" while at Cambridge, which decided him to be a naturalist. In 1831 he went as Government Naturalist on the surveying brig Beadle to South America, where he remained five years and where he collected the material for most of his important works. In 1839 he married his cousin, Emma Edgewood. He was extremely methodical in work, economical of time, imaginative and speculative of intellect; ill of health for years, poor in memory and an omnivorous reader. He was six feet of stature, thin in form, ruddy of complexion, simple and charming in manner, and his numerous works, while not attractive in style, have had an immense influence, whether for good or ill throughout the thinking world. He is popularly, though not correctly, accounted as the author of the "Evolution Theory." In his original edition of the most noted of his works, "Origin of Species," published in 1859, and which was the result of seventeen years of preparation he was extremely orthodox in his views, but these statements he subsequently omitted in later editions. The most important of his other works are "Coral Reefs" published in 1842, "Geological Observations" in 1844, "Fertilization of Orchids" in 1862, "Variations of Plants and Animals under Domestication" in 1868, "Descent of Man, and Selection in Relation to Sex" in 1871, "Expressions of Emotions in Man and Animals" in 1872, "Insectivorous Plants" in 1875, "Effects of Cross and Self Fertilizations in the Vegetable Kingdom" in 1876, "Different Forms of Flowers" in 1877, "Power of Movements in Plants" in 1880, "Formation of Vegetable Mold through the Action of Worms" in 1881.

Thomas Henry Huxley, author, lecturer, born in Ealing, Middlesex, England, May 4, 1825. His father being a teacher in a school at that place, he received his early education at home, save two and one-half years that he spent at Ealing school. In 1842 he entered the medical school of Charing Cross Hospital, receiving the degree of M. B., in 1845, from the University of London, being the second on the honor list. In 1846 he joined the Royal Navy and was stationed at the Haslar Hospital, and then the same year went as assistant surgeon on Captain Stanley's surveying expedition to the South Pacific, making a four years voyage, and gathering much of the material for his work of after years. On his return he published some noted papers, and in 1851 he was elected Fellow of Royal Society; in 1853 he resigned his position in the navy and the following year he succeeded Prof. Edward Forbes as the professor of natural history in the Royal School of Mines. He was also the Hunterian Professor at the Royal College of Surgeons, 1863-9, and the president of the Geological and Ethnological Society, 1869-70. In 1870, president of the British Association of Science, and member of London School Board, 1872, Lord Rector of the University of Aberdeen, and since has been crowned with additional honors as member of learned bodies in various parts of the world. His public lectures on "**Man's Place in Nature**" and "**The Physical Basis** of Life," as well as his published volumes, have attracted marked attention to him as the author of the "protoplasm theory" of life's beginning. Prof. Huxley was the first of learned men to extend the Darwinian theory of natural selection to man.

John Stuart Mill, philosopher, author, born in London, England, May 20, 1806, died in Avignon, France, May 8, 1873. His father, James Mill, was educated for the Scottish ministry and was licensed to preach, but abandoned the ministry and became not only a disbeliever in all religions but an active opponent of them. He supported himself after his change of views by literary work, until, in 1819, he was given a position in the East India House. Mr. Mill, Senior, having adopted the views of Jeremy Bentham, took his son in hand early, and set him, when but three years old, at learning Greek by aid of a Greek-Latin lexicon, and so drilled the child that, before he was eight years of age, he had read all the Greek authors of the University course, being required daily to report and analyze to his father. At eight he began the study of Latin, Euclid and Algebra, then Greek, Roman and English History, and when twelve he took up the study of logic, rhetoric, political economy, and metaphysics, being thoroughly drilled by his father in the systems of Jeremy Bentham, Adam Smith, and Ricardo. For fourteen years the father took the utmost pains to prevent him having any religious ideas whatever, teaching him that men could know nothing of their origin, or of that of the world, or of a God, so that when fourteen he was a shy, timid lad, shut out from associates of his age and ignorant of almost all practical matters and common subjects, but very learned on uncommon and practically useless ones. When fourteen he went with Sir Samuel Bentham (brother of Jeremy B.) to France, where he studied French philosophy and politics and began to write for newspapers and reviews. When seventeen he became clerk in the Examiner's office (in East India House, where his father was assistant examiner), where he remained for thirty-two years, becoming an assistant when twenty-two years of age and examiner in 1856, and when the office was abolished he retired, October, 1858, on an allowance from government. The office afforded him much leisure, so that he continued his literary work, editing, when twenty-one, Bentham's "Rationale of Judicial Evidence," and when twenty-nine was joint editor of the *Westminster Review*. When thirty-seven he published (1843) his "System of Logic," and five years later his "Political Economy," perhaps the best known of his works. In 1865 he was elected to the House of Commons, where he served for three years with great distinction. He was a man of retiring disposition, generous and liberal in spirit, and of a pure life, albeit a worshiper, as he tells us, of Mrs. Taylor, whom he constantly visited for nineteen years during her husband's life, and whom he married in 1851 (Mr. Taylor dying in 1849), and when she died in 1859 at Avignon he built a residence near her grave, where he continued to reside till his death, saying of her in his Autobiography, published the year of his death, "My objects in life are solely those which were hers, my pursuits and occupations those in which she shared or sympathized, and which are indissolubly associated with her. Her memory is to me a religion, and her approbation the standard by which, summing up as it does all worthiness, I endeavor to regulate my life."

Sir Isaac Newton, philosopher, born in Woolsthorpe, Lincolnshire, England, 25th December, 1642, died in (Kensington) London, March 20, 1727. Was born after his father's death (as was the illustrious Kepler) and prematurely in the year that Galileo died as a prisoner at the hands of the Inquisition "for thinking in astronomy," said John Milton, "otherwise than the Franciscan and Dominican licensers thought." When Newton was three years of age his mother again married and gave him in charge to her mother, and he attended the schools at Skillington and at Stoke till his twelfth year, when he was sent to the grammar school at Grantham; being bullied by an older boy he resolved to surpass him in study and was soon at the head of the school. While at school he cared more for making various ingenious mechanical contrivances than for the sports of his school fellows. One of the sun dials he then cut in stone is preserved by the Royal Society. When fourteen, his mother, again a widow, took him to help in carrying on the farm in his native place, but he neglected work for study and his mother sent him back to Grantham, where he fitted to enter Trinity College, Cambridge, in 1661, and was elected scholar in 1664, and the following year took the degree of B.A. During his university course he invented his binomial theorem and fluxions, and began his improvements on the Huygens telescopes shortly after his graduation. The plague compelled him to retire to his native place in 1665, where the fall of an apple, as he sat in the garden, turned his attention to the investigation that at length led to his discovery of the theory of gravitation in 1680-4 and which has made his name immortal. When the plague ceased he returned to Cambridge and graduated M.A. in July, 1668, and, in the autumn of same year, made the first reflecting telescope ever directed to the heavens (Gregory never completed the instrument he invented). Newton's telescope was six inches in length and magnified forty times and enabled him to see Jupiter's satellites and phases of Venus. In 1671 he made another that is now carefully preserved in the library of the Royal Society, in London, and January 11, of that year, was elected a member of the society, and in 1686 at the urgent solicitation of Halley and at Halley's expense, he published his great discoveries in gravitation in his great work the "Principia," that has come down through two hundred years, adding ever new luster to his name. He was elected to represent the university in Parliament in 1689 and 1701. In 1696 he was appointed warden of the mint, and promoted master of the mint in 1699 at a salary of $7,000 a year, holding the office till the end of his life; and for twenty-five years he was annually elected (1703-27) president of the Royal Society. In 1699 he was also made member of Academy of Science at Paris and in 1705 was made Knight by Queen Anne. He wrote and published notable papers, the most important of which were republished by Bishop Horsley in five volumes (London, 1779-85) and by Sir David Brewster (1855-75). He was of medium stature, never married, never wore spectacles, and is said never to have lost but one tooth to the day of his death. He was buried with great pomp in Westminster Abbey, where a monument to him was erected in 1731 and his dwelling house is said to be yet kept in St. Martin's street, London, as a place of pilgrimage.

John Ruskin, author, born in London, England, February 8, 1819. His father, John James Ruskin, began life as a poor clerk, and became a wine merchant, and owner of extensive vineyards in Spain, and by his industry amassed a large fortune, which the son, an only living child, inherited. Both his parents were Scotch, and he was designed by them for the ministry, and carefully educated at home by his mother, a woman of good attainments, and then by a private tutor in his home (Dr. Andrews), who taught him Latin, Greek, mathematics, etc., to fit him for college, and he was then entered as a student at Christ Church College, Oxford, when fifteen years of age, and afterwards spent two years in preparatory work for the college course at the private school of Rev. Thomas Dale, and graduated from Oxford College in 1842, distinguishing himself while there in the year 1839, by gaining the Newdigate prize for English poetry, he having written poetry from his childhood. Immediately after his graduation, Mr. Ruskin devoted himself to the study of art and to water-color painting, and made many visits to various parts of continental Europe, and also spent much time in Italy, especially in Venice, with a view of reforming landscape painting and domestic architecture, and he published notable works illustrated with his own drawings, which awakened much criticisim. In 1867 he was elected Rede lecturer at Cambridge and given the degree of LL. D., and in 1869 elected professor of fine arts in University of Oxford. He has given many courses of lectures to artisans and others, and, beside publishing numerous volumes of illustrated works of more or less merit, has engaged in and established various schemes for the benefit of different classes of society in his native land, and especially seeking to elevate his fellow men.

Herbert Spencer, philosopher, born in Derby, England, 27th April, 1820. His father, W. G. Spencer, was a teacher of mathematics in school in Derby, and Herbert, the only surviving child, being in delicate health, did not learn to read till seven years of age, and when sent to school was a rather dull scholar. In his boyhood he was fond of rearing butterflies and insects and watching their several transformations and making drawings of them, and experimenting. When thirteen he was sent to an uncle, Rev. Thomas Spencer, rector of Hinton, who taught him for three years to prepare him for college, but he refused to take a college course. The uncle was of liberal tendencies, which in after years were manifested in his pulpit. The youth was a good mathematician and when sixteen devised a new theorem in Descriptive Geometry, which was published in the *Civil Engineers' and Architects' Journal*. At seventeen, he was indentured for a few years to Sir Charles Fox, civil engineer, and worked on London and Birmingham Railroad. In 1841 he returned home and spent two years in the study of mathematics and mineralogy and gave attention to experiments and inventions of many kinds from watch springs to electrotyping, and in 1843 went to London to engage in literary work, but not succeeding, returned again to engineering and followed that for some five years. Then from 1848 to 1853, he was engaged in writing for the *Economist* and other journals and published his first volume of "Social Statics," that he afterward withdrew and suppressed. In 1854 he put forth the views on evolution, afterward so extensively developed in his several works. In 1855 he published his "Principles of Psychology," and in 1860 published a prospectus of a universal system of evolution, in biology, psychology, sociology, and morality, and began the preparation of his works which he published from time to time but which met with limited sale, so that when in 1881, his part eight of the series was issued, he stated that, as he had then sunk some $18,000 in the venture, they could no longer be continued. Then Miss Eliza A. Youmans, sister of Prof. E. L. Youmans, read his work, and her brother and others began to take interest in them and a fund of $7,000 was raised for their publication. Mr. Spencer visited the United States in 1882, to the great delight of his friends here, and the year following was elected corresponding member of the French Academy, since which period his works have been translated into various languages —Hungarian, Bohemian, Polish, Swedish, Dutch, Danish, German, French, Russian, Greek, Italian, Spanish, Chinese, and Japanese, and accepted as among the very chief epistles of the doctrine of evolution.

John Tyndall, philosopher, author, educator, born in Leighlin Bridge, Carlow, Ireland, August 21, 1820, died in Haslemere, Surrey, Eng., December 4, 1893. His father was a member of the Irish constabulary, in moderate circumstances, and taught him early the elementary branches and especially instructed him in the Bible, and when a lad sent him to the best schools the district afforded, where he made excellent progress, particularly in mathematics, and at nineteen became a civil assistant in the Irish ordnance survey. Being thwarted by his friends in his plans to go to the United States, he took a situation as civil engineer with a Manchester, Eng., firm in the construction of a railroad, giving up the situation in 1847 to become a professor in the Queenswood College, Hampshire (a new institution, founded by the celebrated Robert Owen and his disciples to inaugurate the millennium and who had cut the letters C. M. (i. e., Commencement of the Millennium) on the front of their Harmony Hall. Here he first met Dr. Frankland, who was the resident chemist at the college, and he now began when twenty-eight those original investigations that gave him at length a world-wide renown. In the following year himself and Frankland went to the University of Marburg, Germany, prosecuting their study and researches under the famous Bunsen and his co-laborers. From thence he went to study in the laboratory of Prof. Magnus at Berlin and returned to England in 1851. In 1853 he was elected F. R. S. and appointed professor of natural philosophy in the Royal Institution (founded 1800, by an American, Count Rumford) succeeding the renowned Prof. Faraday as its superintendent and retaining it till 1887, when he resigned. From 1856–60 he visited each summer the Alps to investigate the glaciers, and in 1859 began his great researches in Radiant Heat, and in 1863 published his famous work on "Heat as a Mode of Motion." In 1872 he delivered thirty-five lectures in the United States, devoting the net proceeds to founding scientific scholarships for original investigations (divided in 1885 among Harvard and Columbia Colleges and University of Pennsylvania, and which amounted to $33,400). In 1872 he awakened much criticism by his proposed "prayer test," which was intensified by his "Belfast Address" when President of the British Association in 1874. During his thirty-nine years of active life as scientist he became greatly distinguished for his researches as to the constitution of light, the phenomena of sound, the nature of the molecules, and of the disease germs, several of his numerous works having a great circulation in the English tongue and being also translated into other languages, that on "Sound" being published in China by that government. In 1876 Prof. Tyndall married Louisa, eldest daughter of Lord Hamilton. Although classed by many as a materialist, in his later years he surely was not such. He was not only among the foremost scientists of his generation, but was also a man of fine literary culture.

AMERICA'S FAVORITE AUTHORS.

William Cullen Bryant, poet and journalist, born at Cummington, Mass., November 3, 1794, son of a cultured physician. Young Bryant was very precocious, is said to have known the alphabet when but sixteen months old, and at five years of age to have learned all of Dr. Watts's poems for children. Before ten years of age was heard to pray that God would give him the gift of poetic genius. His first recorded verses were a translation from Horace, and an address in rhyme recited at the closing of the winter school, at this time being twelve years old. First book was published in 1807; at sixteen, entered Williams College, taking high rank in the classical department. In May, 1811, left Williams, intending to enter Yale; but found himself unable to afford it, and entered a law office. Just before this, wrote "Thanatopsis," which was printed in 1817 in the September number of the *North American Review*, and afterward "The Waterfowl" and other poems appeared in the same journal. In 1821, read a poem before the Phi Beta Kappa Society of Harvard, and on that occasion met Mr. Dana, with whom, for sixty years, he had close correspondence and friendship. Mr. Bryant was admitted to the bar, but did not practice. In 1825, assumed editorial control of the New York *Review*, and not long after became associate editor of the *Evening Post*, remaining in this connection until his death, which occurred June 12, 1878. Of Mr. Bryant's works it is sufficient to say that with them began a new era in American verse, and that they are household treasures in the homes of our country. Of the man, it may with truth be said, that he was a chivalrous gentleman, a sympathetic friend, and a broad-minded Christian; truly, his was a successful life.

Ralph Waldo Emerson, author, lecturer, born in Boston, Mass, May 25, 1803, died in Concord, Mass., April 27, 1882. His father (William) was a clergyman of the Unitarian faith, and pastor of the First Unitarian Church, Boston, when Ralph (the second of his five sons) was born. He entered the grammar school at eight (when his father died), four years later the Latin school, and at fourteen Harvard College, where he was graduated in 1821, having earned his way through by teaching during vacations. After graduation he continued to teach for some five years and studied theology under Dr. William Ellery Channing, and spent one year at the Cambridge Divinity School, and in 1826 was "approbated to preach," by the Middlesex association of his church, and March 11, 1829, ordained as colleague to Henry Ware, Jr., of the Second Unitarian Church of Boston, and that year married Miss Ellen Louise Tucker. Mr. Ware resigned in 1831 and in February of the following year Mr. Emerson's wife died, when he resigned and went to Europe, returning in the fall of 1833. While in Europe he made the acquaintance of Coleridge, Wordsworth, and Carlyle, with the latter of whom he maintained correspondence for thirty-six years (edited by Charles Eliot Norton, 1883). After his return to United States, Mr. Emerson preached for a time at New Bedford, but declined a call, and took up his abode at Concord, Mass., where he remained till his death, preaching for a while at Concord, then at Lexington, but refusing a call, saying, "My pulpit is the lyceum platform." And so for a generation he wrote poetry; prepared and delivered notable lectures on many men and things to more or less appreciative audiences; made two lecturing tours to England receiving homage denied him at home; wrote and published books that waited longer than those of Hawthorne to find appreciative readers; was called a mystic pantheist, atheist; and now termed prophet and seer by the children of those who were wont to denounce him; and is in some circles in danger of being as much overestimated as he was formerly underestimated both for the originality and for the profundity of his thought; while he lived in his thought and purpose in advance of his age, and while he searched after the divine in man, he did not neglect altogther the oppressed, but took a part in the agitation against slavery, albeit nature had not run him in the mold out of which she brings forth her reformers. He was an idealist, dreaming oft unpracticable dreams, rather than the profound explorer of new ways, and of higher, holier thoughts for men; a scholar limited by a creed which while it touches man closely holds his Creator at too profound an angle of distance to be either known or appreciated, and so he missed that greatest sum of all knowledge and hope—Jesus Christ.

Nathaniel Hawthorne (changed by him from Hathorne, the original name), author, born in Salem, Mass., July 4, 1804, died in Plymouth, N. H., May 18, 1864. His father, Nathaniel, was captain of a trading vessel and died at Surinam, when the son was eight years old, leaving beside him two daughters. The mother never recovered from the shock of the husband's death, but thereafter wholly secluded herself. The father was of a melancholy, taciturn spirit, which inheritance came duly to the son. When seven he became a pupil in the school of the lexicographer, Dr. Joseph E. Worcester, and became fond of the English classics, but did not relish school life. A year or two later his mother removed to Raymond, Maine, then a wild country, mainly forest, where his inherited tendency to solitude grew and expanded, and then at fifteen he returned to Salem and privately fitted for Bowdoin College, entering there in 1821, and wrote poor verses, read some novels, mainly Scott's, and "nursed his fancies." At his graduation in 1825, he returned to Salem to his mother's house, where for nine or more years he was a veritable hermit, seldom seeing any but the members of the family and going out of doors at night for long, lonely walks, scribbling sketches by day only to burn them at night. In 1831 Mr. Samuel C. Goodrich published some of his sketches, which led to an acquaintance with Miss Sophia Peabody, whom he married in 1842. In 1837 he published the first of "Twice-told Tales" selling some 700 copies only. Two years later George Bancroft appointed him "weigher and gauger" in Boston Custom House, which he held for two years and on change of administration was ousted. Then in 1841 he published part of "Grandfather's Chair" and joined the noted Brook Farm Colony (1840-7) and invested his $1,000 of savings in it, thinking it was "an Arcady," but found himself he said," up to the chin in a barn-yard." In July, 1842, he married and went to live at Concord, Mass., where he resided for four years supporting himself in part by writing tales for the *Democratic Review*, and on its failure and the loss of his $1,000 at Brook Farm he removed to Salem and became surveyor of that port in 1846, where he remained three years and wrote "Scarlet Letter," publishing it in 1850, selling 5,000 in the first fortnight in the United States, and it had an immense run in this country and England and made him famous. In summer of that year he removed to Lenox, Mass., where he wrote "The House of the Seven Gables" which outsold "Scarlet Letter," and the following year wrote "The Wonder-Book" and "Snow Image," and then in that year he removed to West Newton and wrote "The Blithedale Romance," founded on life and incidents at the Brook Farm. This work also met with enthusiastic reception. In 1852 he bought a residence in Concord, Mass., and the next year was appointed United States Consul to Liverpool, England, and, after the term expired, he traveled on the continent and wrote of his travels and "The Marble Faun," that had also a very great sale. He returned to the United States in 1860 and published sundry other works, the last, "Dr. Grimshawe's Secret," an incomplete story, being published by his son, Julian, in 1882. He died while on a journey to the White Mountains with his close friend, ex-President Pierce.

Oliver Wendell Holmes, author, physician, born in Cambridge, Mass., August 29, 1809, his father, Abiel, being the pastor of the First Congregational Church at that place. He was educated in the schools of his native place, and at a school in Cambridgeport, and fitted for college at Phillips Academy, Andover, and graduated from Harvard in 1829. While at Harvard he contributed numerous poems to the college paper, and gave that at the commencement exercises at his graduation. His lyric "Old Ironsides," published in Boston *Advertiser*, 1830, gave him a name with the public as poet, that his subsequent productions "Evening, by a Tailor," and "The Height of the Ridiculous," much increased. He spent a year at the Cambridge Law School, and then decided to be a physician, and studied medicine under Dr. James Jackson, and in 1833, went to Europe for study, chiefly in Paris, and returned in 1835, and the following year took his degree of M.D., and that year published his first volume of poems, containing, among others, "The Last Leaf," Abraham Lincoln's favorite. In 1839 he was chosen professor of anatomy and physiology at Dartmouth College, and the next year he married Amelia Lee, daughter of Judge Charles Jackson of Massachusetts Supreme Court, and shortly after resigned his professorship and took up the practice of medicine in Boston. In 1847 he was chosen professor of anatomy and physiology at Harvard, succeeding Dr. John C. Warren in that chair, and went before the public on the lecture platform, being in much request. When the *Atlantic Monthly* was established, in 1857, he began to publish his famous serial, "The Autocrat of the Breakfast Table," followed by "The Professor at the Breakfast Table," and later by "The Poet at the Breakfast Table," the series containing many of his best poetical productions. In 1882 he resigned the professorship at Harvard, and devoted himself to literature. In his poems he has run the gamut from serious to gay, and has written famous songs in both moods, the mirth, however, far exceeding the more serious of his moods. He has also published learned medical dissertations, three of which took the Boylston prizes for excellency, and are known, read, and admired in England and on the Continent by vast multitudes, as well as by his own countrymen. His son, Oliver Wendell Holmes, Jr., is a famous jurist and a judge of the Supreme Court of Massachusetts.

Washington Irving, author, born in New York city April 3, 1783, died in Irvington, N. Y., November 28, 1859. Was youngest of the eleven children of his father, who was a Scotchman and a sailor, but settled in New York as merchant trader, and Washington got his education in the schools of the town, mainly in the English branches, with a smattering of Latin, and at about sixteen he entered the law office of Judge Hoffman and studied law. He was a voracious reader of such works of fiction as he could find, and in youth wrote articles for a daily paper under the pseudonym of Jonathan Old Style. When he was twenty-one, his health being frail and threatened by consumption, an elder brother, William, then in business, defrayed the expense of a trip to Europe, where he remained near two years, and on his return took up the law again; and also essayed, with a brother and friend, the publication of a new periodical of the London *Spectator* stamp and called the *Salmagundi*, which soon died. He now turned to writing a more pretentious work, "The History of New York, by Diedrich Knickerbocker," but while engaged on it Miss Matilda Hoffman, daughter of Judge Hoffman, his friend and legal instructor, a young lady whom he devotedly loved, died, and he never loved again, and now sought relief from sorrow in literature, and in 1809 published his History, which had at once a large sale and brought him $3,000 (a large sum for the time). He then took a part interest with two of his brothers in mercantile business, and in 1815 again went to Europe on a visit to relatives and on business of the firm, remaining in England until the firm failed in 1818, and then betook himself to writing his "Sketch Book," published in 1820, and "Bracebridge Hall" (1822), "Tales of a Traveller" (1824), for which works he received some $15,000. During part of these years he was in Paris and then at Madrid as attaché to the American Legation, and at the latter place began his "Life of Columbus," published in London and New York (1828), and which netted him $18,000. His "Conquest of Granada" appeared in 1829

498

and "Tales of the Alhambra" in 1832. In 1829 he was appointed secretary to the Legation at London, and resided in England for three years, receiving there in 1831 the degree of LL.D. from Oxford University. In 1832 he returned (after an absence of seventeen years) to New York and bought "Sunnyside," near Tarrytown, N. Y. He went west with John Jacob Astor and wrote his "Tour on the Prairies," which was published in 1835, and his "Astoria," published the next year. In 1842 President Tyler appointed him Minister to Madrid. In 1846 he returned to America, and 1848-50 brought out a new and very successful edition of his works in fifteen volumes, and added two more, "The Life of Mahomet" and "Life of Goldsmith," and when sixty-nine he began on a "Life of Washington," and at the end of seven years completed the fifth and last volume. Over 600,000 volumes of his works were sold during his lifetime, and he died rich and greatly beloved for his nobility of character, as well as for his genius. A new edition of his works, in twenty-seven 12mo volumes, was issued 1884-6, and it is said that over a million and a half copies of his various productions have been sold in the United States, and he is recognized as one of the most pleasing and successful writers of the century.

Henry Wadsworth Longfellow, poet, born in Portland, Me., February 27, 1807, died in Cambridge, Mass., March 24, 1882. Father a lawyer, member of legislature, and man of means. His mother a daughter of Gen. Wadsworth, and Henry was the second of their eight children. Was studious when a child and fond of reading; at twelve read Washington Irving's "Sketch Book," which made a deep impression on him. At thirteen he sent his first poem to the poet's corner of the Portland *Gazette*. At fourteen entered Bowdoin College, the requisites for admission at that time being very easy, viz., ability to read a little New Testament Greek, and put in lame English a few lines of Virgil and Cicero, and a fair knowledge of the "Walsh Arithmetic" and ' Morse's Geography." But he had some notable classmates, such as Nathaniel Hawthorne, George B. Cheever, William Pitt Fessenden, Franklin Pierce, John P. Hale, Calvin E. Stowe, John S. C. Abbott, S. S. Prentice, and others who made their mark. Longfellow graduated fourth in his class of forty-two During his college course he wrote some fourteen of his poems and published them in the *Literary Gazette* of Boston, none of them being especially brilliant; but he aimed at eminence in literature, for writing to his father while yet at college he said, "Whatever I study, I ought to be engaged in with all my soul, for I will be eminent in something," and in his Junior year, "I most eagerly aspire after future eminence in literature; my whole soul burns most ardently for it, and every earthly thought centers in it. Nature has given me a very strong predilection for literary pursuits, and I am almost confident in believing that if I ever rise in the world it must be by the exercise of my talent in the wide field of literature." After his graduation he tutored for a short time at the college, then entered his father's law office to study law, but the college offering him the chair of modern languages on condition that he first spend three years in study in Europe, in the spring of 1826 he went to France for part of a year, then eight months in Spain, where he first met Washington Irving, then a year in Italy, and after some months in Germany he returned and September 29 he began his new duties as junior professor. Two years later he married Miss Mary S. Potter of Portland, Me., and lived contentedly on his salary of $1,000 a year. When twenty-eight he was invited to the chair of modern languages at Harvard College and again went to Europe for study of Scandinavian languages and at Rotterdam his wife died, and he sought to drown his grief in redoubled application to study. On his return he entered upon the professorship, and in 1838 published his "Footsteps of Angels" and "The Psalm of Life" and the next year "Hyperion" and "Voices of the Night." In 1843 he married Miss Appleton, daughter of Hon. Nathan Appleton of Boston and bought the old "Craigie house" (once Washington's headquarters) where he lived till his death. The most noted of his many poems are "Evangeline" (1847), his best; "Hiawatha" (1855), "Courtship of Miles Standish" (1858) and "Poems on Slavery." In July, 1861, his wife while playing with her children caught her light summer dress on fire and was fatally burned, and this and the trying scenes of the civil war kept his harp silent for six years, and then he sang again in minor lays in volumes that appeared at intervals of a year or more, and translated into felicitous lines the "Divine Comedy" of Dante.

James Russell Lowell, poet and diplomatist, was born at Cambridge, Mass., February 22, 1819, son of Charles Lowell, a Unitarian minister, and his wife, who was a most gifted and intelligent woman. First tuition was received at a private school, and, entering Harvard in his sixteenth year, was graduated when not yet twenty. Was not an industrious student. The first known publication, under his name, was the class poem. Entered Harvard Law School; was graduated and admitted to the bar two years later, at twenty-one; but after one year, in which he had very little practice, the law was definitely and finally abandoned for literature.

SUCCESSFUL MEN AND WOMEN.

In 1841 appeared Lowell's first volume of poems, "A Year's Life." In 1846-48, the "Biglow Papers" appeared, vigorous satire and inventive genius making them acceptable, while moral force and unmistakable prophecy gave them strong influence upon the times. 1851-52 he spent largely in Europe, and, as the fruit of this sojourn, appeared a series of essays on Italian art and literature. In 1855, accepted the professorship of modern languages and literature in Harvard, made vacant by the resignation of Henry W. Longfellow. Held this position for twenty years; and from 1859 to 1862 was editor of *Atlantic Monthly*, also from 1863 to 1872, joint editor with Charles Eliot Norton, of the *North American Review*, and, during his connection with these magazines, the second series of the "Biglow Papers" was published. In 1875 was sent minister to Spain, and in 1880, transferred to the same position in London, which he held until 1885. From 1887 until his death, which occurred August 12, 1891, Mr. Lowell's health was poor; and Elmwood became a permanent residence. As a critic, probably no American could compare with him, unless, possibly, Edmund C. Stedman. The leading characteristic of his work in prose and poetry is moral nobility. Many lines written by him have passed into the people's speech, and will last as long as our language.

Bayard Taylor was born in Kennett Square, Pa., January 11, 1825, of Quaker parentage. During early boyhood he worked on the farm at home and at twelve years began to write short novels, poems, and historical essays. When barely sixteen years of age he published his first poem in the Philadelphia *Saturday Evening Post* (1841). At the age of fourteen studied Latin, French, and Spanish. At seventeen was apprenticed to a printer, but, disliking the trade, bought his time, arranged with the proprietors of the *Post* and the *United States Gazette* for a series of letters from foreign lands, each paper paying $50 in advance; *Graham's Magazine* purchased poems from him, and this raised the poet's funds to $140. He was absent for two years, and by extreme economy and self-denial made the trip on $500. In 1846 he published the collected accounts of his travels under the name of "Views Afoot." Six editions were sold during the year. In 1847 secured a position on the New York *Tribune* as man of all work in the literary department. Two years later published "Rhymes of Travel, Ballads and Poems," and immediately took rank as an American poet of merit. In 1850 his Tribune letters, entitled "Eldorado; or, in the Path of Empire," were published. In 1851 he published "Romances, Lyrics and Songs," and set out again for the continent, visiting Syria, Egypt, Palestine and Asia Minor; then went with Perry's expedition to Japan. Returned to the United States and began lecturing, meeting with pronounced success. In 1854 published "A Journey to Central Africa" and "The Land of the Saracen"; in 1854 also, "Poems of the Orient." In 1855 followed a "Visit to China, India and Japan." In 1855 made his famous journey to Norway and Lapland. In 1862 was sent as Secretary of Legation to St. Petersburg. In 1870 Mr. Taylor was elected Professor of German Literature in Cornell University. In 1877 became Minister to Berlin. Mr. Taylor published many works in addition to those already mentioned. He died in Berlin, Germany, December 19, 1878.

John Greenleaf Whittier, best if not first, of American poets, was born at Haverhill, Mass., December 7, 1807, and died at Hampton Falls, N. H., September 7, 1892. His father, who in his religious belief was a Friend, was a small farmer in moderate circumstances, and from seven years to sixteen John attended for six months in the year the district school. He was fond of reading and devoured the twenty miscellaneous books his father owned, and borrowed from the doctor and neighbors. When he was thirteen, one of the then strolling merchants of the day, spent a night at his father's house and sang to them the songs of Robert Burns, a name new to their Quaker ears. The stirring stanzas made an impression on the susceptible lad that largely determined his future; he too would be a poet. When not at school, and on winter evenings he worked at shoe making and earned enough for a six months' term in the Haverhill academy; then he taught a district school, and with the proceeds took another six months' course, which was all he had. When twenty-two he became editor of a small weekly paper in which many of his earliest verses appeared; but the death of his father shortly compelled him to return to the farm to care for his mother, two sisters, and a brother, and aunt. In 1836 he became secretary of the American Anti-Slavery Society and went to Philadelphia to edit the Pennsylvania *Freeman*, but a mob sacked and burned his office and compelled this man of peace to flee; also at Concord, N. H., where he went with George Thomson, he was again mobbed. He was elected as a member of the Legislature from Haverhill, 1835-6. In 1840 he settled in Amesbury, Mass., where he spent most of his later years. From 1847-59 he was an editorial writer for the *National Era*, Washington, D. C., in which journal Mrs. H. B. Stowe's "Uncle Tom's Cabin" first appeared. During all these years he was writing verses, most of which flamed like beacon fires, or scattered like the lightning's bolts. Of the latter is his "Ichabod" written on learning that Daniel Webster had spoken in Congress in favor of the Fugitive Slave Law. In "School Days" is found the clue to his single life, while the world will not willingly let die "Snow Bound," "My Psalm," and "The Eternal Goodness." An edition of his poems in four volumes appeared during the closing year of his life.

FAMOUS NOVELISTS.

Charlotte Bronte, author, born in Thornton, England, April 21, 1816, died in Haworth, England, March 31, 1855. Her father was a clergyman of Irish descent, an eccentric man, subject to strange outbursts of temper, gloomy, and solitary in spirit, and when Charlotte was six years old her mother died, and two years later she and a sister Emily were sent to school for clergymen's daughters at Cowan's Bridge, near Haworth, where the father was then in charge (the school is the original Lowood in Jane Eyre). They remained here two years and returned home in 1825, and after six years at home she was sent to school at Roe-Head, and in 1835 she became a teacher at that school, and afterward served as governess to a private family, and then went with Emily to Brussels (1842), to learn French and teach English in order to qualify themselves for teaching as a vocation. On her return, in 1844, she found her father had become nearly blind, and her only brother dissipated. Then she and sisters turned to literature for a living, and the three sisters published a volume of poems under the pseudonym of "Currer Bell." It had no sale, and they turned to fiction, and the stories of her sisters Emily and Anne were accepted and published, but her first one could find no publisher to print it. Then she began another, "Jane Eyre," published in 1847, that took the English world by storm, and that continues to be regarded as one of the great masterpieces of literature. Her second story, "Shirley," was published in 1849, and the third and last, "Villette," in 1853. The following year she married the curate of her father's parish, Rev. A. Nicholls, and after a brief married life died of the same disease, consumption, that had already carried off her four sisters and brother.

James Fenimore Cooper, author, born in Burlington, N. J., September 15, 1789, died at Cooperstown, N. Y., September 14, 1851. He was the son of Judge William Cooper, a Congressman who owned large tracts of land in New York state, and the year after the birth of James he laid out the village of Cooperstown on his possession and removed his family there, on the then border of civilization. Here James had limited schooling, and then entered the family of Rev. J. Ellison at Albany, who fitted him for Yale College, which he entered in 1802. Having been well tutored by Mr. Ellison (an alumnus of an English university) young Cooper had much leisure time at Yale, and being guilty of misdemeanors was expelled in his third year. He then resolved to enter the United States Navy and served a voyage to Europe as sailor before the mast and then became midshipman, in 1808 rising to rank of lieutenant. In 1811 he married a sister of Bishop DeLancey of New York, and resigned his commission and resided at Cooperstown until 1817, when he removed to his wife's early home in Westchester county, where, one evening, reading an English novel he declared he could write a good one himself and was urged by his wife to do so, and in 1820 published a tale of English life, which met with but little favor. Urged by his wife and friends he now gave attention to American scenes and topics and in 1821 he wrote "The Spy," which had a wide circulation both sides of the Atlantic, being like many of his seventy odd productions translated into various European and Oriental languages. "The Pioneer," that came in 1823; "The Pilot," 1824, said to be the first sea-story ever written; "The Last of the Mohicans," 1826, gave him great fame. From 1826-33 he was in Europe, much of the time United States Consul at Lyons, France. Political asperities and literary jealousies called forth by some of his productions, led him to institute numerous libel suits against the prominent Whig editors of his state, which being decided in his favor tended to embitter many against him in his later life. Since his death his popularity has increased and he is reckoned among the chief of American novelists, "The Leather Stockings," "Wing and Wing," "Last of the Mohicans," and "The Pilot" being perhaps his best.

Charles Dickens, author, born in Landport, Portsmouth, England, February 7, 1812; died at Gadshill Place, Rochester, England, June 9, 1870. At his birth his father was clerk in the Navy Pay Office. A few years later lost it, and the family came to great poverty when Charles was nine years of age. He was taught by his mother, and was a great reader of the dozen novels his father owned. When ten years of age, he worked in a blacking factory, pasting labels, at six shillings a week. Then the father, "a ne'er-do-well," quarreled with one of the owners of the factory, and took his son away and sent him to the public school. When fifteen, he was chore boy and clerk in a lawyer's office. The father, having moved to London, as reporter for a daily paper, the son again had a little schooling, learning shorthand, and then reported for a law firm, and at nineteen became parliamentary reporter for daily papers for five years, and wrote for the *Morning Chronicle* and the *Monthly Magazine*, his "Sketches of English Life and Character," under the name of *Boz*, that were very popular. When twenty-four he wrote for the proprietors of the *Monthly Magazine* "The Pickwick Papers," and the next year (1837), "Oliver Twist," for *Bentley's Magazine*, as its editor, and the following year "Nicholas Nickleby." Then came "Old Humphrey's Clock," "Old Curiosity Shop," and "Barnaby Rudge," and in 1842 paid his first visit to the United States, as one of the most famous of Englishmen, and on his return wrote his somewhat caustic "American Notes." In 1843 he began "Martin Chuzzlewit," and being in debt went to Italy to save expense, where he finished the story and wrote the "Christmas Carols." On his return to England in 1845 he became editor of the *Daily News* (a new journal), at $200 a week, and it is said came near killing it, and soon left, and wrote "Dombey and Son," in 1846, and at intervals of three years each, "David Copperfield," "Bleak House," and "Little Dorrit," and for nine years (1850-9) he also conducted a periodical of his own, *Household Words*. After Dorrit came his "Hard Times" (1854), "Tale of Two Cities" (1859), then his unfortunate separation from his wife in 1858, after which he wrote "Great Expectations" (1860-1), and "Our Mutual Friend" (1864-5), and in 1870 began "The Mystery of Edwin Drood," which he did not live to finish. For the last ten years of his life he was largely employed on the lecture platform, as reader of his works, making three tours of England and one in America (1867-8), earning enormous sums and adding much to his reputation as a delineator of the characters of his personages. His works in cheap form have had an enormous sale in this country as in England. His "David Copperfield" and "Tale of Two Cities" are generally considered as the best of his works.

Mary Ann Evans (George Eliot), author, born in Griff, Warwickshire, England, November 22, 1819; died in Chelsea, England, December 22, 1880. Her father was a carpenter in moderate circumstances, and shortly after her birth became land agent or farmer on estate of a gentleman in Griff. She was one of three children by her father's second wife and shared the middle class home of her father till twenty-one. When sixteen her mother died, and a year later her older sister was married, and she had charge of her father's house. She was educated at public school at Colton, and also at private schools at Griff, Nuneaton, and Coventry. Being fond of books and knowledge, after her mother's death she had a private teacher at home, and studied French, German, Italian, and music, and a few years after studied Latin, Greek, Hebrew, and Spanish, without being greatly proficient in either language. When she was twenty-one her father removed to Foleshill, near Coventry. Here she made the acquaintance of Mr. and Mrs. Charles Bray, and his wife's brother, Charles C. Hennell, and her character underwent a notable change. The Brays were of some literary ability, and of extreme "liberal views," and the girl, whose family was of the devout Methodist kind, swung at once to the most pronounced skepticism, from which she never after recovered. When she was twenty-five, she undertook to finish for a friend of the Brays, Strauss's "Leben Jesu," that he had begun, and she finished it after three years of to her hard toil, and vowed she would never translate again. It was published by Dr. Chapman of the *Westminster Review*. In 1849 her father died, and she went with her friends, the Brays, to the Continent, visiting Paris and Milan, and spent some time at Geneva, and there continued her study of music, and delighted in reading Proudhon and Rousseau, and in attending lectures on physics. On returning to England, she met at Bray's, Dr. Chapman, who offered her the post of assistant editor on the *Westminster Review*, and she boarded in the doctor's family, where she met Mr. Herbert Spencer, who became her friend, and introduced her to Mr. George Henry Lewes, also Harriet Martineau, George Combe, and other free-thinkers. In 1854 she resigned her position on the *Review*, and formed, with Mr. Lewes, whose legal wife was living, the *liaison*, which history, that, like nature, makes for righteousness, cannot condone, and together they went to Germany, where he collected materials for his "Life of Goethe," and she translated Spinoza Ethics, and wrote magazine articles without signing a name to them, as was then her custom, and read scores of books on scores of subjects, and while at Berlin began to write fiction for first time in 1856, in the "Scenes of Clerical Life," which Mr. Lewes sent to Blackwood, under the name of "George Eliot," the publisher and the public supposing its author was a man. She received $600 for the first edition of it in book form. She then worked on "Adam Bede" for two years, publishing it in 1859 on returning to England, and for which Blackwood paid her $8,000 for copyright for four years, and it was translated into French, German, and Hungarian, and she had become famous, sixteen thousand copies having been sold in England the first year, and was offered $6,000 by an American house for another book. She now devoured, as was her custom, another long list of books, and in 1860 published "The Mill on the Floss," for which Blackwood gave her $10,000 for the first edition of four thousand copies, and Harper & Brother $1,500 for privilege of using it. "Silas Marner" appeared in 1861, and after two years in Europe (mainly in study and reading in Italy), "Romola" was published in 1863, for which the *Cornhill Magazine* paid her $35,000. After much reading of Mill, Fawcett, and other political economists, "Felix Holt" was written in 1866, for which Blackwood gave $25,000. "Middlemarch" came in 1872, bringing her from Blackwood over $40,000 ; and then again reading, it is said, near a thousand books, she brought out in 1876 "Daniel Deronda," and again received $40,000 from Blackwood for it. She was now famous and rich, and in 1878 Mr. Lewes, with whom she lived as wife, died, and her grief was great. A year and a half later she suddenly married John Walter Cross, a rich banker of New York (young enough to be her son), and they went to Italy, and on their return to London, lived at Chelsea. Of their married life and separation Mr. Cross says but little, in his biography of her. After an illness of five days she died of inflammation of the heart, at midnight, December 22, 1880, and she, who when urged to write her autobiography had said, "The only thing I should care much to dwell on would be the absolute despair I suffered from, of ever being able to achieve anything. No one could ever have felt greater despair; and a knowledge of this might be a help to some other struggler," had a name written on the roll of the world's memorable women. A wonderfully receptive, impressible soul, she would have been much greater if her moral nature had been stronger at the parting of the ways. But a world built to run according to the ten commandments can never long accept genius as an excuse for sin, and the one stain on her memory will yet blot out her fame.

William Dean Howells, author, born in Martin's Ferry, Ohio, March 1, 1837. In 1840 father bought weekly newspaper at Hamilton, Ohio, where the family moved, and he learned to set type when child. Nine years after sold out and removed to Dayton, buying the *Transcript*, semi-weekly, of that place, and changed to a daily on which William worked setting type till 11 P. M., and then up at 4 A. M. to "sell papers." It proved unsuccessful, and the family moved to Green County, and for a year "roughed it" in a log house. The next year young Howells worked as compositor on *State Journal* at $4 a week, which went to support the family. Then the father bought the *Sentinel* of Ashtabula, removing it to Jefferson, and William went to work on it. When nineteen he became state capitol correspondent of Cincinnati *Gazette* and wrote also for *Atlantic Monthly*. In 1860 he published a "Life of Lincoln" and with proceeds went to Boston, Mass. From 1861-5 was United States consul at Venice, Italy, marrying in 1862 Miss Elinor G., sister of Larkin G. Mead, the American sculptor. On return to United States he wrote for the *Tribune*, *Times*, and the *Nation* of New York and soon became assistant editor of the *Atlantic Monthly*, and from 1872 to 1881 its editor and resided at Cambridge, Mass. The following year he went to Europe with his family, and then from 1886-91 was one of the editors of *Harper's Magazine* and in the latter year became the editor of the *Cosmopolitan Magazine*. Was brought up in the Swedenborgian faith. Of his many works some twenty are quite as well known and extensively circulated in England as in United States. Is a widely known and successful author and editor.

Victor Hugo was born at Besançon, in 1802, son of Major Hugo of the Neapolitan army. The young Hugo's childish years were passed in Italy, France, and Spain; the education of those early years was in the hands of the mother, an original and self-reliant woman, who gave her three sons, of whom Victor was the youngest, plenty of work and the freedom of a large library; at ten years of age the boy was able to read Tacitus, Homer, and Virgil, and the French classics. In 1812, he entered upon a three years' course of regular study at the Ecole Polytechnique. In 1818, 1819, 1820, three odes presented at the Academie des Jeux Floraux, at Toulouse, received the prize, and with these Victor Hugo entered upon a literary career. Acquired some reputation in succeeding years as a dramatist, but it is in the role of novelist that his genius is most widely recognized. On account of a political difficulty, was banished from Paris in 1851, and retired to the island of Guernsey. Of his most successful books may be noted "Notre Dame de Paris" (1831), "Les Miserables" (1862), and the "Toilers of the Sea" (1865), and "Ninety-Three" (1874). Died May 22, 1885. Few men, even among statesmen, monarchs, and great generals, have had anything like the immense public triumphs the French have accorded to Victor Hugo. And his fame is far from being merely local, is, on the contrary, widespread and pervasive as the love and the demand for good literature.

Charles Kingsley, author, poet, born in Dartmoor (Devon), England, June 12, 1819, died January 23, 1875. His father was a clergyman, and Charles was educated at home, then by tutor, and then attended King's College, London, and afterward Magdalen College, Cambridge, where he took his degree in 1842. After studying law he decided to enter the ministry, and after a course in theology became rector of Eversley in Hampshire, where he remained during most of his life. In 1848 he published his first drama, "The Saints' Tragedy," and a volume of "Sermons," the latter attaining a wide circulation. In 1849 he published what is by many esteemed his greatest work, "Alton Locke." Of his dozen or more other volumes, the best known are "Hypatia" and "Westward, Ho!" Of his poems the most popular are "The Sands of Dee," "The Three Fishers," "To the Northwest Wind." He was canon of Chester in 1869, and of Westminster in 1873, and for a time chaplain to the Queen and Prince of Wales, and from 1860 to 1869 professor of modern history at Cambridge, and in 1872 he became the editor of *Good Words*, and in the winter of 1873–4 made a lecturing tour of the United States. His sympathies, as manifest in "Alton Locke," were always with the toiling masses. His life was published by his wife in 1877 (2 volumes).

Walter Scott, the most popular writer of his era, was born at Edinburgh, August 15, 1771, of respectable and well-to-do parents. Was educated at Edinburgh High School, and at the University; was little distinguished in the ordinary branches of learning, but early secured a store of miscellaneous information. Having completed legal studies, was admitted to the bar in 1792. In 1800 was appointed sheriff of Selkirkshire, and in 1806, principal clerk in the Court of Sessions. Published the "Lay of the Last Minstrel" in 1805, which met with great applause. "Marmion" followed in 1808, and in 1810 the "Lady of the Lake." Greatest celebrity was attained as a writer of historical fiction, of which he produced not less than seventy-four volumes. "Waverley" was published in 1814. "Guy Mannering" in 1815. These were published anonymously, their authorship not being acknowledged until 1827. Also wrote a "Life of Napoleon." Died of paralysis, September 21, 1832. Was distinguished for uprightness of life, simplicity of manners, and benevolence of heart.

William Makepeace Thackeray was born at Calcutta, July 19, 1811, son of an Indian civil service officer. Received education at the Charter House school, and spent a year at Cambridge, leaving without a degree. Intending to become an artist, studied at Paris but without success. Had dissipated his patrimony by unlucky speculations and unfortunate investments, and life for some time was a struggle. In 1837 became connected with *Fraser's Magazine*, in which appeared "Yellowplush Papers," the "Great Hoggarty Diamond," the "Luck of Barry Lyndon," and other masterpieces which ranked him, in the minds of discriminating readers, as, unless Dickens were excepted, the greatest humorist of the day. Began to write for "Punch" in 1842. In 1848 "Vanity Fair" was completed, and placed him at the summit of contemporary fiction. Gave two courses of lectures with success. Later, wrote "Henry Esmond" (1852), "The Newcomes" (1854), "The Virginians," and other works. Became editor of the *Cornhill Magazine* in 1859. Retired from the editorship in 1862, and died December 24, 1863. Was one of the greatest writers of England in his age, its first satirist, and almost its first novelist.

Lewis Wallace, author, born in Brookville, Indiana, April 10, 1827. David Wallace, his father, was educated at the United States Military Academy, became lawyer, judge of court of common pleas, governor of state, and member of Congress, where he gave the casting vote in favor of an appropriation to develop Prof. S. F. B. Morse's telegraph, which vote cost him his re-election. Lewis's mother was daughter of Judge Test, and his parents made much effort to obtain for him an education; but he did not like school, his father saying that, while he paid for fourteen years for him at school, he attended but one year. Upon sending him to college he had no better success, and soon returned. Was passionately fond of reading, drawing, and painting, often caricaturing the congregation by comic sketches when he could be induced to attend church. Studied law with his father, and in 1852 married Miss Susan Arnold, who, like him, is a writer of much note, several of her novels having good sales. After his admittance to the bar he practiced in Covington and Crawfordsville, and was state senator four years; at the breaking out of the civil war was appointed adjutant-general of the State, then colonel of 11th Indiana regiment of volunteers, serving in several battles in West Virginia; was made brigadier-general of volunteers September 3, 1861, and his division led center of Union line at capture of Fort Donelson. Made major-general of volunteers March 21, 1862, and did heroic service in the second day's fight at Shiloh. In 1863 saved Cincinnati from being captured by General Edmund Kirby Smith, and was assigned to command of Eighth army corps, Middle military division, and with 5,800 men fought 28,000, under General Jubal A. Early, July 9, 1864, at the Monocacy, and, though defeated, saved Washington from capture, by giving General Grant time to get General Wright's division from City Point to that city. Was removed by General Halleck, but promptly restored by General Grant; served on court for trial of Lincoln's assassins, and was president of the court that tried and condemned the notorious Captain Henry Wirz, commandant of Andersonville prison. Mustered out in 1865 and practiced law at Crawfordsville. Governor of Utah, 1878-81. United States minister to Turkey, 1881-85. Since has given attention to literature, his most famous works being "The Fair God" (1873), a story of the conquest of Mexico, on which he worked for twenty years; "Ben-Hur" (1880), a tale of the Christ; and the "Prince of India" (1893), a story of the fall of Constantinople and rise of Mohammedanism. His "Ben-Hur" is the most popular religious novel in the English language, over 300,000 being sold in first ten years.

AUTHORS AND JOURNALISTS.

Joseph Addison, son of Dr. Lancelot Addison, born May 1, 1672, at Milston, Wiltshire, England; educated at Charter House, Queen's and Magdalen Colleges, at Oxford. In his twenty-second year, began writing English verse. Instead of taking orders, published a poem, addressed to King William, and later, a poem on the peace of Ryswick, which procured for him a pension of three hundred pounds a year. Traveled in Italy; returned in 1702 and published his travels, which were in such demand that the book rose to five times its original price before it could be reprinted. Was at different times, commissioner of appeals and secretary of state; the latter position he soon resigned. In 1713 the play of "Cato" was produced on the stage, the grand climacteric of Addison's success. Is best known by contributions to the *Spectator*. In 1716, married the Dowager Countess of Warwick. On his retirement from the secretaryship, received a pension of fifteen hundred pounds a year; during this time wrote a "Defense of the Christian Religion." Of Addison's character as a poet and moral writer, too much cannot be said; he was the ornament of his age and country. Died June 17, 1729.

Geoffrey Chaucer, called by Dryden the father of English poetry; born in London, 1328; studied at Cambridge and Oxford; traveled on the continent. Subsequently became Gentleman of the Chamber to the King; his salary was doubled in 1369; was employed to negotiate with the Republic of Genoa for ships for a naval armament; Edward repaid this service by granting him a pitcher of wine daily, delivered by the Butler of England. Subsequently became comptroller of wool customs for London, and ambassador to the French court. Income was £1,000 per year. Embraced Wickliffe's tenets and was imprisoned for a time. During his residence afterward at Woodstock and Downington, devoted himself to poetical writing. Died October 25, 1400. The poetry of Chaucer has smoothness and brilliancy; the sentiments are bold and the characters well supported. Of all his works the "Canterbury Tales" are considered of greatest merit

Samuel Taylor Coleridge, poet, metaphysician, and logician, born October 21, 1772. Youngest of four sons of Rev. John Coleridge; had but little property; was placed in Christ Church Hospital School, London; at nineteen entered Cambridge; was distinguished as an eccentric genius. In 1794 published a small volume of juvenile poems, and soon after commenced a weekly styled *The Watchman*. Was assisted by Josiah and Thomas Wedgewood, who enabled him to complete his education in Germany. On returning to England, became secretary to Sir Alexander Ball, governor of Malta. In 1812, published Essays; "Christabel" appeared in 1816; "Biographia Literaria" in 1817; "Aids to Reflection" in 1825. In conversation Coleridge was peculiarly fascinating; in appearance, striking; in writing, finished and forcible.

William Cowper, poet, was born at Berkhampstead, Hertfordshire, England, in 1731; father was chaplain to George II. Was educated for a lawyer, and at thirty-one was made clerk in the House of Lords. Was unable to occupy the position, owing to nervousness. In 1765 settled at Huntingdon; during retirement here published sixty-eight hymns. In 1782 published a volume of poems; this, being successful, was followed by another in 1785. In recognition of his services to the public the king bestowed upon him a pension of £300 per annum. He was subject to melancholy, and became somewhat deranged. Died April 25, 1800.

Thomas Gray, poet, born in Cornhill, December 26, 1716; educated at Eton and Peter House, Cambridge; went to London, 1738, to study law. Went abroad with Horace Walpole; father died on his return in 1741. Discovering that the property was inadequate to support him in study of the law, returned to Cambridge, where he afterward generally resided. In 1768 was appointed professor of modern history at Cambridge, but, on account of poor health, never filled the place. Died July 30, 1771. A profound and elegant scholar, Gray had read the works of all the English, French, and Italian historians; was well versed in antiquities, morals and politics. His poems, which are few, are elegant and sublime.

Sir William Herschel, one of the greatest astronomers, was born in 1787; son of a

SUCCESSFUL MEN AND WOMEN.

musician and was instructed in that profession. Was successively musician in the band of a Hanoverian regiment, and subsequently in one connected with the Durham militia, then organist at Halifax, and afterwards at Octagon Chapel, Bath. Astronomy formed an occupation for leisure hours; finding the price of a powerful telescope too great, constructed one for himself, and subsequently made others of enormous magnitude. March 13, 1781, discovered a new planet, which he named the Georgium Sidus. Patronized by George III., and assisted by his sister Caroline, continued assiduously in astronomical studies, and in 1816 received the Guelphic order of Knighthood. Among Herschel's discoveries are the lunar volcanoes, sixth and seventh satellites of Saturn, sixth satellite of the Georgian planet, and nature of the various nebulæ. He died August 23, 1822.

Benjamin Jonson was born at Westminster in 1574. Straitened circumstances shortened his stay at the university; being destitute of resources, turned to the stage without success. Attempted play-writing; was at first unsuccessful, but, being befriended by Shakespeare, gained a livelihood. His first printed play was "Every Man in His Humor," which was followed by another every year. In 1603, composed part of the device for the entertainment of King James, as he passed from the Tower to Westminster Abbey, on the day of coronation; during that reign and part of the next, continued to preside over all the amusements and pageantry of the royal household. Being favored of the court, became popular with men of taste and literary talent, among them Shakespeare, Beaumont, Fletcher, Donne, Selden, and others. Visited France in 1613. In 1619 succeeded to the place of poet laureate; and in 1633 his salary was increased to £100. But, through extravagance or carelessness, he was always poor. Died of palsy August 6, 1637.

Samuel Johnson, born at Litchfield, England, September 7, 1709; son of a bookseller; educated at Litchfield school and at Oxford. Exercises in the university showed his superior powers. Was poor, and obliged to leave the university without a degree. Attempted to gain a livelihood by tutoring, but failed. In 1737 visited London and engaged in writing for the *Gentleman's Magazine*; in 1747 began his edition of Shakespeare, and published plan of English dictionary. *The Rambler* was published from 1750 to 1752. In 1759 wrote "Rasselas," receiving for it £100. In 1762 received a yearly pension of £300. In 1781 finished the "Lives of the Poets," a work of great merit, which exhibits sound critical views, vast information as a biographer, and benevolent views as a man. Died December 13, 1784.

Blaise Pascal was born at Clermont in Auvergne, June 19, 1623; was educated by his father, who was president of the court of aids in the province and possessed great mathematical abilities, but forbade his son all treatises on geometry, lest his attention be diverted from belles-lettres. From infancy young Pascal was remarkable, wished to know reasons and causes of everything; was satisfied with none but the most rational. At sixteen, wrote his treatise on Conic Sections. A few years later solved a problem which had perplexed the ablest mathematicians of Europe. Became an ascetic soon afterward, and espoused the cause of the Jansenists against the Jesuits. These letters are models of eloquence and wit, equal to the comedies of Moliere or the orations of Bossuet, and have been frequently published in all the languages of Europe. Pascal died at Paris, August 19, 1662, after a life of exemplary innocence.

John James Rousseau, philosopher, was born at Geneva, June 28, 1712; father was a watchmaker. Left home when very young; and changed his religion in order to procure subsistence. Obtained asylum with Madame de Warens, a charitable lady. Leaving this home later, went to Chambery, where he taught music; thence to Paris, becoming secretary to Montaigne, and going with him to Venice. In 1750 began a literary career; not long afterward retired to solitude and study. Next produced the "Dictionary of Music." In 1761 and 1762, published the "New Heloise" and "Emilius," moral romances; some parts of these offending the public, the author was compelled to leave France. After ineffectually seeking asylum at Geneva, Neufchatel, and Berne, he went to England under the protection of David Hume. Later, was allowed to return to Paris on condition of writing nothing offensive to religion or the government. The last years of his life were spent in company with a few friends. He died July 2, 1778, aged sixty-six.

THE WORLD'S POETS.

Robert Browning, poet, born Peckham, Eng., May 7, 1812, died in Venice, Italy, December 12, 1889. He began to scribble poetry when eight years old. Attended a private school until fourteen, then had a private tutor, attended lectures at University College, London, and then traveled on the Continent. His first poem, "Pauline," was published when he was twenty-one, followed two years later by "Stratford." In 1846

SUCCESSFUL MEN AND WOMEN.

was married to Elizabeth Barrett, settling at Florence, Italy, where his wife died fifteen years later. His collection "Men and Women," was issued in 1855, and in 1863 followed his poetical works in three volumes. Following with several volumes of tragedy, dramatic idyls, and lesser poems, the last, "Asolando," on various subjects, appeared the year of his death. By many admirers he is regarded as the greatest English poet since Milton. As a thinker he far exceeds Tennyson, but lacks the latter's fine musical versification. Many of his poems are gems that will shine for ages.

Robert Burns, chief of Scotland's poets, born near Ayr, Scotland, January 25, 1759, died July 21, 1796. His parents were peasant farmers in very humble circumstances. Robert's shoulders were bowed with hard toil, and he constantly suffered with palpitations, headaches, and melancholy; at fifteen himself and brother Gilbert were hired out to a farmer at $34 a year, and, in accordance with the custom of the times, took stimulants as remedy for bodily ills, which afterwards wrought his ruin. Robert, from a child, was a great reader of what few books were to be had. His first verses were made at sixteen, devoted to one of his boyish loves. When nineteen he went to Kirkoswald school to learn surveying. "Eating at meal time with a spoon in one hand and a book in the other," and while there wrote and had published some poems including "John Barleycorn," "Mailie's Elegy," etc. In 1783 his father died, full of sorrow and fear for his gifted son, and then Robert resolved "to be a better man." The next year himself and brother rented a farm for four years at Mossgiel, where he produced some of his best poems, such as the "Cotter's Saturday Night," "To a Mouse." He issued in 1786 six hundred copies of a book of poems, for which he received $100, and was about to go aboard a ship for West Indies, when he received an invitation to come to Edinburgh, where his book had awakened great interest, and arrange for another edition, was lionized, and returned with $2,500 as proceeds of his book. He married Jean Armour, and was appointed an excise commissioner at $350 a year. But the duties of excise subjected him to added temptations to drink, and at the end of three years he had to abandon the farm. Then in 1791 he went to live in a small house at Dumfries, living on his official stipend and the proceeds of random contributions to magazines, and died in his thirty-seventh year, through drink, exposure, and disappointed hopes, leaving four sons. In his last sickness many persons of rank came to see him, and a vast crowd attended his funeral, for his poems had touched alike the great ones and the small of earth. In 1813 a monument was erected to his memory at Dumfries.

Johann Wolfgang von Goethe, poet, born in Frankfort-on-the-Main, Germany, August 28, 1749; died in Weimar, Germany, March 22, 1832. His father was an imperial councilor, an educated man, stern, cold, pedantic, while his mother was a genial, affectionate woman, fond of poetry and music, and Johann, their first child, inherited, to a marked degree, the peculiarities of both, being, as a child, precocious, lively, sensitive, erratic. Began early to exhibit his talent, writing poems and childish stories before ten years of age. His love escapades in youth and manhood were many. He was inconstant and unwise in his bestowment of affection, partly due to laxity of his time, but more to his lack of moral balance, and this greatest of German poets led an eventful life in keeping with his erratic genius. His love lyrics are many, and generally more sensuous than sensible. In grand, elegant, aristocratic verse he glorified the paganism of which he was an illustrious example. He at length married the woman who for years had been wife in fact, in order to legalize his children by her. Of his numerous works, the "Gotz of the Iron Hand," "Sorrows of Werther," "Wilhelm Meister," and "Faust," are best known to the world.

John Keats, poet, born in London, England, in 1796, died in Rome, Italy, February 27, 1821. At an early age he was sent, with his two brothers, to a school at Enfield, England, where he remained until fourteen. While a great reader, he was not a diligent student. In 1810 he was apprenticed for five years to a surgeon at Edmonton, and at the expiration of the apprenticeship went to the London hospitals for further study, and while there he published a volume of poems that met with no success. Ill health soon obliged him to abandon the profession of a surgeon, and in 1818 the death of a younger brother deeply affected him, and afterward, at a time when his means were nearly exhausted, he was taken with spitting of blood and had a long illness. After a recovery he decided to give himself to literary work, and, greatly loving a young lady of much personal beauty, Miss Brawne, he hoped to make for himself a name among men; but a return of his malady compelled him to go to Italy on advice of physicians. Before going he published a volume containing the "Ode to a Nightingale," "Eve of St. Agnes," and a fragment of "Hyperion." After weeks of suffering with consumption, attended by friends, he passed away, saying, he felt the daisies growing over him, and expressing a hope that after his death he might be among the poets of England, a hope that was realized, albeit his tomb bears the epitaph he dictated for himself: "Here lies one whose name was writ in water."

SUCCESSFUL MEN AND WOMEN.

John Milton, greatest of poets, born in London, December 9, 1608, died there November 8, 1674. His father, a lawyer, who was disinherited in his youth for abandoning the Catholic for the Puritan faith, was a man of wealth, and Milton had the best of educational advantages. He was always constantly, severely studious, from a child studying till after midnight. At twelve he was sent to St. Paul's school, and at sixteen entered Christ's College, Cambridge, to study for the ministry, but soon abandoned that purpose for authorship. His mother died in 1637 and his father sent him to the Continent, where he traveled, especially in Italy, for fifteen months, preparing material for his great poem he had then in mind. Civil war and politics in England, in which he was a leading actor, postponed it for near twenty years. Taught private school in 1643 and suddenly married a daughter of a debtor, a Miss Mary Powell, who left him in a month, refusing to return, because she was fond of company and merriment and did not like his "spare diet and hard study," while he complained that his wife did not talk enough to suit him! Two years later she returned and died in 1653, leaving him three little girls. During the Commonwealth of Cromwell, and before his wife's death, Milton was secretary of state, and nobly defended the cause of religious and civil liberty before the powers of Europe in brilliant letters in Latin but recently discovered. In 1654 he became completely blind through excessive reading and study. In 1656 he married Catherine, daughter of Captain Woodcock, of Hackney, who survived her marriage fifteen months. In 1663 he married Elizabeth Minshull, at the advice of a friend, because his daughters had ceased to treat him kindly. They remained at home six years longer, and amid their daily constant quarrels with their stepmother, with the principles he had for so many years heroically advocated and defended now hopelessly defeated, himself loaded with shame, and shocked by the fearful profligacy of the times, the poor blind man now meditated and dictated his glorious deathless epics, "The Paradise Lost" and "Paradise Regained," selling them at length to Samuel Simmons, bookseller, for £5 in hand and a promise of the same sum on the sale of the first 1,300 copies of each edition, no edition to exceed 1,500 copies. It was two years before he received the second £5; then a second edition was issued in 1674, a third in 1678, and, finally, in 1681, Milton's widow sold all her interest in the work to Simmons for £8! Milton attended no church, belonged to no religious communion, had no family prayers, yet what triumphantly religious monodies he gave the world! He was slight of figure, even girlish in his youthful days, quick of temper, somewhat haughty in spirit, urbane manners, a fine musician, and noble scholar. He died of gout and was buried by the side of his father in the church of St. Giles, Cripplegate.

Edgar Allan Poe, poet, author, born in Boston, Massachusetts, January 19, 1809, died Baltimore, Maryland. His father, David Poe, actor of Baltimore, married Elizabeth Arnold, an English actress, Edgar being born while they were filling an engagement in Boston. Both parents died at Richmond, Virginia, suddenly, leaving three children, who were adopted by sympathetic friends, Edgar being taken by John Allan, a banker, who educated him in England and at classical schools, and by private tutors. In 1826 he entered the University of Virginia, but being expelled he entered the counting house of his father. Finding this distasteful he went to Boston, where he published "Tamerlane and Other Poems" when eighteen years of age. Being penniless he enlisted as private in United States army under name of E. A. Perry; after serving two years his father obtained a substitute, and he was appointed to West Point Military Academy. On asking permission of his father to resign, and not getting it, he got into disgrace, was courtmartialed and expelled. Had a quarrel with his father on his return to Richmond, and renouncing his connection with the family he went to Baltimore, where he fell in love with his cousin, Miss Virginia Clemm, whom four years later he married. After trying various things for a living, he wrote stories for various papers and magazines, but the vice of drink he had contracted began to lead him at times to intoxication and clouded his brilliant talent. In 1835 he went to Richmond as assistant editor of *Southern Literary Messenger*, raising its circulation in one year from 500 to 5000 subscribers. Next he went to Philadelphia on *Graham's Magazine*, increasing its circulation in two years from 5,000 to over 52,000, and in 1841 became its editor-in-chief at small salary. In 1844 he removed to New York, and was an assistant on the *Mirror*, owned by N. P. Willis. In January, 1845, appeared his "Raven," which gave him great fame, and he attempted lecturing with indifferent success. In spring of 1846 being very poor he removed his family to a small house in Fordham, where in 1847 his wife died. A little afterward appeared "The Bells," and then his last, "Annabel Lee." He then went to Philadelphia, to Richmond, Virginia, and returning to Baltimore the end came by delirium at the Washington College Hospital in 1849.

Johann Christoph Friedrich von Schiller, poet, dramatist, born in Marbach, Wurtemberg, Germany, November 10, 1759; died in Weimar, Germany, May 9, 1805. His father was surgeon major in the army. Johann was instructed by the village pastor with a view to the ministry, and attended a Latin school till fourteen, but at command of Prince of Wurtemberg he was sent to a military academy, where he first studied law and finally medicine. From a child he wrote stories and "poems," and the year after he had graduated from the academy and joined a grenadier regiment as surgeon, he published (1781) his first great drama "Die Räuber," but the glorified hero of it being a brigand, his Prince fearing it might encourage brigandage, forbade his further writing, and when he by stealth visited the theater where it was acted his Prince had him arrested. He escaped to Baden and hid at house of schoolmate, afterward connected himself with the Mannheim Theater, as play writer. In 1789 he was appointed professor of history, at Jena, and wrote his celebrated "History of the Thirty Years' War," and in 1790 married Charlotte von Lengefeld. The following year he suffered a pulmonary attack, and thereafter was in delicate health. Wrote incessantly, at times all night, taking stimulants, and further impaired his health. In 1799 he published his great drama "Wallenstein," on which he worked seven years, and in 1804 appeared his last, perhaps noblest drama, "Wilhelm Tell." Schiller's types of womanhood and manhood were more lofty than his time, and portrayed the triumphs of virtue, liberty, and patriotism, moving the hearts of his countrymen as but few have ever done. He had four children, and his countrymen have erected monuments to him in several parts of the empire and greatly revere his memory.

William Shakespeare, greatest of dramatists, was born April 23, 1564, in Stratford-upon-Avon, Warwickshire, England, and died there April 23, 1616. His father, John Shakespeare, who was a man of much character, intelligence, and a chief officer of the borough, was possessed of considerable wealth, which he lost and became bankrupt, and William earned a living in youth as wool-sorter, attorney's clerk, and schoolmaster, having a fair education for his times. He was the third child in the family of eight children, but none of his three brothers gained distinction. He was of a roving disposition and when eighteen he married Anne Hathaway, who was twenty-six, and seems ever after to have regretted it (see "Twelfth Night," act 3, scene 4). She bore him three children, Hamnet and Judith being twins. In 1589 he went to London, and entered upon his life work as playwright and actor, his departure thither being hastened by his having poached a deer, and then lampooned the owner, Sir Thomas Lucy, by a ballad stuck on his park gate. (See his reference to him in first scene of "Merry Wives of Windsor.") He began his dramatic career as an apprentice or chore boy probably at the Blackfriar theater. Actors then wrote plays as well as acted them, and he began to write not for fame but for money that he might return to Stratford and glory before Sir Thomas's face. At twenty-eight he had won much fame, and eight years later bought the largest and best house in Stratford. His incomparable dramas have been the admiration and despair alike of the learned and the unlearned, although the text of most of his thirty-seven plays is now very imperfect and corrupt. The literature concerning his works is immense. Of himself, one of his companions, "that rare Ben Jonson," bears witness that he was "indeed honest and of an open and free nature," and "I loved the man, and do honor his memory on this side idolatry as much as any." Never a great actor, he abandoned the stage about 1604. His family became extinct in the third generation. His house in Henly street is now owned by a corporation, with keepers appointed to entertain visitors. Over his grave on the north side of the chancel of Stratford church is a flat stone, with this inscription said to have been written by himself:

"Good frend for Jesus sake forbeare
To digg the dust encloased heare;
Blest be ye man yt spares thes stones,
And curst be he yt moves my bones."

And he was not disturbed. Against the north wall of the chancel is a monument containing his bust under the arch, and which was erected before 1623.

Alfred Tennyson, poet laureate, born in Somersby, Lincolnshire, England, August 6, 1809, died at Aldworth House, Surrey, October 6, 1892. His father, George Clayton Tennyson, was a finely educated clergyman, proficient in languages, music, painting, and poetry. Alfred and his three brothers studied at Trinity College, Cambridge, and each wrote poetry while there. He gained the Chancellor's medal for his poem "Timbuctoo," which production Thackeray lampooned in the college paper. Tennyson left before graduation, and when Sir Robert Peel was prime minister he was given, at Carlyle's intercession, a government pension of $1,000 a year, and lived in London until forty, when he married Miss Emily Sellwood and lived at Twickenham. When Wordsworth died in 1850 Tennyson succeeded him as poet laureate and removed to Faringford, Isle of Wight. Some years after he bought Aldworth House, near Haslemere. In December, 1888, he was raised to the peerage as Baron Tennyson of

SUCCESSFUL MEN AND WOMEN.

D'Eyncourt. He lived in retirement, and disliked publicity, and once wrote to Sir Henry Taylor that he "thanked God Almighty with his whole heart and soul that he knew nothing, and the world knew nothing, of Shakespeare but his writings, and that he knew nothing of Jane Austen, and that there were no letters preserved either of Shakespeare or of Jane Austen," and he added that they had not been "ripped open like pigs," and so it came to pass that at the end of Tennyson's eighty-three years his countrymen knew but little more of him than the world at large. No other famous Englishman more nearly fitted Novalis's witticism that "every Englishman is an island," than did Tennyson. Carlyle gives, in one of his letters to Ralph Waldo Emerson, a picture of the poet as he was in 1844. "One of the finest looking men in the world. A great shock of rough, dusty-dark hair; bright, laughing, hazel eyes; massive, aquiline face — most massive, yet most delicate; of sallow-brown complexion, almost Indian-looking; clothes cynically loose, free, and easy — smokes infinite tobacco. His voice is musical — metallic — fit for loud laughter and piercing wail and all that may lie between; speech and speculation free and plenteous. I do not meet in these late decades such company over a pipe." Of his poems, "The Lotus Eaters," "St. Simeon Stylites," "Ulysses," "Locksley Hall," and "St. Agnes," are, perhaps, among his best. "In Memoriam," published anonymously in 1850, is an elegy for his friend, Arthur Henry Hallam (son of the historian), who was betrothed to Tennyson's sister, but who died in 1833. The little poem, "Silent Voices," written shortly before his death, in anticipation of that event, was set to music by his widow and sung at his funeral. His body lies in the "Poet's corner," near the grave of Chaucer. A son (Hallam) and daughter (Maud) survive him.

William Wordsworth, poet, born in Cockersmouth, Cumberland, England, April 7, 1770, died at Rydal Mount, Westmoreland, England, April 23, 1850. His father was a lawyer and a man of wealth; his mother, who was of a good family, died when he was five years old, and at eight he was sent to boarding school, and while there his father died when the son was thirteen, and at seventeen he was sent by an uncle to St. John's College at Cambridge, where he graduated in 1791. He then went to France, and while there decided to take part with the French Revolutionists. But his relatives cut off his remittances, and he returned to London. In 1793 he published some indifferent poems. Two years after was given legacy of $4500 by a friend, and then with his sister, Dorothy, he settled at Racedown. In 1797 he made the acquaintance of Coleridge, and they made pedestrian tours through the country, and together brought out a volume of poems, containing Coleridge's "Ancient Mariner," less than 300 copies being sold, and then the publisher gave him the copyright as worthless! In 1802 he had quite a sum of money paid him by a debtor of his father, and in that year married Miss Mary Hutchinson, and in 1813 settled at Rydal Mount, having received a government office worth $4000 a year, publishing at intervals several volumes of poems, but his total income from all his various writings up to 1819 was less than $700. His reputation, however, greatly increased from 1830 to 1840, and in 1843 he succeeded Southey as poet laureate.

NOTED JOURNALISTS AND WRITERS.

Mrs. Margaret Bottome, author, and one of the editors of the *Ladies' Home Journal*, and a writer for various periodicals, is and has been president of the "Order of King's Daughters and Sons" since its organization on January 13, 1886; and which order has a present membership of some 250,000 persons located in nearly every country on the globe. It is a purely religious organization, but entirely undenominational, under the direction and control of Christian women, and has for its object charitable work, in hospitals, by sick beds of the poor, the rescue and teaching of the street waifs of the world, and the alleviation of humanity's wretchedness and want wherever found, the order having two great cardinal principles, viz.: Intense devotion to God, and the service of humanity; its motto being, "In His Name"; and its badge a small silver Maltese cross.

Samuel Bowles, 2d, journalist, born in Springfield, Mass., February 9, 1826, died in Springfield, Mass., January 16, 1878. He was educated in the public and high schools, and at a private school in his native town, and when seventeen began work in the printing office of the *Weekly Republican*, that his father, Samuel Bowles, 1st, had established in 1824. In 1844 Samuel, Jr., persuaded his father to give a reluctant consent to start a daily evening journal, the first number of which appeared March 29 of that year, and which was changed to a morning issue December 4, 1846. The *Republican* was then the only daily in the state outside of Boston, and young Bowles worked night and day to make it a success, and within a year had it paying property. Dr. J. G. Holland was assistant editor with him for ten years, until his retirement from it in 1857, and for years the *Republican* had the largest circulation of any paper in Massachusetts outside of Boston, having become according to the New York *Tribune's* testimony "the best and ablest country journal ever published on this continent." The senior Bowles died in 1851, when the son was twenty-five years of age, and it passed into his hands. In 1857 Samuel, 2d, was for a few months editor of the Boston *Traveller*, and then in the autumn of that year he bought out Dr. Holland's interest in the *Republican*, and was thereafter its editor and proprietor, making his office a famous school for young journalists, some of whom have risen to much distinction through his method of training them. He was a remarkable news gatherer, and the leader in forming the Republican party in Massachusetts, remaining in it till 1872, and thereafter made the paper an independent journal. He was the first editor to advocate giving the ballot to all citizens of the United States, regardless of race, color, or sex. Mr. Bowles constantly refused public office, and gave himself without stint to make and maintain the past and present high character of the paper. He was a keen, pungent writer, and the author of several volumes of entertaining and instructive travels. He left a son, Samuel, 3d, who now conducts the *Republican*, which is yet the great paper of Western Massachusetts.

George William Childs, journalist, publisher, philanthropist, born Baltimore, Md., May 12, 1829; died Philadelphia, Pa., February 3, 1894. Parents poor, and died when he was eight. Began to earn living by selling peanuts. When twelve he had been to school two terms, at thirteen entered United States Navy, remaining fifteen months. In 1844 he went to Philadelphia and walked the streets seeking work, not having a cent in his pocket. At length got place as errand boy in the bookstore of Mr. Peter Thomson, at two dollars a week. Was diligent, rising before daylight, kindling fires, sweeping and washing pavement before other stores were open. Was faithful, working sixteen hours a day, looked after proprietor's interest, who made him when sixteen chief buyer, and he attended the great annual book sales of New York and Boston frequently, shrewdly buying up whole editions. At eighteen he had saved from his small salaries a few hundred dollars and took a small room in "Old Ledger" building and began business for himself, was prospered and at twenty-one became partner, through marriage in the family, of the firm of R. E. Peterson & Co., which changed to Childs & Peterson, publishing many important works, some of which reached a sale of two hundred thousand copies. December 5, '64, he bought the moribund daily paper, the *Public Ledger*, and greatly improved it, elevated the moral tone, put in new features, enlarged news matter, paid well for good work, looked after its character minutely, and soon made it one of the most valuable properties in the United States and netting him an immense fortune. Beginning literally with nothing but a sound body, a stout heart, and an honest spirit, he rose to be one of the leading men of the world, being known in Europe as well as in America for numberless deeds of benevolence privately done.

George William Curtis, journalist, author, lecturer, born in Providence, R. I., February 24, 1824, and died on Staten Island, N. Y., August 31, 1892. His father was a successful business man, and the son was given an education. In 1839 the father removed to New York city, where George served a year as clerk in a mercantile house. But not finding this business to his liking, and being taken with the famous Brook Farm scheme, he, with an elder brother, joined that community in 1842, where they remained eighteen months, and upon the failure of the project they left Roxbury and spent two years at Concord, Mass. (working at farming), so as to be near the famous men of the Brook Farm company. In 1846 he went to Europe, traveling principally in Germany, Italy, Egypt, and Syria, and published the results of his journeys in "Nile Notes," that gave him much fame. Returning in 1850 he joined the editorial staff of the New York *Tribune*, and became also one of the editors and a special partner of *Putnam's Monthly*, and on the failure of the publishers of the latter in 1857 for a large sum, Mr. Curtis, though not legally bound, assumed the obligation and paid the last creditor in 1873. His books of travels were published by the Harpers, and in 1853 he began in *Harper's Monthly* the popular "Editor's Easy Chair" papers, continued for many years, and which brought him great renown. In 1857 he became the editor of *Harper's Weekly*, and was a chief editor of *Harper's Bazar* after its institution, and for near a quarter of a century was one of the most popular of public lecturers. He had many offers of political honors, but declined them, serving, however, as a member of civil service commission, to which reform he was ardently committed. Besides his many extraordinary editorial writings, he was the author of several popular volumes.

Horace Greeley, journalist, born in Amherst, N. H., February 3, 1811; died in Pleasantville, N. Y., November 29, 1872. Father a small farmer, who became bankrupt when Horace was ten, and removed to West Haven, Vt. After Horace's sixth year he was able to attend school only in winter, having to work summers, in order to eke out the family living. Was a famous reader and speller from a child. When fourteen became apprentice to a printer at East Poultney, Vermont, at $40 a year. When he was twenty the proprietor failed and he went to his father, who had removed to the wilds of Pennsylvania, near Erie, and after some months went to New York city, where, after many trials, he succeeded in getting work as a printer in 1831. Two years later he began small job printing and started a daily paper, which failed in three weeks. Later he began a weekly journal that had considerable circulation. In 1838 he was hired to conduct The Jeffersonian, a Whig campaign sheet, and in 1840 published another campaign paper, The Log Cabin, that had great circulation and gave him much celebrity. In 1841 he began the Tribune, that became a great power in the land. He took an active part in the Anti-Slavery contest, and was an uncompromising foe to intemperance, an advocate of women's suffrage and friend of the laboring man and during the war a stanch Union man. He opposed General Grant's second nomination and was himself put in nomination for the presidency against him, by the disaffected Republicans and later by the Democrats, but was overwhelmingly defeated. He was a prolific writer for his journal, and also the author of nearly a dozen volumes, some having a wide circulation, the "History of the American Conflict" being perhaps the most important. He took an active part in all the political movements and reforms of his time. The greatest of American journalists, and one of the most noted men of his century.

Josiah Gilbert Holland, author, editor, born in Belchertown, Mass., July 24, 1819, died New York city, October 12, 1881. Father mechanic, and small farmer, of a roving disposition, and Josiah's educational advantages were confined to a few weeks in district schools in winter. Toiled hard in youth as factory boy, and farm hand. While working in mills at Northampton tried to prepare for college, but health failed. On recovering he taught common schools, writing stories and verses that found no market. Studied medicine with Dr. Thomson, of Northampton, and then went to Pittsfield for course in Berkshire Medical Institute, from which he graduated in 1844, and located in Springfield, Mass., where the next year he married Miss Elizabeth Chapin of that place. Medicine not being very profitable, he started in 1848 a weekly paper which ran six months; then he went to Vicksburg, Miss., as superintendent of public schools. Had great difficulties, having literally to create the schools, and in a year had so succeeded that all the private schools of the city were closed. Insisted on authority to punish pupils, which was given him, and used to say he had "whipped more rebels" than any other man in America! Returned to Springfield in 1850, and began to work on the Republican, and two years later became a partner with Mr. Samuel Bowles, and one of the chief writing editors, and continued with the paper till 1866, writing for that journal his "Titcomb Papers," "History of Berkshire," etc. In 1868 went to Europe with his family, and in 1870 became editor of the new magazine, Scribner's Monthly, in which appeared most of his successful novels. Of his poems his "Bitter Sweet," and "Kathrina," had an extensive sale; his several works aggregating some 350,000 copies.

Whitelaw Reid, editor, born near Xenia, Ohio, October 27, 1837. Father well-to-do. Educated in public schools, and at his uncle's academy in Xenia, and graduated from Miami University in 1856. Then taught for a year, which he abandoned in 1858 for journalism, and established the Xenia News. During the civil war he became a noted army correspondent. In 1868 he accepted the repeated offer of Horace Greeley of a position on staff of New York Tribune and was soon after made managing editor, and when Mr. Greeley accepted the nomination for president he became editor-in-chief. In 1881 he married Elizabeth, daughter of D. O. Mills, and has a son and daughter. In 1889 he was appointed by President Harrison minister to France, 1892 was nominated for office of vice-president on the ticket with Mr. Harrison. He has made the Tribune a very paying property and has amassed considerable wealth.

Mark Twain (Samuel Langhorne Clemens), humorist, writer, born in Florida, Mo., November 30, 1835. Father, farmer, owner of slaves, died insolvent, when Samuel was twelve years old, and he shifted for himself. Apprenticed to printer three years, then journeyman printer in St. Louis, Cincinnati, New York, and Philadelphia, then pilot on Mississippi river. In 1861, proposed to join Confederate army, but his brother being appointed lieutenant governor of territory Nevada, he went there as his secretary, attempted mining and failed, then tried writing for newspapers and was local editor on Virginia City Enterprise, where he first used his pseudonym of "Mark Twain," a Mississippi river pilot phrase for "mark it two." Went to California, where he did similar work in 1864 on the San Francisco Morning Call. Two years later went as correspondent for paper to Sandwich Islands. On return began to give humorous lectures; 1867 went to Europe, through Italy, Mediterranean, Egypt, Palestine, and wrote the "Innocents Abroad," published in 1869, having a great sale. Became editor and part owner of daily at Buffalo, N. Y., where he married a lady of wealth, and shortly removed to Hartford, Ct., where he now resides. In 1872 lectured in England, and in 1874 published "The Gilded Age," which was dramatized. He has written several other books, and contributed to many periodicals, and been often in the lecture field.

Thurlow Weed, journalist, politician, born in Cairo, New York, November 15, 1797, died in New York city, November 22, 1884. No other man for a generation wielded such political power as did Mr. Weed. While not an office seeker or holder, he made and unmade more officials than any other man of his time. Adroit and sagacious to a remarkable degree, he shaped the principles and policy of first the Whig and then of the Republican party "from behind the scenes" for many years, and with Horace Greeley and William H. Seward virtually governed the latter party for a quarter of a century. For sixty years an active politician, his personal character was without stain and it is said of him that he never took a dollar from anyone dishonestly. His father was very poor and when Thurlow was nine years of age he hired as a cabin boy on a sloop plying on the Hudson river, where he remained two years, when the father moved his family to the then wilderness and settled at Cincinnati, Cortland County, and the son worked at clearing the patch of land, and had but one recreation, that of reading, of which he had become passionately fond. But books were scarce and the nearest neighbor three miles away, and illustrative of the way in which poor boys then raised themselves to better things, he heard that the neighbor had a borrowed copy of a "History of the French Revolution" and so one winter morning when he was fourteen years old, he set out barefoot through the snow to borrow it, warming his feet occasionally on a bit of rail fence by the way. Having succeeded in borrowing the book he set out for home, "too happy," he said "to think of the snow or my naked feet," and then after the day's hard work was done he devoured the treasure of knowledge by the light of a pine-knot, his father being too poor to afford the luxury of a tallow dip. Next year his hunger for reading led him to work in a printing office, and the following year being sixteen years old he volunteered as private in war of 1812. At the close of the war he entered a printing office in New York city and in 1819 established a weekly paper at Norwich, New York. During the next ten years he edited several different papers, served a term in the state legislature, 1826 he became an active leader of the Anti-Masonic party. In 1831 he established at Albany the *Evening Journal*, which he edited and controlled for thirty-five years, and though much persecuted and maligned for his Anti-Masonic crusade he succeeded by his great tact in becoming the foremost leader in political affairs, and, outliving the obloquy sought to be put upon him, he became "the power behind the throne" in the management of public affairs and died greatly honored.

MODERN WRITERS.

Mrs. G. R. Alden [Pansy], born in New York in 1841; her maiden name was McDonald; author of a popular series of books called the "Pansy" books, embracing nearly sixty titles, most of which are adapted to Sunday School libraries. Among these are "The King's Daughter," "An Endless Chain," "New Year's Tangles," and "Four Girls at Chautauqua." Mrs. Alden has from the first been identified with the Chautauqua system of education, and has edited *Pansy*, a juvenile paper. Her influence upon young people has been far reaching, and always good.

Edwin Arnold, poet, linguist, and journalist, born in 1832 in England. For a time filled the position of principal of the Sanscrit College at Poona, Bombay Presidency, which he resigned in 1861. Contributed largely to critical journals; is well versed in Eastern subjects, the fruit of which is seen in his Indian poems, the chief of which is "The Light of Asia," an epic of Buddhism, of great literary merit. Popularity of his work among American readers is very marked; has issued many volumes, including "Griselda," "Poems," "Indian Poetry," and "Indian Idylls," from the Sanscrit, etc. He received the distinction of the Companion of the Star of India in 1877; and on behalf of the proprietors of the *Daily Telegraph*, arranged the first expedition of George Smith into Assyria, also the expedition of H. M. Stanley for the finding of Livingstone. One of the best known Englishmen of his day, he represents English literature to thousands of readers.

Edward Bellamy was born at Chicopee Falls, Mass., March 26, 1850, educated at Union College, and in Germany; studied law after returning to America, was admitted to the bar at Springfield, Mass., but did not practice. In 1871 he became an editorial writer for the New York *Evening Post*, and later for the Springfield *Union*. In 1878 published his first novel, "A Nantucket Idyll," followed by two others, and in 1888 by "Looking Backward," a book which has

SUCCESSFUL MEN AND WOMEN.

had an extraordinary circulation, having been translated into German, Danish, French, and other languages, with as large a sale in England as in America. Mr. Bellamy is attempting to build up a party whose aim shall be the nationalization of great industries, and the ultimate conduct of all business by and for the people. Equality of rights, government control of railways, telegraph, and telephone systems, municipal control of all methods of rapid transit, are some of the propositions made; all this is to be brought about by quiet, rational methods. He also advocates raising the age of compulsory education to seventeen years, and supplying aid from the state to such pupils as may need it. As a patriotic American, and thoughtful citizen, he is justly prominent among men of his day.

Will Carleton, born in Hudson, Lenawee County, Mich., October, 1845; graduated at Hillsdale, 1869. In 1878, and again in 1885, visited Europe, spending most of the time in travel. In literature he is best known by his ballads of domestic life, nearly all of which have earned wide popularity. Shortly after leaving college, began lecturing before societies and lyceums, visiting Great Britain, Canada, also most of the northern and western states. His published works are "Poems," "Farm Ballads," "Farm Legends," "Farm Festivals," "City Ballads," and "Young Folks' Centennial Rhymes."

James Freeman Clarke was born at Hanover, N. H., April 4, 1810; grandson of General William Hull. Studied at Boston Latin School, graduated from Harvard in 1829, and from Cambridge Divinity School in 1833. From 1833 to 1840, was pastor of Unitarian church, Louisville, Kentucky; and editor of the *Western Messenger* from 1836 to 1839. Returning to Boston in 1841 he founded the Church of the Disciples, and held the pastorate for forty-five years. Prominent in all educational and reform movements in Boston; overseer of Harvard University, and professor of Christian doctrine and lecturer on ethnic religions. With William H. Channing and Ralph Waldo Emerson, Dr. Clarke prepared the "Memoirs of Margaret Fuller D'Ossoli"; and published twenty-six volumes of his own works, among them, "History of the Campaign of 1812," "Eleven Weeks in Europe," "Orthodoxy, its Truths and Errors," "Thomas Didymus," "Self Culture," and "Anti-Slavery Days." As an ecclesiastical and ethical writer, he has won wide reputation.

Margaret Deland, the author of "John Ward, Preacher," was born in Pittsburg, Pa., February 23, 1857. Her father, Sample Campbell, was a merchant. Her mother was daughter of Major William Wade of the United States army during the war of 1812. Her mother died when Margaret was an infant, and she was brought up by her uncle. She was educated in private schools in Pittsburg, and later at Pelham Priory, New Rochelle, N. Y., at Cooper Art Institute, and was herself a teacher of design in the Normal College of New York city. On May 12, 1880, she was married to Lorin F. Deland of Boston, since then her adviser in literary work. In 1886 she published "An Old Garden and Other Verses"; in 1887, "John Ward, Preacher," a most successful novel; in 1888, "Florida Days." She has also written several short stories and "Sidney," another novel. As an artist and a woman, Mrs. Deland deserves the warm approbation she has received from critics and the general public.

James T. Fields, born at Portsmouth, N. H., December 31, 1817, educated in Portsmouth public schools and at seventeen entered the employ of Carter & Hendee, at that time a noted book house in Boston. In 1839 he was made junior partner of the firm of Ticknor, Reed & Fields, publishers, subsequently becoming head of the firm. From 1862 to 1870, was editor of the *Atlantic Monthly.* Withdrew from business in 1870, and devoted himself nearly up to the time of his death to lecturing, with decided success. Mr. Fields is the author of two volumes of poems and a few literary biographies, but his most distinctive work was that of a publisher, possessing, to a rare degree, the power of judging the intrinsic and money value of manuscripts. He thoroughly understood both the business and the literary side of his occupation; published the works of the New England circle of writers, and was the personal friend of many. His death occurred in Boston, April 21, 1881, at the age of seventy-seven years.

Francis Bret Harte was born in Albany, N. Y., August 25, 1839, of mixed English, Dutch and Hebrew ancestry. He received a common school education. His father, a teacher of much culture, died, leaving his family with little means. In 1854 the family removed to California, where the lad opened a school. This proving unsuccessful, he turned to mining, and, failing in this, became a compositor in a printing office, beginning his literary career by composing his first articles in type while working at the case. He soon became one of the corps of writers; and later, editor of the *Overland Monthly.* At this time appeared several of his best-known stories. In 1870 he was made professor of recent literature in California University. He was United States Consul to Germany in 1878, and remained abroad until 1885. He has resided abroad since that time, devoting

SUCCESSFUL MEN AND WOMEN.

himself to literature. His collected works comprise five volumes, containing stories, novels, and poems. The once obscure typesetter is to-day ranked with the best storytellers, commended by his originality, wit, and pathos.

Jean Ingelow was born at Ipswich, England. Strongly influenced in youth by the poetry of Tennyson and Mrs. Browning; began to write verse, sometimes in ballad form, sometimes didactic or religious. First volume of poems was published in 1850. Later works, very popular for their tender feeling and close study of nature, are "A Story of Doom," "The Little Wonder Horn" "High-tide on the Coast of Lincolnshire" and others. She has also written four successful novels.

Henry James, the subject of this sketch, was born in New York city, April 15th, 1843. His father of the same name was a noted writer upon Swedenborgian doctrines. The son was educated under his supervision, chiefly in Europe, where he spent the years 1855-59. He studied at Harvard law school; began to write for periodicals in 1865, and published several stories in the the *Atlantic Monthly*. He has resided in England since 1869. He, with William Dean Howells, is accounted the leader of the American metaphysical novelists. Some of his best known novels are "The Europeans," "The Bostonians," and "Daisy Miller." His mastery of the French tongue is so complete that stories published by him in that language win the approval of severe French critics. His favorite style of writing introduces both foreign and American characters, drawing contrasts between the life and manners of the two. Latest enumeration gives the number of his books as twenty-seven, including stories, sketches, and essays, many of which are translated into French and German. A genuine American, he has made decided impress upon his generation and upon the reading public in general.

James Parton was born at Canterbury, England, February 9, 1822, but removed to the United States before the age of five years; was educated at White Plains, N. Y. For seven years, taught in New York and Philadelphia; became known as a writer for the *Home Journal* in New York city. His first published work was "Life of Horace Greeley," published in 1855, and noted for its careful research, minute statements, and picturesque incident. Other books, "The Life and Times of Aaron Burr," in particular, were pronounced "almost models." "The Life of Andrew Jackson," "Life and Times of Benjamin Franklin," and an excellent "Life of Voltaire," are among his works. A letter printed in the *New York Critic*, purporting to give Mr. Parton's own estimate of the annual income from the sale of his books for many years, puts it at $8,000; it is improbable that the earnings of any other American author have exceeded this sum. He died in Newburyport, Mass., Oct. 17, 1891.

John Howard Payne, author and actor, was born in New York city, June 9, 1792. Soon after his birth the family removed to Boston; here he became interested in literature and the theater. Returned to New York; was clerk in a counting-room and student at Union College until the age of sixteen, when he appeared at the Old Park Theater as Young Norval, acting remarkably well, and becoming the favorite of the hour. Appeared in Boston, Philadelphia and Baltimore with equal success, tickets sometimes selling for $25 and even $50; in 1813, went to London, remaining in England and in France for nearly twenty years; during his subsequent career wrote more than sixty plays, among them Brutus and Mahomet. He is best known as the author of "Home, Sweet Home"; he died at Tunis, April 19; in June, 1883, his body was brought to Washington, D. C.; a monument has been erected to his memory. The original manuscript of "Home, Sweet Home" is in possession of an elderly lady in Athens, Ga. Himself homeless and poor, he has made an abiding place in the hearts of men, by one immortal song.

Elizabeth Stuart Phelps Ward, born August 31, 1844, at Boston, Mass. When she was four years old, father removed to Andover, being professor in the theological seminary; here she resided until marriage, which occurred in 1888. Engaged in philanthropic work during civil war. Wrote "A Sacrifice Consumed," a war story, for *Harper's Magazine* in 1863, and from that time became a regular contributor. In 1868 published "Gates Ajar," the best known of her books, which has been translated into four languages; has since published "Men, Women, and Ghosts," a collection of short stories. In 1877 delivered an admirable course of lectures before Boston University, upon "Representative Modern Fiction." Was married in Gloucester, October 12, 1888, to Rev. Herbert Ward. Since her marriage, has written in conjunction with Mr. Ward, "The Master of the Magicians," "Come Forth," and "The Lost Hero." Mrs. Ward deals in an earnest and untrammeled manner with momentous questions that have exercised the human mind for centuries.

John G. Saxe was born June 2, 1816, at Highgate, Vt., graduated from Middlebury

SUCCESSFUL MEN AND WOMEN.

College, Vt., in 1839, studied law at Lockport, N. Y., and at St. Albans, Vt., and was admitted to the bar in 1843. He was afterward engaged as states attorney and deputy collector of customs; and was candidate of the Democratic party for governor of Vermont in 1859-1860. He became an editor of the Albany *Evening Journal*, in 1872. Middlebury College gave him an LL.D., 1866. He was very popular as a lecturer and won a reputation as a writer of humorous verse. His first volume appeared in 1846, a larger addition in 1852, and the last in 1860. Up to the time of his death, which occurred at Albany, N. Y., in 1887, his works had passed through forty editions. For many years prior to his decease, his life was wholly devoted to literature and public speaking. From his early career as a young lawyer, he rose to eminence and high literary distinction, and his name became a household word on both sides of the Atlantic.

J. T. Trowbridge was born at Ogden, N. Y., September 18, 1827, the son of a farmer. He was educated in the public schools, and taught himself the rudiments of French, Greek, and Latin; removed to Illinois; remained there for one year, teaching school and doing farm work; subsequently settled in New York city, in 1846, having decided to devote his life to literature. In 1848, removed to Boston, Mass., his present home. Widely known as a writer of popular stories; the first book that appeared over his name was "Father Brighthopes," published in 1853, followed by "Burr Cliff," "The Old Battle Ground," "Neighbor Jackwood," "Cudjo's Cave," and others. Of the last named, 13,000 copies were sold in one week. Mr. Trowbridge was at one time managing editor of *Our Young Folks*, and regularly contributed to many periodicals. From other writers have come many tributes; but not the least of the honors shown him is the strong interest manifested by the public in his writings.

Jules Verne, born 1828. at Nantes; educated at his native town; studied law at Paris; first came before the public as a dramatist, in 1850. His fame mainly rests upon his stories, which have gained an immense circulation throughout Europe, being characterized by wild adventures and scientific possibilities or impossibilities. Among these, "Michel Strogoff," "'Round the World," "Twenty Thousand Leagues Under the Sea," and the "Mysterious Island," are well known. M. Verne is also author of an Illustrated Geography of France.

Charles Dudley Warner was born September 12, 1829, at Plainfield, Mass. He was graduated from Hamilton College in 1851. While in college he contributed to the magazines; at his graduation he won the prize in English. In 1853 he was one of a surveying party on the Missouri frontier. After graduating from the law department, University of Pennsylvania, he practiced four years in Chicago. In 1861 became managing editor of the Hartford *Press* (Conn). In 1884 became an editor of *Harper's Magazine*. He has traveled widely, and achieved great popularity as an author; his writings exhibit grace, humor and versatility. "My Summer in a Garden," "Being a Boy," "Their Pilgrimage," and "Backlog Studies," are among his best known writings. In social and literary topics, Mr. Warner shows cleverness and subtlety, quietly satirizing the follies and foibles of American life.

AUTHORS AND JOURNALISTS.

Thomas Bailey Aldrich, born in Portsmouth, N. H., November 11, 1836. Had nearly completed preparatory studies when the death of his father compelled the abandonment of a collegiate course. Entered the counting house of his uncle, a New York merchant, where he began to write for periodicals. At twenty-one made pronounced impression upon the public mind by the "Ballad of Babie Bell." Entered upon a literary career; became a proof reader, then manuscript reader, contributing to the periodicals meantime. In 1856, while the New York *Home Journal* was still under management of N. P. Willis and George P. Morris, Mr. Aldrich joined the editorial staff, a three years' connection. In 1861 produced "Pampinea, and Other Poems"; two collections of poems in 1863 and 1865. For many years Mr. Aldrich wrote almost exclusively for the *Atlantic Monthly*. During his editorship the magazine took first rank among American periodicals, and introduced to the reading public a majority of the new lights of literature who have become noted during the last ten years. Among his prose works are numbered, "Story of a Bad Boy," "Prudence Palfrey," "Mercedes," and others.

Hans Christian Andersen, Danish novelist, born in 1805, son of a shoemaker of Odense, in the Island of Funen. From extreme poverty, was sometimes compelled to beg; but the father was somewhat educated, and read to Hans, Holberg's comedies and the "Arabian Nights." Was intended for a tailor, but wished to be an actor; wrote a tragedy while very young. At fourteen, having saved thirty shillings, went to Copenhagen "to become famous." Sang for a time at Theatre Royal, possessing a beauti-

SUCCESSFUL MEN AND WOMEN.

ful voice, which unfortunately was soon ruined. A kind hearted man obtained his admission to Slagelse Grammar School, where the philological and philosophical examinations were creditably passed. In 1828 published his first book. Had an intense passion for traveling, and wrote many books of travel; best drama appeared in 1840, entitled "The Mulatto." Best known in England as the author of charming fairy tales; the famous "Ugly Duckling" appeared in 1835. These tales have been translated into most of the European languages, and especially the "Flax," the "Willow Tree," and the "Dream of Little Luk," have become household words. Toward the close of his life, returned to Copenhagen, dying there in 1875, having lived a blameless and innocent life.

John J. Audubon, eminent ornithologist, born at New Orleans, May 4, 1780, of French parentage. Commenced his own active life as a pioneer of civilization and social progress in the West. When thirty years of age he sailed down the Ohio river in an open boat, with wife and child, seeking a suitable location for a cabin. Led a life of bold and fearless adventure, romantic incident and constantly varying fortune. Visited nearly every region of United States; for some years prior to his death, he led a quiet, retired life on the banks of the Hudson, mixing little in society. He left behind him a name and fame which, as legacy to his family and to American science and art, are above all price. He died January 27, 1851.

James Gordon Bennett, journalist, born in New Mill, near Keith, Scotland, September 1, 1795, of French parentage; sent to Aberdeen at fourteen, to study for the priesthood. Convinced that this was not his vocation, determined to emigrate, and in 1819, landed at Halifax, Nova Scotia; attempted to earn a living by bookkeeping. Failing in that, went to Boston and became proof reader. After a time became reporter, paragraphist and contributor of all sorts of articles to the newspapers. In 1825 bought the *Sunday Courier*, but soon abandoned it. Later became assistant editor of the *Courier and Inquirer*, which became the leading American newspaper. Leaving this paper, on account of political differences, he started the *Herald*, which at first sold for one cent a copy. Engaged foreign journalists as correspondents; and was especially apt in news-collecting. The circulation of the paper doubled during the civil war, when sixty-three war correspondents were employed. In 1841, income of the paper was at least $100,000. As a journalist, Bennett was eminently successful, knowing how to select the subject most interesting at the time to the people, and give all the details that could be desired. He died in **New** York city, June 1, 1872.

Thomas De Quincey, most graceful and versatile of English essayists, born at Manchester, England, in 1785; the father, Thomas Quincey, merchant, died when Thomas was but seven years old. The lad was educated at Bath Grammar School, distinguishing himself by Latin verses, also attended a private school at Winkworth, and Manchester Grammar School, from which he ran away, going through with the privations and wanderings immortalized in the "Confessions of an English Opium-Eater." Went to Worcester College, Oxford, in 1803, led an uneventful life there and left in 1808 without a degree. Took a cottage at Grasmere, and became one of the famous circle of Lake scholars. He read voraciously, and with a wonderful retentive power; wrote for *London Magazine* until 1824, then for *Blackwood*. In 1830 removed to Edinburgh, living there until 1837. Acquired the opium habit in 1804, when laudanum was used to cure an attack of neuralgia, and so rapidly did the habit grow upon him that 12,000 drops per day were sometimes used. His works consist entirely of magazine articles, of great subtlety and artistic finish; the essays in literary criticism are the best of their kind. De Quincey died in 1859.

Alexandre Dumas, greatest romance writer of France, born in 1802, son of General Dumas. In 1823 went to Paris to seek his fortune, obtaining a clerkship in the hotel of the Duke of Orleans. Wrote a drama before the age of twenty, offering it to the Theatre Francaise, where it was refused. At the advent of Louis Philippe, a second play was performed, taking Paris by storm; this performance was followed by a series of successes, depicting the life of the sixteenth century. It would be impossible even to attempt a catalogue of Dumas's works in an article, they comprise over 2,000 volumes. Out of these, had he written but "La Reine Margot," "Henri III.," "Les Mousquetaires," and the "Voyage en Espagne," he would still have been justly famous. His death occurred in 1871.

James Harper, founder of the house of Harper & Brothers, publishers, was born in Newtown, L. I., April 13, 1795; father was Joseph Harper, farmer. At sixteen, James, with his brother, was apprenticed to printers in New York, where James became the friend and fellow apprentice of Thurlow Weed. The brothers had a small capital, at the end of their apprenticeship, and, with some addition from the family means, established a printing office in Dover street. First delivered 2,000 copies of Seneca's "Morals," in August, 1817; in 1818, printed

SUCCESSFUL MEN AND WOMEN.

500 copies of Locke's "Essay upon the Human Understanding"; upon this volume appeared, for the first time, the imprint of J. & J. Harper, as publishers. Upon the admittance of two younger brothers, the firm became Harper & Brothers. James Harper was an advocate of temperance and religion, a man of tolerant spirit and kindly manner. Was a Whig in politics; elected mayor of New York city in 1844, a position in which he gained the respect of all. Died March 25, 1869, from the effects of an accident sustained while driving near Central Park.

Thomas Hood, born in London, 1798, son of a bookseller. Commenced his career as a clerk, but afterwards learned the trade of an engraver; next became contributor and assistant editor to the *London Magazine*. Attracted notice mainly by the humor and wit embodied in his productions; was much entitled to reputation as punster and satirist. Of his many poems, "The Song of the Shirt" and "Bridge of Sighs" are most celebrated because of the humor and pathos of common life, displayed in both. Hood lived a life of extreme poverty and suffering; and died in 1845 at the age of forty-five.

Charles Lyell, geologist, born in county Forfar, Scotland, November 14, 1797. Soon after his birth his father, an excellent botanist, removed to Hampshire in England. When nineteen, entered Oxford, remaining three years and then studying law. From childhood had a taste for natural history; while at Oxford studied botany, entomology and geology. In London, where he located, was for the most part occupied with geology. In 1832 began to deliver lectures upon the subject in King's College. Traveled extensively, both in Europe and America, making investigations. Published results of his inquiries have added much to our standard literature in this department. Among his most celebrated publications are his "Principles of Geology and Elements of Geology." Died in 1849.

PREACHERS OF PROMINENCE.

John A. Broadus, D.D., professor of homiletics and interpretation of the New Testament in the Southern Baptist Theological Seminary, was born in Culpeper county, Virginia, January 24, 1827, of Welsh parentage. The family name was originally spelled Broadhurst. The father was a prominent member of the Virginia Legislature for a number of years. Dr. Broadus was educated at the University of Virginia, taking the degree of A.M. in 1850, and in 1851 being elected assistant professor of Latin and Greek in that institution; this position he held two years. Was pastor of the Baptist Church of Charlottesville until 1855; from that date until 1857, served as chaplain of the university, returning afterward to his former pastorate. In 1863 served as chaplain in General R. E. Lee's army. In 1870 published "Preparation and Delivery of Sermons," republished in England, and since used as text-book in theological seminaries of Europe and America. He is author of numberless newspaper articles, of many sermons and reviews, critical papers, and lectures; and ranks with the ablest preachers of his generation.

Russell H. Conwell, clergyman and lecturer, was born at Worthington, Hampshire county, Mass., February 15, 1842, spending his early years on a sterile mountain farm. Kept up with classes in the district school by study during evenings, compelled by manual labor which occupied the time during school hours. Attended Wilbraham Academy, Massachusetts, paying his own way; and in 1860 commenced the study of law, hiring a tutor to instruct him in the academic course. The civil war interrupted his studies in 1862, and took him to the field as a captain of artillery; later, served as a staff officer. Having completed the legal course by private study while in the army, went at the close of the war to Minnesota, and began the practice of law. In 1867 represented Minnesota as emigration agent to Germany; was foreign correspondent for the New York *Tribune*, and the year following was traveling correspondent of the Boston *Traveller*. In 1870 made the circuit of the globe in the employ of these journals. He is a writer of singular brilliancy and power. Was the friend and fellow-traveler of Bayard Taylor. Was ordained to the ministry in 1879, and in 1881 became pastor of Grace Baptist Church in Philadelphia, which has greatly prospered under his ministry. His lectures, "Silver Crown," "Acres of Diamonds," "Lessons of Travel," "Heroism of a Private Life," are models of lyceum lectures, and have made for him national reputation.

Chas. F. Deems, D.D., born in Baltimore, Md., in 1820; father was a Methodist clergyman. Dr. Deems was converted while a mere boy, and chose the ministerial profession, beginning preparation at fifteen years of age, in Dickinson College; graduated in 1836. Was appointed professor of logic and rhetoric in University of North Carolina, occupying this position five years; afterward, became professor of natural science in Randolph Macon College, Va. In 1860, he visited Europe; on his return organized a school in Wilson county, N. C. From this time until 1865, was Presiding Elder of the Wilmington and New-Berne district of that state; preached his first sermon in New York, July 22, 1866, to an audience of fifteen persons; but soon became widely known, among his own and other denominations. In January, 1868, "The Church of the Strangers" was organized with thirty-two members. Cornelius Vanderbilt purchased the Mercer Street Presbyterian Church and gave it to Dr. Deems for the use of the congregation, which greatly increased. Dr. Deems has written several religious books. After many years of earnest and aggressive work, he was called to his reward Saturday, Nov. 18, 1893.

John Hall, D.D., born in County Armagh, Ireland, July 31, 1829, of Scottish descent. Entered Belfast College at thirteen years, and repeatedly took the Hebrew prize. Was licensed to preach in 1849, and engaged at once as missionary in the west of Ireland. Installed pastor of First Presbyterian Church at Armagh in 1852. He was an earnest friend of popular education, and received from the queen the honorary appointment of commissioner of education for Ireland. In 1867 was delegate from the general assembly of the Presbyterian church in Ireland, to the Presbyterian churches of the United States. Received a call to Fifth Avenue Presbyterian Church in New York entering upon his labors Nov. 3, 1867. In 1882 was elected chancellor of the University of the city of New York. He was elected to deliver the funeral sermon of Chief-Justice Chase. Dr. Hall is author of "Familiar Talk to Boys," "Questions of the Day," and "Foundation Stones for Young Builders."

Wayland Hoyt, D.D., was born in Cleveland, Ohio, February 18, 1838. In 1860, was graduated from Brown University; in 1863 from Rochester Theological Seminary. Was ordained over the Baptist Church of Pittsfield, Mass. One year after, he removed to Cincinnati, Ohio, and took charge of the Ninth Street Baptist Church; three years later, took charge of the Strong Place Baptist Church, Brooklyn, a large and influential church, which afforded full scope for his powers, as profound thinker, scholarly writer and able preacher. In the hope of establishing a great Baptist tabernacle in New York city, he accepted a call from the Tabernacle Baptist Church, New York, and commenced services in Steinway Hall, where a favorable beginning was made, but there were insurmountable difficulties, and the enterprise was abandoned. A call to Shawmut Avenue Baptist Church, Boston, Mass., was accepted and, later, he was recalled to the Strong Place Church, his present field of labor. A prolific writer, his contributions are eagerly sought by leading journals of the Baptist denomination. As a preacher, earnest, clear and persuasive, as a platform speaker, ready and forcible, as a pastor, faithful and successful, he has become one of the best known preachers of the denomination.

Edward Judson, D.D., son of Dr. Adoniram Judson, the "Apostle of Burmah," was born at Maulmain, Burmah, December 27, 1844; was graduated from Brown University in 1865. After teaching as principal of a seminary in Vermont, he became tutor in Madison University, and in 1868 was appointed Professor of Latin and Modern Languages. In 1875, was ordained pastor of the church in North Orange, N. J., where between three and four hundred were baptized by him in five years. In 1880, was elected a trustee of Brown University. In later years, has become widely known through work among the poorer classes in New York city, where he built the Judson Memorial Church, in memory of Adoniram Judson; is pastor of this church, and is known in the Baptist denomination as a quiet but impressive speaker, an earnest Bible student, and a hard-working pastor, a worthy son of a great father.

R. S. MacArthur, D.D., was born at Dalesville, Quebec, Canada, July 31, 1841. His parents came from the Scotch Highlands to Quebec; father is Presbyterian, but the mother and other members of the family are Baptists. Was converted at thirteen, and at eighteen began to hold religious meetings and address the people; prepared for college at Canadian Literary Institute, Woodstock, Canada; graduated at University of Rochester, in 1867, taking the sophomore prize for declamation and the gold medal for best written and delivered oration at graduation. He was licensed to preach September 25, 1868; was graduated from Rochester Theological Seminary in 1870. During the seminary course, preached on Sunday evenings at Lake Avenue chapel; many conversions resulted, and a now flourishing church was organized. In June, 1870, accepted the call of Calvary Baptist Church, Twenty-third street, New York city, where he has since labored with marked success; well known as a writer for Baptist periodicals, and as a clear and logical speaker he is one of the leaders of his denomination.

Cardinal Manning, born at Totteridge, Hertfordshire, England, July 15, 1808; son of William Manning, M. P., merchant, of London; was educated at Harrow and Balliol College, Oxford, where he graduated B. A. in first class honors in 1830, and became Fellow of Merton College. Was for some time a select preacher in University of Oxford; was appointed Archdeacon of Chichester in 1840. In 1851 joined the Roman Catholic church, entered the priesthood, and received the degree of D.D., at Rome; was made Prelate to the Pope. Consecrated Archbishop of Westminster, June 8, 1865. Pius IX. created him a cardinal priest in 1875. Has written many ecclesiastical works; is well known not only for his work as Roman Catholic prelate and divine, but as a temperance and social reformer.

Rev. A. A. Miner, LL.D., was born at Lempster, Sullivan County, N. H., August 17, 1814. After studying in various schools and academies until sixteen, taught four winter schools, and then, in 1834, became associate principal of an academy at Cavendish, Vt. One year later took sole charge of a scientific and literary academy at Unity, N. H., remaining there four years. Began preaching in 1838, was ordained as Universalist clergyman in 1839; settled at Methuen, Mass.; three years later removed to Lowell; in 1848 went to Boston, where he was associate pastor with Hosea Ballou, over what is now Columbus Avenue Universalist Church. July 4, 1855, delivered oration before city authorities of Boston. Has been member of school committee of Methuen, Lowell, and Boston, member board of overseers of Harvard, and on state board of education for more than twenty years. Was president of Tufts College 1862 to 1875. A prolific writer, has written much for daily and weekly press. His best known books are "Old Forts Taken," and "Bible Exercises." Dr. Miner is one of the great reformers of our time. Few voices have been so potent as his.

Dwight L. Moody, born in Northfield, Franklin County, Mass., February 5, 1837; received a limited education, and worked on a farm until seventeen years old, then became clerk in a Boston shoe store. United with a Congregational church soon afterward, and in 1856 went to Chicago, where he engaged with enthusiasm in missionary work among the poor; in less than a year established a Sunday-school with more than 1000 pupils. During civil war was employed by Christian Commission, subsequently by the Chicago Y. M. C. A., as lay missionary. A church was built for his converts with himself as pastor. In the fire of 1871, this church and Mr. Moody's house were destroyed; a new and larger church has since been erected. In 1873, accompanied by Ira D. Sankey, visited Europe, holding religious services in England, Scotland, and Ireland, which resulted in great awakenings in the principal cities of these countries. Returning to the United States, similar meetings were organized. A school for boys has been established by Mr. Moody at Gill, Mass., and a school for girls at Northfield. Summer schools for Bible study are held yearly, under his auspices. Mr. Moody has published many religious works, and has been a great influence for good in thousands of lives.

Cardinal Newman, born February 21, 1801, in London; son of John Newman, banker; brother of Francis William Newman, theologian and essayist. Boyhood was passed in Bloomsbury Square, early became interested in theology. After tuition in private school at Ealing, became a member of Trinity College, Oxford. Graduated 1820, was Fellow of Oriel College. In 1824 took orders. In 1828 became incumbent of St Mary's, Oxford, and chaplain of Littlemore. Went abroad in 1833, during this time wrote the hymn, "Lead, Kindly Light." Left the church in 1845 and was received into the church of Rome; was ordained priest; in 1854-8 was rector of the Catholic University at Dublin. In 1864, appeared the "Apologia pro vita sua" and in 1865 the "Dream of Gerontius." In December, 1877, Dr. Newman was elected a Fellow of Trinity College, Oxford. In 1879 was created a cardinal deacon by Pope Leo XIII.; but of late years has led a somewhat secluded life. A collected edition of his numerous works was published in 1877. Died in 1890.

Andrew Preston Peabody, D. D., LL. D., was born in Beverly, Mass., March 19, 1811. Graduated at Harvard, in 1826, studied three years in divinity school, was mathematical tutor one year in university; in 1833 succeeded Rev. Dr. Nathan Parker as pastor of South Parish Unitarian Church in Portsmouth, N. H. Held this pastorate until 1860, when he was appointed preacher to the university, and professor of Christian morals, until 1881, when resigning to give his whole time to literary work, he was given an emeritus appointment. In 1862 and again during 1868-9, he was acting president of the university. He wrote sixty leading articles in the *Whig Review*, was editor of the *North American Review* in 1852-'61 and has contributed to *The Christian Examiner*, *The New England Magazine* and other publications. Some of his books are, "Lectures on Christian Doctrine," "Manual of Moral Philosophy," and "Christianity and Science."

Matthew Simpson, Bishop. Born in Cadiz, Ohio, June 20, 1811. Father died when the boy was two years old, leaving him to the instruction and encouragement of an uncle, Matthew Simpson. Was educated as well as the town afforded, and taught many things by the uncle, who understood Greek and Hebrew, was ten years in State Senate, and seven years judge of the County Court. At sixteen, Matthew became a student in Madison College, Penn., made rapid progress, and was a tutor at nineteen. Studied medicine, but abandoned practice in 1834, entering Pittsburgh conference of the M. E. church, on trial. In 1837 was transferred to Williamsport, and was elected vice-president and professor of natural science in Allegheny College. Was chosen president of De Pauw University in 1839, holding the position nine years. His eloquence made him in great demand, and personal qualities exerted strong influence over students. Was made bishop during the conference of 1852; was delegate to World's Evangelical Alliance at Berlin, where a sermon before the Alliance extended his fame as a pulpit orator throughout the world. President Lincoln considered him the greatest he had ever heard. He died in Philadelphia, June 18, 1884. He was a man of sound judgment a profound scholar, and a wise counselor.

EMINENT PREACHERS.

Lyman Abbott, D.D., author, editor, and clergyman, was born in Roxbury, Mass., December 18, 1835, son of Jacob Abbott. Was graduated from the University of New York, and soon afterward, being admitted to the bar, engaged in practice of law, with his two older brothers. While thus employed, he wrote, in collaboration with them, the two novels, "Conecut Corners," and "Matthew Caraby." But finding the ministry more to his taste than the legal profession, studied theology under his uncle, John S. C. Abbott; was ordained in 1860 a clergyman of the Congregational church. First charge was in Terre Haute, Ind.; remained there until 1865, greatly beloved by the people. Then, becoming discouraged, he laid aside pastoral work and accepted the secretaryship of the American Freedmen's Commission. This work was located at New York city, but visiting Terre Haute, found that his work there had proved very fruitful, so took up ministerial work again, in the New England Church, at New York city, also conducting the "Literary Record" of *Harper's Magazine*, and editing the *Illustrated Christian Weekly*. The last named position was resigned when he became associate-editor with Henry Ward Beecher of the *Christian Union*. Has for some time been editor-in-chief of this journal. October, 1887, was elected temporary successor of Henry Ward Beecher, in the Plymouth Church, Brooklyn, and not long afterward, permanent pastor. His first independent publication was "Jesus of Nazareth" (1869). Later works are, "Old Testament Shadows of New Testament Truths," (1870); "Life of Henry Ward Beecher," and "In Aid of Faith." Is a prominent exponent of the so-called liberal theology; his style is simple, lucid, and possesses deep spirituality.

Henry Ward Beecher, D.D., clergyman, was born in Litchfield, Conn., June 24, 1813, son of Lyman Beecher. Home training was of the severe New England type, alleviated by an irrepressible sense of humor in his father. Was graduated from Amherst College in 1834; did not stand high, being characterized, there and everywhere else, by following his own inclination with zeal and energy. Graduated from Lane Theological seminary (Cincinnati). First parish was the Presbyterian church at Lawrenceburg, Indiana, a small settlement on the Ohio river, the church consisted of twenty persons, nineteen of whom were women. After a year or two, was called to a Presbyterian church in Indianapolis. Here his remarkable oratorical gifts insured a crowded church. After eight years work here, Mr. Beecher was called to the pastorate of the Plymouth church in Brooklyn, N. Y.; entered upon the pastorate, October 10, 1847, remaining there until his death, March 8, 1887. Mr. Beecher was a great pulpit and platform orator, not excelled if indeed, equaled in the American pulpit, or in the Christian church.

Phillips Brooks, D.D., Protestant Episcopal bishop of Massachusetts, was born in Boston, Mass., December 13, 1835; son of a merchant. Had every educational advantage, and was graduated from Harvard at the age of twenty, then studied theology at a Protestant Episcopal seminary. Was admitted to holy orders in 1859, and appointed rector of the Church of the Advent, Philadelphia. Five years later, assumed rectorship of the Church of the Holy Trinity, in the same city, and subsequently, in 1869, of the Trinity Church, Boston, the largest and wealthiest Episcopalian congregation in Massachusetts. Phillips Brooks exercised over the thought and life of his generation a marvelous power; not merely on account of his rich thought, or simple, quietly powerful style, or deep intellectuality, but on account of intense earnestness and profound spirituality and a burning desire to uplift men. Published several books, among them, three volumes of sermons. In 1891, he was elected Bishop of the diocese of Massachusetts. Died January 23, 1893.

William Ellery Channing D.D., was born in Newport, R. I., April 7, 1780; his boyhood was passed in Newport, where strong religious impressions were received from the preaching of Dr. Samuel Hopkins. During college life won the ardent personal attachment of many fellow students, and seemed, even then, to possess remarkable literary powers. After graduation from Harvard, in 1798, was private instructor in Richmond, Va., in the family of D. M. Randolph. Here acquired a thorough abhorrence of slavery; and at the same time became eagerly interested in political discussions growing out of the revolutionary movements in Europe. Returned to Newport, and thence to Cambridge as a student of theology. His first and only pastoral settlement was over the church in Federal street, Boston, June 1, 1803. Was known here, for a style of religious eloquence of rare "fervor, solemnity and beauty." Mr. Channing was practically the leader of the Unitarian denomination in America, in his day, and the sermons left by him constitute the best body of practical divinity that the Unitarian movement in this country has produced. Able addresses on slavery, public education and temperance are also found among his published works. Last public act was an address delivered in Lenox, Mass., Aug. 1, 1842, commemorating the West India emancipation. Best known in America as a theologian and preacher, his influence abroad is chiefly as a writer on social ethics. Died Oct. 2, 1842.

John Hughes, D.D., first Roman Catholic archbishop of the archdiocese of New York, was born at Annaloghan, Tyrone county, Ireland, June 24, 1797, son of Patrick Hughes, a respectable farmer. The family emigrated to America in 1816, and purchased a small farm near Chambersburgh, Penn. Received his early education at a small school in Augher, afterward attending the high school at Auchnacloy. From early childhood, evinced a strong inclination to become a priest, but educational advantages were for a time lacking. Was placed with a friend of his father, learned horticulture, and occupied spare time with study. In 1817 followed the family to America, secured employment at Baltimore, and in 1818 obtained a position at Mount St. Mary's College, Emmittsburg, where in return for services he was enabled to receive private instructions until able to enter the regular classes, and teach the younger scholars. Showed great ability in the philosophical and theological studies; was ordained deacon in 1825, and priest October 15, 1826. Was soon called to Philadelphia, and placed in charge of St. John's Church. Was proposed for the coadjutor bishopric of Philadelphia, when but three years a priest. Father Hughes was brought into great prominence by two debates with Rev. John R. Breckinridge, a Presbyterian minister, on the questions, "Is the Protestant religion the religion of Christ?" and "Is the Roman Catholic religion, in any or in all its principles, inimical to civil or religious liberty?" January 8, 1838, Father Hughes was consecrated titular bishop of Basiliopolis, and coadjutor of the bishop of New York. Two weeks afterward, Father Dubois had a paralytic stroke, and the care of the whole diocese fell upon the young priest, who showed himself eminently well qualified to carry it. In 1838 purchased property at Fordham, N. Y., and founded St. John's College. In 1840-42, was engaged in discussing the public school question. August 15, 1858, laid the corner-stone of the new cathedral of St. Patrick, Fifth avenue and Fiftieth street, New York city. Last public address was delivered during the draft riots July, 1863. Died January 3, 1864.

Theodore Parker, D.D., was born at Lexington, Mass., August 24, 1810, son of a farmer. Had a little instruction at the village school, and somehow acquired a remarkable knowledge of general literature. All the tuition he appears to have had, was one quarter at a school in Lexington, where some mathematics and a little Latin and Greek were taught. But being an indefatigable student, he actually prepared, in time, for college, and entered Harvard in 1830. Even then the study was carried on with the farm-labor, going to the college for examinations only. Obtained a B. A. degree, and taught in the schools of Boston, Watertown and elsewhere for six years. In the mean time, studied in a divinity school, and in June, 1837, was ordained a minister of the Unitarian church, settled at West Roxbury, Mass. By 1841, Mr. Parker had differed from the Unitarian belief, and was afterward excommunicated from the body. In 1846, resigned the pastorate at West Roxbury, and preached before a society of his own, which held services first at Melodeon Hall then at Music Hall in Boston. Mr. Parker's tendencies were humanitarian, his words all in behalf of peace, temperance, morality and the rights of labor; hard work of body and mind at last broke down a constitution naturally strong; and May 10, 1860, the end came at Florence, whither he had gone for change of climate. His writings were quite numerous, most of them appearing in the *Quarterly Review*, of which he was editor.

Charles Haddon Spurgeon, born at Kelvedon, Essex, June 19, 1834; educated at Colchester, Maidstone, and elsewhere, and became usher at a school at Newmarket. Adopted Baptist views, and joined the congregation which had been presided over by Robert Hall, at Cambridge. Subsequently became pastor at Waterbeach, and his fame as a preacher reached London; accepted there the pastorate of the church meeting in New Park street chapel, Southwark. First, preached before a London congregation in 1853, with such success that in two years time, enlargement of accommodations was required; while these were being made, officiated four months at Exeter Hall. Enlargement proved insufficient, and it became necessary to change to Surrey Music Hall and the congregation determined to build. The Metropolitan Tabernacle was opened in 1861. Mr. Spurgeon has published a sermon weekly, since the first week of 1855; at the end of 1889, the series, inclusive of double numbers, had reached No. 2,120, and the weekly circulation had reached about 25,000. The demand for them was not less in the United States than in England, and multitudes felt their uplifting power. Published a number of other works, the chief of which is "The Treasury of David," an exposition of the Psalms, in seven volumes. In 1867, founded the Stockwell Orphanage, since that time enlarged to accommodate 250 boys and as many girls. Founded the Pastor's College, in 1856, which has educated over 800 men; up to 1889, 673 were still engaged in evangelistic or ministerial work. The Metropolitan Tabernacle Colportage Association had at that time about seventy or eighty agents, and sold, annually, about £9,000 worth of pure literature. The church had about thirty mission halls and schools connected with it. Mr. Spurgeon's power over an audience was wonderful, partly due to the strong earnestness and robust spiritual life of the speaker; he was " made for mankind " and to them gave the great store of mind and heart until his death, which occurred January 31, 1892.

Richard Salter Storrs, D.D., clergyman, was born in Braintree, Mass., August 21, 1821; was graduated at Amherst in 1839, and after teaching in Monson Academy and Williston Seminary, studied law under Rufus Choate. Turning to theology, in 1842, was graduated from Andover Seminary in 1845, and ordained October 22 of that year, in Brookline, Mass., where he had been called to the pastorate of the Harvard Congregational Church. In 1846, accepted the pastorate of the new Church of the Pilgrims in Brooklyn, where he has since remained. Received D.D. from Union College (1853), and Harvard (1859), LL.D. from Princeton (1874), and L.H.D. from Columbia (1887). In 1855 delivered lectures before Brooklyn Institute on "The Constitution of the Human Soul," and at Princeton Theological Seminary, the L. P. Stone lectures. Gave the lectures on "Preaching Without Notes," at the Union Theological Seminary in 1875, and in 1881, lectures on "The Divine Origin of Christianity," before Union Seminary and the Lowell Institute in Boston. Has attained reputation as one of the most eloquent pulpit orators in the United States; is well-known for historical studies; and has delivered frequent addresses on public occasions. In 1875 made the seventieth anniversary address before the New York Historical Society, in 1876 the centennial oration in New York city, and in 1881, the Phi Beta Kappa oration at Harvard. In 1887 was elected president of the American Board of Commissioners for Foreign Missions. Was an editor of the *Independent*, 1848-61. Among the published works of Dr. Storrs may be mentioned "Early American Spirit and the Genesis of it" (1875), "Declaration of Independence and the Effects of it " (1876), " Manliness in the Scholar" (1883), "Divine Origin of Christianity " (1884), and " The Prospective Advance of Christian Missions " (1885).

Thomas De Witt Talmage, D.D., was born at Bound Brook, Somerset county, N. J., Jan. 7, 1832, youngest of twelve children of David T. Talmage, a farmer. Preliminary studies were made in the grammar school at New Brunswick, N. J., under Professor Thompson. In early life showed acute observation, remarkable memory, and great bodily vigor. At the age of eighteen, joined the church, and the following year entered the University of the City of New York. The speech made by him at graduation (May, 1853,) met with great enthusiasm, was published in one of the New York papers, the first literary article of Mr. Talmage's ever printed. Studied law three years ; then prepared for the ministry at the Reformed Dutch Church Theological Seminary in New Brunswick, N. J. Was ordained by the reformed Dutch classis of Bergen; accepted a call from Belleville, N. J., remaining three years. Was next settled at Syracuse, N. Y., where he began to be noted. Afterward became pastor of the Second Reformed Dutch Church of Philadelphia; remained seven years; during this period, first entered the lecture platform, laying the foundation of his future reputation. At this time received three calls, one from Chicago, one from San Francisco, one from Brooklyn ; accepted the latter, building up a large church from a small beginning. Two large tabernacles were built, one in 1870 the other in 1873 ; the first was burned December 22, 1872, the second was also burned in 1889. A new tabernacle was completed in 1891. Dr. Talmage has published numerous lectures and addresses, and several books, " Crumbs Swept Up " (1870), " Old Wells Dug Out" (1874), "Night Sides of City Life" (1878), and others. He is a powerful and dramatic speaker.

SUCCESSFUL MEN AND WOMEN.

PREACHERS AND WRITERS.

Richard Baxter was born at Rowton, England, November 12, 1615. By unusual application atoned for a deficient education, and was made master of Dudley Free School, through interest of Mr. Richard Foley of Stonebridge; was soon admitted to orders. In 1640 became a pastor at Kidderminster; but the civil war soon broke out, exposing him to persecution. Charles II. afterward made Baxter one of his chaplains, and Chancellor Clarendon offered him the bishopric of Hereford, which was declined. "The Paraphrase on the New Testament" caused a sentence of two years' imprisonment, which was modified to six months. Died December 8, 1691. His compositions are numerous, and some are very popular, as the "Saints' Rest."

Lyman Beecher, D.D., Presbyterian clergyman, born at New Haven, Conn., September 12, 1775. Took collegiate course at Yale, and graduated 1797. Studied theology under Timothy Dwight, was appointed pastor of the Presbyterian Church, East Hampton, L. I.; in 1810, took charge of First Congregational Church, Litchfield, Connecticut, remaining sixteen years. Became known for his zeal and efficiency. Assisted in organizing the American Bible Society, Connecticut Education Society and others. In 1826 he became pastor of Hanover Street Church, Boston, and in 1832, President of Lane Theological Seminary, Cincinnati. He remained there about ten years; after that time, resided in Boston. Dr. Beecher's published works are for the most part sermons. Died in Brooklyn, January 10, 1863.

John Bunyan, born at Elstow, near Bedford, England. What little instruction he received was quickly obliterated by a vicious career, which was abruptly terminated, say the biographers, by the sudden operation of a heavenly monitor in the soul, which bade him either leave off sin or perish. Established himself as a Baptist preacher at Bedford; was arrested under the laws against conventicles, sentenced to lifelong imprisonment. During confinement wrote several works, and obtained support by making laces. After more than twelve years imprisonment was liberated. Traveled through England and after the publication of Act of Toleration by James II. became a popular preacher. Died of a fever, in London, in 1688. The most celebrated of his writings is "Pilgrim's Progress," a religious allegory, which has passed through more than fifty editions and been translated into various languages.

Jonathan Edwards, born in East Windsor, Conn., Oct. 5, 1703; was educated at Yale College, graduating in 1720. Was six years missionary among the Indians; in 1758 accepted the presidency of Princeton College; was inducted into the office in January and died the March following. Published many works, two of which, the "Treatise on the Will" and the "History of Redemption," are still standard works of literature. He was a wonderful metaphysician, and the only colonial author to reach and maintain a place among the great authors of the world.

Charles G. Finney, born August 29, 1792, in Warren, Litchfield county, Conn.; removed with his father to Oneida county, N. Y.; engaged in teaching when twenty years of age, in New Jersey. Began in Jefferson county to study law, but, becoming converted in 1821, studied theology; was licensed to preach in Presbyterian church, 1824, and began to preach as an evangelist. Met with great success in Utica, Troy, Philadelphia, Boston, and New York. In 1834 became pastor of the Broadway Tabernacle, built especially for him. Mr. Finney accepted a professorship of theology at Oberlin in 1835, and retained it until death. Became pastor of Oberlin Congregational Church. Spent three years in England as a revivalist; in 1851-66 was president of Oberlin. Was an Abolitionist, Anti-Mason, and an advocate of total abstinence. Chief writings were "Lectures on Revivals," translated into several foreign languages, and "Lectures on Systematic Theology." Died at Oberlin, Ohio, August 16, 1875.

Adoniram Judson, D.D., missionary to Burmah, was born in Malden, Mass., August 9, 1788, son of a Congregational clergyman. In 1807, at the age of nineteen, graduated from Brown University with highest honors, and later from Andover Theological Seminary, then just established. With three other students, resolved to become a foreign missionary; there was no missionary society, but one was soon organized. Married Ann Hasseltine, whose devotion and heroism are everywhere well known. Sailed for Calcutta, March, 1812; during the voyage they became Baptists. Began missionary labors in Rangoon, working there for forty years, enduring keenest hardship and suffering, imprisonment and persecution. Dr. Judson acquired a thorough knowledge of the language, translated into it the entire Bible, and other books, and nearly completed a dictionary of the language. He lived to see himself surrounded by a strong corps of evangelists, Burmese and Americans, and

SUCCESSFUL MEN AND WOMEN.

thousands of native converts. Died April 11, 1850, while on the way to America for his health.

Martin Luther was born at Eisleben, November 10, 1483; father was a poor miner. Martin was a promising boy, who early conceived the idea of getting an education. Sang songs beneath the windows of the rich, as one means toward support while in pursuit of education at the University of Erfurt. Joined order of Augustine monks. Was lecturer in Greek and afterward in theology at Wittenberg. Two years later was sent to Rome. In 1517 the Pope inaugurated wholesale traffic in indulgencies, which angered Luther; he boldly denounced the action, and defended his position, at the Diet of Worms. Was imprisoned in Wartburg Castle; there with aid from Melancthon and others, translated the Bible into German. Luther escaped martyrdom, though often endangered, and died peacefully, February 15, 1546.

Cotton Mather, minister in Boston, son of Increase Mather, was born in Boston, February 12, 1663, and graduated at Harvard, 1678. Was ordained colleague of his father in the North Church, in 1684. No person in America read or possessed so many books or retained so much of what he read. So precious was time to him that "Be short" was inscribed over his study door to prevent visits of unnecessary length. Publications amounted to 382. His "Essays to do Good" is a most excellent publication, to which Dr. Franklin ascribes all his own later usefulness. Most celebrated work is the "Ecclesiastical History of New England." No man was so thoroughly acquainted with the history of New England, and he has saved numerous facts from oblivion.

Savonarola, born at Ferrara in 1452, entered Dominican order at Bologna, became an eloquent and popular preacher, after teaching physics and metaphysics for some time. Influence in the pulpit at Florence was so great that for some years he guided the state as its sovereign; but upon denouncing the corruptions of the Church of Rome, and the scandalous life of the pontiff Alexander VI., became an object of vengeance to the Holy See, and neither his popularity nor the purity of his morals could divert its wrath. Was condemned to be hung and burned, and in 1498 suffered the punishment with resignation. Wrote sermons, "The Triumphs of the Cross," and various other theological works, printed at Leyden in six volumes.

William Tyndall, born 1484, in Wales and educated at Magdalen Hall, Oxford, where he imbibed a taste for the doctrines of Luther. Subsequently went to Cambridge, and then settled on the Continent, in order with greater security to print his translation of the New Testament in English. This work was well received in England, though Catholics exerted themselves, with aid of a royal proclamation, to suppress it. Subsequently translated the "Pentateuch," intending to continue his labors, but the Catholics of England were so enraged that they employed a spy, one Philips, to betray him. Was arrested as a heretic at Antwerp; English merchants interceded and Lord Cromwell wrote a release but to no avail. Was strangled, then burned, near Filford Castle, eighteen miles from Antwerp, in the year 1536. A man of persevering spirit and of great zeal as a reformer; was called the Apostle of England.

Isaac Watts, a respectable divine among the English Dissenters, born at Southampton, England, July 17, 1674. Was placed under care of Thomas Rowe, in London, where his studies were completed. In 1696 was tutor in family of Sir John Hartop; in 1702 was appointed successor to Dr. Chauncey in the pastoral office. Though of weak constitution, performed the duties of the office faithfully, also wrote many theological works. In 1728, Universities of Edinburgh and Aberdeen gave him D.D. Among published works are "A Treatise on Logic," "Scripture History," and "Essay on Improvement of the Mind." During the latter part of his life, lived with Sir Thomas Abney. Died November 25, 1748.

Charles Wesley, younger brother of John Wesley, born at Epworth, April, 1708, educated at Westminster, elected to Christ Church College, Oxford, 1726, and after taking degrees adopted and warmly supported the views of his brother, was his companion in the expedition to Georgia. After various adventures with the Indians, returned to England in 1736 and became a zealous preacher among people of his own persuasion. Was well skiled in scripture theology and of a warm, lively character. Died in 1788, aged seventy-nine.

John Wesley, born at Epworth, Lincolnsnire, June 17, 1703; son of Samuel Wesley, a clergyman of the Anglican Church. Attended Christ Church College, where with his brother Charles and some others he was nicknamed Methodist on account of a strict system of pious study and discipline. Was well fitted, by nature and attainments, to form a new sect. Having officiated as curate to his father, set off, in company with Charles, on a mission to Georgia, remaining two years; returning, commenced field-preaching, establishing congregations in Ireland and Great Britain. For a time

SUCCESSFUL MEN AND WOMEN.

was associated with Whitefield, but differed from him on doctrine of election, which Wesley rejected, and they separated. Continued writing, preaching, and journeying until eighty-eight years of age; had preached forty thousand sermons and traveled three hundred thousand miles. His useful and laborious career ended March 2, 1791.

George Whitefield, was born at Gloucester, England, where his mother kept the Bell Inn. Received primary education at the Crypt School of Gloucester, thence entered as servitor in Pembroke College, Oxford, and at the proper age was ordained by Benson, Bishop of Gloucester. Enthusiasm and the love of singularity influenced his conduct. Went to America in 1738 to increase the number of converts. From the controversy between the Wesleys and Whitefield, dated the two distinct sects, Calvinistic and American Methodists. Secure in the good opinion of a great number of adherents and also in the patronage of Lady Huntingdon, to whom he was chaplain, Whitefield built two tabernacles, in London and in Tottenham-Court road, for the commodious reception of followers. Died in 1770, while on a visit to churches in New England; having the satisfaction of knowing that he had many adherents on both continents.

Roger Williams, founder of the Providence Plantations, born in Wales in 1599; educated at Oxford. Being a dissenter, came to America, hoping for religious freedom. Arrived at Hull, February 5, 1631, and was established at Salem, Mass., as colleague of Mr. Shelton, where the peculiarity of his beliefs aroused severe censure. Declared that magisterial interference with religious opinions was wrong, and was banished from the colony in consequence. Land was purchased from the Indians, and a settlement made; Williams gained confidence of the Indians, and went about freely among them. In 1643 was sent to England as agent for both settlements. In 1654 was appointed president of the government. Benedict Arnold succeeded him in 1657. Published a key to the Indian language, and other works; he had a strong, well cultured mind. Died April, 1683.

John Wyckliffe, born about the year 1320, at Ipreswel or Hipswell, Yorkshire, probably descended from the Wickliffes who held the lordship of Wickliff-on-Tees. Attended Baliol College, Oxford; was chosen master of the college some time after 1356. Wyckliffe wrote a variety of scholastic treatises, then, turning to theology, devoted himself to expanding the theory of doctrine of dominion. Was made chaplain to the king. Wyckliffe's teaching with regard to the church had already reached Rome, and a few months later a series of bulls were directed against him by the pope, Gregory XI. The king's death in June delayed execution, and the answer of Wyckliffe to the papal accusation was published meanwhile. Attempts at a trial were unsuccessful, and resulted in simple prohibition to lecture on the offensive subjects. Made the first complete translation of the Bible. Retired, unmolested, to Lutterworth, where he died from paralysis, December 31, 1384.

HISTORIANS AND SCHOLARS.

George Bancroft, historian, born at Worcester, Mass., October 3, 1800, died in Washington, D. C., January 17, 1891. His father was pastor of Unitarian Church at Worcester many years, and George was educated in the common schools and two years at the Phillips Academy at Exeter, N. H., and in 1813 entered Harvard, graduating with honors in 1817. Designed by his parents for the ministry he was sent to Gottingen, Germany, and studied for two years under Eichhorn, Bunsen, and Heeren, the latter inspiring him with a love for history as a vocation, and he made translations of that venerable historian's works, as also of Goethe, Schiller and other German poets, and was given by the university the degree of Ph.D. He traveled in Germany, France, and Italy, and returned to the United States in 1822, and for a year was tutor of Greek in Harvard College. He also preached an occasional sermon and published a small volume of poems. In 1823 founded with Dr. Cogswell at Northampton, Mass., the Round Hill School, on the Eton and Rugby idea. In 1830 he was, without his knowledge or consent, elected to the Legislature, but refused to serve, and in 1834 published the first volume of his "History of the United States." Of his numerous publications the last, his "Life of Martin Van Buren," appeared in 1889. In 1838-41, Mr. Bancroft was collector at Boston, and in 1844 the unsuccessful Democratic candidate for governor of his state, and in 1845 secretary of the navy under President Polk, and from 1846-9 minister to Great Britain. From 1867 to 1874 he was again in Europe as United States minister, first to Russia and then to Germany, and the latter year was recalled at his request, and took up his residence in Washington, D. C., where he resided till his death by old age in 1891. He was made D.C.L. by Oxford University and was a member of many learned societies. He left no children.

SUCCESSFUL MEN AND WOMEN.

John Fiske, author and historian, born in Hartford, Ct., March 30, 1842. His parents' name was Green. His father, who was an editor of a paper, died when the son was ten years of age, and three years later when his mother remarried he went to live with his grandmother, changing his name of Edmund Fiske Green to that of his great-grandfather, John Fiske. He began to study Latin when six years of age and Greek when nine, completed Euclid before twelve, and Calculus soon after. Entered Harvard College as sophomore in 1860, being especially studious in history and philosophy. He graduated from the Law School of Harvard in 1865 and took an office in Boston for six months, and then abandoned law for literature and lecturing, achieving much popularity in the latter both in Great Britain and in this country. From 1869 to 1871 he lectured on philosophy at Harvard College, and subsequently as instructor in history at that institution, and non-resident professor of history at Washington University, St. Louis, Mo., since 1884. As an author he has written several philosophical treatises in exposition of the system of Herbert Spencer, and also some historical works along the same line, and several volumes of essays.

James Anthony Froude, historian, born in Darlington, Devonshire, England, April 23, 1818. His father was a clergyman of the Established church, and archdeacon of Totness. James was the youngest of three sons. Was educated at Westminster school, and entered Oriel College, Oxford, in 1836, taking his degree in 1840, and winning the chancellor's prize two years later, and was elected fellow of Exeter College. Studied for the ministry, and was ordained deacon in 1845, taking part in the so-called Oxford movement, and in 1847 and 1848 he wrote and published two stories that met with ecclesiastical censure at the hands of the University authorities, and he resigned his fellowship, and also a teachership in Tasmania, and (withdrawing from the ministry actually and formally on September 21, 1872) thereafter devoted himself to literature, and for some years wrote mainly for reviews and magazines, his articles on Job being reprinted in pamphlet form. In 1856 the first two volumes of his "History of England" were issued, and covered the period from the downfall of Cardinal Wolsey to the defeat of the Spanish Armada, the last of the twelve volumes being published in 1870, with a supplementary volume on "The Divorce of Catharine of Aragon" in 1892. He gathered his materials mainly from public documents of the time, was painstaking and exhaustive in method, and bold and frank in the expression of his opinion of men and times, and his history has attracted wide attention and awakened much controversy. In 1867 he reprinted his essays under title of "Short Studies on Great Subjects," and in 1869 was installed rector of St. Andrews University, and given the LL.D. In 1872 he went on a lecturing tour to the United States, afterward enlarging the course of lectures into his "English in Ireland in the Eighteenth Century" (1871-4), and had a hot controversy with the Dominican father, Thomas Burke. In 1874 was sent to the Cape of Good Hope by secretary for the colonies to examine and report on Caffir insurrection, returning the following year. In 1881-3, as the executor of Thomas Carlyle, he published the several famous Carlyle books, that again brought much criticism, and 1890 his "Life of Lord Beaconsfield." Beside these he has written several romances, and sundry volumes on miscellaneous subjects, and recently he succeeded the late Professor Freeman as the Regius professor of modern history at Oxford College.

John Richard Green, historian, born in Oxford, England, December 12, 1837, died in Mentone, France, March 7, 1883. During boyhood he was feeble and being debarred from boyish sports took to books. He entered College at Oxford in 1856, graduating in 1860. His ambition was to study law, but was induced by Dean Stanley and other friends to enter the ministry, and was ordained and made a curate, East End, London. During the next ten years of pastoral work he wrote much for the *Saturday Review*, to help make both ends meet. Failing health compelled him to spend his winters in Italy and France, where he wrote many pleasant papers, afterwards collected into one volume, called "Stray Studies." In 1874, he published a thick, closely printed little volume called a "Short History of the English People," which outsold anything of the kind since Macaulay's history appeared, and he was now in easy circumstances, and famous; 30,000 copies were sold in the first year, and the 135th thousand was issued by his widow in 1888, in England. It has also had almost as large a sale in the United States. In 1877, he had enlarged it from a schoolbook to a more comprehensive and stately work, and in that year published the first volume of his "History of the English People," on which his fame as a historian rests, the fourth volume being issued in 1880. Of his other important historical work, "The Making of England," the first volume was issued a year before his death by consumption, and the sequel second volume ("Conquest of England") was published in 1883, after his death, he, by the most incessant work, having succeeded just before he died in completing it by the aid of his wife (*nee* Miss Alice Stopford, daughter of Archdeacon Stopford), whom he had married in 1877, and on whom much of the work of preparing his works devolved. Mr. Green's success as a historian depends, not so much on the great information he conveys, as upon the style in which it is given, it being very readable and attractive.

Thomas Wentworth Higginson, author, born in Cambridge, Mass., Dec. 22, 1823. His father was a merchant; the son was fitted for college in the public schools of his city and entered Harvard when fifteen years of age, graduating in 1841. He then studied for the ministry, and graduated from the Harvard school of theology in 1847 and was ordained pastor of the First Unitarian Church in Newburyport, Mass. Here his ardent advocacy of the cause of the slave gave much offense and in 1850 he resigned his pastorate. From 1852-8 he was pastor of a Free Church (Unitarian) in Worcester, Mass., and distinguished himself by his advanced views on theology and by his advocacy of woman's rights, and his bold opposition to slavery. The latter led to his being arrested in 1854 and indicted in Boston along with Theodore Parker, Wendell Phillips and others for the murder of a United States deputy marshal in the attempted rescue of Anthony Burns, an escaped slave. But the indictment was faulty and they were discharged and never tried. Two years later he served on committee to colonize Kansas with freemen and was appointed brigadier-general on James H. Lane's staff of free-soilers. In 1858 he left the ministry and devoted himself to literature and the lecture platform against slavery, and in September, 1862, became captain of the 51st Mass. regiment, and on Nov. 10, was appointed the colonel of the 1st South Carolina Vols. (afterward called 33d United States colored troops), the first regiment of slaves ever mustered into the nation's service, and captured Jacksonville, Fla. Was wounded in Aug., 1863, and Oct. 1864 resigned because of disability. In 1880-1 was member of State Legislature and in 1881-3 of State Board of Education, and in 1889 was given a five years contract by the state to write the history of the military and naval forces of Massachusetts during the civil war. He has been twice married, his first wife being Mary Elizabeth Channing and the second Mary (Thacher) Higginson, both of whom are known as authors. He has one daughter, born in 1881. Mr. Higginson is well known on both sides of the Atlantic, some of his score or more of works having been translated into French and German.

David Hume, philosopher, historian, and one of the acutest thinkers of the eighteenth century, born in Edinburgh, Scotland, April 26, 1711, died there August 25, 1776. When eighteen he abandoned the purpose to study law in order to be a philosopher, and had written the most important of his philosophic works before he was twenty-five. Are generally superficial and immature. He read much of English, French, Italian and Latin literature. His celebrated argument against miracles, that gave him much of his fame, was produced at the Jesuit College at La Fleche, France, whither he had gone for his health, upon hearing one of the fathers discoursing concerning a recently performed "miracle." Hume's skepticism was for the few only. He was greatly admired in Paris, where he went as attache of the English ambassador, Earl of Hertford, in 1763. He was intensely Scotch, and had a broad, unmeaning face, was clumsy in person and manners, fat and very good-natured. Counted by his countrymen as an "infidel," he was once rescued by an old woman from a bog into which he had stumbled on the condition that he should repeat the Creed and the Lord's Prayer, which the humorous "infidel" did. He never tired of correcting his works, particularly his "History of England," the production that brought him wealth and fame, its dignity of style and clearness of diction being rarely equaled.

Thomas Babington Macaulay, historian, born in Rothley, England, October 25, 1800, died London, Dec. 28, 1859. His father was a West Indian merchant, and, being a man of large wealth, gave him every facility for education, and in his childhood he began to write. When eight he made a compendium of universal history for himself, and wrote much of what he called poetry. He was privately tutored and when eighteen entered college at Cambridge, graduating in 1822. He spent the next four years in leisurely studying law and in 1826 was admitted to the bar, but after a year or two having no success he gave up law and devoted himself to literature, he having written already several ballads, essays, and critiques for papers and the *Edinburgh Review*, that on Milton published in the *Review* gaining him much social distinction, as had his first attempt at public speaking made at an Anti-Slavery meeting in 1824. In 1830 he entered the House of Commons, where he remained for four years and then resigned to accept the appointment of legal adviser to the India Supreme Council at a salary of $50,000 a year. In 1838 he entered Parliament as member from Edinburgh and the next year became secretary for war, retiring in 1841 upon the fall of the ministry. In 1846 he was made paymaster general with nominal duties, and the next year retired to private life and gave himself to complete his "History of England," upon which he had been engaged for nearly fifteen years and pub.

SUCCESSFUL MEN AND WOMEN.

lished the first two volumes in 1848. Its sale was enormous, edition after edition being printed and the work translated almost immediately into German, Polish, Danish, Swedish, Hungarian, Russian, Bohemian, Italian, French, Dutch and Spanish. In 1855 the third and fourth volumes were published. In 1852 Edinburgh without his knowledge or solicitation of friends returned him to Parliament, where he was attacked with heart failure and compelled to abandon active work and life. In 1857 he was raised to the peerage under the title of Baron Macaulay of Rothley, and two years later finished his life and was buried in the Poets' Corner in Westminster Abbey near the statue of Addison.

John Lothrop Motley, historian, born in Boston (Dorchester), April, 15, 1814, died in Dorsetshire, England, May 29, 1877. His father was a merchant, and John was educated at a private school, and entered Harvard College at thirteen years of age, graduating in 1831, and then studied at the Universities of Berlin and Gottingen, Germany. In 1837 he married Mary Benjamin, a lady of great beauty of character. Their three daughters became well known and connected in English society. Mr. Motley when a boy was delicate in person and an insatiable reader and early began writing in prose and verse, publishing his first book, an historical novel, in 1839. Two years later he was appointed secretary of American Legation at St. Petersburg, but soon resigned the position, and in 1845, he published his "Essay on Peter the Great," and the next year began collecting material for his works on Holland that have given him undying fame. He was ten years in writing his great "History of the Dutch Republic," and then found such difficulty in getting a publisher for it, that he at last issued it in 1856 at his own expense. It at once awakened immense interest in Europe and America. It has been translated into various tongues. Mr. Motley spent 1856-8 in his native city and then returned to England, and in 1860 published the first two volumes of his second great work, the "History of the United Netherlands," and in 1868 the two concluding volumes, returning in June of that year to reside in Boston, and in 1874 published two volumes on "John of Barneveldt," the great advocate of Holland, a production that greatly added to his renown. In that year his wife died and he had become disabled by an apoplectic attack in the previous year. Yet he worked on and at the time of his death he was writing a history of the thirty years' war.

William Hickling Prescott, historian, born in Salem, Mass., May 4, 1796, died in Boston, Mass., January 28, 1859. Was son of Judge William Prescott of Superior Court, and was graduated at Harvard College in 1814, and intended to devote himself to the practice of the law, but a fellow student having thrown in sport a hard crust of bread, it struck one of his eyes and practically destroyed it, and this affecting the other, he became virtually blind, and did his great work of after years by aid of helpers and readers, and the stylus for the blind. Beginning in 1819, he gave ten years to the study of ancient and modern literature, and then visiting Europe, he gave ten more years to collecting material and writing his "Reign of Ferdinand and Isabella the Catholic" (three volumes, Boston, 1838), which met with very great success, upon its publication being translated into French, German, Spanish, Russian, and other languages, and being based not only upon works of his predecessors, but to a very large extent, upon many rare and curious documents, and unpublished manuscripts of priceless value in secret depositories and ancient archives hitherto sealed against the historian. Encouraged by the reception given to this work Mr. Prescott resumed his labors, and in 1843 published his "History of the Conquest of Mexico," founded, in addition to preceding historical works of others, upon some eight thousand pages of unpublished manuscripts in the collection of Don Martin Fernandez de Navaretta, besides other manuscripts gathered from all available quarters; and in 1847 he published his "History of the Conquest of Peru," basing it like the others of his works upon unpublished documents and original material gathered at much expense and effort both for him and by him. In 1850 he again visited Europe for study and investigation and gave six years to preparing a "History of the Reign of Philip II.," publishing the first two volumes in 1855, and in December, 1858, the third volume, but did not live to complete it, having experienced in the latter year a slight stroke of paralysis and then on January 28, of 1859, a second, from which he died. He was a writer of rare learning and merit and his name through his works will live long among men, who regret that this rare spirit did not finish the greatest of his works ere death called him.

John Clark Ridpath, historian, born in Putnam county, Indiana, April 26, 1840. He graduated at Asbury (now De Pauw) University, and became professor of history in that institution in 1869, and in 1879 was elected the vice-president of the University, and has become widely known, first by his "Popular History of the United States" (1876), a text-book, in one volume, of which over 600,000 have been sold, and by his "Cyclopedia of Universal History" (four volumes, 1880-5), of which over 100,000 sets have been sold in United States alone. Among his other works of large sales, is his "Life of James A. Garfield" (1881-2), and of "James G. Blaine" (1884).

PROMINENT EDUCATORS.

Elisha Benjamin Andrews, educator, born in Hinsdale, N. H., January 10, 1844. Served during the civil war in First Conn. heavy artillery as private, non-commissioned officer, and second lieutenant from 1861-4 and then studied at Powers Institute, Bernardston, Mass., and at Wesleyan Academy, Wilbraham, and Brown University, graduating from last in 1870, and next two years was principal of Connecticut Literary Institute, Suffield, Conn. Then studied theology at Newton Theological Institution and ordained pastor First Baptist Church, Beverly, Mass., 1874. In 1875 he was president of Denison University, Granville, Ohio, and 1879 professor of homiletics in Newton Theological Institute, Newton, Mass. In 1882 he was elected professor of history in Brown University, and in 1888 elected professor of political economy at Cornell University and in 1889 elected the eighth president of Brown University, where his administration has been eminently successful, in the increase of the faculty, in added numbers of students and enlarged and new buildings and other generous and timely gifts by friends stimulated by his earnest zeal and sterling educational qualities. He was given the honors of LL.D. by University of Nebraska in 1884 and that of D.D. by Colby University the same year.

Samuel C. Armstrong, educator, born in Maui, Hawaii, January 30, 1839. His father, Rev. Richard Armstrong (missionary), was minister of public instruction in that kingdom, and the son studied at Oahu College, and in 1860 came to United States and entered Williams College, where he graduated in 1862, and after graduation joined the army as captain in the 125th N. Y. regiment volunteers, and served to the close of the war, being mustered out as brevet brigader-general, November, 1865, he having commanded for two and one-half years, a regiment of colored troops. In March, 1866, was sent by General O. O. Howard to Hampton, Va., to care for the thousands of colored people, lately slaves, there gathered, and where he established the now famous Hampton Normal and Agricultural Institute, for people of color of both sexes, which is conducted on an undenominational self supporting basis, at a cost per student of $166 per year. The school has fixed property of a value of $600,000, and planing and saw mills, printing office, shoe shops, knitting rooms, laundries, etc., with over 1,000 students (350 being in the primary department), gathered from thirteen states and territories, and 100 teachers and assistants. Of the 700 boarding students some 150 are Indians, and the remainder negroes, nearly half being young women. The United States Government contributes $167 each toward the expenses of the Indian students. The state of Virginia makes an annual grant of $10,000 toward the education of the negroes, who earn yearly about $50,000 by work on the campus and farm, and the yearly deficit of $60,000 has thus far been made up by the voluntary contributions of friends of the institute throughout the country. It has already sent out nearly a thousand negro teachers to the Southern states to those of their color, and nearly four hundred Indians to the West, and is one of the most unique and markedly successful educational institutions of the land, built, developed, and sustained mainly by the untiring industry and faith of its founder, and his charitable friends.

Henry Drummond, educator, author, born in Sterling, Scotland, 1840. His father was judge of the courts and he was educated at schools in his native town and at the University of Edinburgh, and after his graduation he visited Germany and studied at the University of Tubingen, and on his return pursued a theological course at the Free Church Divinity School at Edinburgh and was ordained to the ministry and went to the Island of Malta as pastor of the Mission chapel there, where he remained for a time. In 1873 he became greatly interested in and assisted D. L. Moody in his revival work in Scotland. In 1877 he became lecturer in science at the Free Church College in Glasgow and engaged in home mission work in that city. He then traveled with Prof. Geikie to the Rocky Mountains and to South Africa, in scientific research, and in 1883 went to Central Africa on behalf of the Lake Navigation Company and made further researches in geology and botany and in that year published his celebrated treatise, "Natural Law in the Spiritual World," a reproduction of addresses to students and workingmen, which at once attracted great attention and much criticism and has been translated into various languages of Europe, and has already passed through more than forty editions in English. In 1884 he was elected professor of science in Free Church College and in 1887 again visited the United States, giving a course of lectures at Mr. Moody's school, that were afterward embodied in his "The Greatest Thing in the World" of which over 300,000 copies have been sold. He then went to

Australia on invitation to lecture there, and in 1888 published "Tropical Africa," that, like his other productions, has had a very large sale, and in 1893 he again visited the United States. Prof. Drummond, as he is generally known, not only regularly addresses from week to week 600 or more students from his college, but has large audiences of laboring men in the "Workingmen's Mission" of Glasgow, to whom he regularly discourses. He has been given the titles of F. R. S. E., F. G. S., and LL.D., and is greatly honored throughout the Christian world.

Timothy Dwight, educator, born in Northamptom, Mass., May 14, 1752, died in New Haven, Conn., January 11, 1817. His father was a lawyer, and merchant of Northampton, and his mother, Mary, third daughter of Rev. Jonathan Edwards. He fitted for college at a private school at Middletown, Conn., and entered Yale at thirteen and graduated with but one rival in point of scholarship. For two years he was principal of Hopkins grammar school in New Haven and then for six years was tutor at Yale and studied law, and for a year he served as chaplain in the Continental Army in Parson's brigade Connecticut troops, but the sudden death of his father, in 1778, obliged him to return for the care of the family at Northampton, at which place he remained five years carrying on the farm, teaching a private school, and preaching. In 1782 was a member of the State Legislature, but refused a nomination as congressman, and in 1783 accepted a call to a church in Fairfield, Conn., where he established an academy for both sexes, and became the pioneer of the higher education of women, putting them on the same studies and basis of his male students, and proposed, agitated, and secured the union of the Congregational and Presbyterian churches in New England, and when Dr. Stiles died in 1795 he was called to the presidency of Yale College, and held the office till his death. He effected many changes in the administration and curriculum of the college, trebled the number of students, and wrote and published many volumes, one of which, his "Theology," has gone through more than a score of editions in this country, and over one hundred editions abroad, gaining him great reputation as a theologian. In addition to a wide range of books, he also wrote poems and hymns, that beginning "I love thy kingdom, Lord, the house of thine abode," being now found in all collections of sacred hymnology. Of his eight children, the third, James, is the father of the present Timothy Dwight, D.D., LL.D., the twelfth president of Yale College (where his grandfather had been the eighth), and who, during his incumbency, has seen the school grow to its present magnificent proportions, its increase in new buildings, in numbers of students, in enlarged development of courses of study, and munificent endowments exceeding that of any of his predecessors in the office, nearly two millions of dollars having been given to the college since he succeeded Dr. Noah Porter as president on July 1, 1886.

Charles William Eliot, educator, born in Boston, Mass., March 20, 1834. His father, Samuel Atkins Eliot, was an eminent merchant of that city; its mayor in 1837-9, filled the unexpired term of Robert C. Winthrop when he was elected to the United States Senate, 1850-1, and was treasurer of Harvard College 1842-53, for which institution he was fitted at the Latin school of his native city, and was graduated in the Harvard class of 1853. The following year he was appointed assistant professor of mathematics, and gave himself to the study of chemistry. In 1858 was made assistant professor of chemistry and mathematics, and in 1861 professor of chemistry in the Lawrence Scientific school of the college. Two years later he went to Europe for study of chemistry and to investigate the educational institutions of that continent, and while at Vienna was chosen in 1865 professor of analytical chemistry to Massachusetts Institute of Technology, which post he filled for a period of four years and again went to Europe and spent fourteen months in further investigation, mainly in France. In 1865 the election of overseers of Harvard College was transferred from the Legislature of the State of Massachusetts to the graduates of the college and Dr. Thomas Hill having resigned the presidency, Mr. Eliot was in 1869 chosen to that office, which he has since filled. During his administration many notable changes in the government of the college have occurred, its scope has broadened and a great increase in the number of its professors and students is seen, while its wealth by gifts and benefactions has greatly increased, so that now it successfully competes with the great European universities in its curriculum. Mr. Eliot was given the honors of LL.D. by Williams and Princeton Colleges in 1869 and by Yale in 1870, and is an honored member of many scientific and literary bodies, and has written and, in connection with Professor F. H. Storer, published two excellent manuals on chemistry, besides other notable productions, and is recognized as among the chief educators of his time.

James Ferguson, astronomer, born near Keith in Banshire, England, in 1710, died in London, 1776. His father was very poor, working as a day laborer, who taught his children to read in the evenings, and James learned by hearing the others. His early life was one of hard toil and many privations. When a lad he worked as shepherd for farmers; made models of spinning wheels and mills with a pocket knife, and taught himself portrait painting, and mastered arithmetic without a teacher. Studied algebra, and made himself a terrestrial globe and a wooden clock, and having seen a gentleman's watch afterward made one himself; he constructed a celestial globe, and made important observations and discoveries in astronomy while living a life of great hardship and many sufferings through ill-treatment by some of his employers. At length he was employed by Sir James Dunbar, and at Sir James' sister's suggestion began drawing patterns for ladies dresses at which he earned some money and began to copy pictures with pen and ink, and showed such skill that he was induced to go to Edinburgh to study painting; being too poor to take lessons he studied by himself from living subjects at the suggestion of Rev. Dr. Keith and for twenty-six years was an excellent portrait painter. Meanwhile he pursued his favorite study of astronomy and being shown an orrery by Professor Maclaurin he made some for sale and then went to London to study mechanics and astronomy, and on showing proof of a new truth (that the moon must move always in a path concave to the sun) to Mr. Folks, president of the Royal Society he was brought before that body, and began soon after in 1748 to give public lectures on astronomy that were largely attended by both the nobility and common people, and he now abandoned his portrait painting for lecturing and wrote a number of astronomical treatises that were translated into foreign languages and gained him a distinguished reputation, and was given a pension by George the Third. He was made a member of the Royal Society in 1763, the fees being remitted because of his peculiar eminence, as in the case of Isaac Newton and Thomas Simpson, and he furnishes like the latter a striking example of a literally self-educated man.

Friedrich Wilhelm August Froebel, educator, and founder of the *Kindergarten* (i.e. children's-garden) system of schools, born Oberweissbach, Germany, April 21, 1782, died in Marienthal, Germany, June 21, 1852. His father, a parish clergyman, attended to his parish but not to his family, and the mother dying in Froebel's infancy, the sensitive, thoughtful child suffered from neglect and afterward from a stepmother's rigor, until his mother's brother gave him a home with him for some years at Stadt-Ilen, and where he went to school and passed for a dunce. At fifteen was apprenticed to a forester and in his solitary rambles in the dark Thuringian forest for two years, he observed and studied Nature and her God. Longing for knowledge of Nature's laws, he with great difficulty got permission to attend the University of Jena, and at the end of a year was imprisoned there nine weeks for a debt of thirty shillings, and ended his university education. Then he toiled at farming. His father dying when Froebel was twenty years old, he was left to shift for himself and for three and one half years drifted about to various places trying various things. Then for two years he worked delightedly in a model school conducted after Pestalozzi's system, and from 1807–9 was at the chief school of Pestalozzi near Neufchatel, Switzerland. Served in the Prussian army in campaign of 1813 and next year was curator of Museum of Mineralogy at Berlin under Professor Weiss. In 1816 he went on foot to Griesheim, spending his very last groschen on the journey for food, and there set up his school. Two years later it was removed to Keilhau, a Thuringian village, which became the Mecca of the new system. Here he married, and in 1826 published his book, "Education of Man" (from birth to seventh year). He also published for two years a weekly paper in interest of his system. His wife died in 1839 and his school closed for lack of funds. Some years after he again married and the Duke of Meiningen giving him the use of his mansion at Marienthal he established (1848) a normal school for young ladies, conducted on his system. But the freedom he allowed was considered dangerous and his schools denounced as nurseries of socialism and atheism, and the program of the school of his nephew, Karl Froebel at Hamburg, coming to the attention of the *cultus-minister*—Raumer—he issued an edict forbidding schools to be conducted in Prussia "after Friedrich and Karl Froebel's principles." Friedrich thus misunderstood and suppressed did not long survive the hard blow and was buried at Schweina, a village near Marienthal.

William R. Harper, educator, born in New Concord, Ohio, July 23, 1856. He was studious and fond of reading from his childhood and was educated in the public schools and at Muskingum College in his native town, and was graduated from the latter institution when but fourteen years of age. He then spent three years of study at home, mainly of languages and reading the literature of the German, French, Latin, and Greek classics. Was inclined to music as a profession, but upon advice of parents and friends went to Yale College, where he pursued further the study of languages taking Sanscrit with Professor Whitney, Hebrew with Professor Day, and Greek Gothic with Professor Carter, and at the end of two years received the degree of

Ph.D., being then nineteen years old. At his graduation acting on the advice of Professor Whitney he turned his attention to the Semitic and other Oriental languages in which field his success has since been so marked. After leaving Yale he was employed as teacher in Macon College, Macon, Tenn., and the following year he accepted the professorship of Latin and Greek in Denison University, Granville, Ohio, where he remained three years, and January, 1879, took the chair of Hebrew at the Union Baptist Theological Seminary, Morgan Park, Ill., where he took up and pursued the theological course of that institution, taking the degree of B.D., and began the teaching of Hebrew through the correspondence school, mailing the first lessons, mainly to clergymen, in February, 1881, broadening the work at the institution of the Summer School in Chicago the following July by the introduction of the cognate tongues, the Syriac, Arabic, Aramaic, and Assyrian. The works soon grew until now some thousands of educated men throughout this country are regularly pursuing the study of the Semitic tongue. To facilitate the work Professor Harper established "The American Publication Society of Hebrew," the most important of its early issues being works of his own preparation. Of their value an eminent authority, Professor T. K. Cheyne of Oxford University, England, says, "No better books introductory to Hebrew exist;" they have been introduced into more than sixty institutions of the country. In connection with Professor Paul Haupt of Johns Hopkins University, and Professor Hermann L. Strack of Berlin, Germany, he established the *Hebraica Quarterly*, and edited the monthly journal, the *Old Testament Student*, and conducted the Chautauqua School of Languages with its dozen different tongues, and has projected and issued a series of text-books in Latin and Greek. In 1886 he was called to the professorship of the Semitic languages in Yale College, and in 1892 was called to the presidency of the new Chicago University, Chicago, Ill, where he now resides, and is known on both sides of the Atlantic as one of the foremost scholars of the age.

Mark Hopkins, educator, born in Stockbridge, Mass., February 4, 1802, died in Williamstown, Mass., June 17, 1887. Educated in the public schools and academies at Lenox, Mass., and at Clinton, N. Y., and entered Williams College in 1820, and graduated valedictorian in 1824. He then became tutor in the college in 1825-7 and studied medicine at the Berkshire Medical School at Pittsfield, Mass., and New York city, graduating in 1829, and began practice in the city of New York. In 1830 he was called to the chair of Moral Philosophy and Rhetoric at Williams College and took up the study of theology and was licensed to preach in 1832. In 1836 he was elected president of Williams College, succeeding Rev. Dr. Edward D. Griffin, and became professor also of Moral and Intellectual Philosophy, and pastor of the College Church, and in 1858, taking the professorship of Christian Theology also; and retained the presidency until 1872, when he resigned it and continued his professorship and retained the pastorate of the College Church till 1883. During his sixty-two years' connection with Williams College it grew from humble conditions to be a strong and widely known institution and of the more than seventeen hundred and sixty graduates at the time of his death he had himself taught all of them except thirty. He was given the title of D.D., by Dartmouth College in 1837 and by Harvard in 1841; LL.D., by University of State of New York in 1857, and by Harvard College at its 250th commencement in 1886. President Hopkins was considered one of the foremost teachers of the century, particularly of Moral Science and Philosophy and has embodied his views in his books, "The Law of Love and Love as Law," or Christian Ethics (1869) and "An Outline Study of Man" (1873), which together with his "Lectures on the Evidences of Christianity," delivered before the Lowell Institute and published (1846, new edition 1864) have been extensively used as college text-books throughout the country, his theory of morals having been trenchantly criticised by Dr. James McCosh, to whom President Hopkins made reply. Beside the above works he published "Essays and Discourses" (1847), "Moral Science" (1862), "Baccalaureate Sermons" (1863), "Strength and Beauty" (1874), "Scriptural Idea of Man" (1883), "Teachings and Counsels" (1884).

Mary Lyon, educator, born in Buckland, Mass., February 28, 1797; died in South Hadley, Mass., March 5, 1849. Her father died when she was very young, leaving the family in straitened circumstances. Studied at district schools, and in 1814 taught such school at Shelburne Falls at a salary of seventy-five cents a week, and saving the money she was able three years later to enter as a pupil the Sanderson Academy in the adjoining town of Ashfield, where she studied twenty hours a day, committing to memory Adams' Latin Grammar in three days, and excelling all her classmates. Three years later (1821) she took a further course at the school of Rev. Joseph Emerson at Byfield, Mass., and in 1824 studied chemistry at Amherst, Mass., under Professor Eaton, and then for three years taught at the Adams Female Academy at Derry,

N. H., and during winter vacations teaching at Ashfield and in her native town. From 1828-34 she taught in a girls' school at Ipswich, Mass., and then for two years gave herself to raising funds to found the Mt. Holyoke Female Seminary, laying the corner stone October 3, 1836, and opening the institution the following autumn and served as its president till her death, instructing more than three thousand young women, many of whom became missionaries and teachers in all parts of the world. Her seminary was largely on a self-supporting plan, the students doing work as well as study, the charge for board and tuition being $60 a year. She never would take from the institution anything but board and $200 salary a year, one half of which she gave away to missions and charities. In 1888 the seminary was granted a charter as college, and its early plan has been copied and followed in various parts of the world, and has done more to advance the education of woman than any other institution ever established.

Horace Mann, the great educator, was born in Franklin, Mass., May 4, 1796, and died in Yellow Springs, Ohio, August 2, 1859. His father was a small farmer in very limited circumstances, too poor to even buy the schoolbooks, so that when but a child Horace braided straw for hats in order to earn them. He dreamed even then of a college education, but from ten years of age till twenty he never had more than six weeks of schooling in any year. He said of his instructors in the little district school that they were "very good people but very poor teachers," and of himself, "The poverty of my parents subjected me to continued privations. I believe in the rugged nursing of toil, but she nursed me too much. I do not remember the time when I began to work. Even my play days —not play *days,* for I never had any, but my play *hours*—were earned by extra exertion, finishing a task early to gain a little leisure for boyish sports." When he was thirteen, his father died. Still he toiled early and late, for that education, and at last entered a year in advance and worked his way through Brown University when 23. Then he tutored there a year in Latin and Greek, and the next year entered the law school at Litchfield, Conn., and in 1823 was admitted to the bar and began practice at Dedham, Mass. Was elected to Legislature in 1827 and continued to represent Dedham till his removal to Boston in 1833, where he had Edward G. Loring as his law partner, and is said to have gained four fifths of all his many cases in court, because it was known that he would never undertake an unjust cause. Was elected to State Senate in 1833 and president of that body 1836-7, and from 1837 to 1848 was the secretary of the Massachusetts Board of Education. So eager was he that the poor might have advantages in youth that were denied to him that while the secretary he gave his time wholly to that one cause, working regularly fifteen hours a day and never having a vacation, unless when in 1843 he went to Germany at his own expense, to see how he might improve our school system. He obtained many beneficial changes in the school laws, had established normal schools for training teachers, instituted county conventions, "school registers," published reports of local committees and by his influence banished corporal punishments in school discipline, and did more by securing enactments, by giving gratuitously legal advice and aid, by writings and lectures, to advance the cause of common school education than any other man. In 1848 was elected to Congress to fill vacancy caused by death of John Quincy Adams, and then fought slavery as vigorously as he had fought intemperance, lotteries, and other evils in the Massachusetts Legislature, giving during that session twenty-one successive days to the defense of Messrs Drayton and Sayres, who had been indicted for stealing seventy-six slaves in the District of Columbia. During the session he had a sharp controversy with Daniel Webster for advocating the Fugitive Slave law, and at next nominating convention was defeated by Webster by one vote, but he ran as independent and anti-slavery candidate and was re-elected. In 1852 was nominated for governor of Massachusetts by Free Soil party and defeated, and same year elected president of Antioch College, Yellow Springs, Ohio, carrying that institution successfully through serious financial and other difficulties, and bringing on his death by his untiring labors in its behalf.

Miss Maria Mitchell, astronomer, born in Nantucket, Mass., August 1, 1818, died in Lynn, Mass., June 28, 1889. She was the daughter of William Mitchell, the well known astronomer, from whom she inherited her scientific tastes. In childhood she showed remarkable talent for mathematics and astronomy, and at an early age assisted her father in his investigations, while studying with him. She studied afterward with Professor Charles Pierce, and assisted him in the summer school in Nantucket. For many years she was librarian of the Nantucket Athenæum. She was a regular student of astronomy and made many discoveries of comets and was known as a fine student of the nebulæ. On October 1, 1847, she discovered her first, of a small comet, and on that occasion received a medal from the King of Denmark and one from the Republic of San Marino, Italy. When the

"American Nautical Almanac" was established, she became a leading contributor and her work on that periodical was continued until she was chosen astronomer in Vassar College, Poughkeepsie, N. Y. In 1858, she visited the chief observatories in Europe, and while abroad formed the acquaintance of Sir John Herschel, Sir George B. Airy, Le Verrier and Humboldt. Returning to United States, she was given a large telescope, contributed by the women of this country, headed by Miss Elizabeth Peabody of Boston. In 1865 she began work as professor of astronomy in Vassar College and continued it until 1888, when failing health compelled her to resign; the trustees, however, not willing to accept the resignation, gave her a leave of absence. She made a specialty of studying the sun's spots and the satellites of Saturn and Jupiter. She received the degree of LL.D., from Hanover College in 1852, and from Columbia College in 1887. She became a member of the American Association for the Advancement of Science in 1850, and was made fellow in 1874, and was the first woman elected to the Academy of Arts and Sciences. She was prominent in the councils and associations for the advancement of women, serving as president of the American society in the convention held in Syracuse, N. Y., 1875, and in Philadelphia, Pa., in 1876. She wrote much, her published works being mainly restricted to scientific subjects. The secret of her success in life may be best set forth in her own words: "I was not born with much genius, but with great persistency."

Eliphalet Nott, educator, born in Ashford, Conn., June 25, 1773; died in Schenectady, N. Y., January 29, 1866. Early left an orphan and cared for by a brother. In youth taught school to get means for college course. Graduated at Brown University, 1795, then studied theology and licensed to preach by New London Association of Congregational churches, and sent to wilds of New York as missionary, and established academy and church at Cherry Valley. During 1798-1804 he was pastor of First Presbyterian Church, Albany, N. Y., and in latter year elected president of Union College, and during his incumbency 4,000 students were graduated, and shortly before his death he gave the institution a half million dollars of property. Was an ardent advocate of anti-slavery and other reforms and took out some thirty patents for inventions in heating, the most noted being that of the first stove ever made for burning anthracite coal and which bore his name and was widely used. While he did not found he did almost make Union College.

Francis Wayland, educator, born in New York city, March 11, 1796, died in Providence, R. I., September 30, 1865. His parents were of English birth (the father a currier by trade), and they came to this country in 1792, where the father, soon after his arrival in New York, was given a license to preach in the Baptist ministry, and soon gave himself wholly to that work. The son was fitted to enter the sophomore class in Union College, at the Dutchess County Academy, at Poughkeepsie, N. Y., and graduated at Union in 1813, and began the study of medicine for three years. During this term of study he experienced religion, and, feeling himself called to the ministry, he entered Andover Theological Seminary in the fall of 1816. After a year at this institution he became tutor at Union College for four years, and August 21, 1821, was ordained pastor of the First Baptist Church, Boston, Mass. Here he at once took high rank, not for grace of delivery or fervent oratory, but as an earnest and deep student, and two especially of his sermons attracted wide attention to him as a man of scholarly attainments, one on "The Moral Dignity of the Missionary Enterprise," being translated into many languages. After five years he accepted the professorship of Moral Philosophy in Union, but resigned the following February (1827), to become president of Brown University, which office he filled for twenty-eight years with great credit to himself and profit to the university, taking at once a foremost part in educational reform, and seeking to advance his college to his high ideal; many new buildings and much of its present efficiency being the result of his labors. He was a voluminous writer, and of his seventeen volumes of published works, the three text-books, "Moral Science," "Intellectual Philosophy," and "Political Economy," have now reached a sale of over 200,000 copies. After his retirement from the presidency of Brown in 1855, he served for a year and a half as pastor of the First Baptist Church in Providence, and then devoted himself to literary work, and to religion and humane endeavor, giving much time to the inmates of the reform school, and the Rhode Island state prison.

Andrew Dickson White, educator, born in Homer, N. Y., November 7, 1832. Father in business in Syracuse and wealthy. Mr. White was educated in schools of Syracuse and at Hobart College and at Yale University, graduating from the latter in 1853. He then spent two years in study at Paris and Berlin, and visited many historical sites, and served six months as attache of the American Mission at St. Petersburg and returned home in 1856. He then spent a year at Yale in historical studies and in 1857 was elected professor of history and English literature in Michigan University, resigning in 1862 because of impaired health

SUCCESSFUL MEN AND WOMEN.

and again visited Europe for six months. In 1863 and 1864 he was state senator from his district, and introduced a bill for codifying school laws, creating a new system of normal schools and, with Ezra Cornell, established (with the United States land granted to his native state) at Ithaca a new university on an enlarged plan, known as Cornell University, and he was chosen as its president and professor of history and visited Europe to buy its books and apparatus and served as president till failing health compelled his retirement in 1885.

President White contributed to the institution a valuable historical library of 30,000 volumes, 10,000 valuable pamphlets, and many manuscripts, costing him over $100,000 in addition to a gift of $100,000 in money. In 1871 he served as commissioner to San Domingo at the request of General Grant, and from 1879 to 1881 was United States minister to Germany. He is the author of numerous works mainly of an historical nature, and has been given honorary degrees by Yale, Columbia, Cornell, Michigan University, and Jena.

LEADING STATESMEN

Nathaniel Prentiss Banks, statesman, was born in Waltham, Mass., January 30, 1816. He attended the public schools of his native town but little, having, when a lad, to contribute to the support of the family by working in the cotton mill in which his father was one of the operatives. He afterward learned the machinist trade, and then gave his evenings and leisure time to the study of politics and law, and practiced public speaking at the local lyceum and at temperance gatherings and party rallies, and then became editor of the village paper. Later for a time during President Polk's administration he was given a position in the custom house at Boston, and, patiently continuing his self-education in law, he was at length admitted to the bar, and, after six unsuccessful attempts, he was elected in 1849 representative to the state legislature, and making a notable speech on slavery was re-elected in 1851 and 1852, and the latter year chosen speaker of the House. In 1852 he was elected representative to Congress by American Democrats, but separated from his party (Democrat) on the slavery question. He was president of the convention called to revise the state constitution in 1853, and 1854 was returned to Congress by the Republicans and "Know-Nothings," and again in 1856, when, after an exciting contest of two months, he was chosen speaker of the House on the one hundred and thirty-third ballot. In 1857 he was elected governor of Massachusetts, and again in 1858 and 1859, and in 1860 succeeded Capt. G. B. McClellan as president of the Illinois railroad. May, 1861, he was appointed major-general of volunteers, and assigned to command of fifth army corps, distinguishing himself at battles of Winchester and Cedar mountain, and then was in command of the forces for the defense of Washington. In December, 1862, he succeeded Gen. B. F. Butler in command of the department of the Gulf at New Orleans, and July 9, 1863, took Port Hudson. Early in 1864 he conducted the unsuccessful expedition up the Red river, undertaken against his advice, and was relieved from command in May, 1864, and resigned from the army, and in that year was chosen representative to Congress from Massachusetts, and served four terms, but advocating the election of Horace Greeley for president in 1872, he was himself defeated for Congress, but was returned again as representative from his district by the Republicans in 1874 and 1876. In 1878-9 he was United States marshal at Boston, Mass., and was returned to Congress again in 1888.

James Gillespie Blaine, United States secretary of state, was born at Indian Hill farm, West Broomsville, Pa., January 31, 1830, of Scotch-Irish ancestry. As the schools were then poor, the father attended to James's education until the age of eleven, when he was sent to a select school at Lancaster, Ohio, taught by William Lyons, an Oxford (England) graduate. Two years later, entered Washington College; was graduated in 1847 at the age of eighteen, sharing with a fellow student the first honors of the class. After graduation, Mr. Blaine was for three years instructor at Western Military Institute, in Kentucky. Returned to Pennsylvania and entered upon the study of the law. Next took a position as teacher in the Pennsylvania Institution for the blind, remaining until 1854. Removed during this year, to Augusta, Me.; bought a half-interest in the *Kennebec Journal* and soon, as editor, made himself felt in state politics. Before thirty years of age, was chosen chairman of the executive committee of the Republican organization in Maine. Was a delegate to the first national Republican convention in 1856. Was made state inspector of prisons and reformatories. Was a member of the Maine legislature 1859-1862, and in the last two years was speaker of the House. Was elected to Congress in 1862, and was member of the House of Representatives afterwards, until 1872. During his career in the House, was second to none as debater, and as leader of the party. Was secretary of state under Garfield. Was three times balloted for, as presidential candidate. In 1884-86 published his "Twenty Years of Congress."

SUCCESSFUL MEN AND WOMEN.

Upon President Harrison's accession in 1889, Blaine returned to the secretaryship. As statesman he was energetic and outspoken, as an orator, brilliant and magnetic, and as a man, of generous and manly character. His death occurred in 1893.

Grover Cleveland, twenty-second president of the United States, was born at Caldwell, Essex county, N. J., March 18, 1837. In 1841 the family removed to Fayetteville, N. Y., where the boy received his first schooling, and was clerk in a country store. Obtained further instruction in Clinton, N. Y., so that at seventeen he was appointed assistant teacher of the New York Institution for the Blind. In 1855, read law with the firm of Rogers, Bowen, and Rogers, in Buffalo; in 1859 was admitted to the bar. January 1st, 1863 was appointed assistant district attorney of Erie county. In 1869, joined the law firm of Lanning, Cleveland & Folsom. Was successful and popular; in 1870, was elected sheriff of Erie county, and held office three years. At the close of the term, joined with a Mr. Bissell in forming the firm of Cleveland & Bissell, meeting with wider popularity and success. In 1881, was elected mayor of Buffalo, and in 1882, governor of New York. July 11, 1884, was nominated for president of the United States. Was elected, and inaugurated March 4, 1885. President Cleveland resolutely stood for the protection of the Indians against any encroachments on their territory; insisted that no removals of office-holders, excepting heads of departments, foreign ministers, and other officers charged with the execution of the policy of the administration, should take place without cause. After retiring from public life, Mr. Cleveland resumed law-practice in New York city; besides doing an extensive business in New York courts, was frequently called to Washington to argue important causes before the Supreme Court. Mr. Cleveland was re-elected in 1892, and holds office at the present time.

Henry Laurens Dawes, legislator, born in Cummington, Mass., October 30, 1816. Spent his boyhood on a farm, was educated in public schools and fitted for college and graduated at Yale in 1839. After graduation he taught school for a time and then edited the Greenfield, Mass., *Gazette*, and later the Adams *Transcript*. He in the mean while continued the study of law and was admitted to the bar in 1842 and was elected member of the Massachusetts House of Representatives in 1848-9, and of the Senate in 1850. Again a representative in 1852 and a member of Constitutional Convention of Massachusetts in 1853. District attorney for Western District from 1853-7 and elected representative to the thirty-fifth and succeeding Congresses to the forty-fourth, when he declined a re-election to the House and was chosen United States senator, succeeding Charles Sumner in 1875 and continuing to serve as senator until his retirement from public life in 1893, when notable receptions were given him by his political associates and friends at Boston, Springfield, and at his home at Pittsfield, Mass. During his remarkably long and successful public life, Mr. Dawes originated and carried through many most important measures, such as the system of Indian education, the making Indians citizens and subject to civil laws, the completion of the Washington monument, the severalty, Sioux, and many tariff measures, the *Weather Bureau Bulletin* bill in 1869 (at the suggestion of Prof. C. Abbe). He was during his congressional career one of the leading and most valuable members of Congress, and served as chairman or member of all its important committees, and there are but few if any persons who have rendered such long and valued public service in this country as has he.

George Franklin Edmunds, senator, was born at Richmond, Vt., February 1, 1828, son of a farmer. Received education in the common schools and from a private tutor. At an early age began to study law, was admitted to the bar in 1849, and began practice in Richmond. Two years later removed to Burlington, where the legal talent of the state was concentrated. Soon won pronounced success at the bar, and began also to take decided interest in politics. From 1854 to 1859, represented the Republican party in the Vermont legislature, serving as speaker of the House for three years. March 1866, was appointed by the governor of the state to supply the vacancy in the Senate, caused by the death of Solomon Foot, and subsequently to fill the unexpired term, ending March, 1869; since that time has been successively re-elected four times, taking an active part in all important proceedings. Assisted by Senator Thurman, originated and carried through the Senate, the Pacific railroad funding act. After Mr. Arthur assumed the duties of president, Senator Edmunds was made *pro tempore* president of the Senate. March 22, 1882, introduced a measure for the suppression of polygamy in Utah. In 1866 was delegate to the Loyalists' convention held in Philadelphia. Originated the act passed in 1886, prescribing the manner of counting the presidential electoral votes; and in the same year was a leader in the Senate in the effort to force President Cleveland to show cause for recent removals from office, and furnish all necessary documents bearing on the case. Retired from public life, in 1891. Is quick at repartee, a man of fine parts, and much learning, and possessed of great penetration of mind.

SUCCESSFUL MEN AND WOMEN.

Edward Everett, statesman, orator, born in Dorchester, Mass., April 11, 1794; died in Boston, Mass., January 15, 1865. His father was a clergyman, and Edward was educated in public schools. Entered Harvard College when thirteen, and graduated with the highest honor of his class in 1811. The following year he was appointed tutor at Harvard, and studied theology, and in 1813 was ordained pastor of Brattle Street (Unitarian) Church, resigning at end of thirteen months to accept the professorship of Greek at Harvard, having already won much fame as an orator while in the ministry. He now went to Europe for two years of study at Gottingen, and spent some months afterward in travel, returning in 1819, and filled the chair at Harvard for five years, and then was elected to Congress from his Cambridge district, and served ten years as congressman, being pro-slavery in his sentiments. In 1835 he was elected governor of Massachusetts, and annually re-elected till 1840, when he was defeated by one vote. As governor he sought ineffectually to suppress speech and printing against slavery in the commonwealth. In 1841 President Harrison appointed him minister to England, and in 1845 he was chosen president of Harvard College, which post he held for three years, and resigned, and when Daniel Webster died in 1852 he was appointed secretary of state by President Fillmore, and before the close of the administration was elected, 1853, United States senator to succeed John Davis, and resigned because of ill health in May, 1854. After the recovery of his health he gave himself to the work of raising funds for the purchase of Mount Vernon, giving his lecture on Washington over one hundred and fifty times, and the proceeds of all lectures to that object. He also wrote a weekly article (for one year), to New York *Ledger* for $10,000, which Mr. Bonner also paid to the Mount Vernon Association. In all Mr. Everett raised over $100,000 for that purpose. In 1860 he was nominated for vice-president of United States on the ticket with John Bell of Tennessee, and on the breaking out of the civil war espoused the Union cause, and became a member of the Republican party, and headed the list of electors for President Lincoln in 1864. He was a member of learned societies in Europe and in this country, and was given the highest literary honors by several of the English universities.

James Abram Garfield, twentieth president of the United States, was born November 19, 1831, at Bedford, O., son of a farmer who died while the sons were quite young. James worked on the farm until offered a position as canal driver at $12 per month; this was carried on for a time, when an accident occurred endangering his life. Soon afterward attended the Chester high school, and after two terms found employment as a teacher. In 1850 returned to the Chester seminary. Studied at Hiram, O., and in three years' time prepared for college; entered Williams College, remaining until 1856, when he left for Hiram College; became teacher of ancient languages and literature in this institution, and afterward president. The latter office was abandoned in 1859, upon being elected to the Ohio State Senate. Had in the mean time carried on the study of law. During the senatorial term, secession made its appearance, and upon the commencement of hostilities, Garfield entered upon military life, as colonel of the forty-second Ohio regiment. Did excellent service in many important battles of the war, among them Shiloh, Chattanooga and Chickamauga. December 5, 1863, resigned his commission and returned to political life, soon becoming known as a powerful speaker, delivering speeches upon the confiscation of rebel property, upon a constitutional amendment abolishing slavery, and other important issues. Held various responsible positions, as chairman of the committee on banking and currency, chairman of the committee on appropriations, etc. In 1880 was elected state senator from Ohio for a term of six years. In the Republican convention of 1880, Mr. Garfield was nominated for the presidency. March 4, 1881, was inaugurated. July 2, 1881, while on the way to attend the commencement exercises of Williams College, was assassinated in the Baltimore and Potomac station at Washington, by Charles J. Guiteau and after many weeks of acute suffering death relieved him September 19. President Garfield was a many sided man; as a political leader, brilliant and dashing, possessing great eloquence and powers of debate; and as a man, of sound moral character and strong conviction.

Benjamin Harrison, twenty-third president of the United States, and born at North Bend, O., August 20, 1833, was early placed under private instruction at home. Was sent, in 1847, to a school on College Hill, a few miles from Cincinnati. After two years of preparatory work, entered the junior class of the Miami University, Oxford, O., where he was graduated in 1852. Studied law under Storer and Gwynne, was admitted to the bar in 1854 and began practice at Indianapolis, Ind. Earned his first money as crier of the federal court, at $2.50 per day. Formed a law partnership with William Wallace. In 1860 was chosen reporter of the Supreme Court of Illinois. When the civil war began, assisted in raising the 70th Indiana regiment and became second lieutenant. Returned to the practice of law when peace was declared, and became a leader at the Indiana bar. During

SUCCESSFUL MEN AND WOMEN.

the war, his military record was most creditable, receiving warm commendation from General Hooker, and receiving also the commission of brevet brigadier-general. In 1880 was chairman of the Indiana delegation in the Republican national convention. Was United States senator from Indiana, 1881 to 1887. At the Republican national convention of June 19, 1888, received the nomination to the presidency, was elected in November, and inaugurated March 4, 1889. During the administration, the Behring sea difficulties were adjusted by arbitration; the Pan-American congress held, and by the means, better feeling was produced between the powers represented, and commercial interests promoted; the McKinley law was passed; six new states were admitted to the union (North Dakota, South Dakota, Washington, Montana, Idaho, Wyoming), Oklahoma was opened to settlement, the Indian uprising in the West was quelled with but little bloodshed, and the navy was strengthened by the accession of thirteen new armored vessels.

Abraham Lincoln, sixteenth president of the United States, was born in Hardin county, Kentucky, February 12, 1809. Early education from books was scanty and fitful; he secured the reading of the few books in the settlement, and became known as a hungry reader. First glimpse of the world was afforded in 1828, when he went on a flatboat to New Orleans. In 1830, moved to Decatur, where splitting rails, breaking ground, and doing manual work for anyone who would hire him, busied the president-to-be. In 1831, took charge of a trading-post in New Salem, Ind., where unflinching honesty gained for him the title "Honest Abe" so frequently heard afterward. During all this time, Lincoln was an earnest student of the newspapers, and all other printed matter that came within reach. In 1834, was elected to the legislature, and was returned the following year. In 1837, removed to Springfield, Illinois, and began the practice of law in a modest way; remained in this position until elected to the presidency in 1860. Was elected to Congress in 1846. In 1854, occurred the Lincoln-Douglas debates, in which Lincoln's speeches excited such general interest. June 17, 1860, Lincoln was nominated for president, and elected. Directly following this event, began the secession of the Southern states, and this proceeded until the disaffected states had an organized army and had used every means to arouse Lincoln to resistance, in which all devices failed until Fort Sumter was fired upon, April 12, 1861. Then Lincoln issued a call for 75,000 men. Upon the battle of Bull Run, in July, 1861, followed the long and terrible war that purchased, at so dear a cost, the freedom of an oppressed people, and the final union of the North and South. During this crucial period, the president, though beset by criticisms and complaints, steadily adhered to the course dictated by his judgment and innate conviction of right. September 22, 1862, he issued the emancipation proclamation. November 19, 1863, Lincoln gave the brief address at the battlefield of Gettysburg, which has a permanent place in literature. The second inauguration took place March 4, 1864. Soon afterward the surrender of the Southern army took place. April 14, 1865, at 10.30 P. M., the president was assassinated at Ford's Theater, by John Wilkes Booth, and died April 15, 1865. Few men have lived so worthily and been so sincerely mourned when removed by death as Abraham Lincoln.

Charles Sumner was born in Boston, Mass., January 6, 1811, son of a lawyer of the same name. Was a quiet boy, of a studious bent, became a pupil of the Boston Latin school at eleven, with Wendell Phillips, Robert C. Winthrop, James Freeman Clarke, and others who became distinguished in later years. Excelled in the classics, in general information and in essay writing, but was not considered especially brilliant. Just upon leaving the Latin school for college, he heard President John Quincy Adams speak in Faneuil Hall, and Webster's eulogy upon Adams and Jefferson. September, 1826, entered Harvard, was among the best scholars in classics, history, forensics and belles lettres, but failed entirely in mathematics. Was graduated in 1830, and devoted himself to study and extensive reading; listened to the Boston orators, Webster, Everett, Choate, and Channing. September 1, 1831, entered Harvard Law school, and took up the work enthusiastically; had no apparent ambition except to learn all that was possible, and led a life pure in word and deed. Slavery agitation had by this time begun. In April, Sumner went for the first time to Washington. September, 1834, was admitted to the bar. Was appointed commissioner of the circuit court, and began to teach in the law school during Judge Story's absence. Went to France in 1837, and visited Italy, Germany and England before returning. From 1841 to 1848 was engaged in writing upon public issues, and interested also in prison reform and popular education. Was elected to the Senate in 1850. Here he stood as the uncompromising opponent of slavery, hated and feared alike by the opposition. May 19 and 20, 1856, Sumner delivered a speech which roused the country and by certain personal allusions, led to his being maltreated by P. S. Brooks, a representative from South Carolina. This injury necessitated an absence of nearly four years; on December 5, 1859, returned to the Senate. In 1861, following the secession of the Southern states, Sumner was made chairman of the committee of foreign affairs. During the years between this date and his death, March 11, 1874, Sumner took an active part in public affairs. Both parties acknowledged his sterling worth and great mental endowments.

GREAT STATESMEN.

John Adams, second president of the United States, was born in Quincy, Mass., October 31, 1735, the son of a farmer. It was the custom of the family to send the eldest son to college; accordingly, John was graduated at Harvard in 1755. After taking his degree, took charge of a grammar school at Worcester. In religion was a free-thinker, and adopted the law in preference to the pulpit as a vocation, beginning practice in 1758, in Suffolk county, with his residence at Braintree. Was prominent in the resistance to the Stamp Act. In 1768 removed to Boston. In 1770, served as counsel for Captain Preston and the seven soldiers, at their trial for murder after the Boston massacre. In 1770 was elected as representative to the legislature. Was one of the five delegates from Massachusetts to the first Continental Congress, and afterward chosen member to the Revolutionary Provincial Congress of Massachusetts, convened at Concord. Proposed Washington as commander-in-chief of the Continental Army. By the 15th of May, 1776, Adams was able to carry through Congress a resolution that all the colonies should be invited to form independent governments. June 12, Congress established a Board of War and Ordnance, with Adams as chairman. In 1777, was sent as a commissioner to France. In 1779 was made commissioner of peace to Great Britain; a treaty was signed in 1783. Was minister to Holland in 1780, and by his efforts that country recognized (April 19, 1782) the independence of the United States. Was vice-president under Washington; and was elected president in 1796. After retirement from public life, passed twenty-five years at his home in Quincy, dying July 4, 1826. Among American public men there has been none more upright and honorable.

John Quincy Adams, sixth president of the United States, was born in Braintree, Mass., July 11, 1767. Accompanied his father to France and was sent to school near Paris, where his proficiency in the French language and other studies became conspicuous. In August, 1870, accompanied his father to Holland; after a few months in school at Amsterdam entered the university of Leyden. Two years afterward, Francis Dana, secretary of legation, was appointed minister to Russia, and the boy accompanied him as private secretary. Soon afterward, traveled alone through Sweden, Denmark, and northern Germany, to France. Returned to the United States in 1785, and was graduated at Harvard College in 1788. Studied law, and was admitted to the bar in 1791. In 1794, was sent as minister to Holland, being transferred, two years later, to Portugal. Before his departure for the latter country, John Adams, Sen., became president of the United States, and the son was sent as minister to Berlin. In 1798, made a commercial treaty with Sweden. When Jefferson became president, Adams resumed the practice of law; but in 1802, was elected to the Massachusetts Senate, and next year to the United States Senate. Was concerned in the embargo which was laid upon all the shipping in American ports, and for this position Mr. Adams was subjected to much political unpleasantness. On Madison's election, was made minister to Russia, remaining during the entire administration. In 1814, the treaty of Ghent was signed. Was appointed to conclude a new commercial treaty with England, and this was completed July 13, 1815. Upon arriving in London, May 26, received news of his appointment as minister to England. Was secretary of state under Monroe; was elected president upon the latter's retirement, in 1825. Was president for one term, and, upon retirement, was elected to Congress in 1831, remaining in that body until his death, which occurred February 23, 1848. Mr. Adams was a strong anti-slavery man, and supported his convictions without fear or favor.

James Buchanan, fifteenth president of the United States, was born near Mercersburg, Pa., April 23, 1791. Was educated at a school in his native town, and at Dickinson College, Pennsylvania, where he was graduated in 1809. Began to practice law in 1812; in October, 1814, was elected to the House of Representatives, Pennsylvania legislature. Was elected to Congress in 1820, and remained in the House ten years. Was minister to Russia in 1832, and the mission was successful. Was secretary of state under President Polk. Was minister to England in 1853, under Franklin Pierce, and rendered valuable service. Was chosen to the presidency in 1856, and inaugurated March 4, 1857. While in office he conducted the affairs of the country with prudence and wisdom, and left them in a more hopeful condition than he found them. Many have condemned the policy employed by him in

SUCCESSFUL MEN AND WOMEN.

reference to the states which became disaffected during the administration, but it must be conceded that great injustice was done him, and that loyalty to the Constitution and zeal for the welfare of the Union marked his action. He died June 1, 1868.

Millard Fillmore, thirteenth president of the United States, born February 7, 1800, in Locke (now Summerhill), Cayuga county, N. Y. Working for nine months on the farm, and attending the primitive schools then existing, for the remaining three months, he had an opportunity of forgetting in the summer all that was learned in the winter. Never saw even a map of his own country, until nineteen years of age. Was apprenticed to the business of carding wool and dressing cloth, but remained only a short time, returning home on foot, for a distance of about one hundred miles through the primeval forests. In 1815, resumed the business; and purchased a small English dictionary, which he studied while tending the carding machine. In 1819, began the study of law. Began practice in 1823, as attorney in the court of common pleas; won his first case and a fee of four dollars. In 1827 became counselor of the supreme court of the state. Was afterward partner with N. K. Hall, and Solomon G. Haven, and had a very extensive practice. Served three terms in the New York state legislature, beginning with 1828. Went to Congress in 1832, and was twice re-elected. Retired from Congress in 1843, and was candidate for vice-president. Was comptroller of the state of New York in 1847. In 1848 was elected vice-president, being the seventh furnished by the state of New York. President Taylor died July 9, 1850, and Fillmore succeeded him. During his administration the fugitive slave-law was passed. We are indebted to him for cheap postage, for the extension of the national capitol, for the Perry treaty with Japan, and various valuable exploring expeditions. He was a man inflexibly set for the defense of the truth at whatever cost; willing to be convinced, ready to be advised; possessed a well-balanced mind and a keen sense of justice, while no man who ever held a similar position of trust could show a cleaner record than he. Died March 8, 1874, aged seventy-four.

Benjamin Franklin, printer, scientist, statesman and diplomat, was born in Boston, Mass., January 17, 1706. Son of a tallow chandler; was the seventh of ten children. When eight years old, was sent to grammar school, being intended for the church, but after a year was taken out and soon set to work in the chandlery. Finally, not being successful at those vocations that had been tried, he was apprenticed to a printer. Made good progress, and became acquainted with many good books, which interested him greatly. In 1721, James Franklin began to print the New England *Courant*, third paper published in the United States, and Franklin, the younger, carried the papers through the streets, sometimes even contributing to it. In consequence of a quarrel, left Boston and went to New York, thence to Philadelphia, where he found employment. Went to England when but eighteen years old and worked for one Palmer, a famous printer of London, and afterward with Watts, another printer. October 11, 1726, was once more in Philadelphia and engaged in the printing business; this was carried on for twenty years with good pecuniary profit. Showed an active interest in journalism, science and education. Invented the open "Franklin stove." About 1746 became interested in electricity, and in 1752 made the experiment of the kite which has made his name famous. Franklin became known to every reading person in the old world; and was made a member of the Royal Society. At about this time, too, he became interested in public affairs and in 1757 was sent abroad as a diplomat, to the English court; and later was sent a second time, remaining until May 5, 1775. During a term as envoy to France, the Treaty of Paris was signed in February, 1778. Franklin's long and preeminently useful career closed with his death, April 17, 1790.

Thomas Jefferson, third president of the United States, was born in Shadwell, Albemarle county, Va., April 2, 1743, of Welsh ancestry. His education was well advanced when the father died, leaving him at the age of fourteen, practically without master or guide. In 1760 entered William and Mary College, Williamsburg, Va., and is described as being a tall, raw-boned, freckled, sandy-haired youth, shy and unattractive. Was an earnest student and a fine violinist. Chose the law as a vocation, and at twenty-four was admitted to the bar; gained plenty of cases and handled them in such a manner as to win high praise. In 1769 was elected member of the house of burgesses of which Washington was also a member. By the close of the year 1774, Jefferson's name was among the first of the patriotic leaders. Was one of the committee of thirteen to arrange a plan of defense. Prepared the first draft of the Declaration of Independence. Succeeded Patrick Henry as governor of Virginia, and was re-elected. Was elected to Congress in 1783. For four years held office as minister plenipotentiary at the court of France. In November, 1789, returned on leave of absence, to the United States, to find that he had been appointed by President Washington to the office of secretary of state. Was vice-president of the United

States in 1796. In the election of 1800 was made president. After retiring from office spent the remainder of his days in the effort to secure for Virginia a complete system of education. Died fifty years after the signing of the Declaration, July 4, 1826.

James Madison, fourth president of the United States, was born in Port Conway, Va., March 16, 1751. Education began at an excellent school kept by a Scotch master; preparatory studies were taken at home under tuition of Rev. Thomas Martin, clergyman of the parish. He was graduated at Princeton in 1772, and took one year of post-graduate work in Hebrew. Returning home, was busied with history, law, and theology, and with teaching the younger members of the family. His character was so well known and generally admired, that when the committee of safety was organized, in 1774, Madison became the youngest member; and in 1776 was chosen delegate to the state convention. Was one of the special committee to make the state constitution, and the one to make in it definite provision for entire religious liberty. In 1780, was delegate to the Continental Congress. Was instrumental in bringing about the convention at Philadelphia, at which a scheme of rational state and national government was set forth and with some modifications adopted, transforming our government from a loose confederacy of states to a federal nation. He was elected to the first national House of Representatives. In 1799 Mr. Madison was again elected member of the Virginia assembly; and in 1801 became secretary of state. At the expiration of Jefferson's second term, was elected president of the United States; and was re-elected in 1812. In 1817, at the close of his second term, retired to Montpelier, where he spent nearly twenty happy years with books and friends. As a scholar and a profound, constructive thinker, Madison had few equals. Died June 28, 1836.

James Monroe, fifth president of the United States, was born in Westmoreland county, Virginia, April 28, 1758. Was sent to William and Mary College, but not long after the beginning of his student life, the Revolutionary war broke out. Young Monroe enlisted, as lieutenant of the third Virginia regiment, under Col. Hugh Mercer. Was in the battles of Brandywine, Germantown, and Monmouth. Monroe's civil life began with election in 1782, to a seat in the Virginia assembly. Was next a delegate to the fourth, fifth, and sixth congresses of the confederation. Was envoy to France in 1794, and in 1801, during the last period, by the joint efforts of Monroe and Robert R. Livingston, the vast region then known as Louisiana was ceded to the United States. Monroe was twice governor of Virginia, once in 1799, once in 1811. Was secretary of state under Madison, remaining in this office for six years; in 1814-15 was secretary of war, also. In 1816, was elected president, and in 1821 was re-elected. During the administration, Florida was secured to the United States, and this term of office was also made prominent in the public mind by the "Monroe doctrine," the purport of which was resistance to foreign interference in American affairs. At the close of his second term as president, retired to private life, residing for the remaining seven years of his life, at Oak Hill, Virginia, and in New York city. Died July 4, 1831.

Martin Van Buren, statesman, born in Kinderhook, N. Y., December 5, 1782, died there July 24, 1862. Father a small farmer. He was educated in the public schools of his native village, where he studied also a little Latin and when fourteen entered the law office of Mr. Francis Sylvester and for seven years patiently labored as office boy, lawyer's clerk, copyist of pleas; extemporaneous debater and incipient politician at eighteen, and came at length to be a special pleader in constables' courts, and then when twenty years old went to New York city and studied law with William P. Van Ness, the friend of Aaron Burr, and was admitted to the bar in 1803. Returning to Kinderhook he associated himself in practice with his half-brother, James I. Van Alen. In 1808 became surrogate of Columbia county. In 1812 he was chosen to the state Senate and in 1815 was chosen attorney-general, served again as state senator in 1816, and in 1821 elected to the Senate of the United States, and was re-elected in 1827, but resigned the office to accept that of governorship of his state, to which position he was chosen in 1828. In 1829, secretary of state in cabinet of Andrew Jackson, and in 1832 he was elected vice-president of the United States, on the ticket with Andrew Jackson, and at the close of General Jackson's eight years administration, he was chosen president and entered upon that office March 4, 1836. His administration was made notable by the precipitation into it of the questions of finance and of slavery, the first coming by the "panic of 1837," and the latter by the entrance of slavery as an issue in party politics, by the nomination of a candidate for president by the Abolitionists. He was renominated in 1840 but defeated by the Whig candidate, William Henry Harrison. His name was again proposed in 1844, but James K. Polk secured the nomination and was elected. In 1848 he accepted the nomination of the Free Soil party for the presidency and his candidacy resulted in the election of General Z. Taylor to that office. He now retired from politics and continued in the

SUCCESSFUL MEN AND WOMEN.

practice of law, and made a tour of Europe in 1853-5 and in 1857 wrote his "An Inquiry into the Origin and Course of Political Parties in the United States."

George Washington, first president of the United States, was born near Bridges Creek, Va., February 22, 1732, son of Augustine Washington. Learned reading, writing, and arithmetic in a district school. At the age of sixteen took up land surveying; when but nineteen years old, was a district adjutant general, and showed great ability. On May 10, 1755, was appointed aid-de-camp to General Braddock, and was present at the battle of Fort Duquesne. August 14, 1755, was made commander of a body of 2,000 men, but the reduction of Fort Duquesne terminated the military career of Washington for a time. Three months later took a seat in the house of burgesses, remaining in that body for some years; during this time the stamp act came up for consideration, and Washington, hitherto loyal to the crown, opposed it. June 15, 1775, was made commander-in-chief of the Continental army, on a salary of $500 per month. The conduct of the army under Washington is too well known to need a detailed description. Peace was proclaimed by Congress, January 30, 1783. Washington received the notification of election to the presidency of the United States, April 14, 1789, and was inaugurated, April 30 of same year. Was re-elected in 1793. He died Dec. 14, 1799.

Daniel Webster, secretary of state, was born at Salisbury, N. H., January 18, 1782. Early years were spent on a frontier farm, and early instruction came from his mother. After a year's preparation at Exeter Academy, was sent to Dartmouth College at the age of fifteen. Was a fine student, had a wonderful memory and a keen intellect. At eighteen was selected by the villagers of Hanover to make their annual Fourth of July oration. While a student, devoted more than twelve hours a day to study. Taught school during the college course to eke out an income. On graduation, in 1801, began the study of law, but to aid his brother, Ezekiel Webster, became principal of an academy at Fryeburg, Me., at a salary of $350. Studied law again in the office of Christopher Gore, in Boston. Was admitted to the bar in 1805. In 1808 had acquired extensive practice. In 1812 was elected to Congress, and at once took first rank as debater and practical statesman. In 1816 removed to Boston. Served as representative in the eighteenth Congress, and was elected again in 1823, and 1826; elected to the Senate in 1827. Was secretary of state under President Harrison, in 1841, and under President Tyler in 1843. Perhaps no man born in this country ever impressed his own generation with such a sense of intellectual greatness as did Mr. Webster. He died at Marshfield, Mass., October 24, 1852.

STATESMEN AND JURISTS.

Samuel Adams, born in Boston, Mass., September, 27, 1722. The father, Samuel Adams, was a man of wealth and influence, always a leader; was justice of the peace, deacon of the old South Church, selectman and member of the legislature. Young Adams was educated first at Boston Latin School, then at Harvard, from which he was graduated in 1740. Entered the counting-house of Thomas Cushing; shortly after, received from Samuel Adams, Sen., a gift of a £1,000, wherewith to set up an individual business. Became partner in a brewery business, having lost his own capital, and, at the father's death, carried it on entirely. In 1765, was elected to the legislature. In 1774, arranged for the first meeting of the Continental Congress; and, with John Adams, was delegate. Probably no other man did so much to bring about the Declaration of Independence; he supported the federal constitution, in 1788. Was lieutenant-governor of Massachusetts in 1789, and governor from 1794 until 1797. In all the struggles of the colonies against British oppression, Adams, always brave and tactful, stood at the head. He died October 2, 1803.

Salmon Portland Chase, statesman and jurist, born in Cornish, N. H., January 13, 1808. Was named for an uncle; was the eighth of eleven children of Ithamar Chase, a farmer. When Chase was eight years old, the family moved to Keene; Salmon was sent to school at Windsor, and made good progress in Latin and Greek. In 1820, went to live with an uncle, the bishop of Ohio; spent three years there, attended school, and in 1824 entered Dartmouth as a junior, and was graduated in 1826. At once established a classical school for boys, in Washington, D. C., at the same time studying law with William Wirt. Was admitted to the bar in Washington in 1830, settled in Cincinnati, where he obtained a large practice. In politics did not identify himself with either of the large parties, but was from the first firmly opposed to slavery. When the Liberty party was organized, in 1841, was one of the founders. In 1849 was elected to the United States Senate; in 1855 was elected governor of Ohio; was secretary of the treasury under Lincoln in 1861; in 1864 was appointed chief justice of the United States. In June, 1870, he suffered an attack of paralysis, and from that time until his death was an invalid. Died in New York city, May 7, 1873.

David Dudley Field, jurist, born in Haddam, Conn., February 13, 1805; died in New York city, April 13, 1894. His father was a Congregationalist clergyman, and David was the eldest of his ten children. He was educated at the private school his father taught, and at Williams College, graduating at twenty, the leading scholar of the class of 1825. He then studied law, and was admitted to the bar in 1828, and continued in active practice till 1885. In 1836 he went to Europe and studied the codes of law in England and France, returning in 1837 to his practice, and began to agitate the question of revising the codes in this country, and in 1850 the legislature of New York adopted his Codes of Criminal Procedure, which has since been adopted by nearly all of the other states, and also to a great extent in England and other countries. In 1857 was chairman to prepare for New York a political, penal, and civil code designed to supersede the unwritten or common law, which was completed in 1865, but his state did not adopt the civil code owing to a protest of the Bar Association, but they were adopted entire by California and Dakota. In 1866 he brought before the meeting at Manchester, England, of the British Association of Social Science, a project to reform the law of nations, and was one of a committee of eminent jurists of different nations appointed for that purpose, and seven years later he presented to the Social Science Congress his "Outlines of an International Code," that was translated into French, Italian, and Chinese, which produced an association to reform and codify the laws of nations, and to substitute arbitration for war among the nations of the earth, of which he was made the first president, because, as an eminent chancellor of England said, "David Dudley Field, of New York, has done more for the reform of laws than any other man living." He was an ardent opponent of slavery. Was a brother of Cyrus W. Field of Atlantic cable fame, and acknowledged to be one of the greatest lawyers of the century.

Alexander Hamilton, statesman, born in the island of Nevis, West Indies, January 11, 1757. Parentage uncertain; education was brief and desultory, seeming mostly due to the Rev. Hugh Knox, a Presbyterian clergyman of Nevis, who took great interest in the boy. Before the latter was thirteen years old, he was placed in the office of Nicholas Cruger, a West Indian merchant; showed remarkable precocity; business letters are preserved that would have done credit to a trained clerk of any age, and the employer was wont to go away leaving this mere child in charge of all the affairs of his counting-house. Hamilton also wrote for the local press; was sent by relatives and friends to New York in 1772, found friends and went by their advice to a school in Elizabethtown, New Jersey, where college preparation was made. Entered King's now Columbia College, making rapid progress. Meantime affairs with England were becoming troublesome, and on July 6, 1774, at a field meeting, Hamilton made his first political address, and soon after published two pamphlets, which attracted general notice, being attributed to John Jay and other eminent patriots, but, on discovery of their authorship, the writer became at once a political leader. In 1776, commanded a company of artillery; and soon afterward became one of Washington's staff. Was elected to Congress in 1782, and led a stirring public life during his term and the difficult times succeeding it. In 1789 was made head of the treasury department under Washington. Resigned in 1795, after doing excellent service in the cabinet, and began again the practice of law. During the difficulty concerning the Jay treaty, Hamilton supported Washington to the utmost. During the election when Jefferson was nominated for president, a disagreement arose between Aaron Burr and Hamilton which ultimately led to a duel between them in which the latter was killed; this occurred in July, 1804. Time has only enhanced the fame of Hamilton as a writer and statesman; and has made more apparent his great services to the government of our country; probably no one man has done more than he to secure our permanent institutions.

Joseph Roswell Hawley, statesman, born in Stewartsville, N. C., October 31, 1826, of English-Scotch ancestry; prepared for college at the Hartford grammar school, and at the Cazenovia (N. Y.) Seminary; was graduated at Hamilton in 1847, with high reputation as a speaker and debater. He taught during the winters, studied law at Cazenovia and Hartford, and began practice in 1850; became chairman of the Free-soil committee. The first meeting for the organization of the Republican party met in his office, February 4, 1856. In February, 1857, became editor of the Hartford *Evening Press*, the new distinctively Republican paper. Is said to have been the first volunteer in the state of Connecticut; and raised the Company A, First Connecticut Volunteers, of which he was captain. Did good service in battles of Drewy's Bluff, Deep Run, Derbytown Road, and others. In November, 1864, commanded a picked regiment sent to New York to keep peace during the election. Was brevetted major-general, and mustered out January 15, 1866. In April, 1866, was elected governor of Connecticut.

SUCCESSFUL MEN AND WOMEN.

Having united the *Press* and the *Courant*, resumed editorial life, and entered more vigorously than ever into political discussions. Was president of the National Republican Convention in 1868. Was elected to Congress five times. Is one of the most acceptable orators in the Republic; an ardent Republican, and a believer in universal suffrage.

Sam Houston, the president of Texas, was born in Rockbridge county, Vt., March 2, 1793, of Scotch-Irish descent. The father died and the family moved to Tennessee, settling near the Cherokee territory; the son received little education; was adopted by one of the Indians and spent much time among them. In 1813, enlisted in the seventh United States infantry, soon becoming a sergeant; for bravery in the battle of Horseshoe Bend, was made ensign; soon afterward second lieutenant and finally first lieutenant. Studied law in Nashville, in 1818; became district attorney and adjutant general of the state; in 1821 was elected major general; was sent to Congress in 1823 and re-elected in 1825; was elected governor in 1827, by an overwhelming majority. In 1832 visited Texas and not long after was made general of that section, and commander-in-chief of the army of Texas, which he immediately drilled and put in order for active service, should occasion demand. The Mexicans under Santa Anna invaded Texas soon afterward, but were met and routed by Houston at the head of the Texan forces. On October 22, 1836, he became first president of the Republic of Texas; was re-elected in 1841; in 1838 had taken the first step toward the annexation of Texas to the Union; this finally took place in 1845. When the state was carried for secession Houston refused to take the oath of allegiance to the Confederate states, and was deposed. He retired from public life, and died July 26, 1863.

Andrew Jackson, seventh president of the United States, born in the Waxhaw settlement on the border between North and South Carolina, March 15, 1767. Andrew Jackson, his father, came to America from Ireland, in 1765. The early years of the future president were passed in the home of an uncle; his education was very limited, never learned to write English correctly. In 1781 was apprenticed to a saddler. At the age of eighteen entered the law office of Spruce McCay, in Salisbury. Was much more skilled in sowing wild oats than in the practice of jurisprudence, but was nevertheless appointed public prosecutor for the western district of North Carolina. In 1796 Jackson was member of the convention assembled at Knoxville for making a constitution for Tennessee. The admission of this state to the Union took place in June 1796, and in the autumn Jackson was chosen as its one representative in Congress; in 1798, was senator; resigning in the same year, became judge in the supreme court of Tennessee. He was a great general, as was conclusively shown in the campaign against the Creek Indians in 1813, and the battle of New Orleans in 1814, also the campaign against the Seminoles, in 1818. In 1828 was elected president, having in some respects a stormy administration. Jackson died at his home, "The Hermitage," near Nashville, June 8, 1845.

William Henry Seward, secretary of state, and eleventh governor of New York, was born in Florida, Orange county, N. Y., May 16, 1801, of Welsh-Irish descent. At the age of nine years was sent to an academy at Goshen, N. Y., among whose pupils had been Noah Webster and Aaron Burr. Making rapid progress in his studies, was prepared for college at fifteen. Was received into Union College in 1816, was graduated with honors in 1820. Studied law in New York, with John Anthon, afterward with Ogden Hoffman and John Duer in Goshen. Was admitted to the bar in 1822. Removed, the following year, to Auburn, where he formed partnership with Judge Elijah Miller; had a large and lucrative practice, but turned to the study of political questions. Was one of the committee to welcome Lafayette. In 1830 was elected state senator, and in 1838 governor. In all questions regarding the disposition of fugitive slaves, Seward actively defended them, and procured the passage of an act giving them trial by jury, and counsel at the expense of the state. In February, 1847, was elected to the United States Senate. On the election of Lincoln, he was made secretary of state. In 1867 succeeded in completing the treaty with Russia by which Alaska was ceded to the United States for the sum of $7,000,000. In 1870 he began a journey round the world, accompanied by some of his family. Returning home, he wrote an account of these travels, which was published in 1873. Both in the United States and abroad, Mr. Seward was recognized as a statesman of great brilliancy and spotless integrity. He died October 10, 1872.

Morrison Remich Waite, Chief Justice of the United States Supreme Court, was born at Lyme, Conn., November 29, 1816, son of Henry M. Waite, who was twenty years justice of the superior court, and fifteen years justice of supreme court. The son was educated at Yale College, was graduated in 1837, classmate of William M. Evarts, Samuel Tilden, and other prominent men; studied law and was admitted to the bar in 1839; entered partnership with Samuel L. Young. The firm removed to Toledo, Ohio, in 1850, where it acquired a state reputation; Mr. Waite soon ranked second only to Allen G. Thurman, at the Ohio bar; was elected to Ohio Senate in 1849. In 1871, was selected, with Caleb Cushing and William M. Evarts, to represent the United States before the Geneva tribunal; his quiet but efficient services in this case eventually influenced President Grant to tender the position of chief justice; in 1874 he presided over the Ohio constitutional convention. Although little known outside Ohio, and doubted by the public, when established in office, his ability and judgment as a presiding officer won general approbation and respect. High character and purity of life lent weight to his decisions. Was made LL.D. by Kenyon College in 1874, and by Ohio University in 1879. Died at Washington, March 23, 1888.

EMINENT STATESMEN.

John Albion Andrew, statesman, lawyer, born in Windham, Me., May 31, 1818; died in Boston, Mass., October 30, 1867. His father was a merchant and the son received his education in the public schools and at Bowdoin College, where he graduated in 1837, and then studied law in Boston, being admitted to the bar in 1840, and taking a part in famous slave cases of Burns and Sims in 1850, he came into much renown, and detesting slavery he severed from his party (Whig), in 1848, becoming thereafter antislavery and then an ardent Republican, heading his party's delegation at Chicago in 1860, and was that year elected governor of his state by the largest majority ever given a candidate, and at once set about putting the militia of his state on a war footing, conferring with the governors of the New England states for a like purpose, and was able when President Lincoln issued his Proclamation of April 15, 1861, to dispatch troops at once, for the defense of Washington, the sixth Mass. regiment being the first to suffer the shedding of blood in the war by an attack from a mob while passing through Baltimore on its way to Washington. Governor Andrew was continued in office till 1866 and then refused further services and continued in the practice of law till his death. Because of his heroic service and intense patriotism during the civil war he is lovingly remembered by the citizens of his state as chief of those famous six "war governors," of those dark and trying years.

Thomas Hart Benton, statesman, born near Hillsborough, N. C., March 14, 1782, died in Washington, D. C., April 10, 1858. His father, who was a lawyer, died before Thomas was seven years of age, leaving several children of whom Thomas was the eldest. He attended public school and a grammar school for a time and also studied at Chapel Hill University, but did not graduate, having removed with the family to an extensive land grant of the father's in Tennessee, at what is now Bentonville He afterward studied law and was admitted to the bar in Nashville in 1811 and then served a term in the legislature, and among other reforms obtained the right of a trial by jury for slaves. In the war of 1812 he raised a regiment of volunteers and was aid-de-camp to General Andrew Jackson, their strong friendship being afterward broken by a melee with pistols and knives that darkened the future of both men. In 1813, he removed to St. Louis, Mo., and published a paper, and in 1820 was elected United States senator, which office he held to 1850, when he was defeated by the ultra slavery men of his party, and to break their ascendency in the party he ran as representative to Congress in 1852 and was elected, but was defeated at the next two elections and then he devoted himself to literary pursuits, writing the "Thirty Years' View," "Abridged Debates from Foundation of the Government to 1856," and a "Review of the Dred Scott Case." He was one of the "giants" in Congress, a determined opponent of Calhoun's doctrine, a tireless worker and secured many reforms in the interest of the Great West he delighted in. Of his four daughters the second became the wife Gen. John C. Fremont.

John Caldwell Calhoun, statesman, born in Abbeville district, S. C., March 18, 1782; died in Washington, D. C., March 31, 1850. His father, Patrick, was a native of Ireland, well educated, Protestant in religion, a surveyor by profession, a captain of a company in the frontier times, and for last thirty years of his life a member of the state legislature. He died when John was thirteen years old, and the lad was fitted for college by his brother-in-law, the Rev. Dr. Waddell, and entered Yale in 1802, and after graduation studied law at Litchfield, Conn., and was admitted to the bar in 1807, and the following year was elected member of his state legislature 1808-10, and from 1811-17 was a member of Congress, and the latter year became secretary of war in Monroe's cabinet, December 16, 1817, to March, 1825. He was elected vice-president of the United States by the Congress that elected John Quincy Adams president in 1824, and was re-elected vice-president in 1828, on the ticket with President General Jackson, and resigned in 1832, being that year elected

SUCCESSFUL MEN AND WOMEN.

United States senator, which position he held to March, 1843, and then was secretary of state 1844-5, in President Tyler's cabinet, and from 1845 till his death again United States senator. He was a man of unblemished character, rigid in his morals, simple and unpretending in his manners, of great intellectual force and attainments, honored and almost idolized by the people of his state, bold and fearless in spirit, and an earnest patriot and prince of political philosophers, however astray some of his views may be from the unfoldings of that Providence in history that has regard alone for righteousness. He was the great champion of that doctrine of "state sovereignty" that the civil war annihilated forever.

Lewis Cass, statesman, born in Exeter, N. H., October 9, 1782; died in Detroit, Mich., June 17, 1866. He was educated at the public school and at the academy of his native town, and when seventeen the family removed to Wilmington, where his father, who was major in the United States army, was temporarily stationed, and where Lewis taught school for a time. In 1800 his father settled near Zanesville, O., on land granted him for his services, and Lewis studied law in the office of Governor Meigs at Marietta, O., and in 1803 was admitted to the bar and began practice at Zanesville, and soon acquired a wide reputation as jurist and pleader. In 1806 he was a member of the legislature, and the next year appointed United States marshal of state by President Jefferson, retaining it till 1813. At the breaking out of the war of 1812 he was appointed colonel of the third Ohio regiment volunteers, leading the advance from Detroit into Canada, and was among those surrendered by General Hall, and being paroled, he, in great wrath, carried the first report of the surrender to the United States government. On being exchanged he was made brigadier-general, and took a brave part in the battle of the Thames, and at close of war was appointed governor of territory of Michigan, and explored five thousand miles of the Northwest, made twenty-two treaties with various Indian tribes, and created, organized, and set in motion the machinery of civilized government throughout an immense section of country. In 1831 General Jackson made him his secretary of war, and resigning during the second term because of ill health, he was sent to France as United States minister, and resigned in 1842, and was elected to United States Senate in January, 1845, and being put in nomination for president by the Democrats, he resigned his seat in 1848, but not being successful, was re-elected senator in 1849, and again re-elected in 1851, and then was appointed secretary of state by President Buchanan in 1857. During the preliminary secession movements of 1860 he was in favor of compromise, but resigned when Buchanan refused to reinforce Major Anderson at Fort Sumter, having completed a long term of fifty-six years of public service. During the civil war he sided with the Union, and had acquired much wealth through investments in real estate.

Henry Clay, statesman, born in "the Slashes" district, Hanover county, Va., April 12, 1777, died in Washington, D. C., June 29, 1852. His father, a Baptist clergyman, died when Henry was four years old. He attended a log cabin schoolhouse, and worked on a farm in his early years. Then his mother remarried and went to Kentucky to live, and when he was fourteen he was placed as errand boy in a small retail store at Richmond, Va., and a year later got a place in the office of the clerk of the Court of Chancery, and then was copyist for Chancellor Wythe and read law, and in 1796 studied for several months in the office of the attorney general, and in 1797 was admitted to the bar and removed to Lexington, Ky., where he soon acquired great fame in the conduct of criminal cases, and had an extensive practice. Was elected to the legislature in 1803 and in 1807 and 1808, being speaker of the House in the latter year. He also filled out an unexpired term of several months in the United States Senate in 1806-7 and again one of two years in 1809 and 1810 and at the expiration of this last was elected representative to Congress and chosen speaker of the House 1811-14 and was the leader in inciting war with Great Britain. Re-elected speaker in 1813, he resigned the following January to accept the position of peace commissioner with John Quincy Adams, James A. Bayard, Jonathan Russell, and Albert Gallatin, and as such signed the treaty of Ghent, December 24, 1814, and declining the mission to Russia was re-elected to Congress in 1815-21 and 1823-5, and was five times elected to the chair of speaker of the House. He was a candidate for president in 1824 and on the election of John Quincy Adams by the House he was appointed secretary of state 1825-9. He was then chosen United States senator in 1831 and served until March 31, 1842, and then again was senator in 1849-52. He was candidate for president in 1832, but was defeated by Jackson, and again in 1844 and defeated by Polk. He was noted during his long public life for his great eloquence, his advocacy of what he called "The American system" of a protective tariff, his championship of the South American Republics against European control, his opposition to but vacillating course with human slavery in the South, and his spirit of compromise with that wrong.

547

SUCCESSFUL MEN AND WOMEN.

Stephen Arnold Douglas, statesman, born in Brandon, Vt., April 23, 1813; died in Chicago, Ill., June 3, 1861. His father was a physician and died suddenly when Stephen was two months old, and the mother with her two children lived on a farm near Brandon, where he remained till fifteen, attending school during the winter months and toiling on the farm in summer. Then he set off for himself, and at Middlebury worked eighteen months at cabinetmaking and, abandoning it through ill health, studied a year at the academy at Brandon, and his mother remarrying and moving to the state of New York, he attended the academy at Canandaigua in 1832 and began the study of law, but the mother not being able to give him the long course required in that state he went west in 1833, and after vain wanderings to many places for employment he was at last stranded at Winchester, whither he went on foot, with just 37½ cents in his pockets. He got work as clerk for an auctioneer, and making a good impression as writer and accountant he taught some forty pupils for three months, and studied law at night and practiced before justices of peace on Saturdays, and the following March, 1834, obtained his license and began practice at Jacksonville, Ill., and was that year elected attorney general, but resigned in December of next year, being elected to the House, where he was the youngest member and where his small size in contrast with his mental force and activity led to his being called the "Little Giant," a name that followed him through life. In 1837 he was register of land office at Springfield, and the next year the Democratic candidate for Congress, but his opponent was declared elected by a majority of five votes, albeit some fifty of his were cast out, because his name was slightly misspelled. In 1840 he was appointed state secretary, and in Feb., 1841, elected judge of the Supreme Court. In 1843-6 he was a member of Congress, and from 1847 till his death was United States Senator from Illinois; his last senatorial canvass was made memorable by his joint discussion with Abraham Lincoln on the slavery question, each being then the acknowledged leader of his party in the West. He ran for the presidency in 1860, and received a popular vote of 1,375,157, as against Mr. Lincoln's 1,866,352. He was one of the most brilliant and able men of his day, and might have been president of the United States if he had not yielded to the demands of slavery upon him at a critical hour.

John Hancock, statesman, born in Quincy Mass., January 12, 1737; died there October 8, 1793. His father was a Congregationalist clergyman and died when the son was seven years old, and he was then adopted by his uncle Thomas, a wealthy merchant, who sent him to Harvard College, when he was thirteen and he graduated in 1754, and then was clerk in his uncle's counting house, and at his uncle's death in 1764 he succeeded to his business and inherited a large fortune. Two years later, when he was twenty-nine, he was representative to the General Assembly from Boston with James Otis, Samuel Adams, and Thomas Cushing as colleagues. After the "Boston Massacre" of March 5, 1770, he was chosen member of the committee to demand the removal of the troops from the city, and was selected to give an oration at the anniversary of that event the following year, when his fearless denunciation of the government gave great offense to the officials. In 1774 he was elected with Samuel Adams (the "Father of the American Revolution"), as a member of the Provincial Congress at Concord, Mass., and chosen its president, and the expedition to that town in April, 1775, that resulted in the battle of Lexington on the 18th, was undertaken to secure their arrest; but they escaped and on June 12 of that year General Gage issued a proclamation offering pardon to all the rebels of the colony save Samuel Adams and John Hancock, whose offenses called for "condign punishment." He was a delegate to the Continental Congress at Philadelphia from 1775 to 1780 and 1785-86, and was its president from May, 1775 to October, 1777, and the "Declaration of American Independence" it issued bore at first only his signature as president. Was major-general of the Massachusetts militia in 1776, and a member of the Massachusetts Constitutional Convention in 1780, and governor from that year to 1785 and then from 1787 was re-elected till his death. He was a learned man for his time, and intensely patriotic and liberty-loving, and, though the largest property owner of his city, publicly said, "Burn Boston, and make John Hancock a beggar if the public good requires it." His only son dying in youth, he gave his fortune to benevolent causes, including large gifts to Harvard College, who honored him with the title of LL.D.

Patrick Henry, statesman, born in Studley, Hanover county, Va., May 29, 1736; died in Red Hill, Charlotte county, Va., June 6, 1799. His father was a Scotchman of excellent education, and his mother a devoted Christian woman of Welsh origin. He attended a small country school till ten, and then was taught the classics by his father and an uncle who was a clergyman, and at fifteen became clerk in a country store for a year, and then the father set up an older brother and himself in such a store, but they were not successful. When eighteen he married Mary Shelton, daughter of a small farmer and tavern keeper, and their parents established them on a near-by farm

SUCCESSFUL MEN AND WOMEN.

to get their living, but after two years they failed of success, and selling his half dozen slaves and farm effects he invested in another country store and when twenty-three was again bankrupt, and then set about studying law, and when he applied for admission to the bar in 1760, the majority of the four examiners signed his license with great reluctance and after much entreaty and promise of future study and reading. And so the greatest orator of his time entered on his career. Three years later he distinguished himself by his plea in what was known as the "Parsons Cause," carrying his case with the jury by his eloquence, against law and equity, and then his practice grew immensely. In 1765, he was a member of the Virginia legislature, where his great speech (afterward sown with his seven resolutions broadcast through the colonies) was as General Gates declared "the signal for a general outcry over the continent," and he was thereafter one of the foremost of the country's statesmen, and a member of his state's legislature, till 1774, and then a member of the Continental Congress at Philadelphia, and the following March 23, 1775, made before his state convention that great speech of his life, ending with, "I know not what course others may take, but as for me, give me liberty or give me death." He was delegate to the Second Continental Congress, but left it in July, 1775, to become colonel of First Virginia regiment and commander of the forces of the province, resigning in February, 1776, and then was a delegate to the Virginia Convention again, and on the adoption of the state constitution on June 29 of that year, he was at once elected its first governor, and re-elected 1777, and 1778, and 1784, and 1785, and declining further service resumed the practice of law. President Washington tendered him the position of secretary of state and of chief justice of the Supreme Court, and President Adams that of minister to France, which he refused. He was one of the greatest and best of the great men of his day.

Thomas Brackett Reed, statesman, born in Portland, Me., October 18, 1839. He was educated in the schools of his native city, and at Bowdoin College, where he graduated in 1860, with honors. He then spent some three years in teaching, meanwhile studying law; and during the closing of the war, 1864-5, served as paymaster on a "tin clad," patrolling the Cumberland, Tennessee, and Mississippi rivers, and, on his discharge in 1865, resumed the study of law and was admitted to the bar, and in 1868 elected to the legislature, and re-elected the next year, and in 1870 elected state senator, and was then made attorney general, retiring from that office in 1873. He was then for four years solicitor for the city of Portland, and in 1876 was elected representative to Congress, and has since been continuously re-elected, and has gained much renown by his skill as a debater and parliamentarian, and is now the acknowledged leader of the Republican party in the House, and was elected speaker of the Fifty-first Congress, where his famous counting of a quorum gained him much *éclat*. Mr. Reed has also made some notable contributions to the current reviews, and is prominently mentioned as a candidate of his party for the presidency.

Alexander Hamilton Stephens, statesman, born near Crawfordsville, Ga., February 11, 1812; died in Atlanta, Ga., March 4, 1883. His father died when he was fifteen years old. He was very poor and feeble and sickly, and was given an education first by a gentleman of means in a school taught by the Rev. Alexander Hamilton Webster, and then by the Southern Presbyterian Educational Society, graduating from Franklin College (now Georgia State University) in 1832 with the highest honors, and he then taught school and refunded the expense of his education. He then studied law for two months, and July 22, 1834, passed a perfect examination and was admitted to the bar, and made $400 his first year of practice and lived on $6 a month, and soon had a large practice and afterward was able to buy back his father's old homestead. He was a member of the state legislature from 1836-41, and a state senator in 1842, and the next year was elected representative to Congress, where he remained till 1859, when he refused a re-election. In 1860 he made a great Union speech, and in 1861 voted against the secession of his state from the Union, and that year accepted the vice-presidency of the Confederacy, declaring slavery to be its chief corner-stone. At the downfall of the Confederacy he was confined for five months in Fort Warren, Boston Harbor, being released in October, 1865, on his parole. He was elected United States senator the next year, but not allowed to take his seat, and was elected representative to Congress from 1875-82, resigning in the latter year to become governor of Georgia, in which office he died, having for forty-five years held a foremost place in his state and nation, spite of his self-contradictions of conduct with speech before and during the civil war. He was noted among his acquaintances for his unswerving integrity, great resoluteness of spirit, and enlarged benevolence, he having educated at his expense more than a hundred young men, some of whom are now distinguished citizens of the country.

SUCCESSFUL MEN AND WOMEN.

John Winthrop, statesman, born in Edwardston, Suffolk, England, January 22, 1588; died in Boston, Mass., March 26, 1649. His father was a lawyer, and John entered Trinity College, Cambridge, at fourteen and when eighteen he was made justice of the peace, and married Mary Forth, a young lady of wealth, who died within eleven years leaving him six children; a second wife died after being married a year, and in 1618 he again married, Margaret Tyndall, daughter of Sir John, with whom he happily lived thirty-six years. In 1826 he was appointed an attorney in the court of wards and liveries under Sir Robert Naunton, and on October 30, 1629, was elected the governor of Massachusetts by the company in London, and June 22, 1630, arrived in Salem, Mass., with the charter and company and a fleet of eleven vessels, and soon after went to the site of and settled the city of Boston, and for twelve years he was governor of the Massachusetts colony, to wit: 1629-34, and 1634-40, and 1642-4, and 1646 till his death. He lived to see the Boston which he founded become a large and thriving town; Harvard College organized and incorporated; free schools established; and liberty, civil and religious, enjoyed beyond anything then elsewhere existing; and the state rapidly settled and prosperous; the beginning of the unexampled development, and freedom of the United States of America.

LEADING FOREIGN STATESMEN.

Francis Bacon, statesman, author, Viscount St. Albans and Baron Verulam, born in York house (Strand) London, England, January 22, 1561, died at Highgate, England, April 9, 1626; was youngest son of Sir Nicholas Bacon. Was frail of health, but very precocious when a child, educated at home by his parents and tutors, and entered Trinity College, Cambridge, when twelve years of age, where he remained three years and then went as an attache to English embassy to Paris, and traveled in that country, and his father dying (1579), he returned to England, and studied law, being admitted to the bar in 1582, and eight years later became a counsel extraordinary to the queen, an unexampled distinction to one so young, and awakened the envy of his uncle, Lord Burleigh, who considered him a rival to his son. In 1593, he became member of Parliament for Middlesex and the next year sought the vacant solicitorship but was thwarted by his uncle, and was given an estate at Twickenham, by the then very powerful Earl of Essex, which brought him about $9,000 a year. In 1597 he published ten noted essays. During Elizabeth's reign she would not promote him, alleging that his learning was "not very deep!" He was greatly in debt, was twice arrested for his debts, and twice sought to make a rich marriage and failed. He opposed the course of his friend Essex (Lord Lieutenant of Ireland while in that country), and appeared as counsel against him at his famous trial, thus proving himself, it is claimed, an ingrate. After Elizabeth's death, James made him solicitor general in 1607, and he married Alice Barnham, daughter of a wealthy alderman of London. In 1611 he became judge in knight marshal's court, and the next year attorney general and member of the privy council, and was guilty of torturing at the rack, after the custom of the time, an old clergyman, Peacham, to make him confess to treason in a sermon he never preached. He had now a large income of some $50,000 a year, and in 1616 he resigned the attorneyship and then two years later, in January, was made Lord High Chancellor, and raised to the peerage as Baron Verulam, and in 1621 was made Viscount St. Albans, and in April of that year was charged by his enemies with taking bribes in cases brought before him, and it is claimed that he, to save the honor of the king's court, confessed himself guilty of the twenty-eight charges, and was sentenced to a fine of $200,000, and imprisonment in the Tower during the king's pleasure, banished from court and declared unfit to hold office or sit in Parliament, but the king released him within four days thereafter, remitted his fine, pardoned the offenses, and he came again to court and was summoned to appear at the next Parliament as a member, but thereafter he lived in retirement on his income of $12,000 a year, devoting himself to literature and scientific research. He was one of the greatest of intellects that the world has ever known, the marvel of later generations, as he was the envy of his own times. His "Essays" and the "Novum Organum" are the best known of his writings. An edition of his works in sixteen volumes was issued in London 1825-34, and another in seven volumes, 1858-59, also "Letters and Life," seven volumes, 1862-74.

George Calvert (Lord Baltimore), statesman, born Kipling, Yorkshire, England, 1580, died in London, Eng., April 15, 1632. Graduated at Oxford College when seventeen years of age and became secretary to Earl of Salisbury and acted as attorney general for County Clare, Ireland. In 1617 he was made Sir Knight and in 1619 succeeded Sir Thomas Lake as secretary of state, and was one of the commissioners of the treasury in the following year, with an annual pension of $5,000, and the next year King James I. gave him a grant of 2,300 acres in County Longford, Ireland, and in

1624 he resigned the grant and his office on making a profession of the Roman Catholic religion. The king, however, retained him in his privy council, confirming the grants, and February 16, 1625, made him Baron Baltimore of Baltimore in the County of Longford, Ireland, and gave him a grant of Newfoundland, which he visited in 1625, and 1628 visited the settlements in Virginia, and then in 1632 he obtained a renewal of this Newfoundland grant enlarged to include what is now the states of Maryland and Delaware, the grant being issued by Charles I. to Lord Baltimore's son Cecil, January 20, 1632, and the grant was colonized by two others of his sons, George and Leonard, the latter of whom was the first governor of Maryland, the city of Baltimore taking its name from the founder of the colony, the second Lord Baltimore. Lord Baltimore's colony was distinguished for its principles of religious toleration, being one of the first instances of the kind on record.

Otto Eduard Leopold Bismarck-Schoenhausen, statesman, born in Schoenhausen, Brandenburg, Prussia, April 1, 1815; son of a nobleman, educated at Plamaun Academy, and Frederick William Gymnasium at Berlin, and at University of Gottingen, with a view to a life of jurisprudence; but he had little aptitude for study save history, and delighted in amusements and dueling, having twenty-seven of the latter while at Gottingen. When twenty-one he held a small law appointment in Berlin, and afterward in Potsdam, and at illness of his father took charge in 1839 of the family estates in Pomerania, where his rollicking, drinking habits gave him the appellation of "the mad Bismarck." At his father's death in 1845 he came into possession of Schoenhausen, and in 1847 married Johanna Von Puttkammer, and was that year elected member of the Prussian Landtag, where he at once gained notoriety by advocating extreme monarchical views and measures, and he bitterly opposed the "Revolution of 1848," "the Constitution of 1849," and "the parliament of 1850," and was the leader of monarchists in 1851, when he was made Prussian minister to the Frankfurt Diet; and the following three years went on missions to Vienna and Perth, and the south German states, imbued with his idea of securing Prussian supremacy in Germany. In 1859 he was appointed ambassador to Russia, where he remained three years, and then was sent, May, 1862, to Paris, as ambassador, but was recalled in September, to become minister of foreign affairs and president of King William II. cabinet, and not finding the parliament willing to adopt his measures, he in October closed the chambers, saying the king would get along without them, and treated the next four parliaments in the same way, punishing severely anyone who openly expressed dissent to such despotic measures. He reorganized the army, made government a military despotism, and forced the war with Denmark and later with Austria, and later yet with France, humbling each by turn, and at last secured the dream of his early manhood when in Versailles, France, on January 18, 1871, William II. was crowned Emperor of Germany, and he by his great success as "a man of blood and iron," became henceforth the idol of his countrymen, until what time history shall pronounce her final verdict. Since the consolidation of the Empire, his efforts have been mainly to promote peace among the continental powers. On the accession of William III. to the throne, his relations to that monarch became so strained that on March 20, 1890, he resigned and removed to Friedrichsruhe, where he continues to reside, a notable ovation having been given him on his late visit to the Emperor in 1894, a visit he made at the request of his sovereign.

John Bright, statesman, born in Rochdale (Lancashire), England, November 16, 1811; died in Rochdale, March 27, 1889. His family for generations were Quakers, and his father worked as weaver in a cotton mill at six shillings a week until two years before John's birth, when he bought an old cotton mill and began to amass a fortune for his eleven children, who as fast as they were old enough worked in the mill. John being of delicate health was sent to Friends' School at Ackworth, and later at York and Newton, and at sixteen began work in his father's factory. Gave his evenings and spare hours to reading, and writing speeches and rehearsing them to one of the workmen for his criticism, speaking on temperance, death penalty, church rates, and parliamentary reform, and took delight in reading books of travel, and having saved some of his earnings he went in 1833 to the Holy Land, Greece, and Egypt. In 1838 he took a prominent part in the anti-corn law movement, and the following year married and two years later his wife died, at which time Cobden visited him, and after words of condolence told him: "There are thousands of homes in England at this moment where wives, mothers, and children are dying of hunger. Now when the first paroxysm of your grief is past I would advise you to come with me, and we will never rest until the corn law is repealed," and thereafter he was known as the great reformer, and mightiest orator of his day. Was chosen to Parliament from the city of Durham in 1843–47, and then as a member from Manchester till 1857, and thereafter from Birmingham until his death. He was a most earnest advocate of free trade, of the repeal of the game laws, of the removal of Jewish disabilities, of freedom for Roman Catholics and Dissenters, of freedom for the press, and of the Irish disestablishment and land bills, and of the Indian and Parliamentary reforms, restricting House of Lords and extending suffrage. He opposed the Crimean war energetically, and constantly advocated the Union cause in the American civil war, held office under the Gladstone administration of 1868, resigned in 1870 because of ill-health, again a member of Gladstone's ministry in 1872, and again in 1880, resigning in 1882 because opposed to the bombardment of Alexandria, Egypt. His second wife, whom he married in 1849, died in 1878, leaving a family of seven children, all of whom survived him. His body was followed to its Quaker burial by an immense concourse of the working people for whom he had battled, and by great numbers of the titled and honored people of his land. His "Life and Speeches," with portraits, were published in 1884 (5 vols.).

Edmund Burke, statesman, born in Dublin, Ireland, January 1, 1730, died in Beaconsfield, England, July 7, 1797. His father was a lawyer. He graduated at Trinity College, Dublin, in 1748, Oliver Goldsmith being one of his fellow students. Two years later he went to London and studied law, but soon abandoned it for literature and when twenty-six published some essays that attracted much attention. From 1761-4 he was clerk for Hamilton, secretary to Lord Halifax, the lord lieutenant of Ireland, and the following year was appointed private secretary to the prime minister, Marquis of Rockingham, and in 1766 was a member of Parliament for Wendover, where his great eloquence at once made him famous and where for nearly thirty years (1766-94) he was one of the great figures, distinguishing himself by his masterly defense of the American colonies before and during the War of the Revolution, by his pleading for religious toleration and freedom, by his opposition to slavery, and by his great speeches at the impeachment trial of Warren Hastings, the first at the opening of that memorable seven years' trial, occupying four days in its delivery and the latter lasting over nine days. He was not only celebrated for his oratory, but was greatly distinguished for his sense of public justice, refusing when paymaster general, to make the office a source of private revenue, but sacrificed all its perquisites, and at his retirement from public service was given a vote of thanks by the House of Commons, and given at the request of the king pensions of $18,000 yearly. A new edition of his works was published in 1866. He is distinguished above all the men of his time for his power as orator, and his keen political forecast, and conversational gifts.

Marie Francois Sadi Carnot, statesman, born in Limoges, France, August 11, 1837, and is grandson of the great War Minister Carnot. Was educated at the Ecole Polytechnique as civil engineer. Became prefect of the Seine at the siege of Paris in 1871. Was member of the Assembly from 1871-80 and then head of the Jules Ferry cabinet in 1880 and minister of finance in 1882, and again in 1885 under M. de Freycinet retiring December, 1886. He was then re-elected to the Assembly and when President Grevy resigned in December, 1887, M. Carnot was elected president of the Republic of France on the third of that month and now fills that office, the term expiring the present year.

Benjamin Disraeli, statesman, author, born in London, December, 21, 1804; died there April 19, 1881. His father was a writer of note, and carefully educated the son privately and then articled him to an intimate friend, a lawyer, who intended to make him heir to his great practice and considerable wealth; but he disliked the law and betook himself to writing fiction, his first venture, " Vivian Grey," published in 1826-7, creating a great sensation and being translated into many of the languages of Europe. He then made an extended tour through the East, returning in 1831; and then publishing three more novels. He betook himself to politics and made three unsuccessful attempts to gain a seat in Parliament, and when thirty-two years of age was elected for Maidstone in 1837, and made his first attempt at a speech in a bombastic, high flown style of words and gestures and was jeered down by his fellows, saying as he took his seat, " I have begun several times many things, and I have often succeeded at last. I shall sit down now; but the time will come when you will hear me." And it did. The following year his colleague, Wyndham Lewis, a wealthy gentleman died, and in 1839 Mr. Disraeli married his widow, and he now gave serious attention to parliamentary rules and to oratory, and in 1849 he began to take an active part in the debates of Parliament, having during this decade written and published three more of his novels. In 1852 Earl Derby appointed him minister of finance and he served with honor and credit to himself and country. The following year witnessed a change of ministers and then in 1858 he served a second time under Lord Derby as the chancellor of the exchequer, and retired the following year, and then led his party in the Commons for seven years, returning again with Derby in July, 1866, and when Derby resigned in February, 1868, he became prime minister and resigned in December, when his wife was made Viscountess Beaconsfield by Queen Victoria, as reward for his services, and died in 1872. In 1870 he published

SUCCESSFUL MEN AND WOMEN.

"Lothair," and in 1874 succeeded Mr. Gladstone as prime minister; and in 1877 took his seat in the Lords as Earl of Beaconsfield, and remained premier till 1880, when he was retired at the elections in favor of Mr. Gladstone, his last work of fiction "Endymion," being published in that year. He furnishes the only example in England's history of a person of Jewish birth being premier of the realm.

Honorable William Ewart Gladstone, late prime minister of the British Empire, was born in Liverpool, England, December 29, 1809. He was educated at Eton School and at Christ Church College, Oxford, and elected to the House of Commons in 1832, when but twenty-three years of age. He is the only man who has been prime minister of England four times, having been called to that position in 1868, in 1880, in 1886, and again summoned by Queen Victoria to be premier on August 15, 1892, as the result of the Liberal victory at the election of that year. His chaste, simple, and abstemious habits have made him to be even now at his great age as hale and hearty, physically and mentally, notwithstanding his enormous labors, as most men are at fifty. But few have continued so long and nobly in public life as he. By far the most prominent personage in England, he is also known throughout the civilized world, both for the greatness of his intellect and for his earnest Christian character. He resigned the premiership February, 1894, and declined the peerage tendered him by Queen Victoria on that occasion.

Robert Peel, statesman, born in Bury (Lancashire), England, February 5, 1788; died in London, Eng., July 2, 1850. His father, Sir Robert, was a cotton manufacturer and the son inherited the estate of ten millions at his father's death. He was educated at the Harrow school, and at Christ Church College, Oxford, graduating at the latter in 1808, and the next year entered Parliament as member for the Irish borough of Cashel, and in 1812 was chief secretary for Ireland, and created the Irish constabulary system of police, afterward extended throughout Great Britain (whence came their nickname of "Peelers" and "Bobbies"). In 1817 was member for Oxford and the next year resigned his secretaryship. In 1822 he became Home secretary, and reformed the criminal laws, and retired in 1827 on the downfall of the Liverpool ministry. In 1828 he took the same office again under the Duke of Wellington, and in his speech of March, 1829, renounced his former bitter opposition to Roman Catholic emancipation, and advocated it and was rejected by the electors of Oxford University, but was returned for Westbury, and in 1830 for Tamworth, which constituency he thereafter represented till his death. In 1834-5 he was for a few months premier at the dissolution of the Melbourne ministry, and again after six years in the opposition, he became premier in September, 1841; he modified and finally repealed the corn laws and introduced the income tax, and largely increased the free trade lists, and being defeated on the Irish coercion bill he resigned June 29, 1846, and made his last speech in opposition to Palmerston's foreign policy in June 28, 1850, and the next day was thrown from his horse and died. He refused the peerage and in his will solemnly enjoined his children not to accept such honor. Originally a high tory, rigid ecclesiastic, and protectionist he became an earnest advocate of liberal measures and was regarded with much gratitude by the middle classes and the working people for whom he pleaded.

William Pitt, Jr., statesman, born in Hayes, Kent, England, May 28, 1759; died in Putney, England, January 23, 1806. He was the son of the famous prime minister, William Pitt, Sr., but he became at twenty-five the greatest of Englishmen, whether of his own or of many generations, if considered as a statesman. As a child he was precocious and sickly, trained by his father for public speaking, and was educated at home till fifteen, when he entered Cambridge University, distinguishing himself by his great proficiency in the classics and in mathematics. On leaving the university he studied law, and was admitted to practice in 1780, and was sent to Parliament the same year as member for Appleby, and the next year made his first speech in favor of Burke's plan of reform, that gave him much renown, and at the next meeting of the Parliament delivered another oration that directed attention to him as one of England's most promising statesmen. When twenty-two he was offered the vice-treasuryship of Ireland, but declined it. When twenty-three he became chancellor of the exchequer and first lord of the treasury, and in four months was beaten in sixteen divisions of the House on his measures, but at the election of 1784, one hundred and sixty of the opposition lost their seats in Parliament, and he was thereafter for seventeen years the great statesman of England, if not of Europe. He was a vigorous advocate of free trade, opposed slavery, pleaded for liberal treatment of Ireland and the Roman Catholics, strenuously opposed "the Man of Destiny," Bonaparte, was a man of great honesty, so far as public money and bribery were concerned, refusing to prostitute his great office for private gain, was greatly addicted in later life to use of port wine, and died overwhelmed with private debts, Parliament voting after his death $200,000 to the relief of his creditors.

SUCCESSFUL MEN AND WOMEN.

Sir Walter Raleigh, statesman, author, born in Hayes (Devonshire), England, 1552; died by being beheaded at Old Palace yard, Westminster, England, October 29, 1618. His father was one of the English gentry, and Walter was educated at Oriel College, Oxford, and also attended it is said at the University of Paris in 1569, but left there to serve under Conde and Coligny in defense of the Huguenots, and later in the Netherlands under William of Orange, and then was a captain of a troop to suppress the Desmond rebellion in Ireland in 1780. He then became an attache to the English embassy to France and afterward to Duke of Anjou at Antwerp. Queen Elizabeth gave him an extensive grant and he sent out two ships, which explored some of the shore of North Carolina and gave such glowing accounts of the country on their return that the virgin queen called the land Virginia and conferred the order of knighthood on Raleigh. In 1585, he was member of Parliament for Devonshire, and was given a grant of 12,000 acres of forfeited land in Ireland, and that year he sent a colony to Virginia which returned in 1586, disheartened, bringing the potato and some tobacco, which were then introduced into Europe. He then sent out another colony which perished. In 1587, he was lieutenant general in command in Cornwall and member of council of war, and the following year served in his own ship against the Spanish Armada. He brought Edmund Spenser from Ireland to present Elizabeth the three books of his "Faerie Queen." He was with Frobisher in a fleet Raleigh fitted out and captured a great Spanish prize. Was one of the ambassadors to Netherlands in 1600, and then the death of Elizabeth three years later brought his ruin. On the accession of James he was stripped of his preferments, convicted on the slightest evidence of treason, condemned, reprieved, sentenced to the Tower for thirteen years and his estates given to Carr, afterward Earl of Somerset. During his imprisonment he wrote his "History of the World," the best then produced in England. March, 1615, he was liberated by James but not pardoned, and being commissioned as admiral he fitted out a fleet of fourteen ships and sailed to Guiana in 1617, and destroyed the Spanish settlement of St. Thomas, his son being killed in the action. A Spanish fleet scattered his ships, his sailors mutinied and he returned to England in 1618, and, on the demand of the Spanish ambassador, the suspended sentence was carried out and he was executed. He was a man of extensive knowledge and many accomplishments and dauntless courage, and wrote several volumes and treatises and a few poems. His complete works were published at Oxford, 1829 (six volumes).

William Wilberforce, statesman, born in Hull, England, August 24, 1759; died in London, England, July 29, 1833. His father was a wealthy merchant, who died when the son was nine years of age, and he was sent to school at Wimbledon, where an aunt, who was a devoted Christian, greatly influenced his character. His mother disapproving, removed him to another school, and when he was seventeen he entered St. John's College at Cambridge, where he graduated in 1776, and then came into possession of a large fortune and entered on a political career, being elected to Parliament in 1780 from Hull, and four years later was elected member from York, and in that year made a tour of the continent with the Dean Milner of Carlisle and the serious impression of his youth revived and he abandoned his life of gayety and in 1787 entered on the great struggle for the abolition of human slavery and in 1789 offered his first bill for the suppression of the slave trade in the House of Commons; he was powerfully opposed and defeated there, but was aided throughout the country by the herculean efforts of George Thompson, Thomas Clarkson, and others. After fifteen years of agitation he succeeded in 1804 in getting his bill through the Commons, but it was defeated in the Lords, and in that year he published a book on the slave trade that powerfully affected public opinion. Renewing his bill the next year, it was lost in the Commons, and then in 1806 Mr. Fox's resolution to abolish the slave trade at the next session was adopted by the Lords and by the Commons in 1807. He now began to agitate for the total abolishment of slavery and continued it until his death. In 1825 he was compelled, by ill health, to retire from Parliament, intrusting his cause to Sir T. Fowell Buxton, and three days before Wilberforce's death news was brought him that the abolition bill had passed its second reading and he gave God thanks that he had lived to see his countrymen spend $100,000,000 for emancipation of the slaves. He was honored with a burial in Westminster Abbey as a public benefactor. He was the author of a "Practical View of Christianity," translated into many tongues, and also wrote many essays and pamphlets and a book of "Family Prayers" of large circulation. He left a large family, some of whom have come to fame.

SUCCESSFUL MEN AND WOMEN.

PROMINENT LAWYERS AND JURISTS.

Charles Francis Adams, statesman, born in Boston, August 18, 1807; died there, November 21, 1886. When two years old he went with his father, John Quincy Adams, then just appointed United States minister to Russia, where he learned the Russian, French, and German languages, and, soon after Napoleon's fatal Moscow campaign, the father went to Ghent as one of the United States peace commission to treat with Great Britain for the closing of the war of 1812, and shortly after the mother and son made the journey to Paris in a private carriage, and that year (1815) the father being appointed United States minister to England he was there placed at an English boarding school, and after his return to America he attended the Boston Latin school and Harvard College graduating at the latter in 1825, and shortly after his father's inauguration as president of the United States. After two years in Washington he returned to Boston and studied law in the office of Daniel Webster and was admitted to the bar of Suffolk in 1828. From 1831 to 1836 he was a member of the state legislature, but like his grandfather and father he was very independent of party rules and platforms and soon separated from the Whig party and became in 1848 the Free Soil candidate for vice-president; and then in 1850 and 1860 the Republican party to which the Free Soilers had grown elected him to Congress, and in the spring of 1861 President Lincoln appointed him United States minister to England, a post his father and grandfather had filled before him,—one at the close of the Revolutionary War with that country, the other at the close of the war of 1812 with the same government, and he during and at the close of the civil war in this country, a war that England had secretly and at times openly abetted. His career as minister from 1861 to 1868 was one attended by great difficulties and grave responsibility; but he discharged the obligations upon him with so signal ability, as to make that career to be cited among the foremost triumphs of American diplomacy. After his return to this country he was for a number of years president of the Harvard College board of overseers and edited the works and memoirs of his grandfather and father (twenty-two volumes), and published a number of his own addresses and orations, and 1872 he was named as candidate for president by the Liberal Republicans but the arduous task finally fell to Horace Greeley.

Schuyler Colfax, statesman, born in New York city, March 23, 1823; died in Mankato, Minn., January 13, 1885. His father died a few weeks before the son's birth, and when he was ten years of age his mother remarried, and he then served two years in his stepfather's store and removed with the family to New Carlisle, Indiana, in 1836, where he continued as clerk in the father's store till his retirement from business in 1839; and then young Schuyler wrote for the county paper and read law. In 1841 his father was elected county auditor and removed to South Bend, where the son served as deputy for eight years, and united with a temperance organization and reported for the Indianapolis *Journal* for two years, and in 1845 bought the *Free Press*, changing it to *St. Joseph Register*, quadrupling its subscription and making it the most influential Whig paper in his section of the state, and vigorously opposed, in 1859, the clause in the state constitution prohibiting free colored men from settling in the state. In 1851 he held a joint debate as candidate for Congress throughout his district with his Democratic opponent on slavery question, and though defeated at the election, he was in 1854 elected to Congress as the candidate of the newly formed Republican party, and in 1856 made a speech in Congress on the slavery question that gave him great renown, more than half a million copies having been circulated as a campaign document in the Fremont campaign, and he had at this time established a mail route to San Francisco via mining camps, whose letters had hitherto cost them $5 an ounce by express companies. He was continuously re-elected to Congress till 1869, and December 7, 1863, was elected speaker, and twice re-elected to that office, gaining great praise as a presiding officer. In 1868 he was nominated and elected vice-president on the ticket with General Grant, who offered him in 1871 the secretary of state office for the remainder of the term, which he declined, as he did in December, 1872, the editorship of the New York *Tribune*. His enemies implicated him in the "Credit Mobilier" scandal, but he stoutly denied the accusation and maintained his innocence. In his later life he became well known on the lecture platform and at his death of heart disease, public honors were given him by Congress and by his state.

Samuel Sullivan Cox, statesman, born in Zanesville, O., September 30, 1824; died in New York city, September 10, 1889. After attending the public schools he entered the Ohio University at Athens, and then attended Brown University at Providence, R. I., graduating at the latter in 1846, having paid his way through college largely by doing literary work and taking during his course prizes in classics, history, literary criticism, and political economy. He then studied law, and after admission to the bar of Cincinnati he abandoned law for journal-

555

ism and literature and went to Europe for three years, 1850-3, and published his first book, named "The Buckeye Abroad," and on his return edited the *Statesman* at Columbus, where a gorgeous article in sophomore style gained him the sobriquet of "Sunset" Cox. He went to Peru as secretary of legation in 1855 for a year, and on his return he was elected to Congress, serving from 1857-65, and in the latter year removed to New York city, and in 1868 was returned to Congress from the sixth district, and again went on a short trip to Europe. He was re-elected in 1870 over Horace Greeley, but defeated in 1872, and on the death of James Brooks was again elected, taking his seat December 1, 1873, and was continuously re-elected to 1885, when he went to Turkey as United States minister and resigned at end of a year, and was again elected to Congress to fill a vacancy in the ninth district and re-elected in 1888. He was a general favorite as a man of humor among even his political adversaries, and was an able debater and the author of important measures in Congress, and wrote nearly a dozen volumes of various topics, some of which have had a large sale.

Chauncey Mitchell Depew, lawyer, born in Peekskill, N. Y., April 23, 1834, of French Huguenot ancestry. His father was a farmer, and his boyhood was spent on the farm, and at the public school, and he then fitted for college, and at eighteen entered Yale, graduating in 1856, and then studied law with Hon. William Nelson at Peekskill, and was admitted to the bar in 1858, beginning practice the following year, but the exciting times drew him into politics almost constantly as a stump speaker for the Republican party, and in 1861 he was elected to the legislature, and re-elected the following year, and in 1863 he was elected secretary of the state, having made, each year, a remarkable personal canvass, frequently speaking twice a day during the campaigns. Deciding to go out of politics he accepted the office of attorney for the New York and Harlem Railroad tendered him in 1866 by Cornelius Vanderbilt, and on the reorganization of the Vanderbilt interests in 1869 was continued as its attorney, and became a director in the several roads of the corporation known as the New York Central and Hudson River Railroad Company, and in 1882 he was made second vice-president on the retirement of his friend, William H. Vanderbilt, and then at the death of Mr. James H. Rutter in 1885, he became the president of the company. In 1888 he was a prominent candidate of his party before the Chicago Convention for the presidency of the United States, but withdrew in the interest of harmony. Mr. Depew is a man of wide reading and culture, and noted for his geniality of disposition, and for his force as an orator, and is in great request as speaker on notable occasions; but his immense railroad interests almost wholly engross his time and attention, and so the public know him only as one of the great business men of the age.

John Adams Dix, lawyer, soldier, born in Boscawen, N. H., July 24, 1798; died in New York city, April 21, 1879. He was educated at the public schools and at Phillips Academy, and at Salisbury Academy, and at the College of Montreal, and in 1812 was appointed cadet, and joined his father,—who was a major in the army at Baltimore,—and studied at St. Mary's College, and served in the army till 1828, when he resigned, having for the previous five years studied law, and being admitted to the bar in Washington. He now practiced at Cooperstown, N. Y., and at Albany, and from 1833-40 was secretary of New York state, and superintendent of common schools. In 1841 he was a member of the legislature, and then spent the next two years in Europe, and in 1845 was elected United States senator, and in 1848 was the candidate of the Free Soil Democrats for governor against Hamilton Fish, but was defeated. He was appointed secretary of the treasury by President Buchanan, January 10, 1861, on petition of New York bankers, and as such telegraphed his famous order to New Orleans to the captain of the revenue cutters, "If anyone attempts to haul down the American flag, shoot him on the spot." When President Lincoln issued his first call for troops, he organized and sent forward seventeen regiments, and was commissioned major-general volunteers in June, 1861, and stationed at Baltimore, where his energetic efforts prevented that state from joining the Confederacy. In 1862 he was in command at Fortress Monroe, and in 1863 at the draft riots in New York city; he was stationed there until the close of the war. In 1866 he was made naval officer of that port, and the same year appointed minister to France, and in 1872, was elected governor of New York on Republican ticket, but defeated in 1874. He was connected as president with several railroads, was a man of culture, speaking fluently several languages, was prominent in the Episcopal church with which he was connected, and the author of several well known volumes.

Hannibal Hamlin, statesman, born in Paris, Me., August 27, 1809; died in Bangor, Me., July 4, 1891. He was given a common school education, and then fitted for college at Hebron Academy, but unable to go to college he began teaching school, and so bought law books and began to fit himself for the law, when the death of his father obliged him to forego the study and take charge of the home farm. Two years after the father's death he bought an interest in a weekly paper, but soon sold it to his partner and resumed the study of law, and was admitted to the bar in 1833, and began to take an interest in political affairs as a Democrat, and in 1836-40 was a member of the state legislature, being speaker of the House for three of the years. He was then elected to Congress in 1842, and again in 1844. Was in the legislature in 1847, and on the death of Senator Fairchild he was elected United States senator to fill that vacancy in 1848, and in 1851 was re-elected. In 1856 in a notable speech in the Senate he separated from his party on the slavery question, and in that year he was elected governor of his state by the Republican party, and resigned his seat in the Senate in 1857; but within a fortnight thereafter he was re-elected United States senator, and on advice of his party accepted that position. In 1860 he was elected vice-president of the United States on the ticket with Abraham Lincoln, and resigning his seat in the Senate he presided over that chamber till March 3, 1865. When Lincoln was renominated the party leaders decided that the exigency of the party demanded a southern Union man as candidate for vice-president, and the place was given to Andrew Johnson of Tennessee. In 1865 Mr. Johnson made him collector of the port of Boston, and in 1868 and again in 1875, he was chosen to the United States Senate; and in 1881-3 he was United States minister to Spain; resigned in the latter year after near fifty years of public service, and retired to private life.

John Marshall Harlan, jurist, born in Boyle county, Kentucky, June 1, 1833. He was graduated from Centre College, Tennessee, and then fitted for the bar at Transylvania University under the distinguished jurists, George Robertson and Thomas A. Marshall, and afterward continued his study with his father, the attorney general of Kentucky, and in five years after his admission to practice he was elected judge of Franklin county, Kentucky, and in 1859 was Whig candidate for Congress in the Ashland district, represented by John C. Breckenridge, and failed of election by sixty-seven votes. He then went to Louisiana and at the beginning of the civil war returned and enlisted in the Union army as colonel of Tenth Kentucky regiment, and was in active service till the death of his father in 1863, when he resigned with rank of brigadier general, and at once became attorney general of his state, serving till 1867, when he returned to practice at Louisville, Ky. In 1871, and 1875, he was against his wishes nominated by his party (Republican) for governor, and declined a foreign mission offered him by President Hayes, but served on the Louisiana commission in 1877, and then was appointed by President Hayes as one of the chief justices of the United States Supreme Court, and commissioned November 29, of that year (1877), at the age of forty-four, and has since become noted as one of the most eminent jurists of his time. For many years he has filled the chair of constitutional law at the Columbian University, Washington, D. C., holding to the opinions of the great John Marshall on constitutional questions, and is an ardent advocate of freedom for all irrespective of color, and a stanch upholder of our free institutions, both civil and religious.

John MacLean, jurist, born in Morris county, N. J., March 11, 1785; died in Cincinnati, O., April 4, 1861. His father, a poor man with a large family, emigrated to the west when John was three years old, and after sundry removes finally settled on a farm in Warren county, O., in 1799, where he attended the log schoolhouse in winter and toiled on the farm until he was sixteen, and then for two years took private lessons in Latin, and at eighteen went to Cincinnati to study law, supporting himself by writing in county clerk's office, and was admitted to practice in 1807 and settled at Lebanon, O., and in 1812 was elected to the legislature by the Democratic party over two competitors in a sharp campaign, and was almost unanimously re-elected in 1814. He refused a nomination for the United States Senate the next year, and in 1816 was elected judge of the supreme court of his state, retaining it till he was appointed commissioner of the land office by President Monroe in 1822. In the following year he was made postmaster-general and continued in that office through the next administration, that of John Q. Adams, to 1829, when Jackson requested him to remain but he refused, not being willing to remove faithful employees for spoilsmen. After declining the war and then the navy departments, Jackson named him as associate justice of the United States Supreme Court, which he accepted January, 1830, and became distinguished for great legal ability and eloquence and gained immortal renown in the Dred Scott case, being one of the two dissenting judges to Chief Justice Taney's decision; and then declared in his opinion given on the case that slavery had its origin solely in power, that it was contrary to the law of righteousness, and was, and could be, sustained only by local law. In the Republican convention at Philadelphia in 1856 he received 196 votes to 359 for John C. Fremont as candidate for president. He was the author of six volumes of United

States Circuit Court reports, and also published a number of addresses, and a eulogy on James Monroe.

Thaddeus Stevens, statesman, lawyer, born in Danville, Vt., April 4, 1792; died in Washington, D. C., August 11, 1868. He was the child of poor parents, and was lame and sickly, but delighted to read, and the father dying early, his mother toiled hard to give him an education. Graduated at Dartmouth College, 1814, then he studied law at Peacham, Vt., and afterward went to York, Pa., to teach an academy, and continued his law studies and was admitted to the bar and established himself at Gettysburg and gained much fame. In 1833-5, he was a member of the legislature, defeating in the latter year the bill to abolish the recently established common school system, and afterward he gave a farm to Mrs. L. J. Pierson, whose poems had helped in that contest for education for the poor. In 1836, he was a member of the state Constitutional Convention but refused to sign the constitution prepared because it gave the franchise only to the whites. He was again a member of the legislature in 1837, and 1838 being the most prominent man of his party (Whig) in the House. In 1848 and 1850, he was elected to Congress and sturdily opposed Henry Clay's compromise measures and the fugitive slave law, and then for five years he toiled at the bar. In 1858, he was again sent to Congress by the Republican party, where he remained until his death, being the leader of the radicals of his party, the great champion of emancipation for the blacks, and lovingly called "the great commoner" by the friends of freedom; his force of character and great oratorical powers justly earning him the title. He proposed the impeachment of President Johnson. In his will he stipulated that his body be buried in a cemetery which he had given for all races, that he might continue to illustrate the principle he had advocated in life, "equality of man before the Creator." He founded by his will an orphan asylum for children of all races.

Samuel Jones Tilden, statesman, lawyer, born in New Lebanon, N. Y., February 9, 1814; died in Westchester county (Greystone), N. Y., August 4, 1886. His father was a farmer and country merchant and Samuel was the fifth of his eight children. When eighteen he entered Yale College, but ill health prevented his continuing through the course. Resuming his studies in 1834 at the University of New York, at his graduation he began the study of law, and his father having been an ardent Democrat he was early drawn into politics. Locating in New York city, he soon became eminent as a corporation lawyer so that "from 1855 onward more than half of the great railway corporations north of the Ohio and between the Hudson and Missouri rivers were at some time clients of Mr. Tilden." He was a member of the legislature in 1845 and of the constitutional convention in 1846 and took part in the Free Soil revolt in his party (Democrat) in 1848, and during the civil war devoted himself to business rather than to patriotism, not approving the methods of the government, and by 1868 he had become the virtual leader of the then Democracy in his state. He, however, did noble work in his city against "Boss Tweed" and his plunderers after their exposure in the columns of the *Times*, July, 1871, and in 1874 he was elected governor of New York, over Gov. John A. Dix, when his message concerning the dishonest management of the state canals created a great sensation, and during his administration the state capitol building was begun, costing over $18,000,000. In 1876 he was nominated by his party for the presidency, and received one hundred and eighty-four electoral votes to one hundred and eighty-five for Mr. Hayes, according to the final returns of the electoral commission that was appointed to try the contested cases; the popular vote as counted being Tilden 4,284,265; Hayes 4,033,294; Cooper 81,737; Smith 9,522. Thereafter he was accounted the great leader of his party and was urged in 1880 and again in 1884 to become their candidate, but steadily refused, devoting his time almost wholly to his enormous practice. He never married and at his death left the greater part of his fortune, then estimated at five millions, to found and endow a free public library in the city of New York, which was not carried out owing to his will being contested and annulled by his relatives.

Elihu Benjamin Washburn, statesman, born in Livermore, Me., September 23, 1816; died in Chicago, Ill., October 22, 1887. His father was a farmer, and after a country school education he began life as printer's apprentice at seventeen, and after a year, taught a district school, and then spent another year in a newspaper office; and deciding when twenty to study law he spent a year at Kent's Hill Seminary, and then entered the law office of John Otis at Hallowell, who assisted him financially, and in 1839 he became a student at Harvard College Law School, and on his admission to the bar in 1840 went to the west, settling in Galena, Ill., and soon acquired an extensive practice. In 1848 he was an unsuccessful candidate for representative to Congress, but was elected in 1852, serving thereafter as congressman from December 5, 1853, to March 6, 1869, and held the chairmanship of the committee on commerce

SUCCESSFUL MEN AND WOMEN.

for ten years. He was called the "Father of the House," because of his long, continuous service, and also the "Watch dog of the Treasury," from his opposing all extravagant expenditures, grants of public lands to railroads and other bodies, and the "log rolling" of river and harbor bills, and his persistent insistence that the finance of the government should be conducted on a strict economic business basis. President Grant made him his first secretary of state in his first administration; but he did not serve out the term, being appointed minister to France before its close, where he gained great renown by his prudent, patriotic course during the Franco-Prussian war and the reign of the commune, taking charge, with the permission of the French government, of the German archives, and acting as the representative of the several German states and other foreign governments, and sturdily remained at his post during the siege of Paris and the days of the commune, and labored hard, but in vain, to save Archbishop Darboy from the mob bent on his murder, and was given for his extraordinary services by the Emperor William, the Order of the Red Eagle, but declined it under the United States Constitution's provision, and on his resigning the mission in 1877, the Emperor of Germany, Bismarck. Thiers, and Gambetta, each sent him their life-size portraits as tokens of their esteem for him. On his return to America he settled in Chicago, and refused to be the candidate of the Republican party for president in 1880. He wrote his "Recollections of a minister to France in 1869-1877," which was published at New York in 1887 (two volumes), and gave his extensive collections of pictures, documents, and autographs to the city of Chicago for free exhibition to the public.

EMINENT LAWYERS AND JURISTS.

George Nixon Briggs, jurist, born in Adams, Mass., April 13, 1796; died in Pittsfield, Mass., September 12, 1861. His father was a blacksmith in humble circumstances, and the son was early obliged to toil hard to eke out the family living, and on the death of his father in his boyhood, he was apprenticed, when twelve years of age, to a hatter at White Creek, N. Y., where he remained three years, and then an elder brother gave him a year's schooling, and with five dollars he had earned at haying, he started to study law at Pittsfield, Mass., and was admitted to the bar in 1818, and practiced successively in Adams, Lanesborough and Pittsfield, and was register of deeds for his county 1824-31, and gained a wide reputation as a criminal lawyer in 1827 by his defense of an Indian of Stockbridge on trial for murder. From 1830 to 1843 he was a member of Congress, where he became prominent as an eloquent debater, and from 1843 to 1851 he was governor of Massachusetts and refused to commute the sentence of the murderer of Dr. Parkman, notwithstanding the great efforts made to influence him. He was made judge of the court of common pleas in 1851, and served as such till the reorganization of the courts in 1856. He was member of the state Constitutional Convention in 1853, and in 1861 was a commissioner to adjust claims with New Granada, but was accidentally shot in that year before entering on his duties. He was not only an able lawyer and patriot, but a prominent Christian and the president of many religious associations and charitable societies. A memoir of him under the title "Great in Goodness," was published in Boston, 1866.

Horace Binney, lawyer, born in Philadelphia, Pa., Jan. 4, 1780; died there August 12, 1875. His father was a surgeon in the Revolutionary army, and died when Horace was seven years old, and the next year he was sent to a classical school at Bordentown, N. J., remaining three years, and when thirteen entered Harvard College, dividing the honors with a classmate at his graduation in 1797. In November of that year he began the study of law and in 1800 was called to the bar, where his untiring industry and great study brought him to be at length a leader. In 1806 he was chosen to the legislature and declined a renomination, his professional engagements having then become very large. In 1830 his health being impaired and being opposed to President Jackson's course on the banking question he accepted a nomination to Congress and was elected, but refused a second term. He prepared and published the six volumes of Pennsylvania supreme court decisions that bear his name and are regarded as almost perfect models. His great argument in the Girard case of 1844 is the subject of much admiration, both in this country and in Europe, for its vigor of reasoning, fullness of research, and force and beauty of language.

Aaron Burr, statesman, born in Newark, N. J., February 6, 1756; died on Staten Island, N. Y., September 14, 1836. His father was president of Princeton College. His mother was the daughter of Rev. Jonathan Edwards, D.D. His parents died in his infancy leaving him and his sister Sarah a handsome fortune and he was placed in the care of his uncle, Rev. Timothy Edwards, and was given every advantage of education and was fitted to enter Princeton College when eleven, but was not admitted till in his thirteenth year because of his youth, and then he entered the Sophomore class; was a great reader, impulsive, and mischievous, and small in stature and a general favorite, and graduated in 1772 with much distinction. Just before graduating he was greatly moved by a revival in the town, but was discouraged from yielding to its influence by the president of the college, Dr. Witherspoon, and the next year still troubled in mind by religious questions he went to live with Rev. Dr. Bellamy of Bethlehem, Conn., and while there threw off his convictions and adopted the infidelity then rife in Europe and America. In 1774 he studied law and in 1775 at breaking out of Revolutionary war he entered the army, against the commands of his guardian, and went with Colonel Benedict Arnold to Quebec, returning with the rank of major for gallant conduct, and became aid to General Putnam and July 7, 1777, was made lieutenant-colonel, and commanded a regiment and distinguished himself at the battle of Monmouth, resigning in 1779 on account of ill health and resumed the study of law and was admitted to the bar in 1782 and began practice at Albany but soon removed to New York city and devoted himself to his profession for eight years, having but one rival as a lawyer, Alexander Hamilton. In 1789 he was appointed attorney general of his state and in 1791 was elected United States senator and served with marked ability. In 1800 he was elected by the House of Representatives the vice-president, after a fierce conflict of seven days, with Thomas Jefferson as president. Shortly before the term expired he became candidate for governor of New York, but was defeated by Morgan Lewis through the unceasing aid of Alexander Hamilton and then the bitter political and professional feuds and rivalry of years culminated after the fashion of the times in a duel at Weehawken, N. J., 7 A. M. July 7, 1804, where Hamilton was mortally wounded and Burr fled before the coroner's verdict of murder to his daughter in South Carolina, who had become the wife of Joseph Alston, a wealthy planter, and after a time he returned and served out his term as vice-president. In 1805 he undertook the project of conquering Texas and Mexico, as a kingdom for himself and grandson, but was denounced by a presidential proclamation. In 1807 was arrested in the Mississippi territory but, escaping, was again arrested in Alabama and taken to Richmond, Va., where the great trial for treason began and continued for six months and resulted in a verdict of not guilty as to treason. He then went to England for a time and was expelled from the country for his schemes that he still was trying to carry out. He then visited Sweden, Germany, and France, being under the surveillance of the government and reduced to great sufferings through poverty, and went to England again for a year and a half, a homeless outcast and beggar, and, grown desperate, disguised himself and came to Boston under the name of Arnot, and after a time returned to New York city, where his friends rallied around and he began practice of law when stunned by the death of his only grandchild at eleven years of age and then in Jan., 1813, Theodosia, the idol of his life, went to an unknown death at sea. He was now fifty-seven and had considerable practice though shunned by society. When seventy-eight he married a rich widow. whose fortune he squandered in riotous living and they separated, he being dependent for a home in his last days on the charity of a Scotch lady, a friend of his former years. Though he was counted an infidel he was not a scoffer, and in his last hours bore this testimony to the Scriptures whose counsels he had not followed, "They are the most perfect system of truth the world has ever seen."

Rufus Choate, lawyer, born in Essex, Mass., October 1, 1799; died in Halifax, N. S., July 13, 1859. His father died when he was nine years of age. He was fond of reading and devoured most of the books in the town library before he was ten, and delighted to memorize Bunyan's "Pilgrim's Progress" and the Bible. He graduated valedictorian at Dartmouth in 1819, and was led to the study of law by hearing Daniel Webster's plea in his college's case in 1818. He was tutor a year after graduating and then entered a law school at Cambridge and in 1821 studied with William Wirt (United States attorney general), at Washington, D. C., and returned to Massachusetts in the autumn of 1822 for further study and was admitted to the bar in 1823 and practiced at Danvers for five years, and in 1828 removed to Salem and from 1830–4 was member of Congress, resigning in latter year to resume practice in Boston, and in 1841, when Daniel Webster became secretary of state in President Harrison's cabinet, Mr. Choate was chosen United States senator, and he distinguished himself by several brilliant speeches. In 1845 he returned again to his practice in Boston, and in 1850 traveled extensively in Europe and died suddenly while on a second journey thither for his health. He was one of the most scholarly of American public men, and one of its chief forensic advocates, having an amazing power over his audience, and is frequently styled the American "Lord Erskine." His writings with a memoir were published in Boston in 1862 (two volumes).

Benjamin Robbins Curtis, jurist, born in Watertown, Mass., November 4, 1809; died in Newport, R. I., September 15, 1874. He fitted for college in the schools of his native town and graduated at Harvard in 1822. He then studied law and was admitted to the bar in 1832 and practiced first in Northfield and then in Boston, where he soon became eminent in the profession. In 1851 he became a member of the state legislature and in that year was appointed by President Fillmore an associate justice of the Supreme Court and won much renown in the celebrated "Dred Scott" case, being one of the two dissenting judges to that infamous decision, his powerful argument awakening an earnest response throughout the North. He resigned from the bench in 1857 and resumed practice in Boston, frequently appearing before his former court in important cases, and was one of the counsel for President Johnson in his impeachment trial in 1868, and was the author of numerous reports of law.

John Jay, jurist, born in New York city, December 12, 1745; died in Bedford, N. Y., May 17, 1829. His parents were of French Huguenot ancestry, the father being a wealthy West India merchant. The son was educated at a boarding school at New Rochelle, and when fifteen entered King's (now Columbia) College, and on graduating in 1764, served four years as apprentice at law in office of Benjamin Kissam, the consideration being $500 paid Mr. Kissam. On his admission to the bar he became partner with Robert R. Livingstone, afterward chancellor of New York. He was a member of the Continental Congress of 1774, and wrote one of its three famous addresses (that to the people of Great Britain), and was a member of the secret committee of safety, and in 1777 drew up the draft of the constitution for the state of New York (which remained its organic law for forty-five years till revised in 1822), and acted as chief justice of that state *pro tempore* and wrote appeals in behalf of the Revolution, then in progress. December 1, 1778, he was president of the Continental Congress and went to Spain as minister from Congress, reaching there January 22, 1780, but was not received as such. In 1782 he went to Paris as one of the peace commissioners, where he was the chief personage in securing the treaty with Great Britain, and on his return in 1784 was elected secretary of foreign affairs, holding it till the adoption of the United States Constitution, when on President Washington offering him his choice of office, he chose that of chief justice of the United States Supreme Court, being the first to hold that office. He retained it till 1795. In 1794 he was sent to England by Washington to settle peaceably, if possible, the vexing boundary question, and succeeded to the dissatisfaction of his party associate (Federalist), but subsequent benefit of his countrymen, and his party in consequence nominated in 1797 John Adams rather than Jay as the next president. In 1795 he was elected governor of New York, and again in 1798, and during the six years as governor dismissed no person from office on account of his politics. In 1801 he was renominated and reconfirmed as chief justice of the United States Supreme Court, but declined to accept and spent the remaining twenty-eight years of his life at his country-seat, inherited through his mother, his last offices held being president of an anti-slavery society and of the American Bible society. He was a noble man, of great intellect, pure morals, and blameless character, an ardent patriot, and an earnest Christian.

Franklin Pierce, statesman, born in Hillsborough, N. H., November 23, 1804; died in Concord, N. H., October 8, 1869. He was the son of a farmer, who gave him an education at the academies of Hancock, Francestown, and Exeter, N. H., and at Bowdoin College, Brunswick, Me., being graduated at the last institution in 1824, the third in his class. He then studied law at Portsmouth, N. H., a year, and at a law school at Northampton, Mass., two years, and in the office of Judge Parker at Amherst, N. H., being admitted to the bar in 1827. In 1829-32 he was a member of the legislature of his state, the last two years being the speaker of the House, and in 1833 was elected to Congress, and in 1837 was elected to the United States Senate, being the youngest of the senators. He resigned his seat in 1842, and resumed the practice of law at Concord, N. H., and refused nomination for governor by his party and refused attorney generalship of United States tendered him by President Polk in 1845, and in that year had a notable debate with John P. Hale on slavery, Mr. Pierce openly supporting that wrong. In 1847 he enlisted as a private in the war with Mexico, and on March 3 was made brigadier general by President Polk, and served till the close of the war in December, 1847, and then resumed the practice of his profession and gained great distinction in his state as its leading lawyer. Being a most zealous Democrat, he supported and defended his party's compromises with slavery, and advocated the Fugitive Slave law, and at the National Convention at Baltimore, Md., June, 1852, he was first named on the thirty-fifth ballot as candidate, and nominated on the forty-ninth ballot by 282 to 11 for other as president, and at the election carried all the states but four and had 254 electoral votes to 42 for General W. Scott. In his inaugural he denounced agitation against slavery and declared his purpose to defend it by the then laws. But the decision of Chief Justice Taney, and the bid of Stephen A. Douglas for the next Democratic nomination for president in his "Kansas and Nebraska bill," which Mr. Pierce signed the 31st of May, giving as he then supposed the final victory for slavery, was but the precursor of its destruction, and the remainder of his term was embittered by sectional strifes, riots, and bloodsheds in Kansas, whose Free Soil party he strove in vain to subdue in the interest of what he and many of the great men of his time mistakenly termed patriotism and right. Those who lived through those troubled days and knew of his great kindness of heart, his hatred of injustice and oppression when it was practiced on the white man, are aware that his course toward the brother with the black skin was due wholly to his political and religious training, and his inherited prejudices. After the expiration of his term he failed of a renomination, and then spent three years in Europe, and thereafter lived in retirement at Concord.

Joseph Story, jurist, born in Marblehead, Mass., September 18, 1779; died in Cambridge, Mass., September 10, 1845. His father was a surgeon in the Revolutionary army, and one of the famous "Boston tea party." He was an immense reader in his youthful days, was educated at the public schools and at Harvard College, graduating at the latter in 1798, and studied law under Samuel Sewell and Samuel Putnam, and in 1801 began practice at Salem, Mass., and soon came to eminence in his profession, having made a profound study of the old English law, and of law relating to property. In 1805 he was elected to the legislature, and was the acknowledged leader of his party. In 1808 he was elected to Congress, and secured the repeal of the "Embargo Act," as injurious to New England. In 1811 he was again member of his state legislature and speaker of the House, and November of that year he was appointed by President Madison associate justice of the Supreme Court, his circuit embracing Maine, New Hampshire, Massachusetts, and Rhode Island. He occupied this position for thirty-three years, the reports of his judicial life filling thirty-five volumes. In 1829, when Nathan Dane founded the law professorship at Harvard, Judge Story was elected to fill it at an annual salary of $1000, and for sixteen years he resided in Cambridge as the famous teacher, drawing students to him from all parts of the land; he wrote more text-books than any other writer of his day, dividing with Chancellor Kent the honor of founding the American system of equity jurisprudence. In 1819 he boldly denounced before grand juries the slave trade then carried on from New England ports, and though denounced by the press as deserving "to be hurled from the bench" he continued to express his abhorrence of that inhumanity, which opinions prevented him from becoming, on the death of John Marshall, the chief justice of the Supreme Court. His twelve treatises on various subjects of jurisprudence are recognized both in this country and in Europe as of the highest authority, and have gone through many editions and been translated into various languages. As a teacher his geniality, sympathy, bubbling humor, and great conversational powers, no less than his vast acquirements of legal lore, put him at the head of teachers of the law.

Roger Brooks Taney, jurist, born in Calvert county, Md., March 17, 1777; died in Washington, D. C., October 12, 1864. Was the son of a planter, a man who had been educated at a college in France. He was instructed by his father at home, and when fitted entered Dickinson College, where he graduated in 1795, and then read law and, admitted to the bar in 1799, began to practice in his county, and the same year was elected to the Maryland House of Delegates, being the youngest member. In 1816 was sent to the state Senate. In 1819 he said of slavery, "while it continues, it is a blot on our national character." In 1823 he removed to Baltimore, and was at the head of the bar for six years, being attorney general of his state in 1827, and of the United States in 1831, and on September 24, 1833, he was appointed by President Jackson, secretary of the United States treasury, and carried out Jackson's purpose to remove the deposits from the United States bank, a proceeding that brought on a "panic," and then, when on June 23, 1834, the president, for the first time sent his name to the Senate for confirmation, that body rejected him on the next day, the first case on record of such rejection, and he resigned the position, and the next January was nominated for judge of Supreme Court by Jackson, but again rejected by the Senate; and on the death of Chief Justice Marshall that same year (1835), the President nominated him for the position, and he was confirmed March 15, 1836. In 1837 he began to preside over the full bench, and became noted for reversing the opinions of Judge Marshall on the United States Constitution, and for his construction of the United States Constitution in behalf of slavery; the most famous of such decisions being that of 1857, known as the Dred Scott case, wherein he declared the negroes could not become citizens, saying they had for more than a century before been regarded as beings of an inferior order, and altogether unfit to associate with the white race, either in social or political relations, and had no rights which the white man was bound to respect, and that the negro might justly and lawfully be reduced to slavery for his benefit. In this decision he further declared that the laws of Congress and the Missouri Compromise prohibiting slavery in the territories were unconstitutional, and the next year he affirmed the constitutionality of the "Fugitive Slave Law," which decision immensely intensified the conflict with slavery throughout the North, and brought about the election of Abraham Lincoln in 1860, and the civil war. He died on the very day that his native state of Maryland abolished slavery.

LAWYERS OF FAME.

Benjamin Franklin Butler, lawyer, born in Deerfield, N. H., November 5, 1818; died in Lowell, Mass., January 11, 1893. His father, a coasting trader and captain, died when Benjamin was five months old leaving his widow poor and with two babes (one an older brother of Benjamin's) to care for. He was in youth small of size, frail, sickly, and his principal recreation was reading, of which he was very fond. His mother was a devoted member of the Baptist church, and early instructed him in the Bible. When he was ten years of age his mother removed to Lowell, Mass. (then a town of 2,000 inhabitants), and kept a boarding house. Here he attended the public schools and having a taste for military life wished to go to West Point Military Academy, but his mother designed him for a Baptist clergyman and so sent him when sixteen to Waterville, Me., to what is now Colby University, where he paid his way in part by working in a chair shop. The school was new, the teaching almost wholly religious, discipline strict, and Butler came near being expelled for non-attendance at prayers. Had intended near close of his school life to be a physician, but by accident was at court and listening to the lawyers resolved then and there to study law. At his graduation in 1838 he was in miserable health, weighed but ninety-seven pounds, was poor and in debt for schooling and, with no one to look to for help, his prospects were not very bright. Just then an uncle, who was a fisherman, invited him to go on his schooner to Labrador on condition he took fisherman's fare and did full work. He went, spent the season, was made well and strong, and did not have another sick day for twenty-five years. When twenty years of age he returned to Lowell and studied law, teaching school to pay his way and earn clothes, often working eighteen hours a day; was admitted to the bar in 1840 and the next year began practice in Lowell, where he soon won much renown by his vigorous measures in behalf of factory girls and others: was an indefatigable worker, toiling regularly from opening of court at nine till midnight, and, having a remarkably retentive memory, he soon became the most successful lawyer of New England; his regular practice yielding him, at the time he left for the war, over $18,000 a year (a large sum for that period), and he being then at the opening of war retained in over five hundred coming cases at court; was a member of Massachusetts House of Representatives in 1853 and of Senate in 1859 and Democratic candidate for governor in 1860. When President Lincoln issued call for troops April, 1861, Mr. Butler was brigadier-general of state militia and on 17th of that month marched with Eighth Massachusetts regiment to Annapolis, Md., and was given command of that district and May 13 entered Baltimore with 900 men, occupying that city, and on the 16th was made major-general and assigned to command of Fort Monroe and Department of Eastern Virginia, where his order making slaves "contraband of war" gained him much renown. In August, 1861, he captured Forts Hatteras and Clark in North Carolina, and returned to Massachusetts to recruit an expedition to the Gulf of Mexico and the Mississippi, and on March 23, 1862, reached with his command Ship Island, and April 17 went up the Mississippi river, co-operating with Admiral Farragut's fleet, the fleet passing the forts on April 24 and virtually capturing the city of New Orleans, La. General Butler, on May 1st, took command there, where his vigorous and exceeding salutary administration caused great consternation among the enemy, so that in December, 1862, Jefferson Davis, president of the Confederacy, by public proclamation, declared him an outlaw, and he was then through secret intrigues of Louis Napoleon, emperor of France (then engaged in his Mexican schemes and who feared General Butler's opposition), recalled from his command in December, 1862. Near the close of 1863 he was given command of the army of the James. In October, 1864, was sent with a force to New York city to prevent an anticipated riot, and in December of that year commanded an unsuccessful expedition against Fort Fisher, and was then removed from its command by General Grant. In 1866 he was elected by the Republicans of his district as representative to Congress and (with exception of one term) he served until 1877; was principal manager in impeachment proceedings against President Andrew Johnson in 1868, and the unsuccessful Republican candidate for governor of Massachusetts in 1871 and of the Greenback party in 1878 and 1879 but in 1882 the

Democrats also uniting on him he was, after an intense personal and exciting canvass, elected governor of Massachusetts, though the rest of the ticket was overwhelmingly defeated. Was candidate the following year, but defeated, and in 1884 was Greenback and Labor party candidate for president of the United States. He married in 1842 Sarah, daughter of Dr. Israel Hildreth of Lowell, and three children survive him.

John Griffin Carlisle, lawyer, born in Kenton county, Kentucky, September 5, 1835. His father was a farmer with a large family and able to give him but meager advantages, save that of work; so he toiled hard by day; and, as lad, read and studied by night, eager for an education. His schooling was poor and brief, comprising but a few weeks in a year at a country school. When seventeen he taught such school, reading law at night. Then taught in Covington, Kentucky, where he read law with J. W. Stevenson and W. B. Kinkead, and was admitted to the bar in 1858, and at once became very successful. In 1859-61 was elected to the legislature, and in 1867 and 1869 to the state Senate. From 1871 to 1875 he was lieutenant-governor of his state, and in 1877 was elected representative to Congress, and chosen thereafter to same office for six terms, becoming the leader of his party (Democrat), and the speaker of the House, in 1883-5-7, was chosen United States Senator in 1890, and appointed by President Cleveland member of his cabinet (secretary of treasury) in 1892. Mr. Carlisle married Miss Mary Jane, daughter of Major John A. Goodson of Covington, Kentucky, January 15, 1857, and has two sons living, William K. and Libbon L.

William Maxwell Evarts, born in Boston, February 6, 1818. Fitted for college at the Latin School and entered Yale when fifteen, graduating in 1837. Took course in Harvard Law School and read law in the office of Daniel Lord of New York, and was admitted to the bar of that city in 1841. A diligent student and hard worker, he, like Rufus Choate, made it a point to read some law every day. Became noted constitutional lawyer, and was employed upon most of the great cases of his time, such as the Cuba "Cleopatra Expedition" case, the "Metropolitan Police Act" case, the "Lemmon Slave" case, the "Maratine Prize" case, the "National Bank" case, the "Parrish" and "Gardner" will cases, and many other notable trials. He was the United States counsel for the prosecution of Jefferson Davis for treason, and defended President Andrew Johnson in his "impeachment trial," and was the leading lawyer for the defense in the six months' case of Henry Ward Beecher. He was the United States counsel before the "Alabama commission," and counsel for President Hayes before the "Electoral commission." Was United States attorney general under President Johnson and United States secretary of state under President Hayes, and United States senator from New York in 1885-91. His fees as in the "Berdell mortgage" case frequently amounted to twenty-five and even fifty thousand dollars for an opinion. He has a fine residence in New York city, and a summer home in Vermont.

George Frisbie Hoar, lawyer, statesman, born in Concord, Mass., August 29, 1826. His father was an eminent lawyer and legislator, and gave his son every advantage. After the common school course he studied at the Concord Academy and at Harvard College, graduating from the latter in 1846. He then took a course at the Harvard Law School, and on graduating there removed to Worcester and soon acquired an extensive practice. In 1852 he was elected representative to the legislature and a member of the Senate of Massachusetts in 1857, and in 1869 was elected representative to Congress and served as such till 1877, when he was elected senator from Massachusetts, and re-elected in 1883, and each successive term to the present time. Mr. Hoar is, as he has been since entering public life, a great leader among men, because of his great intellectual ability and his sterling integrity. He is a prominent member of many educational societies and but few men of his time have had such a long and successful political career, and been so highly and constantly honored by their fellows as has George F. Hoar.

William McKinley, Jr., lawyer, born in Niles, Trumbull county, Ohio, February 26, 1844. He pursued his studies at the public schools till seventeen, when the call of his country induced him to enlist as a private in the Twenty-third Regiment, Ohio volunteer infantry, and he served with it until the close of the war, being mustered out as captain and brevet-major, being then twenty-one years old. He at once entered upon the study of law, becoming widely known and successful in his profession, and for two years served as prosecuting attorney for Stark county; at close of this service he was elected representative to Congress, serving for six terms and up to March 4, 1891, and becoming greatly known and loved by his party and associates. During his last term he was chairman of the committee, framing the tariff measure that bears with the public, his name, and so has become one of the most noted and prominent men of his time. In 1891 he was elected governor of Ohio, and again in 1893.

George Dexter Robinson, lawyer, born in Lexington, Mass., January 20, 1834. Father was a successful farmer, and George spent his early years on the farm, attending school according to the custom, in the winter season. When sixteen he entered the academy at Lexington. He afterwards studied at the Hopkins Classical School at Cambridge, and at Harvard University, where he graduated in 1856. At his graduation he became principal of the high school at Chicopee, Mass., which position he retained nine years, and in 1865, went to Charlestown, Mass., and studied law in the office of his brother and was admitted to the bar in 1866, and returned to Chicopee, where he at once took high rank in his profession. In 1873 he was elected representative to the legislature, and two years later was elected to the Senate. He then served four terms in Congress, and was then nominated for governor against General Butler and elected, serving as governor from 1884 to 1887, and on retirement from governor's chair, declined further political honors and resumed the practice of law at Chicopee, where he now resides, and has a large and lucrative practice.

John Sherman, United States senator from Ohio for six terms, is brother of Gen. William T. Sherman, and the eighth of his father's eleven children. He was born in Lancaster, Ohio, May 10, 1823. His father was Charles Robert Sherman, lawyer, who came to Ohio from Connecticut in 1810, and became judge of Ohio's supreme court. The father died suddenly when John was six years old, leaving the family in straitened circumstances. John was sent to a cousin's, who gave him four years of schooling. Then he attended an academy for two years. Compelled by poverty to forego a much cherished college course, he began at fourteen to earn his way as rodman for public surveyors on the Muskingum river, but was discharged at seventeen for political reasons, and thereupon resolved to become a lawyer, and studied with his brother, afterward Judge Charles T. Sherman. He was elected to the Thirty-fourth Congress in 1855, and has been in public life since. He became secretary of the United States treasury, under President Hayes, and has led a stirring and eventful life. This once poor boy, genial, prudent, studious, methodical, has won a competence for himself, and has become a great leader among men.

Allen Grauber Thurman, lawyer, born in Lynchburg, Va., November 13, 1813. His father was a clergyman of the Methodist church and his mother a daughter of Colonel Nathaniel Allen of Ohio. When he was six years old, his parents removed to Chillicothe, Ohio, where he was educated first in the public schools and by his mother (a woman of fine talents), and then studied at the Chillicothe Academy. When eighteen he became assistant surveyor of land, and when twenty-one was private secretary to Governor Robert Lucas. The following year he studied law in the office of his uncle Governor William Allen, and was admitted to the bar in 1835 and soon became noted as an able and successful lawyer. In 1844 he was elected to Congress by the Democrats of his district but declined a renomination. In 1851 he became one of the judges of the supreme court of Ohio, and from 1854 to 1856 its chief justice, his decision attracting much distinction. March 4, 1869, he took his seat at Washington as United States senator, succeeding Benjamin F. Wade, and continued to serve as such till March 4, 1881, when the vicissitudes of politics relegated him to private life. During his senatorial career he was not only the leader of his party, but was also highly respected by those not of his political faith. In 1888 Mr. Thurman was the candidate for the vice-presidency of the United States on the ticket with Grover Cleveland.

Henry Wilson, statesman, lawyer, born in Farmington, N. H., February 16, 1812; died in Washington, D. C., November 22, 1875. His father was a farm laborer and a poor man and the family had hard fare, and when Henry was ten years old he was apprenticed to a farmer till twenty-one, and during the eleven years he had less than twelve months schooling all told, but he read over a thousand volumes he had borrowed of the neighbors. When twenty-one he had his name of Jeremiah Jones Colbaith changed by act of legislature to that of Henry Wilson, by which he is now known. Shortly after coming of age he went to Natick, Mass., and learned the trade of making shoes, toiling incessantly and saving all he could in order to gain an education for the law, but through the failure of one to whom he had intrusted his savings he had to cut short his academy course, and he returned to Natick and again engaged in the shoe business as manufacturer, amassing some property, and studying as he had opportunity. Was elected as representative to Massachusetts legislature for years 1840-3, and from 1845-8 as senator. Then for two years he was editor and chief owner of the Boston *Republican*, a weekly journal and leading organ of his Free Soil party. From 1850-3 was again senator and president of that body. The latter year was candidate of his party for governor, but was defeated, and in 1855 was by aid of American (Know Nothing) party elected to United States Senate, succeeding Edward Everett, but that year the American party adopting in its national platform resolutions countenancing slavery, he withdrew and took an active part in forming the Republican party, of which he was thereafter a leading member, serving as United States senator for eighteen years, for eight years being chairman of that most important committee on military affairs. In 1861 he recruited the 22d Regiment Massachusetts volunteers, and went to the field as its colonel, and served as aid on staff of General George B. McClellan till Congress reassembled. In 1872 he was elected vice-president of United States on ticket with U. S. Grant, having 286 out of 354 electoral votes. In the following year he was stricken with paralysis, and remained very infirm till his death, that came by apoplexy. During all the years of his public life he stood boldly, unflinchingly, for the right, and died at the post of duty, as he had always lived, rich alone in his integrity and self-respect, and the esteem of good men, and the gratitude of the down-trodden and oppressed, for whom he had unceasingly labored.

TEN GREAT REFORMERS.

William Booth, general of the Salvation Army, born at Nottingham, England, April 10, 1829, and educated at a private school in that town. Studied theology with the Rev. William Cooke, D.D., became a minister of the Methodist New Connection in 1850, and was mostly employed in evangelistic services. Coming to the East End, of London, observed that the vast majority of the people attended no place of worship; and in July, 1865, started the "Christian Mission." This became a large organization formed on military lines, and received the name of the "Salvation Army" and in 1885, it had 1,322 corps at stations in the United Kingdom, France, United States, Australia, India, Cape of Good Hope, Canada, and Sweden; 3,076 officers or evangelists were then entirely employed in and supported by this army, and are under General Booth's absolute control. The general has published several books. Every member of his family is actively employed in some branch of the army's service. In November, 1890, General Booth published "In Darkest London," a volume containing a scheme for the enlightenment and industrial support of the lower classes, which has met with almost universal approval.

Dorothea Lynde Dix, author and philanthropist, born in Hampden, Maine, April 4, 1802; died in Trenton, N. J., July 19, 1887. Her father was a visionary, wandering man, and when fourteen she began teaching a private school in Worcester, Mass., then she went to Boston to live with her grandmother, and for study, and her father dying in 1821, she established in Boston a school for girls at her home. In 1830, inheriting a modest competence from her grandmother and learning of the then neglected condition of the criminal classes and the unfortunate, and encouraged by Rev. Dr. Channing and other friends, she began to visit public institutions and to investigate their condition and minister to their inmates. In 1834 she went to Europe to learn by personal observation the treatment of prisoners, paupers, and the insane, and on her return in 1837 visited all the states east of the Rocky mountains and by her personal exertions succeeded in establishing thirty-two asylums for the unfortunate and insane in this and other lands. Twice she petitioned Congress for appropriations of public lands wherewith to endow hospitals for the indigent insane, and in 1854 succeeded in getting an appropriation of ten million acres for this purpose, which President Pierce vetoed. July 10, 1861, she was made superintendent of nurses in the United States Army hospitals, and during the civil war had entire charge of their appointment and assignment to duty, and herself served without salary. At the close of the war she again took up her labor for the insane and unfortunate. She also wrote a volume on "Prison Discipline," several tracts for prisoners, and documents on philanthropic subjects, and some miscellaneous volumes of wide circulation, her "Conversations on Common Things" having gone through more than sixty editions. But few philanthropists have done as much for suffering humanity as did Miss Dix.

Frederick Douglass, orator, reformer, born a slave in Talbot county, Md., February, 1817, to Captain Aaron Anthony, agent of Colonel Edward Lloyd's estate. Father a white man, mother mulatto. At eight he was sent to Baltimore, where he learned the alphabet of a white woman, and then, when that was forbidden him, learned of white boys in streets and on the wharves, and spelled the sign boards and bills on the walls. At eleven was set to work in ship-yard, and practiced writing on boards. When fifteen sent to farm of Edward Covey and harshly treated, and at last rebelled at being brutally flogged and attempted to escape, and was put in prison, and then returned to Mr. Covey's brother in Baltimore, where he worked in a ship-yard for two years and a half, and then escaped September 2, 1838, and went to New Bedford, Mass., where he worked as stevedore and was asked to speak at anti-slavery meetings His speeches attracted great attention, and in 1841 he was induced to take the platform in behalf of his people, and traveled through New England, and west to Indiana, having his right hand broken by one of the frequent mobs in the latter state. In 1844 he wrote his narrative, and had to go to England to escape arrest as a runaway slave, and lectured in England, Ireland, Scotland, and Wales, and was then ransomed of his old master by Mrs. and Miss Richardson of Newcastle-on-Tyne, for $750, and returned to the United States and published a paper at Rochester, N. Y., from December, 1847-63, and lectured throughout the Northern states. At the John Brown raid, 1859, was indicted and fled to England. During war took part in raising the Fifty-fourth and Fifty-fifth Massachusetts regiments colored troops, two sons being in the regiments. At close of war edited a paper for two years at Washington, D. C. In 1871 sent by President Grant commissioner to St. Domingo. In 1872 presidential elector from New York, and 1877 appointed United States marshal for District of Columbia, by President Hayes, and in 1881 recorder of deeds of District by President Garfield, and in 1889 appointed minister to Hayti by President Harrison, resigning in 1891.

Neal Dow, reformer, born March 20, 1804, in Portland, Me. Father (Josiah) was a prosperous tanner. The son was educated at public and private schools in Portland, and at Friends' Academy, New Bedford, Mass., and trained to business pursuits. He began in youth to oppose the use of intoxicants, then well-nigh universal, and when James Appleton made his report to the Maine legislature of 1836-7 advocating the prohibition of the sale of intoxicants by law, Mr. Dow espoused the cause, being stirred to action by an appeal of the wife of a friend ruined by drink, and he therefore devoted himself to the task of creating a public sentiment in favor of suppressing the sale of liquors in Maine. He spent many years in canvassing the state, lecturing, holding mass-meetings, scattering temperance documents by the scores of thousands, enlisting everybody whom he could in the work, and in 1846 secured the first prohibitory act, that, through defects, accomplished but little. Nothing daunted, he continued his agitation throughout the state until he secured the election of a legislature pledged to enact prohibition, in 1851, and being then the mayor of his native city, he drafted what he called, "a bill for the suppression of drinking houses and tippling shops," which he submitted to the leading temperance people of his city, who objected to its radical character and predicted its defeat. Undiscouraged he went to Augusta, the capital, April 29, 1851—two days before the legislature was to adjourn—and the next morning asked for the appointment of a committee to consider his bill and give a hearing in the afternoon, which was granted. A dense crowd attended the hearing; he spoke for more than an hour in favor of the bill, explaining its features. The committee reported unanimously in its favor, it was printed that night by a rumseller, laid on the desks of the members the next morning, and that day passed (April 30) by a vote of 86-40 in the House, and 18-10 in the Senate, without a change of a word, was at once signed by the Democratic governor, and the now immortal Maine law went into the pages of history to bless, by saving men. Notwithstanding repeated attempts to repeal it and nullify it, it yet remains as his monument and the most beneficent act of legislation of the century. In 1884 the people of his state put prohibition into the constitution by an amendment having a majority of 47,075 votes, and an affirmative more than three times that of the negative. Mr. Dow was elected member of the legislature in 1858-9, and December 31, 1861, appointed colonel of the 13th Maine regiment volunteers, and joined General Butler's expedition to the Gulf, was commissioned brigadier-general volunteers April 28, 1862, and given command of forts at the mouth of the Mississippi, and later of the district of Florida. He was twice wounded in the attack on Port Hudson, May 27, 1863, and taken prisoner while lying in a house near by and carried to Mobile, and to Libby prison, Richmond, Va., and after eight months exchanged; he resigned his commission November 30, 1864. He was twice mayor of his city, has made three visits to England on behalf of prohibition and numerous visits to Canada, and traveled extensively throughout the United States, giving a multitude of addresses in behalf of his reform. On March 20, 1894, his birthday was celebrated in all the four quarters of the globe, including a meeting in Jerusalem in the Holy Land, more than two hundred separate meetings in England, and thousands in this country, he receiving on that day thousands of messages of congratulation and many hundreds of telegrams from all parts of the world, and addressing an immense throng in his city, opening with the ancient gladiators' cry, "I who am about to die, salute you."

William Lloyd Garrison, reformer, born in Newburyport, Mass., December 10, 1805; died May 24, 1879, in New York city. His father, a native of Nova Scotia, was a sea captain of intelligence and ability, who, unfortunately, ruined himself by the drink curse and disappeared when William was some six years of age. His mother was a woman of sterling character and strong moral convictions, which were imparted to her boy and markedly distinguished him through life. When he was nine years old he went to Lynn to learn shoemaking, but being small and frail had to abandon it. Then for a time he worked for a cabinet maker, and when thirteen was apprenticed to the publisher of Newburyport *Herald* for seven years. Here he began writing for the paper. At end of his apprenticeship he published the *Free Press* at Newburyport, a reform journal to which Whittier contributed anonymously. The paper failed, and he worked for a time on *National Philanthropist* at Boston, then went to Bennington, Vt., on *Journal of Times*, and in 1829 to Baltimore, Md., on Benjamin Lundy's *Genius of Emancipation*, where he continued to write against slavery, and was under the state laws arrested therefor, and imprisoned in the jail, his fine being at length paid by an unknown friend, Arthur Tappan, a wealthy merchant of New York city. As soon as released he began lecturing against slavery, and then, January 1, 1831, he founded at Boston, Mass., *The Liberator*, a weekly journal, which he edited for thirty-five years, announcing in his first issue his ultimatum, " I will be as hard as truth, and as uncompromising as justice. On this subject I do not wish to think, or speak, or write with moderation . . . urge me not to use moderation in a cause like the present. I am in earnest; I will not equivocate; I will not excuse; I will not retract a single inch; and I will be heard." So he made his appeal, not to the passions, but to the consciences of men and was heard and persecuted, was mobbed, held up to public scorn as a fanatic and incendiary, outraged, and efforts made to suppress his paper. The whole land was speedily filled with excitement and turmoil, for his colaborers gathering courage by his example wrought mightily for the truth and liberty. The state of Georgia offered $5,000 reward for his arrest and conveyance there, while in 1835 an angry mob dragged him through the streets of Boston with a rope around his neck, intent on hanging him, and he was only saved by his friends lodging him in jail under pretense of punishing him. Those who lived through those troublous days remember vividly how slavery raged and punished all whom it could reach who dared even to speak against it. As a sample—a theological student, Amos Dresser, selling Bibles in Nashville, Tenn., was publicly whipped in the city square because, unknown to him, some of his books had been wrapped by the shippers in cast-off anti-slavery papers! While in the North, Marius Robinson was (with great cruelty) tarred and feathered in Ohio by a mob for having lectured against slavery; and at Alton, Ill., the Rev. Elijah P. Lovejoy had his paper and press twice destroyed by a mob, and at length was cruelly murdered by them in 1837, as though the right was ever dangerous, or could be destroyed by angry men! In 1844 Garrison became convinced that slavery's prime defense was in the United States Constitution, and, borrowing Isaiah's words he thereafter denounced it as " an agreement with death and a covenant with hell," and unterrified by almost daily threats of violence, often denounced by friends as well as foes, this man of the vanguard, wrote, lectured, labored, until January 1, 1863, when he saw his work crowned by the Emancipation Proclamation of President Lincoln, and slavery died the death of violence at its own defenders' hands. After the civil war the leaders of the Republican party and personal friends contributed a purse of $30,000 to him, and he ended his days in peace, ease, and honor, and Boston, at his death, erected a bronze statue to the memory of him whom once it sought to hang. Perhaps it will yet be confessed that Wendell Phillips's eulogium of him at his burial was not overwrought—"noblest of Christian men, leader, brave, tireless, unselfish. The ear that heard thee, it blessed thee. The eye that saw thee, gave witness to thee. More truly than it could be uttered since the great patriot wrote it, 'the blessings of him that was ready to perish are thine own eternal, great reward.'"

John Bartholomew Gough, temperance reformer, born in Sandgate, Kent, England, August 22, 1817. Received early education from his mother; was sent to the United States when but twelve years old. Arrived in New York in August, 1829, and went to Oneida county remaining on a farm there for two years. Obtained a situation in a publishing house in New York city, learning the trade of a bookbinder. The mother and sister joined him, but in 1833, during a financial depression, he lost the situation, the family was reduced to destitution, the mother died and the son drifted into dissipation. For some years he obtained a precarious living by singing and giving comic impersonations, about drinking shops. Had always a passion for the stage and once or twice attempted to become an actor, but, owing to bad habits, met with little favor. In 1839, became an independent bookbinder. In 1842, while on the verge of delirium tremens, a kind Quaker influenced him to sign the pledge. From this time, was possessed of an irresistible desire to work for the cause of temperance; carpet bag in hand, the new apostle of temperance set forth to tramp through the New England states, glad to obtain even seventy-five cents for a lecture. An intense earnestness, derived from experience, with the power of imitation and expression, gave great power over audiences. During the first year, spoke three hundred and eighty-six times, and thenceforward, for seventeen years, spoke only upon temperance, addressing not less than 5,000 audiences. Visited

England in 1853, by invitation of the London Temperance League, and by the first lecture at Exeter Hall produced a great sensation. Was busied there for two years, returning to America and to his former work, in 1855. In 1857, made another journey to England, lecturing for three years. Made a considerable fortune by public speaking. An apoplectic stroke terminated his life, February 18, 1886.

John Howard was born at Hackney, England, in 1726. Was apprenticed to a grocer, but purchased indentures, and having considerable means, made a tour through France and Italy. Resided in England for a few years, after returning from this tour; then sailed for Lisbon, to see the ravages of the great earthquake. The frigate in which he embarked was captured by a French privateer, and the rigorous confinement endured in French prisons originated that sympathy for suffering captives, destined to bear fruit in later days. In 1773, having purchased an estate at Cardington, near Bedford, filled the office of sheriff, and thus became more intimately acquainted with the sufferings of prisoners. Visited the jails of England with the purpose of administering relief and suggesting improvement; and received the thanks of the Commons. He then traveled on the Continent, inspecting the prisons; passed three times through those of France, four times through the German, five times through the Holland, twice through the Italian, and once through those of Spain and Portugal, between the years of 1775 and 1787. Proposed a similar visitation in Russia and the East, but became infected with malignant fever and died Jan. 20, 1790.

Francis Murphy, temperance lecturer, born in County of Wexford, Ireland, April 24, 1836, was youngest of seven children. His father lost his little home by debt, and they moved to a cottage on the seashore, where, shortly before Francis's birth, the father and five children died of scarlet fever, and the widow and her remaining children saw deep poverty for years. He had but little schooling, and when a small lad was servant to a nobleman, who was often intoxicated, and who, after the customs of the country, taught his servant to drink. When sixteen he begged his mother's permission to come to America, and landing in New York soon spent the little money he had in drink and then spent two years there in want and suffering through drunkenness, and, finally was driven out of the city by a drinking Scotchman in order to save him, and he got work with a farmer and led a sober life for six years. When eighteen he married, and his brother having come to America also, when Francis was twenty-two they went to New England, and at length to Portland, Maine, where they kept a hotel, and sold liquors contrary to the law. Some time after the brother left and Francis took to drinking with his customers, lost his property, and sank to keeping a low groggery and lodging-house, the wife struggling to keep her children from starving. On July 30, 1870, he was arrested and lodged in jail, when Capt. Cyrus Sturdevant visited the prisoners holding meetings on the Sabbath, and Mr. Murphy was converted in the jail and was released on the 30th of October, before the expiration of the sentence, through the intercession of Captain Sturdevant and friends, and found his family at the point of starvation. Three months later the wife died of her sorrows and sufferings. After his release from prison Mr. Murphy supported his family by sawing wood until at the invitation of Captain Sturdevant and others he began to address the public on the subject of temperance, giving on April 3, 1871, his first temperance lecture in the city hall, in Portland, and thought he had made a most miserable failure as a speaker, but was given over a half-hundred invitations to lecture ere he left the hall, and thereafter gave himself to the work of reform, giving some forty consecutive lectures in that city and then repeating through the state the tragic story of his life and rescue. He then went to Rhode Island for four months, where many hundreds signed his pledge. He next spent a year in New Hampshire, and in September, 1874, delivered his famous lecture, "Real Life," at the National Temperance camp meeting at Old Orchard Beach, Me., before an audience of 15,000 people, and became known throughout the country, and the following November went to Chicago and gave a series of thirty-two lectures to immense audiences, multitudes taking his pledge. And he afterward labored in Illinois, Michigan, and Iowa, having 1,300 applications for his services within a year. In the winter of 1876 he labored in Pittsburgh, Pa., where more than 50,000 persons signed his pledge of total abstinence, and in that city, as a result of his labors, there was organized on February 22, 1877, the National Christian Temperance Union, that in the following October reported over three million signers to what is known as Mr. Murphy's pledge. Mr. Murphy continued for many years to labor in his chosen field with most remarkable success, moving his vast audiences as but few men have ever done. Of late years his son Edward T. has taken up the father's work, with similar success, both laboring on what is known as gospel temperance lines, or moral suasion efforts against the drink traffic.

Wendell Phillips, orator, reformer, born in Boston, Mass., November 29, 1811; died in

Boston, February 2, 1884. His father, John, was the first mayor of Boston, and for thirteen years previous to the time of his death, a member of the state Senate, and for ten years its president. Wendell was educated in the public schools and at the Latin school and at Harvard College, graduating from the latter in 1831 with Motley, the historian. He was converted under Dr. Lyman Beecher's revival ministry, and remained always evangelical in his faith. After graduation at Harvard he gave a year to study of English history, and then spent three years at Harvard Law School, being admitted to the bar in 1834, resolving "if clients do not come, I will throw myself heart and soul into some good cause and devote my life to it," and the "good cause" calling on him first as he looked out of his office window October 21, 1835, it was the most gifted orator of Massachusetts, who thenceforth gave it the devotion of his life. On that day a mob of "gentlemen of property and standing" were collected in Washington and State streets to break up an anti-slavery meeting of ladies and "snake out that infamous foreign scoundrel, Thompson" (George), and "bring him to the tar-kettle before dark,"—the man of whom John Bright declares, "I have always considered him the liberator of the slaves in the English colonies; for, without his commanding eloquence, made irresistible by the blessedness of his cause, I do not think all the other agencies then at work would have procured their freedom,"—the Thompson of whom Lord Brougham spoke in the House of Lords, when the Act of British Emancipation was passed, "I rise to take the crown of victory from every other head and place it upon his. He has done more than any other man to achieve it,"—the Thompson whom a mob in Springfield, Mass., burned in effigy on the public square. But this mob of "gentlemen" not finding him, found William Lloyd Garrison, whose *Liberator* for four years had been a stench in their nostrils, and so they proceeded to drag him through the streets with a rope around his waist, intent on hanging him and were only kept from their purpose by the desperate ruse of the mayor and a few friends who arrested Garrison and lodged him in jail, and so saved his life. This act fired Phillips's soul, and when a few months later, 1837, Elijah P. Lovejoy was murdered at Alton, Ill., for his anti-slavery opinions, Phillips openly announced himself an abolitionist, and was henceforth the most eloquent and noted advocate of freedom. How untiringly, loyally, heroically he wrought, during his life for the liberty of the black man, for suffrage for women, for the righting of the Indians' wrongs, for the overthrow of the legalized liquor traffic, for justice to labor, we have not space to tell.

As an orator, he stood foremost as the people's favorite speaker, and in the days when he was deluged with calls to lecture at an hundred dollars and more a night, he would always stipulate that he would lecture for nothing if he might speak against slavery. Loved by friends of freedom, hated by those of slavery, as no other man of his time was, he lived to see the negroes free, and himself as greatly honored as he had formerly been despised. In 1870 he was the Prohibition candidate for governor of Massachusetts, and at his death was followed by a vast multitude to Fanueil Hall, where his remains lay in state. A collection of his speeches, letters, and lectures, revised by himself, were published in 1863.

John P. Saint John, reformer, born in Brookville, Indiana, February 25, 1833. He received his education in a shackling log schoolhouse, his early years being darkened by the drink curse in his home. When a lad worked in a country store as clerk and chore boy, at six dollars a month, until nineteen, when he went to California; not finding fortune there he went to Mexico, South America, Sandwich Islands, and returning to the United States took part in the then Indian war in California and Oregon. In 1859 left the Pacific coast and resided at Charleston, Ill., where he was prosecuted under the infamous "Black laws," for having given food to a hungry colored boy. He pleaded guilty and was acquitted. He then studied law and was admitted to the bar in 1862. Enlisting in the Union army as private, he served two years and was commissioned as captain, major, and lieutenant-colonel of his regiment. In 1864 he left the army and practiced law for four years at Independence, Mo. In 1869 removed to Olatho, Kansas, where he has since lived. Was state senator in 1872 and elected governor by the Republican party in 1878 and re-elected in 1880 by a greatly increased majority and carrying the constitutional amendment which declares that "the manufacture and sale of intoxicating liquors shall be forever prohibited except for medical, scientific, and mechanical purposes." In 1884, when his party refused to take the defense of the temperance cause, he left it and was nominated as candidate for president by the Prohibition party, receiving 150,676 votes and was denounced and burned and hung in effigy in various places as the cause of defeating his old party, as the candidate of the Abolitionist or Free Soil party (Martin Van Buren) was treated in 1848 for causing the defeat of Lewis Cass. Mr. St. John has since been actively engaged throughout the country upon the lecture platform, being a powerful and convincing speaker in behalf of his loved cause.

SUCCESSFUL MEN AND WOMEN.

FAMOUS WOMEN.

Louisa May Alcott, author, born in Germantown, Pa., November 29, 1832, on anniversary of her father's (A. Bronson Alcott, "the sage of Concord") birthday, and died at Boston, Mass., March 6, 1888, two days after her father's death. Her father was a distinguished lecturer and teacher, residing at Concord, Mass., Louisa being the second of his four daughters. She began to write "poems" when eight years old. Her teacher aside from her father, was that eccentric genius, Henry Thoreau. At sixteen she began to teach a school, and during a period of fifteen years continued at it, varying it by serving as nursery governess, and anon sewing for a living, helping in the support of her parents. Wrote stories for various publications, but, like many other authors, found her work discouraging. In 1862 she served in army hospital at Washington, D. C., and came near dying from overwork and a fever she contracted. In 1863, she went to Europe as companion to an invalid lady, traveling in Germany, Switzerland, France, and England. The several volumes she published met with poor reception, until, in 1868, she published her "Little Women" (two volumes), a story founded on incidents in the lives of her sisters and herself at Concord. This work made her famous, it reaching a sale of over 87,000 copies in three years. Her "Little Men" (1871) had orders in advance of publication from dealers for 50,000 copies, and more than a half million of her numerous works have been sold in the United States.

Susan Brownell Anthony, reformer, born at South Adams, Mass, February 15, 1820. Her father, Daniel Anthony, was a cotton manufacturer and a Friend, who, having married a Baptist lady and wearing on the occasion a comfortable coat was disciplined therefor, which proceeding naturally alienated the family. Susan received a good education, and at seventeen, her father having failed in business, she began to make her own way by teaching school for $1.50 a week and board around. For thirteen years she followed teaching with ever-growing indignation at seeing men who had but a tithe of her qualifications getting three times as much as she for the same work, and at length made her first public speech at the New York State Teachers' Association, where they were discussing the question, "Why the profession of the teacher was not considered as honorable as that of the minister, the doctor, and lawyer?" Asking permission to speak, she put to them this pointed question, "Do you not see that so long as society says a woman has not brains enough to be a lawyer, a doctor, or a minister, but has ample brains to be a teacher, that every man of you who condescends to teach school tacitly acknowledges before all Israel and the sun that he hasn't any more brains than a woman?" In 1849 she began to publicly lecture for the temperance cause, but after two years of effort she became convinced that if the cause succeeded woman must have the ballot, and from that time to the present she has constantly advocated the cause of woman's legal emancipation. From 1856 to the overthrow of slavery she gave her time largely to lecturing against that crime, and circulated and presented petitions to Congress against it. For two and a half years she was editor and proprietor of *The Revolution*, published weekly at New York, and though an able journal, through the prejudices of the time it failed and she was $10,000 in debt, which sum with interest she paid by public lectures, speaking during 1870-80 five to six times a week in all parts of the country, constantly advocating equal political rights for woman. In 1872 she voted at presidential election in order to test the validity of the statutes; was arrested, and her counsel, wishing to save her from imprisonment, gave bail and so lost her opportunity to carry her case to the United States Supreme Court, a proceeding she always after regretted; at the time she was simply fined, but has steadily refused to pay it. In 1880 she made her plea for equal suffrage before the United States Senate judiciary committee, a plea that Senator Edmunds pronounced unanswerable and a credit if given before the Supreme Court; and though she has not yet realized the fulfillment of her desires, she has lived to see many of the wrongs of women abolished and her right to the ballot conceded in part by several of the states of the Union, and in full by a few, and a constantly developing sentiment in favor of woman suffrage, especially among all intelligent communities.

Elizabeth Barrett Browning, the first of female poets, born at Burn Hall, Durham, England, March 6, 1809; died at Florence, Italy, June 30, 1861. Was eldest daughter of Edward Moulton, who afterward took the name of Barrett, and removed to his country house at Hope End, Herefordshire. She was educated with great care, and began to write for periodicals at a very early age. When fifteen, trying to saddle her pony alone in the field, she fell and injured her spine, having thereafter to remain for years lying upon her back. In 1838 her delicate health was further impaired by rupture of a blood vessel and soon after a brother accidentally drowned while on a visit to her, and then for years she never left her room, but lay hovering between life and death. In 1843 she wrote the "Cry of the Children," so often quoted, and the next year the collected edition of her poems appeared in two volumes and contained "Lady Geraldine's Courtship" with its graceful compliment to the poet, Mr. Robert Browning, whom she did not personally know. Mr. Browning called to express thanks, the acquaintance ripened into love, and in 1846, her health being improved, they were married and went to the Continent and soon to Italy and settled in Florence, where their boy was born in 1849. Her beautiful idyls, "Sonnets from the Portuguese," due to her husband's calling her "his Portuguese," appeared in the second edition of her poems in 1850. In 1851 she published "Guidi's Windows" and in 1856 "Aurora Leigh." The "Poems Before Congress" appeared in 1860, and "The Last Poems" were published (after her death) in 1862. Of her person Hawthorne said after visiting her: "It is wonderful to see how small she is, how pale her cheeks, how bright and dark her eyes. There is not such another figure in the world, and her black ringlets cluster down into her neck and make her face look whiter." After her death her husband and son resided in London. Mr. Browning, who was born at St. Giles, London, May 7, 1812, and who began to write poems when but eight years of age, and was an extensive writer of great merit, in drama and lyric, died in Venice, Italy, December 12, 1889.

Clara Louise Kellogg, opera singer, born in Sumterville, South Carolina, July 12, 1842. Her father, George Kellogg, was inventor, and her mother a fine musician and a clairvoyant physician, Clara being only child. Her childhood was spent in Birmingham, Conn. Her musical talent seems to have been an inheritance like many another's genius, for when nine months old she could hum tunes correctly. She was given a good education, and, on the removal of her father to New York in 1856, she applied herself to the study of music, both French and Italian methods, and in 1860 made her debut as "Gilda" in the Academy of Music of that city. In 1864 she won much renown as Marguerite in Gounod's Faust, and after singing in various cities of United States, she went to London, where her rendering of Marguerite at once placed her in the front rank of famous singers. On her return in 1868 she made, with Max Strakosch, a concert tour of the United States, and afterward spent three seasons in Italian opera, in New York city. She then organized a company to sing in English during 1874-5, singing in a single season one hundred and twenty-five nights. In 1880 she sang in Italian in Austria and Russia with a German company, and in 1889 gave her last concert tour. She was the first American singer to gain renown in Europe, and has amassed a large fortune; her list of operas including some forty-five casts. Her voice in youth was high soprano, with range from C to E flat. Is wife of Carl Strakosch.

Jenny Lind-Goldschmidt, singer, born in Stockholm, Sweden, October 6, 1820; died Wynd's Point, Malvern, England, November 2, 1887. When three years old she delighted her friends by her fine singing, and when nine years of age was admitted by Count Puke to the musical academy at Stockholm, and made such progress that in a year she appeared on the stage in juvenile parts, and for two years performed to the delight of Stockholm audiences at the Court Theater. Then the upper notes of her voice became harsh and clouded and her friends abandoned the idea of fitting her for grand opera. For four years she was forbidden to exercise her voice, but when sixteen was called on to take a small part in Meyerbeer's opera, and discovered that her voice had returned to her, and then she was for some years the prima donna of the Stockholm opera. In 1841, feeling that her naturally harsh and unbending voice was not under her control, she went to Paris for study under Garcia, then the first singing master in Europe. He gave her but little encouragement, but for nine months she bent herself unswervingly to reach her ideal, and then Meyerbeer went to hear her; was delighted, and predicted a brilliant career for her. In August, 1844, she went to Berlin and studied German, and in September sang in Stockholm at the crowning of King Oscar, and returned the next month to Berlin, singing there and in Hamburg, Cologne, and Coblentz, Leipsic, Copenhagen, and Vienna. May 4, 1847, she made her first appearance in London at Her Majesty's Theatre in Robert le Diable and in Alice, to immense and wildly enthusiastic audiences, and reappeared there for each of the next two years, and on May 18, 1849, abandoned finally the stage for the concert room. In 1850, she was engaged by P. T. Barnum to make a most memorable tour of the United States, and arrived there in 1850, and remained for near two years; and on February 5, 1852, married at Boston, Mass., Mr. Otto Goldschmidt, the pianist and composer. On her return to Europe, she traveled through Holland and Germany, and to London, England, in 1856, where she continued to reside till her death, becoming the mother of a family and appearing frequently in oratorios and concerts, and maintaining to the last her interest in music, her last public services being from Easter, 1883, to Easter, 1886, when she served as professor of singing at the Royal College of Music (London). Her voice was a remarkable, bright, sympathetic, and rich soprano, having a compass of somewhat over two and one-half octaves, ranging generally from D to high D, and at times two notes above, and which voice she had so trained as to be able to execute some most marvelous passages in oratorio, E in alt, and which made her one of the most remarkable singers the world has ever known. Mrs. Goldschmidt was attractive in person and manner, and a woman of rare purity of spirit, and of great benevolence, having built at her expense a hospital at Liverpool and part of another in London, besides endowing many art-scholarships, and other charities in her native land, the whole of the vast proceeds of her American tour going toward the last enterprise.

Christine Nilsson, operatic singer, born in Wexio, Wederslof, Sweden, August 20, 1843. Her father was poor, and conducted a small farm on the estate of Count Hamilton. (The little farm called Sjoabal she bought, after the death of her parents, with her first professional earnings, and gave to her eldest brother.) She early showed great aptitude for music, and while a small girl became proficient on the violin and flute, and visited fairs and other gatherings, singing for a living, and while at a fair at Ljungby, in June, 1857, her extraordinary voice attracted the attention of Mr. F. G. Tornerhjelm, a gentleman of influence who was instrumental in rescuing her from her vagrant life, and she was given some lessons by Baroness Leuhusen, herself a singer of note, and went to school at Halmstad and then studied at Stockholm under Franz Berwald, and in six months was able to sing before the Court of Sweden. She then went to Paris, France, with the Baroness Leuhusen, and studied under M. Masiet and M. Martel, and made her debut at the Theatre Lyrique, October 27, 1864, as Violetta, in a French version in La Traviata, and was then engaged at the Lyrique for nearly three years, and afterward went to England, appearing at Her Majesty's Theatre, June 8, 1867, as Violetta, and subsequently as Lady Henrietta, Elvira, Don Giovanni, and as Margaret in Faust, singing also in the Crystal Palace and Birmingham Festival. The following year she sang in Italian opera in England and then went to Baden-Baden, and Paris. In 1870-72 she first appeared in the United States, singing in concert and Italian opera, under M. Strakosch, and netting her $150,000 the first year. In 1872, she returned to Drury Lane, London, and on July 27 of that year was married at Westminster Abbey, to M. Auguste Rouzaud, an eminent merchant of Paris, France. In 1873 and 1874, she was again in the United States, and in 1876 made her first professional tour of her native land, meeting with extraordinary success, and has frequently appeared at St. Petersburg, Moscow, Vienna, Berlin, and other capitals of Europe. Her first husband, M. Rouzaud, dying at Paris, February 22, 1882, she was again married in March, 1887, to the Count Casa de Miranda, and the following year gave her farewell concert and retired to private life. Mme. Nilsson is charming in manner and appearance, of slight physique, and her voice, while of moderate power, is one of great sweetness, evenness, and brilliancy in all its register, having a compass of two and one-half octaves from G natural to D in alt.

Alice Elvira Freeman Palmer, educator, born in Colesville, N. Y., February 21, 1855, being eldest of five children. During her childhood her parents lived on a farm, but her father's health being delicate and farm work uncongenial, he went to Albany and studied medicine, her mother carrying on the farm. After his graduation and when Alice was ten years old Dr. Freeman went to Windsor, N. Y., to practice his profession. Here the daughter studied diligently and when seventeen entered Michigan University, graduating in 1876. She became professor of history in Wellesley College, Massachusetts, in 1879, its acting president in 1881, and accepted the presidency of that institution in 1882, continuing till 1888. Was given the degree of Ph.D. by Michigan University in 1882 and of Doctor of Letters by Columbia College in 1887, marrying that year, Prof. George Herbert Palmer of Harvard University, and then resigned her most active and public duties. She was the Massachusetts commissioner of education to World's Fair, Chicago, president Woman's Educational Association, member Massachusetts State Board of Education, trustee of Wellesley College for women, and president of Collegiate Alumnæ. Her home is in Cambridge, Mass.

Mrs. Bertha Palmer, wife of Potter Palmer, born in Louisville, Ky., where her girlhood was spent. She was given a fine education, and after study in her native city, took a course in the convent school at Georgetown, D. C. Her maiden name was Bertha Honore. Shortly after her graduation she became the wife of Mr. Potter Palmer of Chicago, Ill., where she has since resided, her home being a marvel of luxury, and she a leader of fashion in her city, her husband a man of great wealth. Mrs. Palmer was chosen president of the Board of Lady Managers of the Women's Department of the Columbian Exposition, and in 1891 visited Europe in its interest, and to her was largely due the great success of that department of that notable World's Fair. She is slight in person, tall, having dark eyes and hair, is a fine musician and an accomplished linguist, of good executive abilities, of beautiful form and features, and a woman of many personal graces.

SUCCESSFUL MEN AND WOMEN.

Lucy Stone-Blackwell, woman suffrage reformer, born in West Brookfield, Mass., August 13, 1818; died in Boston, Mass., February, 1894. Her father was an enterprising, prosperous farmer, who, while sending his sons to college, refused in accord with the prejudice of the times to send his daughter, because women did not need an education, that boon being reserved to men only. So this girl in summer picked berries, cherries, and chestnuts, and sold them to buy her books, and studied at night, and, as soon as able, she taught a public school until twenty-five, to earn the money to go to Oberlin College, Ohio, then the only one admitting women. She earned her way through college by teaching in the primary department, and doing work in the ladies' boarding hall at three cents an hour, and cooked her own food in her room and boarded herself at fifty cents a week, and had but one new dress, a cheap print, during her college course, and did not go home once during the four years. She graduated as an honor student and was requested by the faculty to write a graduating essay, they insisting that it be read by one of the faculty, inasmuch as it would be contrary to Scripture for a woman to publicly read her own essay. So Lucy refused to write. In year of her graduation she gave her first lecture on woman's rights in her brother's pulpit at Gardner, Mass., and same year was engaged by Massachusetts Anti-Slavery Society as their lecturer, and consented on condition that she be allowed also to speak on her own chosen reform, and they compromised by allowing her to speak on woman's rights week evenings, and on anti-slavery on Saturdays and Sundays. So she arranged her own meetings, tacked up her own hand-bills, and took her own collections. She headed the first call for a National Woman's Rights Convention, and in 1855 was married to Dr. Henry Blackwell, of Cincinnati, they having to send thirty miles to Worcester, Mass., in order to get a clergyman, Rev. T. W. Higginson, better known as Colonel Higginson, who was willing to omit the word "obey" from the marriage ceremony. With her husband's approval, she retained her own name. While they lived in New Jersey she let some property be sold for non-payment of taxes, and with her child on her knee wrote her pamphlet against "Taxation Without Representation." In 1870 she became associate editor of the *Woman's Journal*, Boston, and two years later its editor, writing and lecturing constantly, and taking most active part in many suffrage amendment campaigns throughout the Union. Was a woman of many attractions of intellect and person, and a born leader.

Harriet Elizabeth Stowe, author, born at Litchfield, Conn., June 14, 1811. She was the sixth of her father's (Rev. Dr. Lyman Beecher) children, her mother dying when Harriet was four years old. When ten years old was a student in Litchfield Academy, where she wrote notable compositions for one of her years, "and read everything she could lay her hands on." In 1832 her father removed to Cincinnati, O., as president of Lane Theological Seminary, and while living there she became greatly interested in the slave by her visits to Kentucky. In 1836 she was married to Prof. Calvin E. Stowe of Lane Seminary. When the anti-slavery paper, *The Philanthropist*, established and conducted by James G. Birney of Alabama, and Dr. Gamaliel Bailey, was destroyed by a mob set on by Kentucky slave owners, she began to write against slavery. From 1840–50 she passed through severe trials and much poverty, her husband's health being very precarious, and he obliged to leave his family. On his return from Europe he became professor in Bowdoin College, Brunswick, Me., whither she removed. The fugitive slave law was just enacted, and stopping at Boston on her journey to Maine she was urged to action against it, and on getting an urgent letter from a sister-in-law entreating her to write she was stirred in spirit and determined to do something, and in April, 1851, sent the first chapter of her great story, "Uncle Tom's Cabin," to the *National Era*, an anti-slavery paper at Washington, D. C., edited by Dr. Gamaliel Bailey and John G. Whittier, and it appeared in the issue of June 5, 1851, and continued to April 1, 1852, she receiving $300 for it, it being then pronounced the most powerful production that had ever appeared in magazine literature, and its author was put in the front rank of writers. Meanwhile John P. Jewett, publisher, of Boston, contracted with her to bring the story out in book form, she to have ten per cent. royalty on all sales. The first edition appeared in the latter part of March, 1852, 3000 copies being sold on day of issue; the next week a second edition followed, and the next week a third; 120 editions appearing within a year, aggregating 300,000 copies, she receiving in first four months $10,000 as royalty, and was the most famous woman in America. In August of that year it was dramatized, and continues to win popularity. In that same year eighteen publishing houses in London were kept busy supplying the demand for it there, more than a million and a half copies having been sold in England and colonies up to 1889. Next to the Bible it is perhaps the most widely read book of the world, having been translated and published in Armenian, Bohemian, Danish, Dutch, Finnish, Flemish, French, German, Hungarian, Illyrian, Italian, Polish, Portuguese, Roman, Greek, Russian, Servian, Spanish, Wallachian, and Welsh languages. In 1853 Mrs. Stowe went to Europe and had a remarkable reception. On her return she published her "Key to Uncle Tom's Cabin," giving facts on which it was founded. Then till 1863 lived at Andover, Mass., where her husband was professor in Theological Seminary, at which time he took a position at Hartford Seminary, and in which city he died in 1886. Mrs. Stowe's publications embrace a list of thirty-two volumes.

TALENT AND GENIUS.

Emma Abbott Wetherell, opera singer, born in Chicago, Ill., December 9, 1849; died in Ogden, Utah, January 4, 1891. Her father was a music teacher in poor circumstances, and when she was a child trained her to play on guitar and sing at entertainments he gave in the region about Peoria, whither he had removed. Her education was derived at the public schools of that place, and at sixteen she taught school to aid the family living, and on Saturday sang in the synagogue at that place. The next year she joined a concert company, to gain the family's support and traveled through the West, and when the company disbanded was left moneyless and friendless at Grand Rapids, Mich., and with her guitar began to give concerts in hotels and elsewhere alone and so worked her way to New York city, hoping for a musical education, but failing of notice, she went to the West again, touring it with her guitar, and at Fort Wayne pawned her guitar to get to Toledo to see Clara Louise Kellogg; at a private interview told her ambition to Miss Kellogg, who gave her money to pay her fare to New York, and gave her a letter to Professor Errani and Rev. Henry Ward Beecher, who gave her admission to his choir and she soon learned to read music for the first time. She then obtained a situation in Madison Avenue Baptist Church at $600 a year, and later at Dr. Chapin's church at $1,500 a year, and there met her future husband, Mr. Eugene Wetherell. In 1872 Mr. Lake, Mr. Beecher, and others raised $10,000 to send her to Europe for a musical education. At Paris she made the acquaintance through her instructor, Wartel, of the Baroness Rothschild, who on hearing her sing gave her $2,000 and offered to pay her bills for tuition. After studying under Wartel and Sadie at Paris and also Don Giovanni at Milan she made an engagement with Manager Gyr to sing in London, but refused on moral grounds to appear in the opera "La Traviata," and being supported in the refusal by her husband, whom she had privately married in Europe, she canceled her London engagement and returned to the United States in 1876, and organized a company under the direction of her husband and Charles Pratt and sang throughout this country, and at length amassed a fortune of several millions of dollars, by her great industry, perseverance, and good temper under storms of ridicule and abuse. After providing for her relatives by her will, she distributed her estate to various charities and gifts to those who befriended her in her early struggles, Plymouth and Madison Avenue churches, devoting her gift to them in remodeling their organs and putting up memorial plates to her memory.

Mary Anderson, Mrs. Antonio F. De Navarro, actress, was born at Sacramento, Cal., July 28, 1859. In 1860 her parents removed to Louisville, and the father entered the Confederate service, dying at Mobile, Ala., in 1863, aged twenty-nine. When the daughter was eight years old, Mrs. Anderson married Dr. Hamilton Griffin of Louisville. Mary was educated at the Ursuline Convent and the Academy of the Presentation Nuns. Began to read Shakespeare and other dramatic authors, before ten years of age; saw Edwin Booth act, and was filled with ambition to go on the stage. Her stepfather realized the genius hidden under a retiring manner, and promoted it in every possible way. Her naturally fine mind was trained by diligent study; and in November, 1875, she made a successful debut at the principal theater in Louisville, in the part of "Juliet." From that time on success was assured. First appearance in New York was in November, 1877, at the Fifth Avenue Theater, where she played "Parthenia," "Juliet," "Bianca," and other leading parts. In 1878 made a European tour, appearing in the great capitals and in Stratford and Verona. Her great beauty and blameless life made her a great favorite in society, but she continued modest and retiring. June 17, 1890, was married in Hampstead, to Antonio de Navarro; and spent the following winter in Venice. In March, 1891, abandoned the stage, having sold all her stage dresses, theatrical scenery, and stage properties.

Phineas Taylor Barnum, showman, born in Bethel, Conn., July 5, 1810; died in Bridgeport, Conn., April 7, 1891. His father kept a country store and tavern, and died poor when Phineas was fifteen. After the father's death the son, who had an ordinary district school education, wandered about for a few years, trying his hand at various things in New York, Brooklyn, and elsewhere, and having saved a little money he returned to his native place, opened a small store, sold lottery tickets for Groton Monument Association, took a larger store and failed. Went to New Jersey with a young lady of Bethel, in 1829, and was secretly married, and soon after his return, started a weekly paper, *Herald of Freedom*, and was imprisoned two months for libel, and failed. He then went to Philadelphia in 1834, and bought, for $1,000, a colored slave, Joyce Heth, reputed to be one hundred and sixty-one years old, and the nurse of General Washington, and exhibited her, his receipts soon averaging $1,500 a week. She died a year later, her longevity being much disputed, and Barnum continued in the exhibition business in various parts of the country, and returned to New York city in 1839, reduced again to poverty. For some time he barely subsisted by petty jobs from day to day, and by occasional articles for newspapers. In 1841 he bought, on credit, Scudder's Museum, added new features and specialties, called it Barnum's Museum, worked untiringly, and paid his indebtedness within a year. In 1842 he bought out Charles S. Stratton, the dwarf ("Gen. Tom Thumb"), whom he exhibited to great crowds, and with much profit, through the chief cities of the United States, Great Britain, and France, and whom he subsequently had married with great eclat to Lavina Warren, also a dwarf, in Trinity Church, New York. In 1849 he engaged Jenny Lind for a concert tour of one hundred and fifty nights in the United States, the gross receipts of the nine months' concert tour made in 1850-1 being over $712,000, and she received $176,000. In 1855 wrote his autobiography (revised 1869), and 1856-7, having indorsed notes for nearly $1,000,000, which went to protest, his property was again swept away save what he had previously settled on his wife, and in the latter year he went to England again with Tom Thumb and gave lectures. His museum in New York was burned in 1865, and also a larger one he had built was burned in 1871. In 1865-69 he was member of his state's legislature, and in 1874-5 mayor of his city. He subsequently established his "Greatest Show on Earth" with Bailey and Hutchinson as partners, and exhibited in United States and England, introducing to the gaping, gullible public, his "woolly horse," "what is it?" with many freaks and curiosities, such as Commodore Nutt, Admiral Dott, and a Giant, together with many really excellent zoological exhibitions, and gaudy, glittering panoramas, and specialties and curios, and amassed another and larger fortune, $600,000 of which he gave before his death to the Bridgeport Scientific and Fairfield County Historical Societies, besides many gifts for public improvements to his city, and by his will bequeathed handsome legacies to charitable, religious, and literary bodies.

Lawrence Barrett, born in Paterson, N. J., April 4, 1838, son of a poor Irish mechanic, Thomas Barrett, who removed to Detroit when Lawrence was a young lad. As soon as age would permit, was forced to find employment for himself, and was clerk in a dry goods store; leaving the store, hired as call boy at the Metropolitan Theater. Was at this time unable even to read or write, but soon learned and began to declaim Shakespeare and other dramatists until he was noticed and given a place. First appearance was made as Murad, in the French Spy. Began acting in New York in 1857, at Burton's Theater, contemporaneously with Forrest, Wallack, Cushman, Laura Keene, and Booth. In 1858 played leading parts in Boston, thence went to Philadelphia at the time when the civil war was coming on, making his appearance as Cassius, destined to become his greatest role. Played in New Orleans, Washington, Cincinnati, in Liverpool, Eng., and in San Francisco. Here a new theater was built for Barrett and McCullough, with whom he had formed a partnership, which continued through a brilliant season of twenty months. In 1871, played Cassius, in New York; the play had a run of eighty-three nights. Another important part played by Mr. Barrett was King Lear. In the summer of 1887 began the remarkable Booth-Barrett combination, which continued with almost unvarying good fortune till Mr. Barrett's death, March 20, 1891. He was a most able and versatile actor and an excellent man of business.

Edwin Booth, tragedian, born at Bel Air, near Baltimore, Md., November 13, 1833, son of Junius Brutus Booth the elder. Had few educational opportunities, but the few were improved, with the result that while yet a lad he was very well informed. First appearance on the stage was in 1849, at Boston Museum, playing the minor part of Tressel in Richard III. Was now devoted to the profession and worked hard to succeed in it. For two years continued with his father, making the first appearance in New York, on September 27, 1850, at the National Theater, Chatham street, as Wilford. The elder brother of Edwin, Junius Brutus Booth, Jr., was a manager in San Francisco, and thither went the others; so that the three played together. In 1854, Edwin played in Australia, with Laura Keene. Returned to California and played at Sacramento, presenting Richelieu for the first time. Went to Baltimore in 1857, and played also in Boston and New York, arousing greatest enthusiasm by his splendid impersonations. Played in London 1861, also in Liverpool and Manchester. In 1863, entered upon a five years' management of the Winter Garden Theater.

SUCCESSFUL MEN AND WOMEN.

York city, and during this period, the three brothers appeared together, in Julius Cæsar, Edwin playing Brutus, Junius Brutus playing Brutus, and John Wilkes, Mark Antony. Booth's Theater, New York city, was opened February 3, 1869, and ran thirteen years, presenting in the most superb manner ever known, all the great plays in his repertoire; closed his last season June 14, 1873. The panic of September forced him into bankruptcy, and after the panic subsided, it was necessary to retrieve the shattered fortunes. Beginning in 1876, in fifty-six weeks, Mr. Booth earned nearly $200,000. Made a second trip to Europe in 1880, being received with greatest favor. Died June 7, 1893; and by his death the world lost one of the greatest actors of modern times.

Ole Bornemann Bull, violinist, was born at Bergen, Norway, February 5, 1810. Played the violin without instruction, at five years of age. At twelve, took lessons of a Swedish musician. His father, an actor, intended to make a Protestant minister of the boy, so sent him at eighteen to the University of Christiania, to study theology; was expelled soon afterward for taking temporary charge of the orchestra at one of theaters. Next the young genius went to Cassel, in Germany, to take lessons of the celebrated violinist, Ludwig Spohr, but being coldly received, went to Gottingen, undertaking there the study of law. Returning to Christiania after a short time, pursued musical studies, giving occasional concerts, until, after a year or more, he acquired sufficient funds to go to Paris; was there robbed of everything, even the violin, and attempted suicide, but was rescued and through royal patronage was once more in comfortable circumstances. Made a tour of the principal cities of Italy, then returned to Paris, appearing in grand opera. Then followed a tour in Great Britain, Ireland, Belgium, Holland, Russia, and Germany, received everywhere with utmost enthusiasm. In 1843 visited the United States and Canada, and the West Indies. Amassed a considerable fortune. From 1869 until his death, the winters were passed in America, and the summers in Europe. He died at Bergen, Norway, August 18, 1880. Not only was he remarkable as a musician, but was also a man of rare cultivation, broad intellect, and great social charm.

Charlotte Saunders Cushman, actress, was born in Boston, Mass., July 23, 1816, daughter of Elkanah Cushman, a West India merchant. As a child the future actress displayed great imitative faculty. In school was remarkable for elocutionary talent. Was a promising singer and made her debut as such, but soon lost voice, and by the advice of a friend decided to become an actress. Made her first appearance in New Orleans as Lady Macbeth, meeting with success. Appeared in New York and Albany, Buffalo and Philadelphia. Made her appearance in Liverpool, February 14, 1845, with immediate success, receiving offers from Birmingham, Edinburgh, Manchester, and Dublin. Made the acquaintance of many noted people, among them Thomas Carlyle and wife, the Brownings, and members of royalty. Spent the winter of 1856-7 in Rome. Often appeared in America for the benefit of the sanitary commission, and the net proceeds of these benefits were $8,267.29. Made her final appearances in New York, at Booth's Theater, October 19 to November 7, 1874, playing Queen Katharine, Lady Macbeth, and Meg Merrilies. Received a splendid ovation, and was crowned with laurel. Miss Cushman died February 18, 1876.

Edwin Forrest, actor, born in Philadelphia, March 9, 1806, of Scottish ancestry. Was educated at the common schools in Philadelphia, and early evinced a taste for the theater, quite against the wishes of his parents. In 1820 first appeared on the stage as Douglas, in Home's tragedy of that name, with immediate success. In November, 1826, made the first metropolitan experiment as Othello, in the old Bowery theater. The success met in New York was repeated in every city visited, and after a few years of profitable labor, he visited Europe, being received with courtesy and honor by actors and scholars. In 1836, he repeated the tour professionally, making the first foreign appearance as Spartacus in the tragedy of The Gladiator at Drury Lane Theater, London, and afterward playing King Lear, Othello, and Macbeth. Returned to Philadelphia in 1837. In 1853 played Macbeth at the Broadway Theater for four weeks, with great success, and then retired from the stage for several years, became interested in politics, and did not return to professional life until 1860, when he appeared at Niblo's Garden, as Hamlet, and played the most successful engagement of his life. Played the last New York engagement in February, 1871. Soon after, retired from the stage, and died at Philadelphia from a stroke of paralysis, December 12, 1872.

Joseph Jefferson, actor, born in Philadelphia, February 20, 1829; was the third of his name coming of a race of actors. Was brought up in the precincts of a theater from earliest infancy. As an infant, was sometimes employed in child parts, appearing first as the child in Rolla at about three years of age. Went to Mobile in 1842, and here the head of the family died of yellow fever. Mrs. Jefferson opened a boarding house and the son acted with Macready and the elder Booth. After a tour through Mississippi, Texas, and Mexico, Mr. Jefferson took up residence in Philadelphia, appearing at the Arch Street Theater. During the next six or seven years, was engaged a part of the time as actor, and part as stage manager, in different cities. In June, 1856, went to London, thence to Paris, and from the latter city returned to America. Was engaged for leading parts at the opening of Laura Keene's Theater in Broadway, New York, in September, 1857. During the season of 1858–59, played Asa Trenchard, in Our American Cousin, which ran more than 150 nights. It is doubtful if any American actor has played any one of Jefferson's great characters with his careful excellence, while, with the exception of one or two, no English comedian has ever excelled him in either of them. Played with great success in Australia. In 1859, the idea of dramatizing and playing Rip Van Winkle first occurred to him, and Boucicault wrote the drama as it is at present. It was first performed at the Adelphi Theater, September 5, 1865, and had a run of 170 nights. First produced in America at the Olympic Theater, New York, September 3, 1866, and became the most taking card in Mr. Jefferson's collection. In later years, Mr. Jefferson has spent his winters on a Louisiana plantation near the Bayou Teche, and the summers in New Jersey. Aside from stage reputation, has gained recognition as an artist of decided ability in the impressionist school. In acting, an absolute truth to nature, coupled with rare originality, marks his work.

Ignace Jan Paderewski, pianist, born in Podola, Russian Poland, 1860. Father a farmer of no musical tastes, the lad's inheritance coming from his mother, who was a good performer on the piano. From his infancy he had an "ear for tones" and at three would steal to the piano to ring the keys and listen. He knew the pitch of all sounds he heard. At six he began to study, taking lessons of a performer on the fiddle. Two years later he had another teacher, no better, who gave him and his little sister lessons. They could play better than the teacher and they were then left alone. At twelve he went to the Conservatory of Music at Warsaw and studied under Roguski and Janotha, where he wrote musical compositions of his own, and studied those of the masters, and when sixteen made a tour through Russia and used mainly his own compositions; then he returned to Warsaw, at his father's request, and studied six months more and took his diploma. At eighteen he became professor of music in the conservatory at Warsaw and studied general literature at night after the day's work was over. When nineteen he married, and his wife dying the following year, he gave himself to music to drown his grief, and went to Berlin and studied composition under Kiel and Heinrich Urban. When twenty-three he became professor of music in the conservatory of Strasburg. Resolving to become a virtuoso, he in 1886 studied under Leschetitzky for seven months and made his debut at Vienna, Austria, in 1887, and has since traveled in concert in various parts of the world, and is popularly known as the "piano king," his performances being confined to that instrument. It is his custom before giving a concert to practice many hours, and often the entire night previous. In 1893 he made an American tour, that brought him $160,000. He began writing music when but seven years of age, and in 1882 published his first volume of compositions in Berlin.

Adele Juana Maria Patti, soprano opera singer, born in Madrid, Spain, February 19, 1843. Her father was an Italian singer, her mother a Spanish singer of note, Adeline, as she is known in the United States, being their youngest daughter. When a child, her parents removed to the United States, residing in New York, where she was carefully trained by Maurice Strakosch, who had married her sister, Amelia. When but a girl she sang with great acceptance at entertainments, but made her first entry on her life work as Lucia, in New York, November 24, 1859, and was very successful. Her first appearance in London was as Amina at the Covent Garden, May 14, 1861, repeating the part eight times, and, though unknown, became at once famous. She has since appeared there every year as well as in America. In 1870 she went to Russia, and was given Order of Merit by Emperor Alexander, and appointed first singer at Imperial Court. In 1888 sang in Argentine Republic in twenty-four entertainments, the receipts being over $350,000, she having one-half. Was married in May, 1868, to Marquis de Caux, equerry to Napoleon III., but divorced from him, and in 1866 married Signor Nicolini. Her voice is of moderate power, but great compass, reaching F in alt, with finished and brilliant execution. She appears in more than 30 casts, chiefly of Italian, and is charming in person and manners. Her earnings have amounted to millions. Has fine estate in Swansea valley, Wales, Eng., having a private theater costing $30,000, and lives in regal state. Is small in person with dark hair and eyes. Has a rare ear for music and is said never to have sung a false note.

SUCCESSFUL MEN AND WOMEN.

HONORED SOLDIERS.

George Armstrong Custer, soldier, born at New Rumley, Ohio, December 5, 1839, son of a blacksmith who became a farmer in later years. George was a bright lad and a quick student, but disliked study. Received a fair district school and academy education, and then, receiving from John A. Bingham, congressman from that district, an appointment to the United States military academy, entered West Point in 1857. Was graduated in 1861 and sent at once to Washington, D. C. (July, '61), and intrusted with dispatches to Generals Scott and McDowell, which he delivered and then entered the battle which was the first at Bull Run. Served in various capacities during the war, sometimes as assistant to the chief of engineers, again as scout, when for bravery he was made aid-de-camp to General McClellan, with the rank of captain. Took the first color captured by the army of the Potomac. When McClellan was relieved of the command, Custer was made first lieutenant in the Fifth United States Cavalry (July, 1862). At Aldie, Va., won a star as brigadier-general, and this promotion took him to Maryland, to command the Michigan cavalry brigade. Was in action at Gettysburg, and during all the remainder of the war more than sustained the high reputation already won. Had first experience in Indian fighting under General Hancock against the Cheyenne Indians. In July, 1874, it was found that a large portion of the Sioux tribe had confederated against the United States government, and Custer's regiment was a part of the force sent against them, under command of General Terry of the United States regular army. Was directed to take the regiment up the Rosebud river (tributary to the Yellowstone), to the headwaters of the Little Big Horn, and down the latter stream to join the column of Captain Gibbon, who was en route for the mouth of the Big Horn. At 8 A. M., June 25, 1876, Custer determined upon an attack, and, dividing the forces into three commands, proceeded. Receiving no support from the two divisions under Captain Reno and Captain Barber, was overwhelmed by a large force of the Sioux, and every man of the command was killed. The character of General Custer was marked by truth, honor, sympathy, piety, and temperance, and a desperate bravery.

David Glasgow Farragut, Admiral of the United States Navy, was born at Kimball Station, near Knoxville, Tenn., July 5, 1801, father was in cavalry service of the United States, and a friend of General Jackson. The boy's early life was passed on the frontier, not without a considerable experience with Indians. At the age of nine, became a midshipman, his first service being on board the Essex, under Com. David Porter. Was the engagement resulting in the capture of the British ship Alert, and in the engagement in the bay of Valparaiso, March 28, 1814, when the Essex surrendered to the Phœbe and Cherut. At close of the war with England, made a cruise to the Mediterreanean on the Independence. In 1825 received a commission as lieutenant. In the mean time, was cruising for pirates, under Commander Porter; from 1834 to 1851, was employed on the West India station, at Norfolk navy yard, or with the home squadron, 1851 to 1853 was assistant inspector of ordnance. In 1855 received a commission as captain in the United States navy, and three years later took command of the steam sloop Brooklyn. Was residing at Norfolk, Va., at the time the state seceded, and immediately went North with his family. First active service was the capture of New Orleans, and opening of the Mississippi river. This was in 1862. Sailed up the river under a terrible fire, delivering broadsides of grape shot as he passed. Met and destroyed a fleet of twenty armed steamers, four ironclad rams, and many fire rafts. Thence proceeded to Vicksburg. In autumn his squadron captured Corpus Christi, Sabine Pass, and Galveston. Until July 9, when the garrison surrendered, aided the army in its investment of Vicksburg. The following summer, took Mobile, winning a victory almost as important as that of New Orleans; and was created vice-admiral, December 21, 1864. July 25, 1866, was created admiral. In 1868, went to Europe, and commanded the European squadron for a year. Died at Portsmouth, N. H., August 14, 1870.

John Charles Fremont, soldier and explorer, was born at Savannah, Georgia, January 21, 1813, of French descent. Had the best educational advantages circumstances could permit, and in 1828, entered the junior class of Charleston College; there acquired more than an ordinary knowledge of the classics, and showed special aptitude for mathematics. Was restless and high-spirited, however, so that he frequently broke away from studies, and this, with a disregard of college regulations, finally led to expulsion by the faculty. Gained a livelihood, thereafter, by teaching mathematics, in Charleston; was given a degree by Charleston College. Became assistant engineer under Capt. W. G. Williams of the United States topographical corps, and engaged in exploring mountain-passes in North Carolina and Tennessee, and making military reconnoissance of the Cherokee country. Early in 1838 was made assistant of the celebrated Nicollet, who was engaged by the United States war department, to make a map of the wild country, from the upper waters of the Missouri.

579

to the British line. Was appointed second lieutenant of the topographical corps. In this capacity, Fremont did efficient service, and it was largely through the efforts of these expeditions under his leadership, that the great West was opened to settlement and cultivation. In 1846 took possession of California for the United States, holding it against the rule of Mexico, and from the English, who also were endeavoring to gain possession; was elected governor by the American settlers in California, in 1846. Was senator from that state in 1850. Visited Europe in 1852 and received many honors. In 1855 took up residence in New York city. Was nominated by the Republican party for president, in 1856, but defeated by Buchanan. Was made major-general in the United States army at the beginning of the civil war, but, owing to some dissatisfaction with his command, was relieved. Was governor of Arizona in 1878-81. In 1890 Congress authorized an appointment to be major-general, and a place on the retired list, with a salary of $5,625 per annum. Mr. Fremont was a unique character, possessed of high moral and physical courage; but eccentric to a degree. He died in New York city, July 13, 1890.

Ulysses S. Grant, soldier, and eighteenth president of the United States, was born at Point Pleasant, Ohio, April 27, 1822, eldest of six children of Jesse Grant. As a lad, worked about the farm; showed no special intellectual promise, but displayed courage and resolution. Attended school during the winter. At seventeen was appointed to a cadetship at West Point; was proficient in mathematics and the best horseman in his class. Was graduated in 1843, and assigned to the infantry as brevet second lieutenant, and sent to Jefferson Barracks, St. Louis, Mo. May, 1844, was sent to Louisiana, and in September, 1845, commissioned second lieutenant. Joined the army under Zachary Taylor, the same month, and was in all the battles of the Mexican war in which any one man could be. In 1847 was made quartermaster of his regiment. For conduct in the battle of Monterey, was brevetted first lieutenant, at Chapultepec, captain; and at the occupation of the city of Mexico, was promoted to full first lieutenancy. In 1852, went to California, where the gold excitement rendered troops necessary. After the commencement of the civil war, he became at first brigadier-general of volunteers, then commander of the twenty-first Illinois volunteer infantry. After his troops were augmented by General McClernand's brigade, took possession of Paducah, Ky. In 1862 aided by Commodore Foote with a gunboat fleet, captured Forts Henry and Donelson. It was at this time that Grant's terms with the enemy gained for him the sobriquet of "Unconditional Surrender." For this exploit, was made major-general of volunteers. In July, 1862, Grant was made commander of the department of the Tennessee. May 3, 1863, surprised Pemberton at Vicksburg and July 3, received the latter's surrender. Afterward took a leader's part in the battles of Chattanooga, Lookout Mount, Orchard Knob, and Missionary Ridge. After appointment as commander-in-chief, fought the battles of the Wilderness and captured Richmond and Petersburg. April 9, Lee surrendered at Appomattox and the war was at an end. In the election of November, 1868, the nation manifested its gratitude and esteem to Grant by electing him president, the inauguration taking place March 4, 1869; was re-elected in 1872. In 1884 was attacked by the disease which ended in death July 25, 1885.

Winfield Scott Hancock, born at Montgomery Square, Pa., February 14, 1824, of English ancestry. Was sent to Norristown Academy while a small boy, and here organized a military company, of which he was captain. In 1840, at the age of sixteen, entered West Point, was graduated June 30, 1844, and brevetted second lieutenant of the sixth infantry, July 1. Was on duty in the Indian country, on the border of Texas, until 1846. Joined the army under Scott, and was brevetted first lieutenant for gallant conduct in the battles of Cherubusco and Contreras. Served in the Seminole war of 1855, then in the Kansas troubles. Was on duty in California at the time of the secession of the Southern states; reached New York city, September 4, 1861, and reported for service, at Washington. Was placed in charge of a brigade. First met the enemy at Lee's Mills, April 16. Was engaged in the fighting at Williamsburg and Frazier's Farm, and in the Maryland campaign. Commanded the first division of the second army corps, at the battle of Antietam. In the battle of Fredericksburg, commanded the first division, second army corps, in the attempt to storm Marye's Heights. Fought at Chancellorsville and Gettysburg, fixing the locality for the latter conflict, in the consultation that preceded it. July 3, commanded the left center, the main point assailed by the Confederates. Fought at the Wilderness and at Spottsylvania, Cold Harbor, and Petersburg. August 12, 1864, was appointed brigadier-general in the regular army. November 26, 1864, was called to Washington to organize a veteran corps of 50,000 men. February 26, 1865, was assigned to command of the military division, ordered to Winchester, Va. After the death of Lincoln, was stationed at Washington, having charge of the defense of the capital. July 26, 1866, was appointed

SUCCESSFUL MEN AND WOMEN.

major-general of the regular army. Was engaged again in Indian warfare. In 1868, was appointed commander of the division of the Atlantic, remaining in this command until his death, February 9, 1886. In 1868 and 1872, was a candidate for the presidency of the United States, but was defeated by Garfield. Last appearance in public was on the occasion of General Grant's funeral, for which he made the arrangements. He was the embodiment of chivalry and devotion to the highest duties of a soldier.

Oliver Otis Howard, born at Leeds, Me., November 8, 1830. Worked on a farm, attended district school, and at the age of nine, after the death of his father, lived for two years with an uncle, John Otis, of Hallowell. Prepared at Monmouth and Yarmouth, and at sixteen entered Bowdoin College; was graduated in 1850. Became a cadet at West Point and was graduated in 1854. Stood fourth in the class and was assigned to the ordnance department, with the brevet rank of second lieutenant. First service was at Watervliet, N. Y., and Kennebec arsenal, Me. Served in Florida as ordnance officer, under General Harney; The following year was promoted to first lieutenant and was made acting professor of mathematics at West Point, holding the position until the civil war. In the mean time received the degree of M. A. from Bowdoin College. In 1861 volunteered for service and was made colonel of the third regiment Maine volunteers. Commanded the third brigade of the third division during the battle of Bull Run, and was created brigadier-general of volunteers. Participated in the advance against Richmond. Was wounded in the battle of Fair Oaks, and lost an arm owing to this injury. Returned to his command in less than three months, and participated in the battles of Bull Run (second), Antietam, Fredericksburg, Chancellorsville, Gettysburg, Chattanooga, and Atlanta. Reached the rank of brevetted major-general of the regular army. May 12, 1865, was assigned to duty in the war department in the bureau of refugees, freedmen, and abandoned lands. In 1877 commanded a successful expedition against the Nez Perces Indians, and, the following year, against the Bannocks and Piutes. In 1881-82 was superintendent of the United States military academy; 1882-86, commanded the department of the Platte, at Omaha, Neb. Was commissioned major-general in 1886, and placed in command of the division of the Pacific. After the death of Sheridan was commander of the division of the Atlantic. Received the degree of LL.D., four different times, and was made chevalier of the Legion of Honor by the French government in 1884. Was author of "Donald's School Days," "Chief Joseph, or the Nez Perces in Peace and War," and other works.

Robert Edward Lee was born at Stratford, Va., January 19, 1807, son of "Light Horse Harry" Lee, of Revolutionary fame. At eighteen, entered West Point military academy, obtaining a thorough technical education. Was graduated in 1829, receiving a commission on the corps of engineers. At the outbreak of the Mexican war, had risen to a captain's rank; and served in that war with credit, under Scott. Was brevetted colonel for gallant conduct at the siege of Chapultepec. Was appointed superintendent at West Point in 1852. Three years later, returning to active service, it was an open secret that General Scott offered to recommend him for the chief command of the Union forces, if he would remain true to the old flag. Resigned command after Virginia had passed the ordinance of secession, and became commander-in-chief of the Virginian troops, but was later recalled by Jefferson Davis. But when Joseph E. Johnston was defeated and wounded at Fair Oaks, Lee was put in command, and a great strengthening of the Confederate army was at once apparent. How effective was Lee's action is at once shown by the fact that while only a month before, the Washington government had considered its forces in the field adequate to all demands, upon the battle of Mechanicsville, followed a hasty call for 300,000 men. Lee also won the battle of Chancellorsville with 60,000 men to Hooker's 100,000. That nine months should have intervened between the time of Grant's advancing before Petersburg and the capture of that city and of Richmond, bears unmistakable testimony to Lee's power to make the most of a hopeless situation, and achieve great results with small resources. Not many months after the surrender at Appomattox, Lee was made president of Washington and Lee University at Lexington, Va., and remained in that office until his death in 1870, on the 12th of October. Not only was Lee a great general, but he was also a man of modest nature and high moral worth.

Winfield Scott, born near Petersburg, Va., June 13, 1786, son of William Scott, farmer, was left an orphan at seventeen. After the usual preparatory studies, entered the high school at Richmond, Va., then passed two years in William and Mary College, in the study of law. Completed legal studies in the office of David Robertson, and was admitted to the bar in 1806. In 1807 emigrated to South Carolina, intending to practice the law in Charleston. But as a hostile feeling between the United States and England was abroad and the army was being increased, Scott obtained a position as captain of light artillery. When the war of 1812 was fairly begun he was commissioned lieutenant-colonel and sent to the Niagara frontier, and took part in the battle of Queenstown. Was engaged in the battles of Chippewa and Lundy's Lane, displaying great bravery and shrewdness. In 1814 declined the position of secretary of war. On returning from a trip to Europe in 1815 was made commander of the seaboard, with headquarters at New York city. In 1814 received from Congress the appointment of brigadier-general, and a gold medal. In 1835 was again engaged in active service, in the Seminole war. In 1841 was made commander-in-chief of the United States army. Was the Whig candidate for president, in 1852. Was engaged in the Mexican war, winning notable victories. In 1859, as commissioner to England, settled the northwestern boundary question. At the outbreak of the civil war was again called into service remaining until November 1, 1862, when, at the age of seventy-five years, he retired. After making another tour in Europe, settled at West Point and there died, May 29, 1866.

Philip Henry Sheridan, soldier, born in Albany, N. Y., March 6, 1831; died in Nonquitt, Mass., August 5, 1888. Graduated at West Point, July 1, 1853, the thirty-fourth in class of fifty-two; Gen. James B. McPherson (killed before Atlanta) being at the head, and Gen. John M. Schofield of Union, and Gen. John B. Hood of Confederate army, among his classmates. At breaking out of civil war he was captain in thirteenth infantry; appointed colonel of second Michigan cavalry, May, 1862; July 1, brigadier-general volunteers; December 31, major-general of volunteers. At battle of Stone River he saved General Rosecrans from defeat by his brilliant manœuvre, but at the wreckage of his own division, losing 1,630 men, and he played a most important part in the battle of Missionary Ridge, attracting the attention of General Grant, who transferred him (April 4, 1864) to Virginia, and put him in command of the cavalry corps of the army of the Potomac, where, having under him the kindred spirits of Generals Merritt, Custer, Wilson, and Gregg, he made many astonishing and successful raids on the Confederate flanks and rear. August 7 was put in command of army of Shenandoah, the middle military division, and gained great renown by his defeat of General Early's army, in three pitched battles in thirty days, snatching victory from the very jaws of defeat at Cedar Run by his famous twenty-mile ride from Winchester, rallying his flying troops on the way. November 8 made major-general in United States army, and on February 9, 1865, received the thanks of Congress for his brilliant exploits. In February and March, with 10,000 cavalry he made a colossal raid from Winchester to Petersburg, fighting almost constantly, and at length by his famous and decisive battle of Five Forks compelled Gen. Robert E. Lee to evacuate Petersburg and Richmond, which resulted in Lee's surrender. In 1869 was made lieutenant-general; in 1870 went to Europe to witness Franco-Prussian war, and was with German staff at battle of Gravelotte; and in 1883 became the general-in-chief (nineteenth) of the United States army. Was below middle height, powerfully built, a born soldier, who was never defeated, cool and daring, a splendid cavalry man, and affectionately called "Little Phil," by his army. In 1879 he married the daughter of Gen. Daniel H. Rucker of United States army, and wrote and published his "memoirs" (two volumes), in 1888.

William Tecumseh Sherman, general United States army, born in Lancaster, Ohio, February 8, 1820, died in New York city February 14, 1891. Was sixth of his father's children and after the father's death was adopted by United States senator Thomas Ewing. Graduated at military academy, West Point, N. Y., in 1840, sixth in a class of forty-two. Sent second lieutenant with regiment to California on breaking out of war with Mexico, reaching Yerba Buena (San Francisco) in 1847. Had chance to enrich himself by securing gold property for almost nothing, but thought it of small account. Was urged to buy lots in San Francisco at $16 each, but considered the venture foolish! In 1850 returned to Washington, D. C., and married Miss Ellen Boyle Ewing, daughter of Thomas Ewing, secretary of the interior. In business in California and elsewhere until in 1860, then superintendent of military academy at Alexandria, La. Resigned in 1861 when state seceded and commissioned as colonel of thirteenth United States infantry and took part in first Bull Run battle. In October succeeded Gen. Robert Anderson in Department of Cumberland, but relieved by General Buell in November and transferred to Department of Missouri under General Halleck. Organized a division of new troops and took part in the bloody battle of Shiloh, holding heroically right of line near Shiloh church and for it promoted major-general of volunteers. In 1862 when Halleck went as military adviser to President Lincoln, he came under General Grant's command and took conspicuous part in stirring events leading up to capture of Vicksburg on July 4, 1863, and was then made brigadier-general in regular army. In October took charge of the Department and Army of the Tennessee and was again conspicuous by defeating the armies of Generals Bragg and Longstreet, and February 19, 1864, was given thanks of Congress for services in the Chattanooga campaign, and assigned by Grant to Division of Mississippi, and in a bloody campaign defeated successively the army under Gen. Joseph E. Johnston and Gen. John B. Hood, and September 1, captured Atlanta, Ga.; then after much difficulty persuaded President Lincoln and General Grant to consent to his proposed march of three hundred miles to the sea, and to prevent being countermanded had all telegraph wires cut, and years after learned that the authorities had tried to recall him by telegraph and failing supposed "the enemy had cut the wires." November 12, his army of 60,000 veterans set forth and nothing more was known of him till near Christmas, when he appeared before Savannah, and on December 21 took that city. He then marched northward through the state of South Carolina to Durham Station near Raleigh, North Carolina, where the Confederate army, under Gen. Joseph E. Johnston, surrendered to him. His great march brought the downfall of the confederacy, and May 24, 1865, his army passed in grand review at Washington and a week later he took leave of it in a farewell order. Was made lieutenant-general of the army, July 25, 1866, and general of army March 4, 1869. In 1871-2 made tour of Europe, and put on retired list, February 8, 1884, and from 1886 till death resided in New York city. His "Memoirs" written by him were published in 1875 (two volumes). He could easily have been president of the United States if he had accepted proffered Republican nominations, and is, perhaps, the only man that ever refused that office. His funeral was a great military pageant, witnessed by scores of thousands of people. Buried at St. Louis, Mo., by side of his wife, who died a year earlier.

George Henry Thomas, soldier, born Southampton county, Va., July 31, 1816; died in San Francisco, Cal., March 28, 1870. Was educated at home and in the Southampton academy, and when twenty entered the office of an uncle who was clerk of the county, with a view to the law, but having an offer of a cadetship at West Point military academy, N. Y., he entered there in 1836, graduating twelfth in a class of forty-two in 1840, and commissioned second lieutenant in Third United States artillery, and served in Florida till close of the Seminole war. He also served under General Taylor in the Mexican War, being brevetted major for gallantry in action. He then served three years as cavalry instructor at West Point, and five years with the Second United States cavalry in Texas, and in 1860, when the most of his fellow-officers renounced their allegiance to the United States government on the breaking out of the civil war, he remained true. While on his way home he was injured in the spine by a railroad accident, and to this was doubtless due his "slow" riding and deliberate movements, adversely commented on during the progress of the war. He was colonel of second cavalry, and promoted to command of a brigade in the first Shenandoah campaign, and commanded a division in the battle of Mill Spring, where his sterling qualities as commander first directed national attention to him. He was now promoted to the command of the right wing of the army of the Tennessee at the siege of Corinth, and during much of 1862 was in full command of that army. He commanded the center of army of the Cumberland, and did noble work at Murfreesboro; and then had charge of the Fourteenth army corps in the campaign in middle Tennessee during 1863. At the battle of Chickamauga his heroism gained for him the title of "the Rock of Chickamauga." He commanded the army of the Cumberland at battle of Missionary Ridge, and took part in the Atlanta campaign of 1864 up to the capture of that city, and on December 15 of that year won the battle of Nashville, Tenn., one of the most splendid achievements of the war, and was promoted major-general in regular army, and given a vote of thanks by United States Congress, and a gold medal by the state of Tennessee. In 1865-67 he commanded military division of Tennessee, and 1867-9 the third military district, and from May 15, 1869, till his death the division of the Pacific, with headquarters at San Francisco. He was buried at Troy, N. Y., where in 1852 he had married Miss Frances Kellog of that city. He was affectionately called "Old Reliable" and "Pap Thomas" by his men, and has the glory of never having lost a battle when in independent command. A monument has been erected to his memory at Washington, D. C., and, if not fully appreciated by the civil authorities at the time, it will come to pass as he was wont to say to his most intimate friends, "History will do me justice."

PROMINENT SOLDIERS.

Gustavus Adolphus, surnamed the Great, was born at Stockholm, Sweden, in 1594; ascended the throne in 1611, and though so young, evinced great sagacity in the choice of able ministers. Was fond of military glory, and soon acquired renown in battles against the Danes, Muscovites, and Poles. By heroic valor and judicious policy, made an honorable peace with the first two, and obliged the latter to evacuate Livonia, when forming an alliance with the Protestants of Germany, he overran, in two years and a half, all the countries between the Vistula, the Rhine, and the Danube. Tilly, the imperial general, was twice defeated, and the pride of Austria humbled; but the battle in the plains of Lutzen, in 1632, proved fatal to the life of the brave monarch. It is said that he fell by the intrigues of Richelieu, or by the hand of the Duke of Saxe-Lauenburg, his cousin, who was bribed by Emperor Ferdinand. Gustavus Adolphus patronized literature, founded academies and universities. Before his reign, the Swedes were indifferent soldiers, but he always had an army of 80,000 well-disciplined men.

Napoleon Bonaparte, Emperor of France, born August 15, 1769, at Ajaccio, in Corsica, of noble parentage. Educated at the military school of Brienne; entered the artillery service as second lieutenant in 1785; served at the sieges in Lyons and Toulon, and subsequently displayed high talents in the French army which assailed Piedmont, on the Genoese frontier. Early in 1796, was placed at the head of the French army in Italy, where he began a career of glory. Subjugated Egypt and Malta, and invaded Syria. Hearing of the reverses his countrymen had sustained in Europe, went to France, overthrew the Directory and was raised to the position of first consul. Having restored order in the kingdom, he led an army over the Alps, fought the battle of Marengo, and recovered the whole of Italy. Austria and Russia being leagued against him, the battle of Austerlitz was fought dissolving the coalition. Prussia sent an army against him, at the battle of Jena, and was defeated. Invaded Russia and took possession of Moscow, but was obliged finally to make a disastrous retreat. Another confederation against him compelled abdication; the invasion of France in 1815 proved a failure, and, throwing himself upon the generosity of the British government, he was exiled to Saint Helena. Died May 5, 1821. Being a most consummate general, and possessed of splendid talents, Napoleon might have held a throne throughout life, but for a fatal and selfish ambition.

Oliver Cromwell, the protector of England, was born at Huntingdon, England, April 25, 1599; received education at grammar school, in his native town, and at Sidney College, Cambridge, where he paid small attention to study and a great deal to play; was sent to Lincoln's Inn to study law, with as little success. When twenty-one, married and settled at Huntingdon, becoming a zealous Puritan. Appeared in Parliament in 1625. Was prevented from emigrating to America, by a royal proclamation, which the misguided monarch afterward had reason to repent, for Cromwell opposed him in the House, and, when the Commons decided on resistance, raised a troop of horse, most admirably disciplined. This became enlarged to a regiment of one thousand men, and he was a most conspicuous leader. Was instrumental in the execution of the king, and formed one of the council of state, after the death of Charles. Was three years Lord Governor of Ireland. In 1650, defeated the Scots, at Dunbar. Having, in 1653, forcibly dissolved the Long Parliament, assumed supreme authority, under the title of Lord Protector. The severity of mental labor at last undermined his health, and he died of a slow fever, September 3, 1658.

Stephen Decatur, naval officer, born in Sinnepuxent, Md., January 5, 1779, son of Stephen Decatur, also a naval officer. In 1798, Stephen, the younger, was appointed a midshipman in the United States navy; cruised in the West Indies on the frigate United States, distinguishing himself as a youth of unusual talent and bravery. Was promoted to be lieutenant in 1799. Was first lieutenant of the Essex, one of four vessels sent against the bey of Algiers; and when the Philadelphia was captured and carried into the harbor of Tripoli, Decatur entered the harbor and destroyed her, retreating unharmed, to his own ship, under fire of 141 guns. In recognition of this service, was created captain on May 22, 1804. During the war of 1812, Algiers violated treaty with the United States, and in 1815, two fleets, one under Bainbridge, one under Decatur, were sent to demand reparation. Decatur met and captured two Algerian vessels, and forced the bey to sign a treaty in which he agreed to levy no more tribute on the United States, and to release all the Christians whom he held captive. Later, similar agreements and indemnity for their encroachments on American commerce were obtained from Tunis and Tripoli. In January, 1816, was appointed member of the new naval commission, to which he devoted his energies for four years. In 1820, was challenged to a duel, by Com. James Barron, accepted the challenge, and was mortally wounded. Died March 22, 1820.

Nathaniel Greene, Revolutionary soldier, was born at Warwick, R. I., May 27, 1742, son of a Quaker preacher; the sect being opposed to literary attainments, at the age of thirteen Nathaniel could only "read, write, and cipher"; but later was taught Latin and geometry. Made small toys of iron, and, with the proceeds of their sale, bought books. Went to Coventry, R. I., to look after a part of the

SUCCESSFUL MEN AND WOMEN.

family estate, and here his remarkable qualities became recognized; was soon chosen to represent his new home in the general assembly; first act was to move the establishment of a school. In 1774 was one of a committee to revise the militia laws. Entered the Kentish Guards, and in 1775, when the battle of Lexington had been fought, he was made brigadier-general of the army of 1,500 raised by order of the Rhode Island legislature. In August, after the appointment of Washington as commander in chief of the army, Greene was appointed as one of the four major-generals. Was joint commander with General Sullivan, at the battle of Trenton; and was a close friend and valued counselor of Washington, during the entire war. In all the principal battles of this time, Greene's bravery and skill were conspicuous. After the establishment of the army at Valley Forge, was appointed quartermaster. Succeeded Gates as commander of the Southern army, which he found disorganized and inefficient, a state of affairs that was soon changed. So effective was his service, that he was called the "Savior of the South." Died from sunstroke, June 19, 1786.

Thomas Jonathan Jackson, born at Clarksburgh, W. Va., January 21, 1824. Father died when Thomas was three years old, leaving the family without property. When six years of age was sent to live with an uncle; attended school and was a good mathematician. Was made county sheriff when only eighteen years old. Entered West Point in 1842, deficient in preparation; studied very hard, and graduated seventeenth in a class of seventy. On graduation entered the American army, under Winfield Scott. For good conduct during the Mexican war was made major. When the civil war broke out he was made colonel of the Virginia forces, and ordered to take command at Harper's Ferry. It was during the battle of Manassas Junction that General Jackson earned the sobriquet "Stonewall," that clung to him ever afterward. The campaigns that followed displayed his great skill in military tactics, and made him alike the admiration of the confederacy and the dread of the federal forces. During the attack upon Lee at Fredericksburg by Burnside, Jackson was severely wounded and pneumonia set in, from which he died May 10, 1863.

Lafayette was born in the chateau of Chavagnac, in that part of France then known as the Province of Auvergne, September 6, 1757. Was educated by relatives, up to the age of twelve, when he was removed to the College du Plessis, Paris; soon after came into complete personal possession of great wealth; was a page at court, and a commissioned officer of the king's regiment of musketeers. Was anxious for political liberty and the regeneration of France. Meeting Silas Deane, in Paris, became determined to go to the aid of the colonists; Efforts were made to prevent this, and he was finally compelled to adopt a disguise; this was successful, and in due time Lafayette, with Baron de Kalb and eleven other officers, landed at Georgetown, S. C. Rode nearly 900 miles on horseback to Philadelphia, where he was made a major-general in the continental army. Fought in the battle of Monmouth, and displayed bravery on many other occasions. Went to France on a mission in 1779, and, as a result, Count de Rochambeau was sent out with 6,000 men, in July, 1780; himself returned and engaged again in active service under Washington. After the close of the Revolution he held various honorary positions in France; becoming implicated in political troubles, he was imprisoned at Olmutz, in Austria, for several years. Upon release was again appointed to positions of honor and importance. He died in Paris, May 20, 1834.

George B. McClellan was born in Philadelphia, Pa., December 3, 1826; son of a physician; was educated in the public schools and the University of Pennsylvania. Entered the United States military academy in 1842, was graduated second in class of 1846, the largest that had ever left the academy, and he was first in the class in engineering. Distinguished himself under General Scott in battles of Cherubusco, Molino del Rey, and Chapultepec; was commissioned second lieutenant, and brevetted captain. Volunteered for service on the outbreak of the civil war, and after serving as commander of the department of the Ohio, and commander of the army of the Potomac, was made commander-in-chief of the Union forces, November 1, 1861. Finding the army in poor condition to engage in the long war which was to be, he set about organizing thoroughly; but being indifferently supported, was unable to carry out cherished plans. August 30, 1862, was superseded by Pope, with disastrous effect; being reinstated, fought the battle of Antietam, one of the greatest Union victories of the war. Was nominated by the Democratic party for president, in 1864, but was defeated. Was offered the presidency of California University, and the year following, of Union College, but declined both. Was governor of New Jersey from 1877 until 1881. There has been much dispute concerning McClellan's true status during the war, but certain it is that the men he led would follow him as they followed no other man. He died October 29, 1885.

SUCCESSFUL MEN AND WOMEN.

George Gordon Meade, soldier, was born in Cadiz, Spain, December 31, 1815, son of Richard Worsam Meade, merchant of Philadelphia, who established himself at Cadiz. The family was eventually sent back to Philadelphia, when young Meade attended school. Was graduated from West Point in 1835, with the rank of second lieutenant. Served in the Seminole war in Florida. Was engaged in military surveying until the war with Mexico broke out, when he joined the staff of General Zachary Taylor, at Corpus Christi, Texas. For bravery in the battle of Monterey, was made first lieutenant. When the civil war began, Meade was made brigadier-general of volunteers; commanded a brigade in battles of Mechanicsville, Gaines' Mills, and Newmarket Cross Roads; at the second battle of Bull Run, rejoined the army, after being severely wounded. When Lee invaded Maryland, Meade commanded the Pennsylvania Reserves, and was at the battle of South Mountain; commanded the first corps at Antietam. November 29, 1862, was made major-general. June 23, General Meade relieved Hooker in command, just before the battle of Gettysburg. For his admirable conduct of this battle, was appointed brigadier-general in the regular army. Was in every campaign of the army of the Potomac, and in all its battles except two. August, 1864, was appointed major-general. Died in Philadelphia, November 6, 1872.

Philip John Schuyler, Revolutionary soldier, born at Albany, N. Y., November 22, 1733, of Dutch descent. When eight years old, lost his father; was the eldest of five children, and came into possession of the paternal estates, also the estate of an uncle, situated at Saratoga. At fifteen, entered school at New Rochelle, N. Y.; manifested a preference for mathematics and the exact sciences, also acquiring full knowledge of French. Later, engaged in those wild trading and hunting expeditions with Indians, in which most young Albanians were then engaged. No other man, except Sir William Johnson, exercised so great an influence over the easterly tribes of the Iroquois confederacy. Was engaged in the last French and Indian war; served under Bradstreet in 1756. At the time of the difficulties between England and the colonies was delegate to the Continental Congress; was appointed one of the four major-generals of the army, being assigned to the control of the Northern department. The misconduct of the troops, his own wretched ill-health, and the pecuniary straits of the army, hampered and discouraged him; resigned from the army in 1777, remaining, however, the trusted friend and adviser of Washington. Was interested in many public works, and did much for the prosperity of New York. He died November 18, 1804, at his mansion in Albany.

John Stark, born at Londonderry, N. H., August 28, 1728; boyhood passed in Derryfield, N. H. April 28, 1752, when on a trapping excursion, was taken prisoner by Indians, kept six weeks and liberated only upon payment of $103 ransom. From 1753 to 1755, was employed as scout. During the latter year, was made a lieutenant, engaged in the French and Indian war, and, for gallant conduct, was made captain; was in the battle of Ticonderoga. Was afterward created colonel, and enlisted eight hundred men in one day. Fought the battle of Bennington, a complete victory for the American forces. Was twice appointed to the command of the northern department; and on retirement was given a pension of $60 per month. Died May 2, 1822.

Zachary Taylor, twelfth president of the United States, was born in Orange county, Va., September 24, 1784. In 1808 was appointed lieutenant in the seventh infantry, and made captain in 1810. In 1812 took command of Fort Harrison on the Wabash, where, after several successful campaigns, he was brevetted major, and afterward attained that rank by commission. With a brief interval, remained in the army until elected to the presidency. Was engaged in the second Black Hawk campaign, and received the surrender of that chief; fought in the Seminole war, and gained the notable victory of Okeechobee. Anticipating the annexation of Texas, he was directed to prepare her defense against Mexico. Went to Corpus Christi with 1,500 men, in July, and by November had 4,000. After victorious encounters with the Mexican troops, Taylor was commissioned major. With a regiment of riflemen, a mounted company of Texans, a squadron of dragoons, and three batteries that had seen service, the rest of his army being raw recruits, met Santa Anna, the Mexican general, at the head of a fine army of 21,000 men and routed him completely. After his return home, he was elected president, being nominated by the Whigs, June 8, 1848. He was a patriot rather than a partisan, and regarded office as a public trust. Died July 9, 1850.

Joseph Warren, soldier, born at Roxbury, Mass., June 11, 1741; was graduated at Harvard in 1759, and became master of Roxbury grammar school, in 1760. In 1764, having studied under Dr. James Lloyd, began the practice of medicine. Wrote a series of articles on the stamp act, for the Boston *Gazette*, which attracted general attention and led to prosecution of the proprietor, by Governor Bernard. Soon after this, became the warm friend and one of the

SUCCESSFUL MEN AND WOMEN.

most trusted lieutenants of Samuel Adams. When in August, 1774, Samuel Adams took his seat in the Continental Congress, Dr. Warren became leader of the Patriot party in Boston. Was author of the "Suffolk Resolves," which were approved by the Continental Congress, and placed the colony of Massachusetts in open rebellion against the British government. When the Massachusetts Provincial Congress met in October, 1774, Dr. Warren was appointed chairman of the committee of safety, and entered actively upon the work of arming and drilling the militia. May 31, he was made president of the Provincial Congress, and on June 14, was appointed second major-general of the Massachusetts forces. While attempting to rally the militia, at the close of the battle of Bunker Hill, was shot in the head and died instantly.

Arthur Wellesley Wellington, one of the greatest generals of the age, was born at Dangan Castle, county of Meath, Ireland, May 1, 1769; received classical education at Eton, and military education at the military college of Angers, in France. Entered on a military career when only eighteen, and promotion followed promotion with great rapidity, until in 1796, when he was commissioned colonel and ordered to India, his name had a prominent place on the roll of military honors. On returning, was knighted and received a general's commission. For services in Spain, received the titles of Baron and Viscount, a vote of thanks from Parliament, and a pension of £2,000 per year. In 1813, made a triumphal entry into Madrid, and was appointed generalissimo of the Spanish armies, and in the same month received the titles of Marquis and Duke. July 3, 1815, Paris capitulated to Wellington and Blucher, after a short and bloody conflict. After the evacuation of France, November 1, 1818, he returned to England and devoted the remainder of his life to offices connected with the British government. Whether in field or cabinet, the Duke was bold in conceiving and had gigantic powers for carrying out his projects. Died at Walmer Castle, September 14, 1852.

MANUFACTURERS.

Andrew Carnegie, manufacturer, born in Dunfermline, Scotland, November 25, 1835, son of a weaver in humble circumstances, whose ambition, joined with ardent republicanism, led him to emigrate to the United States with his family in 1845. Family settled at Pittsburgh, where Andrew began his career, two years later, by attending a small stationary engine. Dissatisfied with this, became a telegraph messenger with the Atlantic and Ohio company, and subsequently, an operator. Was one of the first to read telegraphic signals by sound. Afterward met Mr. Woodruff, inventor of the sleeping car, and joined in the effort to have it adopted; the success of this venture gave the nucleus of his wealth. Was superintendent of Pittsburgh division of Pennsylvania railroad, and member of a syndicate that purchased property on Oil Creek, which cost $40,000 and yielded in one year over $1,000,000 cash dividends. Was associated with others in establishing a rolling mill, from which has grown the most extensive and complete system of iron and steel industries ever controlled by an individual. He long owned eighteen English newspapers, which he controlled in the interests of radicalism; has devoted large sums to benevolent and educational purposes. Has published numerous books.

Jerome I. Case, manufacturer, was born in Williamstown, Oswego county, N. Y., December 11, 1818; father was a pioneer settler in New York; the son had only a common school education until after his majority; worked on the farm during the summer. The father bought a one-horse threshing machine of which Jerome, having a taste for mechanics, was put in charge, successfully operating it on their own and other farms. In 1839 entered the academy at Mexicoville. In 1842 bought from an eastern manufacturer six one-horse threshing machines, mainly on credit, and went to Wisconsin, where he sold all but one of the machines; by studying the defects of the old one, produced, during the winter of 1843–44, a new combined threshing and winnowing machine. In 1847 was able to erect on his own ground, a large, well-equipped shop, which the first year after sent out eleven machines, the next year one hundred, and within ten years was putting on the market sixteen hundred machines per year; at present furnishes twenty-five hundred per annum, and employs nine hundred persons. Mr. Case was also interested in the J. I. Case plow works, and in the Northwestern Life Insurance Company of Milwaukee, in which he was shareholder. In 1871 organized, with other parties, the Manufacturers' National Bank of Racine, becoming president. The same year established the First National Bank of Burlington, Wis., became president of that also, and retained the presidency of both until his death. Was also identified with the First National Bank of Crookston, Minn., the First National Bank of Fargo, Dakota, the Pasadena National Bank of Pasadena, and the Granite Bank of Monrovia, Cal. Was at one time a large owner of California lands.

SUCCESSFUL MEN AND WOMEN.

Owned many fine horses, among them Jay-Eye-See, and had a large stock-farm. Was mayor of Racine in 1856, re-elected in 1859, and passed one term in state Senate. His only son, Jackson I. Case, served one term as mayor of Racine. Mr. Case died on the 22d of December, 1891.

Peter Cooper, manufacturer and philanthropist, born in New York city, February 12, 1791; father and grandfather served in the continental army; former was a hatter and the son became familiar with the trade; afterward worked at brickmaking, and in the brewing business. Acquired such knowledge as was possible by half days during a single year. In 1808 was apprenticed to John Woodward, a carriage maker, remaining until he became of age. Invented a serviceable device for mortising hubs of carriage wheels. Settled at Hempstead, L. I., and for three years manufactured machines for shearing cloth, ultimately buying the right of the state of New York for a cloth-shearing machine. After the war, began making cabinet ware, later entered the grocery business, and afterward manufactured glue, oil, whiting, prepared chalk, and isinglass. In 1828 erected the Canton iron works. He was a mover in the laying of the Atlantic cable. In 1829 manufactured a steam engine that would operate successfully. Was Greenback candidate for president in 1876. Took great interest in public education. Cooper Institute, founded by him in 1854, with its ample endowment, is a monument of his goodness. He died April 4, 1883.

George Henry Corliss, inventor and manufacturer, born in Easton, N. Y., June 2, 1817. Father was a physician and moved to Greenwich, N. Y., where the son attended school until fourteen. Spent several years as clerk in a cotton factory, then three years in Castleton Academy, Vermont; in 1838 opened a country store in Greenwich. First showed mechanical skill in rebuilding a bridge that had been washed away by a freshet, after such structure had been declared impracticable. Afterward constructed a machine for stitching leather, before the invention of the original Howe sewing-machine. Moved to Providence, R. I., in 1844, and two years later began developing improvements in steam engines, for which he received letters-patent, March 10, 1849. The improvements made by Corliss are said to have revolutionized the construction of the steam engine. In introducing the new engine, the inventor and manufacturers adopted the novel plan of offering to take as pay, the saving of fuel for a given time, which, in one year, amounted to $4,000. In 1856, the Corliss Steam-Engine Company was incorporated, with works covering acres of ground, and hundreds of the engines in use. Medals have been awarded at Paris, Vienna, and in America. Mr. Corliss has also invented a machine for cutting the cogs of bevel-wheels, an improved boiler for marine engines, and pumping engines for water works.

George Mortimer Pullman, inventor, born in Chautauqua county, N. Y., March 3, 1831. At fourteen entered the employment of a country merchant, and at seventeen joined an elder brother in the cabinetmaking business, in Albion, N. Y. At twenty-two, successfully undertook a contract for moving buildings along the Erie canal. In 1859 removed to Chicago, undertaking the then novel task of raising entire blocks of brick and stone buildings. In 1858 his attention was first directed to the discomforts of long-distance travel, and the determination arose to offer the public something better. The attempts when tested, created a demand, and in 1863 he began to construct a sleeping car upon the now familiar model; it was named the "Pioneer," and cost about $18,000. From this, ideas were continually developed, till now Pullman cars are known all over the world. The Pullman Company, of which he is president, was organized in 1867, and now operates over 1,400 cars on more than 100,000 miles of railway. In 1887 he designed and established the "vestibuled trains," which practically make the entire train, a single car. In 1880, founded the town of Pullman, now containing over 11,000 inhabitants, 5,000 of whom are employees of the company's shops. Mr. Pullman has been identified with various public enterprises, among them, the Metropolitan elevated railway system of New York, constructed and opened to the public by a corporation of which he was president.

John D. Rockefeller, born in Moravia, Cayuga county, N.Y., 1839. John inherited $3,000 from his father's estate. He was educated at the common schools of his native town, and in 1863 went to Cleveland, O., where he became clerk in a small commission house, $25 a month salary. The petroleum business was then in its infancy, and the firm employing him were refining a few barrels of oil a day, but lacked capital to enlarge, and he offered his money for an interest and became a partner, and in 1865 they were refining one hundred and fifty barrels a day; Mr. Rockefeller being the shrewd, pushing member of the firm. In 1870 they reorganized as Clark, Payne & Co., increasing their refineries and enlarging operations, and for the next decade made enormous profits, through stock speculation and buying up or driving out competitors. In 1880 the company was again reorganized or merged into what is now known as the Standard Oil Company with a nominal capital of $6,000,000, and three years later M. B. Clark and S. Andrews retired from the firm, Rockefeller buying the former's interest at a profit to himself of over $600,000, and then William H. Vanderbilt entered the company, taking $1,500,000 worth of stock. In 1885 the capital was increased to $72,000,000, and in 1890 was $153,000,000, controlling the oil product of the country, and owning vast properties and paying a dividend of 30 per cent. profits on the capital. Mr. Rockefeller's wealth is variously estimated at from $150,000,000 to $200,000,000, the result of his thirty years of speculation in oil. He has contributed largely of his wealth to the benevolent objects of the Baptist denomination, with which he is connected. He established and heavily endowed the Chicago University.

Cadwalader Colden Washburn, lawyer and manufacturer, was born in Livermore, Me., April 22, 1818, worked on a farm in summer and attended school in winter until about 1835, when he went to Hallowell and was employed in a store, also served in the post office, and in the winter of 1838-9 taught in Wiscasset. In the spring of 1839, went west, settling in Davenport, Ia.; there joined the geological survey under David Dale Owen. Entered law office of Joseph B. Wells; was admitted to the bar March 29, 1842. In 1844 turned his attention to dealing in public lands. Was an honored officer in the civil war, performing acts of signal skill and bravery. Was member of Congress in 1867-1871, and governor of Wisconsin for two years. After retirement from politics, engaged largely in lumber trade. In 1876 erected a flouring mill in Minneapolis, where first in this country was introduced the "patent process" and Hungarian system. Was also one of the largest owners in waterpower at St. Anthony's Falls, and a heavy stockholder in the Minneapolis and St. Louis railroad. Founded in connection with the Wisconsin State University, Washburn observatory, which, with equipment, cost more than $50,000. To other institutions he gave the sum of $445,000. Died at Eureka Springs, Ark., May 14, 1882.

Ichabod Washburn, manufacturer, born in Kingston, Mass., August, 1798; died in Worcester, Mass., December 30, 1868. Father died when he was two months old, leaving no property. His mother supported herself and three children by weaving, teaching them what she could, and sending them to school part of the winters. When nine years he was apprenticed to a saddler for five years; he was a harsh master, and the lad went cold from lack of clothing, and often suffered greatly. When fourteen he went to work in a cotton factory, and when sixteen was apprenticed for four years by his guardian to a blacksmith near Worcester, Mass. There he spent his after life. He bought books by working over time forging pot hooks, although his daily task was from sunrise to sunset in summer; and from sunrise to nine P. M. in winter. When twenty he began to make plows, and afterward served in an armory near Worcester, and later manufactured lead pipe, and in 1831 began the making of wire, in which business he continued till his death. Previous to his time an English house had made all the piano wire used for eighty years, by a secret process only known to them. He invented new processes and new machinery, and increased the daily product of a machine from fifty pounds a day, to 2,500 pounds a day, and at his death was making over twelve tons of wire daily, having built up with his brother Charles an immense industry, the largest in the world, now known as the Washburn & Moen Manufacturing Company at Worcester, Mr. Moen being his son-in-law, employing over 3,000 persons. During his life Mr. Washburn gave many hundreds of thousands of dollars to charitable objects, and by his will distributed $424,000 to benevolences, including $100,000 for a home for aged women and widows, $100,000 for a free hospital and dispensary, and $110,000 to Free Institute for Industrial Science at Worcester, Mass.

Daniel B. Wesson, manufacturer, born in Worcester, Mass., May, 1825. His father was a farmer, and the son who was one of ten children spent his early life on the farm and at the common schools till eighteen, when he went to learn the gunsmith trade with an elder brother Edwin at Hartford, Conn., where he remained until 1849, when he began to manufacture pistols on a small scale at Grafton, Mass., and in 1851 became superintendent of the Leonard pistol factory at Charlestown, Mass., for two years. He then began with Horace Smith as partner to manufacture pistols at Norwich, Conn. In 1856 they removed to Springfield, Mass., and established the well-known Smith & Wesson works, now grown to large proportions, its product going to all parts of the world, and where both the members of the firm amassed a very large fortune. In 1874, Mr. Smith retired from the firm, since which time Mr. Wesson and his sons have carried on the business.

SUCCESSFUL MEN AND WOMEN.

PROMINENT MERCHANTS.

Samuel Appleton, merchant, philanthropist; born in New Ipswich, N. H., June 22, 1766, died in Boston, Mass., July 12, 1853. His father was a farmer and he was the third of twelve children, and was given a common district school education of a few weeks in the year, which he so improved that when seventeen he was called to teach in his own and the neighboring towns, and when twenty-two took up new land in Maine and farmed for two years, and then returned to his native town and served in country store for two or three years, and at twenty-eight began business as a dry goods merchant at Boston, Mass., and afterward as importer, wholesaler, and manufacturer till his death, being a silent partner for the last twenty years of his life. He spent several years in Europe in the interest of his house, and in connection with his brother and others established cotton factories at Waltham and what is now the city of Lowell, introducing the first power looms ever used in the United States. After retiring from active business he gave his whole income to charities, placing large sums in the hands of physicians, clergymen, and missionaries to help the destitute. At his death he left an estate of a million dollars, and is said to have given away as much during his life. By his will he distributed an additional $200,000 to benevolent purposes.

Philip D. Armour, millionaire and philanthropist, born at Stockbridge, Madison county, New York; educational advantages were limited. At the age of twenty went to California, where travel and observation revealed the opportunities which he subsequently mastered. Took the brothers from New York farm, and they became commanders only less great than their chief. Mr. Armour is not only the richest man in Chicago, but the greatest trader in the world, one of the greatest manufacturers of this or any country, employer of twelve thousand persons, paying six or seven millions of dollars in wages, yearly; is owner of largest number of grain elevators owned by a single person in either hemisphere. He is also owner of a glue factory turning out a product of seven millions of tons yearly, and is actively interested in a great railway enterprise. Is founder of Armour Institute, a technical school of large accommodations, where nearly all branches of science and domestic art are taught; six hundred pupils were enrolled at the institute opening. Mr. Armour's very successful life is due to sound judgment, application, and judicious habits which have been followed from boyhood. The training of the coming generation for usefulness, through his beneficence, will be a lasting tribute to one of America's worthiest citizens.

John J. Astor, born in Waldorf, Germany, July 17, 1763. Father was a butcher; the son worked with him until sixteen years of age, when he became employee in flute factory of Astor & Broadwood, London. In 1783, he sailed for Baltimore, with small invoice of musical instruments to sell on commission. Entered employ of a Quaker furrier in New York, and, having learned the trade, began private ventures, opening a shop in Water street; later, visited London, formed business connections, and became American agent for Astor & Broadwood. Became first regular dealer in musical instruments, in United States. At the end of fifteen years, he possessed a fortune of $250,000. In 1809 conceived a scheme of colonization in the northwest, which was thwarted by the war of 1812; but trade was initiated with many countries, including China. Invested his gains in real estate. Lived in retirement for last twenty-five years of his life. Left $400,000 to found the Astor library. Fortune at the time of his death was about $20,000,000. His judgment was sagacious, habits industrious, and his memory remarkably tenacious.

William Earl Dodge, merchant, born in Hartford, Conn., September 4, 1805; died in New York city, February 9, 1883. Father a merchant and manufacturer, building the first cotton mill in the state of Connecticut, and later removed to New York city, where the son, when fourteen, began life as clerk in a wholesale dry goods store, then served as clerk at father's store at Bozrahville, Conn., and later in New York, and when twenty-two began for himself in Pearl street, New York, as dry goods merchant, and fifteen years afterward formed a partnership with his father-in-law, Anson G. Phelps, in the metal business, with a branch house in Liverpool, Eng., and became very wealthy. He also invested largely in timber lands in various states and in Canada, and in iron and copper mines and properties, and built and conducted a number of furnaces and rolling mills, and was a leading builder of several railroads. Was a member of the 34th Congress; president of national temperance society from its foundation till his death; the originator of numerous charities, and for many years gave away annually over $100,000 to benevolent objects, and for support of the many benevolent and religious institutions of which he was a member. It was said of him at his funeral obsequies: "Benefactions so diversified, so lavish, so incessant, and yet so sagaciously bestowed, this city (New York) has seldom, if ever, witnessed."

Marshall T. Field, born in Conway, Franklin county, Mass., in 1835; son of John

SUCCESSFUL MEN AND WOMEN.

Field, a farmer. Worked on the farm until seventeen; had two terms in the district school; was fond of mathematics, and intended to become a merchant. At seventeen became clerk in dry goods store at Pittsfield, commencing the mercantile career which has made him the largest dry goods merchant on the globe, and possessor of a fortune estimated in excess of $30,000,000. Remained in Pittsfield three or four years; is remembered as active, industrious, and devoted to business. Decided to go west, having in mind either St. Louis or Chicago; finally settled in the latter; had no money, other than what was necessary while seeking work. Was engaged by the leading dry goods firm of Palmer, Farwell & Co.; was set about packing and unpacking goods; advanced to higher positions. Later, Henry and Joseph Field, his brothers, engaged with the same firm. Palmer leaving the firm to become a builder and dealer in real estate, and Farwell to found another house, Mr. Field founded house of Field, Leiter & Co., and later, with his brothers, that of Marshall Field & Co. Henry Field died some years ago, and Joseph is head of a great dry goods branch house at Manchester, England. Mr. Field frequently visits his Massachusetts home, and has made munificent gifts to Conway. The greatest merchant of the world is a slender man of medium height, of dignified presence, active, alert, but quiet in manner. The secrets of his success are said to be: He never gives a note; never buys stock on margins; never borrows; buys for cash, and gives not more than sixty days' credit.

Stephen Girard, born near Bordeaux, France, May 24, 1750; son of a sea captain; at an early age, with scant education, sailed as cabin boy to West Indies, thence to New York. Became mate, then captain; made several voyages; then became part owner of the ship. In 1769 established himself in trade; was alternately shipmaster and merchant, till the Revolutionary war. During Haytian insurrection, planters deposited their treasures with him, but were massacred by negroes, and the property of $50,000 remained in his hands. In 1812 purchased old Bank of United States. Was a man of enigmatic character, had but few friends, and, though generous in public matters, was somewhat penurious in private life. He gave thousands to churches, schools, hospitals, and for city improvements. The bequest to Girard College was $2,000,000 and land for the erection of college buildings; college is entirely nonsectarian, no minister can hold connection with the institution, by provision of Mr. Girard's will. He died at Philadelphia, December 26, 1831.

Johns Hopkins, merchant, philanthropist, born in Anne Arundel county, Md., May 19, 1795; died in Baltimore, Md., December 24, 1873. His father was a farmer, and Quaker in religion, and the son spent his youth till eighteen on the farm, getting only the common school education. He then became clerk in the wholesale grocery store of an uncle in Baltimore, where his industry and aptitude for business soon brought him into notice and advancement, and in six years he had saved enough to begin trade in the same line with a partner, and then three years later he retired from the firm and founded with two of his brothers in 1822 the firm of Hopkins & Brothers, where he amassed large wealth, and retired from the grocer trade in 1847 and engaged in banking and railroads, being till his death president of the Merchants' Bank, and director in many others, and in life insurance companies, warehouse and coal and mining companies, and transportation lines to Europe, and held 15,000 shares of the Baltimore & Ohio railroad, saving the latter from disaster in the panics of 1857 and 1873. In the latter year gave property valued at four and a half million dollars to found a free hospital for all persons regardless of creed, or race, or color, and presented his city with a public park, and donated three and a half millions of dollars to the founding of the Johns Hopkins University, which was duly opened in 1876, at Clifton, his country residence, and by will, the balance of his ten millions of property for the benefit of the institution.

Abbott Lawrence, born at Groton, December 16, 1792, fifth son of Deacon Samuel Lawrence. Attended district school in winter, worked on a farm in summer, until he was apprenticed to Amos Lawrence; when he worked by day and studied by night. Coming of age in 1814, formed a copartnership with his brother, only broken by death. Firm engaged in importation and sale of foreign manufactures, standing at the head in its department. Mr. Abbott Lawrence was for years successfully engaged in the Chinese trade. In 1834 was elected to the twenty-fourth Congress, by the Whig party; served on the committee of ways and means; was re-elected, but resigned. In 1842 was commissioner on the boundary question, state of Massachusetts. Mr. Lawrence satisfactorily settled this question with Lord Ashburton, representative of Great Britain. Lacked but six votes to have become vice-president with General Taylor. Went minister to Great Britain, in 1849. In 1852 returned to America and to private life. In 1847, gave $50,000 to the scientific school at Harvard, which bears his name. Harvard gave him LL.D. in 1854. Married Katherine, daughter of Timothy Bigelow.

SUCCESSFUL MEN AND WOMEN.

Lawrence died August 18, 1855, after a pre-eminently useful career.

Amos Lawrence, merchant, was born at Groton, Mass., April 22, 1786. The progenitor of the family in America, John Lawrence, emigrated from Wissett, England, about 1630, was, it is thought, one of Governor Winthrop's company; was one of the original proprietors of Groton. Their lineage can be traced back twenty-two generations. Amos Lawrence was the son of Samuel Lawrence, a hero of the Revolution, and Susanna Parker. Attended public schools and Groton Academy. In 1799 engaged as clerk in a country store; at twenty-one, went to Boston; was a clerk in a prominent business house. Firm was liquidated, and Lawrence appointed to settle affairs, which he did satisfactorily. December 17, 1807, opened a shop on Cornhill; in 1818, took Abbott Lawrence as his apprentice; business was very successful. In 1830 established a cotton factory at Lowell. Retired in 1831; and devoted the remainder of his life to philanthropy. Between 1829-52 he expended $639,000 in charity. Gave $40,000 to Williams College, a large sum to Groton Academy, founded the library, gave the telescope, willed to it all his works of art, and added to its landed estates. At the time of his death was raising $50,000 for the college. In 1846, the name of Groton Academy was changed to Lawrence Academy. He gave to many other institutions, and gave $10,000 toward completion of Bunker Hill monument; distributed a great many books. Was a sagacious, liberal-minded man, prominent in commerce and manufacture for upwards of forty-four years. Died at Boston, Mass., December 31, 1852.

George Peabody was born in Danvers, Mass., February 18, 1795; descended from an old English family, whose ancestor, Francis Paybody, settled in New England, in 1635. Taught to read and write in the Danvers schools, became clerk at eleven years of age; afterward went to Georgetown, D. C., and assumed management of a store belonging to his uncle, John Peabody. Entered partnership with Elisha Riggs, in dry goods house, subsequently became head of firm, and in 1837 established banking house in London. In 1852 gave $10,000 to the second Grinnell expedition, under Dr. Kane, sent in search of Sir John Franklin. In 1857 founded Peabody Institute, Baltimore, Md. Donated largely to various other institutions. Was offered a baronetcy by Queen Victoria, but declined, asking instead, a letter from her hand, which together with a portrait of herself may be seen in the institute at Danvers. In 1869, made the last visit to his native land. His obsequies were celebrated in Westminster Abbey. Death occurred November 4, 1869. Being unmarried, his property remaining, $5,000,000, was bequeathed to relatives. He was the most liberal philanthropist of ancient or modern times.

A. T. Stewart, born at Lisburn, Ireland, October 12, 1803; descendant of Scotch emigrant to north of Ireland, and only son of a farmer; father died while Stewart was a mere lad. Studied for the ministry, but abandoned the idea and came to New York in 1823. Taught in select school in the city; returned to Ireland, took possession of his modest fortune, bought stock, laces, linens, etc.; opened a store at 283 Broadway in 1825. Capital invested was about $3,000. Ultimately removed to 257 Broadway. Became owner of many mills and manufactories; during the war his income was nearly $2,000,000. In 1867 was sent as chairman of honorary commission sent to Paris exposition. In 1871 gave $50,000 to relief fund, after the Chicago fire. At the time of his death, Stewart was completing the home for working girls on Fourth avenue, New York. Wealth was estimated at $40,000,000. Mr. Stewart's property was not used according to directions left in the letter of advice written to Mrs. Stewart, to whom was left the bulk of the property. His death occurred in New York city, April 10, 1876. It is said with truth that he was "the first of American merchants and philanthropists."

Arthur Tappan, merchant, reformer, born in Northampton, Mass., May 22, 1786; died in New Haven, Conn., July 23, 1865. Father was a merchant and farmer. The son was educated at the schools of his town, and when fourteen went to Boston as apprentice (as was the custom) to a merchant friend of the family. On coming of age, he went to Montreal, engaging in business for himself and on breaking out of war of 1812 returned to Boston, and later to New York city, and engaged in wholesale and importing dry goods trade and amassed a large fortune. Was an earnest Christian, having a room for daily prayers in his store to which his help were welcomed. Was the financial head of the anti-slavery cause, giving a thousand dollars a month to it, and aiding fugitive slaves to escape to Canada. He was several times mobbed in New York, and a reward of $10,000 offered for his capture by state of Georgia. Was a man of such integrity that southern merchants, while denouncing him for his opinions on slavery, preferred to buy goods of him because they could trust his statements as to their quality and cost. He was one of the leading originators and founders of the American Tract Society and the American Bible Society. Was the founder of Oberlin College. Endowed Lane Theological Seminary at Cin-

SUCCESSFUL MEN AND WOMEN.

cinnati, Ohio, and a chair in Auburn, N. Y., Theological Seminary. Founded the New York *Journal of Commerce*, and established the *Emancipator* in 1833, and paid the fine of William Lloyd Garrison at Baltimore, and established him in his anti-slavery work. In 1837 the panic caused his suspension and crippled him, so that five years later he went into bankruptcy, surrendering all his property even to his watch and other personal belongings for benefit of creditors. His brother Lewis published his "Life" in 1871.

John Wanamaker, ex-postmaster-general, United States, born in Philadelphia, July 11, 1837. Grandfather was John Wanamaker, farmer, descended from the Palatines who left Germany during religious persecution of 1730–48. Subject of this sketch was eldest of seven children. Attended public school until fourteen; entered retail store as errand boy on $1.50 per week, and rose to higher positions in the same establishment. April, 1861, formed partnership with Mr. Nathan Brown, with joint capital of $3,500. At Mr. Brown's death, the firm was generally known. May, 1869, established house of Wanamaker & Co., Chestnut street, placing his brother Samuel in charge. 1871, enlarged the "Oak Hall" clothing house. Has spent millions in advertising. For eight years of his mercantile life, did not lose a single day from business. Held important position on finance committee of Centennial exposition. Was nominated for congressman-at-large, for Pennsylvania, in 1882; for mayor of Philadelphia in 1886; but refused both. In 1888 became postmaster-general in Harrison's cabinet. Is member of Presbyterian church; in 1858 organized on South street, Philadelphia, a Sunday-school with twenty-seven members, now the renowned "Bethany" with 2,600 scholars and one hundred and twenty-eight teachers and officers. As postmaster-general he provided quicker transmission of mails, established sea post-offices, whereby foreign mails are distributed and made up on board ship, ready for immediate transmission to inland cities; improved the immediate delivery system and urged establishment of the postal telegraph.

PROMINENT INVENTORS.

Samuel Colt, inventor of the Colt revolver, was born in Hartford, Conn., July 19, 1814. When quite young entered his father's factory, remaining there and at school until fourteen, was then sent to boarding school at Amherst, Mass., but ran away and went on an East Indian voyage. Returning, was again placed in the factory and became a practical chemist, then traversed the Union and British America, lecturing under an assumed name, drawing crowds by his skill as an experimenter. The proceeds of these lectures went to experiments in firearms, and when twenty-one years of age he took out the first patent for revolving firearms. Many doubts were entertained by officers of the government, army, and navy, as to the practicability of the weapon, but at last, during the Seminole war, they proved so useful as to be adopted by the troops. They were again brought into use in the Mexican war, and afterward in the emigration to California and Australia. They were adopted by the army as a regular weapon, and were used in the Indian and Crimean wars. In 1852 and 1861 Colonel Colt erected factories in Hartford, dwellings for the employees, a public hall, library, and other buildings. Besides the manufacture of arms, machinery for their manufacture elsewhere is also constructed, and is in use at the armory of the British government at Enfield, England, and the Russian government armory at Tula. Colonel Colt died January 10, 1862.

Thomas Alva Edison, inventor, was born at Milan, Erie county, O., February 11, 1847; mother was a school teacher and most of his education was gained from her. Was very enterprising, and was at various times newsboy, proprietor of a news stand, a book store, and a vegetable market. At fifteen, buying old type and plates, issued the *Grand Trunk Herald,* the only newspaper ever published on a railway train. Learned telegraphy from a station master, set up a private wire from station to town and sent messages for ten cents each. After various experiments went to Memphis, where he earned $125 per month and rations, but all his money went for experiments. Here perfected a repeater, and was first to bring New Orleans and New York into direct communication. While visiting his parents at Port Huron, Mich., made direct connection with Sarnia, across the river, and was repaid by a pass to Boston; secured work there, but as before, experimented until all his money was gone. In 1871 came to New York, and by repairing the machinery which operated the gold indicators in Wall street, obtained a position as superintendent at $200 per month. Experimented for nine years before the incandescent light was in working order. At Paris exposition in 1878 Mr. Edison first exhibited the phonograph, which ultimately sold for $1,000,000. Much as electrical illumination is employed in the United States it is more in use elsewhere; there are more electric lights in Berlin than in New York. Edison has taken out over 400 patents. Was created a commander of the Legion of Honor in 1889, where his exhibit cost at least $100,000.

John Ericsson, engineer and inventor, was born in Langbanshyttan, province of Wermland, Sweden, July 31, 1803, son of a mining proprietor. Boyhood was passed among mines and iron works; earliest instruction came from a German engineering officer and a Swedish governess. Before the age of eleven, constructed a little sawmill, and soon afterward, a pumping engine. At fourteen, was engaged to lay out the work of a section on the Gotha ship canal, employing six hundred soldier operators. At the age of seventeen, entered the Swedish army as ensign, and was soon made lieutenant. He produced the instrument for taking sea soundings, a hydrostatic weighing machine, tubular steam boilers, self-acting gunlock, and the steam engine "Novelty," which made thirty miles an hour. But the most important invention of Ericsson, the one which revolutionized navigation, was that of the screw-propeller. The first boat was used as tow boat on the Delaware river for a quarter of a century. He invented the caloric engine, of which hundreds are used in New York city for pumping water into private dwellings. The "Monitor," iron clad war ship, which defeated the Merrimac at Hampton roads, was also due to him. The sun-motor, which succeeded in developing a steady power, obtained from the supply of mechanical energy stored up in the sun's rays, was another peculiar invention. Ericsson belonged to many royal orders, and received many decorations. He died March 8, 1889.

Thaddeus Fairbanks, inventor of platform scales, was born at Brimfield, Mass., January 17, 1796; removed with his father to St. Johnsbury, Vt., aiding in the running of a saw and grist mill, and the making of carriages. Had an aptitude for mechanics, and while dressing hemp, remarked the rudeness of the prevailing methods of weighing it. The result was his invention of the platform scale, for which a patent was received June 21, 1831. Platform scales were not then wholly unknown, but little used. Improvements covering fifty patents have been made, and the Fairbanks scales are now used in all parts of the world; have received medals at eight international expositions. Mr. Fairbanks died April 12, 1886.

Robert Fulton, civil engineer, born at Little Britain, Penn., in 1765, of Irish descent. From a child, was obliged to maintain himself. Cultivated the art of drawing, hoping to become a painter; and at the age of seventeen went to practice as painter of portraits and landscapes, in Philadelphia; was quite successful. When twenty-one, had accumulated sufficient means to buy a small farm in Washington county, Pa. Went to England and became a pupil of Benjamin West. While there, met the Duke of Bridgewater, the father of that vast system of inland navigation which reaches every accessible part of England. At his suggestion, Fulton became a civil engineer. In 1793, met James Watt, who had just given his steam engine a form adapted to universal application as a prime mover. Fulton made several inventions, at this time, among them a torpedo boat; but the triumph of his genius was yet to come. The invention of a vessel propelled by steam was looked upon as an utter impossibility, but in 1807, on the 11th of August, the Clermont made the first passage by steam from New York city to Albany, a distance of nearly 150 miles, in thirty-two hours. The passage was ordinarily made in about four days, by sloops. The public crowded the new boat and regular trips were made till the end of the season. In the closing years of his life, Fulton devised a system of ferriages, the first of which was established between New York and Brooklyn. Before he died, there were five steamships on the river. Died February 24, 1815.

Richard Jordan Gatling, inventor of the Gatling gun, was born in Hertford county, N. C., September 12, 1818; son of a planter in easy circumstances, the owner of a large tract of land and several slaves. Every educational advantage was improved by him, and at seventeen, he was well advanced. Worked in a county clerk's office during sixteenth year; afterward worked upon an invention for sowing cotton seed and one for thinning the plants. Invented a screw propeller, but found Ericsson had already done the same, so turned his attention to a machine for sowing rice or sowing wheat in drills. While working in a store in St. Louis, in 1844, employed a skilled mechanic to construct the machines, which found ready sale. In 1850 invented a machine for breaking hemp. The idea of the machine gun was conceived in 1861, and in the spring of 1862 the inventor tested it in the presence of army officers and private citizens. Three hundred and fifty shots per minute were discharged with ease. While six guns were being manufactured by the firm of Miles, Greenwood & Co., Cincinnati, the factory took fire, and guns, plans, and patterns were burned, so Dr. Gatling had to begin over again. The government finally adopted the guns; one hundred were made and delivered in 1867. They have been used in Alaska and on the expeditions of Stanley, as well as elsewhere all over the globe.

SUCCESSFUL MEN AND WOMEN.

Charles Goodyear, inventor, was born at New Haven, Conn., December 29, 1800, son of Amos Goodyear, pioneer in the manufacture of American hardware. The son was educated in New Haven public schools; the family removed to Naugatuck, and in 1807 the father began to manufacture the first pearl buttons made in America; in the war of 1812, supplied the United States government with metal buttons; also took out patents for making steel pitchforks. Young Goodyear exercised his inventive genius by making improvements on the farm implements. In 1816 was apprenticed to Rogers Bros., Philadelphia, to learn the hardware business; at majority, returned to Connecticut entering partnership with Goodyear, Sen., in that trade. About 1831 became interested in the manufacture of India rubber, just begun in the United States. No means had then been found to prevent the rubber from melting under exposure to heat, this Mr. Goodyear set himself to discover. The firm having failed, much of this investigation was carried on in prison; and many were the failures and discouragements that ensued; but in 1839 he discovered that a high degree of heat applied to rubber previously coated with sulphur produced vulcanization of the raw material, so that it remained elastic in all temperatures. The first patent was taken out in 1844. In six years from this time, the companies which held the right of manufacturing shoes alone, under his patent, paid Daniel Webster $25,000 for defending Mr. Goodyear's title to the invention. Before his death, July 1, 1860, vulcanized rubber was put to nearly five hundred different uses.

Johann Gutenburg, the inventor of printing, was born at Mentz, in Germany, about 1400. In 1450 entered into partnership with John Faust, a citizen of Mentz, in conjunction with whom he printed a vocabulary called the "Catholicon," by means of letters engraved on blocks of wood. Types of copper or tin were soon afterward substituted for wood, and with these a Latin Bible was printed, at great difficulty and expense. Gutenburg was appointed by the archbishop, elector of the city, and a noble of the court. A bronze monument by Thorwaldsen was erected to his memory in Mentz in 1837. He died in 1468.

Robert Hoe, mechanical engineer, and manufacturer of printing machinery, head of the firm of R. Hoe & Co., of New York and London, was born in New York city, March 10, 1839, grandson of Robert Hoe, who constructed and introduced into America the first iron and steel printing presses. Has been identified for the last thirty years with the progress of the art of printing. With his partners, has greatly enlarged what were already considered extensive works. Those fronting on Grand, Sheriff, Broome, and Columbia streets, New York, have floor room equivalent to five acres. The London works are proportionately well equipped, and fifteen hundred skilled workmen are employed. The apprentices, averaging 200, are instructed in the firm's night schools.

Elias Howe, inventor of the sewing machine, was born at Spencer, Mass., July 9, 1819; father was a farmer and miller. At six years of age, the lad worked at sticking wire teeth into the strips of leather for "cards" used in the manufacture of cotton. In 1835 went to Lowell to work in a manufactory of cotton machinery, earning fifty cents per day. Afterward worked in Cambridge and Boston. In 1839, by a chance conversation, his thoughts were turned to the construction of a sewing machine; and this he set about. The first device was a needle pointed at both ends, with an eye in the middle, but afterward the idea of a curved needle with an eye near the point, and a shuttle to carry the thread, occurred to him. In 1845 he had completed a machine, and made two suits of clothes, one for his partner, Mr. Fisher; and the sewing of both outlasted the cloth. The tailors of Boston stoutly opposed this innovation, and made the inventor much trouble. February 5, 1847, Mr. Howe went to England, thinking to find more hopeful reception, but here, also, he met with much trouble and little encouragement, though a London machinist bought the single machine that was taken over to England, paying $250 for it. Returning to America, found that infringements upon the patent had been made. The rights were secured to Mr. Howe by action of the courts, and he ultimately realized a revenue of more than $200,000 per annum. In 1863, erected a large factory at Bridgeport, Conn. Up to the close of the year 1866, the whole number of machines manufactured in the United States was about 750,000. Died at Brooklyn, N. Y., October 3, 1867.

Cyrus McCormick, inventor of the reaping and binding machine, was born in Walnut Grove, Va., February 15, 1809; was educated at the common schools, and then worked for his father on the farm and in workshops. At the age of twenty-one invented two new and valuable plows, but his chief invention was the reaping machine, of which he built the first really practical one. As early as 1816 the father had attempted to construct a reaper, but it was a failure; the son worked in an entirely different channel. The reaper was patented in 1834. In 1847 removed to Chicago, and built large works; was awarded several medals, and made officer of the Legion of Honor; was also elected member of the Academy of Sciences, "as having done more for the cause of agriculture than any other living man." Reverdy Johnson said, in 1859, "The McCormick reaper has already contributed an annual income to the whole country of $55,000,000 at least, which must increase through all time." In 1859, Mr. McCormick gave $100,000 to found the Presbyterian Seminary of the Northwest in Chicago; also, endowed a professorship in Washington and Lee University, Va. Died in Chicago, May 13, 1884.

Samuel F. B. Morse, founder of the American system of the electro-magnetic telegraph, was born at Charlestown, Mass., April 27, 1791, eldest son of Rev. Jedediah Morse, Presbyterian clergyman. Was educated at common schools, and Yale College, where he was graduated in 1810. In that institution received his first instruction in electrical science. Became an artist, was pupil of West and Copley, and produced some works of decided merit. Returned home in 1815, and in 1818 invented an improved pump. It was during the voyage from Havre that the idea of an electro-magnetic telegraph first occurred to him; in 1835, after three years of untiring labor, completed the first instrument. Two years later, had two instruments in operation at the ends of a short line, and was able to send and receive messages. After striving in vain for help and recognition from our own government and those of Europe, after suffering for the barest necessities of life, an appropriation was at last made by Congress for an experimental line between Washington and Baltimore. The line was completed and its workings displayed to an admiring company of government officials and distinguished men, May 24, 1844. By July, 1862, there were 150,000 miles of telegraph lines in operation. Before his death, Mr. Morse witnessed the adoption of his invention by France, Germany, Denmark, Sweden, Russia, and Australia. In October, 1842, he laid the first sub-marine telegraph line ever put down, across the harbor of New York and later gave generous aid to Peter Cooper and Cyrus W. Field, in their enterprise. Died in New York city, April 2, 1872.

George Stephenson, an English civil engineer of extraordinary ability, was born of humble parentage in 1787; his first recorded employment was picking turnips at two pence per day. When a boy was a trapper in the coal workings, and early in life became a brakeman, thus learning the laws of motion on railways. Was next assigned the care of a steam engine, and attracted notice by being able to repair defects in the valve-gear of the engine. The invention of a safety-lamp for miners placed him in the first rank among original mechanics. Though an illiterate man, was fully aware of the value of an education, and sent his son to college. After the latter's graduation, they had a large engine factory, and on the opening of the Darlington railway, Stephenson's engines traveled ten miles an hour. When appointed engineer of the Liverpool and Manchester railway, Stephenson entered the field of his great fame, and for twenty-five years occupied the foremost position among railway engineers. He amassed great wealth and did much good. Died August 12, 1848.

James Watt, distinguished by his improvements in the steam engine, was the son of a tradesman at Greenock, and was born in 1736. Was brought up as a maker of mathematical instruments; in that capacity became attached to the University of Glasgow, remaining there until 1763. In 1764 adopted the profession of a civil engineer, and was frequently employed in making surveys for canals, etc. In 1774 removed to Birmingham, where, in partnership with Mr. Boulton, he made improvements in the steam engine, eventually bringing it to great perfection. Mr. Watt was Fellow of the Royal Society there and at Edinburgh. Various inventions of great practical utility originated from his ingenuity. Died Aug. 25, 1819.

Eli Whitney, inventor of the cotton gin, was born in Westborough, Mass., December 8, 1765. Family were in humble circumstances, and, at the time of the Revolution, Eli was making nails by hand, to earn a livelihood. Was an apt mechanic, and saved money enough to attend Yale College, where he was graduated in 1792. On leaving college, obtained a situation as tutor, in a private family in Georgia, but, upon arrival, found the place already filled; was offered a home on the plantation of the widow of Nathaniel Greene. While here, became acquainted with the difficulty and slowness of cleaning seed cotton, and set to work upon an invention to remedy this. In 1793, exhibited his machine, which was a success; it was found that with this machine one man could clean as much cotton in a day as he formerly was able to do by hand in a whole winter. Not long after the invention of the machine, it was stolen, and before a model could be made and patented, it had been copied. Lawsuits induced by this cost him much money; the South Carolina legislature paid Mr. Whitney $50,000, and North Carolina paid a royalty on the use of the gin, but no just compensation was ever received. The use of the machine brought the exportation of cotton up from 189,500 pounds, in 1791, to 41,000,000 pounds in 1803. He died in New Haven, Conn., January 8, 1825.

SUCCESSFUL MEN AND WOMEN.

RAILROAD MAGNATES.

Oakes Ames, manufacturer, born in Easton, Mass., January 10, 1804; son of Oliver Ames. After obtaining a public school education, entered his father's workshops and made himself familiar with every step of the manufacture; became a partner in the business and with his brother, Oliver, Jr., established the firm of Oliver Ames & Sons. This house carried on an enormous trade during the gold excitement in California, and again a few years later in Australia. During the civil war they furnished extensive supplies of swords and shovels to the government. Were directly interested in the building of the Union Pacific railroad and obtained large contracts, which were transferred to the Credit Mobilier of America, a corporation in which Oakes Ames was one of the largest stockholders. In 1861 was called into the executive council of Massachusetts. His relations with the Credit Mobilier led to an investigation, which resulted in his being censured by a vote of the House of Representatives, of which he was then a member. After withdrawal from political life he resided at North Easton, Mass., where he died of apoplexy, May 8, 1873.

Oliver Ames, manufacturer, born in Plymouth, Mass., November 5, 1807; was a member of Massachusetts state Senate during 1852 and 1857. Was largely interested with his brother in the development of the Union Pacific railroad and was its president *pro tem.* from 1866 to 1868. Was formally elected president of the company, March 12, 1868, and continued as such until March 8, 1871. He was connected with the Credit Mobilier, and in 1873 succeeded his brother as head of the firm. He died in North Easton, March 9, 1877.

Sidney Dillon was born in Northampton, Montgomery county, N. Y., May 7, 1812; son of a farmer; had a common school education. He became an errand boy on the Mohawk and Hudson railroad, extending from Albany to Schenectady, and later, on the Saratoga and Rensselaer road; was then overseer under the firm of Jonathan Crane and John T. Clark, who took a contract at Sharon on the Boston and Providence railroad. Remained about two years, until the completion of the road; was afterward foreman and manager on the Stonington railroad. During a term as manager of a difficult piece of road-building, notice was attracted to him, and, through the influence of others, he took up contract work; this was continued and always satisfactorily done. In 1865, became interested in the construction and management of the Union Pacific railroad, an interest which was kept up throughout his life; was also interested in the Connecticut Valley, Council Bluffs and Omaha, Chillicothe, Canada Southern, Morris and Essex roads. Became president of the board of directors of the Union Pacific road, and was closely associated with Jay Gould in his enterprises. Was a director of Western Union Telegraph Company, Manhattan Elevated road, Missouri Pacific, Pacific Mail Steamship Company, and others, also a director in Mercantile Trust Company. His fortune has been estimated at $10,000,000. He was greatly esteemed in business circles as a man of good judgment, keen insight, and sterling moral worth. Mr. Dillon died June 9, 1892.

Cyrus W. Field, promoter of submarine telegraphy, was born at Stockbridge, Mass., November 30, 1819, third son of Rev. David Dudley Field, D.D., and grandson of Capt. Timothy Field, officer of the Revolutionary army. Of four sons, Cyrus alone did not receive a collegiate education. Early schooling was acquired in his native town. At fifteen, entered employ of A. T. Stewart & Co., on salary of fifty dollars per year. Was afterward in prosperous business for himself. In 1853 partially retired, traveling for several months in South America. In the same year met Frederick N. Gisborne, a Canadian inventor, who had attempted to lay a subterranean telegraph line across Newfoundland, a distance of four hundred miles. Gisborne had secured legislative authority, surveyed the route, organized the company, and in 1853 set to work. Some forty or fifty miles having been laid, his bills were dishonored, and the work brought to a standstill. Mr. Field's attention was secured, and the idea occurred to him that the telegraph might be made to span the Atlantic ocean; the task was undertaken. For twelve years his time was exclusively given to the "cable"; went to England thirty times. After five unsuccessful and discouraging attempts, the first message passed over the completed and satisfactory ocean telegraph, July 27, 1866, and the inventor was made hero of the hour. Was interested in the elevated railway system of New York city, and devoted much time and money to its establishment. Mr. Field died July 11, 1892.

Jay Gould, financier, born in Roxbury, Delaware county, N. Y., May 27, 1836; spent childoood on the farm; entered Hobart Academy at fourteen, and kept the books of the village blacksmith. On leaving school found employment in making the surveys for a map of Ulster county, which was so accurately done, that the late John Delafield applied to the legislature for aid that Mr. Gould might complete a topographical survey of the whole state. This work brought $5,000. After some time became acquainted with Zadoc Pratt, and with him carried on a large lumbering business. In 1857 became the largest stockholder and a director in the Stroudsburg, Pa., bank. Shortly after bought the bonds of the Rutland and Washington railroad, at ten cents on the dollar, abandoning all other interests to put his entire capital into railroad securities. For a long time was president, treasurer, and general superintendent of this company; brought about consolidation of the Reussaelaer and Saratoga roads, and with the proceeds removed to New York city in 1859, established as a broker and invested heavily in Erie railway stock, making large investments also in stock of many other roads. On consolidation of Atlantic and Pacific Telegraph with Western Union, he organized the American Union. In December, 1880, official records showed that Mr. Gould controlled 10,000 miles of railroad, more than one ninth of the mileage of the country. Once showed stock certificates to the amount of $53,000,000 face value, offering to show $20,000,000 more. Mr. Gould died December 2, 1893.

Collis Potter Huntington, railroad builder, born in Harwinton, Litchfield county, Conn., October 22, 1821. Educated in a local school, secured freedom from his father when fourteen years old, promising to support himself. Engaged in mercantile business, spent ten years traveling through the south and west, subsequently settling with an older brother in Oneonta, Otsego county, N. Y. In October, 1848, the brothers made a shipment of goods to California, which Collis followed in March. After spending three months in trade on the isthmus, began business in a tent in Sacramento, dealing in the necessities of a miner's life. Afterward opened a hardware store in the city, became associated with Mark Hopkins in business, and in 1860 matured a scheme for a transcontinental railroad. Five men organized the Central Pacific Railroad Company, of which Mr. Stanford was president, Mr. Huntington vice-president, and Mr. Hopkins treasurer. In addition, Mr. Huntington planned and perfected the whole California railroad system, extending over 8,900 miles of steel track, built on Atlantic system, and developed an aggregate of 13,900 miles of steam water lines, including the route to China and Japan.

Leland Stanford, senator, born in Cedar Valley, Ohio, March 9, 1824. Ancestors settled in the Mohawk valley about 1720. Was brought up on a farm, and when twenty years old began the study of law. Was admitted to the bar in 1849, and the same year began to practice at Port Washington, Wis. In 1852, having lost his law library and other property by fire, removed to California, and began mining for gold at Michigan Bluff, Placer county, becoming associated with his three brothers, who had preceded him to the Pacific coast. In 1856 removed to San Francisco, and engaged in mercantile pursuits on a large scale, laying the foundation of a fortune since estimated at more than $50,000,000. In 1860, made his entrance into public life as delegate to the Chicago convention that nominated Abraham Lincoln to the presidency. He was an earnest advocate of a Pacific railroad, and was elected president of the Central Pacific company on its organization in 1861. The same year was elected governor of California, serving from December, 1861, till December, 1863. As president of the Pacific road, superintended its construction over the mountains, building 530 miles in 293 days. In 1885 was elected to the United States Senate for the full term of six years. In memory of his only son, Mr. Stanford gave to the state of California $20,000,000 to found Leland Stanford Jr. University, at Palo Alto, with both classical and business curriculum. Died June 21, 1893.

Cornelius Vanderbilt, financier, born near Stapleton, Staten Island, N. Y., May 27, 1794; father, a farmer in moderate circumstances, who conveyed produce to market in a sailboat, which the son early learned to manage; the latter was hardy and practical but cared nothing for education. At sixteen, purchased a boat in which he conveyed passengers and baggage between New York city and Staten Island; at eighteen, was owner of two boats and captain of a third; at nineteen, married and removed to New York city. For twelve years worked on salary as captain of a steamer running between New York and New Brunswick, N. J. Later his success as boat builder and manager caused the title of "Commodore" to be attached to his name. Was worth $500,000 before forty years of age. In the time of gold-excitement, established a passenger line by way of Lake Nicaragua, which yielded large profits. In course of eleven years accumulated $10,000,000 by this business. Carried on transatlantic trade during the Crimean war; withdrawing on account of European competition, transferred his interests to railway enterprises. First important railway venture was in 1836; bought a large part of the stock of New York and Harlem railroad; began in the same year to purchase the Hudson River railroad shares, intending to consolidate the two. Rival parties concocted a plan to prevent this and cause loss to Vanderbilt and his associates; but the scheme ultimately worked to the latters' advantage. He had interests in many other roads; erected the

SUCCESSFUL MEN AND WOMEN.

Grand Central Station in New York city, half the expense being borne by the city. Founded Vanderbilt University at Nashville, Tenn. Had a fortune generally estimated at $100,000,000. He died January 4, 1877.

William H. Vanderbilt, son of Cornelius Vanderbilt, was born in New Brunswick, N. J., March 8, 1821; educated at Columbia grammar school. Left school at seventeen, engaging in business as a ship chandler; one year later became clerk in a banking establishment, of which Daniel Drew was senior partner. Owing to failing health, settled in New York, Staten Island, on a small farm, his father's gift; this he cultivated successfully. Was made receiver of the Staten Island railroad; later, had the business management of Commodore Vanderbilt's ventures in that line. Avoided a protracted war of rates and a strike of laborers, by conciliation and compromise. Between 1877 and 1880 obtained control of the Chicago and Northwestern road. He distributed $100,000 among the laborers and trainmen of the New York Central, when they refrained from striking in 1877. Added $200,000 to endowment of Vanderbilt University, gave $110,000 for library and theological school in connection with the university. Paid $103,000 for removal and erection in Central Park, of the obelisk given by Khedive Ismail to the United States. Bequeathed $10,000,000 to each of his eight children, besides other provisions. Died in New York city, December 8, 1885.

SOME PROMINENT BANKERS.

Alexander Brown, born at Ballymena, county Antrim, Ireland, November 17, 1764. In early life was engaged in commercial pursuits in Ireland. In 1796, leaving three sons to be educated in England, emigrated with family to Baltimore; became at once prominent as importer of Irish linen; and gradually extended the business to general commission and banking. He soon built up an extensive foreign trade. In the year 1811, organized in Baltimore the firm of Alexander Brown and Sons. Had a phenomenal genius for business, and his unassailable integrity made the name of his house respected in every financial center of the world. Died December 17, 1834.

Henry Clews was born in Staffordshire, England, August 14, 1840; father was an able business man, manufacturing for the American markets. A Cambridge education and the ministry of the established church were his ambitions for his son; but a visit to America determined the younger Clews's residence there, where securing a junior clerkship with Hunt & Co., importers of woolen goods, he rose to a position of responsibility. Was always ambitious to become a banker, became a member of firm of Stout, Clews & Mason. Supported government during civil war; was agent for loans issued to meet expenses of the war. Mr. Clews was originator and organizer of the "Committee of Seventy" that deposed from office the entire "Boss Tweed Ring." Became the largest negotiator of railroad bonds in America or Europe. Present firm of Henry Clews & Co. was established 1877 for commission business, under agreement not to take speculative risks. Mr. Clews is author of "Twenty-eight Years in Wall Street," was for some years treasurer of the American Geographical Society, and Society for the Prevention of Cruelty to Animals. His verdict is looked upon as authority in business circles.

James Herron Eckels, comptroller of the currency, was born at Princeton, Ill., November 22, 1858; attended the public schools of his native town, graduating from the high school at Princeton in 1876. Studied law in the law department of Union University at Albany, N. Y., in 1879 and 1880, and after graduation practiced law at Ottawa, Ill., from October, 1881, until April, 1893, when appointed comptroller of the currency by President Cleveland; entered upon the duties of that office April 28, 1893.

Lyman J. Gage, president of the First National Bank of Chicago, Ill., who has been called the first citizen of Chicago, began a business career as cashier of a small bank. From that position he has risen to others of increasing importance, and stands to-day at the head of the second largest financial institution of the greatest country in the world; and is reckoned among the millionaires, as a result of careful saving and shrewd investment. Not only is Mr. Gage one of the ablest financiers of America, but as a man he is splendidly endowed; is a clear and forcible writer, a ready and able speaker on economic and philosophic subjects, and a man of broad and liberal views, all of which bespeaks for him acknowledgment as one who realizes the necessity of accumulating mental and moral as well as material wealth.

John Jay Knox born at Knoxboro, N. Y., March 19, 1828; received a liberal education, and was graduated from Hamilton College in 1849. Began a business career in the Bank of Vernon at Vernon, N. Y., of which his father had been president for more than twenty years; assisted in organizing banks in Syracuse and Binghamton, N. Y. From

1857 to 1862 conducted an independent banking business in St. Paul, Minn. In 1866 was sent to San Francisco to examine the United States branch mint in that city, and his report was published with highly complimentary notice by the secretary in the finance report of that year. In 1866 was placed in charge of the mint and coinage correspondence at the Treasury Department, Washington, and in 1867 appointed deputy comptroller of the currency; in 1872 was promoted to the comptrollership. The bill known as the "Coinage Act of 1873" was prepared by him. Was reappointed to the comptrollership by President Hayes, and later by President Arthur; the last appointment, however, he resigned, to become president of the National Bank of the Republic, New York city. As comptroller of the currency he made twelve annual reports to Congress, which have become standard authorities on financial questions and have had wider circulation than almost any other public documents. Mr. Knox died February 9, 1892.

John Pierpont Morgan, financier, born in Hartford, Conn., April 17, 1837. His father, who was a native of Holyoke, Mass., was a banker associated as partner with George Peabody, which firm after Mr. Peabody's retirement has become known as Drexel, Morgan & Co., and ranks as one of the great banking institutions of the world. John Pierpont was educated at the English High school in Boston and at the University of Gottingen, Germany, and on his return to the United States in 1857, entered the firm of Duncan, Sherman & Co., of New York, and seven years later became partner in the firm of Dabney, Morgan & Co., and in 1871, became a member of the Drexel, Morgan & Co. banking house, whose immense transactions now extend into all parts of the world.

Levi P. Morton, ex-vice-president of the United States, born at Shoreham, Vt., May 16, 1824, son of Rev. Daniel Oliver Morton. Received a public school and academic education; entered country store at fifteen; commenced mercantile business at Hanover, N. H., in 1843. After engaging in business in Boston and New York, became a banker in 1863 under the name of L. P. Morton & Co. Was twice sent to Congress; and made minister to France by Garfield in 1881; accepted the Bartholdi statue for his government, on July 4, 1884. Was inaugurated vice-president March 4, 1889. He proved a model presiding officer, dealing with justice and fairness.

George Gilbert Williams, financier, born in East Haddam, Conn., October 9, 1826. His father was a physician and he was educated at the schools of his village, and fitted for college at Brainard Academy, Haddam, and when fifteen, a gentleman, pleased with his home training and good habits, procured him a situation as assistant to the paying teller in the Chemical Bank, New York. Here, shunning bad habits and evil acquaintances, he gave his spare time to reading and study, and when twenty, was made paying teller, being then the youngest person so employed in that city. He was next made discount clerk, and in 1855 cashier, and when John Q. Jones, the president of the bank, died, January 1, 1878, the board of directors chose Mr. Williams the president on the following day. The original $100 shares of this bank are now quoted at private sales as worth over $5,000. It has a surplus of many millions, and is the depository of many of the wealthiest men of the land, and under Mr. Williams's administration the bank has steadily grown in prosperity, being considered the greatest banking institution in this country.

Of the 39 pages of portraits, 32 pages are special inserts and not included in the number of pages shown at the foot of this page.

Some Leaders of the New South.

BIOGRAPHIES WRITTEN ESPECIALLY FOR THIS WORK.

By Prof. William M. Baskerville, A.M., Ph.D. (Leipsic),
Vanderbilt University, Nashville, Tenn.

Marion Butler was born near Clinton, Sampson county, North Carolina, May 20, 1863. He spent the early years of his life on his father's farm. He graduated A. B. from the University of North Carolina in 1885. After his graduation he taught school for a few years, then he became editor of the country paper at Clinton. A short time afterward he became president of the Farmers' County Alliance, and a little later was elected president of the State Alliance. This was soon followed by his election to the State Senate, which was accomplished by a vigorous campaign in which his political talents were fully tested and demonstrated. He became United States Senator in 1893, being elected for the long term, expiring in 1901. He has been for many years in the journalistic field, being editor of the *Caucasian* at Raleigh, the organ of the Populist party in North Carolina. Mr. Butler has all through his political career been closely identified with the agricultural interests of his state and nation, having held the presidency of the National Farmers' Alliance since 1895. In the Senate he has been active in promoting every measure which could be helpful to the common people. Probably one of his best pieces of legislative work is the Postal Savings Bank Bill, which he introduced and the passage of which he was largely instrumental in securing. He has been one of the most prominent figures in the development and growth of the Populist party, and is at present chairman of its national executive committee. He married Miss Florence Faisson of Elliott, N. C., Aug. 28, 1893.

Wilbur F. Crafts was born at Fryeburg, Me., Jan. 12, 1850. He is wont to say that he was born a twin of the Maine law; in the same state, in the same year and almost of the same father. Mr. Crafts' father, a preacher, was the writer of one of the rallying songs of Neal Dow's first campaign, and also a fearless opponent of slavery, therefore Mr. Crafts was a reformer born, rich in an inheritance of moral heroism received through heredity and the environment of a state in which in all his childhood he saw neither saloon nor drunkard. He graduated at Middletown, Conn., in 1869, studied theology in Boston University, and became a preacher in 1870. Mr. Crafts' activity in reform as a pastor down to 1883 was chiefly as a temperance writer and speaker. On becoming pastor of a Presbyterian church in New York city in 1883 he planned a series of sermons on "The Sabbath." That series of sermons grew into his best known book, "The Sabbath for Man." Mr. Crafts continued his New York pastorate for five years, giving to reform only such aid as a busy pastor might. The American Sabbath Union grew out of a petition circulated by Mr. Crafts among the leaders of Sabbath reform, by which in the spring of 1888 the various ecclesiastical bodies were induced to combine in an official union, organized to defend the Sabbath against its foes. On Jan. 1, 1889, Mr. Crafts was elected field secretary of the American Sabbath Union. Sabbath reform led Mr. Crafts to discuss labor reform and from that to the anti-lottery crusade. In the fall of 1891 he became the editor of *The Christian Statesman*, a paper devoted to the whole circle of Christian reform.

John Warwick Daniel was born at Lynchburg, Va., September 5, 1842. His father was judge of the supreme court of appeals of Virginia. At the opening of the war, John was at Dr. Gissner Harrison's school in Albemarle county, Virginia. He volunteered as a private soldier, became second lieutenant in the Stonewall brigade and was wounded at the first battle of Manassas. Later, he became adjutant of the eleventh Virginia infantry, was wounded at Boonsboro, near Antietam, was appointed major in the Confederate States army and adjutant of General Early's division. While serving in the last capacity he was permanently crippled by a wound received in the battle of the Wilderness. After the war he studied law at the University of Virginia and entered upon its practice at Lynchburg. He began his political career as a member of the Virginia House, where he served one term of two years, and continued it in the Virginia Senate from 1875 to 1881. In 1884 he was elected a member of Congress and, in 1885, succeeded General Mahone in the United States Senate. He has been twice re-elected to the Senate, member of various Democratic National Conventions, temporary chairman of the Chicago Convention, 1896. He has wide reputation as an advocate. He has published "Attachments," and "Negotiable Instruments."

John B. Gordon was born in Upson county, Georgia, February 6, 1832. He was educated at the State University of Georgia, where he was graduated in 1852 at the head of his class. He read law and practiced a short time in Atlanta, but soon gave up the profession to aid his father, who was mining coal in Georgia and Tennessee. He was married in 1853 to Miss Fanny Haralson. He was mining when the war began, but enlisted at once and served heroically to the close, becoming, in succession, captain, major, lieutenant-colonel, colonel, brigadier-general, major-general, and lieutenant-general in command of one wing of the army in Virginia. His personal daring in war was remarkable. He was wounded eight times. He settled in Atlanta after the war. He was elected United States senator in 1873, and re-elected in 1879. He resigned in 1880 and raised the money to build the Georgia Pacific Railroad. He was elected governor of Georgia in 1886 and re-elected in 1888, and in 1890 was elected United States senator. General Gordon was one of the illustrious generals of the Confederate army and won an international fame as a soldier. Mr. Gordon has been all his life a model of social worth and an ardent Christian worker. For many years he has been commander-in-chief of the United Confederate Veterans.

Henry Woodfin Grady was born in Athens, Georgia, May 17, 1851. He graduated at the State University of Georgia in 1868, and took a post-graduate course at the University of Virginia until 1870, when he returned to Athens. While at college in Virginia he wrote a letter for publication signed "King Hans." That letter, written by Mr. Grady, then a youth of nineteen, had the marks that signalized him in the maturity of his powers, the sparkle, rare vein of thought, affluent diction, descriptive verity, delicious humor, and luxuriant imagination, and the editor, recognizing the talent of the writer, published the letter, and invited more, and the boy became the leader of a galaxy of fine contributors. Soon after leaving school he took up journalism. In 1871 he moved to Atlanta and became the Georgia representative of the New York *Herald*. In the same year he bought an interest in the Atlanta *Herald*, and in 1880 he bought a fourth interest in the Atlanta *Constitution*, and remained a part owner and editor of that paper until his death. He held high rank as an orator. His editorials, articles, and addresses did much toward the upbuilding of the South. His oration on "The New South," before the New England Society in 1886, gave him a national reputation. He vigorously championed the new era. His writings and speeches have been collected in the "Life of Henry W. Grady." Mr. Grady was a great journalist, author, and philanthropist. He had genius of the highest order. In October, 1872, he married Julia King at Athens, Ga. His death occurred December 23, 1889, at Atlanta, and the expression of regret was universal over the country. The citizens of that city have erected a monument in his honor

Gen. Wade Hampton was born in Columbia, S. C., in 1818. He was graduated from the University of South Carolina and for a short time studied law but never practiced his profession. He was elected a member of the legislature of his state, but did not serve long in that capacity as his political opinions made him unpopular with his fellow citizens. When the war broke out he enlisted as a private soldier, but subsequently raised "Hampton's Legion" which he commanded throughout the war and greatly distinguished himself. For his services at the battle of Seven Pines he was raised to the rank of brigadier-general of cavalry. At the battle of Gettysburg, Hampton fought with splendid bravery and received three wounds. He was appointed major-general to date from August 3, 1863. He was assigned to Lee's cavalry in August, 1864, with the rank of lieutenant-general. At the close of the war, Hampton retired to his plantation. He was elected governor in 1876. In 1878 he was elected to the United States Senate, where he has always been a stanch Democrat of the conservative stripe, believing firmly in sound currency. He has been twice married, his first wife being Margaret, youngest daughter of General Francis Preston ; his second wife was the daughter of Senator George McDuffie of South Carolina.

Fitzhugh Lee, born in Clermont, Fairfax county, Virginia, November 19, 1835. Of the famous Lee family of Virginia — nephew of Robert E. Lee. Graduated from United States Military Academy, 1856. Commissioned second lieutenant in second cavalry. Saw service on the Indian frontier. Made instructor of cavalry at West Point, May, 1860. Entered Confederate army in 1861. Adjutant-general of Ewell's brigade until September, 1861. Colonel of first Virginia cavalry until July 25, 1862, when he was made brigadier-general. Became major-general September 3, 1863. At the battle of Winchester in 1864, he was severely wounded and had three horses shot from under him. In March, 1865, he was appointed to the command of the whole cavalry corps of the Army of Northern Virginia. In 1874 he made a celebrated Bunker Hill speech. In 1882-3, he made a tour of the Southern states in interest of the Southern Historical Society. Elected governor of Virginia in 1885. Appointed consul-general at Havana by President Cleveland and retained in that position by President McKinley. He has proved himself discreet, able, and fearless.

James Longstreet was born in South Carolina, June 8, 1821. He graduated from West Point in 1842 and was assigned to the 4th Infantry. In 1861 he resigned to join the Confederate army, of which he was immediately appointed brigadier-general, and won distinction in the first battle of Bull Run. At the second battle of Bull Run he commanded the first corps of the army of Northern Virginia. He led the right wing of the army of Northern Virginia at Gettysburg, and tried to dissuade Lee from ordering the disastrous charge on the third day. In the battle of the Wilderness he was so prominent that he was wounded by the fire of his own troops. Throughout the army he was familiarly known as "Old Pete," and was considered the hardest fighter in the Confederate service. Gen. Longstreet took up his residence in New Orleans after the war, and established the commercial house of Longstreet, Owen & Co. He was appointed surveyor of the port of New Orleans by President Grant, and was afterwards surveyor of internal revenue in Louisiana, and postmaster at New Orleans. In 1880 he was sent as United States minister to Turkey, and under Garfield he was United States marshal for the district of Georgia.

Dr. Hunter Holmes McGuire was born at Winchester, Virginia, October 11, 1835. His professional studies were begun in the Winchester Medical College, from which institution he received his degree in 1855. In 1856 he matriculated in both the University of Pennsylvania and Jefferson Medical College of Philadelphia, but was taken ill and compelled to return home before the end of the session. In 1857 he was elected professor of anatomy in the Winchester Medical College, but after one year's service he resigned his position and relinquished a growing practice to return to Philadelphia. In 1859, in consequence of John Brown's raid into Virginia, Dr. McGuire was the leader of a movement among the students to return to Richmond. In 1860 Dr. McGuire went to New Orleans, but, after the secession of South Carolina and other states, he hastened home to offer his services to Virginia. He volunteered in Company F, second Virginia regiment ; he afterwards became medical director of the Army of the Shenandoah. He was afterward medical director of the second army corps. While in this capacity, Dr. McGuire inaugurated the plan of releasing captured medical officers. After the fight at Winchester, eight Federal officers were set free upon the simple condition that they would endeavor to procure the release of the same number of Confederate surgeons, and, a few weeks after this, all the medical officers who had been confined by both the Confederate and Federal armies as prisoners of war, were released and returned to their respective commands. After the war, Dr. McGuire in 1865 removed to Richmond, having been elected to fill the chair of surgery in the medical college of Virginia. This position he held until 1878, when the demands of an extensive practice compelled him to resign it. In 1887 the degree of Doctor of Laws was conferred on Dr. McGuire by the University of North Carolina. He organized St. Luke's Home for the Sick, with training school for nurses, in Richmond. In 1886 he was married to Mary Stuart of Staunton, Virginia. He has published various important papers in medical journals. Contributed to Ashhurst's "International Cyclopedia of Surgery," William Pepper's "System of Medicine" and American edition of "Holmes' Surgery."

John Tyler Morgan was born at Athens, Tennessee, June 20, 1824. He received an academic education, and became a good Latin scholar before he was nine years of age. In 1845 he was admitted to the bar, and practiced his profession until he became United States senator. When the war broke out he entered the army and served as private, major, lieutenant-colonel, colonel and brigadier-general of infantry, resigning in 1863 to rejoin his regiment, whose colonel had been killed in battle. He subsequently acted as brigadier-general of cavalry to the end of the war. He was elected United States senator in 1876, 1882, and again in 1886. His war service was gallantly active; as a lawyer, he has shown himself learned and profound, a skillful pleader, and an eloquent and successful advocate. As a senator, he has taken the highest rank.

Benton McMillin, born in Monroe county, Kentucky, September 11, 1845. He received his early education at Philomath Academy, Tennessee. Afterwards attended Kentucky University at Lexington. Read law in a private office and began to practice in 1871 at Celina, Tenn. Was elected to National House of Representatives in 1874. Tilden and Hendricks elector in 1876. Commissioned by the governor as a special judge of circuit court in 1877. He has represented the Fourth District of Tennessee in Congress for ten successive terms, serving on the most important committees of that body. He is a popular party leader and well known in national councils. At present writing he is a candidate for the governorship of Tennessee.

Matt Whitaker Ransom was born in Warren county, North Carolina, October 8, 1826. He was graduated at the University of North Carolina in 1847 and admitted to the bar the same year, and was presidential elector on the Whig ticket in 1852. For the subsequent three years he was state attorney-general, and then joining the Democratic party was a member of the legislature in 1858 and in 1861, and one of the three North Carolina commissioners to the Confederate Congress in Montgomery, Alabama. He did his utmost to avert the war, but on the secession of his state volunteered as a private in the Confederate service and was at once appointed lieutenant-colonel of the first North Carolina infantry. He was chosen colonel of the thirty-fifth North Carolina infantry in 1862, participated with his regiment in all the important battles of the army of Northern Virginia, was severely wounded in the seven days' fight around Richmond, and was promoted brigadier-general in 1863 and major-general in 1865, but the fall of the Confederacy prevented the receipt of the latter commission. He resumed his profession in 1866, was elected to the United States Senate in 1872, and served until 1895.

James Elwell Brown Stuart was born in Patrick county, Virginia, February 6, 1833. In 1848 he entered Emory and Henry College and in 1850 he obtained an appointment to the United States military academy at West Point. He was graduated from West Point in 1854, thirteenth in a class of forty-six members, and was at once commissioned brevet second lieutenant in the regiment of mounted riflemen serving at that time in Texas. He served in the United States army until the outbreak of the civil war, but as soon as Virginia seceded he sent in his resignation as an officer of the United States army, which was accepted, and he at once joined the Confederate army, being commissioned a lieutenant-colonel of infantry. He was afterwards brevetted colonel of cavalry, brigadier-general, and commissioned a major-general. Gen. Stuart's cavalry in 1861 contained but 21 officers and 313 men, yet such was his efficiency and activity that a front of over fifty miles was closely guarded and every important movement reported. At Bull Run he did much toward gaining the victory for the Confederates. In June, 1862, he conducted the reconnoissance to the rear of McClellan's army known as the "Chickahominy raid." He took an active part in the seven days' fight around Richmond. He was a conspicuous figure during the whole war. He was mortally wounded in a battle against Gen. Sheridan at Yellow Tavern on the 12th of May, 1864. Noticing the retreating ranks of his disorganized men, he cried to them as he was being carried from the field, " Go back! Go back! and do your duty as I have done mine, and our country will be safe. Go back! Go back! I had rather die than be whipped." These were the last words he uttered on the battlefield. He died at Richmond, Virginia, June 12th, 1864.

Robert L. Taylor, governor of Tennessee, born at Happy Valley, Carter county, Tenn., July 31, 1850. Descended from distinguished Revolutionary ancestors who came originally from Virginia. Educated at Pennington, N. J. Married a cousin of Senator Vance in 1878. Began life as a clerk in a store. Afterwards engaged in making iron by the old trip hammer process. Read law in Jonesboro. His oratorical abilities early showed themselves. Licensed to practice in 1878 and within two weeks was nominated by the Democrats for Congress. Won the election by seven hundred votes over Judge Pettibone in a district which had a Republican majority of over five thousand. He was defeated in 1880 by Pettibone, elector-at-large on the presidential ticket of 1884. Elected governor in 1886, over his brother, Alfred Taylor, after a most interesting canvass. Re-elected in 1888. Has won fame as a unique and eloquent lecturer. Was elected governor in 1896 and now holds that office.

Benjamin Ryan Tillman was born in Edgefield county, S. C., August 11, 1847. He received his education at an "old field" school. He left school in 1864 to join the Confederate army, but was prevented by a severe and prolonged illness, which resulted in the loss of an eye. In 1867 he removed to Florida, but, returning in 1868, married Miss Starke and devoted himself to farming. At this time he took but very little active part in politics; gradually, however, his attention was directed to the depressed condition of the farming interests in his state and he began to study the larger questions connected therewith. He made his first public address in this line in August, 1885. The boldness of his utterance startled the conservative and official classes and a war of denunciation was begun against the innovator, who was contemptuously styled the "Agricultural Moses." He established the

SUCCESSFUL MEN AND WOMEN.

Clemson Agricultural and Mechanical College at Fort Hill. He was elected governor on the farmers' ticket in 1891 and re-elected by an overwhelming vote in 1892. The famous dispensary laws of South Carolina were enacted during his term of office, and lynch law, against which he took a decided stand, has disappeared from the state. The Winthrop Normal and Industrial College for women was established during his term of office. He was elected to the United States Senate in 1895 by the Democratic party. He is widely known as a fiery and brilliant debater.

Zebulon Baird Vance was born in Buncombe county, N. C., May 13, 1830. He was educated at Washington College in Tennessee, and at the University of North Carolina, at Chapel Hill. He commenced to study law, and was admitted to practice in 1852. In 1856 he was elected to the Thirty-first Congress. He was re-elected in 1858, and became an active participant in the stormy scenes in Congress preceding the outbreak of the war. Like many of the best men of North Carolina, he was opposed to secession, but when the step was taken followed the fortunes of his native state. He entered the Confederate army in May, 1861; was commissioned captain, and three months later was promoted to the rank of colonel. In 1862 Colonel Vance was elected governor of the state, a position which he held four years, being re-elected in 1864. By reason of his activity in procuring supplies for the Confederate troops in his state, he was known as the war-governor. In May, 1865, when he saw that resistance to the victorious Federal troops was no longer possible, he issued a message counseling peace, and advising the citizens of the state to accept the results of the war. He was arrested on order from Washington by a detachment of Kilpatrick's cavalry, but was released after a few months. In April, 1867, he was pardoned by the president, and for several years retired to private life. He was elected to the United States Senate in 1870, but could not take his seat on account of political disabilities, which were not removed by Congress until 1872. He practiced law in Charlotte until 1876, when he was elected governor. He was again elected to the United States Senate in 1879, where he served until his death in 1894. His wit and eloquence made him exceedingly popular in all circles.

Thomas E. Watson was born in Columbia (now McDuffie) county, Georgia, September 5, 1856. He had a common school education and entered Mercer University, Macon, Georgia, in 1872, as freshman, but, for want of means, left college at the end of the sophomore year and taught school and studied law until admitted to the bar in 1875. He has practiced law successfully since and farmed on a large scale. He was elected a member of the Georgia legislature in 1882-3. Was Democratic elector for the state-at-large in 1888. He afterwards joined the People's party. He was a member of the Fifty-second Congress and contested a seat in the Fifty-third Congress but failed to gain admittance. He was nominated by the People's party in convention at St. Louis on July 25, 1896, for the office of Vice-President of the United States. While in Congress he was a vigorous debater and a stanch advocate of Populist principles. He married, in 1878, Georgia Durham and has two children.

Leading Southern Writers.

BIOGRAPHIES WRITTEN ESPECIALLY FOR THIS WORK.

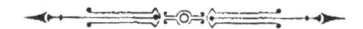

By Prof. William M. Baskerville, A.M., Ph.D. (Leipsic),
Vanderbilt University, Nashville, Tenn.

James Lane Allen was born in 1849, on a small farm near Lexington, Ky. Mr. Allen's childhood was spent on the farm. He attended school but little, but was drawn to literature under the guidance and through the influence of his mother. After spending seven years at Kentucky University, he graduated at the head of his class. He then taught for several years, and, while thus teaching, took a post-graduate course in Spanish, Italian, and French. He became professor of Latin at Bethany College, West Virginia. He was the first non-resident student to enroll himself for the degree of Ph.D. from Johns Hopkins University. Finally he abandoned teaching, and began the pursuit of literature, one of his first attempts being an essay, which was printed in the *Critic*. He spent three years in New York, and during that period contributed sketches to *Harper's*, *The Century*, *The Critic*, and other magazines. He then returned to Kentucky, and began a series of descriptive articles which appeared in *Harper's* and *The Century*. For the last three or four years he has spent most of his time in Cincinnati. A clear eye, a firm hand, with abundant local knowledge and sympathy, are evident in his "King Solomon," "Two Gentlemen of Kentucky," "Posthumous Fame," "The White Cowl." and "Sister Dolores," gathered in a volume, which took the name from one of its component parts, "Flute and Violin." These studies gave their author rank as one of both promise and performance. He has also written several other stories. Though recognition has been tardy, the tributes which his work has called forth have always been of the highest character. He has also published "The Blue Grass Region of Kentucky," "A Kentucky Cardinal," "Aftermath," "A Summer in Arcady," and "The Choir Invisible."

George W. Cable, author, was born in New Orleans, La., October 12, 1844. At fourteen years of age, owing to the death of his father, he was obliged to leave school to help support the family. He worked as a clerk until 1863, when he entered the Confederate army as a volunteer in the fourth Mississippi cavalry. He served through the remainder of the war, employing his leisure in studying Latin, mathematics, and the Bible. Returning to New Orleans, and being forced by straitened circumstances to take up with the first work that presented itself, he became an errand boy in a mercantile house. Later he studied civil engineering, and practiced it for a short time, but was forced to abandon it on account of malarial fever. His first literary work was contributed to the New Orleans *Picayune*, and was so well received that in 1869 he became one of the editors of this journal. In a few months, however, he lost this position by positively refusing, on an urgent occasion, to edit the theatrical column, owing to his scruples against the stage. He then entered the employ of a large cotton firm as accountant and corresponding clerk, remaining with them until 1879, when the success of "Old Creole Days" emboldened him to adopt literature as a profession. Mr. Cable has written several books, among which are "The Grandissimes," "Madame Delphine," "The History of New Orleans," "Dr. Sevier," "The Creoles of Louisiana," and "The Silent South," all of which aroused considerable antagonism in the sections of which they treat. As a novelist, Mr. Cable stands as the first and (up to the present) the foremost exponent of the Creole life. His present home is Northampton, Mass. He is interested in prison reforms and Bible studies, and is prominent on the platform as a lecturer and reader.

Joel Chandler Harris, born in Eatonton, Putnam county, Georgia, December 9, 1848. His early education was obtained in Eatonton Academy, and as a typesetter on the "*Countryman*," a backwoods newspaper. First writings were boyish contributions to the "*Countryman*." Compositor on Macon *Daily Telegraph*; private secretary to editor of *Crescent Monthly*, New Orleans. Editor of Forsyth *Advertiser*; associate on staff of Savannah *Daily News*, 1871-1876. Since 1876 on editorial staff of *Atlanta Constitution*. Does daily journalistic work. Unsurpassed as a writer of negro folk-lore and dialect stories. Published works are "Uncle Remus: His Songs and Sayings" (1880), "Mingo and Other Sketches" (1883),

"Nights with Uncle Remus" (1884), "Daddy Jake, the Runaway" (1889), "Balaam and His Master" (1891), "Uncle Remus and His Friends" (1892), "Free Joe and Other Stories" (1888), "On The Plantation" (1892), "Evening Tales" (1893), "Sister Jane" (1896), "The Story of Aaron" (1896), "Little Mr. Thimblefinger" (1896), "Aaron in the Wildwoods" (1897), "Stories of Georgia" (1896).

Constance Cary Harrison, novelist and short story writer, born in Vaucluse, Fairfax county, Virginia, about 1835. Married Mr. Burton Harrison, a Virginia lawyer, in 1867. Afterwards moved with him to New York, where she now lives. She has written for most of the prominent magazines. She has traveled much, and is cosmopolitan in her tastes. Some of her stories are Southern in color and sentiment, but for the most part the subject matter of her novels is international. She has published "Golden Rod" (1880), "Helen Troy" (1881), "Woman's Handiwork in Modern Homes" (1881), "Old Fashioned Fairy Book" (1885), "Bric-a-Brac Stories" (1886), "Flower de Hundred" (1890), "A Daughter of the South" (1892), "Sweet Bells Out of Tune" (1893), "An Errant Wooing" (1894), "A Bachelor Maid" (1894), "The Merry Maid of Arcady" (1896), "A Virginia Cousin" (1896), "A Son of the Old Dominion" (1897), "Good Americans" (1898). In addition she has adapted many plays from the French.

Richard Malcolm Johnston, author and editor, was born in Hancock county, Ga., March 8, 1822. The early years of the boy were spent upon his father's farm. He was graduated from Mercer University, Georgia, in 1841, with the first honor of his class. He taught for a year and then studied law, was admitted to the bar and began to practice in 1843. In 1857 he accepted a professorship of belles-lettres in the State University. This position he held until the outbreak of the civil war in 1861. He established a boys' school at Sparta, Ga., and afterwards one near Baltimore, Md., where he now lives. He has published "Georgia Sketches," "Dukesborough Tales," "Old Mack Langston," "Two Gray Tourists," and others. Of his later stories the most important are "The Chronicle of Mr. Bill Williams" and "Their Cousin Lethy."

Grace Elizabeth King, born in New Orleans, La. Educated at home and in the French schools of her native city. Her first contributions to literature were published in 1886 in the *New Princeton Review*. Her knowledge of Louisiana life is very complete, and her acquaintance with Creole and Catholic customs is minute. Her works, mostly short stories, are "Bonne Mamam" (1886), "Monsieur Motte" (1888), "Earthlings," (1889), "One Woman's Story" (1891), "Balcony Stories" (1893), "New Orleans, The Place and Its People" (1896).

Sidney Lanier, poet, was born at Macon, Georgia, February 3, 1842. At the age of fourteen he entered the sophomore class at Oglethorpe College, Midway, Georgia, and was graduated at eighteen with honors. Immediately on graduation he became tutor in the college, remaining there until the outbreak of the civil war. In April, 1861, he enlisted in the Confederate army and served as a private to the close of the war, having three times refused promotion in order that he might not be separated from his younger brother, to whom he was tenderly attached. Was taken prisoner near the close of the war. In December, 1867, he was married to Mary Day. In the spring of 1868 he returned to Macon, where he remained studying and practicing law with his father until 1872, when he visited Texas in search of health and subsequently in the autumn of 1873 settled in Baltimore, Md. Often for months together he was too ill to work and obliged to visit different parts of the country, hoping the change of climate would benefit his health. On his birthday in 1879 he received notice of his appointment as lecturer in English Literature at the Johns Hopkins University, which gave him his first assured income since his marriage. He developed a theory of the reconciliation of music and poetry. Of his poems it has been said that "one thread of purpose runs through them all. This thread is found in his fervid love for his fellow men and his never ceasing endeavors to kindle an enthusiasm for beauty, purity, nobility of life, which he held it the poet's first duty to teach and to exemplify." After a time he removed to Lynn, N. C., and died there September 7, 1881. His works are "Tiger-Lilies," a novel; "Florida," "Poems," "The Boy's Froissart," "The Boy's King Arthur," "The Science of English Verse," and others.

Mary N. Murfree, known by the pen name "Charles Egbert Craddock," was born in 1850, at Grantlands, near Murfreesboro, Tennessee, a town named in honor of her great grandfather. Miss Murfree was an indefatigable student, and as she was incapable of taking part in childish pastimes, because of a lameness which came from an accident, her natural bent had ample chance to develop, and she read everything that came in her way. She was educated in Nashville. She lived several years in St. Louis, but afterward returned to Grantlands. She spent her summers for fifteen years in the mountain region of eastern Tennessee, becoming thoroughly familiar with the inhabitants, and mastering their dialect. Her writings were first published in the *Atlantic Monthly*, her identity being so carefully concealed, that her reputation was well established before even her publishers were aware that the masculine name, penmanship, and vigor of style, hid the personality of a very feminine woman. Her first book was "In the Tennessee Mountains." Her other works are, "Where the Battle was Fought," "Down the Ravine," "The Prophet of the Great Smoky Mountains," "In the Clouds," "The Story of Keedon Bluffs," "The Despot of Broomsedge Cove," and others.

Thomas Nelson Page, author and lawyer, was born in Hanover county, Virginia, April 23, 1853, at Oakland, a part of the old family estate. The civil war sadly interfered with any systematic education for the lad, but materially increased his knowledge of human nature. The war left the family impoverished, which still further delayed his education, but the time was by no means lost. He finally entered Washington and Lee University, but there, like many another literary genius, neglected the curriculum of the college for the debating society and the college magazine, of which he was editor. He afterward attended the law school of the University of Virginia, where he took his degree in one year. He was admitted to the bar and practiced in Richmond, devoting his leisure to literary work and the lecture field, but never neglecting his profession for these pursuits. For one year he was connected with the editorial staff of *Harper's Magazine*. He now lives in Washington, D. C. His works follow one another in rapid succession, among which are, "Marse Chan," "Meh Lady," "Unc Edinburgh's Drowndin," "Polly," "Two Little Confederates," "Elsket," and "Among the Camps." Some of his later works are "Social Life in Old Virginia," "The Old Gentleman of the Black Stock," and "Red Rock."

Samuel Minturn Peck, poet, was born at Tuscaloosa, Ala., November 4, 1854. His earliest education was received in the public schools of the South and West, being graduated at the University of Alabama in 1876, when, in obedience to the wishes of his family, he studied medicine, and was graduated at Bellevue Hospital Medical College in New York, but having an aversion to the profession, never practiced it. When about twenty-four years of age his taste for literary composition developed, and he contributed his first work, a lyric entitled, "The Orange Tree," to the New York *Evening Post*. His verse was successful from the first, and found ready acceptance in the various magazines. He has also written a number of songs which have proved great favorites with the musical composers. The chief collections of his verse are "Cap and Bells," "Rings and Love Knots," and "Rhymes and Roses."

Mrs. Margaret J. Preston, poet, was born in Philadelphia, Pa., about 1820. Her father was Rev. George Junkin, D.D., a Presbyterian clergyman, known as one of the most distinguished educators of his day. She received her early education from her father and from private tutors at home. She read Latin when only ten years of age, and Greek at twelve. She early developed a taste for literary pursuits. In 1857 she married Prof. John T. L. Preston, a professor in the Virginia Military Institute at Lexington, Va. Her first contribution to the press in 1849 was received with great favor. In 1856 she published a novel entitled, "Silverwood," which appeared anonymously, refusing to allow her name to appear, even though offered double price for her consent. She was an enthusiastic sympathizer with the South, and published, in 1865, her most sustained poem, called, "Beechenbrook; a Rhyme of the War." This poem won for her wide popularity from the Potomac to the Gulf. Her second volume of poems appeared in 1870, under the title, "Old Songs and New," and won high praise from the leading critics. She also wrote "Cartoons," "For Love's Sake," "Centennial Poem for Washington and Lee University," "Volume of Travels," "Colonial Ballads," and a "Semi-Centennial Ode for Virginia Military Institute." Her prose, which in grace and diction is fully equal to her poetry, is not, however, as well known. Mrs. Preston died at the residence of her son, Dr. George S. Preston, in Baltimore, Md., March 28, 1897.

Ruth McEnery Stuart, story-writer, born in New Orleans, La. Descended from aristocratic ancestry. She married Mr. Alfred O. Stuart in 1879, and moved to southwestern Arkansas. There she became thoroughly familiar with the old plantation life. She has written plantation verses of pleasing rhythm, but it is to her stories that she owes her fame. They are noted for humor and realistic accuracy, and are charmingly told. She is among the few women that read their own works on the platform. Her first story, "Uncle Mingo's Speculations," appeared about nine years ago in *The New Princeton Review*, to which and to *Harper's Magazine* she contributed much of her work. Among her published works are, "A Golden Wedding" (1893), "Carlotta's Intended" (1894), "The Middle Hall" (1895), "The Story of Babette" (1895), "Solomon Crow's Christmas Pockets" (1896), "The Unlived Life of Little Mary Ellen" (1896), "A Slender Romance" (1896), "Sonny" (1897).

Lights of Canada.

Sir Oliver Mowat, born in Kingston, Ont., July 22, 1820. He was educated in Kingston, subsequently studied law, was called to the bar of Upper Canada in 1841 and was created a Queen's Council in 1856. He represented South Ontario in the Canada Assembly from 1857 till 1864; North Oxford in the Ontario Parliament since 1872; was provincial secretary in the Brown-Dorion government in August, 1858, and held many other public offices until he was appointed a member of the executive council and attorney-general of Ontario, October 31, 1872, and since then has been leader of the Ontario government. Sir Oliver is the author of many important legislative measures in the Provincial Parliament, among which is the judicature bill and an act for the fusion of law and equity in the courts of Ontario. He is a Liberal in politics, an effective public speaker, and has been a cautious, intelligent, and successful administrator of the government of his native province, in which his popularity is very great. He was knighted in 1892.

Sir John A. MacDonald, born in Glasgow, Scotland, January 11, 1815. He was educated at the Royal Grammar school, adopted the law as his profession, and was called to the bar of Upper Canada in 1836. Ten years later he was appointed Queen's Council, but it is as politician and statesman that he won his place in Canadian history. In 1844 he was elected to represent Kingston in the Canadian Assembly and sat for this constituency almost continuously until his death. He assumed office for the first time, May 21, 1847, entering the cabinet as receiver-general; became commissioner of crown lands and was attorney-general for Upper Canada from September 11, 1854, to July 29, 1858, when, as prime minister, he and his cabinet resigned; after this he was reappointed attorney-general, a position he held until the defeat of the administration, May, 1862, when he and his colleagues again retired from office. On July 1, 1867, he was called upon to form the first government for the new Dominion and was appointed minister of justice and attorney-general of Canada, an office which he held until he and his ministry resigned on the Pacific Railway charges, November 6, 1873. The measures which Sir John carried through Parliament comprise the most important features of Canadian legislation from 1854 up till the period of his death in 1891.

Hon. Joseph Howe was born near Halifax, Nova Scotia, December 13, 1804. He was apprenticed to a printer, and in 1828 became sole editor and proprietor of the *Nova Scotian*. As an outspoken Liberal and friend of responsible government, he was involved in a vexatious libel suit, and fought a duel with Mr. Haliburton. As a member of the Provincial Parliament, colonial agent in England, provincial secretary, etc., he was long one of the most prominent men in Nova Scotia, and was one of the founders of responsible government in the province. He resigned his office of provincial secretary to superintend the construction of the railway from Halifax to Quebec. He was (1869–72) secretary of state for the provinces in the Dominion government, and superintendent of Indian affairs He was afterwards lieutenant-governor of Nova Scotia. Died at Halifax, June 1, 1873.

Hon. Wilfrid Laurier, born in St. Lin, Quebec, November 20, 1841. He was educated at L'Assomption College, and admitted to the bar in 1865. He was a member of the Quebec Assembly, 1871–74, and since 1874 has been a member of the Dominion Parliament, and was minister of inland revenue, 1877–78. He is an eloquent speaker, and, since the retirement of Mr. Blake, has been the leader of the Canadian Liberals. He is an earnest advocate of temperance, and was a delegate to the Dominion prohibitory convention at Montreal in 1875.

Sir John William Dawson was born in Pictou, Nova Scotia, October 13, 1820. Was educated at Pictou College and the University of Edinburgh, and afterwards devoted himself to the study of the natural history and geology of the Provinces of Nova Scotia and New Brunswick. His studies in the lower forms of animal life, both recent and fossil, have been numerous and valuable; and he is the discoverer of the oldest known form of animal life, the *eozoon Canadense* of the Laurentian limestones. In 1850 he was appointed superintendent of education for Nova Scotia, in which position he reorganized the schools of that province. In 1855 he was appointed principal and professor of natural history in the McGill University at Montreal, of which he has since become vice-chancellor. He also organized the Protestant normal school for the Province of Quebec. Dr. Dawson has the degree of LL.D. from McGill University, and is a fellow of the Royal and

Geological Societies of London, and a member of many other learned societies.

Sir John Sparrow David Thompson, born at Halifax, Nova Scotia, November 10, 1844. He was educated at the common school and the Free Church Academy at Halifax, studied law, was called to the bar in July, 1865, and appointed a Queen's Council in May, 1879. He was in turn a member of the House of Assembly of Nova Scotia, attorney-general of the province, premier and attorney-general of the same until July 25, 1882, when he was appointed a judge of the supreme court of Nova Scotia; resigned September 25, 1885, to become minister of justice and attorney-general of Canada and was elected to the Parliament of Canada. He was appointed premier of Canada upon the resignation of Sir John C. Abbott. He was a member of the senate of the University of Halifax, held several other offices, and was knighted for his services in 1888. Died at Windsor, England, December 12, 1894.

Sir Richard John Cartwright was born at Kingston, Ontario, December 4, 1835, and was educated at his native place and at Trinity College, Dublin, Ire. He entered Parliament as a Conservative in 1863, but in 1870 formally severed his connection with the Conservative party. He voted against his old party on several questions, but was re-elected in 1872. He then identified himself thoroughly with the reform party and in 1873 accepted office as minister of finance and was sworn of the privy council. On May 24, 1879, he was knighted. Sir Richard is a leader of the Liberal party and a keen critic of the financial policy of his political opponents.

Hon. Alexander Mackenzie, born in Logierait, Scotland, January 28, 1822. Was educated at the public schools and, after following for a time the trade of a mason, became, like his father, an architect and builder. In 1842 emigrated to Kingston, Canada. He had been a Whig in Scotland and naturally, soon after his arrival in Canada, allied himself with the Liberal party. In 1861 he was elected to Parliament for Lambton and represented it until 1867; he represented the same constituency in the Dominion Parliament, sat for West Middlesex in the Ontario Assembly, 1871-72, and was treasurer of the province during that period. On November 5, 1873, upon the resignation of Sir John A. MacDonald, Mr. Mackenzie was called upon to form a new administration, which he succeeded in accomplishing November 7, 1873, taking the position of premier and minister of public works, which he held till he and his cabinet resigned in 1878 in consequence of the Conservatives being returned to power. His administration was productive of the most important legislation. Among the measures that were enacted were a stringent election law, the abolition of the real estate qualifications for members of Parliament, the enactment of the marine telegraph law, the establishment of a Dominion military college, and many others. He was three times offered the honor of knighthood, which he declined. Died at Toronto, April 17, 1892.

Sir Charles Tupper, born at Amherst, Nova Scotia, July 2, 1821; graduated as a physician at Edinburgh in 1843. He was appointed governor of Dalhousie College, Halifax, by act of Parliament in 1862, was president of the Canadian Medical Association from its formation until 1870, and is director of the London board of the bank of British Columbia. He was a Conservative in politics, but took no active part in public matters until 1855, when he was elected to the provincial legislature for the county of Cumberland. At once Tupper took a marked position in the legislature, and when, in 1856, the Johnston cabinet was formed, he became provincial secretary of Nova Scotia, serving till 1860, and identified himself with such measures as the abolition of the monopoly in mines and minerals, representation by population and consolidation of the jury law. In 1864 Dr. Tupper became prime minister of Nova Scotia, which post he held until 1867. During these three years he passed the free school law, which is still in operation in Nova Scotia. He held many other public offices, and in 1879 was knighted, and became a baronet in 1888. He was largely instrumental in securing the assent of the Maritime provinces to confederation, and other important legislation.

John Campbell Hamilton Gordon, seventh Earl of Aberdeen, was born August 3, 1847. He succeeded to his title January 27, 1870. He began political life as a Conservative; was in 1875 a member and later the chairman of a royal commission to investigate the subject of railway accidents. In 1880, having become a Liberal, he was appointed lord-lieutenant of Aberdeenshire, and, for the years 1881-85, he was high commissioner to the General Assembly of the Church of Scotland. Appointed Lord Lieutenant of Ireland by Mr. Gladstone in 1886. He became extremely popular with the Irish people in his mission of carrying out the Home Rule policy of that time, and his departure on the fall of the Gladstone Cabinet was the occasion for much popular demonstration.

Well Known Men.

Charles Henry Parkhurst was born in Framingham, Mass., April 17, 1842. Until the age of sixteen he was a pupil of the Clinton, Mass. Grammar School. Then for two years he was a clerk in a dry-goods store. At the age of eighteen he began his preparation for college, pursuing his studies at Lancaster Academy, three miles from Clinton, walking to and from the place each day. In 1862 he went to Amherst from which he graduated in 1866. In 1867 he became principal of the Amherst High School, remaining until 1870, when he visited Germany with the intention of pursuing a course of study in philosophy and theology. Illness in the family caused his early return from his meditated European studies and he became a professor of Greek and Latin in Williston Seminary, Easthampton, Mass., where he remained two years. During this period he married Miss Bodman, a pupil of his while teaching in Amherst. He then, accompanied by his wife, made his second journey to Europe, and devoted two years to study in Halle, Leipsic and Bonn. Upon his return to this country he spent a number of months at his old home devoting himself particularly to the study of Sanscrit. In the spring of 1874 he received a call to the pastorate of the First Congregational Church in Lenox, Mass., and in the same year was installed over his charge. As pastor he gained a reputation as a pulpit orator, and on March 9, 1880, became pastor of the Madison Square Presbyterian Church, New York city. He began to take a lively interest in city and national politics, and used his sermons as a vehicle for publicly expressing his views. A sermon on municipal politics preached by him in 1890, attracted the attention of Dr. Howard Crosby, President of the Society for the Prevention of Crime, and he was invited to become not only a member but a director in the society. He accepted the invitation and at once entered heartily into the work of the society. A few months later the presidency of the society becoming vacant by the death of Dr. Crosby, Dr. Parkhurst was chosen to be his successor. His work in this position has been fearless, and he has twice been summoned before the grand jury to prove charges he had made in his sermons, and as a result of his statements and of their own investigations, a strong presentment was made by that body charging the police authorities with "incompetency or corruption," in view of their failure to suppress flagrant exhibitions of crime.

Dr. Parkhurst has published "The Blind Man's Creed and other Sermons" (1883), "The Pattern on the Mount and other Sermons" (1885), "Three Gates on a Side" (1887), and others.

Winfield Scott Schley was born near Frederick, Maryland, October 9, 1839. He was appointed an acting midshipman in 1856, and was graduated from the U. S. Naval Academy in 1860. He served in the U. S. frigate "Niagara" in China and Japan after carrying the Japanese embassy back to their own country in 1860-61. He was promoted to master in 1861 and ordered to the U. S. frigate "Potomac." When the Potomac was turned into a store ship he was ordered to the gunboat Winona of the West Gulf blockading squadron, and after several months of service in the Mississippi was ordered to the steam sloop Monongahela and subsequently to the steam sloop Richmond. He was commissioned as lieutenant on July 18, 1862, only two years after leaving the naval academy. From 1834 to 1866 he was attached to the steam gunboat Wateree as executive officer in the Pacific squadron. He was commissioned a lieutenant-commander in July, 1866, and upon his return from the Pacific was ordered to the U. S. Naval Academy where he remained until 1869 when he was appointed to the U. S. ship Benicia and served in her until 1872. He was commissioned a commander in 1874 and was ordered to command the U. S. ship Essex in 1876, and served in her on the North Atlantic, west coast of Africa and South Atlantic stations until 1879. When the Greely relief expedition was organized in 1884 he was sent in command of it to the North Polar regions, and on June 22d rescued Lieutenant Greely and six survivors, at Cape Sabine, and brought them home with great promptitude. Partly as a reward for this service he was promoted by President Arthur to Chief of Bureau of Equipment and Recruiting in the navy department, and resigned from the office in 1889 when he was ordered to command the cruiser Baltimore.

He proved himself worthy of trust and confidence when in command of the American forces in the Pacific at the time the Chilians made the assault upon the sailors from the Baltimore.

Upon the outbreak of the present war he was placed in command of the "Flying Squadron" and with it bottled up Cervera in Santiago harbor.

William T. Sampson was born in Palmyra, N. Y., February 8, 1840. He entered the Naval Academy in 1857 and graduated first in his class three years later. His first cruise was made in the frigate "Potomac" in 1861, and in 1862 he was commissioned a lieutenant. In 1874 he was made a commander, and in 1889 was promoted to the rank of captain, and in the next year was placed in command of the cruiser "San Francisco." In 1892 he was made Inspector of Ordnance, and in 1893 Chief of the Bureau of Ordnance. He held this position until the "Iowa" was ready to be commissioned when he was detailed to that vessel. When the fleet was sent to Havana, Captain Sampson was placed in command and raised his flag on the cruiser "New York." The authorities showed their confidence in him by promoting him from captain over the heads of Commodore Schley and others, to Acting Rear-Admiral and the command of the fleet. His conduct, since hostilities broke out, has shown that the confidence of the authorities was well placed. He is popular with his men; they thoroughly respect him and have the utmost confidence in his skill and ability.

He is counted the highest authority in the United States on the subject of ordnance:

William Jennings Bryan was born in Salem, Illinois, March 19, 1860. He spent his early life on his father's farm in the outskirts of Salem, went to the public schools, prepared for college in the Whipple Academy at Jacksonville, Illinois, and at the age of seventeen entered Illinois College in that town. He was a good student and graduated with honors in 1881, appearing at commencement as the orator of his class, a position that he had earned by gaining the second prize in an intercollegiate contest held at Galesburg while he was a senior. Upon graduation he immediately began the study of law, entering Judge Lyman Trumbull's office in Chicago, and at the same time pursuing the course of the Union Law College. He began his professional career in Jacksonville, and a year later married Mary E. Baird, the only daughter of a prosperous merchant of Perry, Illinois. In 1870 he removed to Lincoln, Nebraska, where he formed a partnership with a lawyer named Talbot, and opened a law office in the autumn of that year. Mrs. Bryan took up the study of law, was admitted to the bar, and gave effective aid to her husband in his law practice.

In May 1888, Bryan was elected a delegate to the Democratic State convention which met at Omaha, to elect delegates for the National convention at St. Louis. In 1890, he was elected to Congress, and was placed on the Committee of Ways and Means. His speeches in Congress were so eloquent and effective that he was retained as a member of the Ways and Means Committee when it was reconstituted by the Forty-third Congress, to which he was elected. In 1894 he was a candidate for U. S Senate, but was defeated by John M. Thurston. He was the Democratic candidate for president in 1896, but was defeated by the Republican nominee, William McKinley.

John H. Vincent was born February 23, 1832, in Tuscaloosa, Ala. At his birth the child was consecrated to the ministry, and he was taught from infancy what was hoped for him. Even when very young he seems to have accepted the idea for before he was five years old he began his career by gathering the children in the neighborhood into his play ground and expounding the gospel to them, keeping them in order meantime with a whip. When he was six years of age the family left Alabama for Pennsylvania, and the boy was given a governess. Then came several years in the best schools of the neighborhood. When fifteen years of age he became a school teacher. He had the usual plain little country school-house, and he wanted to make the hours less wearisome; beside the school-house was a grove; with the aid of his pupils he enclosed part of the grove by a rail fence and put up seats, and there on warm days the lessons were studied and recited. He had been licensed to "exhort" when eighteen years old, and the same year had been made local preacher. He gave up the thoughts of a college course, but he resolved that he would make up for what he had missed by a course of self culture. In 1874, Dr. Vincent and Lewis Miller of Akron, Ohio, originated the Chautauqua Sunday School Assembly on the shores of Chautauqua Lake. Methods of teaching every grade of pupils from the baby in the infant class to the the grey-haired elder in the adults' Bible class were discussed. The Assembly met with a hearty public response and it grew steadily in attraction and usefulness until in 1878, a feature was introduced which has given it a world-wide fame. This was the Chautauqua Literary and Scientific Circle, which has grown to a world-wide reputation and usefulness.

George Dewey was born in Montpelier, Vermont, December 26, 1837. He first attended the Washington County Grammar School in Montpelier. At fifteen he went to the Norwich Military Academy in Norwich, Vt., and it was while there he conceived a strong taste for a military life and expressed a desire to go to Annapolis. This was greatly against his father's wishes, but it had never been his policy to thwart his children and so he consented. Dewey entered the class of '54, at the age of seventeen. He was graduated in 1858, fifth in his class. As a midshipman he was sent to the European station, cruising for two years in the Mediterranean in the Wabash. In 1860 he returned to Annapolis to be examined for a commission, showing his ability by leading his fellows. This stand, combined with that of his graduation, gave him a final rating of third in his class. Dewey was at home in Montpelier when Sumter was fired upon. A week afterward he secured his commission as a lieutenant and was ordered to the steam sloop Mississippi of the West Gulf squadron and served during the Civil War with great bravery and heroism, and was raised to the rank of lieutenant commander. After the war he served for two years on the European station. In 1870 he received his first command, that of the Narragansett. In 1875 Lieutenant-commander Dewey was advanced to a commander and was assigned to the Light-House Board. Next he was in command of the Jianiata of the Asiatic squadron. He was honored in 1884, upon attaining his captaincy, by receiving the Dolphin, which was among the very first vessels in our new navy, then known as the "White Squadron." From the Dolphin in 1885 Captain Dewey went to the Pensacola. Since 1888 he has occupied various responsible positions on shore. At his promotion to be commodore he went to the head of the Board of Inspection and Survey. When war broke out between this country and Spain, Commodore Dewey, at Hong Kong, found himself in a singular and trying position. He was forced to leave British waters, and with no coaling station nearer than Honolulu there was but one thing to do — take Manila. The taking of Manila involved first the capture and destruction of the Spanish fleet, which Dewey proceeded to do, and practically annihilated the enemy's fleet, forts and all in two hours. He didn't lose a ship nor one of his brave men

QUEEN VICTORIA.

VICTORIA ALEXANDRINA, Queen of Great Britain and Ireland and Empress of India, only child of Edward, Duke of Kent, was born at Kensington Palace, May 24, 1819.

Her father died when she was but eight months old. Her education was conducted by competent instructors under the direction of her mother. Until within a few weeks of her elevation to the throne, her life was spent in comparative retirement.

Queen Victoria succeeded her uncle William IV., June 20, 1837, as Victoria I., and she was crowned in Westminster Abbey, June 28, 1838.

In 1840 she married her cousin, Prince Albert of Saxe-Coburg and Gotha, and the union proved a most happy one. His sudden death in 1861 has colored the whole of the queen's later life, and in a great degree prevented her from appearing in public.

She has had four sons and five daughters.

Her character is most exemplary and greatly admired. It is a source of great pride to her subjects, that not only in her own vast dominion, but throughout the civilized world, Her Majesty's name is never mentioned save in terms of sympathy, affection, and respect, as a Christian woman and as a queen.

She has enjoyed a reign of peace and prosperity unexampled in the annals of England.

Among the events of her reign have been the repeal of the corn laws; the Irish famine and emigration to the United States; the Crimean war; the Indian mutiny; the assumption of the direct government of India, forming an empire; the Reform Bill; the introduction of the ballot; the creation, rapid growth, and organization of the Australasian colonies; and the prolonged agitation of the subject of home rule in Ireland.

The "Victorian period" bids fair to be chiefly remarkable for the material prosperity of the British people and for the magnificent scientific discoveries which have changed the face of modern civilization.

The fiftieth year of her reign was celebrated by a Jubilee in 1887.

The sixtieth anniversary of her elevation to the throne was celebrated in June, 1897, the civilized nations of the world joining Great Britain in an expression of esteem and admiration for her noble queen.

WELL KNOWN MEN.

ENGLISH LEADERS IN SOUTH AFRICAN AFFAIRS.

The Marquis of Salisbury, Prime Minister of England, was born at Hatfield, February 3, 1830, and educated at Eton and Oxford. Always a Conservative in politics he was first elected to Parliament for the Stamford division in 1853. In 1866-67 and again from 1874 to 1878 he was Secretary for India and President of the Indian Council. He was Special Ambassador for the Conference at Constantinople, 1876-77; Plenipotentiary at the Congress of Berlin, 1878. In 1885 he was first elected Prime Minister, occupying that position until the elections of 1886 when the Conservatives were returned to power with Lord Salisbury as their leader. He is also Secretary of State for Foreign Affairs, which position he also occupied from 1878 to 1880; 1885-86; 1887-92, and since 1895. He was not born with "a silver spoon in his mouth." On the contrary, as a young man, his income consisted principally of the money he earned as a leader writer for the great London newspapers.

Gen. Lord Roberts was born in 1832. He was educated at Eton and Addiscombe. His first appointment was that of Lieutenant in the Bengal Artillery in 1851 in which he became Captain and in 1860 Brevet-Major. His services in the Indian Mutiny brought him the Victoria Cross. In 1868 he took part in the Abyssinian war as Assistant Quartermaster-General. He became Quartermaster-General in India in 1875 with the local rank of Major-General; and in the Afghan war of 1878 commanded the column detailed to operate through the Kuran valley. On the investiture of Candahar by Ayoub Khan, after the disaster of Maiwand, he rapidly performed a march from Cabul to Candahar, one of the most brilliant feats of modern times, and utterly defeated the Pretender. He was created a baronet in 1881 and again advanced to G. C. B. and C. I. E. In 1881 he was dispatched to the command of the forces against the Boers in South Africa. He succeeded Sir Donald Stuart in the command of the Indian army in 1885 and was created a peer in January, 1892. In 1895 he was appointed Field Marshal and Commander-in-Chief of the English forces in South Africa during the South African rebellion.

Gen. H. H. Kitchener was born in 1850. He was educated at the Royal Military Academy, Woolwich, and then joined the Royal Engineers in the Palestine and Cyprus surveys. He served as a Major of Cavalry in the Egyptian army in 1882, with the Nile expedition in 1884, and became Governor of Suakin in 1886. For his bravery when he led the Egyptian troops against Osman Digna, he was made Aid-de-Camp to the Queen. From 1888 until 1892 he held the rank of Adjutant General in the Egyptian army, and in the latter year was appointed Sirdar. After the taking of Dongola in 1896, he was made K. C. V., and subsequently organized a final irresistible advance against the Khalifa, which resulted in the latter's utter defeat at Omdurman in September, 1898. For this he was awarded a peerage, as Baron Kitchener of Khartoum and of Aspall in the County of Suffolk. Oxford University honored him with the degree of D.C.L., in 1899.

Rt. Hon. Joseph Chamberlain was born in London, July, 1836. For many years he devoted himself to the manufacturing business in which his father was engaged, his spare time being given up to the study of politics. He was thrice elected Mayor of Birmingham. In 1876 he was elected a member of Parliament from Birmingham, which seat he retained until 1885. From 1880 to 1885 he was President of the Board of Trade, in 1886 President of the Local Government Board, with cabinet rank. He was appointed General Commissioner to Washington for the settlement of the dispute between the United States and Canada on the fisheries question. In June, 1895, Mr. Chamberlain took office under Lord Salisbury as Colonial Secretary. In 1896 he had to deal with the Ashanti and Transvaal difficulties. In 1898 he made the famous "long spoon" speech, and declared himself strongly in favor of an alliance with the United States. The negotiations with the Transvaal, which ended in war, occupied him fully during 1899. Mr. Chamberlain was educated in University College, London, and has received doctorates in law from both Cambridge and Oxford.

Rt. Hon. Cecil Rhodes, after taking his M.A. degree at Oxford, went to South Africa, where he at first met with but little success. When the DeBeer's mine was anything but prosperous, he combined various Kimberly mines and amassed a large fortune. Cape politics attracted him and he represented West Barkly for a short period and held a position in the Ministry of Sir T. Scanlon. On the fall of the Spriggs Ministry, the new government, with Mr. Rhodes as Prime Minister, took office at the Cape, July 17, 1890. He remained in office from that time until June, 1896, when he resigned in consequence of the Jameson raid into the Transvaal. Mr. Rhodes, in 1896, was chairman of the British South African Company. In 1895 he became a member of the Privy Council. After resigning office at the Cape in 1896 he devoted himself to the development of Rhodesia and also became a leader in elections to the Cape Parliament. During 1898 he was returned for two constituencies. He holds the honorary degree of D.C.L. from Oxford, an honor which was given him in 1892 and publicly conferred in June, 1899.

Gen. Sir Redvers Buller was born in 1839 and entered the 60th Rifles in 1858. In 1860

WELL KNOWN MEN.

he served in the campaigns in China, in 1873-74 in those of Ashanti, and in 1878-79 in South Africa, when he commanded the Frontier Light Horse in the Zulu war. He won his Victoria Cross in Egypt in 1882-84, and Soudan, 1884-85. He has received four medals with seven clasps and five other decorations. All his regimental services have been in the 60th King's Royal Rifles. He has held twelve staff appointments, and was Quartermaster-General of the army in 1887-90 and Adjutant-General of the army, 1890-97. He was Under Secretary for Ireland for a short time in 1887; in 1889, at the beginning of the Transvaal troubles, he was appointed to chief command of the British forces in South Africa.

Gen. Sir George S. White was born in July, 1835. He was educated at Sandhurst and entered the army in 1853. He had a brilliant career and won his Victoria Cross at Charasiab in 1879, and at Candahar, September, 1880, by his conspicuous personal bravery. He served in the Mutiny, in the Afghan campaign 1879-80, in the Nile expedition 1885, and in the Burmese expedition 1885-87 as commander of the forces there, when he gained the rank of Major-General. In 1893 he succeeded Lord Roberts as Commander-in-Chief in India. He was appointed Quartermaster-General of the army in 1898, and in 1899 was sent out to take command of the British forces in Natal, in connection with the Transvaal troubles. The troops under his command gained some brilliant victories early in the struggle; but he was afterward closely invested at Ladysmith.

Lieut.-Gen. John D. P. French was born in 1852. In 1874 he joined the army as Lieutenant in the 19th Hussars. His promotion was rapid for one who had seen little active service, and when the war broke out he held the rank of Major-General. His services as an Assistant Adjutant-General on the Headquarters Staff, and later as commander of the cavalry brigade at Aldershot stamped him as a soldier of more than ordinary ability. He was promoted to Lieutenant-General. He is one of the finest swordsmen in the British army, but, curiously enough, a bad rider.

Col. Robert S. S. Baden-Powell, Lieutenant-Colonel in the British army, commanding the Fifth Dragoon Guards since 1897, was born February 22, 1857. He was educated at Charter House and joined the 13th Hussars in 1876. He served as Adjutant with that regiment in India, Afghanistan, and South Africa and from 1887 to 1889 was a member of the staff as Assistant Military Secretary of South Africa. From 1890 to 1893 he was Assistant Military Secretary of Malta. In 1897 he was promoted from the 13th Hussars to command of the 5th Dragoon Guards, after military service in Ashanti and Matabeleland. Since the beginning of the war in South Africa, Col. Baden-Powell has been a prominent figure in the campaigns.

CANADIANS PROMINENT IN SOUTH AFRICAN WAR.

Lord Strathcona (Donald Alexander Smith), was born at Morayshire, Scotland, in 1820, but emigrated to Canada in 1838, and entered the employ of the famous Hudson's Bay Company. Promoted step by step he eventually became a Chief Factor, and finally Resident Governor and Chief Commissioner for the Company in Canada, a position which he still holds. In 1870 he was appointed a member of the first Executive Council of the Northwest Territory, and from 1871 to 1874 was the member for Winnipeg and St. John in the Manitoba Legislature. In 1871 he was also returned to the Dominion House of Parliament for Selkirk, retaining the seat during 1872, and again from 1874 to 1880, being then defeated in a by-election. In 1880 he was returned to the House of Commons for Montreal West, and was re-elected in 1891. During 1896 he retired from political life in Canada, and was appointed Canadian High Commissioner to London, by the Laurier government. The Queen made him a knight of the most distinguished Order of St. Michael and St. George in 1886; and in 1897 raised him to the peerage as Baron Strathcona and Mount Royal. He has given enormous sums to educational institutions, and equipped a picked body of horse, known Strathcona's Horse, which has done much service in the South African campaign under command of Lieut.-Col. Steele.

Lieut.-Col. Samuel B. Steele, commanding Strathcona's Horse during the South African campaign, was born at Medonte, Ontario, January 5, 1849. As ensign, he served with the Thirty-fifth Battalion, "Simcoe Foresters"; and in 1870 served in the Red River expedition commanded by Col. Wolseley, now Lord Wolseley, and Commander-in-Chief of the British army. Afterwards he served with "A" Battery, Royal Canadian Artillery, and the Northwest Mounted Police. During the Northwest Rebellion of 1885 he commanded the cavalry and scouts of the Alberta Field Force. In 1887 he commanded "D" division of the Northwest Mounted Police, when the Indians of the Kootenay district of British Columbia attacked the government agency and released some Indian murderers. Before the South African war broke out he was in command of the Northwest Mounted Police division in the Yukon district, and subsequently accepted the command of Strathcona's Horse. Lieut.-Col. Steele is a typical rider of the plains, cool, alert, daring, and resourceful.

WELL KNOWN MEN.

Capt. Robert K. Barker, in command of the "C" Company, Royal Canadian Regiment, during the South African war, is thirty years of age, and was born at Kingston, Ontario. He is a lawyer, and was educated at Toronto University, and Osgood's Law College. He enlisted in "K" Company, Queen's Own Rifles (Toronto), formed exclusively of university students. He rose step by step, until, on July 15, 1897, he attained the captaincy. On the government's offer of a contingent for active service being accepted by the Imperial authorities, Captain Barker was offered and accepted the command of the company recruited from Toronto's militiamen, and known as "C" Company. His selection met with hearty approval. The officers and men of "C" Company were the first of the regiment to take any part in the actual fighting.

Lieut.-Col. William D. Otter, commander of special service battalion of the Royal Canadian Regiment in the South African war, was born December 3, 1843. In 1861 he enlisted in the Queen's Own Rifles of Toronto, as a private, and rose steadily, until in June, 1874, he attained command of the regiment. He saw some active service on the Magard frontier during the winter of 1864-65, and the Fenian raid of 1866. He commanded the Queen's Own Rifles, and did effective service during the "pilgrimage riots," in Toronto, 1875; and the Grand Trunk Railway riots, Belleville, 1877. In 1883 he was appointed commandant of the School of Infantry, Toronto, and organized "C" Company, of what is now known as the Royal Canadian Regiment of Infantry. During the rebellion in the Northwest Territory, 1885, Lieut.-Col. Otter commanded the second column. When the Canadian government decided to send a first contingent to South Africa, he was the one officer who Canadians considered would be given the first chance to accept the command. The government's choice therefore met with universal approval.

Hon. Frederick W. Borden, Canadian Minister of Militia, was born at Cornwallis, Nova Scotia, May 14, 1847. He graduated from King's College, Windsor, Ont., in 1867, and continued his medical studies at Harvard Medical School, Boston, U. S. A., receiving his M.D. degree in 1868. He was first elected to the House of Commons for King's county, Nova Scotia, in 1874. He was defeated in 1882, but in 1887 regained his seat. Upon the formation of the Laurier government, in 1896, he was called to the cabinet and appointed Minister of Militia.

LEADING BOERS.

Paul J. Kruger, president of the South African Republic, was born near Colesburg, Cape Colony, on October 10, 1825. When about nine years old he took part in the Great Trek over the Vaal, and is one of the few survivors of that time. While still young he was appointed a Field Cornet, and afterwards chosen to command the Boer forces. In 1872 he was chosen a member of the Executive Council of the Transvaal, President Burgers being then at the head of affairs. After Majuba, he was one of the leaders of the rebellion which ended in the convention of 1881. In 1882 he was elected president for the first time. In 1883 he was re-elected for five years, and in 1888, after a contest with General Joubert, he was again chosen president. Since then he has been twice re-elected, the last time in 1898.

Gen. Petrus Jacobus Joubert, late Commander-in-Chief of the Boer army, was born in Cape Colony in 1831, and died in 1900, during the siege of Ladysmith. He came from a French Huguenot family, long resident in South Africa, which had intermarried with the Cape Dutch. It was by him that Sir George Colley was defeated at Majuba Hill during the war of 1881-82. It was to his effective organization of the fighting men of the republics that gave the Boers success in 1881, and their later successes in the present South African war. In 1893, and again in 1898, General Joubert stood for the presidency of the Transvaal Republic, but was easily defeated by President Kruger. The surrender to Dr. Jameson, in 1896, was mainly due to him.

Gen. Pietrus Arnoldus Cronje, who surrendered to Lord Roberts at Paardeburg on February 27, 1900, was the most respected of all among his own people. Born in the Transvaal some sixty-three years ago, he first attracted the attention of his countrymen in the war of 1881, so disastrous to British arms, and popularly known to the Transvaalers as "The War of Independence." In this war he commanded the Boers, besieging the British force at Potchefstroom. On January 2, 1896, he defeated Dr. Jameson and his raiders at Doorn Kop. That event placed him on the topmost pinnacle in the hearts of his countrymen. They named him "The Lion of the Transvaal," and always greeted him as "Commandant." In the same year he was made Superintendent of Natives, and a member of the Transvaal Executive. He was not a success as legislator. On the outbreak of the present war Cronje was made Commander-in-Chief of the Free State forces.

Martinus Theunis Steyn, Ex-President of the Orange Free State, was born at Winburg, Orange Free State, October 2, 1857. He was educated for the legal profession at Grey College, Bloemfontein, and in Holland. Mr. Steyn is entitled to practice his profession in England, having been called to the English bar (Inner Temple), in November, 1882. He was appointed State Attorney in 1883, and a little later was raised to the bench as second puisne judge. He was elected president of the Orange Free State in 1896.

INDEX.

	Biography	Portrait		Biography	Portrait
Abbott, Lyman	521	24 G	Broadus, John A.	518	24 I
Adams, Chas. F.	555	24 M	Bronte, Charlotte	501	24 T
Adams, John	540	24 C	Brooks, Phillips	521	24 G
Adams, J. Q.	540	24 C	Brown, Alexander	599	24 A2
Adams, Samuel	543		Browning, Elizabeth B.	571	24 D2
Addison, Joseph	505	24 O	Browning, Robert	506	24 S
Adolphus, Gustavus	583	24 E	Bryant, W. C.	496	24 V
Agassiz, L. J. R.	491	24 N	Buchanan, James	540	24 C
Alcott, Louisa May	571	24 D2	Bull, Ole	577	24 V
Alden, Mrs. G. R.	513	24 Q	Bunyan, John	524	24 H
Aldrich, T. B.	516		Burke, Edmund	552	24 E2
Allen, James Lane	606	24 C2	Burns, Robert	507	24 S
Ames, Oakes	597	24 Z	Burr, Aaron	559	24 L
Ames, Oliver	597	24 Z	Burritt, Elihu		24 F
Anderson, H. C.	516		Butler, B. F.	563	24 K
Anderson, Mary	575	24 V	Butler, Marion	601	24 B2
Andrews, E. B.	530	24 J			
Andrew, John A.	546	24 A	Cable, George W.	606	24 C2
Anthony, Susan B.	571	24 D2	Calhoun, John C.	546	24 A
Appleton, Samuel	590	24 Y	Calvert, George	550	24 E2
Armour, P. D.	590	24 Y	Cannon, H. W.		24 A2
Armstrong, S. C.	530	24 J	Carleton, Will	514	24 Q
Arnold, Edwin	513	24 Q	Carlisle, John G.	564	24 K
Arnold, Matthew	491	24 N	Carlyle, Thomas	491	24 N
Astor, John J.	590	24 Y	Carnegie, Andrew	587	24 X
Audubon, J. J.	517		Carnot, President	552	24 E2
			Cartwright, Sir Richard J.	610	24 F2
Bacon, Francis	550	24 E2	Case, Jerome I.	587	24 X
Bancroft, George	526	24 R	Cass, Lewis	547	24 A
Banks, N. P.	536	24 B	Channing, W. E.	521	24 G
Barnum, P. T.	575	24 V	Chase, Salmon P.	543	
Barrett, Lawrence	576	24 V	Chaucer, Geoffrey	505	24 O
Baxter, Richard	524	24 H	Childs, G. W.	511	24 P
Beecher, H. W.	521	24 G	Choate, Rufus	560	24 L
Beecher, Lyman	524	24 H	Clark, J. G.		24 X
Bellamy, Edward	513	24 Q	Clarke, J. F.	514	24 Q
Bennett, J. G.	517		Clay, Henry	547	24 A
Benton, Thomas H.	546	24 A	Cleveland, Grover	537	24 B
Binney, Horace	559	24 L	Clews, Henry	599	24 A2
Bismarck-Schoenhausen,			Coleridge, S. T.	505	24 O
O. E. I.	551	24 E2	Colfax, Schuyler	555	24 M
Blaine, J. G.	536	24 B	Colt, Samuel	593	24 W
Bonaparte, Napoleon	584	24 E	Conwell, R. H.	518	24 I
Booth, Edwin	576	24 V	Cooper, J. F.	501	24 T
Booth, William	566	24 F	Cooper, Peter	588	24 X
Bottome, Mrs. Margaret	510	24 P	Corliss, G. H.	588	24 X
Bowles, Samuel	510	24 P	Cowper, William	505	24 O
Briggs, George N.	559	24 L	Cox, Samuel S.	555	24 M
Bright, John	**551**	**24 E2**	Crafts, Wilbur	601	24 F

SUCCESSFUL MEN AND WOMEN.

Name	Biography	Portrait
Cromwell, Oliver	584	24 E
Curtis, B. R.	560	24 L
Curtis, G. W.	511	24 P
Cushman, C. H.	577	24 V
Custer, Geo. A.	579	24 D
Dana, C. A.	492	
Dana, J. D.	492	24 N
Daniel, John W.	601	24 B2
Darwin, C. R.	493	24 N
Dawes, Henry L.	537	24 B
Dawson, Sir John William	609	24 F2
Decatur, Stephen	584	24 E
Deems, C. F.	518	24 I
Deland, Margaret	514	24 Q
Depew, Chauncey M.	556	24 M
De Quincey, Thomas	517	
Dickens, Charles	501	24 T
Dillon, Sidney	597	24 Z
Disraeli, Benjamin	552	24 E2
Dix, Dorothea L.	566	
Dix, John Adams	556	24 M
Dodge, William E.	590	24 Y
Douglass, Frederick	566	
Douglas, S. A.	548	24 A
Dow, Neal	567	24 F
Drummond, Henry	530	24 J
Dumas, Alexandre	517	
Dwight, Timothy	531	
Eckles, James H.	599	24 A2
Edison, T. A.	593	24 W
Edmunds, G. F.	537	24 B
Edwards, Jonathan	524	24 H
Eliot, Charles W.	531	24 J
Emerson, R. W.	497	24 U
Ericsson, John	594	24 W
Evans, Mary Ann	502	24 T
Evarts, William M.	564	24 K
Everett, Edward	538	24 B
Fairbanks, Thaddeus	594	24 W
Farragut, D. G.	579	24 D
Ferguson, James	531	24 J
Field, C. W.	597	24 Z
Field, David D.	544	
Field, Marshall T.	590	24 Y
Fields, James T.	514	24 Q
Fillmore, Millard	541	24 C
Finney, C. G.	524	24 H
Fiske, John	527	24 R
Forrest, Edwin	577	24 V
Franklin, Benjamin	541	24 C
Fremont, John C.	579	
Froebel, F. W. A.	532	24 J
Froude, J. A.	527	24 R
Fulton, Robert	594	24 W

Name	Biography	Portrait
Gage, Lyman J.	599	24 A2
Garfield, James A.	538	24 B
Garrison, W. L.	567	24 F
Gatling, Richard J.	594	24 W
Girard, Stephen	591	24 Y
Gladstone, Hon. W. E.	553	24 E2
Goethe, J. W. von	507	24 S
Goodyear, Charles	595	24 W
Gordon, John B.	602	24 B2
Gordon, John C. H.	610	24 F2
Gough, John B.	568	24 F
Gould, Jay	597	24 Z
Grady, H. W.	602	24 B2
Grant, Ulysses S.	580	24 D
Gray, Thomas	505	24 O
Greeley, Horace	511	24 P
Green, J. R.	527	24 R
Greene, Nathaniel	584	24 E
Gutenberg, Johann	595	24 W
Hall, John	519	
Hamilton, Alexander	544	
Hamlin, Hannibal	556	24 M
Hampton, Gen. Wade	602	24 B2
Hancock, John	548	24 A
Hancock, W. S.	580	24 E
Hardy, A. S.		24 T
Harlan, John M.	557	24 M
Harper, James	517	
Harper, William R.	532	24 J
Harris, Joel Chandler	606	24 C2
Harrison, Benjamin	538	24 B
Harrison, Mrs. Burton	607	24 C2
Harte, Francis B.	514	24 Q
Hawley, J. R.	544	
Hawthorne, Nathaniel	497	24 U
Henry, Patrick	548	24 A
Herschel, Sir William	505	24 O
Higginson, T. W.	528	24 R
Hoar, G. F.	564	24 K
Hoe, Robert	595	24 W
Holland, J. G.	512	24 P
Holmes, O. W.	498	24 U
Hood, Thomas	518	
Hopkins, John	591	24 Y
Hopkins, Mark	533	24 J
Houston, Sam	545	
Howard, John	569	24 F
Howard, O. O.	581	24 D
Howe, Elias	595	24 W
Howe, Hon. Joseph		24 F2
Howells, W. D.	503	24 T
Hoyt, Wayland	519	24 I
Hughes, John	522	24 G
Hugo, Victor	503	24 T
Hume, David	528	25 R
Huntington, C. P.	598	24 Z
Huxley, T. H.	493	24 N

618

SUCCESSFUL MEN AND WOMEN.

	Biography	Portrait		Biography	Portrait
Ingelow, Jean	515	24 Q	Monroe, James	542	24 C
Irving, Washington	498	24 V	Moody, D. L.	520	24 I
			Morgan, J. P.	600	24 A2
Jackson, Andrew	545		Morgan, John T.	603	24 B2
Jackson, T. J.	585	24 D	Morse, S. F. B.	596	24 W
James, Henry	515	24 Q	Morton, L. P.	600	24 A2
Jay, John	561	24 L	Motley, J. L.	529	24 R
Jefferson, Joseph	577	24 V	Mowat, Sir Oliver	609	24 F2
Jefferson, Thomas	541	24 C	Murfree, Mary N.	607	24 C2
Johnson, Samuel	506	24 O	Murphy, Francis	569	24 F
Jonson, Ben	506	24 O			
Johnston, Richard Malcolm	607	24 C2	Newman, Cardinal	520	24 I
Judson, Adoniram	524	24 H	Newton, Isaac	494	24 N 24 O
Judson, Edward	519	24 I	Nilsson, Christine	573	24 D2
			Nott, Eliphalet	535	24 J
Keats, John	507	24 S			
Kellogg, Clara Louise	572	24 D2	Paderewski, I. J.	578	24 V
King, Grace Elizabeth	607		Page, Thomas Nelson	608	24 C2
Kingsley, Charles	503	24 T	Palmer, Alice E. F.	573	24 D2
Knox, John J.	599	24 A 2	Palmer, Mrs. B.	573	24 D2
			Parker, Theodore	522	24 G
Lafayette,	585	24 E	Parton, James	515	24 Q
Lanier, Sidney	607	24 C2	Pascal, Blaise	506	24 O
Laurier, Hon. Wilfrid	609	24 F2	Patti, A. J. M.	578	24 V
Lawrence, Abbott	591	24 Y	Payne, J. H.	515	24 Q
Lawrence, Amos	592	24 Y	Peabody, A. P.	520	24 I
Lee, Fitzhugh	602	24 B2	Peabody, George	592	24 Y
Lee, Robert E.	581	24 D	Peck, Samuel Minturn	608	24 C2
Lincoln, Abraham	539	24 B	Peel, Robert	553	24 E2
Lind-Goldschmidt, J.	572	24 D2	Phillips, Wendell	569	24 F
Longfellow, H. W.	499	24 U	Pierce, Franklin	561	24 L
Longstreet, James	603	24 D	Pillsbury, Hon. J. S.		24 X
Lowell, J. R.	499	24 U	Pitt, William	553	24 E2
Luther, Martin	525	24 H	Poe, Edgar Allan	508	24 S
Lyell, Charles	518		Prescott, W. H.	529	24 R
Lyon, Mary	532	24 J	Preston, Mrs. Margaret. J.	608	
			Pullman, G. M.	588	24 X
MacArthur, R. S.	519	24 I			
Macaulay, T. B.	528	24 R	Raleigh, Sir Walter	554	24 E2
MacDonald, Sir John	609	24 F2	Ransom, Matt	604	24 B2
Mackenzie, Hon. Alexander	610	24 F2	Reed, T. B.	549	24 A
MacLean, John	557	24 M	Reid, Whitelaw	512	24 P
Madison, James	542	24 C	Ridpath, J. C.	529	24 R
Mann, Horace	534	24 J	Roberts, Chas. G. D.		24 F2
Manning, Cardinal	519	24 I	Robinson, George D.	564	24 K
Marshall, John		24 L	Rockefeller, John D.	588	24 X
Mather, Cotton	525	24 H	Rousseau, J. J.	506	24 O
McClellan, G. B.	585	24 E	Ruskin, John	495	24 N
McCormick, Cyrus	595	24 W			
McGuire, Dr. Hunter	603	24 B2	Savonarola,	525	24 H
McKinley, William	564	24 K	Saxe, John G.	515	24 Q
McMillan, Benton	603	24 B2	Schiller, J. C. F. von	508	24 S
Meade, G. G.	586	24 E	Schuyler, P. J.	586	24 E
Mill, John S.	494	24 N	Scott, Walter	504	24 T
Mills, B. F.		24 I	Scott, Winfield	581	24 D
Milton, John	508	24 S	Seward, William H.	545	
Miner, Rev. A. A.	520	24 I	Shakespeare, William	509	24 S
Mitchell, Miss Maria	534	24 J	Sheridan, P. H.	582	24 D

619

SUCCESSFUL MEN AND WOMEN.

Name	Biography	Portrait	Name	Biography	Portrait
Sherman, John	565	24 K	Van Buren, Martin	542	24 C
Sherman, W. T.	582	24 D	Vance, Z. B.	605	24 B2
Simpson, Matthew	520	24 I	Vanderbilt, Cornelius	598	24 Z
Spencer, Herbert	495	24 W	Vanderbilt, William	599	24 Z
Spurgeon, C. H.	522	24 G	Vernes, Jules	516	24 Q
Stanford, Leland	508	24 Z			
Stark, John	586	24 E	Waite, M. R.	545	
Stephens, A. H.	549	24 A	Wallace, Lew	504	24 T
Stephenson, George	596	24 W	Wanamaker, John	593	24 Y
Stevens, Thaddeus	558	24 M	Ward, E. S. P.	515	24 Q
Stewart, A. T.	592	24 Y	Warner, Charles D.	516	24 Q
Stewart, J. E. B.	604	24 D	Warren, Joseph	586	24 E
St. John, J. P.	570	24 F	Washburn, C. C.	589	24 X
Stone-Blackwell, Lucy	574	24 D2	Washburn, E. B.	558	24 M
Storrs, R. S.	523	24 G	Washburn, I.	589	24 X
Story, Joseph	562	24 L	Washington, George	543	24 A
Stowe, H. E.	574	24 D2	Watson, Thomas	605	24 B2
Stuart, Ruth McEnery	608	24 C2	Watt, James	596	24 W
Sumner, Charles	539	24 A	Watts, Isaac	525	24 H
			Wayland, Francis	535	24 J
Talmage, T. DeWitt	523	24 G	Webster, Daniel	543	24 C
Taney, R. B.	562	24 L	Weed, Thurlow	513	24 P
Tappan, Arthur	592	24 Y	Wellington, A. W.	587	24 E
Taylor, Bayard	500	24 U	Wesley, Charles	525	24 H
Taylor, Robert L.	604	24 B2	Wesley, John	525	24 H
Taylor, Zachary	586	24 E	Wesson, Daniel B.	589	24 X
Tennyson, Alfred	509	24 S	Wetherell, E. A.	575	24 V
Thackeray, W. M.	504	24 T	White, A. D.	535	24 J
Thomas, G. H.	583	24 D	Whitefield, George	526	24 H
Thompson, Sir John S. D.	610	24 F2	Whitney, Eli	596	24 W
Thurman, A. G.	565	24 K	Whittier, J. G.	500	24 U
Tilden, Samuel Jones	558	24 M	Wilberforce, William	554	24 E2
Tillman, B. R.	604	24 B2	Williams, G. G.	600	24 A2
Trowbridge, J. T.	516	24 Q	Williams, Roger	526	24 H
Tupper, Sir Charles	610	24 F2	Wilson, Henry	565	24 K
Twain, Mark	512	24 P	Wilson, W. L.		24 K
Tyndale, William	525	24 H	Winthrop, John	550	24 A
Tyndall, John	496	24 W	Wordsworth, William	510	
			Wyckliffe, John	526	24 H

WELL KNOWN MEN.

Name	Biography	Portrait	Name	Biography	Portrait
Bryan, William Jennings	612	24	Sampson, William T.	611	24
Dewey, George	612	24	Schley, Winfield Scott	611	24
Parkhurst, Charles Henry	611	24	Vincent, John H.	612	24

ENGLISH LEADERS IN SOUTH AFRICAN AFFAIRS.

Name	Biography	Portrait	Name	Biography	Portrait
Baden-Powell, Col. R. S. S.	615	23	Rhodes, Rt. Hon. Cecil	614	23
Buller, Gen. Sir Redvers	614	23	Roberts, Gen. Lord	614	23
Chamberlain, Rt. Hon. Jos.	614	23	Salisbury, Marquis of	614	23
French, Lieut.-Gen. J. D. P.	615	23	White, Gen. Sir Geo. S.	615	23
Kitchener, Gen. H. H.	614	23			

CANADIANS PROMINENT IN SOUTH AFRICAN WAR.

Name	Biography	Portrait	Name	Biography	Portrait
Barker, Capt. Robt. K.	616	22	Steele, Lieut.-Col. Samuel B.	615	22
Borden, Hon. Fred'k W.	616	23	Strathcona, Lord	615	22
Otter, Lieut.-Col. Wm. D.	616	22			

LEADING BOERS.

Name	Biography	Portrait	Name	Biography	Portrait
Cronje, Gen. Pietrus Arnoldus	616	22	Kruger, Paul J.	616	22
Joubert, Gen. Petrus Jacobus	616	22	Steyn, Martinus Theunis	616	22